Germany, America, Europe

Germany, America, Europe

Forty Years of German Foreign Policy

Wolfram F. Hanrieder

Yale University Press
NEW HAVEN AND LONDON

Published with assistance from the Louis Stern Memorial Fund.

Designed by James J. Johnson and set in Palatino Roman type.
Printed in the United States of America.

Library of Congress Cataloging-in-Publication Data

Hanrieder, Wolfram F.
    Germany, America, Europe : forty years of German foreign policy /
Wolfram F. Hanrieder.
        p. cm.
    Bibliography: p.
    Includes index.
    ISBN 0–300–04022–9 (alk. paper)

    1. Germany (West)—Foreign relations. I. Title.
DD258.8.H37 1989
327.43—dc19   88–30356
                                                                   CIP

The paper in this book meets the guidelines for permanence and durability of the Committee on Production Guidelines for Book Longevity of the Council on Library Resources.

10 9 8 7 6 5 4 3 2 1

for Lani

Caelum, non animum, mutant qui trans mare currunt.
—HORACE

Contents

Preface
The Approach

Germany, for centuries merely a geographical expression and between 1871 and 1945 the strongest power in Europe, is today divided into two parts. This book is about one of these parts—West Germany, the Federal Republic of Germany—and how it became embedded in a European political order that is itself divided, and emplaced in a transatlantic security compact that is itself insecure.

In the course of four decades, West Germany has become a potential balancer in the equilibrium of power between East and West; it has grown into an economic giant and a major force in the European state system; it supports the largest conventional troop contingent in Western Europe; and its abiding concern with the question of German unity lends a somewhat unsettled quality (for some, an unsettling one) to its diplomatic dealings with the Soviet Union, Eastern Europe, and East Germany.

The Federal Republic is a product of the Second World War and the Cold War, and its security and welfare remain inextricably tied to the international circumstances that have shaped its short history. Its achievements and failures, its strengths and weaknesses—all of which are considerable—are the result not only of the Germans' own exertions but also of large forces beyond West Germany's borders and beyond its capacity to change in fundamental ways. Delineating these large forces is essential to understanding how the Federal Republic is situated in its time and place, in the coordinates of necessity and choice that define the limits and opportunities for German foreign policy.

This book attempts such a delineation. It is not a diplomatic history of the Federal Republic or even a history of its foreign policy. The range of such an undertaking would most likely require a collective effort,[1] the archival materials for a full historical treatment of even select aspects of German foreign policy are not yet available, and we are in any event too close to the recent past to speak with assurance of events the meaning of which is still unfolding. Contemporary history consists of stories for which there are no conclusions, only postponements. But the foreign policy aspirations of the Federal Republic, and the restraints placed on them, are characterized by a remarkable continuity. Their historical antecedents retain immediacy and relevance for current events and policies, and the issues of the present obtain their fuller meaning only when connected with the past and tentatively with the future.[2]

This book is also not a case study to test a particular theory of international politics or foreign policy. Like any other book that deals systematically with human events, it contains hidden theories: in this case about the nature of politics and power, the connections between foreign and domestic policies and between politics and economics, and the sources of political conduct in the Federal Republic and other countries. I have dealt with such matters explicitly elsewhere,[3] and my view of them has no doubt influenced the analytical judgments presented here. But I did not wish this book to carry a heavy methodological burden; nor did I intend my theoretical orientation to yield precisely defined hypotheses or propositions that are amenable to testing, replication, or prediction. My analytical temperament—through which runs my "axis of reality," as William James would say—shies away from translating politics into science, aspirations into mathematics; and I am perhaps equally distant from approaches that provide a detailed accounting of how decisions were made, from what institutional setting they emerged, and how their proclaimed or masked purposes were compromised in the corridors of bureaucracies and the daily routines of diplomacy. Rather, I chose to look at the historical record and extract what I perceived to be its meaning and portent, striving for the "abbreviation of reality" that Ernst Cassirer saw as the essence of theory.

In some respects, the historical record abbreviated itself. Though I deal with large concepts—containment, deterrence, interdependence, integration, to mention a few—they attain their prominence from sustained diplomatic use, not by virtue of theoretical invitation or analytic manipulation. These concepts are themselves "abbreviations of reality," the condensed representation of political purposes and diplomatic intentions. They are not theoretical but political abstracts, imposed on diplomatic parlance and the public debate by the makers and not the observers of historical events.

But examining the complementary and conflicting relationships among these concepts is a theoretical task that the historical record does not on its own undertake for us. Such a task requires the oversimplification of complex events, always unwarranted and always unavoidable.

There can be no evenness of attention for the historian, who cannot avoid distilling from the available record those events that have for him a special analytic density, leaving aside others that appear crucial and indispensable when seen from a different perspective and intended to serve a different analytic purpose. Anything that is said is likely to do some injustice to the things that are left unsaid. Historical accounts are partial, in both senses of the word; and the evidence we adduce is almost always circumstantial and should be treated with the same reserve with which this kind of evidence is treated in the law. It is a question of choosing among conflicting modes of description, recognizing and accepting that each holds its distinctive promise and that each is afflicted with its own distortions.[4]

This then is the view of theory that I intended to govern the outlines and conclusions of the story that follows: guarded toward its possibilities of objectivity, modest in denying it scientific validity, assertive in claiming for it relevance as a principle of historical judgment.

Like most stories about human endeavors this is a convoluted one, and the largest difficulty for the narrator is how to tell it. We must choose a suitable analytical syntax that provides momentum and organization (as should any form of syntax). And here the insistent and insidious questions of method reappear, disguised as problems of organization: every question we raise circumscribes its possible answers, the punctuations and spaces with which we interrupt a chronicle contain a hidden theory, and the sequence in which we arrange chapters and topics conceals judgments about cause and effect and about the emphasis we accord distinct and yet related areas of events. This is the inevitable consequence of a mode of explication that must proceed in a sequential manner (like words and sentences), and that does not allow the analyst to be everywhere at once. Analysis, to paraphrase Goethe's remark about opera, consists of examining significant situations in an artificially arranged sequence.

This book, like any other, is such a sequence. Its arrangement is inevitably contrived and cut into parts, whereas the significant situations themselves were real and whole. Many of the political, strategic, and economic developments with which I deal unfolded concurrently, shaping one another in complementary as well as conflicting ways, their own meaning a consequence of the multiple connections among them. Important things happened at the same time, their separate significance compounded by their conjuncture. Security and arms control, West Germany's policies toward the other Germany and its partners in the East, the political and economic dimensions of the Federal Republic's involvement in Western Europe—these were for the Federal Republic overlapping and amorphous territories of concerns and aspirations, with unmarked boundaries between military and political dimensions, politics and economics, domestic and foreign policies.

The Federal Republic's postwar foreign policy was an encompassing existential experience for those who made it, and for those who felt its consequences in their daily lives. Constrained as it was, their diplomacy became for the Germans a matter of immediate and practical importance, a glaring and constant demonstration of how their present and future security and welfare depended on the outside world. This sense of the significance of international politics for the routines of daily life was sharpened by historical experience. In the postwar years, many Germans attributed their past personal and collective misfortunes to foreign policy events, and they saw how current foreign policy issues were once again reaching into every aspect of domestic life, though with the hope of happier consequences. The cumulative results of foreign policy became deeply embedded in the Federal Republic's social, economic, and political order. They resist being uprooted as isolated issues—security, welfare, unity—that we can analyze separately and then reassemble in a historiographic synthesis.

But even more compelling are the reasons why the Federal Republic's major foreign policy aims should be accorded their own distinct analysis, why the contours of these separate domains should be traced separately and then placed over one another to yield a cumulative topography of Germany's political landscape.

In the first place, these aims varied in kind. Laying claim to lost territories in the East and to the other German state was a goal fundamentally different, morally as well as practically, from that of promoting economic and political integration in the West. As the major issues of German foreign policy evolved over the decades—military strategy, economic and monetary matters, the Federal Republic's European and Eastern policies—they acquired their own self-contained and sometimes conflicting political and historical logic. They resisted attempts by successive German governments to render them mutually supportive and to gather them into a coherent foreign policy program. Each area of concern, as it developed, obtained its own political imperatives, its own foreign and domestic constituencies, its own habits of mind and conduct. Each set of issues evoked different political and psychological responses from the West Germans and their allies and opponents, each required its own material, intellectual, and moral efforts, and each met with different obstacles and opportunities on the international and domestic political scenes.

Equally important, the foreign policy aims of the Federal Republic reached into an international setting that was itself an ensemble of different components. The postwar world order turned into a combination of the old and new, an uneasy mix of the old territorial-geostrategic mode of international relations, of a new military-strategic mode shaped by nuclear weapons, and of a modern economic-interdependent mode that seemed impervious to considerations either of territory or of the nuclear balance. Each of these three major strata of the world order began to exhibit its own power relations, superpowers, political and ideological compulsions, formal and informal institutions, rules of conduct, and historical lineage and contemporary relevance.[5] They became the major levels on which political, strategic, and economic demands were contested and resolved in different ways, where one state's strengths and weaknesses met with those of other states in an interplay of conflict and cooperation. The distinguishing feature of the modern state system is its multidimensionality, each dimension characterized by its own configuration of power and purpose, each holding its own and distinct challenge for national statecraft and diplomacy.

On these three great plateaus the major foreign policy aims of the Federal Republic were pursued and contested. But none of these aims was unambiguously situated on one alone. The Federal Republic's security problems were the product both of traditional, territorial concerns and modern, nuclear ones. They stemmed from the perennial hazards of geographical proximity—the weak fearing the threatening presence of the strong—but also from the novel need to rely on the nuclear protection of a distant ally whose own population and territory became totally vulnerable. Similarly, the issue of Germany's reunification, though transformed from an issue of enlarging territory into an issue of enlarging human contacts, has nonetheless retained territorial connotations, geostrategic implications, and historical memories that cannot be eradicated. The state itself has remained a territorial organization, and there persists an irreducibly territorial mode of contemporary international relations, even though the boundless reach of nuclear weapons and the intrusions of modern economic interdependence have permeated the territorial boundaries of the traditional nation-state.[6] The Germans' security concerns, foreign and domestic economic policies, and preoccupation with the division of their country straddled the multiple levels of the modern state system. German foreign policies were both traditional and modern, contradictory as well as complementary, embracing a territorial mode of thinking in one context and rejecting it in another, accepting as well as resisting the tides of historical change that shaped the second half of this century.

On all three layers of power the United States emerged from the Second World War as a superpower. They became the great arenas in which the United States implemented the three central principles of its postwar global and European strategies: containment on the territorial-geostrategic layer, deterrence on the nuclear-strategic layer, and hegemony on the economic-interdependent layer. Inevitably, American policies engaged the Federal Republic (and Western Europe) on all three layers, with German-American relations taking a more complicated and contentious turn when American power began to diminish in relative terms on all three levels as Germany's leverage increased (principally on the economic level) and when the day-to-day diplomatic saliency of military-strategic matters yielded to economic and political matters.

All these reasons urge that the issues of the Federal Republic's security, Eastern policies, and political economy each be treated on its own analytical terms and followed diachronically along its separate continuities, although we recognize that the larger meaning of the issues lies in their synchrony. But this historiographic procedure is as contrived as any other. The sequence of analysis is as artificial when it is governed by diachronic analysis, which traces issues and events along their own, longer time, as it is when it gives primacy to synchronic conjuncture, which highlights the interconnectedness of events within a narrower and foreshortened time.[7] In either case we impute relationships of cause and effect, embrace chronology (whether short or long), and plot a vertical path through time even as we see events spread and linked on a horizontal plane of time, their significance a function of their separate pasts as well as of their conjoined present.[8]

There is yet another obstacle to an even, sequential flow of narrative, this one governed by a spatial rather than a temporal metaphor. This is the confluence of the Federal Republic's domestic and foreign policies, of its external and internal political space.[9] The political and military commitments that the German government made to the Western alliance in the early 1950s—commitments that were the precondition for restoring sovereignty and economic reconstruction—not only restricted the future choices of German foreign policy but also shaped the content of West Germany's internal political and economic order. As a consequence, the makers and opponents of West Germany's foreign policies were convinced, especially in the formative years of the republic, that the outcome of foreign policy issues would determine what kind of society would ultimately prevail in Germany. Their confluence often held foreign and domestic policies in anguished tension: disagreements over the Federal Republic's external relations were at the same time disputes over what constituted a desirable internal political order. Kurt Schumacher, the postwar leader of the German opposition, the Social Democratic Party, noted that "the contest over foreign policy is at the same time the contest over internal policy and the social content of the political order . . . [because] foreign policy sets the limits to the possibilities of our economic and social policy."[10] Chancellor Konrad Adenauer and his supporters similarly expected that the results of foreign policy would help prepare the ground for the political and social values they hoped to nurture in West Germany.[11]

Rather then being another demonstration of the *Primat der Aussen-politik*, which assumed the possibility of drawing clear distinctions between foreign and domestic policies, this was an example of their inextricable meshing.[12] Yet another example of this meshing, which affected the politics of most West European states in the postwar period, was provided by the emerging institutions of West European integration: they promulgated policies that were in their reach and effect simultaneously domestic and foreign and that broke through the barrier of sovereign prerogatives with which the nation-state had traditionally surrounded itself. This was especially important for the Germans, because the aspirations reflected in the idea of an integrated Western Europe allowed them to define and advance their political, economic, and even moral rehabilitation in terms of Europe rather than a discredited German national interest. The integrative institutions of Western Europe were an indispensable bond between the Federal Republic and the West, and they laid the foundations for German political and economic reconstruction in the postwar era. Second only to the transatlantic security compact, German membership in the European Community shaped the direction of German foreign policies and the content of the Federal Republic's domestic political and economic order. America and Europe became the dual pillars that sustained, energized—and inhibited—the course of postwar German diplomacy.

The confluence of domestic and foreign policies, and the Atlantic and West European context in which this confluence was embedded, had a decisive impact on the course of West Germany's political and socioeconomic reconstruction, leaving an indelible imprint on the political institutions and economic structures of the Federal Republic and the code of conduct that sustained them. Ultimately, foreign policy outcomes contributed to the domestic political stability of the Federal Republic even as they occasioned contentious and often abrasive disagreements between the government and opposition.

Considerations of synchronic and diachronic time and of external and internal political space stem from the need to gather and compress into a sequential narrative the unruly and crowded universe of historical events that shaped West Germany's foreign policy. Yet these events can be connected in a variety of combinations, each yielding a different meaning in response to a different analytical query, each serving its own historiographic purpose. How then is the narrator to deal with such tensions of form, knowing that they imply prejudgments about historical causation, that each mode of assemblage informs and deceives in its own fashion, that categorization is theory in disguise?

I have sought to have it both ways. In the first segment of the book I present by way of an introduction an overview of the relationships among the Federal Republic's major foreign policy aims during the past four decades, tracing their complementarities and contradictions across three time frames (of about a decade each) and stopping short of current events. This is an interpretive essay, undisturbed by notes and not slowed by the qualifications of nuance that the historical record puts in our way. Its broad sweep is intended to demonstrate the interrelatedness of German foreign policy goals and their remarkable continuity over the decades. It can be read either as an introduction or as a conclusion.

The ensuing chapters consider in more detail the issues that are dealt with in their conjoined relationships in the introduction. Issues of security and arms control (part I), of the Federal Republic's Eastern policies (part II), and of the German political economy and its domestic political repercussions (part III) are treated on their own analytical terms, developed chronologically and then connected with the contemporary configurations of the European and transatlantic political order, bringing the reader within hailing distance of current events. In these parts I do not shy away from a technical discussion of the complexities of military-strategic, economic, and political-legal issues whenever this seems necessary for a fuller understanding of German policies. Political themes reign supreme, however, and I try to protect them from being overwhelmed by intricate technicalities. In part IV, I turn to the confluence of German foreign and domestic policies, which is the essence of the Federal Republic's political experience.

The arrangement of these parts may be likened to that of sliding panels: the parts are interchangeable and can be read in different sequences. This is more than an intellectually playful suggestion or an analytical foible. Rather, I point to this option (unlikely as it may be that a reader will exercise it) to emphasize that a successive narrative mode cuts apart and therefore distorts historical situations that were whole and real. Reading the parts of this book in different sequences offers different slants on interconnected issues, suggests somewhat different causal connections, and rearranges the inevitable distortions that attend historical discourse.*

---

*The narrative content can of course compensate for these distortions, but they are ineradicable in the narrative form. The reader who follows the parts of the book along the course in which they are presented—security issues first, the division of Germany second, Germany's political economy third, the domestic politics of foreign policy last—is quickly confronted with the sharp conflict between the Federal Republic's security policies in the West and its reunification policies in the East (parts I and II), and will be guided to a smooth transition between the closely connected subjects of economics and the domestic context of foreign policy (parts III and IV). Alternatively, reading part III (economics) before part II (Eastern policies) provides an immediate and strong sense of the combined weight of Germany's Western policies, which obtained their political density from the close connection between security and economics. In that case, however, there would be a somewhat jarring transition from the considerations of Germany's Eastern policies (part II) to the discussion of the domestic context of German foreign policy (part IV). The other sequential alternatives, which I need not spell out, similarly would provide a somewhat different perspective on historical connections.

The largest reason for pointing to the relative analytical self-sufficiency of the various parts of the book (though we recognize their interrelatedness) is to highlight their connections with the major layers of the modern state system—the nuclear, military-strategic, the territorial-geopolitical, and the economic-interdependent—that have had such a profound impact on Germany's security, its place in the European political order, and its political economy. Each of these layers (and each part of this book) opens up different perspectives on past events and on the future possibilities of German foreign policy; each has in its own way reshaped the nature of German foreign policy goals, providing alternative settings for Germany's diplomatic exertions and confronting the Germans and their allies with dilemmas that may yet escape solution. Together they suggest the multidimensionality of the postwar state system, and the conflicting as well as complementary pulls it has exerted on German diplomacy.

To help sustain also the connections among themselves, the various parts of the book refer whenever necessary to one another, each touching on themes at the core of its adjacent parts. Economics surfaces in the discussion of security issues and Eastern policies (and vice versa); considerations of détente appear in the treatment of both arms control and Ostpolitik; the Federal Republic's integration into the West emerges as a major theme, seen from different perspectives, in all parts of the book. The book contains a variety of internal links and short recapitulations— variations on themes that indicate the multiple connections among issues, which a sequential order of narrative conveys so inadequately. I have let them speak clearly and insistently, and they are brought together in the Overview and the Epilogue. As much as possible, I have aimed to achieve a suitable internal proportion among the various parts and topics of the book. Each would of course warrant volumes of its own, an even more nuanced historical treatment, an even more extensive presentation of source materials. Inevitably, I have been forced to compromise.

In the sequence of its chapters, the book's geographic and analytical center of gravity first moves eastward: from the transatlantic security relationship to the Federal Republic's dealings with the East. As the chapters proceed on their eastward course and then return to the political economy and domestic setting of German foreign policy, their constant companion is the weighty presence of the United States. The political order of Europe, and the Federal Republic's development within it, have been shaped in fundamental ways by the imperial power across the Atlantic, so distant in space yet over the decades so close in its impact.

The closeness of the German-American connection is also embodied in the narrator of these events, and I shall conclude these prefatory remarks with a personal observation. In 1969, on accepting Germany's Inter Nationes prize, Hajo Holborn said: "One of the finest experiences in my career was that I could always act in the fullest identity with both my American responsibilities and my German past."[13] But times have changed, and this enviable sense of identity can no longer be as full for those who view the state of German-American relations with growing concern. Today, those of us who combine American responsibilities with a German past face a more anguished task: explaining to both sides what has gone wrong, hoping that what remains right will survive and grow, applying a method of historical analysis that blends, in Walt Whitman's metaphor, tenderness with remorseless firmness, as of some surgeon operating on a beloved patient.

This is an ambivalent and unhappy responsibility. The chronicler of past and current strife and herald of future discord brings unwelcome tidings to both courts. It is of no consolation that they are even more unwelcome to himself. The only full identity we are permitted today must lie in the determination to combine the pessimism of the intellect with the optimism of the will.

Research for this book was supported by the Volkswagenstiftung; Christoph Hanterman and Mary M. McKenzie, untiring and uncomplaining, have helped to bring it to conclusion.

Introduction and Overview
Restraints and Opportunities
in the Postwar Decades

> *Between the ages of twenty and forty we are engaged in the process of*
> *discovering who we are, which involves learning the difference between*
> *accidental limitations which it is our duty to outgrow and the necessary*
> *limitations of our nature beyond which we cannot trespass with impunity.*
> *Few of us can learn this without making mistakes, without trying to be-*
> *come a little more than we are permitted to be.*
>
> —W. H. AUDEN

Over the decades the Germans have learned, at times reluctantly, that politics is the art of the necessary as well as the art of the possible. At forty the Federal Republic has reached political maturity, and the limits placed on its foreign policy may appear less confining than in the beginning. But they were of an order in the 1980s perhaps different from that of the 1950s. In its early years the Federal Republic, weak and under the tutelage of the Western allies, was incompetent both in law and in power to conduct its own foreign policy. When the postwar European order was still in flux and not yet hardened by the full inclusion of the two Germanies in their respective alliances, there may have existed genuine alternatives that were foreclosed to the Federal Republic because of external and internal constraints.

In its later years, after the restoration of sovereignty in 1955, the Federal Republic achieved an increase of influence and legitimacy that elevated it to the status of a middle power, centrally involved in the Atlantic alliance and the European political order and capable of ex-

1

ercising political choice. But by then there were no longer genuine alternatives. The dynamics of historical developments had created political and economic circumstances both inside and outside the Federal Republic that appeared, at least for the foreseeable future, to be as confining as the legal and political restrictions that had been placed on the Federal Republic at the time of its establishment. For the Germans, it was not so much a narrowing of choices—they had few—as a deepening of the consequences of choices made by others.

In the 1980s the range of maneuver available to the Germans remained limited, their targets of design needed to be reduced to targets of opportunity, their foreign policy options more often than not were determined by circumstance rather than choice. The Federal Republic's foreign policy retained a somewhat tentative, irresolute, and reactive quality, often guided more by a sense of what not to do than by a clear view of what to do.

There can be no question that in the beginning of the Federal Republic necessity overwhelmed choice. The German government and the German people were faced with predicaments and dilemmas that seemed beyond solution or even attenuation. The defeat of Nazi Germany, the years of political impotence and economic deprivation during the postwar occupation, and the Cold War not only raised West Germany's foreign policy issues but also apparently mapped or foreclosed the paths toward their resolution. The Federal Republic owes its very existence to the disagreements between East and West (and within the West) that prevented the four occupying powers from jointly administering Germany after the Second World War and that made control of Germany the central issue of the Cold War. Even in defeat Germany remained the epicenter of European politics. The "German problem" was cause as well as effect in the origins of the Cold War, and the creation of the two German states in 1949 seems in retrospect a logical if not necessarily inevitable conclusion to the contest among the victors over the nature of the postwar European order.

Throughout the history of the Federal Republic its foreign policy aims have remained remarkably constant: security, reunification, and political rehabilitation and economic reconstruction in the context of Western Europe and the Atlantic alliance. Even though they have been modified (especially the goal of reunification) in the light of failures and successes and in response to changes in international and domestic politics, the major foreign policy preoccupations of West Germany are characterized by persistence and continuity.

This continuity is in large measure a consequence of the durability of the postwar European order. For although the intense, ideologically inflamed political contest of the Cold War abated in the decades of coexistence and détente, the central features of the East-West conflict in

Europe have proven remarkably constant: the political and economic division of the European continent and of Germany; the mostly unrelieved confrontation of the two military alliances at the border between the two German states; and the regional manifestations in Europe of the continuing global rivalry between the United States and the Soviet Union. Continuity as well as change have characterized the postwar history of Europe.

The remarkable endurance of the postwar European state system took root amid fundamental changes in the global configuration of power. Whereas the broader global world order reflected deep transformations— the decline of American economic hegemony and nuclear-strategic preponderance, the rise of Japan and other major trading states on the rim of the Pacific, the new triangulation of diplomacy among America, China, and the Soviet Union, the uneven and tentative development of Third World countries—it seemed as if Europe, although itself undergoing change, nonetheless remained an island of stability amid the turbulent shifts of the larger international state system.

We are still too close to these developments to speak of them with assurance. Their sources are manifold and complex, their consequences diffuse and not easily traced. The shifting weights in the international balance of power remain ill-defined and difficult to calibrate, and we cannot yet confidently appraise how the evolution of a new international order will affect the fortunes of the Federal Republic, Western Europe, and the United States. But we do sense that these developments have left a profound imprint on the foreign policies of all industrialized states, and that they have deeply transformed the relations between the Federal Republic and its European neighbors and transatlantic partner.

As the political, strategic, and economic configurations of power changed over the decades, so did the mix of restraints and opportunities confronting German foreign policies. Necessities became coupled with possibilities. In retrospect, three distinct phases emerge, during which the complementarities and contradictions among German foreign policy goals were shaped in significantly different ways.

In the first phase, the formative years from 1949 to the late 1950s, the Cold War contest between the two power blocs, the historical burdens of the past, and the Federal Republic's lack of sovereignty presented it with the most severe restraints and led to fundamental contradictions between West German foreign policy goals in the West and the East. Within the confines of the West, the Germans achieved security, sovereignty, prosperity, and a stable democratic political order. But their success in the West further removed them from the East and sealed the partition of their country and people.

In the second phase, from the late fifties to the late sixties, an additional set of contradictions was placed on German policy, leading to a fragmentation of its previously coherent Western policy. As the Soviet Union reached for nuclear parity with the United States and sought to legitimize rather than alter the European status quo, Gaullist France was determined to gain a global role for a Europe led by the French, even at the expense of Atlantic unity. This compelled Bonn to make choices between its central security interests in the Atlantic alliance (which it saw no longer fully accommodated in the transatlantic security compact) and its central economic interests and political aspirations in Western Europe (which it saw no longer fully accommodated in the European Community). These choices carried with them important ramifications for Bonn's Eastern policy as well.

In the third phase, the 1970s and 1980s, the restraints, contradictions, and opportunities affecting German foreign policy goals were again rearranged for several reasons. First, the elements of international power and its overall configurations changed considerably, diminishing the relative power of the United States and making for a much more complicated global and European political environment, which provided less stark alternatives and thus demanded less clear-cut choices from German foreign policy makers. Second, Chancellor Willy Brandt's Ostpolitik, although its dynamics were largely spent by the mid-seventies, had obtained a more active role for German diplomacy. It was the centerpiece of efforts at East-West détente, and it had become an integral part of the security policy of NATO and Germany because it meshed the dual principles of NATO's Harmel Report of 1967: deterrence coupled with détente, military preparations coupled with political negotiations. Third, although the emerging primacy of economic and monetary matters and the ramifications of global economic interdependence increased the Federal Republic's political leverage, they further complicated German-American relations in the 1970s and 1980s—relations that were already burdened by conflicting assessments of the meaning of détente, the infirmities and ambiguities of Washington's security and arms control policies, and mutual recriminations over diplomatic style as well as political substance.

The Formative Phase: The First Decade

In the first phase of West German foreign policy, from 1949 to the late 1950s, the restraints and opportunities affecting West German foreign policy goals were the most visible. The period is characterized by a sharp contrast between the failure of Bonn's reunification policy and the remarkable success that the Federal Republic achieved in the areas of security and political and economic recovery. This contrast developed from the impossibility of pursuing both goals simultaneously in a Cold War setting in which the cross-purposes of East and West were sharply polarized. The very success of Bonn's pro-Western security and recovery policy, through which the Federal Republic became the bulwark of Washington's containment policy in Europe, solidified the Cold War alliances in Central Europe and further deepened the division of Germany.

Turning toward the West

It is doubtful whether the Federal Republic, faced with a hostile Eastern bloc and restrained by political and contractual commitments to the Western alliance, had a genuine choice of incompatible alternatives.

In its early years the Federal Republic had neither the power nor the legitimacy to conduct its own foreign policy. The Second World War had destroyed the power base of German foreign policy, and Hitler's Third Reich had destroyed the legal, moral, and psychological foundations of German foreign policy. When the Federal Republic was created in 1949, it was not a sovereign state: this did not come about until 1955, when the Federal Republic joined NATO, and even then it was hedged with significant restrictions. The Allied High Commission, which succeeded the military governors of the occupation regime, for all practical purposes controlled the Federal Republic's political and economic relations with other countries and also had the power to regulate or at least supervise domestic political and economic developments. The German government had only limited and provisional authority over domestic and foreign policy. The first, indispensable foreign policy aim of the Federal Republic was therefore to obtain its sovereignty and with it a legal and political base for German diplomacy.

Although the Western powers were ready to make political and economic concessions in return for West Germany's willingness to rearm, these concessions did not allow Bonn to pursue an independent or flexible foreign policy. A central feature of Allied and especially American policies toward the Federal Republic in the postwar era was the intention, only superficially a paradox, to make the West Germans free and at the same time not free: free with respect to the personal liberties and constitutional safeguards that are the essence of a democratic political order, but not free to formulate and implement an independent foreign policy.

The Western allies had the power and authority to implement both intentions. Between 1949 and 1955, when the United States and the Soviet Union struggled over what may still have been a malleable European political order, the foreign policies of the Federal Republic were constrained by the legal and political controls that had been placed over it, and its domestic development was closely supervised. During these years, the gradual incorporation of the two German states in their respective Cold War alliances hardened the division of Germany and Europe, clearly drew the boundaries of the American and Soviet spheres of influence, and became the central feature of the postwar political, economic, and military-strategic European order.

The restraint of the Federal Republic through international organizations and treaties was at the core of Washington's postwar European policy of double containment: the containment of the Soviet Union at arm's length, and of West Germany with an embrace. Every major event in the postwar history of Europe follows from this: the rearmament and economic reconstruction of the Federal Republic within the restraints of international organizations, the development of NATO from a loosely organized mutual assistance pact into an integrated military alliance, American support for West European integration, and the solidification of the division of Germany and Europe. So long as the two components of America's double containment were mutually reinforcing, America's European diplomacy was on a sure footing. In later years, when tensions and contradictions developed between the two components, German-American relations became increasingly strained.

From the perspective of the German government, and especially of Chancellor Konrad Adenauer, "diluting" gains of sovereignty by joining integrative organizations was intrinsically unobjectionable. His sense of priorities inclined him in the same direction. Adenauer's version of the goal of political recovery—the irrevocable integration of the Federal Republic in a tightly knit Western European community—could be achieved even with the curtailing of Germany's freedom of action. In fact, this was probably the only way it could be guaranteed. Integration and equality became and remained the central precepts of the Federal Republic's Western policies. The creation of integrative West European and Atlantic institutions thus had a decisive influence on the speedy political recovery of West Germany. They provided mechanisms for controlling Germany and made the restoration of sovereignty less risky for the Western powers. In turn, the mounting pressures to grant West Germany political and economic concessions provided a powerful impetus for establishing integrative organizations that could supervise the Federal Republic.

Adenauer's Europe-oriented policy, implemented by a close alignment with the West and the decision to rearm, was not only compatible with the goal of political recovery but a prerequisite to it. The quest for security and the aim of political recovery, with the meaning attached to recovery by Adenauer, were mutually reinforcing.

The cutting characterization of Adenauer as "the chancellor of the Allies" by the Social Democratic opposition was therefore impertinent (in both senses of the word), for what was involved was not a nefarious plot or a collusion between the German and Allied governments at the expense of German interests, but rather Adenauer's assent to a course of Western diplomatic action that he favored himself. German compliance stemmed not from a complicity of persons but from a concordance of attitudes. For Adenauer, choice coincided with necessity. The German chancellor, deeply skeptical about the political maturity and circumspection of his compatriots, was determined to tie them to the West and thus prevent his successors from following a policy of neutrality between East and West. America's policy of double containment was complemented by German self-containment.

Moreover, the pro-Western course the German government charted could count on the political assent and electoral support of the Federal Republic's citizens, in large part because Adenauer's policies promised rapid progress toward economic reconstruction and political rehabilitation. Although rearmament was not popular and was vehemently opposed by the Social Democrats, it was widely (and correctly) perceived as the cornerstone of Adenauer's Western policy that enabled the Federal Republic to gain immediate economic and political benefits.

Indeed, economic and political recovery were themselves highly complementary. A weak West German economy would have been a liability for the Western alliance, undermining political stability and opening up opportunities for Soviet maneuvers. Because of the integrative features of the Western alliance, the faltering economy of one partner in the alliance would have weakened all, with negative consequences also for military preparedness. The tensions of the Cold War created an atmosphere in the West that was generally in sympathy with German aspirations to restore a viable economy.

Economic recovery was skillfully complemented and underpinned by Bonn's policy on political recovery, and by extension its policy on security and rearmament, on which the whole construct rested. In such mixed political and economic ventures as the European Coal and Steel Community and later the European Economic Community (EEC), political and economic gains went hand in hand and were achieved through a coordinated strategy that advanced German demands in the name of European and Atlantic unity rather than of a discredited German nationalism.

The German government's determination to liberalize domestic and international trade was in the long run advantageous politically as well as economically, for it demonstrated and reinforced Bonn's commitment to political internationalism. By forgoing traditional protectionism Bonn rejected both economic and political nationalism—a policy strongly supported in Washington. As a consequence, there existed during the 1950s, in the formative stage of the Federal Republic's development, a striking correspondence between the principles of Germany's domestic economic order and the principles of the international economic order guided by the United States and supplemented by the institutions of West European integration. The German penchant for monetary stability, budgetary discipline, and trade liberalization was reciprocated in the United

States; the Bretton Woods monetary regime came to full implementation in the late 1950s with the free convertibility of currencies, introducing a period of equilibrium between past dollar shortages and future dollar gluts; and the establishment of West European integrative institutions promised to advance the Federal Republic's economic as well as political aims in Europe. In addition, the personality traits of German and American leaders, and their attitudes on how to contain the Soviet Union, were more congenial than at any time afterward.

Facing the East

Whereas Bonn's foreign policy aims in the West were characterized by diplomatic consistency, political complementarity, and above all a supreme sense of the possible (as was clearly reflected in the interlocking elements of the Paris Agreements of 1954), Bonn's goal of unifying Germany was of an entirely different order. Although the sharp dualism of the postwar European political order helped advance the Western policies of the Federal Republic, it was the very success of these policies that destroyed any remaining chances that the division of Germany could be eased or overcome. The logic of this political reality was so incontrovertible that it raised the question of whether the German chancellor was genuinely interested in Germany's unification, leading to abrasive conflicts between the German government and the Social Democrats, who followed a drastically different order of priorities and viewed unification as the precondition for establishing the domestic order they favored for Germany.

Chancellor Adenauer's long-range unification policy was based on two central assumptions: first, that Washington and Moscow held the key to the German question, and that the existing balance of power between East and West meant that unification could be achieved only with the consent of both Cold War camps; second, that with the passage of time the balance of power between the two Cold War blocs would shift in favor of the West, thus allowing negotiations "on the basis of strength," which would induce the Soviet Union to settle the German question on terms acceptable to the West. The first of these assumptions was correct, the second, false.

Adenauer realized that the Western powers viewed the prospect of a unified Germany with apprehension, a realization which underlay the first assumption of his reunification policy and which required that Bonn enlarge its political leverage within the Western alliance: to gain for reunification the support of the Western powers, especially the United States; to ensure that the West would not trade off the German issue in an overall settlement of the Cold War; and to solidify politically the legal and moral commitment of the Western powers (incorporated in the Paris

Agreements) to support reunification and acknowledge Bonn as the only legitimate spokesman for all of Germany. Yet the only way that Bonn could increase its leverage within the Western alliance was by becoming an indispensable partner in it, a quest that necessarily took the form of seeking legal and political equality and the restoration of sovereignty. This partnership was however directed against the Soviet Union and thus ill suited for inducing Moscow to settle the German question on terms acceptable to the West.

As a consequence, Adenauer's reunification policy toward Moscow was much more passive and negative than his policy toward Washington—it became merely a formalistic appendage to his Western policy. It was in essence a policy of denial, couched in legal terms, through which Bonn refused to recognize the German Democratic Republic and the loss of German territories in the East—in short, the existing state of affairs in Central and Eastern Europe. Bonn's diplomacy in the East was leached of vitality and imagination and encrusted by legalisms, and it inevitably appeared rigid, especially in contrast with the political acumen, shrewdness, and tenacity displayed by Adenauer in his Western diplomacy.

But aside from Adenauer's own determination to tie Germany, united or not, to the institutions and values of the West, the Western powers most likely would have obstructed German overtures to the Soviet Union at the height of the Cold War—a point that is almost always ignored by those who speak of the "missed opportunities" of the early 1950s. Further, a more dynamic Eastern policy would have jeopardized the entire treaty structure that was to restore sovereignty to the Federal Republic. This would have undermined the Federal Republic's political power base in the West, from which Adenauer expected to deal with the Soviet Union at some future date, calling into question the central premises of his reunification policy.

At crucial junctures in the shaping of Bonn's rearmament policy, Moscow held out the prospect of unification if West Germany would abstain from forming military, economic, and political ties with the Western powers. But the Soviet Union demanded in effect that the West accept a power vacuum in the heart of Europe (as in the notes of March 1952 and the disengagement proposals of the mid- and late 1950s), at a time when clearly drawn spheres of influence seemed most promising for Washington's policy of double containment. The implementation of forward containment through alliances led by America was precisely what the United States sought to establish on all Cold War fronts with a series of interlocking security treaties. The United States saw no advantages in replacing a tolerable and stable status quo in Europe with the uncertainties and ambiguities that would have followed if Moscow's proposals had been implemented. The West and Adenauer had to weigh the uncertain and risky prospect of a neutralized Germany against the certainty of increasing Western power at a crucial stage in the Cold War.

By 1955, when the Federal Republic joined NATO and the German Democratic Republic became a member of the Warsaw Pact, the Western orientation of Bonn's policy had proven remarkably successful. Germany had achieved an astonishing economic revival, Bonn's political leverage within the Western alliance had increased enormously since 1949, and the Western powers were legally committed to support the cause of German reunification. But the very success of this policy, through which the Federal Republic became the European centerpiece of Washington's global containment policy, had further accentuated the Cold War division of Europe and sealed the partition of Germany. Unless circumstances changed, Bonn could not hope to improve the chances for reunification by pursuing a policy of integration with the West.

Chancellor Adenauer was fully aware of this. His long-range calculations (at least as he expressed them in public) anticipated different political circumstances, when the balance of power would have shifted in favor of the West—the second central assumption of his reunification strategy.

The single most important development that scotched these expectations (leaving aside the question of the Allies' sincerity in claiming to support German unification) was the Soviet Union's acquisition of a nuclear capability, which made increasingly remote the possibility of exerting diplomatic pressure on the Soviet Union. The consolidation of Nikita Khrushchev's position in the Kremlin, the improvement of the Soviet Union's military-strategic position, and the tendency of the German question to help contain centrifugal forces in Eastern Europe were soon reflected in Moscow's policy toward Germany.

The opposite of Adenauer's premise for a policy of strength in fact occurred. Instead of becoming more conciliatory with the passage of time on the German question, the Soviet Union's attitudes stiffened. After failing to prevent the Federal Republic's membership in NATO, the Soviet Union shifted to a "two Germanies" policy, symbolized in the Kremlin's readiness to establish diplomatic relations with Bonn. By 1955 the Soviet Union had come to accept the status quo in Central Europe, and from then on a major aim of Soviet diplomacy was to solidify the existing state of affairs politically and contractually—a process that culminated two decades later in Bonn's Eastern treaties and the Helsinki Accords of the Conference on Security and Cooperation in Europe (CSCE).

This shift in Moscow's policy toward Germany had important consequences for the Western base of Bonn's reunification policy—a base that Adenauer saw eroding as the Western powers sought to move away from Cold War confrontations toward competitive coexistence. As the Soviet

Union began to support the territorial status quo in Europe rather than threaten it, fear of direct Soviet military aggression waned in the West, with a corresponding readiness to seek a political accommodation with the Soviet Union and turn to arms control measures and European security arrangements as an actual as well as a symbolic step toward relaxing tensions between East and West.

This placed Bonn in an awkward political and psychological position. After 1955 Bonn's major efforts at unification necessarily became limited to denying the Soviet Union and East Germany a de jure recognition of the existing state of affairs (there was little hope of bringing about unification itself), and Bonn expected its allies to support this policy of denial diplomatically. On the verbal level this support was generally forthcoming, especially from the United States. But Adenauer remained suspicious. He perceived a readiness in the West to reach a modus vivendi with the Soviet Union on the basis of the status quo in Europe and at the expense of what he perceived as vital German interests; and by the late 1950s Bonn's reunification policy, weak in substance and brittle in its formalism, had not succeeded in either its Eastern or its Western dimension.

To put it in even starker terms, by 1955 Washington's policy of double containment had been fully implemented. The Soviet Union had become contained within the political and geographical limits of influence it had gained at the end of the Second World War, and the Federal Republic had become an integral part of the Western alliance. The same was true for the German Democratic Republic in its own alliance. Given the democratic principles that prevailed in the Federal Republic and the opportunities they afforded the West Germans to express their political preferences in free elections, the incorporation of the Federal Republic into the Western alliance took place in political and moral circumstances fundamentally different from those that attached the German Democratic Republic to the Eastern bloc of socialist countries. But in terms of Realpolitik, the consequences of integrating the two German states in their respective Cold War alliances were similar and mutually reinforcing. The division of Germany and hence of Europe became a major stabilizing element in the global contest between the United States and the Soviet Union, which neither side was ready to question fundamentally lest the regional and global balances of power be upset.

Transitions and Incongruities: The Second Decade

The central dilemma in the second stage of the Federal Republic's foreign policy development (the decade from the late 1950s to the late 1960s) was the necessity of making difficult choices between Washington and Paris—choosing between Bonn's security interests and its desire to construct a viable European community, navigating between John F. Kennedy's transatlantic Grand Design and Charles de Gaulle's design for a "Europe from the Atlantic to the Urals."

The 1960s saw the first signs of the unraveling of the striking complementarities that existed in the 1950s between the goals of security and of political and economic recovery—complementarities that rested on Bonn's willingness to rearm and that became the foundation of the Federal Republic's emplacement in the Western alliance. Tensions developed between Bonn's security policy, oriented toward Washington, and its Europe policy, oriented toward Paris; the connections between German security policy and economic policy, although as close as in the first decade, were becoming politically troublesome; the economic and monetary controversies within the Atlantic alliance resulted in awkward and costly diplomatic maneuvering; and the correspondence between American and German monetary policies began to dwindle. These tensions affected not only Bonn's Western policy but also its Eastern policy. Washington and Paris pursued divergent policies toward the Soviet Union and Eastern Europe, and Bonn found it difficult to adjust its rigid Eastern policy to the more accommodating stance of the Western powers. Above all, neither Washington nor Paris pursued foreign policy programs congruent with German interests, forcing Bonn to choose between alternatives that were intrinsically flawed.

Choosing between Washington and Paris

To be sure, the disagreements between Washington and Paris did not begin with General de Gaulle's return to power in 1958; they had posed serious problems for Adenauer from the very beginning. Whereas Washington wanted to bring the Federal Republic into the Western military alliance and an integrated Western Europe as quickly as possible, France was reluctant and sought to curtail West German influence in these international bodies. At the same time, Adenauer's long-range political goals—a European union and reconciliation with France—required France's sympathetic cooperation.

Although this situation was at times awkward for Bonn, it was still manageable so long as the Western alliance was fairly cohesive, the United States could threaten France with "agonizing reappraisals" of American diplomacy, and Bonn could advance its interest in the name of an integrated Western alliance. But these problems of the early years foreshadowed the much more serious dilemma that the German government had to face later, after de Gaulle returned to power, when taking sides with either the United States or France sharpened the developing tensions within the Atlantic alliance.

For Bonn taking sides was frustrating, because neither the American nor the French design for Europe fully accommodated German interests.

Opting for Washington meant supporting a strategic posture that the German government no longer viewed as fully serving German security interests; and opting for Paris meant supporting a European order that fell far short of Bonn's preferences. Moreover, neither Washington nor Paris pursued Eastern policies that satisfied Bonn and that could have allayed Bonn's suspicions that the German viewpoint was insufficiently represented by its major allies.

Although the security of the Federal Republic in the 1960s depended as inextricably on the United States as it had in the 1950s, it was subject to increasing strains. During the 1960s, as American nuclear superiority began to diminish with the development of Soviet nuclear strategic capabilities, an intense doctrinal debate took place within NATO that revolved essentially around the question of how the credibility of the American nuclear commitment to Western Europe could be sustained now that the United States was gradually becoming vulnerable itself.

This issue (which remains to this day) had special significance for the Federal Republic because of Germany's exposed geographical and political position, and because Bonn depended increasingly on the deterrent capabilities of NATO over which the Germans had no control. Moreover, the Kennedy administration aimed for a more flexible American strategic doctrine, which was designed to multiply Washington's strategic and tactical options and required a buildup in conventional forces on the part of the European NATO allies.

This doctrine of "flexible response," which NATO officially adopted in 1967, required higher German defense expenditures at the same time as it seemed to undermine the credibility of the American willingness to extend its nuclear umbrella over Western Europe. Implementing the new doctrine was more expensive at the same time as it was less reassuring on strategic grounds. Bonn no longer saw its central security interests effectively represented in Washington—a feeling that was strengthened when President Lyndon Johnson canceled the Multilateral Nuclear Force scheme, creating significant political problems for Chancellor Ludwig Erhard—at a time when the economic and political costs of Germany's military buildup were increasing. Although the Federal Republic had no real alternative to its security partnership with the United States, which became the backbone of NATO after the French withdrawal of 1966, it became increasingly clear in the 1960s that the security interests of the United States and the Federal Republic were no longer as congruent as they had appeared to be in the 1950s.

But opting for Paris (which was not seriously considered on security issues) meant opting for a French foreign policy agenda that conflicted with German purposes on a number of centrally important questions, including the future shape of the European order. Konrad Adenauer and Charles de Gaulle had quickly established a remarkable rapport, but even though the general was prepared to implement the economic provisions of a European economic community he was vehemently opposed to the political aspirations embodied in its founding document, the Treaty of Rome. Both Adenauer and de Gaulle preferred a "little Europe" as an integrative structure, but de Gaulle opposed genuine political integration because this would curtail the national independence of France, and he expected Germany to help the French regain their position in world politics by providing economic and political support. De Gaulle wanted the economic benefits of the Common Market without paying a political price, whereas Adenauer was ready to pay an economic price for political benefits. De Gaulle sought a European base for his global political ambitions; Adenauer sought an Atlantic base for his European ambitions.

The conflicts that developed between the Anglo-American powers and France during the late fifties and early sixties immensely complicated Adenauer's aim of integrating the Federal Republic into a cohesive West European community. Although the United States remained the indispensable partner of Germany's security policy, France, the indispensable partner for Germany's European policy, was determined to shut out Anglo-American influence on the Continent after de Gaulle's proposal for French participation in a three-power "directorate" of NATO had been rejected by President Eisenhower. This meant that during the 1960s Germany's security policy no longer meshed with its Europe policy, in contrast to the 1950s, when the complementarity of Bonn's Atlantic and European policies provided the cornerstone of Adenauer's foreign policy program. But the difficult choices between Washington and Paris imposed on Bonn were not choices between policy alternatives that Adenauer favored: Bonn's interests were not fully supported either in Paris or in Washington. Personality clashes further complicated Bonn's diplomacy. Whereas President Kennedy benefited from the avuncular attitude of British Prime Minister Harold Macmillan and admired the histrionic grandeur of de Gaulle's diplomacy, he tended to view Adenauer (and his ambassador in Washington, Wilhelm Grewe) as inflexible remnants of the Cold War who could not be expected to appreciate the sophistication and managerial rationality of the New Frontier.

By this time there were in effect two German foreign policies. The first was Adenauer's, which resulted in the Franco-German Friendship Treaty of 1963 and allowed de Gaulle to blackball Britain's membership in the Common Market, with Germany's implicit acquiescence. The second policy direction was preferred by Economics Minister Ludwig Erhard and Foreign Minister Gerhard Schröder, who advocated a more flexible course and tended to support the Anglo-American position not only on the Common Market and the Atlantic alliance but also on a more imaginative Eastern policy.

When Erhard succeeded Adenauer in fall 1963, the policy differences between France and Germany were leading to a major confrontation, if not a crisis. Almost every item on de Gaulle's agenda opposed German foreign policy at a time when the new chancellor in Bonn was much less sympathetic to French projects than Adenauer had been. The crisis of 1965 over the political future and membership of the Common Market pitted Bonn against Paris (it ultimately strengthened Germany's position in the Community), and Franco-German disagreements over political fundamentals were further aggravated by clashes over economic and monetary specifics. The NATO crisis of 1966, resulting from France's withdrawal from the organization's command structure, not only affected German security interests, but raised the touchy political and legal question of how French troops could remain in Germany (as Bonn hoped they would, for reasons of deterrence) once they were transferred from NATO control to French national control.

Erhard's relations with Washington were troubled as well. The ill-considered proposal of the Multilateral Nuclear Force (MLF), which had no military-strategic value and was designed primarily to give European members of NATO the appearance of nuclear ownership without actually providing it, led to serious tensions between Bonn and Washington when the Johnson administration scrapped it in 1965 to further the overriding American interest in obtaining a nonproliferation treaty with the Soviet Union.

Economic and monetary controversies within the Atlantic alliance also compelled Bonn to make choices it wished to avoid. At issue between the Europeans and Americans were a wide range of questions: the enlargement of the Common Market, the European Community's plan to achieve monetary union, and the overall political, strategic, and economic relations between the United States and Europe.

As American hegemony declined relative to Europe and Japan, America's allies, especially France, felt increasingly restive about American political, economic, and monetary privileges and began to push for an alteration of the framework within which these political and economic arrangements had been made (such as the Bretton Woods international monetary regime). Washington's displeasure with the practices of the EEC was also manifold and focused largely on three related areas: the Community's preferential trade agreements with an increasing number of countries, which tended to violate the most-favored-nation principle; its protectionist agricultural policy; and the unloading of the Community's large agricultural surpluses in markets traditionally favorable to the United States, especially in the Far East and North Africa. The Europeans felt that the central economic issue between them and the United States was money rather than trade, especially because the United States enjoyed a consistently favorable balance of trade with the Community. In the European view, the United States was acting irresponsibly and self-

ishly in not taking steps to remedy its chronic balance-of-payments problems and in shifting a major part of the resulting burden of adjustment
onto its European partners. As the American balance of payments deteriorated in the postwar decades, the Bretton Woods monetary system
became highly inequitable, because American deficits allowed transfers
of foreign resources to the United States, which many Europeans resented because they felt compelled to finance American foreign military
operations and control of European industrial resources.

All this put the Germans in an awkward position. France insisted on
Germany's support for the Community's Common Agricultural Policy
(CAP) because it was the keystone of the economic compact Paris and
Bonn had made upon entering the Community framework, which provided that France would accept an open-market arrangement for German
industrial goods in return for agricultural price supports. The United
States insisted on Germany's monetary support (including military offset
payments, military purchases from the United States, and other bur-
densharing arrangements within NATO) to alleviate the tensions that had
developed among the Bretton Woods system's three central principles:
the dollar-gold parity, fixed exchange rates, and free convertibility of
currencies. The myth that Bretton Woods still worked could be maintained only because the German Bundesbank committed itself not to
convert dollars to gold and refrained from otherwise shaking the regime,
as the French did with great relish. What had developed was a relationship of mutual dependency. The United States supplied the Germans
with security benefits (which Washington considered a major source of
its balance-of-payments problem), and the Germans reciprocated with
direct and indirect monetary support until the formal offset arrangements were terminated in the mid-1970s.

Small Steps toward the East

The central dilemma of the Federal Republic's Eastern policy in the
1960s was Bonn's inability to reconcile the political and legal aspects of its
reunification policy. The Germans realized that international developments (in Western as well as Eastern Europe, Washington as well as
Moscow) called for a revision of Bonn's sterile Eastern policy, but the
legalistic inhibitions that had been placed on this policy in the 1950s stood
in the way of responding adequately to the political imperatives of the
1960s—an impediment that also explains why Bonn's Eastern policy
could not be attuned to that of its major allies.

From the German perspective, American diplomacy was too conservative and French diplomacy too innovative. Washington's European
policy in the 1960s was too conservative in that it seemed to favor a
legitimization of the European status quo. American policy was based on
the assumption that the shared dangers and responsibilities of the two

nuclear superpowers required stabilizing the nuclear military balance and that the stability of the European order required continuing the Soviet as well as American spheres of influence on the Continent. For Washington, the gradual loosening of the Warsaw Pact (a process that was arrested in August 1968) was a cause less for exultation than for concern. The fragmentation of the Soviet empire in Eastern Europe might at worst lead to a major international crisis and at best unravel the relatively stable and tolerable postwar European order: in short, it would lead to the dissolution of Washington's policy of double containment. The Kennedy administration had revamped NATO strategy despite German misgivings, showed little resolve during the Berlin crisis of 1961, and apparently aimed at an accommodation with the Soviet Union in Europe even at the expense of German interests. The policies of the Johnson administration were hardly more reassuring. The president himself seemed uncomfortable with European matters and tended to ignore them, and he became increasingly preoccupied with Vietnam and with fashioning an arms control arrangement with the Soviet Union, all of which made Washington a politically and psychologically distant ally for the Federal Republic. The possibility that the United States would assent to legitimizing the division of Europe and Germany—the central foreign policy aim of the Soviet Union in the 1960s—was a nightmare for both Adenauer and Erhard and a continuing source of concern during the years of the "Grand Coalition" government of Kurt Georg Kiesinger and Willy Brandt, although the coalition itself represented conflicting views on the German question.

Where American policy was too conservative for Bonn because of its implicit readiness to solidify the European status quo, French policy was too innovative and dynamic because it aimed at bottom at dissolving the American and Soviet spheres of influence in Europe. Deeply suspicious of American motives, Adenauer felt obliged to turn to Paris for support of Bonn's rigid Eastern policy, although de Gaulle had recognized the Oder-Neisse frontier in 1959 (a prerequisite for his overtures toward Eastern Europe), and although the chancellor must have known that de Gaulle could support a solution of the German question only if it fell short of actual reunification.

To be sure, de Gaulle wanted the German issue defused because he considered it the major cause (and justification) of the superpowers' continued presence in Europe, a cause that would evaporate with a solution of the German question, leading to the dissolution of the two Cold War military alliances and speeding American and Soviet withdrawal from Europe. De Gaulle's "Europe from the Atlantic to the Urals," led by France, would supplant the dual hegemony that the United States and the Soviet Union had imposed on the postwar European order. But de Gaulle, in reaching out toward Eastern Europe and the Soviet Union, went far beyond what the Bonn government thought appropriate; and the fundamental shift of French policy toward the Soviet Union and the implied Franco-Soviet accommodation had a profound impact on Franco-German relations, which were already soured in the area of transatlantic and European politics. De Gaulle's course called into question a long-standing premise of Bonn's reunification policy—that Bonn would as much as possible support France's Atlantic and European policies if France would support Bonn's Eastern policy—and served notice to Bonn that de Gaulle intended to exploit the new international circumstances, at Germany's expense if necessary. Moreover, the loosening of the Western alliance and of the Soviet bloc had increased France's importance in resolving the German question. There was an increasing realization in Bonn, though the German government did not manage to act on it, that reunification could be accomplished only in the context of a larger European settlement and that in this context France was (along with the United States) a crucial partner for Germany's opening to the East.

In short, Washington's policy undermined the political dimensions of Bonn's Eastern policy because it implied the solidification of the existing spheres of influence in Europe and portended their future legitimization, and French policy undermined the legal dimension of Bonn's Eastern policy because, in contrast to Bonn, it approached Eastern European capitals as full diplomatic partners and also conflicted with Bonn's NATO-oriented security policy.

The rigidity and formalism of Bonn's Eastern policy during the 1960s clearly stood in the way of a dynamic approach to the question of German unity. The apparent loosening of the Warsaw Pact, which French policy sought to accelerate and exploit, and the dynamics of the bilateral accommodation between Washington and Moscow, which American policy sought to sustain, made it appear imperative that the Germans themselves take some initiative on an issue the resolution of which was after all of interest primarily to them. But this was difficult to accomplish, for the legal dimensions of Bonn's policy clearly stood in the way of acting on the political recognition that the Federal Republic should develop a more dynamic Eastern policy.

During the last years of Adenauer's administration and throughout Erhard's, Bonn did initiate steps to respond to the political developments in Eastern Europe by moving toward a gradual normalization of relations. But the obstacles to Bonn's "policy of movement" were formidable, no less so because some of them were self-imposed. Bonn's efforts did not move far or fast enough and were constantly limping behind French policy toward the East. Bonn expressed its good intentions toward East European capitals and set up trade missions in Eastern Europe, but it did not revise its opposition to codifying the European status quo or modify its implacable rejection of the East German regime. The cause of German unity became beclouded with withered aspirations, weakened by a view of the past that was at the same time resentful and nostalgic, and devoid of a plausible program for the future.

For the West Germans, even a partial modification of their position appeared risky. Compromising one part would have compromised the whole, and scrapping one of its essential features would have weakened the legal and political foundations of Germany's Eastern policy. As a consequence of Bonn's rigidity, the Federal Republic's Eastern policy took on an increasingly anachronistic quality, standing in the way of fundamental developments in global and regional politics and suffering from erosion in the West as well as the East. Not only had Bonn become the only European power to question the territorial status quo in Europe, opening itself to charges of revanchism from the East, but it invariably felt compelled to reject arms control proposals because of their political and juridical implications for the German question. On both counts— resistance to accepting the status quo and resistance to arms control—the Federal Republic not only complicated its relations with the East but began to lose support in the West. For a fuller understanding of Bonn's Eastern policy in the 1960s it is essential to realize that its legalistic cast was directed as much against the West as against the East. The dispiriting realization that their Eastern policy was failing on political grounds compelled the Germans to safeguard as much as possible the legal codification of the political commitments that Western allies had made on the German question.

In sum, the choices between Washington and Paris that were imposed on the governments of Adenauer, Erhard, and Kiesinger in the 1960s were not really choices between policy alternatives that these governments themselves favored. In contrast to the 1950s, when Bonn could implement only one of two mutually exclusive but inherently desirable alternatives—a viable Westpolitik and a viable Ostpolitik—the alternatives of the 1960s amounted to a choice between an eviscerated European option and an equally tattered Atlantic one, and between American and French policies toward the East that were for different reasons equally objectionable to the German government.

The Federal Republic as a Middle Power in the Seventies and Eighties

In the 1970s German diplomacy was dramatically revitalized. The coalition government of the SPD (Sozialdemokratische Partei Deutschlands) and FDP (Freie Demokratische Partei) under Chancellor Willy Brandt and Foreign Minister and Vice-Chancellor Walter Scheel, which had come into office in fall 1969, was determined to make a more realistic Eastern policy the centerpiece of its foreign policy agenda, and the new leaders

were convinced that a general rapprochement with the East required
Bonn's formal acceptance of the status quo in Europe.

A New Ostpolitik

Dynamic as Brandt's Ostpolitik was in many ways, it was nonetheless
fundamentally a policy of resignation, designed not so much to bring
about changes for a foreseeable future as to leave open possibilities for an
unforeseeable one. Ostpolitik combined continuity with innovation. The
legal positions with which the Bonn government approached the East
had been prepared over the years by previous administrations and
sharpened by use against both Bonn's opponents in the East and its allies
in the West. Unease and dissatisfaction with the stale policies of the 1960s
ranged over the entire German political spectrum. In that sense, and
without meaning to diminish its historic significance, one could say that
the new Ostpolitik was less a product of an imaginative energy than the
result of a readiness to acquiesce in a political and moral necessity.

Even so, Brandt's Ostpolitik pushed German foreign policy in a direction where it obtained its greatest diplomatic density—in the Soviet
Union, in Eastern Europe, and in East Germany. In important respects,
Bonn's Ostpolitik matched a central diplomatic concern of the Soviet
Union that had preoccupied Moscow since the mid-1950s: obtaining
international recognition of the Soviet sphere of influence in Eastern and
Central Europe. As a consequence, the treaty package that ultimately
resulted from Bonn's Ostpolitik was an essential step toward the Conference on Security and Cooperation in Europe that culminated in the
Helsinki Accords of 1975, the capstone of détente. These accords would
have been little more than diplomatic symbols if the preceding treaties
between Bonn and the East had not lent them political substance.

Germany's Ostpolitik was indispensable from the perspective of the
West as well: for the first time since its establishment, a government of
the Federal Republic was willing to join its allies in an Eastern policy that
accepted the existing state of affairs in Europe. Attuning German diplomacy to the Western powers' policies of détente was not an easy matter,
however. There was always the question of whether Ostpolitik was
merely the remnant of former efforts at reunification—the sum of past
subtractions, as it were—or the beginning of an evolutionary process
intended to change the status quo by formally recognizing it. As a result,
German intentions were questioned the more intensely in private the less
they could be questioned openly. Both Bonn and Washington came to
realize that even between allies, confidence is suspicion asleep.

For the West, a central feature of détente was its implied meshing of
the military-strategic requirements of deterrence and the political possibilities of East-West accommodation. This anticipated complementarity
was already embodied in NATO's Harmel Report of 1967, which stressed

the need to approach the East on the basis of a "two-pillar" approach that incorporated détente as well as defense.

In Western Europe, détente referred to one part of a dual strategy: that of conveying to the Soviet Union and Eastern Europe a readiness for dialogue, negotiations, and cooperation (economic as well as political), while at the same time securing an acceptable military balance between NATO and the Warsaw Pact—preferably at a reduced level achieved through negotiations on both nuclear and conventional armaments. In addition to its intrinsic importance, Ostpolitik was connected with Germany's security policy because Bonn's readiness to accept the territorial status quo confronted German security problems at their political roots and thus became a complementary political part of Germany's and NATO's policy of deterrence. Ostpolitik overcame the stark contradictions of the fifties and sixties, when Bonn's security policy conflicted sharply with its Eastern policy. By recognizing the territorial and political realities stemming from the Second World War, the Germans meshed their security and Eastern policies, developed a more constructive attitude toward arms control, and adjusted West German foreign policy to the dynamics of détente.

The Germans obtained political benefits as well. They were the main beneficiaries of the détente processes of the 1970s, whereas both the Soviet Union and the United States were disappointed—a situation that led in the late 1970s and throughout the 1980s to frictions in German-American relations. The expectations of the superpowers, had they been fully articulated, would have been shown to be contradictory to begin with. On the other hand, Bonn's expectations of enlarged and intensified human contacts between the Federal Republic and the German Democratic Republic were at least partly fulfilled, and the Federal Republic enhanced its international prestige as well as its diplomatic leverage. Consequently, throughout the 1970s and 1980s the Germans remained committed to the evolution of a European order that would secure and broaden these benefits, while neither the United States nor the Soviet Union shared the benefits or the commitment. Thus détente sharpened and reflected a central paradox: for many Europeans détente meant a chance to overcome or at least ameliorate the division of Europe, whereas for the Soviet Union and the United States it meant solidifying the European status quo.

Frictions with the West

These differing assessments of the purpose and prospects of détente came at a time when the evident vulnerability of the United States to Soviet attack had forced Washington to qualify the automaticity of its nuclear guarantee to Europe, impaired the credibility of the guarantee, institutionalized nuclear parity of the United States and the Soviet Union in strategic-arms agreements, and ultimately brought the strategically distinct positions of America and Europe into clear focus. Although doctrinal debates within NATO were less strident in the 1970s than in the 1960s, the willingness of the United States to sustain a forward strategy on NATO's central front became even more questionable.

These concerns among European leaders were discussed less openly than in the sixties. Other problems had become more pressing, the European perception of the Soviet threat had changed, and it was assumed that public airing of these concerns would in itself aggravate them. But tensions persisted. Whereas the European members of NATO, above all the Federal Republic, saw their security interests best maintained by threatening the early use of nuclear weapons, the United States wanted their use postponed as long as possible. Although NATO planners had all along questioned the military feasibility of defending Western Europe along the West German border with the East, it was politically imperative to assure the Germans with the principle of forward defense that their geographical position would not condemn them to being the first and perhaps only victims of a conventional war or limited nuclear war.

Even more important, during the years of Carter and Reagan, Bonn began to doubt the political circumspection and reliability of American diplomacy and what effect these shortcomings might have on American security policies. When Chancellor Helmut Schmidt raised the issue of the Eurostrategic nuclear balance in 1977, he was less concerned about the physical military threat posed by the Soviet Union than about lack of American resolve in dealing with the political implications of the Soviet preponderance in intermediate-range nuclear weapons.

In addition to the problems caused by the diverging security interests of the United States and the Federal Republic, in the 1970s and 1980s a series of conflicts between Washington and Bonn erupted on economic and monetary matters. The world monetary crises of the early 1970s not only led to the collapse of the Bretton Woods monetary regime but also sharpened American attacks on the exclusionary trade practices of the European Community, signifying the abrogation of a tacit transatlantic agreement between the United States and Western Europe that had been forged in the postwar era. The essence of this bargain was that the United States, based on its hegemonic economic and monetary position in the postwar period, would be willing to make marginal economic sacrifices in return for political privileges and to advance European integration and America's double-containment policy in Europe. As American hegemony declined during the sixties, the United States wearied of the burdens of global leadership and Western Europe, increasingly restive about American privileges, pushed for an alteration of the framework within which the postwar political, economic, and monetary arrangements had been made. The need to alter this framework was made the more pressing by the emerging primacy of economic and monetary matters over military-strategic issues, by growing economic interdependence, and by the special political and economic difficulties posed by the enlargement of the European Economic Community and its arrested integrative dynamics. The 1970s brought a fundamental reconfiguration of the global and regional balance of power, placing a heavy strain on the historic transatlantic security compact and the economic, political, and psychological foundations that had sustained it in the postwar decades.

Although these developments increased German diplomatic leverage, their ramifications became especially troublesome after Helmut Schmidt took over the chancellorship from Willy Brandt in 1974. This was not so much because of the change in German leadership (although Schmidt could not resist the temptation to lecture Western leaders, especially on economic matters and especially in Washington), but because German Ostpolitik had largely run its course, and because oil price increases and the worldwide recession brought economic matters to the foreground. Although the Schmidt government took great pride in having successfully adjusted the German economy to the oil price shocks and general economic turbulence of the 1970s, this impressive performance complicated West Germany's relations with both the United States and the European Community. The Bonn government resisted American suggestions for a political and economic "axis" between Washington and Bonn or a locomotive role for the German economy; it complained about American monetary policies; and it generally took a dim view of the style and substance of Washington's foreign policies. Bonn also took a much tougher stand regarding the European Community than had previous German governments, calling on the member states to exercise fiscal responsibility and support reforms of the Community's entrenched bureaucracy. Although Schmidt was willing to be a "good European"—his generally harmonious relationship with French President Valéry Giscard d'Estaing enabled France and Germany to launch the European Monetary System—he also believed that the economic and monetary plight of some members of the EEC was in large part due to fiscal and political irresponsibility and that the sense of drift in the Community could be overcome only by political leadership that faced up to the challenges of the future and resisted the day-to-day pressures of political expediency.

In the 1980s Western European countries were not as preoccupied with the dramatic "high politics" of the previous decades as they were with the much more technical economic and political tasks that confronted them: economic growth and monetary stability, dealing constructively with the Third World, adjusting the structures of the Community to implement much-needed reforms and accommodate new members, and preparing the way for a genuine common market by 1992.

In all these tasks, which required coordinated and therefore incremental steps, it became apparent that economic policy played a steady, fundamental, and perhaps decisive role, with large opportunities for the Federal Republic to translate economic and monetary capacity into political leverage. The changing ground rules of the world monetary regime, the growing importance of economic matters, and the absolute and relative increase in the Federal Republic's economic and monetary capacity doubly benefited the Federal Republic, for these developments shifted elements of power in a direction where the major sources of German capacity were situated. The growing strength of the Federal Republic was applied to every aspect of German foreign policy and energized every facet of German diplomacy. German economic weight obtained for Bonn a powerful and perhaps decisive voice in plans for a more fully integrated West European economic community; it was an important source of influence in Eastern Europe, the Soviet Union, and East Germany; it enlarged Bonn's role in dealing with the Third World; and it served to advance the subtle but persistent diplomacy of the Germans in international organizations. For Bonn, economics became the continuation of politics by other means.

The translation of German economic power into political leverage was less successful in the area of security and arms control policies. When Chancellor Helmut Kohl sought to provide continuity in Bonn's Eastern policies in the 1980s, while President Ronald Reagan took a strongly confrontational course with his own policies toward the Soviet Union, it also became clear that the Federal Republic's increased leverage in economic matters could not be significantly extended into the area of security policies, where Germany's dependence on NATO and the United States remained as pronounced and diplomatically confining as it had been all along. As security and arms control issues reemerged in the 1980s as major concerns in German-American relations, it was apparent that these concerns reflected and portended as always political purposes that went far deeper than those of weighing the regional or global military balance and redefining the meaning of security for the 1980s and beyond.

For example, the issue of the Eurostrategic balance, important as it was in its own right, took on a meaning that went far beyond its military and technical import and extended into fundamental questions about the future shape of the transatlantic alliance and the European political order. German attitudes were formed, or hardened, on the issue of the Eurostrategic balance and related security questions in a way that reverberated and extended into other issues of German-American relations. The highly technical discussions over arms control measures and the highly emotional response these discussions evoked were closely related to fundamental political attitudes (in Western Europe as well as the

United States) about the nature of the East-West conflict, the fluctuations of American diplomacy, and the shape of a desirable regional and global world order. At the end of the 1980s, as the Federal Republic and its allies sought to come to terms with the flexibility and sophistication of Mikhail S. Gorbachev's diplomacy and as Bonn prepared to deal with the new administration in Washington, it again became clear that the limits defining arms control were at the same time the boundaries that contained the possibilities for the evolution of a new European order.

These political, economic, and military-strategic transformations of the 1980s may have appeared incremental, subtle, and technical, but they nevertheless called into question long-standing assumptions and premises of the Federal Republic's foreign policies in the areas of security, welfare, and relations with the East.

I

The Politics of Security, Arms Control, and Strategic Doctrine

Is war not merely another kind of writing and language for political thinking? Its grammar may be its own, but not its logic. If that is so, then war cannot be divorced from politics, and whenever this occurs in our thinking about war, the many links that connect the two elements are destroyed and we are left with something pointless and devoid of reason.

—CARL VON CLAUSEWITZ, *On War*

Since the establishment of the Federal Republic, its security has depended on NATO and through it on the United States and American national security policies.

In the late 1940s and early 1950s NATO had little with which to deter the Soviet Union except America's nuclear weapons, nor could the Germans make a contribution. No West German forces were established in significant numbers until the late 1950s, and until the Federal Republic became sovereign in 1955 even the formal responsibility for the defense of West German territory rested with the Western powers, for they had retained final authority over West Germany's foreign policy as well as domestic policy. In later years too, as France and Britain developed and modernized their own nuclear arsenals and the German Bundeswehr became a mainstay of NATO's conventional forces, Germany's security ultimately rested on the American commitment to guarantee it.

But the term *security* is misleading. At no time did anyone perceive Germany's rearmament and subsequent contribution to NATO merely in terms of the military balance between East and West. Political implications overshadowed those of military strategy from the beginning. Underlying the Western security policies of the postwar decades was an ever-present but hidden premise that the Federal Republic's military exertions were required not only to check a military threat from the East but also to serve fundamental political interests of the West.

Security policy always has two dimensions, arms and diplomacy, and the Germans and their allies and opponents have always been acutely sensitive to this dual purpose. The term *security* itself became the metaphor for a larger political purpose, the condensed representation of

29

diplomatic intentions. Politics was continually quoting the language of arms. Large political calculations were refracted in the technical details of military preparations and in the carefully weighed nuances of strategic pronouncements. There was a blurring even of idioms—as in the German term *Sicherheitspolitik,* in which the distinction between politics and security evaporates, or the concept of "economic security," with which the Western powers expressed their concern about the energy crises and economic dislocations of the 1970s.

The translation of political purpose into the grammar of war was most succinctly accomplished in the language of American strategic doctrine. American strategic doctrines of the postwar era (such as massive retaliation and flexible response) were political symbols, directed both toward allies and toward opponents. From the beginning of the Cold War, the United States acted as the spokesman of the Western allies in expressing political purpose in terms of military doctrine. In the postwar period, the West Europeans' fear of the Soviet Union and their military, economic, and political dependence on the United States did not allow them to deviate substantially from the strategic directives issued in Washington or express their own political intentions in the language of military strategy. So long as NATO was relatively cohesive and the United States the unchallengeable Western superpower, Washington's political and strategic guidelines were generally followed by the Western alliance. The United States created the military diction of the postwar world.

Throughout the history of NATO, the core principle of Western security policy was the doctrine of deterrence: the threat to respond with nuclear retaliation to a Soviet attack on allied territory.[1] For the United States, deterrence was the military-strategic complement to the political doctrine of containment. Together, containment and deterrence were the principal elements of a global American strategy that faced, at the divide of Europe and the periphery of the American empire, toward both East and West. Implemented by political containment, strategic deterrence, and economic hegemony, America's global strategy in the postwar era sought to restrain the Soviet Union at the same time as it established in Europe and Asia the geopolitical base on which the American empire and the American Cold War effort could be securely emplaced.

In Europe, American containment policy embodied two components: one directed toward the Soviet Union, the other toward the Federal Republic. So did deterrence: while one component of American deterrence policy was aimed at the Soviet Union, threatening the Soviets with unacceptable consequences in case of aggression, another was aimed at America's West European allies, reassuring them that their security requirements were adequately met by the first component and that the United States was prepared to initiate nuclear war on their behalf. Together, the threat of punishing the opponent and the corresponding reassurance of American allies became the core of the transatlantic security partnership.[2] Deterrence symbolized America's determination to contain the Soviet Union and its commitment to extend its protection to Western Europe.

Throughout the 1950s Washington's policies of double containment and of deterrence and reassurance were complementary and mutually reinforcing. (They were in addition sustained by America's hegemonic position in the world economy and bipartisan political support at home.) The Soviet Union was contained and deterred; West Germany was contained and reassured. This dual thrust of America's European strategy lent to postwar American diplomacy a compelling political logic and an extraordinary clarity of purpose. Better still, it could be implemented with the same policies. Integrative transatlantic and West European institutions, military as well as political and economic, bound the Federal Republic to the West at the same time as they laid the foundation for a concerted Western containment effort against the East. In the military-strategic area, deterring the Soviet Union and reassuring the Western allies were equally compatible. America was invulnerable, and its nuclear superiority lent credibility to the threat to initiate nuclear war in case of Soviet aggression against American allies. The complementarity of containment and deterrence, and of the dual components of each (containing the Soviet Union while containing Germany, deterring the Soviet Union along with reassuring American allies) became the foundation of America's European policy in the postwar decade. The vitality and plausibility of America's European diplomacy derived from the striking reciprocity of its Russian and German policies.

In the 1960s these interlocking elements of American strategy began to lose their complementarity. What had been fungible assets of American diplomacy, interchangeable and reinforcing in their intended political and strategic purchase, became in their disjuncture serious liabilities. The dual components of containment and of deterrence began to diverge and, in a development of even larger significance, the overarching strategies of containment and deterrence themselves became less complementary. As tensions developed over the decades between containing the Soviet Union and containing West Germany, between deterring the Soviet Union and reassuring the allies, and between containment and deterrence themselves, Washington's European policy became immensely more complicated and German-American relations increasingly strained. Most problems that have beset NATO and the German-American security relationship during the last decades are the result of the fractious dynamics that rent the component parts of double containment and of deterrence and reassurance. (These strategic-political dilemmas were sharpened by the concurrent decline of American economic hegemony and of domestic support for American foreign policy, an important theme that is treated in part III.)

With respect to double containment, problems developed for American diplomacy when a growing number of Germans began to question its implications for the continued division of Europe and Germany. Over time, many Germans became convinced that both the United States and the Soviet Union regarded the partition of Germany as a major element of stability in the postwar European order and that neither had a genuine interest in overcoming it. They began to consider that the American policy of containing the Soviet Union by containing the Federal Republic was outdated; they realized that America's unremitting pressure on the Soviet Union also perpetuated those strictures of containment that were directed toward themselves; and they suspected that the United States was using its security partnership with the Federal Republic to retain American control over German foreign policy. They developed a strong interest in détente and grew resentful when they saw its prospects threatened by American security policies and nuclear diplomacy.

These were the deeper concerns that underlay the controversies over arms control and related military matters in the 1980s. Everyone understood that such issues as NATO's double-track decision of 1979, the double-zero accord on Eurostrategic arms of 1987–88, and the plans of the Reagan administration for a defense-dominated American strategy were at bottom political issues couched in military-strategic terms. Both proponents and opponents of these and similar measures realized that what was ultimately at stake was the future shape of the European political order.

The tensions that began to afflict America's policy of double containment were sharpened by military-strategic developments that called into question the continuing complementarity of deterrence and reassurance. The gradual loss of American invulnerability inevitably brought with it the gradual loss of the West Europeans' confidence that the United States would risk the destruction of its people and territory for the sake of the alliance. Extended deterrence became less credible. In some respects, it became easier to deter an opponent than reassure an ally.[3] The complementarity of deterrence and reassurance, which had sustained the Atlantic security community, began to diminish.

Again, West Germany was the most affected. Dependent for its security on the United States, precluded from obtaining its own national nuclear deterrent, and handicapped by the singularity of its political, geographical, and historical position in Europe and the alliance, the Federal Republic was obliged to pay increasing political and economic costs for decreasing strategic benefits. This issue was at the core of the German-American frictions that developed in the 1960s over a wide range of issues in the area of security policies. In the early 1970s the widening gaps between deterrence and reassurance and between the components of America's policy of double containment were briefly bridged by the short-lived expectations and policies associated with détente, only to emerge with even greater clarity during the years of Carter and Reagan.

In the 1980s, the geostrategic complementarity that had in the early postwar decades connected the politics of containment with the strategies of deterrence was itself called into question. Containment and deterrence, each weakened by its own infirmities, appeared to be drifting apart. This did not come about suddenly. Over the years American strategic thought and weapons development seemed to have slipped away from political guidance, taking on their own institutional, economic, intellectual, and political life, and creating powerful and stubbornly supportive constituencies. American leadership seemed to be forgetting that strategy should be subordinate to politics, that the imperial contest between the United States and the Soviet Union in the postwar era was not so much about territorial security or gaining an edge in the military balance as about political spheres of influence, obtaining and keeping allies, shaping the global state system in ways that furthered American national and imperial interests.[4] America began to suffer from a gradual disconnection between political purpose and its military-strategic implementation, leading to a militarization of American diplomacy and a corresponding depoliticization of American foreign policy. By the 1980s American diplomacy seemed to be the continuation of the arms race by other means.[5]

In Europe also there came about a paradoxical disjuncture of politics and arms. Although the high tensions of the Cold War abated over the decades and the West Europeans' fear of Soviet military aggression dissipated, there was no letup in the military confrontation between the alliances. Both continually increased or modernized their nuclear and conventional capabilities, and both seemed to cling to the sterile stability of the military balance the more they failed to come to terms with the political, economic, and social changes that were transforming Europe. Washington and Moscow apparently saw in the military division of Europe the most solid and permanent element of the postwar partition of the Continent, and seemed determined that the most reliable guarantee of their double hegemony over Europe, military alliances, should endure.

This began to change in the mid-1980s. After Mikhail S. Gorbachev's accession to power in Moscow, it was precisely the skillful use of arms control policies that energized the Soviet Union's European policies and challenged the orthodoxy of Western security policies. Accustomed to a Soviet diplomacy that was stodgy, comfortably predictable, and centered on a narrow definition of security, the Western alliance saw itself increasingly challenged to respond with an energetic and imaginative diplomacy of its own.[6] But NATO, torn by the conflicting interests of its members and suffering from the perennial incongruity between its declaratory strategy and the actual disposition of its forces, seemed ill prepared politically, institutionally, and intellectually to face the problems of the late 1980s and the challenges that lay beyond. By pointing the way toward ridding Central Europe of nuclear weapons, Soviet diplomacy not only appealed to deeply held popular sentiments (especially in Germany) but increased the pressure on the already weakened foundation of America's European policies: the corroded principles of double containment and of deterrence and reassurance.

On the American side of the equation there was contradiction and confusion. Like all its predecessors, the Reagan administration entered office reaffirming the American commitment to the historic policy of containment and the necessity of implementing it with an engaged American presence in Europe. Indeed, some critics complained that the administration overextended containment geographically, overstated it ideologically, oversimplified it intellectually, and overburdened it financially. At the same time, however, a tempting set of contradictory calculations began to inform American strategic thinking. In subtle but powerful ways there developed in Washington a sense that the American nuclear commitment to the defense of Europe had grown into more of a liability than an asset; and that present and future American interests might be better served by a more detached and qualified strategic association with Europe, coupled with a political and economic tilt toward the Pacific and an appropriately supportive American maritime strategy. Irrespective of whether the Reagan administration's plans for a Strategic Defense Initiative would be implemented by its successor, the driving ideas behind them not only aimed to reverse the historic principle of deterrence but also flirted with the possibility of a more unilateralist American diplomacy.

As a consequence, fundamental if hidden and unarticulated tensions developed between the principles of political containment and strategic deterrence. Political containment clearly required a deep and sustained American engagement in the affairs of Europe—both to contain the Soviet Union and to contain the Federal Republic. But on the military-strategic level an equally plausible rationale seemed to call for a measure of American disengagement from Europe. Political imperatives suggested a continuing American involvement in Europe. Strategic imperatives suggested a less entangling relationship with American allies, a narrower definition of American national interests, and perhaps a return to American unilateralism.

The closeness of the German-American security relationship made it inevitable that such large political and strategic developments as the erosion of double containment, deterrence and reassurance, and containment and deterrence would reach into every element of Germany's foreign policy agenda. Throughout the history of the Federal Republic, security issues not only affected the entire range of Germany's Western policies but also its relations with the Soviet Union, Eastern Europe, and East Germany. Given the close connection between German foreign and domestic politics, security issues reshaped the domestic political discourse as well.

The Federal Republic was both subject and object in these developments. It contributed to their origins and dynamics, and it felt their consequences more directly than did other American allies, primarily in four areas. First, the decline of double containment raised troubling questions about the political control of the Federal Republic's military contribution to the alliance, the political purposes that underlay it, and the strategic directives that guided it—an issue that takes us back to the origin of the Federal Republic. Second, that of deterrence and reassurance called into question the credibility of the American nuclear commitment to Europe and the extent to which German security interests remained adequately served by the transatlantic alliance; this question had emerged as early as the 1950s. Third, the corrosive politics of arms control stemmed from the close connection between considerations of double containment and of deterrence and reassurance, creating tensions and raising issues that affected every aspect of East-West diplomacy, the Western alliance, and German-American relations. This set of problems can be traced back to the disengagement proposals of the 1950s. Finally, the diminishing complementarity between containment and deterrence raised fundamental questions about the present and future American role in Europe, the geostrategic implications of an American defense shield, and how the Federal Republic and its neighbors would adjust to a more detached American involvement in the European political order.

1

Security for Germany, Security from Germany: Institutional Control, Strategic Guidelines, and Nuclear Diplomacy

> *We [Germans] ourselves cannot do without* NATO. NATO *after all is the cloak under which the German-American alliance becomes tolerable not only for France but also for our smaller neighbors and, last but not least, for the Soviet Union itself.*
>
> —HERBERT BLANKENHORN, 1959

The issue of how to control the Federal Republic's military contribution to the Western alliance was from the outset more important than a narrow consideration of Germany's or Western Europe's security.

From the perspective of the West, the political containment of the new German state required above all that it become "entangled and integrated" in the transatlantic and West European political order—militarily, economically, and diplomatically.[1] Integrative institutions, strategic guidelines, and the nuclear diplomacy of the United States became the most effective and durable ways to create and perpetuate this entanglement in the military sphere. Even after West Germany became an economic superpower and enlarged its political influence, its continuing dependence on the United States for its security afforded Washington ample opportunity for influencing the course of German foreign policy, in the East as well as in the West. Washington's postwar European strategy of double containment proved most enduring in the area of German security policies and East-West nuclear diplomacy.

The military integration of West Germany was a precondition for restoring sovereignty to the Federal Republic, and was in later years an important restraint on German security policies and therefore on German diplomacy. Throughout the concurrent histories of NATO and the Federal Republic, the necessity of maintaining a sturdy institutional framework for Germany's military integration had a large effect on the shape and purpose of the alliance itself. The need to tie the Federal Republic to the United States and Western Europe transformed NATO from a loose security pact into an integrated military alliance, helped hold the alliance together, and reflected the common interest of the United States and its West European allies in keeping the Bundeswehr under international supervision. NATO and the Federal Republic were literally made for one another. The political purposes that the Western allies sought to advance by establishing and rearming the Federal Republic were those of NATO itself, because NATO's primary function also was political reassurance rather than military deterrence: "NATO was not created to marshall military power, either in being or potential, in order to deter an imminent attack on Europe. Like Russia's huge army, it was intended to provide political and psychological reinforcement in the continuing warfare of the Cold War. There was no significant fear of a massive Russian invasion."[2]

From Bonn's perspective, political considerations were paramount as well. Chancellor Konrad Adenauer entertained no promilitary sentiments or attitudes. He viewed rearmament primarily in political terms, and fully appreciated the diplomatic and political leverage he could obtain from it.[3] Although a number of years would pass until German armed forces were finally established, the German government's decision in 1949–50 to assent to rearmament had immediate as well as far-reaching consequences. West Germany's chances of achieving its major foreign policy goals—security, political sovereignty and economic recovery, and reunification—were directly affected, both positively and negatively, by the decision to join the Western military alliance.

For Bonn, rearmament was the nexus between the international diplomatic environment, which was characterized by severe Cold War tensions, and the whole range of German foreign policy goals. Without the Cold War, there would have been little reason for the Western powers to arrange for West Germany's rearmament a few years after the end of the Second World War and a few years after an intense American re-education effort had sought to persuade the Germans that arms were incompatible with their progress toward democracy. Without the need to rearm Germany, a need that the German government exploited skillfully with the appropriate diplomacy, there would have been much less of an incentive for the Western allies to accommodate the Germans in their pursuit of political sovereignty and economic recovery and to lend verbal support to their aspirations for German unity. Rearmament offered the Germans the diplomatic opportunities to exploit the Cold War. It became the anchor of Adenauer's diplomacy and the underlying cause for both the successes and the failures of Bonn's foreign policy. From the beginning the link between German rearmament and restoring sovereignty was so clearly acknowledged that it was obvious the Federal Republic "was to pay for its sovereignty by being irrevocably bound to the Western military alliance . . . on which the validity of the whole arrangement rested."[4]

The Western powers were not interested only in West Germany's military potential, which gave Bonn more effective bargaining power than did rearmament alone. A German military contingent could perhaps have been established by conscripting West Germans under the command of Allied occupation authorities. But this would not have permanently integrated West Germany into the Western alliance. Merely "deputizing" a German army under Western command, as France had in effect suggested at the beginning of the rearmament debate, would have placed a West German military contribution in a sociopolitical and economic void. The United States wanted to integrate the Federal Republic in the Western alliance in more fundamental ways: by committing the Germans to Western values through political supervision and the interdependence of economies, and by creating domestic consensus and political stability. Moreover, the Western orientation of Adenauer's diplomacy soon obtained a solid domestic political base (although the major opposition party, the SPD, feared the detrimental consequences of this policy for Germany's reunification and opposed it strenuously), without which the Federal Republic's integration in the Western alliance would have remained a formalistic and tenuous pact among governments. Given the close connections between German foreign and domestic policies, it prepared as well the internal conditions for the political and economic development of the new republic (which was yet another reason why the Social Democrats opposed it, for it pointed this development in a conservative socioeconomic and political direction). German rearmament not only was the basis for Bonn's Western diplomacy but laid the groundwork for the future dynamics and content of the Federal Republic's internal political and economic order.

In December 1949 Adenauer announced that if German troops were to be raised it would have to be in the context of a European army and on terms of equality—articulating for the first time what became Bonn's diplomatic doctrine in its dealings with the Western powers, the twin concepts of integration and equality.[5]

Bonn's Security Diplomacy: Integration and Equality

In these early years, Bonn's call for integration was not yet a source of political disappointments and diplomatic problems. It matched and energized a complementary Western interest in creating institutional restraints on German military contingents, and the alliance, under the

unchallengeable tutelage of the United States, was still sufficiently cohesive to instill some meaning in the idea of integration.

The German demand for equality was always more problematic. During the long negotiations over the European Defense Community (EDC),
France consistently opposed the participation of Germany as an equal,
and when the Federal Republic joined NATO and the West European
Union (WEU) after the idea of an integrated European army proved abortive, it was not strictly speaking on terms of equality.[6] Although the
Federal Republic's membership brought with it the restoration of sovereignty, as part of its accession to the WEU Bonn renounced the manufacture of atomic, biological, and chemical weapons on German soil, and
accepted other restrictions on German sovereignty. The WEU fixed the
upper limits of the German military contribution, and the twelve divisions that Germany agreed to provide were put wholly under NATO's
command. Both the WEU and NATO were in their intended effect arms
control limitations on the Federal Republic.[7]

In the early and mid-1950s, when the Bundeswehr was only at the
planning stage, there were already indications that along with American
troops stationed in Germany it would become the mainstay of NATO's
conventional forces and of America's nuclear presence in Europe—in
part because other West European members allowed these developments
to unfold by defaulting on their own commitments to NATO, in part
because the support functions assigned to a German army that did not
yet exist were already intended to sustain America's nuclear strategy in
Europe. Both factors gradually narrowed NATO to an essentially bilateral
German-American security connection and thus called into question
Bonn's aims of equality and integration; and both entangled for years to
come the security policies of the Federal Republic in the nuclear diplomacy of the United States.

The first reason why Bonn's military contribution increased in importance was that NATO's ambitious force goals of the early 1950s proved
unrealistic. Implementation would have been costly and politically controversial at a time when economic reconstruction was Europe's highest
priority. France and Britain in particular were remiss in meeting their
obligations to NATO. They were financially overburdened, their troops
were required to sustain colonial ambitions in Africa and Asia, and their
first military priority was to retain a nuclear capability (in the case of
Britain) and obtain one (in the case of France). The United States too
sought to save money and manpower and, as part of the Eisenhower
administration's New Look strategy, reduced its conventional forces in
Europe and supplanted them with tactical nuclear weapons.

Once the decision to deploy these weapons in Europe had been
reached, NATO planning became officially based on the principle that

tactical nuclear weapons would be used to counter almost any type of aggression, and NATO's contingency plans were formulated on this basis. Accordingly, at the meeting of the NATO Council in December 1954, the conventional force goal of ninety-six divisions that had been set in 1952 was scaled down to thirty standing divisions, to be deployed in NATO's central sector. Nuclear arms were designated as NATO's sword, conventional forces as its shield, intended to carry out brief holding actions.

For many West European governments the shift in NATO strategy was attractive. They regarded conventional forces primarily as a trip-wire that would trigger an immediate American nuclear response if Europe were attacked (an assumption for which the Eisenhower administration's doctrine of massive and instant retaliation seemed to provide the necessary reassurance), and they perceived no pressing need to take the unpalatable economic and political steps that extensive conventional rearmament would have required. On the contrary, West European governments believed that providing NATO with large ground forces would undermine the credibility of massive retaliation and increase the risk that Europe would become a battlefield in a conventional war. Better not to provide too many conventional forces: doing so might enable and encourage their use.

By contrast, Washington considered it essential that Western Europe build up its conventional forces. Basically, the United States and Western Europe began to perceive the purpose of NATO in different ways. For the United States, the transformation of NATO from a guaranty pact to an integrated military organization—in large part the consequence of Germany's accession to it—meant that NATO had become the major instrument for redressing the military balance between East and West in Europe. For the Europeans, NATO remained the visible commitment of the United States to come to their defense, as it had been before the Korean War. Consequently, "to her allies the United States seemed unnecessarily preoccupied with military considerations at the expense of accommodating divergent political interests in Western Europe and relieving the tensions of the Cold War; while to the United States, who had entered the alliance to help Western Europe defend itself, her allies now seemed less interested in assuming the responsibility for their self-defense than she."[8]

Amid these conflicting perceptions of NATO's role, the military functions assigned by American planners to the Bundeswehr were expanding. Under America's New Look strategy, German conventional forces were needed even more than before. The twelve divisions that Bonn had agreed to provide were now assigned two tasks: one was to carry the major burden in defending the central sector (especially because the other members of NATO were not meeting their force goals), the other to provide a strong forward position of ground troops, which was required by the new strategy to force the enemy to attack in concentration so as to make tactical nuclear counterstrikes efficacious.

This was an important development, because it substantially enlarged the importance of Germany's military contribution to Western defense. In addition to enlarging Western ground forces, the planned German contingents had now become an indispensable element of Washington's attempt to reinforce the American strategic nuclear position. Without having proceeded beyond the planning stage, the significance of rearming the Federal Republic had increased dramatically (even the planning stage had been held hostage in the French National Assembly until the EDC treaty was finally voted down in August 1954). German rearmament, which initially had been regarded only as complementing American nuclear superiority, had become an integral part of sustaining a new nuclear strategy in Europe.[9]

Reaching for Nuclear Co-management

Soon after Germany joined NATO, Bonn began to reappraise its security policy.[10] In summer 1956, when a bill for conscripting German soldiers was presented to the Bundestag, the government still argued for a buildup of conventional forces, and Chancellor Adenauer called NATO's change of emphasis from conventional forces to nuclear arms a mistake. The government now shifted, however, from arguing that German rearmament would help deter Soviet aggression to stressing that it would help in deterring nuclear war. There were domestic political reasons for this shift as well. Having failed to prevent the Federal Republic's rearmament and accession to NATO, the Social Democrats focused their opposition on the deployment of nuclear weapons in Germany. In that respect, Bonn's "shift in emphasis corresponded to a modification of general apprehension. In the early fifties, at the beginning of the rearmament debate, German politicians had to deal with the fear of Soviet aggression. In 1955 and 1956, this fear had abated and had been replaced by the fear of nuclear weapons."[11] In September 1956 the cabinet announced the reduction of the conscription period from eighteen months to twelve (which meant that West Germany's total force goal would be reduced from 500,000 to 325,000), and at the end of the year Bonn for the first time expressed an interest in equipping West Germany's armed forces with tactical nuclear weapons and in obtaining a voice in the nuclear management of the alliance.

To explain his new policy, Chancellor Adenauer argued that a nonnuclear response by NATO to a Soviet attack was no longer likely in light of the ramifications of Washington's new strategy, the French transfer of troops to Algeria, British reliance on nuclear defense, and Belgium's reduction of its period of conscription. In effect, Bonn implied that the

West could continue to rely on nuclear deterrence, and that Western Europe's conventional capabilities were so depleted that NATO had no choice but to use tactical nuclear weapons to respond to a Soviet attack. The Germans were joining their major West European partners in NATO in playing down the importance of conventional forces and highlighting the significance of nuclear arms.

Behind Bonn's somewhat oversimplified announcements lay a fundamental lack of confidence in NATO's ground forces. But the confidence in the American nuclear commitment to Europe was waning also. Bonn became concerned about the distinction between Germany's responsibilities to NATO (providing conventional forces) and those of the United States (providing nuclear protection): the less the conventional forces of West Germany's allies were involved in the early stages of a Soviet attack, the less likely or the more delayed might be American nuclear retaliation. German co-management of nuclear weapons was expected to reinforce the Western nuclear presence at the German border by extending Washington's nuclear commitments more unequivocally to cover the Federal Republic. Even more important were political considerations. Bonn feared the political consequences of an expanding nuclear club from which Germany would be excluded, and hoped to derive leverage for its Eastern policies from the sharing of nuclear control.

The revamping of Bonn's defense policies met with little enthusiasm. NATO members criticized the reduction of the German defense contribution and were even less supportive of Bonn's ambitions for nuclear control sharing. In December 1956 Bonn was saved from a politically embarrassing situation when the British carried the brunt of the argument and proposed in the NATO Council that the United States institute nuclear sharing by providing European forces with tactical nuclear warheads. In April 1957 the United States agreed to provide tactical nuclear weapons systems (with the nuclear warheads remaining under American control), thus fully implementing the revision of NATO strategy, and later in the year Bonn began to show interest in deploying American intermediate-range ballistic missiles (IRBMS) in West Germany, which Washington viewed as a counterbalance to the rapid Soviet development of intercontinental missiles, dramatized by the flight of Sputnik.[12]

NATO's new defense strategy meant that West Germany and other European allies were becoming increasingly dependent on weapons over which they had no control and the use of which was being called into question by the improvement of Soviet nuclear capabilities. The warheads of the tactical nuclear weapons, which were deployed in increasing numbers with ground forces in Germany, were kept under tight American control, and Bonn was largely excluded from the planning for their use and deployment. Bonn's misgivings over the efficacy of this arrangement were shared in other European NATO capitals. France in particular was interested in ultimately developing its own strategic nuclear capability, which would permit it to join the special Anglo-American atomic entente as an equal partner. Before General de Gaulle returned to power, France and Germany also reportedly discussed during 1957–58 the establishment of some type of nuclear partnership between the two countries. It is not certain whether France was unwilling to share control and secrets, or whether Bonn felt the time had not come to engage in such a politically controversial venture and burden German-American relations in the process. In any event nothing came of the discussions.[13]

For Bonn the logical middle course between obtaining independent nuclear capabilities (which was out of the question) and having no control over nuclear weapons at all was an integrated nuclear alliance with equal sharing of control. West Germany now aimed to increase its military and political influence by stressing the need for the political and military integration of the alliance and for a larger German share in the control of nuclear weapons. In fall 1960 Bonn began to express interest in an integrated NATO *force de frappe* as an alternative to the national French *force de frappe* favored by de Gaulle.

In this instance as in others, Bonn sought to advance its national interests in the name of those of the alliance, applying its diplomatic concepts of integration and equality. But this was becoming inefficacious, because the members of the alliance no longer had congruent interests. By the late 1950s and early 1960s their diverging foreign policies led the principal members of NATO to seek very different solutions to NATO's military and political problems. The Suez war of 1956 had left France and Britain with a deep distrust of the United States, the U-2 incident and abortive Paris summit meeting raised further questions about American leadership, and Hungary and Sputnik demonstrated the changing balance of power. While the United States struggled to avert the fragmentation of NATO, the West Europeans themselves developed quite distinct bilateral relations with both Washington and Moscow, and they explored conflicting alternatives to the nuclear hegemony of the United States in the alliance—all of which deprived the German diplomatic program of "integration with equality" of real meaning.

The American "solution" to NATO's problems consisted of reassuring America's allies that the American nuclear commitment to Europe remained intact, that responsible crisis management demanded a single center of nuclear decision making in the alliance, and that the Europeans were in principle misguided in viewing national nuclear arsenals as a more convincing alternative to NATO's collective nuclear protection. The French solution was to do precisely that: create a national nuclear force de frappe, in part because of the diminishing credibility of the American nuclear commitment, but at bottom primarily for the political purpose of escaping from American diplomatic tutelage. The British solution was to prolong the life of its independent nuclear arsenal by extending Britain's special political and historical relationship with the United States into the area of military strategy. This was accomplished at the meeting of December 1962 in Nassau between President Kennedy and Prime Minister Harold Macmillan, when the United States agreed to sell to Britain Polaris submarine missiles with the proviso that these submarines be assigned to a NATO command as the nucleus of a NATO nuclear force (if one were ever established).[14] Inevitably, the German solution was to seek a NATO solution: an integrated NATO nuclear force, with equal German participation. Precluded from any other plausible arrangement, Bonn again took recourse to the principles of integration and equality. When this failed and created a major diplomatic embarrassment for Bonn, the Germans were obliged to accept the American solution, the status quo.

Strategic Illusions and Political Realities:
Bonn and the Multilateral Nuclear Force (MLF)

The so-called multilateral nuclear force was a hapless scheme. Floated at the end of the Eisenhower administration and reluctantly revived by President Kennedy, it envisaged the creation under a multilateral NATO authority of a seaborne nuclear force consisting of a British contribution of four or five Polaris submarines, an equal or larger American contribution, a French contingent, and a number of surface ships owned by NATO to be manned and financed by the non-nuclear members of NATO willing to join in the arrangement. The Federal Republic was willing.

On military-strategic grounds, the MLF was difficult to justify. It was defended with the arguments that NATO needed to offset the large number of medium-range missiles that the Soviet Union had aimed at Western Europe, and that the American Polaris submarines stationed off the coasts of Europe should be placed under NATO command to give the Europeans greater reassurance[15]—antecedents of the "Eurostrategic" arguments that appeared two decades later, with equally troublesome consequences for the cohesion of the alliance.

But the military-strategic imbalance in Europe was not the real issue; had it been, the MLF could not have addressed it. It was difficult to imagine how the MLF could have reassured the alliance and fostered a feeling of "interdependence" in Western Europe.[16] Not only would the United States have retained a veto over use, which made it improbable that the MLF could enhance the credibility of a nuclear response by NATO, but the military adequacy of surface deployment at sea was widely questioned by European and American experts, and America's own reliance on submarines rather than the less expensive surface ships clearly implied that the latter were inferior in Washington's eyes.

The MLF was intended by the Kennedy administration to serve not a military function but a political one. The president considered the MLF "something of a fake,"[17] and saw it as a device to counteract the disarray of NATO, promote the transatlantic Grand Design and the integration of Western Europe, and prevent a nuclear pact between Paris and Bonn. Even though Bonn had shown an early interest in the creation of a collective nuclear force and later became its only enthusiastic supporter, American support for the MLF was designed not to satisfy West Germany's alleged desire to become a nuclear power but to forestall it; and although Germany was presumably the beneficiary of the project, German-American relations suffered severely as a result of the MLF.[18]

The problem was that although the Kennedy administration did not take the MLF seriously, the Germans did. Far from being a harmless palliative (Arthur Schlesinger, Jr., called it "a rather transparent public relations attempt"), the MLF proposal turned out to be a troublesome liability for American diplomacy. It ultimately placed a serious strain on German-American relations, further cooled Franco-American relations, and jeopardized the nonproliferation treaty a few years later. It also burdened Franco-German relations further (which were strained throughout the years of Chancellor Ludwig Erhard, who had succeeded Adenauer in 1963), because de Gaulle wanted a European defense structure under French leadership and was adamantly opposed to German participation in nuclear ventures that would tie Bonn more closely to the United States.

In the first place, after Bonn had committed itself fully to the MLF (in 1964 it looked as if Bonn and Washington would proceed with it bilaterally)[19] the scrapping of the proposal by the Johnson administration in 1965 caused Chancellor Erhard considerable embarrassment on both the domestic and international political scenes. This was especially serious because Erhard, in the face of strong French objections, had consistently supported American policy (on NATO and the Atlantic community, on Vietnam, and by responding to Washington's call for higher conventional troop levels for Central Europe), and had relied heavily on President Johnson's readiness to reciprocate by supporting the MLF. The demise of the MLF, coupled with the president's refusal in fall 1966 to accept a reduction of German offset purchases for American troops stationed in Germany, thus dealt a serious blow to Erhard's prestige.[20] It added to the foreign and domestic policy problems that already beset Bonn, and by providing additional ammunition for the domestic opposition to Erhard contributed to his forced resignation late in 1966.

Second, the political ramifications of the multilateral force, which were the ones that really mattered in that the MLF hardly enhanced German security interests, magnified rather than papered over the conflicts between Germany and the United States. Throughout the period when the MLF was considered, an important reason for the Germans' interest was the symbolic quality that joint ownership of nuclear forces would have provided. It would have indicated to the Germans' allies, to their opponents, and to themselves the continuing centrality of their contribution to the alliance, which they saw diminishing as the intense Cold War confrontations of the 1950s (which culminated in the Cuban missile crisis of 1962) eased into the period of coexistence in the 1960s. (In those years Bonn, isolated in its Eastern policies and frustrated by its weakening political influence in the alliance, was especially susceptible to psychologically charged diplomatic ventures. The MLF was one example, the monetary crisis with France another; see chapter 9).

Bonn also hoped that the MLF would provide bargaining leverage to help the cause of German reunification. Foreign Minister Gerhard Schröder made this explicit in summer 1965, when he declared that the Federal Republic would renounce its nuclear ambitions only if the Soviet Union would not obstruct German reunification. This anticipated leverage, illusory to begin with, obviously required continued and forthright American support for the MLF, especially because de Gaulle had indicated that German participation in the MLF would stand in the way of a "European solution" to the German question (the only kind of solution he would support), because it would tie Bonn too closely to Washington.[21] But it was precisely the implied anti-Soviet dimension of Bonn's interest in the MLF that forced the Johnson administration to back away from the project. Vital American interests were at stake—a détente with the Soviet Union, an arms control agreement, and the need to nurture Soviet-American relations amid the abrasions of the war in Vietnam—and they required Moscow's cooperation. Sacrificing the MLF was relatively easy for Washington, for neither Britain nor France wanted to see Germany admitted to nuclear policy making, and most members of NATO had shown no real interest in the MLF.[22]

The Germans felt of course that their deep-seated suspicions about a possible Soviet-American deal at their expense were confirmed by Washington's about-face on the MLF. In pushing for the MLF, Bonn had further isolated itself on its Eastern policy for the uncertain prospect of gaining no more than a token of joint nuclear control. What had been intended as a demonstration of Bonn's political importance turned into a demonstration of Bonn's diplomatic weakness.

The German government found it difficult to realize that the political circumstances of the 1960s were fundamentally different from those that had sustained German-American relations in the 1950s (or, if it did, it could not act on its realization). The German-American diplomatic accord fashioned in the 1950s, which encompassed a comprehensive understanding not only on security issues and Germany's status in the alliance but also on a common Eastern policy, had eroded. Adenauer's long-held suspicions about American willingness to make arrangements with the

Soviet Union, if necessary over the head of the West German government, were becoming a reality under his successor. In committing themselves to the MLF, the Germans had acted on assumptions about the
reliability of their American partner that may have been justified in the
1950s but had clearly become illusory in the 1960s.[23] The German chancellor's expectations of American diplomacy seemed based on grievous
misconceptions about American intentions and policies.

Aside from the bitterness and mutual recriminations that were engendered by this "misunderstanding," the Germans were compelled to rethink the central political and diplomatic principles that had guided their
Western policies in the 1950s: equality and integration. The corrosion of
NATO also signified the corrosion of the institutional, political, strategic,
and ultimately psychological context in which the Germans had pressed
their demands for integration and equality. As NATO was weakening, as
Britain relied on its special relationship with the United States, and as
France left NATO's institutions, the Germans' claim to equality was deprived of real meaning. The question became: Equal to whom? This
situation might have been tolerable if Bonn could have continued to rely
on its transatlantic partner. But as Adenauer's ambassador to Washington, Wilhelm Grewe, had pointed out: "German and American security interests are in part coterminous—but only in part. Important
differences existed, which could not be removed through discussions or
compromise. It followed that the interests (and the strategic plans and
dispositions which implemented them) of the stronger prevailed, and
that the weaker had to accept them and try to live with them. Nor could
we afford reactions of spiteful defiance (*Trotzreaktionen*) as did the
French."[24]

The meaning of integration also was eroding. As the transatlantic
security compact began to shrink to a German-American connection, the
opportunities that the integrative features of the alliance provided for
American control became even more clearly visible and again pointed
unmistakably to the Federal Republic. Integration, which in the 1950s
had been the foundation of the political and economic reconstruction of
the Federal Republic and the basis for its security arrangements with the
West, turned in the 1960s into the symbol and reality of Washington's
security control over Bonn. Noting how the Germans had been given no
choice but to accede to NATO under the principle of integration, in 1965
Grewe (then West Germany's ambassador to NATO) wrote to Foreign
Minister Schröder that "integration is without doubt an effective hegemonial instrument of the most powerful in the alliance."[25] These were
strong words indeed coming from a German conservative: for the Germans, equality and integration, the anchors of Bonn's Western diplomacy in the 1950s, had in the 1960s become eviscerated symbols, not of
alliance cohesion or of a politically secure and equitable German status in

the alliance, but of the continuing American control of the Federal Republic's security policies.

Nor was Bonn assuaged by the American proposals for joint nuclear consultations. The Germans considered institutionalized nuclear consultations a consolation prize for the collapse of the MLF,[26] and although they welcomed the opportunity to participate in nuclear planning (primarily because it seemed to ensure the early use of nuclear weapons through explicit contingency planning), they also made clear that they did not regard this arrangement as a substitute for an allied nuclear force.[27] In December 1966 NATO's Nuclear Planning Group (NPG) was established,[28] and in October 1968 the group's members assigned the task of drawing up defense guidelines for the alliance to Britain (the leading European nuclear power) and the Federal Republic (the West European country with the largest conventional forces).[29] But even when the Nuclear Planning Group was supplemented by the so-called Eurogroup in 1968, the West Europeans did not obtain genuine nuclear co-management: the Eurogroup concentrated its efforts on joint training, the coordination of tactical concepts, doctrines, and force structures, and on weapons standardization and joint procurement.

In later years the NPG, augmented by various subcommittees, the Special Consultative Committee (1977), and the "High Level Group" (1978), provided a forum in which to articulate the German viewpoint in NATO, and it was instrumental in preparing for NATO's double-track decision on Eurostrategic weapons in 1979.[30] But the NPG was never intended to be more than a palliative, unlikely to dissipate the allies' concerns. As a former senior official in the Defense Department put it in 1979, "during most of its life, the NATO Nuclear Planning Group was so inhibited by the US that it might sometimes have better been called the Nuclear 'Unplanning' Group. The US initiated it as a sop to Allied concerns. It could have been a far more useful body."[31]

A major reason why NATO could not establish genuine joint control over nuclear weapons was the conflict in Washington between those who supported the dispersal of control over nuclear weapons and those who supported its concentration. Those who supported dispersal, largely to meet the political requirement of reassurance, justified their position in part by pointing to the deterrent effect of multiple centers of Western nuclear decision making. The MLF, the Nassau agreement, and bilateral "nuclear sharing" or "dual key" arrangements were consistent with this view. Those who supported concentrated control over nuclear weapons in a single center (that is, in Washington) argued that nuclear sharing arrangements designed to enhance political reassurance could have disastrous consequences in the event deterrence failed, that the sharing was more illusory than real (given command-and-control arrangements), and that the proliferation of control over nuclear weapons was in principle dangerous and should be opposed. It was the latter view that ultimately prevailed.[32]

Strategic Doctrines as Political Guidelines: Germany and the Language of Arms

Over the decades NATO's institutional control of Germany's armed forces and American political control of German security policies were consistently augmented by the strategic directives issued by the United States and NATO. Throughout the history of the alliance, NATO's strategic posture and doctrinal announcements (which were not always congruent) were formulated largely in Washington and adjusted not only to changes in the regional and global military balance but also to shifts in relations between East and West, intra-alliance politics, and American domestic politics. Both political and technical considerations led to periodic alterations of military policy and strategic doctrine, alterations to which the Federal Republic was especially sensitive and responsive because its military command structure was fully integrated in NATO, and because the military tasks, deployment, and equipment of the Bundeswehr needed to be coordinated with NATO headquarters. Strategic doctrines were at the same time military directives and political guidelines.[33]

When the Eisenhower administration announced its doctrine of massive retaliation in January 1954, it aimed not only to enunciate a military strategy but also to convey a political purpose. The tough language of massive nuclear retaliation was designed to signal a more assertive American attitude toward the Soviet Union, reassure European allies, revitalize America's containment policy with a more "dynamic" dimension, and save resources by denying the Soviet Union the opportunity to challenge America at times and places of Moscow's choosing, which would have compelled Washington to build a costly, across-the-board, "symmetrical" deterrence posture.[34]

When the Kennedy administration switched from the principle of massive retaliation to that of flexible response and graduated deterrence, it meant to convey as well that it intended to move beyond what it considered the outmoded and entrenched Cold War positions of its predecessor. A more flexible strategy was a signal of a more flexible diplomacy. Again, when NATO formally adopted the principle of flexible response in 1967–68 (with some reluctance and after considerable delay), it connected it to the political and diplomatic principles of NATO's Harmel Report, through which the alliance expressed its intention to pursue a policy of détente as well as of defense, to seek a political accommodation in the East at the same time as it remained determined to uphold the military preparedness of the West.[35]

The fluctuations of American declaratory national security doctrines were especially troublesome for the Federal Republic, for reasons of military strategy as well as politics.[36] The Germans disliked the qualification of the principle of extended deterrence that was reflected in Washington's transition from massive retaliation to flexible response; they believed that the ideas behind flexible response implied the divisibility of deterrence (both geographically and on the ladder of escalation) and highlighted the singularity of Germany's position in the alliance; and they worried about the more accommodating policy toward the Soviet Union that accompanied Washington's shift in strategic doctrine.

On more technical grounds, changing military doctrines required the Germans to adjust their contingency planning and the force posture of the Bundeswehr. Between 1956 and 1958, when Bonn sought to implement its NATO commitments by establishing a conventional army, Washington adopted the New Look and the German government, in the face of strong domestic opposition, had to shift its planning from conventional defense to tactical nuclear defense; from 1958 to 1961, when the Germans gradually adjusted to NATO's new strategy, there was a good deal of international as well as domestic opposition to equipping the Bundeswehr with the weapons systems that this strategy required (primarily tactical nuclear carrier weapons); from 1961 to 1963, when the Bundeswehr had already been partly equipped with these weapons, the Kennedy administration introduced the conventional force option and applied pressure on the European allies to raise conventional troop levels.

This situation improved somewhat in the following years with more extensive consultations among the allies, but the decision in 1967 by NATO to make "flexible response" official policy was not entirely out of character. It took from 1963 until 1968 and required hard negotiations before NATO ministers accepted the document incorporating the conventional options that made up the core of flexible response (MC 14/3). Although successive German governments generally did not raise objections in public, some critics were less reluctant and more outspoken. In 1965 Franz-Josef Strauss argued that European doubts about whether the United States could be relied on "to incinerate themselves in a nuclear holocaust for the sake of Europe's freedom" were enhanced by "the frequent changes in American strategic doctrines. . . . We have had the Radford Doctrine, which was a modified John Foster Dulles Doctrine. We have witnessed the introduction of nuclear weapons into the alliance by giving the allies the means of delivery for tactical nuclear weapons and retaining control and custody in American hands. Then came the McNamara Doctrine, from countercity strategy to counter-force strategy, the theory of a pause on the threshold, and now an increased trend back to massive retaliation, not automatic as at the time of the Radford Doctrine, but in the case of extended military operations or to halt an aggressor when he has reached a certain line."[37] The official *White Paper 1970* of the

German Defense Ministry managed to put the matter in terms both more succinct and more delicate: "The modalities of the U.S. commitment in Europe are subject to change, even though the fundamentals of that commitment are not in question."[38]

These doctrinal shifts, coupled with the inevitable delay in the rethinking and replanning required in Bonn and at NATO headquarters, led to serious discontinuities, as when Bonn embraced the concept of massive retaliation at a time when it was already seriously questioned in the United States. There were complementarities as well, mostly imposed by the United States, as when the Federal Republic raised its troop levels and extended military service after the Berlin crisis of 1961 and the United States raised its nuclear deployment in Europe substantially—at a time when the doctrinal differences between the United States and the Federal Republic were intense. A similar situation developed between the Federal Republic and France when their defense policies were no longer congruent, although their strategic conceptions were not all that dissimilar.[39]

The necessity for Bonn to adhere to the political as well as to the military aspects of the strategic guidelines promulgated by Washington was of course precisely what the Western powers had intended when Germany became a member of NATO. But this adherence became increasingly problematical for Bonn, because NATO's political and military purposes were much less compatible than they had been during the 1950s, when Washington's containment and deterrence policies were mutually reinforcing, and when deterring the Soviet Union with American nuclear capabilities still reassured American allies. The more NATO's preoccupations shifted from military to political matters, and the more the alliance suffered from centrifugal tendencies (both changes having been propelled by the superpowers' nuclear standoff and the perceived lessening of the Soviet military threat), the more difficult became the position of the Federal Republic. Bonn was forced to choose between Paris and Washington, and the Germans were required to apportion their diplomatic loyalties and energies between sensitive, watchful partners. In the process, they incurred the displeasure of France as well as of the Soviet Union, for the Federal Republic was unable and unwilling to loosen its indispensable security ties to the United States.

As the cohesion of the alliance weakened and the United States continued to issue in strategic language what were essentially political guidelines, the allies responded in kind and began to use issues of nuclear strategy to express what were at bottom political dissatisfactions with successive American administrations.[40] What developed in the 1960s was a conflicting set of strategic doctrines, most prominently those of the United States and France, through which the Western powers formulated national nuclear strategies that reflected fundamentally conflicting global and regional political aspirations. There emerged a rivalry of competing doctrinal languages in which the Federal Republic, although it was affected, had to remain moot by virtue of its non-nuclear status and its security dependence on the United States, which made it difficult for the Germans to participate in the general trend of articulating political purpose in the language of arms. (Britain, which had European and global policies less succinct than those of the United States and France, was therefore also less prone to express its diplomatic purposes in the language of strategic doctrines. It did so, however, in the language of arms control and European security arrangements; see chapter 3.)

This made for a striking contrast between France and Germany on this matter. Throughout the 1950s and 1960s France and the Federal Republic had distinctly different bilateral relations with the United States and the Soviet Union, and France began quite early to enunciate its goal of diplomatic independence in the idiom of strategic language. The force de frappe was a supremely political instrument, and its doctrinal justification, the principle of "all-round" defense, practically amounted to a stance of armed neutrality.[41]

But it was not only their different geographies of risk and the differing degree of their security dependence on the United States that distinguished France and Germany in the political use of strategic doctrine. History, politics, and psychology imposed distinctions as well. Because of Germany's past, had the Germans followed General de Gaulle's example of couching political aspirations in terms of arms they would have been accused of being unreconstructed militarists. Especially sensitive was the question of any kind of German association with nuclear weapons—the German finger on the nuclear trigger. Whenever German policy touched on nuclear matters (talks about a Franco-German nuclear consortium, German participation in the proposed multilateral nuclear NATO force, Bonn's procrastination on the nonproliferation treaty) anxiety levels rose in the West as well as in the East. The Germans had to speak softly indeed.[42]

In some tentative ways, the Germans did use strategic language and issues of military strategy to advance what were basically political purposes, especially in the delicate matter of sharing nuclear control within the alliance.[43] More important, the Federal Republic's geographical and political location on the periphery of the Western alliance entitled it to a "mini-doctrine" of its own, the principle of forward defense, which shared with other doctrines the conveying of political intent and the lack of military plausibility. Fundamentally, the idea of "forward defense" was intended to express NATO's determination to stand up to the Warsaw Pact's armies at the West German border and not permit the territory and population of the Federal Republic to be overrun in case of an attack. The principle of forward defense was in a sense the Federal Republic's answer to NATO's doctrine of flexible response—an answer through which the Germans sought to deny NATO at least the flexibility of geography even if they could not deny it the flexibility of what weapons systems to choose in meeting a Soviet attack.[44] Although NATO planners had all along questioned the military feasibility of defending Europe along the Federal Republic's border with the German Democratic Republic and Czechoslovakia (indeed, Germany's insistence on forward defense antedated the American enunciation of flexible response in the early 1960s), it was politically imperative to assure the Germans that their geographical position would not condemn them to being the first and perhaps only victims of a conventional war.[45] Political and symbolic necessities were expressed in military fiction.

The connections between flexible response and forward defense became clearly visible after France left NATO's integrated command in 1966,[46] for it was after this event that the United States (in the person of Defense Secretary Robert S. McNamara) pressed upon NATO the doctrine of flexible response, and that the idea of forward defense, which had always appeared rather impracticable, became further undermined by the loss of French troops, airspace, and territory.[47] Spokesmen in Washington now implied that the French withdrawal might compel NATO to resort to nuclear arms in a major conflict earlier than otherwise anticipated because "we are removing a part of the defense in depth which is useful." Persons making such statements "could not have had in mind how the Germans might respond to such a remark. For it means simply that West Germany could be considered expendable before nuclear weapons were used."[48]

The French withdrawal from NATO clearly precluded the possibility of establishing a closer Franco-German security compact, which the Kennedy administration had sought to obviate by supporting the idea of a NATO nuclear force. This possibility seemed quite remote, however. Throughout the 1960s Franco-German relations were burdened for a variety of reasons having to do with conflicting Eastern policies, highly charged monetary disagreements, and totally opposed views of the purpose of West European integration. There was little likelihood that Paris and Bonn could arrive at a common security arrangement, because each side saw security matters as closely connected to its overall foreign policy program.

When Charles de Gaulle returned to power in 1958, his quest for a national nuclear force de frappe reflected much more than the attempt to fashion a more convincing nuclear deterrent for France: it became the symbol for the political independence of French diplomacy. The French were deeply frustrated by having all the attributes of a great power except power itself, doubly sensitive to real or imagined slights at the hands of the United States and Britain, and determined to escape the dependencies in economics, finance, and military strategy that had characterized Franco-American relations in the Fourth Republic. De Gaulle was convinced that being a nuclear power would energize a French diplomacy that put a premium on independence and flexibility, regardless of whether the cost of a small national force de frappe was justified on purely strategic grounds. As Charles Burton Marshall noted, "France's problem was not how to gain security but how to regain a lost significance."[49]

Against this background, France's larger political aims were much more important than the technical arguments for a French nuclear capability (that it might trigger an American nuclear response, or compensate in the credibility of its use for what it lacked in size and sophistication).[50] De Gaulle intended that a national nuclear arsenal should help France escape from the grip of the superpowers, the superiority of which had paralyzed the nation's foreign policy in the postwar period, and regain for France diplomatic maneuverability in dealing with its allies as well as its opponents. When France left the integrated command structure of NATO in 1966, it was merely the last logical step in a series of diplomatic events that had their origin in de Gaulle's determination to restore independence to French diplomacy.

For all these reasons and others, Paris could not have been a suitable partner for Bonn's security policies. Bonn simply would have exchanged its security dependence on the United States for a security dependence on France. There was no likelihood that de Gaulle would offer the Germans genuine equality on security matters.[51] On the contrary, the French nuclear program was in some fundamental respects directed against the Federal Republic, with the French seeing in their nuclear status a compensating feature for the Germans' growing influence in economic and monetary matters. Both Washington and Paris realized that whoever controlled German security policy would control German diplomacy as well. As a high German official put it, the Germans had the choice of serving either as a glacis for France or as a missile ramp for America.[52]

U.S. Conventional Troops in Europe

It is in this context that American conventional forces in Europe (particularly those based in the Federal Republic) obtain their significance. In addition to American nuclear weapons, American troops have contributed importantly to the dynamics of double containment, extended deterrence, and political reassurance. They have done so precisely because their role cannot be viewed in isolation from that of nuclear weapons. The American soldiers stationed in West Germany have always enhanced the credibility of extended nuclear deterrence, both because American ground forces serve a "hostage" function that ensures the prompt engagement of the United States in the early stages of a

European conflict, and because American ground forces enlarge NATO's capacity for non-nuclear defense of the central front, thereby raising the nuclear threshold to a more credible level and diminishing the problem posed by America's "self-deterrence."[53] In psychological terms these forces have constituted for West Europeans a tangible manifestation of the American political commitment to the future of the Continent.

Just as important, they have in Soviet eyes been evidence that the duopolistic Soviet-American division of Europe remains efficacious, since their presence checks the instabilities that might result if West Europeans (and especially the West Germans) were left to their own devices.[54] It is unlikely that Washington's European policy of double containment, its strategic posture of deterrence and reassurance, or its effort to stabilize the political and strategic relationship with the Soviet Union could have been sustained without the large-scale presence of American conventional forces on German soil. That this presence in Germany was not drastically reduced in conjunction with the Eisenhower administration's doctrine of massive retaliation indicates perhaps that the stationing of American troops was justified not only by the nature of the Soviet military threat, but primarily by the political requirements of double containment, reassurance, and stabilizing the alliance.[55]

The calculus of West European military security began to change in the 1960s. As the United States itself became vulnerable to nuclear attack, American decision makers became increasingly nervous about any commitment to the early use of nuclear weapons. Secretary of Defense McNamara made it clear early in the Kennedy administration that he wanted an enhanced conventional force capability for NATO, and that the quid pro quo for nuclear sharing arrangements such as the MLF would be agreement by Europe, and especially West Germany, to a strategy that embodied a larger, more active role for conventional forces. Despite European fears that an increased emphasis on such forces would undermine nuclear deterrence, the role of NATO's conventional forces continued to be intimately linked to tactical nuclear weapons and the American strategic deterrent.

By the mid-1970s, as the onset of nuclear parity between the superpowers placed the United States at considerable risk and undermined the credibility of extended deterrence, the nature of the relationship between conventional and nuclear forces became more controversial: "With the emergence of strategic nuclear parity and the Allies' manifest lack of enthusiasm for tactical nuclear weapons, the importance of the conventional element in the overall deterrence equation . . . increased significantly."[56] In Washington's view, American conventional forces in Germany (along with the Bundeswehr) now had a role that extended beyond their strategic and political link to nuclear weapons. Increasingly, they had deterrent value in and of themselves. This position seemed to be supported by the analyses of the conventional force balance in Central Europe, which sought to demonstrate that NATO was quite capable of deterring or blocking a conventional assault without recourse to nuclear weapons.[57] Such arguments stressed of course the military dimensions of the East-West confrontation in Europe, while ignoring the larger political purposes that conventional and nuclear forces served in the relationships between (and within) the two alliances.

In the 1980s American analysts and their counterparts at NATO took the case for strengthening conventional forces still further, often with the support of Gen. Bernard Rogers, until 1987 the Supreme Allied Commander in Europe (SACEUR), who argued that in case of attack he would otherwise need to resort to nuclear weapons quite quickly. They pointed to new operational concepts that by capitalizing on emerging military technologies would preserve flexible response and forward defense, enhance the efficacy of conventional forces, and diminish early reliance on nuclear weapons while relieving NATO governments of the economic and political burdens of large-scale conventional deployments. These new concepts included follow-on forces attack (which envisaged wide-range, deep interdiction of the Warsaw Pact's second echelon forces), the U.S. Army's AirLand Battle doctrine (which called for rapid, highly maneuverable, unpredictable, and disorienting operations behind the enemy's front line), and Counter-Air 90 (which envisaged the use of conventionally armed ballistic missiles to destroy the Warsaw Pact's air bases far behind the battle area). In short, the new orientation was intended to enhance deterrence with non-nuclear means by denying the opposing side the sanctuary of its own territory. (See also chapter 4.)

Many Germans found much to object to in all of this, as always torn between conflicting considerations. While they valued the presence of American troops, they also tired of Washington's periodic threats to reduce it, expressed skepticism about the technical feasibility and reliability of these highly complex modern battle doctrines, felt uncomfortable with a more aggressive conventional force strategy that envisaged the destruction of both Germanies, and viewed Washington's emphasis on conventional forces as a transparent attempt to compensate for diminishing American nuclear commitments. Moreover, there was a glaring contradiction between preparing NATO for a more aggressive force posture while demanding at the same time that the Warsaw Pact restructure its troop deployments to render them capable only of defensive and not of offensive actions. In the 1980s NATO's tendency toward divorcing planning for conventional and nuclear forces seemed to have brought the thinking of the alliance full circle, back to the days when conventional and nuclear capabilities and doctrines were not articulated and coordinated with each other.[58] Although prominent Americans saw the American strategic protection of Western Europe as "a classic case . . . of doctrinal confusion and pragmatic success," Germany's former chancellor Helmut Schmidt wrote in 1985 that "Europeans are profoundly skeptical of the amount of careful thinking that lies behind the Grand Strategy of their most important ally and friend. They see, and worry about, a pattern of volatility and discontinuity in American strategy."[59]

To the extent that American conventional forces in Germany contributed to double containment and political reassurance by being a linkage with American nuclear weapons (both in the United States and in Europe), the logic of the American conventional presence would have to be reoriented in the late 1980s and early 1990s. A Soviet-American condominium based on the virtual elimination of intermediate-range nuclear forces (coupled perhaps with a reduction of strategic nuclear forces) would demand a different rationale for the continued presence on German soil of large-scale American ground forces. Paradoxically, the superpowers' effort to militarize the essential dynamics of their relationship would remain intact, and West German attempts to overcome the division of East and West by political and economic means would face an uncertain future. Although the Soviet arms control initiatives of the late 1980s (both conventional and strategic) made it appear imperative that NATO respond with a militarily coordinated, strategically consistent, and politically defensible reorganization of its overall deterrence and defense posture, there was little evidence that it could do so. When the former German defense minister Manfred Wörner became NATO's secretary general in summer 1988, his most urgent task was to help in effecting a plausible restructuring of NATO's institutions, strategy, and political purpose.

The Federal Republic and the Nuclearization of East-West Diplomacy

In addition to being checked by NATO's integrative institutions and American strategic guidelines, German security policies were most fundamentally restrained by the imperatives of the East-West nuclear balance and the nuclear diplomacy of the United States.

When the Cold War was intense and the nuclear balance not yet sufficiently even to encourage either superpower to codify it in arms control agreements, the nuclear weapons deployed on West German territory were an important element of NATO's nuclear arsenals and a powerful base for America's nuclear diplomacy. In the 1960s and 1970s, as the contest between the superpowers moved from Cold War to coexistence to détente, the peculiar and singular nuclear status of the Federal Republic—full of nuclear weapons, devoid of nuclear control—became even more visible and significant for the conduct of East-West nuclear diplomacy. As the Western alliance weakened under the impact of political and military-strategic developments, as the perceptions of the Soviet threat changed, and as the superpowers sought to stabilize the nuclear balance with arms control arrangements, the nuclear weapons deployed in West Germany and East Germany became major stakes in superpower diplomacy. (See chapter 3.)

Paradoxically, the advent of strategic parity between the United States and the Soviet Union (and the superpowers' corresponding willingness to stabilize their relations through arms control and détente) enlarged rather than narrowed the opportunities for using nuclear diplomacy for the purposes of alliance management. Restrained by the perils of the nuclear balance of terror and by their mutual vulnerability, the superpowers began to realize that their extensive nuclear arsenals obtained little political leverage in their direct contest with one another. Weapons that could not be used were not very effective for exerting military or political pressure on the opponent or gaining advantage in bilateral diplomacy: "The paradox . . . is that arms-related substitutes for war, such as deployments, competitive arms races, sales of arms, and even arms control negotiations and related transactions, tend to multiply to compensate for the dearth of opportunities for effective diplomacy backed by force. These substitutes contribute to the illusion of prenuclear international politics as usual."[60]

But although nuclear weapons provided little diplomatic leverage anywhere else, they remained powerful instruments for managing the superpowers' military alliances, especially in Europe where these alliances confronted one another. From the American perspective this leverage applied especially to the Federal Republic, which in contrast to France and Britain had no independent nuclear arsenal or independent security policy; from the Soviet perspective this leverage applied especially to the German Democratic Republic, which served the Warsaw Pact as the forward base for the emplacement of its nuclear capabilities. The nuclear saturation of both German states had a number of important consequences: it tied the two German governments even more closely to their respective superpower protectors and their views of the East-West conflict, it provided bargaining chips in the politics of arms control, it stabilized the division of Europe and checked what might otherwise have been less controllable attempts to overcome it, it narrowed the range of diplomacy available to both German governments and constrained their political mobility, and it supported the essentially conservative European policies pursued by the United States and the Soviet Union.[61]

To be sure, the continuing centrality of military issues in superpower diplomacy may also be attributed to the intractability of fundamental political issues between East and West. But it was primarily the limited utility of nuclear weapons in adversary diplomacy that made them prime instruments for alliance diplomacy, especially when directed toward partners such as the Federal Republic that were handicapped by their non-nuclear status. Debilitating as it became for German-American relations and for the cohesion of the alliance, the use of nuclear diplomacy for tying the Federal Republic to NATO remained at the core of American strategic policy in Europe in the 1970s and 1980s. Washington's political use of nuclear diplomacy and arms control policies continued to have a profound effect on the limits and possibilities of West German diplomacy.

But this was fraught with risk. Nuclear weapons are illsuited as a symbolic substitute for political trust in addressing the controversies that have beset American relations with Western Europe and Germany. As most disagreements within NATO have demonstrated in the past, the political and symbolic use of nuclear weapons for managing the alliance can cut both ways: it can demonstrate the continuing commitment of the United States to risk its own security for the sake of the alliance, but it can also raise the fear among allies that a nuclear war might be limited to Europe.[62] Even on purely political grounds, nuclear issues play a negative role in the alliance. They are most prominent when the political health of the alliance is most infirm; they are the symptoms of NATO's political malaise, which they in turn aggravate. Political problems announce themselves in the guise of strategic problems. "When Europeans are tolerably confident of American purpose and leadership, nuclear matters will be less salient; when they are not, specific issues . . . will emerge as surrogates for concern about the ultimate reliability of the American nuclear guarantee."[63]

Nuclear diplomacy as an instrument for managing the Western alliance is also damaging because it inevitably emphasizes the different security interests of the allies and their different political and legal status in the alliance. For reasons of history, politics, and geography, the foreign policy interests of the Federal Republic, France, and Britain are not congruous. Although they are allies, these countries have distinctly different relations with Washington and Moscow, and a distinctly different political and institutional status in the transatlantic security compact. Nuclear diplomacy affects them in different ways, not only because they either have or lack nuclear arsenals of their own, but because all parties have become accustomed to the translation into the language of nuclear arms of what are at bottom political purposes. Nuclear diplomacy is divisive diplomacy.

Moreover, the militarization of East-West diplomacy is by and large disadvantageous to the West. It confers on the Soviet Union the distinction of being a superpower equal to the United States, which is of great symbolic and political importance to Moscow, the more so because it is undeserved in most other respects. For example, participation in the SALT process made the Soviet Union something of a silent partner in the nuclear-strategic deliberations and arrangements of the Western alliance at the same time as the Federal Republic's Ostpolitik gave Moscow more of an indirect influence on German politics, both foreign and domestic.

Both superpowers can use security issues to accelerate or brake the dynamics of détente.[64]

The nuclearization of diplomacy also tends to erode domestic political support for the Western alliance. Again, this applied with special emphasis to the Federal Republic.[65] In the 1980s there was a growing perception among Germans that American security policies were intended both to provide them with security and keep them politically controlled. Second only to Germany's restraint by NATO, the saturation of West Germany with nuclear weapons drew the limits of German diplomacy. West Germans have long understood that the nuclear superpowers exploit their nuclear status for political purposes, use their nuclear-strategic preponderance in an attempt to compensate for diplomatic, political, and even economic infirmities, and generally translate geostrategic intentions into nuclear diplomacy. Indeed, Bonn's own policies significantly contributed to creating this leverage. Bonn's decision in the 1950s to permit and in some cases encourage the deployment of American nuclear weapons on German soil had a profound and persistent effect on the entire range of German foreign policy goals, in the East as well as the West, because most of them became entangled with the issue of nuclear arms on German territory. Because of the Federal Republic's security dependence, each successive German government has been centrally interested in the American nuclear presence in Europe, and Bonn's quandary in the mid- and late 1980s with respect to eliminating medium- and shorter-range nuclear weapons again pointed to the Germans' fundamental dilemma of reconciling their strategic security interests, which seemed to call for an unambiguous American nuclear presence in Europe, and their political interests in détente in Europe, which seemed to call for a reduction or at least a qualification of the American nuclear presence—a possibility consistently suggested by the opposition in Bonn.[66]

As it was, one of the transatlantic security community's strongest bonds in the 1980s was the need, present from the beginning, to secure the allegiance of the Federal Republic in an integrative Western security compact. It was precisely the mounting European doubts about the ability of the United States to contain the Federal Republic through durable security commitments that led France in the late 1980s to forge independent military ties with Bonn, which involved reconfiguring the role of French tactical nuclear weapons for the forward defense of West Germany (a departure from prior French doctrine), and a European role for the French Rapid Deployment Force (RDF).[67]

To be sure, there were other powerful bonds as well. The durability of the alliance amid shifting doctrinal orientations and tilting weights in the military balance can also be attributed to political and bureaucratic inertia, the visceral reluctance to effect change, lack of leadership and of plausible institutional alternatives, and the powerful political and symbolic orthodoxies that have grown around NATO as the historic and most visible embodiment of containment and deterrence. The Soviet Union also has helped to keep NATO alive through its habitual inclination to define its basic security interests primarily in terms of arms (which appears diminishing under General Secretary Mikhail S. Gorbachev), eliciting in Western Europe the belief, justified or not, that its own defense efforts were insufficient and required transatlantic augmentation and guarantees.

Nonetheless, from the American perspective the primary reason for sustaining the existing framework of NATO was the continuing imperatives of double containment, embodied in the institutional arrangements of the alliance and directed toward both the Soviet Union and the Federal Republic. These imperatives were apparently as compelling to American planners in the 1980s as they had been in the 1940s and 1950s. For the West Europeans too, although they would like to stretch NATO's existing security framework to accommodate their distinct regional security interests, the integrative structures of NATO remain the most effective way of dealing with the "German problem." Any fundamental change in NATO would reopen the issue of how to contain the Federal Republic within the Western alliance and within Europe. It is still difficult to perceive NATO and the Federal Republic, which were created and have matured together, as separate entities. There persists "a solid allied consensus that because the Soviet Union poses at least a serious *latent* threat to the security of Western Europe, an alliance with the United States is indispensable. Equally important, there is consensus that an alliance with the United States is indispensable in making the Federal Republic of Germany's contribution to European security politically acceptable both to Germans and to Germany's allies. The strength of this two-fold consensus has enabled the allies to surmount numerous crises in Atlantic relations."[68]

2

German Security Interests and the Devolution of Extended Deterrence

Perhaps even today, but surely in the 1980s, the United States will no longer be in a strategic position to reduce a Soviet counterblow against the United States to tolerable levels. . . . And therefore, I would say, which I might not say in office, the European allies should not keep asking us to multiply strategic assurances that we cannot possibly mean, or if we do mean, we should not want to execute because if we execute, we risk the destruction of civilization.

—HENRY KISSINGER, 1979

"Flexible response" has never presupposed genuine flexibility. Instead, it has always implied a quick escalation toward very early first use of nuclear weapons by the West. But it is unrealistic to believe that West German soldiers would fight after the explosion of the first couple of nuclear weapons on West German soil. . . . Western nuclear weapons are necessary and valuable only in order to deter the Eastern side from a first use of Soviet nuclear weapons. . . . Nuclear weapons must not be perceived as an instrument to deter limited war or even large scale conventional attack. What we do need in order to discourage and deter an adversary from limited aggression . . . are credible conventional forces.

—HELMUT SCHMIDT, 1987

The most fundamental question to be raised about the Federal Republic's security concerns is whether they were plausible to begin with. Was West German security threatened by the Soviet Union or its allies at any time during the postwar era?

A fully persuasive answer to this question is of course not possible. History does not disclose its alternatives, and even in retrospect we cannot fully discern the motives and intentions of the Soviet Union in the postwar period. There can be no incontrovertible proof or refutation of the claim that NATO and the American deterrent secured the peace of postwar Europe and prevented the Red Army from extending its sway from Eastern Europe to the Atlantic. It is in the very nature of a successful deterrence policy that its success cannot be attributed unambiguously to the policy itself: "The more we are inclined to believe that Soviet policy-makers had expansionist intentions and might have been willing to use force if the calculus of risk and advantage was ever right, the more we must credit them with cautious behavior in face of a deterrent which, in its various forms, the Western governments themselves over the years constantly—and publicly—undervalued."[1]

But for the West the narrow question of territorial security was in any case subsumed by the larger question of political security. Over the decades the Germans too drew connections and comparisons between the measure of political control exerted over them and the measure of security extended to them. The more they perceived a weakening of the American nuclear commitment to them, accurately or not, the more they sought a larger voice—a *Mitspracherecht*—in the nuclear management of the alliance. And the more they saw other allies, especially France, slip away from their nuclear dependence on the United States, the more sensitive they became to the restrictions placed on them. As the alliance's principle of equality weakened and its principle of integration turned into an instrument of American dominance, the Germans became increasingly aware of the political limitations and military-strategic liabilities that their special status in the alliance entailed. The Germans felt they were entitled to strategic reassurance so long as they accepted political containment and augmented it with self-containment.

But the American postwar nuclear strategy of deterring the Soviet Union and reassuring American allies became unconvincing once the Soviet Union obtained nuclear weapons that posed a threat to the United States itself. While central deterrence, which seeks to deflect an attack on America itself, remained intact, extended deterrence, which entails the commitment to initiate the use of nuclear weapons on behalf of an ally, progressively weakened. Increasingly, the requirements of deterrence as the Germans saw them called for political commitments and military measures that Americans perceived as immensely risky and ultimately unacceptable. To an ever greater degree, steps taken to enhance NATO's deterrence posture posed the risk that a nuclear response might actually be used in a severe crisis—a risk the United States needed to avoid in light of its own vulnerability.

In the nuclear age, the main purpose of military policy must be to avert war rather than win it. An opponent or potential aggressor must be persuaded that the anticipated benefits of initiating military action are incommensurate with its costs, and that it is likely that these costs will be inflicted. But one of the paradoxes of the nuclear age is that a politically constructive posture of deterrence requires that the opponent to be deterred must also be reassured. In circumstances of nuclear parity and mutual assured destruction, the nuclear protector of an alliance, such as the United States, must reassure not only its allies but also its opponent that its deterrence policy is both responsible and credible, firm yet circumspect, governed by loyalty to the alliance as well as the prudence imposed by one's own vulnerability.[2]

This is not an easy task. What develops between opponents in the nuclear age is an *alliance entre ennemis*, as Raymond Aron called it many years ago, with a corrosive effect on the security compact between friends. What reassures an opponent is not necessarily what reassures an ally. The nuclear protector of an alliance is entrapped in the convoluted and insidious dialectic that results from having to provide central deterrence, extended deterrence, double reassurance, and (should deterrence fail) defense—each requiring its own diplomatic exertions and military-strategic implementation, each being in conflict with the others. Once the Soviet Union reached nuclear parity with the United States, Washington became obliged to accept Moscow as an equal, a necessity reflected in strategic doctrine as well as in the readiness to stabilize the nuclear balance through arms control. Yet as long as Western Europe felt inferior in the area of conventional capabilities (perhaps because it preferred to), the security of Western Europe could be convincingly assured only on the basis of an implied American invulnerability or nuclear superiority.[3] A realistic American strategic relationship with the Soviet Union must rest on a balance of terror, whereas the American guarantee of West European security rests in the end on an implied imbalance of terror in favor of the United States—especially if the alliance contemplates the first use of nuclear weapons should deterrence fail and the tide of conventional battle turn against the West.

As a consequence, American policies intended to stabilize the Soviet-American strategic balance and create mutual assurance between the adversaries often conflicted with American policies intended to enhance the security of American allies and give them more reassurance. "The real efficacy of extended deterrence is in keeping allies, not just deterring adversaries. There is a nagging asymmetry about nuclear protection: it takes more credibility to keep an ally than to deter an adversary."[4]

Throughout the history of NATO, the principle of extended deterrence has remained official doctrine of the alliance. Extended deterrence embodied America's nuclear commitment to its allies, which was reaffirmed by every American administration since the 1950s and signified the indivisibility of Western security even as the alliance superpower was separated from its partners by the Atlantic. In the course of decades the idea of deterrence was supplemented by a number of subdoctrines—such as massive retaliation, flexible response, graduated deterrence, assured destruction, mutual assured destruction, to mention just a few—which expressed (or obscured) in increasingly technical language what remained fundamentally political concerns and intentions. In effect, all doctrinal changes of the last decades, beginning with flexible response, amounted to a qualification of the principle of extended deterrence. Extended deterrence became a fiction: a myth of the alliance that had to be protected from the rough and unpalatable realities of the East-West nuclear balance and the inevitable reconsiderations of the American national interest that these realities brought with them.

Whatever problems plagued NATO because of waning American nuclear superiority always were felt more keenly in Bonn than in other West European capitals. Each infirmity of NATO tended to highlight the unique position of the Federal Republic in the Western alliance. Bonn's concerns were always sharpened by the recognition that security conflicts existed not only between the United States and Western Europe but also between Western Europe and the Federal Republic. The security interests of the United States, Britain, France, Italy, and the Federal Republic were not congruous, especially not at the lower levels of provocation, which were most likely to involve West Germany because of its forward geographical position and unresolved political issues with the East. For the Germans, the question of whether the defense of the Atlantic alliance was indivisible was compounded by the equally troublesome question of whether the defense of Western Europe was indivisible.

All this underlined that the Federal Republic's geography, history, legal status, and political interests made it from the beginning a NATO member with special inhibitions, obligations, and frustrations. Although they resented and fought it, the Germans were condemned to their position of "singularity" in the alliance. Even as successive German governments rejected the existence of "differentiated zones of security" in NATO's geography of risk, they could not avert the diminishing salience of equality and integration in the Western alliance.

The Waning of Reassurance

Several years before Germany joined NATO in 1955 and many years before the Soviet Union reached nuclear parity with the United States, the Germans were already uneasy about the implications for their security of NATO's defense posture and strategy.

When the EDC Treaty was signed in 1952 by the Federal Republic, France, Italy, and the Benelux countries, the question of German rearmament had become even more pressing, which was one reason why the demise of the EDC in the French National Assembly caused such consternation in Washington. From the beginning, NATO planners had operated on the basis of several defense plans. In addition to stopgap emergency plans, they had formulated a long-term requirements plan based on the contingency of a main Soviet thrust across the north German plain, which spelled out the force levels required to meet the threat and defend Europe in a major war. By 1952 there was a feeling of increased urgency among NATO members to put these plans into effect, for the Soviet Union had already exploded nuclear devices and it was expected that American strategic nuclear superiority would gradually diminish. Thus at the NATO Conference of February 1952 in Lisbon, the North Atlantic Council agreed on a force goal of ninety-six divisions, of which thirty-five to forty were to be battle-ready on the line, the remainder capable of mobilization within a month after D-day.[5] Given these force requirements, it was not surprising that the Council members "reaffirmed the urgency, for the defense of Western Europe, of establishing at the earliest possible date a militarily effective European Defense Force, including a German contribution."[6]

There was no intention, however, of matching Soviet conventional forces in Europe. The decision to equip NATO with a conventional army powerful enough to sustain a prolonged engagement with Soviet ground troops was intended to compensate for the diminishing advantage of the American nuclear deterrent rather than to provide a conventional alternative. The primary purpose of a large NATO army was to prevent the Soviet Union from effecting a fait accompli with a conventional attack while threatening a nuclear strike against Western Europe. Because the Soviet Union was not yet capable of threatening the United States with nuclear destruction, a Soviet threat to attack Western Europe could be credibly countered by an American threat to retaliate with nuclear weapons.[7]

The implications of the strategy devised in Lisbon aroused misgivings in Bonn that foreshadowed the much more serious concerns voiced in later years: the Germans were worried that the large force goals envisaged at Lisbon implied the possibility of a limited war in Europe, during which the Federal Republic would necessarily suffer the most. But this was not the time to raise in public concerns about NATO strategy. The Bonn government was reluctant to weaken its argument for rearmament and German membership in the EDC at a time when the debate over rearmament was at its height in Germany, and when the opposition was accusing the chancellor of recruiting German foot soldiers for the Western alliance. Nor was it the time to place on the important political negotiations with the Western allies the burden of German reservations about American military planning—a point that should also be borne in mind by those who see in the famous Soviet notes of March 1952 large missed opportunities for German unification.[8] The political concessions that Bonn expected to gain through rearmament were still held in abeyance. Dean Acheson described the situation as follows: "The major problems that remained after Lisbon were of two general types—those of high policy and those that, while involving policy, also involved vast and complicated detail. Of the first type, so far as the contractual arrangement was concerned, were the extent of allied reserved power to declare an emergency and resume authority in Germany and the extent to which a future all-German government should or could be bound by the present government; of the latter type, the division of the German defense budget between German military effort and allied troop support, and the review of items that might properly be charged to German support of allied troops stationed there."[9]

When Germany joined NATO in 1955, the principle of extended deterrence was already weakening, even though the United States still enjoyed nuclear supremacy and the measure of trust between the American and German governments was higher than at any time afterward.

Bonn was greatly concerned when the Eisenhower administration, as part of its New Look, augmented Washington's strategy of massive retaliation with a plan to use conventional troops to deal with minor aggression and prevent the Soviet Union from mounting a limited attack. This dual purpose of NATO planning, which prepared for the contingency of conventional defense at the same time as it tried to sustain the credibility of nuclear deterrence, appeared troublesome to the Germans. The concept of mobile strategy and elastic defense had already stirred up a lively debate in the German press and among German military experts because it seemed to accept the possibility that an attacker would penetrate deeply into West German territory, subjecting the Germans to the risk of being first overrun and then "liberated." In Western capitals, there were already doubts whether a full-blown American response could be relied on in light of the Soviet nuclear arms buildup. The gap between deterring the Soviet Union and reassuring the allies was opening.

But opening as well was a gap between two increasingly conflicting German attitudes on the role of NATO's conventional troops. While the Germans kept insisting that the United States maintain a large number of troops in Europe, they could not fully reconcile themselves to the conventional military mission for which these troops were designed. Full-fledged preparations for a conventional response, enhanced by the presence of a strong American conventional force, suggested that an American nuclear response would not be automatic and might be delayed.

It was widely believed in the Federal Republic and elsewhere in Europe that preparation for a conventional response would increase the likelihood of war by undermining the credibility of massive retaliation, and would in fact encourage American nuclear disengagement from Europe.[10] Because even a limited engagement with conventional forces would make Germany a battlefield, from Bonn's perspective it seemed better not to extend the range of retaliatory options and thus weaken the automacity of a nuclear response. Owing to its forward position, the prospect of deterring Soviet ground forces with Western ground forces had little attraction for West Germany. Whether it was rational or not in light of the overall East-West military balance, the deployment of tactical nuclear weapons (which Washington defended as serving deterrence rather than defense) held some attractions for Bonn.

On the other hand, there was the implication that in case deterrence should fail the two Germanies would become a nuclear battlefield. The consequences of this possibility were illustrated by NATO's atomic exercise Carte Blanche in June 1955, which simulated 335 atomic bombings on German soil, with casualties estimated to have exceeded five million. NATO and the Federal Republic were now faced with the question of whether tactical nuclear weapons should be viewed primarily as an instrument of *defense* or as an instrument of *deterrence*, and it was not clear how those two functions could be made reinforcing and complementary.

The role of conventional forces was also unclear. Spokesmen for NATO stressed that the thirty divisions planned for the central sector would be there primarily to implement NATO's commitment to a forward strategy in case of an all-out war, a calculation that stemmed from the expectation that a nuclear war would probably be of short duration, and thus would not provide time for mobilizing reserve contingents. At the same time, some German planners resisted the implications of tactical nuclear weapons for Germany's defense and called for a more "national" solution.[11] Even more disturbing, although Washington sought to persuade the Germans that tactical nuclear weapons were to enhance deterrence, there was talk of the possibility and desirability of a "limited" nuclear war (for which Henry Kissinger provided the rationale, later retracted),[12] creating anxieties that burdened the German-American security relationship for decades and that reemerged with renewed intensity in the 1980s during the Reagan administration.

From Massive Retaliation to Flexible Response

The American commitment to initiate nuclear war in case of Soviet aggression against West European territory—the principle of extended deterrence—found its most unqualified expression in the Eisenhower administration's strategy of massive retaliation. But when Washington announced this strategy in 1954 in public, it had already been questioned in private. In August 1953, after a warning by a study group in the Air Force that the United States would soon find itself in a "militarily unmanageable" situation in light of the Soviet Union's emerging nuclear capability, the president wrote to his secretary of state, John Foster Dulles, that a situation might develop where America's security would rest on its ability "to inflict greater loss against the enemy than he could reasonably hope to inflict on us." This was, in effect, an early statement of the principle of mutual assured destruction. The president even contemplated preemptive nuclear war to avoid this dilemma: "If the contest to maintain this relative position should have to continue indefinitely, the cost would either drive us to war—or into some form of dictatorial government. In such circumstances, we would be forced to consider whether or not our duty to future generations did not require us to initiate war at the most propitious moment we could designate."[13]

Before long there was a review of the strategy of rapid nuclear escalation, in which conventional NATO troops were primarily a "trip-wire" that would trigger the tactical phase of a nuclear war. In 1957 NATO adopted a study (MC-70) that redefined the strategic and political relationship between conventional and nuclear weapons and in effect qualified the sweeping American commitments undertaken in the strategy of massive retaliation. The study called for a "shield" of conventional forces, which was designed not to fight an extended conventional war (this would have been unacceptable to countries such as the Federal Republic) but rather to force the enemy to pause after the initial stages of an attack and reconsider the consequences of continuing it. The thinking reflected in MC-70 assumed that the Soviet Union might contemplate only limited intrusions on NATO territory rather than an all-out drive to the English Channel; it clearly required a higher level of conventional NATO forces than the previous "tripwire" strategy; and it envisaged a "firebreak" between the outset of hostilities and the unleashing of an American nuclear response. Even before the United States and the Soviet Union reached nuclear parity, the thinking reflected in MC-70 pointed to the widening gap between the security interests of the United States and its West European NATO partners, above all the Federal Republic.

The idea of a firebreak, which suggested that the escalation to strategic nuclear weapons would be delayed, could hardly reassure the Federal Republic, which was on the forward line of defense: it raised the possibility of what would later be called "decoupling" the American nuclear guarantee from Western Europe. Firebreaks, a rational and understandable requirement from the viewpoint of the United States, weaken the cohesion of the alliance, because coupling across geography and between levels of weapons and warfare is the indispensable core of a security alliance.[14] But the necessity of establishing firebreaks was the essence of the revamping of American strategy that took place during the Kennedy administration, which was intent on reversing the reliance on nuclear weapons that had characterized NATO planning during the Eisenhower administration, and which began to stress a more flexible and therefore more credible American response to military threats. Based on Defense Secretary Robert S. McNamara's maxim that "one cannot fashion a credible deterrent out of an uncredible action," the West was to be fully prepared on all levels to avoid having to choose between nuclear war and accepting the political consequences of doing nothing at all. Washington wanted to provide itself with a credible retaliatory response to every possible level of provocation.

By 1962 the president and his secretary of defense had fully articulated and partly implemented a "doctrine of flexibility," which involved contingency planning that tacitly admitted the feasibility and acceptability of a limited conventional war in Europe.[15] In December 1962 McNamara suggested that because of the shifting nuclear balance of power, nuclear arms had become NATO's shield and conventional arms NATO's sword (thus completely reversing the strategic principles of the Radford Plan), and implied that a nuclear strike countering a conventional attack might be "delayed."[16] Even more clearly than the implications of the Radford Plan, the so-called McNamara Doctrine seemed to reduce the chances of escalation, which Bonn sought to enlarge for reasons of deterrence, and increase the chances that conventional aggression would be met with a conventional response. From the European perspective, a "graduated response" by the United States "came to be regarded exclusively as a defense against escalation, against the spread of hostilities to Soviet and American territories, rather than being regarded *at the same time* as a means to restore psychological *plausibility* to the American deterrent" (italics in original).[17]

In broad terms, the new strategy implied that the United States would not use nuclear weapons at the outset of hostilities except in reply to a nuclear attack, that small-scale attacks would not elicit a nuclear response at all, and that even in case of a massive attack NATO would initially respond only with conventional forces to allow time for negotiations with the opponent and consultations among the allies about the initial use of nuclear weapons. Central to the new strategy was the concept of "graduated deterrence," which postulated an initial Soviet attack without nuclear weapons (presumably on the Federal Republic), and envisaged a series of controlled steps of escalation ranging from the use of conventional forces, to the "selected and limited use" of tactical nuclear weapons, to a more general use of these weapons, and ultimately to the threat of a strategic nuclear attack on the Soviet Union.[18] Henry Kissinger may have been right when he argued that "those Europeans who believe that emphasis on local defense reduces the credibility of the deterrent are confusing cause and effect"; he also noted the ambiguity of Washington's strategic doctrine, however, which did not envisage a buildup in conventional forces sufficient to meet a Soviet challenge on any level of violence (for that thirty divisions were not nearly enough), but instead "justified the build-up of conventional forces in a more technical sense, as providing a capability for a last warning before implementing a counterforce strategy." This posture made Washington's assertions that "an increase in the shield forces was designed to make a counterforce strike more likely" appear "as a subterfuge for our reluctance to face nuclear war. The need for flexibility of response in Europe cannot be used to justify a counterforce strategy but to reduce our reliance on it."[19]

On both strategic and political grounds, flexible response was anathema in Bonn. German-American relations were already burdened by personality clashes, conflicting diplomatic styles, and disagreements over the handling of the Berlin crisis connected with the building of the wall. These problems were compounded by the revamping of Washington's strategic doctrine, intensifying German suspicions that a flexible American strategic stance also signaled a flexible American diplomatic stance, that America was ready to seek political accommodation with the East at the expense of German interests.

Changes in the deployment and tactical disposition of NATO's defenses added to Bonn's security concerns. The emphasis of NATO's defense planning during the Kennedy administration gradually shifted to a tactical doctrine of "fluid defense" and mobility, with designated but not otherwise prepared defense positions. This defense doctrine required not only time to assess the opponent's major thrusts and direct counterforces to critical sectors of the front but also space, and both commodities would be crucial for Germany in case of an attack, because time and space would determine the extent of destruction on German territory.

The Kennedy administration also tried to strengthen the credibility of the nuclear deterrent by stressing the feasibility of controlling nuclear war and of preventing "spasmic," irrational nuclear exchanges. Again, this created a conflict of interest in the alliance, because the Germans believed that they could gain most by "emphasizing the uncontrollable nature of nuclear war, in order to preserve the credibility of such deterrent power as [was] available on the continent."[20] Further, the Cuban missile crisis and the Test Ban Treaty strongly pointed to a common Soviet-American interest on nuclear questions. To Bonn the Test Ban Treaty, which followed the allies' exclusion from Washington's deliberation on the Cuban confrontation, indicated that in the case of a major European crisis the two nuclear superpowers might settle the issue bilaterally, and that Washington would complement the Pentagon's doctrine of strategic flexibility with political and diplomatic flexibility.

In the mid-1960s, when the Soviet Union obtained an assured destruction capability (that is, a counter-city capability) vis-à-vis the United States and Western Europe, the growing vulnerability of its nuclear forces compelled NATO to plan for preemptive strikes on a broad scale, giving a generally undesirable, hair-trigger character to NATO forces and reducing the measured options that Washington wanted to retain for its strategy of extended deterrence. As a consequence of this and other technical, budgetary, and political considerations, Secretary McNamara announced in February 1965 a declaratory strategy of assured destruction. This doctrine rejected counterforce options and indicated that the United States would seek a stable strategic balance by convincing the Soviet Union that the United States could retain a sufficient second-strike capacity to devastate the Soviet Union, and that extended deterrence remained viable because a nuclear conflict in Europe would escalate and ultimately lead to an American attack on the Soviet population and economy.

After changes in the Soviet force structure that reflected a rapid move toward nuclear parity, Secretary McNamara supplemented the precept of assured destruction with the term "mutual" in September 1967. The principle of Mutual Assured Destruction (MAD) was to convey to the Soviet Union that the United States accepted its vulnerability and, along with it, the realization that a significant use of strategic or theater nuclear weapons could result in nuclear escalation that would destroy both the United States and the Soviet Union. As a result, the United States "ended its era of superiority in assured destruction capability without any clear plan for executing strategic strikes in support of extended deterrence. If anything, she regarded the improvement of NATO conventional forces as a much higher priority for ensuring the overall deterrence of Warsaw Pact aggression than any possible action she could take to improve the capability of either her own nuclear forces or NATO's."[21]

In the late 1960s and early 1970s two major aspects of the military balance became significant: the competition over antiballistic missile (ABM) defense, and the introduction of missiles with independently targetable warheads (MIRVs)—although the administration failed to grasp the significance of multi-warhead missiles for both strategy and arms control, as Henry Kissinger was to admit later. Between 1970 and 1974 the number of American ICBM and SLBM warheads that could be aimed at the Warsaw Pact increased threefold (from fewer than 2,000 to about 6,000, in later years to rise to about 9,000), with a much smaller growth on the Soviet side until 1974, when the growth became significant. The Nixon administration perceived itself to be in the lead with both MIRV and ABM technology—a perception that held important implications for the German-American security compact: "This analysis of the balance had several major effects for extended deterrence. First, the perceived US lead again reassured a new Administration that there was no real urgency about further improving either the strategic or theatre nuclear balance, particularly in the absence of any doctrine for making use of the latter capabilities. Second, it reinforced President Nixon's initial view on coming to office that NATO theatre systems did little more than increase the risk of accidental war or threaten loss of US strategic control. Third, it meant that the Administration felt it was free to concentrate on SALT I and the Vietnam issue."[22]

The Security Concerns of the 1970s: Old Issues with New Meanings

By the late 1960s the Soviet Union was approaching parity with the United States in long-range missile capabilities. Given the advent of nuclear parity and the growing vulnerability of NATO's nuclear protector, it would appear that the security of Western Europe and the Federal Republic was much more precarious than it had been in the late 1940s or during the 1950s. But the meaning of security and the Europeans' perception of how it was threatened had also changed during the intervening decades. The likelihood of invasions and of direct military aggression by the Warsaw Pact seemed even smaller than it had in the 1950s (the military prowess of the Soviet Union was felt more keenly by its partners than its adversaries, as the events in East Germany, Hungary, and Czechoslovakia had demonstrated), and this appeared especially pertinent in areas of the world such as Europe, where existing borders were unambiguous and uncontested. For a variety of reasons, highly industrialized countries present an unattractive target for military aggression and territorial occupation, and the Soviet Union had consistently demonstrated since the mid-fifties that it was interested in the political and legal solidification of the European status quo rather than in overthrowing it by military means.

Ironically, the Soviet Union contributed as much as the United States to the feeling of reassurance on which the German-American security relationship ultimately rested: the perception of the Soviet threat diminished at the same time as the American nuclear guarantee became more qualified by the advent of nuclear parity. Changed European perceptions were in part a response to changed Soviet strategy, which in turn responded to Moscow's new assessment of changed perceptions and intentions in the West. In the 1950s and early 1960s Soviet defense planners apparently assumed that a conflict in Europe would escalate to a strategic nuclear war, and that emphasis should therefore be placed on developing superior Soviet nuclear forces. By 1967 Soviet planners were more drawn to the idea that a European war might not escalate and could remain conventional. Soviet strategy began to embrace the notions that significant nuclear superiority was unattainable, that Soviet nuclear weapons were useful principally to deter NATO's first use of nuclear weapons, that stabilizing nuclear parity through arms control might be desirable, and that conventional superiority would increase in importance.[23]

Most fundamentally, the risks of nuclear war had made it imperative for the Western powers to calibrate Soviet intentions as well as Soviet capabilities, aiming to return politics to its primacy over the arcane debates of strategic numerology.[24] By and large, West Europeans became much more sensitive to the political dimension of strategic deterrence

and less sensitive to the quantitative and technological relationship between the opposing strategic forces of East and West.[25]

As the immediacy and intensity of the Soviet threat diminished in the
eyes of both Americans and Europeans, their governments shifted priorities from matters of military strategy to political and economic ones.
The breakdown of the Bretton Woods monetary system, the developing
trilateral economic balance of power among the United States, Western
Europe, and Japan, the need to secure essential energy supplies in the
wake of the oil crisis of 1974, and a variety of other economic and
monetary developments suggested that the industrialized countries sup-
plement their military-strategic definition of security with considerations
that were soon to be labeled "economic security."

In NATO and especially the Federal Republic, the intense debates of
the 1960s over how the alliance should adjust to the waning American
nuclear superiority began to abate during the Nixon administration. On
the German side, there was less of an incentive to question the American
commitment to Europe. The perception of the Soviet threat had changed,
and the government of Willy Brandt and Walter Scheel was not about to
burden German-American relations with security disputes at a time
when it needed to demonstrate unequivocally its continuing loyalty to
the alliance in order to allay the suspicions that its Ostpolitik had initially
raised in Washington.[26] Bonn refrained from pressing the United States
for commitments that would not in any case become more firm by being
reiterated, and it managed to approach East-West arms control with a
much more constructive attitude than its predecessors, precisely because
it saw in it a supplementary element of its Ostpolitik rather than a
conflicting one.

On the American side too, President Nixon and his national security
adviser, Henry Kissinger, espoused a view of international politics and of
the balance of power that proved reassuring to Europe. Nixon and Kissinger intended to conduct American diplomacy according to the perennial principles of Realpolitik and on the basis of carefully weighed central
American national interests. Where previous administrations had taken
pride in the "management-oriented" implementation of national security
policy, the new administration played its diplomatic cards close to the
chest and deplored the bureaucratic tendency to compartmentalize problems. Above all, Nixon and Kissinger recognized the multidimensional
nature of political influence, accepted the evolving multipolar configurations of power and determined to use them to America's advantage, and
sought to concentrate the American diplomatic effort where it seemed to
matter most.

The geopolitical and historical perspective of Henry Kissinger nurtured the awareness that there were definite limits to American power

(an awareness for which the process of extricating the United States from Vietnam provided constant reminders), and that nuclear parity also implied the decreasing applicability of nuclear weapons. A central aspect of American diplomacy toward the Soviet Union became the effort to institutionalize nuclear parity through arms control arrangements, to create the foundations for the relaxation of tensions that came to be known as détente, and to connect the whole range of Soviet-American issues through the principle of linkage (an attempt to influence Soviet behavior by denying to Moscow benefits in one area of contention unless it restrained itself in others).

Confronted with the unavoidable implications of nuclear parity, the Nixon administration managed its security policy with a remarkable mixture of caution and self-assurance, which translated into a larger measure of reassurance of American allies. As a consequence of the restoration of Sino-American relations and of the administration's more measured view of the military challenges to the United States, the administration scaled down the conventional force requirement it had inherited from its predecessors (reducing it from a "two-and-a-half-war" to a "one-and-a-half-war" capability) and approached nuclear weapons development with relative restraint.[27]

This did not mean of course that the underlying contradictions that had plagued the German-American security relationship had gone away. But it did demonstrate that the reassurance aspect of American deterrence policy could be sustained with the appropriate diplomacy even after the advent of nuclear parity, precisely because that reassurance depended increasingly on political rather than predominantly military assessments by the Germans of Soviet intentions and American diplomacy. This meant also that strategic issues could be shielded from other issues facing the alliance. The disagreements within the alliance occasioned by the monetary shock of 1971, when America's gold window was closed, the "year of Europe" and the Yom Kippur War in 1973, and the oil price shock of 1973–74, generally did not spill over into strategic and organizational disputes centered on NATO.[28] The Nixon administration managed to narrow the gap between deterring the Soviet Union and reassuring its allies by making clear that it worked with a more narrow definition of American vital interests, differentiated between varieties of threats, and considered it futile to reach beyond nuclear sufficiency to the elusive and destabilizing goal of restoring American nuclear superiority.

A New Counterforce Strategy

Even so, some important (although highly technical) security concerns persisted. By the late 1960s and early 1970s the deficiencies of NATO's conventional forces and the diminishing plausibility of extended strategic deterrence began to weaken NATO at both ends of the military spectrum, narrowing NATO's range of military options and prompting the United States to formulate a doctrine, named after Secretary of Defense James R. Schlesinger, that placed a heavy stress on an American counterforce capability and in effect envisaged a limited nuclear war in Europe.[29]

The Schlesinger Doctrine was at bottom an attempt to reintroduce a measure of flexibility into the constraints that had narrowed NATO's doctrine of flexible response, and to compensate through a strategy of limited nuclear war for NATO's inability to maintain conventional forces at a level sufficient to demonstrate their own deterrent potential.[30] As Secretary Schlesinger stated in his report to Congress for fiscal year 1975, "What we need is a series of measured responses to aggression which bear some relation to the provocation, have prospects of terminating hostilities before general nuclear war breaks out, and leave some possibility for restoring deterrence."[31]

According to the new doctrine, American nuclear responses would become more measured by being aimed at the Warsaw Pact's military support facilities and other military installations, with the implied message to the Soviet Union that American missiles were also sufficiently accurate for a counterforce strategy, and thus implement a more selective retaliatory doctrine that might limit damage as well should deterrence fail. President Nixon had pointed out as early as 1970 that he did not want to "be left with the single option of ordering the mass destruction of enemy civilians, in the face of the certainty that it would be followed by the mass slaughter of Americans,"[32] and the more considered steps envisaged in the new doctrine seemed to strengthen deterrence by being more credible, in turn providing the opponent with an incentive for a measured response that could avert the mutual annihilation of a counter-city nuclear exchange. Entrapped between the destabilizing consequences of a counterforce strategy and the demoralizing consequences of a countervalue strategy, Washington sought to arrive at a more complementary meshing of American diplomacy and American nuclear strategy, and to fashion a counterforce capability susceptible to control in wartime.

Although Secretary Schlesinger claimed that "the reaction in Europe to change in targeting [had] been uniformly welcoming, even joyous, because they recognize that this means U.S. strategic forces are still credibly part of the overall deterrent for Europe,"[33] the official German White Paper, 1975–76 noted rather dryly that the "risks associated with the NATO strategy are not the same for the European allies as they are for the transatlantic parties. By using strategic nuclear weapons the United States risks having its own territory exposed to similar effects from enemy weapons. By contrast, Western Europe and, above all, the Federal

Republic of Germany would be a battlefield in any war, whether conducted with conventional or possibly even tactical nuclear weapons, even prior to escalation to the strategic nuclear stage."[34]

The disproportionate consequences of a nuclear exchange for Western Europe and the United States were necessarily underlined by a nuclear strategy such as the one expressed in the Schlesinger Doctrine.[35] If a nuclear exchange were limited to tactical nuclear weapons and narrowed by selective targeting, the opponent would have a large incentive to strike only at targets in Western Europe: "[Europeans] prefer a strategy of U.S.-European deterrence indivisibility whereby American strategic forces would be unequivocally joined in the defense of Europe through an escalatory risk sufficient to deter any form of aggression. The United States, although formally endorsing the security indivisibility concept for both political and strategic reasons, emphasizes a regionally differentiated deterrence and defense strategy which it believes enhances deterrence while maximizing the prospects for keeping a European war, should it occur, at arm's length from the United States."[36]

This created a dilemma for which neither the United States nor the Europeans could be blamed, nor from which they could escape. Nuclear parity between the two superpowers led to conflicts of interest between the United States, which now needed to delay or otherwise qualify the use of nuclear weapons, and its partners in NATO at the forward line of defense (such as the Federal Republic), which were prohibited from obtaining a national nuclear capability but could not accept a strategy that implied sustained conventional warfare at the expense of their territories and populations. The central dilemma of NATO could not be resolved: the United States, in seeking to limit the arms race and arrive at a stable nuclear balance, was compelled to deal with the Soviet Union on the basis of parity, as was reflected in the arrangements of the Strategic Arms Limitation Talks. At the same time, Washington could not convincingly guarantee the security of Western Europe except on the basis of an implied American nuclear superiority. As a consequence, West Germany's initial misgivings about NATO's doctrine of flexible response were increased by the advent of nuclear parity. The West Germans feared that deterrence would be weakened by the inclination of the United States to avoid or postpone nuclear intervention, that the idea of flexible response would add to the Warsaw Pact's geographical advantage with respect to deployment and resupply, and, most insidious, that the thinking behind flexible response implied the "divisibility" of deterrence, that Europe would become a battlefield while the United States remained a sanctuary.

Helmut Schmidt and Jimmy Carter

Although the security implications of the Schlesinger Doctrine were hardly reassuring to the Germans, Helmut Schmidt's government (which replaced Brandt's in 1974) retained its predecessor's reluctance to engage in doctrinal debates with the United States and NATO. The chronic irritations between Chancellor Schmidt and President Carter revolved less around doctrinal disputes than over what the Germans viewed as Washington's ineptness in handling specific issues, such as its waffling over an enhanced-radiation weapon (known as the neutron bomb), American reluctance to deal with the evolving Eurostrategic imbalance, and the president's inability to fashion a consistent policy toward the Soviet Union.

The reemerging transatlantic security debate of the later 1970s also revolved around the perennially troublesome question of forward defense. Although President Carter reaffirmed the American commitment to the principle of forward defense and did not exclude the use of tactical nuclear weapons on principle, the central question—the timing of a tactical nuclear response—remained as ambiguous as ever. Many German military figures viewed tactical nuclear weapons as an essential link in the chain of escalation from a conventional response to a strategic nuclear exchange between the Soviet Union and the United States, and they regarded American ambivalence as to when (or if) tactical nuclear weapons would be used as undermining NATO's "escalation dominance," leading to a decoupling of the American nuclear guarantee for Europe.

Whereas NATO's European members and above all the Federal Republic saw deterrence best maintained by the threat to use nuclear weapons in the early stages of a conventional war (in itself a paradox, because the short range of NATO's tactical nuclear weapons implies their use on German territory, East or West) the United States wanted their use postponed as long as possible. European strategists saw American tactical nuclear weapons as the essential link between American strategic nuclear forces and American theater capabilities in Europe, symbolizing Washington's determination to risk escalation for the sake of its European allies; American strategists saw tactical nuclear weapons as a backup should NATO's conventional defenses fail, and as a means of limiting conflict to the Continent and preventing escalation.[37]

These differing perspectives of the United States and the Federal Republic were underlined by the flap caused within NATO when President Carter vacillated over the decision to develop and deploy neutron weapons, which could be used effectively against tanks and armored vehicles, because some European strategists saw such enhanced-radiation weapons as a compensation for NATO's weakness in the area of conventional forces.[38] Nor were the Germans reassured (in fact Chancellor Schmidt was furious in private) when American columnists published excerpts from the so-called Presidential Review Memorandum 10, which included a suggestion to President Carter that among other options Western Europe might not be defended along the border between West

Germany and East Germany but along the Weser and Lech rivers in the Federal Republic.[39] Because 30 percent of West Germany's population and 25 percent of its industrial capacity are within a hundred kilometers of its border with the Warsaw Pact region, a defense along the Weser and Lech would mean sacrificing about one-third of the Federal Republic in the early phases of an attack. In addition, the memorandum implied that even if the perimeter defined by the Weser and Lech were breached, the use of tactical nuclear weapons would by no means be assured—of course, at that stage the use of tactical nuclear weapons on the battlefield would in any case involve the West German population and could hardly reassure the Federal Republic.

The Demise of Extended Deterrence

In his much-noted address to American and European strategists in Brussels in September 1979, Henry Kissinger in effect told the Europeans that they could no longer rely on the American nuclear commitment to their defense.[40] Although Kissinger did not specifically elaborate on it in Brussels, the question of "first use" of nuclear weapons became inevitably connected with the diminished plausibility of extended deterrence, for it was the American willingness to initiate nuclear war that had become less credible. The principle of first use had been questioned for decades, most forcefully in an article by McGeorge Bundy, George F. Kennan, Robert S. McNamara, and Gerard Smith, in which the authors present a powerful and well argued case for the renunciation of the first use of nuclear weapons in Europe.[41] Like Kissinger's argument, theirs rested on the consequences of the diminished credibility of the American nuclear commitment to Europe and led to the prescription, again quite similar to Kissinger's, that the conventional forces of the alliance be strengthened to provide a more plausible deterrent on the conventional level and thus raise the nuclear threshold in Europe.[42]

But there was a certain avuncular quality to these arguments. They were friendly in their intentions toward Europe, basically unquestioning of the continuing political centrality for the United States of the Euro-American connection, and perhaps even somewhat patronizing in their underlying theme of "how to save the Europeans from themselves."

But there also developed in the 1980s a school of American strategic analysts who were equally concerned with the shrinking validity of the American nuclear commitment to Europe, but did so more from the perspective of "how to save ourselves from the Europeans." In their view, the transatlantic alliance and its commitment to collective security are more of a strategic liability for the United States than an asset.[43] Seen from this perspective, it is extended deterrence rather than central (or essential) deterrence that has proved most troublesome for the United States both strategically and politically, and that should therefore be reexamined in its premises and consequences. A central point in this line of argument is that extended deterrence requires an American strategic posture fundamentally different and immensely riskier than would be required by central deterrence alone, primarily because extended deterrence entails a counterforce posture. This is said to be so because in the absence of a protective umbrella over the United States, only a counterforce strategy can limit damage and provide a measure of invulnerability for the American people. Because extended deterrence implies that an American president is willing to risk an attack on the United States, for such a deterrence posture to remain credible there must be sufficient protection for the American people, as distinct from protection of American missiles.

According to this argument, a counterforce strategy is expensive and risky: expensive (and complicating to arms control) because it requires a "hard target kill" capacity and therefore a large number of warheads and delivery systems, risky because it implies a preemptive first-strike strategy and undermines stability in a crisis with the insidious logic attached to nuclear weapons—"use them or lose them." In short, a counterforce strategy's main and perhaps only purpose is its contribution to societal invulnerability. To obtain this invulnerability, the United States can develop defensive systems to obviate, neutralize, or at least complicate a Soviet attack, rely on a counterforce strategy, or renounce its commitment to extended deterrence. Earl C. Ravenal summarizes this view as follows:

> A mostly indirect but very significant requisite of societal invulnerability is the acquisition of a nuclear counterforce capability, specifically hard target kill. Counterforce contributes to damage limitation in several related and mutually reinforcing ways, both indirect and direct. . . . Counterforce "makes sense," then, as an attempt to fulfill some of the requisite conditions of damage limitation or societal invulnerability, and, in turn, of extended deterrence—but, it is fair to say, *only* as such. Thus our willingness to protect our allies rises and falls, generally, with our ability to protect our own society from nuclear attack, and, more specifically, with the prospective viability of counterforce. If there is any explicit doubt—technical, economic, political—that we will achieve that invulnerability, or that we should pursue counterforce, then to that extent there is implicit doubt that our extensive nuclear commitments, especially to Western Europe, can survive. (Italics in original.)[44]

This chain of reasoning inevitably leads to two conclusions, which tend to be mutually reinforcing: the necessity for an American defense shield (such as that envisaged in the Strategic Defense Initiative proposed by President Reagan), and the more general political stance that the United States itself would not face a serious or fundamental security threat were it not for its commitment to come to the nuclear defense of an ally. Because a direct and initial attack on the United States by the Soviet Union is considered much less likely than the outbreak of conventional war in Europe, and because the United States would retain a sufficient second-strike capability against Soviet civilian and industrial targets even after having suffered an attack, central or essential deterrence would according to this line of thinking remain unimpaired. It is because of its commitments to the alliance that the United States runs unacceptable and basically implausible risks.

All this brought into sharp focus the central paradox of the West Europeans' (and especially the West Germans') attitude toward their nuclear protector: they seemed equally afraid that the United States would use nuclear weapons and that it would not, that it would lack both circumspection and resolve, that it favored global confrontation with the Soviet Union at the same time as it flirted with unilateralism and disengagement from Europe. Europe wanted to be coupled to the United States but not too closely; it feared entrapment as well as abandonment.[45]

Were it not that the Soviet Union for its part had been unable to fashion a sophisticated European policy, and above all to define its security in terms other than military ones, the transatlantic connection would be even weaker than it already is.[46] But it might be worthwhile for American policymakers to consider that "confidence-building measures" should be addressed to allies as well as opponents (especially in light of the more sophisticated leadership in Moscow in the late 1980s), and that the widening gap between deterrence and reassurance can be narrowed only by an appropriately measured diplomacy. This necessity had prompted Henry Kissinger to urge President Nixon to pursue a circumspect policy toward the Soviet Union:

> We had to remain sober in our own dealings with the Soviet Union. If we became too impetuous the European nations would grow fearful of a U.S.-Soviet deal. This would cause them to multiply their own initiatives, perhaps beyond the point of prudence, to protect themselves by making their own arrangements with the USSR. But paradoxically, the same would happen if the United States stayed in the trenches of the Cold War. In that case European leaders would be tempted to appear before their publics as "mediators" between bellicose superpowers. The United States had to conduct a careful policy toward the Soviet Union: sufficiently strong to maintain the interest in the common defense; sufficiently flexible to prevent our allies from racing to Moscow.[47]

3

The Political Dimensions of Arms Control

As the modifying principle gains hold on military operations, or rather, as the incentive fades away, the active element gradually becomes passive. . . . The art of war will shrivel into prudence, and its main concern will be to make sure the delicate balance is not suddenly upset in the enemy's favor and the half-hearted war does not become a real war after all.

—CARL VON CLAUSEWITZ

The U.S. and the Soviet Union are in a paradoxical and unprecedented position. Their irreconcilable differences prevent them from making real peace; nuclear weapons prevent them from making war. Partly for that reason, arms control has emerged as the new coin of the realm, which the two sides use to measure progress toward a reduction of tension. The superpower rivalry is so profound that it defies systematic accommodation in all areas except one: regulation of the military competition. The game of nuclear one-upmanship is the outward manifestation of their essentially political conflict. Instead of using nuclear weapons to fight, the two sides have learned to use them to maneuver for political advantage and, at the same time, to diminish the danger of catastrophic conflict. That peculiar exercise in sublimation is what arms control is all about.

—STROBE TALBOTT, 1986

Nowhere do the themes of double containment and deterrence and reassurance merge more clearly and insistently than in the area of arms control and its impact on German policy.

The reason for this is that arms control inevitably occurs in a political context. The intentions that drive or brake arms control negotiations go beyond avoiding war or stabilizing the military balance. They derive their larger and deeper meaning from political purposes—global, regional, and domestic.[1] In the nuclear age, arms control has become the political

83

sublimation of nuclear weapons that cannot be used, and of rivalries between East and West that are so profound and intractable that they cannot be ameliorated except in regulating the military balance. Arms control has become the "new coin of the realm,"[2] which is used by all parties to test the degree of East-West tensions and the limits of political accommodation.

For the United States and the Soviet Union, as well as for their allies, arms control has always had fundamental implications for the nature of East-West relations, for the management of their security alliances, and hence for the shape of the global and European political order.[3] Arms control is the prototypical confluence of arms and politics in the nuclear age, an example of how the disposition of nuclear weapons (both in deployment and reduction) is at the same time political diplomacy of the highest order. Ever since nuclear weapons were deployed in Europe in the 1950s, all contestants in the conflict between East and West, superpowers as well as allies, have turned either for or against arms control to make political use of weapons that are so destructive that they cannot be applied to any rational military purpose. Arms control policies are nuclear diplomacy par excellence.

For the United States and its allies, this has meant that America's European political and military strategies, double containment and deterrence and reassurance, coalesced in its arms control policies. The congruent (and over time increasingly conflicting) American intentions that underlay these strategies were invariably reflected in arms control. For decades, a central purpose of American arms control negotiations has been to sustain both its policy of double containment and its strategy of extended deterrence. Arms control is multilateral alliance diplomacy as well as bilateral adversarial diplomacy.

German attitudes toward arms control have always been complex. Because of Germany's troubled past, its European neighbors have expected of the Federal Republic that it demonstrate a special moral and political sensibility with respect to military matters, both conventional and nuclear, and it would have enhanced the effectiveness of German diplomacy in the 1950s and 1960s if successive governments in Bonn could have developed a more constructive attitude toward arms control. But there were powerful obstacles. Above all, Bonn's tortuous responses to the arms control proposals of the fifties and sixties stemmed from misgivings over their repercussions for Germany's division and from the attempt, by and large unsuccessful, to obtain a larger German influence in the institutional arrangements of NATO and the nuclear management of the Western alliance.

Arms Control and the European Order in the 1950s
The various proposals for arms control, disarmament, and European security arrangements put forth in the 1950s by the East and West played

an important role in the superpowers' diplomacy on the German question and on the configuration of the European political order. They were invariably laden with implications for Bonn's Eastern policies that the Germans found distasteful or outright unacceptable. The need to assess the implications of arms control for the German question has been a characteristic feature of Bonn's foreign policy since the 1950s. Its concern with the issue of German unity, its non-nuclear status, and its geographical location and security dependence on the United States distinguished the Federal Republic from other European members of NATO and strongly shaped German attitudes on arms control.

The Federal Republic's relations with its Eastern neighbors were burdened by large, unresolved issues. Aside from their historical and political roots, these issues stemmed primarily from the refusal of successive West German governments to recognize the German Democratic Republic and the Oder-Neisse border between Poland and the German Democratic Republic. Because most arms control proposals of the 1950s and 1960s implied the recognition of the European status quo and in some cases were specifically intended to serve that purpose, the Germans responded to them with caution ranging on suspicion, with hesitation ranging on procrastination and rejection.

In the mid- and late 1950s a variety of proposals known by the general term *disengagement* were put forth by Warsaw Pact governments as well as by official and unofficial proponents in the West.[4] To mention only the most prominent examples, at the summit conference in Geneva of July 1955, Britain's foreign minister, Sir Anthony Eden, suggested creating a "demilitarized area between East and West," in fall 1957 George F. Kennan held his much-noted "disengagement" lectures for the BBC, and in 1957 and 1958 Foreign Minister Adam Rapacki of Poland proposed a "denuclearized zone," prohibiting the production, stationing, and use of nuclear weapons and reducing conventional forces in Poland, Czechoslovakia, the Federal Republic, and the German Democratic Republic. In 1957 Nikita Khrushchev formally endorsed Eden's idea of a demilitarized zone and Rapacki's plan for prohibiting the stationing and production of atomic weapons in a Central European zone. The idea of a "denuclearized" Europe is an old one. It was revived in a somewhat different form many years later in the so-called Palme Report of 1982,[5] and figured prominently in the Eurostrategic arms control debate in the 1980s.

From the perspective of the Soviet Union and Eastern Europe, the proposals of the 1950s were made essentially for two reasons, which also explain why the Federal Republic and the United States rejected them.

A first, large reason why disengagement proposals were put forth in both West and East was in response to the impending deployment of American nuclear weapons in Europe and Bonn's developing interest in the sharing of nuclear control: disengagement would have kept American nuclear weapons out of the Federal Republic and in the process have

defused the issue of German nuclear co-management. An equally important reason for Moscow's interest in military disengagement and a nuclear-free zone in Europe was connected with the German question.
After the German states were integrated in their respective military alliances, the Soviet Union had shifted to a "two Germanies" policy and
subsequently sought to solidify the European status quo and Soviet
hegemony in Eastern Europe by gaining the Western powers' recognition
of the German Democratic Republic and the existing borders in Eastern
Europe. Most disengagement proposals would have served that purpose
at least indirectly, for they provided for the participation of the German
Democratic Republic as an equal and implied its de facto if not de jure
recognition by the Western powers. Generally, the Soviet Union began to
lay a heavy emphasis on questions of disarmament and arms control,
relating them to the question of German unity and the status of Berlin.

The disengagement proposals of the 1950s are a perfect illustration of
the political implications that attach to arms control negotiations and
agreements. Accepting disengagement proposals would have solidified
the *political* line of division in Central Europe (reflecting the Soviet interest in legitimizing the territorial status quo) and at the same time blurred
the *military* boundary between East and West running through Germany
(reflecting the Soviet interest in denying the West the conventional military power of the Federal Republic and the opportunity to deploy nuclear
weapons at the periphery of the Warsaw Pact). Disengagement would
have ended plans for a cohesive West European political arrangement
and by prying the Federal Republic from the Western alliance undermined NATO's forward strategy, which the United States sought to
strengthen for its symbolic effect and to make nuclear deterrence more
credible.

With these considerations in mind, the United States and the West
German government were agreed that these proposals were unacceptable. Neither Bonn nor Washington was ready to jeopardize the progress
toward a transatlantic security compact and a West European economic
community for the uncertain prospect of an untested European political
order. Above all, Bonn fought the possibility that the East German government could fully participate in disengagement negotiations and obtain indirectly the international recognition Bonn sought to deny it at all
cost. Adenauer was deeply worried that the United States would at some
point arrive at an understanding with the Soviet Union, over the heads of
the Germans and contrary to what Adenauer perceived to be German
interests, and he was afraid that a serious consideration of disengagement plans by the West would water down carefully crafted legal positions to which the Germans clung the more desperately the less they
could exercise genuine diplomatic leverage on the German question.

Chancellor Adenauer deeply distrusted the West's interest in arms control proposals, because it seemed to be based on a need to bring about a lessening of East-West tensions and to explore possibilities for arms control, not on an interest in German unity.[6] The Germans were becoming nervous about "a certain readiness in the free world to come to an understanding with the Soviet Union on the basis of the status quo," and they reacted with dismay when Great Britain (in a second version of the Eden Plan) proposed to solve the German issue by offering a demilitarized zone in Central Europe, an agreement to curtail armaments, and a European mutual security pact. Generally, the coupling of the German question with arms control measures caused apprehension in Bonn because "for the first time these . . . areas of negotiations, sharply separated until then, were brought in contact with each other. For the first time also it was officially indicated by British and French statesmen that the demarcation line between the zones of Four Power occupation in Germany could serve at least temporarily as a basis for arms-control arrangements between the Four Powers."[7]

In light of Soviet suggestions that Bonn "needed" a failure in arms control negotiations, the Germans made it a point to impress on their Western allies and the Soviet Union that disarmament would not have to be accompanied by Germany's unification.[8] Before the summit conference held in Geneva in 1955, Chancellor Adenauer declared that disarmament should have priority over the German issue, a view he reiterated in 1958 in an interview with William Randolph Hearst. This however was more a tactical and political consideration. Adenauer resisted John Foster Dulles's ideas of linking arms control and the German question, precisely because he feared that German interests regarding reunification would be traded off against progress on arms control.[9]

The German government's rejection of nuclear disengagement in Central Europe was a momentous turn of events, which had consequences extending into the 1980s and beyond. From then on, the German question and the shape of the European political order became inextricably tied to the global and regional nuclear arms race and to the attempts to restrain it through arms control. For decades to come, the resolution of one issue became hostage to the resolution of the other, compounding the difficulties that already stood in the way of achieving a negotiated settlement in either. By linking the nature of the European political order to the global and regional nuclear balance, the nuclear powers (including France and Britain) obtained even greater leverage on the German question than they had before—an ironic development in that this link was forged by Bonn as well. In terms of its long-range consequences for the German question, the deployment of nuclear weapons on German territory was second in importance only to the Federal Republic's accession to NATO.

But Adenauer, always fearful of proposals that implied the neutrality of Germany and determined to safeguard the Federal Republic's legal claims on the German question, seemed curiously insensitive to the implications that postwar nuclear diplomacy held for the conduct of traditional political diplomacy. The Germans underestimated the political consequences of deploying nuclear weapons on German territory, a grave miscalculation also of the intentions of their allies and of their opponents. In his memoirs, George F. Kennan recalls the opposition to his call for nuclear disengagement and a neutralized Germany in 1957:

> I quite failed to realize . . . the intensity of the fear that the specter of a reunited Germany aroused in Western countries, the depth of attachment there to the programs already evolved for uniting Western Germany economically with the rest of Western Europe and militarily with the Atlantic Community. . . . This was a project that assumed the continuation of a divided Continent; and for this reason any views, such as my own, that envisaged even the possibility of a removal of the division were bound to appear dangerous and heretical. I was dealing here, in my critics and in the offended statesmen, with people who would not have considered the withdrawal of a single American battalion from Western Germany even if the Russians had been willing to evacuate all of Eastern Germany and Poland by way of compensation.[10]

Arms Control in the 1960s: European Security Pacts

In the mid- and late 1960s a number of proposals were put forth for a European security pact between East and West and other measures for military détente in Western and Eastern Europe, which ranged from suggestions for mutually reducing the level of conventional and nuclear forces to calls for dissolving NATO and the Warsaw Pact.[11] With an attempt to check the arms race, most of these proposals entailed a readiness to accept a European political settlement, which is why the German government continued to view them with deep reservations.

These proposals, not dissimilar in intent and format from those of the 1950s, reflected a limited European consensus within both blocs that the relevance of NATO and the Warsaw Pact was diminishing as a consequence of changing political and strategic circumstances, and that a formalized military détente would be mutually advantageous.[12] Several of these proposals not only stressed the desirability of creating immediate arrangements for controlling and managing conflict, but pointed out opportunities for finally resolving conflict. In other words, military security arrangements were expected to facilitate political reconciliation through increased contacts between East and West and cooperative economic and diplomatic endeavors, thus holding out the hope that the unresolved political problems of Europe (such as the division of Germany and the unsettled frontier questions) would become more manageable.[13]

Ever since the disengagement proposals of the 1950s, these two distinct aspects and purposes of a European arms control arrangement—the military aspect, conflict control, and the political aspect, conflict resolution—had posed a dilemma for Bonn. Although conflict control and crisis management were even more important to the Federal Republic than to its allies because of Germany's forward position, Bonn invariably felt obliged to reject proposals for European arms control arrangements, because they seemed to portend the legitimization of the status quo in Central Europe, including the division of Germany.

The East bloc's proposals of the mid-1960s carried the same implications. They were in addition coupled with the argument that any German association with nuclear weapons (such as that which the MLF would have provided) would stand in the way of the nuclear nonproliferation treaty, which soon became a centerpiece of American nuclear diplomacy. Beginning with the 23d Party Congress, the Soviet Union and its allies renewed their proposals for a European security pact as an alternative to the Warsaw Pact, but their concept of "European security" clearly looked toward the dissolution of NATO and the withdrawal of the United States from Europe as well as toward legitimizing the German Democratic Republic.[14]

In contrast with the 1950s, when the Federal Republic could count on the support of the Eisenhower administration for its opposition to disengagement proposals, Bonn now found itself diplomatically isolated. The fundamental agreement between Bonn and Washington in the 1950s on arms control matters began to dissipate in the 1960s. When the Kennedy administration showed interest in arms control arrangements with the Soviet Union and concurrently pursued security policies and Germany policies that were in Bonn's view insufficiently firm and loyal, German-American relations began to suffer considerably. Not even the Test Ban Treaty of 1963, which on the surface seemed unrelated to the issue of German unity, escaped Bonn's wary attention. The German government strongly objected to the Soviet suggestion that the treaty be supplemented with a nonaggression pact between NATO and the Warsaw Pact, fearing that this would lead to the "legal perpetuation of Germany's partition," and Bonn was concerned that article 3, which allowed other powers to become signatories to the treaty, amount to a de facto recognition of the German Democratic Republic if it acceded to it.[15]

In the mid-1960s the postwar European order was shifting, and Bonn's policies were becoming outdated and isolated.[16] As the immediacy and intensity of the Soviet threat diminished in the eyes of Europeans and Americans, political and economic issues appeared more pressing than military ones (although the United States remained mired in Vietnam), and centrifugal pressures could not be contained in the Western alliance except in the area of German-American security arrangements, where American diplomacy retained its powerful leverage. American planners still saw NATO's primary function as military, but they no longer considered an assault by the Warsaw Pact on Western Europe probable and were devoting most of their attention to Vietnam. Gradually Washington supplemented its Cold War policy of "forward containment" in every region of the world (of which the war in Vietnam was a misguided example) with attempts to reach a bilateral accommodation with the Soviet Union on matters of mutual interest, such as stabilizing the nuclear balance of power. Assertive containment at the periphery of the American empire (or, depending on one's perspective, at the periphery of the Soviet bloc) was augmented by a core of accommodation, as was exemplified in the attempt of the Johnson administration to salvage a measure of Soviet-American cooperation at the same time as American troops were containing "communism" in Vietnam and Soviet troops were protecting "communism" in Czechoslovakia.

West Europeans in turn began to see the primary function of NATO as political: that is, ensuring a continued American commitment to the political and economic future of Europe and thus ultimately guaranteeing the Continent's military security as well. As the West Europeans found that the new atmosphere enabled them to make their own political and economic arrangements with the Eastern bloc, intra-European détente and its dynamics for overcoming the division of Europe sometimes conflicted with the more static strategic détente between the two superpowers (which merely stabilized the division). Given the prevailing balance of power, the United States had to deal with the Soviet Union on the basis of recognizing the status quo in Europe, although many Europeans on both sides of the dividing line were seeking to overcome it.

These strategic, political, and psychological developments had a profound impact on the meaning of national security and the purposes and instruments of arms control. There developed an intense interest in both Western and Eastern Europe in institutionalized European security arrangements that could overcome the sterile, costly, and dangerous confrontations of the Cold War and make coexistence more tangible. As the likelihood of war in Europe diminished, the Western powers could afford to use military terms to express political concerns. Security policies and arms control proposals became saturated with purposes that were essentially political rather than military, with large implications for the future shape of the European political order. The logic of politics and power was being expressed in the language of security and arms control.[17]

The trend toward translating political purposes into the language of military strategy and arms control posed special problems for Bonn, because in this area the Germans had to be especially circumspect and reticent. This was a mode of political and diplomatic communication in which the Federal Republic was for historical, legal, and psychological reasons at a distinct disadvantage. But because all European states as well as the two superpowers had begun to resort to the idiom of arms, the Federal Republic was compelled to follow suit, both when it assented to a policy or (more often) when it balked. Bonn's implied (and explicit) threats to carry a big stick by seeking joint nuclear control met with strong opposition from Germany's allies and opponents, and the thorny issue of the nonproliferation treaty provided yet another example of how the Federal Republic risked diplomatic isolation unless it could fashion a more constructive attitude toward arms control. The issues connected with the treaty were important in their own right to the Germans, but like many other issues of the Federal Republic's association with military matters they became a metaphor of what were essentially political intentions and resentments.

The Nonproliferation Treaty (NPT)

The Federal Republic's opposition to a nonproliferation arrangement stemmed primarily from Bonn's determination to keep open major options for German foreign policy, all of which seemed in danger of being foreclosed or narrowed by the NPT:[18] German participation in a jointly owned NATO nuclear force and in NATO's nuclear planning and crisis management, the creation of a European nuclear force, and the possibility of retaining (or obtaining) bargaining leverage in future negotiations on the German question.[19]

In German eyes the NPT suffered in the first instance from its unfortunate connection with the abandoned idea of a NATO multilateral nuclear force. Throughout 1965 the issue of the MLF and the proposals for a nuclear nondissemination treaty were closely related. The Soviet side repeatedly emphasized that any German association with nuclear weapons except consultative arrangements would stand in the way of the NPT; on the American side, President Johnson was urged by his advisers to drop the MLF because it would jeopardize the treaty.[20]

This led to an intense German campaign to ensure that the United States would not trade the MLF for Soviet flexibility on the NPT. Foreign Minister Gerhard Schröder urged the establishment of a joint nuclear deterrent force because of the threat posed by Soviet missiles aimed at Western Europe, and insisted that the Federal Republic would forgo the acquisition of its own nuclear weapons only if such a force were set up. Schröder indicated that Bonn had a "very precise" conception of the minimum requirement that the West's joint nuclear force would have to meet before the Germans considered unnecessary the development of a West German nuclear force. The German government also tied the renunciation of nuclear capabilities to the German question, arguing that although Bonn was not seeking to acquire nuclear weapons at that point, it would renounce the right to acquire them later only if Germany's security and eventual reunification were guaranteed.[21]

These tough demands raised the specter of a nuclear Federal Republic or a non-nuclear, united Germany (neither of which found support in the West or the East) and could not possibly have gained the support of the United States, because conflicting and important American interests were at stake.[22] The United States was thoroughly committed to non-proliferation efforts (which appeared especially pertinent after China had exploded nuclear devices), and an agreement with the Soviet Union on nonproliferation was expected to nurture Soviet-American cooperation at a time when the escalation of the Vietnam conflict had strained relations considerably.

There was a growing suspicion in Bonn that the NPT was directed mainly against the Federal Republic and that the United States was unwilling to support the Germans' opposition to the treaty. For the first time, it was being clearly demonstrated to Bonn that overriding Soviet-American interests took precedence over the German-American partnership, and that Bonn's view of a desirable European political order lacked support not only in the East but in the West. In essence, the Germans' recalcitrance on the nonproliferation treaty was directed at the United States as well as the Soviet Union. Many Germans viewed Washington's insistence that the Federal Republic accede to the treaty without gaining any concessions on unification as a further indication that Washington had shelved the German question, perhaps indefinitely.

Considering the far-reaching repercussions of such an arrangement for German foreign policy, Bonn was probably justified in complaining that it had been insufficiently consulted, and the unfortunate connection between the episode surrounding the MLF and American nonproliferation efforts was hardly designed to put to rest German fears of a Soviet-American deal made over the heads of the German government. Even more awkward for Bonn's diplomacy was that its opposition to arms measures highlighted the tensions between American and West German interests and underlined the congruence of interests between the Soviet Union and East Germany. "Adherence of both West and East Germany to the Limited Test Ban Treaty in 1963 caused difficulties between Washington and Bonn, but none between Moscow and East Berlin. . . . Soviet arms control policy [was] a useful complement to its Germany policy, while the United States . . . obtain[ed] the benefits of the Test Ban and Non-Proliferation Treaties only at a cost in terms of its relations with West Germany."[23] A situation had arisen where American interests were in effect more congruent with those of East Germany than with those of West Germany, which did not sit well with Bonn.

Bonn was adamant, however, about taking part in a nuclear force.[24] In light of their experiences with Washington, the Germans must have viewed the likelihood of gaining co-ownership of nuclear weapons as remote. But the connections perceived between the nonproliferation treaty and the possibility of forcing some progress on the question of reunification go a long way toward explaining Bonn's reluctance to accede to an arms control arrangement. Reservations about the nonproliferation treaty stemmed not so much from a desire to own nuclear weapons as from a reluctance to be deprived of the threat of acquiring them.

Considering the widespread apprehensions about a German finger on the nuclear trigger, the value of keeping open this possibility was doubtful. But the Germans were reluctant to relinquish an opportunity to extract concessions on the issue of reunification, because they had had so little bargaining leverage on this question in the past, and because it was clear that all along Moscow's main purpose in negotiating the treaty had been to deny the Federal Republic an association with nuclear arms.[25] "From the Soviet point of view, there [was] a striking parallel between the proposal for a nonproliferation treaty and the proposal for a European security system. The first [was] meant as a bilateral enterprise with the United States against their nonnuclear friends and allies; the second as a continental enterprise with the Europeans against the United States. In both cases, however, the opponent against whom the project [was] really directed [was] Germany."[26]

The Grand Coalition government that replaced the Erhard administration in December 1966, when the cdu's Kurt Georg Kiesinger became chancellor and the spd's Willy Brandt vice-chancellor and foreign minister, was split on the question of Germany's accession to the treaty. The chancellor saw in the treaty "a kind of atomic complicity" between Washington and Moscow, former chancellor Adenauer called it "a Morgenthau Plan to the nth degree," and Finance Minister Franz-Josef Strauss, head of the csu, called it "a Versailles of cosmic proportions" and maintained that the treaty would deprive Bonn of leverage on the German question and endanger nato, the eec, and Germany's "equal partnership" with the United States. Foreign Minister Brandt, on the other hand, supported accession to the treaty, placing the issue in the larger context of a European security arrangement.[27] Brandt was convinced that a constructive German attitude toward European security proposals would benefit German diplomacy in both East and West (he acted on this conviction when he became chancellor in 1969) and that the Federal Republic should not obstruct efforts at détente that were finding such a wide and supportive echo in all of Europe.

Although the Grand Coalition government could not speak with one voice on the npt, there were some significant shifts in emphasis and direction. Like its predecessor, the new government was not indifferent to the implications that a nonproliferation agreement held for German reunification and for the issue of joint ownership of an allied Atlantic nuclear force, but its persisting objections focused primarily on the implications of such an agreement for the creation of a European nuclear force and German participation in joint nuclear planning.[28] In fall 1968 Brandt declared that Germany would sign the nonproliferation treaty only if the treaty obliged the nuclear powers to reduce their arsenals through arms control and did not endanger the security of Germany, delay the integration of Europe, or inhibit the peaceful application of nuclear energy. Bonn obtained written assurances from Washington that the nonproliferation treaty would not preclude the formation of a European nuclear force if a politically united Europe came into being, and the West German government was also careful to stress that German participation in NATO's Nuclear Planning Group should not be regarded as a substitute for a German role in such a European nuclear force.[29]

Bonn's misgivings about the nonproliferation treaty were further strengthened by the Soviet invasion of Czechoslovakia in August 1968. Most other NATO members also expressed concern. NATO's non-nuclear forces had been cut back for several years, particularly on the forward line in the Federal Republic, and the invasion of Czechoslovakia seemed to invalidate the prevailing Western view that Soviet leadership after Stalin had become too sophisticated to resort to large-scale force to further political aims.[30] Even so, Washington's deep interest in a reduction of Soviet-American tensions and an accommodation with the Soviet Union in arms control was so compelling that a few weeks after the invasion Washington was ready to resume negotiations with Moscow.

Nor had the invasion diminished the West European powers' interest in arriving at a modus vivendi with the East, an interest that required the Federal Republic to accept the restrictions of the nonproliferation treaty and not impede the progress of détente. When the government of Brandt and Scheel came into office in fall 1969, it acceded to the treaty without further delay (although ratification did not take place until February and March 1974), which not only reassured Washington but helped create a better climate for Bonn's dynamic initiatives toward the Soviet Union, Eastern Europe, and the German Democratic Republic.

But the issue of the NPT also left a legacy of bitterness in Bonn, especially among German conservatives, who saw in the treaty a serious "downgrading" of the Federal Republic. Bonn's former ambassador to Washington and to NATO wrote in his memoirs:

> In drawing a balance sheet, one cannot avoid some sobering facts: the equality (*Gleichberechtigung*) which the Federal Republic obtained by the Paris Agreement of 1954 and by German rearmament has been lost with the nonproliferation treaty. This is especially grave for the future prospects of the European Community, which cannot survive

without the principle of equality. The sense of solidarity among the Atlantic alliance partners was damaged through the collusion of the leading power of the alliance with Moscow. . . . In particular, the Soviet Union obtained, without a quid pro quo, an additional element of the European order of the status quo it favors. . . . Perhaps the Federal Republic was not strong enough to obviate this development. Without doubt, her position was weaker in the second half of the 1960s than in the mid-1950s, when the West believed that it could not do without her defense contribution. . . . In the meantime, it has become fully clear how naive it was to see in this treaty in the first instance an effective instrument for the prevention of a nuclear war. It was and is in the first instance an instrument of the superpowers.[31]

Antiballistic Missile Defense
In addition to Bonn's concerns about the nonproliferation treaty and in connection with it, the Germans became apprehensive about the issue of antiballistic missile (ABM) defense. In the mid-1960s both the Soviet Union and the United States had started deploying "light" ABM systems, but there remained sufficient doubt on the American side as to whether these systems would work and what a full deployment by both sides would imply for the strategic balance, crisis stability, the prospects for arms control, and managing the alliance.[32] The issue was complicated by the work being done by both sides toward perfecting multi-warhead strategic missiles (the United States was far ahead in research and development), which suggested that defensive systems could be overwhelmed by a large number of incoming missiles.[33] By 1967 the Johnson administration was convinced that an ABM system would not significantly reduce the vulnerability of the United States, and the president and his defense secretary, Robert S. McNamara, gradually persuaded the Soviets that their own interests would be advanced by forgoing ABM systems, which ultimately led to the portion governing ABM systems of the SALT I treaty of 1972.

The prospect of developing extensive ABM systems had not been received well in Europe in the mid-1960s, for reasons that were reiterated twenty years later and that foreshadowed the tensions in the alliance raised by the Reagan administration's Strategic Defense Initiative. France and Britain worried about the continuing effectiveness of their nuclear arsenals; many Europeans feared that developing even a limited ABM system would induce the United States to develop an isolationist strategy and become a "fortress America"; and the European members of NATO were not fully reassured when Secretary McNamara (a skeptic on ABM himself) sought to allay their concerns during the meeting in Ankara of NATO's Nuclear Planning Group in September 1967.[34] There was also concern that antimissile defenses could upset the relative stability of the nuclear balance by creating uncertainties about their effectiveness, which in turn would lead to the development of new offensive weapons in an attempt to maintain or restore deterrence. In other words, Europeans perceived a contradiction between the "vertical proliferation" that might result from an accelerated development of strategic countermeasures against ABM systems and the prohibition against horizontal proliferation embodied in the nonproliferation treaty.[35]

Yet at the same time as European NATO allies were expressing concern about a renewed arms race and especially about the production of multi-warhead missiles, Bonn entertained reservations about the Soviet-American strategic arms limitation talks that had long been projected, fearing that they might damage German interests.[36] Again, Bonn's position was linked to the German question. Chancellor Kiesinger wanted to tie the resolution of outstanding European problems (such as the division of Germany) to Soviet-American arms control arrangements, and it was also clear that Kiesinger intended to postpone further West Germany's accession to the nonproliferation treaty to retain some bargaining leverage. Many Germans perceived in the ABM issue and the NPT an attempt by the superpowers to create a Soviet-American condominium in Europe, a perception later heightened by the Soviet-American agreement of 1973 on the avoidance of nuclear war. Pierre Hassner pointed out at the time:

> Without being a specific or binding "no first use" agreement, the agreement to prevent nuclear war does make the use of nuclear weapons by the United States much less credible and does have a decoupling effect between theater and strategic deterrence. On the other hand, while consultation and cooperation between the superpowers in nuclear matters does not imply a political condominium, cooperation to prevent conflict between third powers erupting in the first place, or otherwise ending up in "unilateral advantage" to one superpower, does mean a political priority of the bipolar concern over other ties, and a preference for the joint management of the status quo. It is an agreement against revolution and, possibly, against peaceful change, to the extent that the latter, by modifying the diplomatic or even the domestic position of a given country or region, affects the balance between the two coalitions and their leaders.[37]

The Twin Pillars of Détente: The European Status Quo and Arms Control

At the end of the 1960s and in the early 1970s the preconditions and foundations for a plausible policy of détente existed primarily in two areas of the East-West conflict: arms control and the readiness to stabilize the European political order. These two central precepts of détente were connected (indeed had been connected for more than a decade) and mutually reinforcing. With the advent of nuclear parity between the United States and the Soviet Union, both antagonists began to share an interest in stabilizing the existing balance of terror and formalizing the inhibitions created by the prospect of mutual annihilation. This led to the codification of the principle of mutual assured destruction (in the provision governing ABM systems in the SALT I Treaty of 1972) and to the partial freezing of offensive systems (in the SALT II Treaty of 1979, which went unratified).[38] The superpowers shared an equally strong interest in stabilizing the existing European political order. This understanding culminated in 1975 in the final accords of the Helsinki Conference on Security and Cooperation in Europe (CSCE) and in the solidification of the Western position in Berlin, to which the Federal Republic made its own indispensable contribution: the set of treaties negotiated in the early 1970s by Bonn with Moscow, Warsaw, and East Berlin. In both areas, arms control and the European political order, the United States and the Soviet Union perceived a common interest and a rough equilibrium in power, which led to a corresponding willingness to codify the balance with an explicit set of understandings.

Moreover, the nature of the issues that were negotiated allowed a relatively explicit codification, as even a casual reading of the SALT treaties and the Helsinki accords would demonstrate. This is not to say that the formal understandings reached on arms control and stabilizing the European order did not contain ambiguities, uncertainties, and large opportunities for differing interpretations of their content and meaning. Nonetheless, the codification of these understandings was far more specific than some of the conflicting assumptions and aspirations that attached to détente in the Third World and other areas of conflict, which ultimately led to the corrosion and demise of détente in the late 1970s.[39]

Most important, the two core elements of détente were complementary and mutually reinforcing. Strategic parity had created a powerful set of restraints, which made it difficult to conceive of direct conflicts between the United States and the Soviet Union that would challenge the credibility of their respective postures of central deterrence. Each side could inflict unacceptable damage on the other, as was reflected in the principle of mutual assured destruction, and neither had any real reason to question the plausibility of the bilateral "core" deterrence that protected its home country. Rather, the risks of military confrontation and of an escalation to a nuclear war were situated at the periphery of both empires, in regional areas of competition such as Europe. A mutual interest in stabilizing the political circumstances of Europe, based in essence on its continued division, was a logical complement to the necessity to stabilize the rough equilibrium between the global powers in nuclear strategic weapons. For both sides, considerations of politics and military strategy went hand in hand.

The linkage between these two central components of the détente of the early and mid-1970s was clearly acknowledged in Nixon's and Kissinger's diplomacy: as a condition to assent to what amounted to solidifying the European status quo (a major Soviet aim since the mid-1950s) the United States demanded a solidification of the Western position in Berlin and progress on nuclear as well as conventional arms control. A stabilizing arms control package, extending from the conventional end of the spectrum to the nuclear, was to be connected to a stabilization program for the European political order.

The Germans were fully aware that both the United States and the Soviet Union were pursuing an essentially conservative European policy. Herbert Blankenhorn, then the German ambassador in London, noted in 1969: "It is certain that the Americans want to discuss arms control matters with the Soviet Union. . . . Whether these discussions will be used by the Americans to raise questions about a new political order (*Neuordnung*) in Europe, I am not so sure. I lean more toward the view that the American government also does not want to touch upon the European status quo at this point. The result of such considerations is that neither of the two world powers is at this time urgently interested in a solution of European issues." Noting the Soviet Union's interest in stabilizing the European status quo, Blankenhorn continued: "The interest of the United States is today directed primarily toward the consolidation of the situation at home and toward the new political circumstances in Asia that will follow . . . American troop withdrawals. A new initiative on the German question, which perforce would lead to a confrontation with the Soviet Union in Europe, would not be welcome to the United States at the present moment."[40]

The complementarity perceived in Washington between strategic arms control and the political stabilization of Europe had a profound significance for the plausibility and coherence of America's European policies and their effect on the German-American security relationship. In stabilizing the bilateral strategic military balance with the Soviet Union and legitimizing the European status quo, the United States simultaneously acknowledged its strategic vulnerability and reaffirmed the division of Germany. At the same time as the United States implicitly disavowed the principle of extended deterrence in SALT I (for what else could the acknowledgment of its own vulnerability imply?), its assent to the European status quo reaffirmed its policy of double containment (for what else could stabilizing the status quo entail for America's policies toward Germany and the Soviet Union?). To put it another way, while the United States sought to retain the complementarity of its double containment policy, it could not prevent the widening gap between the double components of America's deterrence policies, reassuring allies while deterring the opponent. No wonder German conservatives felt doubly betrayed by American diplomacy: for them sacred political and strategic principles were traded away simultaneously. But no wonder either that the SPD-FDP coalition in Bonn found this arrangement basically acceptable: the German government was itself ready to stabilize the European status quo (perhaps in the hope that this would permit changing it in the distant future), and it could condone the implied erosion of extended deterrence precisely because it felt more reassured by the political circumspection it saw embodied in Nixon's and Kissinger's diplomacy than by the mechanics of the superpowers' military balance.

Given the premises and intentions of its new Ostpolitik, the Federal Republic could for the first time fully subscribe as well to the principles of NATO's Harmel Report of 1967 (deterrence coupled with détente), which had become the centerpiece of Western Europe's diplomatic agenda in dealing with the East. Whereas previous German governments had carried the burden (largely self-imposed) of always needing to criticize or reject arms control measures because they implied a hardening of the European status quo (a diplomatic stance that had strained Bonn's relations with its allies as well as with its opponents), Brandt's government could act on its conviction that German political interests would be ill served by stalling arms control or European détente. On the contrary, Bonn perceived large political advantages in backing détente and arms control, for the goals of German Ostpolitik required a more conciliatory attitude toward the East in any case. For the Germans, arms control and Ostpolitik became the substance and symbol of détente. In the process, Brandt's Ostpolitik also became complementary to the Federal Republic's security policies, not because it lessened the Federal Republic's strategic dependence on the United States or allegiance to NATO, but because Bonn's readiness to accept the territorial status quo tackled German security problems at their political roots. Whereas in the fifties and sixties Bonn's security policy had conflicted sharply with its Eastern policy, Ostpolitik reduced these stark contradictions. By recognizing the territorial and political realities stemming from the Second World War, the Germans meshed their security policy and their Eastern policy, developed a more positive attitude toward arms control, and adjusted West German foreign policy to the dynamics of détente.

In light of these fundamental political considerations, and given the West Europeans' changing perception of the Soviet threat, Bonn managed to approach the major arms control initiatives of the 1970s with a constructive sense of support. It became an active and constructive participant in what became seemingly endless discussions between NATO and the Warsaw Pact on the mutual and balanced force reductions on the conventional level (MBFR), supported the SALT I agreement, by means of which the United States and the Soviet Union sought to institutionalize the principle of mutual assured destruction, and welcomed the attempt to check the strategic arms race, which was at the core of the SALT II agreement.

Mutual and Balanced Force Reductions (MBFR) and the Conference on Security and Cooperation in Europe (CSCE)

The East-West negotiations on conventional force reductions that began in fall 1973 were on the surface intended to address the problems posed by the massive peacetime confrontation of NATO and Warsaw Pact forces on the central front, with the objective of achieving mutual reductions in these forces.[41] These discussions, which extended inconclusively into the late 1980s, were from the beginning burdened by asymmetries of geography and political purpose, and led to stagnation on several major issues: in the data base, because the West insisted on reaching agreement on troop strength in the area of MBFR before agreeing to troop reductions; in so-called flanking measures, because of the difficulty of connecting confidence-building provisions to verification provisions; and in establishing ceilings, because the West called for collective ceilings whereas the other side called for national ones. From the West's standpoint, MBFR was basically intended to bring about a more equal and stable balance of conventional forces by stipulating greater reductions for the Warsaw Pact than for NATO, thereby reducing the East's numerical advantage. The Soviet Union of course did not see the agenda in quite this way, and called for "equal reductions" rather than "equal ceilings" of conventional forces, thus striving to preserve the East's advantage at a lower aggregate level. In short, the Soviet Union objected to the Western definition of "balanced" and preferred the acronym MFR.[42]

From the beginning, however, the talks between NATO and the Warsaw Pact had more to do with the political balance between the two alliances (and within the Western alliance), although their ultimate effect would be on the military balance. From the perspective of the Federal Republic, these political purposes were aimed in three directions: toward the Federal Republic, toward the United States, and toward the Soviet Union.

Talks on MBFR were in the first instance directed toward the Federal Republic when it appeared during 1966–67 that the country would reduce its forces considerably and thus weaken the mainstay of NATO's conventional defense on the central front.[43] The situation became reversed quite quickly, however, and the Germans began to see in MBFR a check against unilateral American troop reductions. The Europeans were deeply worried about the substantial support given in the U.S. Senate to the proposals for deep cuts of American forces in Europe by Sen. Mike

Mansfield of Montana. The long-term implications of the withdrawal called for by Mansfield were deeply troubling to Bonn, which saw it as signaling a diminution of the American political commitment to Europe and as compromising the American nuclear guarantee. Although the Nixon White House fought hard against the Mansfield Amendment, there was a widespread feeling in Washington that European NATO members were not carrying a fair share of their burdens in the alliance, and European NATO members feared that the Nixon Doctrine (which called for a larger participation of America's allies in the common defense effort) would be applied to Europe as well as Asia. Both in Bonn and in Washington, MBFR negotiations were seen as the best way to defeat the Mansfield measure, because the Senate could be persuaded not to withdraw unilaterally American forces that would be bargaining chips in the negotiations and thus undercut the Western bargaining position.[44]

From the German viewpoint, MBFR negotiations were also aimed in the direction of Moscow. The opening of the talks in 1973 was the culmination of diplomatic maneuvers between East and West and within NATO that had their origins in the early and mid-1960s.[45] By 1967–68 NATO had decided to seek mutual force cutbacks (strongly opposed by France, which was of course no longer a member) as the first step toward détente in Europe, while the Warsaw Pact advocated a comprehensive political settlement before dealing with the East-West conventional military balance in Europe. These different approaches, which on the Soviet side could be traced back to the political purposes of the disengagement proposals of the 1950s, could in effect not be reconciled until the early 1970s, when the Federal Republic's new Ostpolitik accepted the political status quo in Europe and when the SALT I agreement and Four Power agreement on Berlin had laid the foundation on which the positions of the two sides could converge. By late 1972 both sides agreed that MBFR and the Conference on Security and Cooperation in Europe (CSCE) should proceed on parallel tracks and that progress on the political and military dimensions of European security should be linked together—a linkage which was at the core of NATO's Harmel Report of 1967.[46] CSCE stemmed from a series of initiatives put forth by the Warsaw Pact and reluctantly accepted by the West, whereas MBFR stemmed from an initiative by NATO.

As a consequence of this linkage (which the West did not manage to sustain), the Brandt government saw MBFR negotiations as an integral part of its Ostpolitik. The connections between MBFR and CSCE were especially significant, for Bonn was obliged to take a position on the security conference that was at least initially somewhat ahead of that of its NATO partners: it agreed to support actively CSCE in a declaration of intent attached to the German-Soviet treaty of August 1970. (This declaration was the so-called "Bahr paper," named after Egon Bahr, Bonn's chief negotiator with Moscow.) In turn, the Brandt government announced that it would present the treaty to the Bundestag for ratification only if there was a satisfactory outcome of the Four Power negotiations on Berlin, followed by an agreement on Berlin between East Germany and West Germany. During his visit to the Soviet Union in September 1971, Chancellor Brandt pledged to "accelerate" efforts to arrange a security conference, and General Secretary Leonid Brezhnev in turn implied his country's willingness to accede to Western demands that any reductions of military forces in Europe would have to be genuinely balanced and mutual.

The various quid pro quos that linked the major elements of détente in the early 1970s led the Western side to believe that it could extract concessions from the Soviet Union in the complicated area of conventional force reductions, an expectation that was not met successfully. The subject matter of MBFR was extraordinarily complex and intractable, and eluded solution even in the 1980s. Neither Washington nor Bonn was ultimately prepared to uphold the linkage between progress on MBFR and other elements of détente such as SALT I, a Berlin agreement, and the convening of CSCE. This greatly annoyed German conservatives, who insisted that a linkage be maintained between MBFR and CSCE, hoping that lack of progress in MBFR (which was to be expected) would stall the convening of the Helsinki security conference, which they strongly opposed because it would lend legitimacy to the European status quo and might turn into a propaganda triumph for the Soviet Union. As Wilhelm Grewe noted later in his memoirs: "The calculation that MBFR would help avert unilateral [American] troop reduction was successful. The other aim of MBFR politics—to obviate or retard the European Security Conference, or at least guide it in directions that would correspond to Western interests—led to failure." Clearly implying that the Brandt-Scheel government wanted to send an inconvenient critic into diplomatic exile, Grewe writes: "In Bonn the linkage between MBFR and general questions of security and cooperation in Europe was pressed forward (vertreten) only temporarily, tentatively and uncertainly. When and why this linkage was dropped, is not known to me. I had been sent to Tokyo [in 1971 as German ambassador] ahead of time."[47]

SALT I and SALT II

Although the strategic arms control negotiations were a central element of détente, this did not mean that the Germans supported SALT I and II without reservations.[48] The Germans were concerned that SALT I did not encompass the medium-range missiles in the Western part of the Soviet Union that were aimed at Western Europe, a concern that spilled over into the SALT II negotiations as well. In the American negotiating position during SALT I, there were already indications that the United States recognized the strategic and political logic of the Soviet demand to include forward-based U.S. systems and British and French arsenals in future negotiations, especially if such negotiations would result in lowering the central strategic systems deployed on American and Soviet territory to such a level that U.S. forward-based systems would become an important element of the American threat to the Soviet Union.[49] For differing reasons this prospect caused concern in Paris, London, and Bonn which reemerged during SALT II and even more strongly during the START and INF negotiations in the 1980s. For Bonn it provided a powerful incentive for seeking more effective consultative procedures in the alliance and for obtaining a stronger influence on Washington's arms control policies—an attempt at co-managing the alliance that was by and large unsuccessful.

Aside from political considerations having to do with détente, the support given by Brandt's and Schmidt's governments to Soviet-American strategic arms control was predicated on a basic assumption: that after an agreement between the superpowers on limiting ABM systems and intercontinental nuclear forces in SALT I and II, the United States would seek to stabilize in SALT III the Eurostrategic, intermediate-range nuclear balance on the Continent.[50] The Germans were anxious to move on toward negotiations that to them mattered most. Postponed during the years of the SALT I negotiations, the Eurostrategic issue became even more pressing when in the mid-1970s the Soviet Union started modernizing its intermediate-range nuclear forces aimed at Western Europe, which created a serious imbalance in these weapons between NATO and the Warsaw Pact. The Germans were concerned that SALT II, by excluding the Eurostrategic imbalance from consideration, would highlight and aggravate it, and that the treaty could stand in the way of sharing nuclear control and modernizing NATO's intermediate-range nuclear arsenal, especially with respect to land-based cruise missiles. The fear that Moscow would soon obtain a credible first-strike capacity against the United States renewed the perennial concern in Bonn that Washington would not honor its nuclear commitment or would seek to limit a nuclear exchange to Europe. As always, the American performance in negotiating arms limitation was "to Europeans a constant lie detector test of the U.S. commitment to the defense of Europe."[51]

Nonetheless, Bonn officially remained strongly supportive of SALT II. The Germans did not want to add to the president's difficulty in obtaining ratification by the Senate, because they were greatly worried about the negative political consequences if the treaty fell by the wayside. Chancellor Schmidt (who had replaced Willy Brandt in 1974) told Americans that failure or nonratification of SALT II would mean "that the world would lapse back not only into a full-scale arms race between the East and West but also into another cold war,"[52] and even such vociferous German opponents of SALT II as Manfred Wörner (then the security spokesman of the opposition CDU/CSU) felt that rejection by the Senate would be "inappropriate."[53] All parties concerned swallowed some of their misgivings in light of the overarching political importance attached to the treaty. For the Germans the political consequences of rejection included the possibility of Eastern pressures on Berlin, reduced human contacts between East and West Germany, and domestic political difficulties for the governing coalition, which had fully committed itself to continuing détente.[54]

The most important political reason for supporting the treaty, however, stemmed from the Germans' doubt about American resolve and trustworthiness. Leopold Labedz was entirely correct when in testimony before a U.S. Senate committee he described as follows official endorsements of SALT II by West European NATO members:

> Paradoxical as it may seem, [they are] an indication of the undermined European political morale in the face of growing Soviet threat. . . . Many Europeans, such as Chancellor Schmidt, feel that a failure to support SALT II by the Europeans may result not in a resolution by the Americans to reverse the unfavorable trend in the balance of power between the United States and the Soviet Union, but in a growing American isolationism which will totally undermine European security. They are ready therefore to support SALT II in spite of negative features from the European point of view. They think, on plausible if not necessarily realistic grounds, that the alternative is even more dangerous.[55]

The crucial difference between the arms control negotiations of the early 1970s and of the late 1970s, and the Germans' response to them, was the political purposes that were to be served by the negotiations and the political contexts that either sustained or weakened them.

During the early 1970s both Washington and Bonn saw SALT I in the broader context of détente, and the meaning that both governments attached to arms control was an important bond between them. The Germans could fully subscribe to the view expressed by Henry Kissinger on May 29, 1972, in Kiev when he said: "To put the central armaments of both sides for the first time under agreed restraint is an event that transcends in importance the technical significance of the individual restrictions that were placed on various weapons systems. . . . In traditional diplomacy the aim was . . . to gain a qualitative edge over other countries. In the nuclear age, the most dangerous thing to aim for is a qualitative edge over your major rivals."[56] This thoroughly political view of arms control reassured many Europeans, who were always more concerned with the political commitment of the United States to retain a military presence in Europe than with purported asymmetries in the East-West military balance. This may also explain why the West Europeans showed relatively little concern over the growing Soviet strength in intercontinental ballistic missiles that developed between 1967 and 1971.[57] They were less concerned about the adequacy of American military strength than about the reliability of the American commitment to exercise it on behalf of Europe. For the same reason West Europeans, and Germans especially, assessed arms control negotiations less in terms of their specific results (although they of course mattered too) than as a political symbol that the United States and its European partners were engaged in a common and constructive dialogue with the Soviet Union.[58]

In the mid- and late 1970s it became increasingly difficult to sustain the dialogue. The supportive political context for arms control that détente had provided in the early 1970s gave way to the mutual disappointments and recriminations that increasingly beclouded Soviet-American relations at the end of the decade. Absent also was such a powerful complement to arms control as the mutual interest of East and West in the late 1960s and early 1970s in codifying the European status quo. The most dramatic and important feature of détente—the treaty package resulting from Bonn's Ostpolitik—had run its course and had been capped with the Helsinki accords of 1975, which amounted in effect to a substitute peace treaty for the Second World War. Over the next decade no East-West issue emerged that could have incorporated and symbolized a common interest of equal magnitude and that could have served as a supportive complement to arms control. As a consequence, in the second half of the 1970s the American approach to détente became highly "SALT-ocentric," placing a burden on arms control that could not be carried without supplemental political support.[59] Washington's arms control policies became heavily oriented toward the numerical aspects of the military balance, seemingly less concerned with geostrategic consequences or considerations of alliance management.[60]

Although the Germans retained a fundamental interest in keeping détente alive, they no longer had the political leverage that their own Ostpolitik had obtained for them in the early 1970s. Hoping to retain the benefits of détente for intra-German relations, Bonn argued for the divisibility of détente at the same time as Washington insisted on its global indivisibility. This highlighted again the tensions between two central aspects of Bonn's diplomacy, its security interests and its political interests in Europe. For at the very time that Bonn called for the divisibility of détente, it also kept insisting on the indivisibility of deterrence.[61]

This contradiction, which allowed of no fundamental solution, could at best have been attenuated by a close and mutually trusting relationship between the German and American governments. But this proved to be impossible. Owing to monetary and other issues German-American relations became increasingly tense; and for a variety of reasons having to do with both style and substance, personalities as well as issues, Helmut Schmidt found it difficult to establish close ties with Washington after

President Carter succeeded President Ford. With respect to arms control, the Germans were deeply annoyed that they had been insufficiently consulted during the SALT II negotiations and unable to comment on the treaty's framework and major provisions before the United States had settled on them. Washington's handling of the entire SALT process (and the controversy over the neutron bomb) undermined Bonn's confidence in the circumspection and trustworthiness of the Carter administration (especially those of the president himself and of his national security adviser, Zbigniew Brzezinski), and left a deep rift between the German chancellor and the American president.

In essence, Bonn had to be content with urging the United States to develop a more circumspect, constructive, and consistent policy toward the Soviet Union and to give fuller consideration to the interests of its West European allies. By the late 1970s arms control was deprived of its earlier political support (both in the larger context of East-West relations and in the narrower one of German-American relations), setting the stage for the severe tensions that afflicted the German-American security compact in the 1980s.

4

The Eurostrategic Balance, Arms Control, and SDI

The . . . conflict between the United States and the Soviet Union is not really about the number or kinds of American nuclear weapons . . . stationed in Europe. Even the Soviet missiles targeted against Western Europe are not the true heart of the matter. This is terrain over which the contest is being waged. The fundamental issue is the continuing struggle over the future of Europe: whether Western Europe will continue to seek its security through close dependence on the United States, or will gradually move toward a more autonomous position; whether the United States is capable of both reassuring its allies and sustaining a credible deterrent against the Soviet Union.

—WILLIAM G. HYLAND, 1984

One compelling reason why we could not avoid intervening in previous wars was because of balance-of-power considerations. A hostile power in Europe, we calculated, might ultimately pose a threat to our physical security. . . . This reasoning, though, seems no longer relevant. It applied to a pre-nuclear world and to a balance-of-power system. In such a system a surfeit of defensive and deterrent power was practically unachievable. This being so, a great object of diplomacy was to avoid isolation. In this respect, as in so many others, nuclear-missile weapons have affected a revolution in international politics.

—ROBERT W. TUCKER, 1984

There is a striking continuity in the Federal Republic's concerns with matters that are roughly but inadequately described by the term *security*. The issues of the 1980s were all rooted in the 1950s: the diminishing credibility of the American nuclear guarantee for Europe, the suspicions aroused in Bonn by revisions of Washington's strategic doctrine, the political costs of Germany's security dependence on the United States, the implications for military strategy and politics of arms control, the political repercussions of shifts in the Eurostrategic balance.

The possibility of limiting a nuclear war to Europe was not discovered by Jimmy Carter or Ronald Reagan: it emerged in the 1950s and was explained to the Germans by Gen. Alfred Gruenther and Gen. Lauris Norstad, both Supreme Allied Commanders in Europe, even before it became an implicit part of the Kennedy administration's doctrine of flexible response.[1]

The issue of the Eurostrategic balance did not originate with the massive deployment of Soviet SS-20s in the mid- and late 1970s, but stems from the deployment of Soviet intermediate-range nuclear weapons in Europe in the 1950s, which contributed to the rationale for considering a NATO joint nuclear force in the 1960s.

European concerns over American deployment of antimissile defenses did not begin with the announcement of the Strategic Defense Initiative in 1983, but can be traced to the 1950s, when the United States began research on ABM systems, long before Secretary of Defense Robert S. McNamara entertained (and rejected) the possibility of deploying them in the 1960s.

Arms control issues were from the mid-1950s inseparable from political considerations that touched on the cohesion of the Western alliance, German policies in the East, and the leeway of Bonn's diplomacy in pursuing German interests.

The basic reason for these continuities is fairly simple, perhaps because it is also somewhat tautological. It is to be found in the remarkable durability of the military division of Europe, which was solidified and sharpened in the mid-1950s with the integration of the two German states in their respective military alliances and the introduction of nuclear weapons to Europe. From then on, there developed an enduring connection between the global and regional nuclear balance, arms control, management of the alliance, and the shape of the European political order.

Intertwined all along, these issues became rearranged in the 1980s in ways that again compounded their separate significance and lent them a special diplomatic density. The dialectic of security and politics, which for decades had been the distinctive feature of the European state system and the European balance of power, retained its powerful pull on East-West diplomacy and forced a reconsideration of the historic American policies toward Europe of double containment, deterrence and reassurance, and containment and deterrence. Precisely because the United States had come to rely so heavily on implementing political containment with military strategy, any drastic alteration of the latter would inevitably also alter the former. America's policy of double containment in Europe had become so closely enmeshed with its strategy of deterrence that modifying deterrence also meant modifying containment. Inevitably it also meant that the Federal Republic would be affected profoundly.

The Eurostrategic Political Balance in Europe
In the mid-1970s the twenty-year-old issue of the nuclear balance in Europe, which had been dormant since the MLF debacle of the mid-1960s, became reconnected with the equally old issues of forward defense, the timing of an American nuclear response, and the general reliability of the American nuclear commitment to Europe. Also renewed were the political controversies that had always been attached to the Eurostrategic nuclear balance and had always been more important than the military ramifications. In its more recent manifestation, from the late 1970s to the late 1980s, the Eurostrategic debate again reflected and exacerbated political differences between Bonn and Washington, and again demonstrated Bonn's limited influence in nuclear diplomacy, in arms control, and in the co-management of the Atlantic security pact.

In the late 1950s and early 1960s, when the United States deployed intermediate-range nuclear missiles in Britain, Italy, and Turkey, it intended them (in contrast to tactical nuclear weapons) as an interim measure until American intercontinental missiles covered the Soviet targets Washington thought necessary. By 1964, when the United States had obtained this capability, the missiles were withdrawn. The Soviet Union, which also had deployed a number of IRBMs in the 1950s, similarly viewed them as a compensatory device, mostly because technical problems had slowed the Soviet intercontinental missile program. But it did not withdraw them once it had reached strategic parity with the United States, and began to augment and modernize them in the 1970s by extensively deploying SS-20 missiles (tipped with three warheads, mobile, and highly accurate).[2] The deployment of these missiles and the development of a new intermediate-range bomber obtained for the Soviet Union a Eurostrategic preponderance to which NATO's nuclear-armed aircraft, Germany's Pershing I missiles (equipped with nuclear warheads controlled by the United States), and the French and British national nuclear capabilities seemed an insufficient counterweight.

The security problems that arose from the European nuclear imbalance stemmed basically from the distinction between Eurostrategic and global-intercontinental issues. The major reason for this lies in the difference between the requirements of central deterrence and extended deterrence. Central deterrence rests on the capability and readiness of the United States to respond with a nuclear strike in case America should sustain a nuclear attack; extended deterrence, which encompasses America's allies, rests on the capability and readiness of the United States to make first use of nuclear weapons in case of a conventional attack on allied territory.[3] Over the decades central deterrence has by and large remained unimpaired; extended deterrence has become substantially weakened.

Issues of the Eurostrategic balance raised the perennial question of whether the United States would risk its own survival for the sake of its allies or rather seek to contain a nuclear war to Europe. This issue was sharpened in the 1970s because American ICBMs were gradually becoming vulnerable (making it less plausible that an American president would authorize the first use of nuclear weapons in Europe), and because the SALT I and SALT II negotiations had excluded intermediate-range nuclear forces in Europe, drawing attention to NATO's shortcomings in this area.

Among Europeans it was most prominently Chancellor Helmut Schmidt who expressed concern over the growing Eurostrategic nuclear imbalance in a much-noted speech in London in October 1977, in which he argued that nuclear parity, as institutionalized in the Strategic Arms Limitation Talks, had "neutralized" the strategic nuclear capabilities of both sides and therefore magnified the significance for Europe of the disparities between East and West in shorter-range nuclear and conventional weapons.[4]

The Carter administration was not enthusiastic about complicating the SALT II negotiations with the issue of Eurostrategic weapons, and it considered the military-strategic implications of the Eurostrategic imbalance not very important.[5] In response to German pressures, however, the United States agreed to modernize NATO's nuclear weapons, a decision coupled at the Western Summit Meeting in Guadaloupe of January 1979 with the idea of seeking arms control measures at the same time. This culminated in December 1979 in NATO's so-called double-track decision: to begin deploying in 1983 in Europe 108 American Pershing II missiles and 464 ground-based cruise missiles capable of reaching the Soviet Union, and to seek at the same time an arms control agreement with the Soviet Union that would make the first part of the decision unnecessary. All the Pershing missiles were to be deployed on German territory but only 96 of the cruise missiles would be, reflecting the determination of the German government, based largely on political grounds, that the Federal Republic would not be the sole West European NATO member to accept weapons that the Soviet Union considered a major strategic threat.[6] As always, their aversion to "singularity" was a neuralgic point for the Germans.

As in many instances in the past, for the Federal Republic's security interests NATO's decision to deploy modernized intermediate-range nuclear weapons carried contradictory implications and could be perceived in different ways.[7] On the one hand one could argue that an imbalance on an important rung of the ladder of escalation, such as that of Eurostrategic systems, needed to be redressed. It had created a gap in the flexible response posture of NATO, weakened its "escalation dominance" and strengthened that of the Warsaw Pact, and generally threatened NATO's deterrence strategy. Should NATO fail in checking a Soviet attack with conventional forces and resort to battlefield, tactical nuclear weapons, the accuracy and reduced yield of the Soviet SS-20s would allow Moscow to escalate the conflict by striking NATO's nuclear-equipped aircraft capable of reaching the Soviet Union, presenting the United States with the choice of doing nothing or resorting to intercontinental nuclear weapons. In short, a continuing East-West imbalance on the Eurostrategic nuclear level might have a decoupling effect, especially if U.S. strategic forces were limited by arms control.[8]

On the other hand one could argue with the same set of facts that restoring the Eurostrategic nuclear balance could actually lead to a different kind of decoupling of the American strategic deterrent from Europe: by substantially improving NATO's capability to strike the Soviet Union from Western Europe, modernizing NATO's nuclear forces might give the United States the option of limiting a war to Europe.[9]

Both trains of thought were equally plausible on purely logical grounds; both implied unverifiable political assumptions about Soviet intentions and American circumspection; both rested on unprovable judgments about an American president's reactions in a crisis and his readiness to go the brink for the sake of Europe and the Western alliance.

For the German government, the technical discussion of whether Eurostrategic nuclear parity would help couple the American strategic nuclear commitment to Western Europe or whether it would on the contrary enhance American opportunities for limiting a nuclear war to Europe was somewhat theoretical and academic. NATO had not managed to establish a clear doctrine either for its overall strategy or for its nuclear forces based in Europe, which left the double-track decision unconnected to NATO's nuclear planning;[10] and Helmut Schmidt, who prided himself on his pragmatism, considered the question of when and how an American president might use nuclear weapons to be not only unanswerable but improperly posed, because it postulated the most extreme, incalculable, and unlikely crisis.

For the German chancellor, who had become increasingly skeptical about the quality and consistency of American diplomacy in general and of the Carter administration in particular, the question of the Eurostrategic balance was primarily a political matter. Beneath its technical, military-strategic ramifications, the Eurostrategic nuclear balance became what nuclear issues had so often become in the past: a test of alliance management and a probing on both the German and American sides of the political limits imposed on the Federal Republic by the transatlantic security compact. In a sense, the double-track decision became a symbol and test of the extent to which the control of the Federal Republic through the Western alliance, intended from the time West Germany had acceded to NATO, was still operative.

For Helmut Schmidt, restoring the Eurostrategic *military* balance, whether by deploying modernized NATO weapons or (preferably) by reducing Soviet weapons, was the essential prerequisite for sustaining the European *political* balance and retaining an important German voice in the management of the Western alliance. The chancellor feared that the Soviet Union could convert its Eurostrategic nuclear advantage into political pressures, and worried that the United States might not resist such pressures firmly enough.[11] The German government called for restoring the Eurostrategic balance less in response to a threatening Soviet military strategy than in response to what it perceived as an incompetent American diplomacy.[12]

The Germans had wanted all along to see the Soviet-American strategic balance that was codified in SALT II extended to the Eurostrategic balance, and they had urged the Ford and Carter administrations to include Eurostrategic nuclear weapons in the SALT II process. Having failed in that, the German government sought to retain a measure of influence in the SALT II negotiations and placed its hopes in a subsequent round of arms control negotiations (already labeled SALT III) that might stabilize the Eurostrategic balance.

But these expectations failed to materialize when the Soviet Union continued to deploy SS-20s, making a codification of the Eurostrategic balance increasingly difficult, and when President Carter's political fortunes in Washington fell so drastically that he needed to shelve consideration of the SALT II treaty by the Senate. SALT II, the basis for SALT III, never materialized in a formal sense. Helmut Schmidt became stuck with the political liabilities of NATO's double-track decision, which he had urged in circumstances far different from the ones that prevailed at the end of Carter's administration and the beginning of Reagan's and which he was obliged to defend in the face of mounting criticism at home— directed at him mostly from his own party, the left wing of which strongly opposed deploying additional nuclear weapons on German territory.[13]

The German chancellor was closely identified with the NATO decision of 1979. Not only had he publicly expressed concern over the Eurostrategic imbalance, but the double-track decision marked the first time in NATO's history that the alliance undertook collective responsibility for procuring weapons: allies were asked for a commitment to deploy Pershing II missiles and cruise missiles before the new weapons were produced. Before that, procurement decisions had been made by the United States alone (or by France and Britain, for their respective arsenals), and allies were approached subsequently about their interest in deployment. The first time this arrangement was changed was in connection with the neutron bomb project, contributing heavily to its demise and straining German-American relations in the process when President Carter abandoned the project after Chancellor Schmidt had been persuaded to accept it.[14] When the idea of taking joint responsibility for production and deployment was resurrected in the NATO double-track decision, it necessarily tied the Federal Republic, and especially the German chancellor, very closely to the political liabilities, foreign and domestic, that accompanied the decision of December 1979.

The two novel aspects of the Eurostrategic issue—joint decisions on procurement and deployment, and linking the implementation of the decisions to the outcome of Soviet-American arms control negotiations—turned into heavy liabilities for the German chancellor. Although Helmut Schmidt shared the increasingly burdensome political responsibility for the first track of the decision of 1979 (deployment), he had practically no influence over the second (the arms control negotiations that were to make the first track unnecessary). It was in the very nature of the double-track decision that the United States gained an even larger leverage over alliance politics and in particular over the German-American security relationship.[15]

Arms Control and German-American Relations in the 1980s

From the German viewpoint, the double-track decision of 1979 obligated the United States to demonstrate an equal commitment to both tracks. The German government expected that the American government would in the course of its negotiations with the Soviet Union be firm in safeguarding the political and strategic calculations underlying Bonn's interest in the deployment track, but also protective of German interests in the arms control track. They hoped American diplomacy would be sensitive to the special mix of German security requirements and political requirements, and that American arms control policies would reflect a balanced consideration of Germany's need for both strategic security and political détente. In short, Bonn expected Washington to help implement the dual principles of NATO's Harmel Report of 1967—military security and alliance solidarity, but also search for political solutions and détente. As it turned out, from the German perspective American diplomacy failed to accommodate either dimension: ultimately it jeopardized both German security interests and German interests in détente.

During the twenty-two months in which their terms in office overlapped, President Reagan and Chancellor Helmut Schmidt could not establish sufficient personal rapport or agreement on substantive issues to improve German-American relations, in part because Schmidt became increasingly preoccupied with the political tensions that ultimately collapsed his coalition government with the Free Democrats in October

1982. During this period some major political liabilities of the NATO decision emerged, which became the focal point of German-American tensions toward the end of Schmidt's government and remained during Helmut Kohl's, which took office in October 1982 and was returned to office by general elections in 1983 and 1987.

One major obstacle to improving German-American relations was the Reagan administration's inability to convince its European allies (and their electorates) that it was seriously interested in arms control. The talks in Geneva on intermediate-range nuclear forces (renamed INF negotiations by Washington to avoid the tainting continuity implied in the term SALT III) commenced ten months into the President's term, and then it seemed only at the insistence of the U.S. Congress and of European leaders, who were themselves pressed by the expressions of public concern over the impending deployment of Pershing II and cruise missiles.[16] The talks in Geneva on strategic arms reductions, renamed START, began seventeen months after the president took office and again only after there had been extensive expressions of concern over the delay, in the United States as well as abroad. The administration placed known opponents of the SALT II treaty in key positions in its arms control agencies and negotiating teams, and the president postponed indefinitely the negotiations on a comprehensive test ban treaty, arguing the need for more nuclear testing. The president provided no succinct guidelines for the American negotiating position and created doubts as to whether he understood it, and the major decisions on arms control were apparently made at the subcabinet level, allowing undersecretaries to project their personal disagreements and bureaucratic rivalries onto the discussions in Geneva.[17]

Moreover, the Reagan administration provided itself with a powerful rationale for avoiding arms control. Washington argued that the United States was inferior to the Soviet Union in intercontinental strategic capabilities—an argument that the Schmidt government found implausible and that the Kohl government chose to ignore in public—and that this "window of vulnerability" should be closed as quickly and tightly as possible.[18] Its determination to modernize and augment the American nuclear arsenal hardly predisposed the Reagan administration to arms control measures that might impede these goals: there is little incentive to engage in arms control negotiations if one perceives oneself to be inferior.

During its first term the Reagan administration generally viewed arms control as a strategically unprofitable and politically hazardous digression that would only stand in the way of quantitative and qualitative improvements of America's strategic triad, and by raising unjustified hopes among Western electorates for the revival of détente would also stand in the way of the tough confrontation with the Soviet Union that the administration favored. Washington contended that in the past

American policy had played into Soviet hands by attaching too much importance to arms control, and that some linkage should be established between progress on arms control and progress on resolving outstanding issues in Third World conflicts and human rights.[19]

The strategic calculations underlying the Reagan administration's distaste for arms control were strengthened by its ideological inclinations. Washington's strident anti-Soviet rhetoric and its black-and-white view of the East-West conflict seriously burdened Soviet-American relations, with the consequence that the main prerequisites of successful arms control—a mutual sense of a balanced power relationship and a conducive political context—were absent. Arms control in the 1980s was deprived of the political base that the mutual interest of East and West in solidifying the European status quo had provided in the early and mid-1970s, nor was there any prospect in the 1980s that another major East-West issue would lend itself to a similarly supportive role. The Reagan administration was fundamentally hostile to the Soviet Union, disillusioned by what it considered the negative results of SALT I, SALT II, and détente, sensitive to real or imagined asymmetries in the East-West military balance, torn between conflicting views on how to deal with the Soviet Union, and responsive to different domestic political constituencies. For reasons both of foreign and of domestic policies, the administration could not fashion a diplomacy that would have given arms control or détente a central place in its foreign policy agenda.

Washington's hostility toward arms control and toward the renewal of détente did not reassure the Germans. One of the heaviest burdens placed on the transatlantic alliance was the failure of the Reagan administration to develop an attitude toward the Soviet Union (not to speak of a policy) that would have conveyed anything but confrontational hostility.[20] Characterizing the Soviet Union as an "evil empire" and elevating the contest between West and East to a messianic crusade between the forces of light and darkness elicited among Europeans not only disdain but also the fear that this Manichaean struggle would be acted out on their territory. Perhaps most disturbing, the administration raised discussions about "protracted" nuclear and conventional war, warned against the "short war fallacy" and stressed the need to prepare for a long struggle of the dimensions of the Second World War, and told the Europeans that they were not living in a postwar period but in a prewar period.[21] No wonder Europeans spoke of the beginning of a "second cold war" and developed the nagging suspicion, fueled by injudicious American statements and Washington's promilitary budget priorities, that the United States aimed to achieve nuclear superiority over the Soviet Union by retarding arms control, eviscerating the ABM treaty, and deploying a strategic defense shield.[22] In the wake of the disappointing American performance during the SALT II negotiations in the Carter administration, the West Germans saw in the disarray of American arms control policies during the first Reagan administration another example of Washington's insensitivity to their concerns.

These concerns were heightened by the administration's disdain for East-West détente. The Federal Republic had been the main beneficiary of the détente of the 1970s, which revitalized Bonn's diplomacy and eased inter-German contacts; and both Schmidt's and Kohl's governments continued to see in arms control a practical as well as a symbolic indicator of the nature of East-West relations. They also regarded American arms control policies as an indicator of Washington's sensitivity to the concerns of the Federal Republic. The range of Bonn's Eastern policy (especially its inter-German component) was inevitably delimited by the general climate of East-West relations, in which arms control remained of central importance, and both German states pressed against this delimitation to keep improving their bilateral relationship. As a consequence, the Reagan administration's distaste for arms control placed a major burden on German-American relations.

But Chancellor Helmut Kohl was determined to establish a more harmonious relationship with Washington than the one that had prevailed during the last phase of Schmidt's government—in part out of conviction and reflex, in part because the deterioration of German-American relations had been a major rationale for bringing down Chancellor Schmidt. In particular, the new government intended to demonstrate Bonn's continuing commitment to the Western alliance by reaffirming German support for deploying modernized Pershing missiles and cruise missiles (which continued to be opposed by the SPD, now the party in opposition), should the negotiations in Geneva on Eurostrategic weapons fail to come to a satisfactory conclusion.

When the negotiations did fail, the German government, making the deployment decision an issue of loyalty to the alliance, was nonetheless determined to see it implemented and succeeded in doing so.[23] But many West Germans, although supportive of NATO and not inclined toward neutralism, were not eager to see additional nuclear weapons installed on their territory. Relative to its size, the Federal Republic already contained more nuclear weapons than any other country,[24] many Germans saw no compelling need to add to them, and the political constituency in Germany that opposed deployment, although concentrated mostly at the left of the political spectrum, reached also into the political center, where the charge of neutralist or anti-American tendencies lacked credibility. For Bonn, progress on arms control remained centrally important, for reasons of domestic as well as foreign policy, and Chancellor Kohl felt obliged to remind the president in public of the urgency to maintain the arms control dialogue with the Soviet Union.

But the president nonetheless burdened German-American relations when he discovered his interest in some form of arms control during his second term, arguing that the purported strategic inferiority of the United States had been redressed during his first, and inspired perhaps by the desire to enter history as a peacemaker. The relative ease with which the United States and the Soviet Union apparently agreed at the Reykjavík Summit in 1986 on a "zero" solution of the Eurostrategic issue attested further to the relative insignificance of that issue for the East-West military balance, to its paramount significance for the political balance, and to Bonn's lack of influence in either dimension. Reservations in the Federal Republic, in NATO, and among the Joint Chiefs of Staff about a zero solution for Eurostrategic weapons in the absence of concurrent reductions of shorter-range missiles and conventional forces were either swept aside or, more likely, did not even enter into the president's calculations. In general, the ill-considered negotiating agenda in Reykjavík, where central and historic elements of NATO strategy were put on the table, further reminded the Germans of how excluded they had been from consultations and how little their basic security concerns seemed to matter to the president.

The lack of Bonn's influence was glaringly demonstrated in summer and fall 1987, when Chancellor Kohl (but not his foreign minister, Hans-Dietrich Genscher) strongly opposed the double-zero proposals for Eurostrategic arms control, which linked a zero solution for intermediate-range Eurostrategic missiles to a zero solution for shorter-range missiles. Faced with the prospect of bearing the onus for obstructing an East-West arms control agreement (which the Reagan administration chose to interpret as a major success because more Soviet systems would be removed than American ones), the German government ultimately agreed to the Western negotiating position even as it saw its central security interests neglected and its diplomatic position undercut. When the superpowers arrived at a double-zero agreement in late 1987, which was formalized at the summit in Moscow, May 1988, the Germans were not only compelled to agree to the withdrawal of American Pershing II missiles and cruise missiles, the stationing of which had burdened their relations with Moscow and caused them the most serious domestic political problems, but were obliged in the bargain to assent to the scrapping of their own intermediate-range Pershing missiles (the aging Pershing 1A missiles, tipped with nuclear warheads controlled by the United States).

These developments were a serious matter indeed for the Germans. Even before Chancellor Schmidt's speech in London in 1977, the Germans had viewed the modernization of NATO's intermediate-range nuclear forces not simply as a compensatory military requirement to offset the deployment of Soviet SS-20s, but as a political requirement, assuring them that they would not have to face down a Soviet nuclear threat on their own. American INF forces, capable of reaching the Soviet Union,

118 SECURITY, ARMS CONTROL, AND STRATEGIC DOCTRINE

were seen as a guarantee of the American commitment to Europe. The Reagan administration's preoccupation with eliminating entire categories of nuclear weapons in Europe rather than merely reducing them was thus in direct conflict with what Bonn perceived to be important German interests, and moreover amounted to an unintended and indirect American endorsement of the antinuclear and neutralist sentiments expressed in Germany by the opposition on the Left. In the face of overriding American and Soviet interests, both domestic and foreign, the Germans were again forced into retreat on an issue of major practical and symbolic importance to them, demonstrating the limits of their diplomatic influence within the alliance on fundamental security matters. The entire issue of modernizing NATO's Eurostrategic arsenal had turned into an unrelieved diplomatic nightmare for Bonn that lasted a decade: taking the missiles out proved almost as troublesome as putting them in, and the Germans had lost their own in the process. Moscow had succeeded in driving a major wedge between Washington and Bonn, abetted by an American administration singularly unconcerned about the consequences of its arms control decisions for the cohesion of the alliance. Coming or going, Eurostrategic missiles strained the German-American security compact.

There was also the implication that the double-zero accord of 1987–88 served Washington as a political substitute for a more significant but unattainable strategic arms control arrangement. The administration's obsession with a strategic defense shield checked progress in the START negotiations (as did the Pentagon's inability to decide what land-based missile systems it wanted after a drastic reduction of strategic weapons); and Washington seemed determined to reach for more readily obtainable alternatives (once the Soviet Union had dropped its demand for linkages), such as the INF treaty. Wanting or needing an arms control agreement, infatuated with the drama of abolishing entire sets of arms rather than merely reducing them, and determined to hang on to SDI, Washington was almost inevitably pointed in the direction of seeking an agreement on Eurostrategic systems that left unimpaired what Washington perceived to be central American interests even as it threatened those of American allies. In its waning days, the Reagan administration appeared determined to compensate for its shaky foreign policy record with an arms control agreement and to cap its two terms in office with the symbolic satisfactions of at least superficially successful Soviet-American summits.

Twenty years after the MLF debacle, the circumstances surrounding the INF accord demonstrated again Bonn's inability to influence Washington's nuclear diplomacy and arms control policies. In both instances, the real issue was political and not military; in both instances the Germans aimed for political symbols rather than genuine nuclear co-management; and in both instances they suffered major diplomatic embarrassment. By the late 1980s it had again become clear that nuclear issues in general and arms control in particular had taken on a meaning far beyond their military and technical import and extended into fundamental questions about the future shape of the alliance and the European political order. Attitudes on nuclear weapons were connected on both the domestic and international scenes with the present and future course of East-West relations. Political calculations were much more important than military and strategic calculations.[25]

Toward a Post-INF Europe

But the matter did not end with the conclusion of the INF double-zero accord. Equally divisive for the alliance was the prospect that the double-zero INF treaty might in the future be enlarged to a triple-zero arrangement, encompassing the short-range tactical battlefield nuclear weapons deployed mostly in the Federal Republic and the German Democratic Republic.

In 1988 both the Soviet Union and East Germany hinted that a future East-West arms accord might include such weapons (at the same time as the Pentagon was pressing for their modernization and augmentation), raising a dilemma for the alliance and for the Federal Republic for which there seemed no ready solution. On the one hand, removing the remaining battlefield nuclear weapons would for all practical purposes make Central Europe a nuclear-free zone, a prospect long favored by the Soviet Union (and the German Left) and long opposed by successive German governments as well as by the Federal Republic's allies. From the German perspective, the continued presence of tactical nuclear weapons was a reminder to the Soviet Union that an attack might risk nuclear escalation, and the German defense ministry was not averse to American plans for their modernization, although the German foreign ministry was opposed. If the remaining battlefield nuclear weapons were removed, the deterrent elements of NATO's strategy would shrink to U.S. bombers based in Europe (which the Pentagon wanted equipped with modernized air-to-ground missiles), the strategic nuclear forces of the United States (both at home and at sea), and of course conventional forces. NATO's flexible response posture and its escalation dominance would be seriously undermined, in effect highlighting the erosion of the principle of extended deterrence, if not its demise.

But there were conflicting considerations. The Bonn government (and, significantly, the right wing of the CDU) felt uneasy about the battlefield nuclear weapons remaining on German soil after the double-zero accord was implemented. The continuing presence of short-range battlefield nuclear weapons, disconnected from American intercontinental systems by the removal of Eurostrategic intermediate-range forces, meant in effect that the Germans were expected to support a NATO nuclear strategy that threatened primarily Germans, again raising among other sensitive issues the delicate matter of Germany's position of "singularity" in the alliance.[26] This concern was captured in the slogan "the shorter the range, the deader the Germans." The Reagan administration's implicit suggestion that battlefield nuclear weapons could be substitutes for medium-range missiles simply raised again the Germans' fear that the United States was ready to limit a nuclear war to European territory (indeed, more specifically, to German territory), and that their West European allies, in opposing the withdrawal of these short-range weapons and urging their modernization, were similarly determined to keep using German territory as a forward glacis for their own security posture. The political implications of their allies' support for keeping nuclear weapons on German territory were equally distasteful to the Germans. For it was difficult to avoid the conclusion that the Western powers were reasserting their political interest in seeing the Federal Republic tied to the West through the continuing deployment of nuclear weapons on German soil, thus also curtailing Bonn's diplomatic room of maneuver.[27]

The Germans' unease with having to face yet another nuclear issue was spread across the political spectrum and reflected a clear sense of an important national interest, which ran directly counter to their allies' interest in modernizing the remaining short-range nuclear weapons. In February 1988 U.S. Secretary of Defense Frank C. Carlucci urged a reluctant Bonn government, which was also concerned about the domestic political implications of such a move, to follow through on NATO's decision of 1983 (the so-called Montebello agreement) to modernize the short-range Lance missiles in the wake of the double-zero INF accord or else risk an erosion of the American security commitment to Europe.[28] The question of the Eurostrategic balance was already creating new problems as it expanded from a double-zero to a triple-zero issue, putting the German government in a difficult position: although it did not favor the denuclearization of Central Europe and feared its adverse consequences for German security interests, it could hardly support a NATO force posture that singularized the Germans by highlighting their unique geographical and political situation in the alliance. As always, questions about the indivisibility of the transatlantic security compact were for the Germans compounded by equally troublesome questions about the indivisibility of the West European security compact. By 1988–89, the double-zero accord had already created new problems for Bonn's security policies, highlighted the clashing interests of NATO allies, and called into question the consistency and circumspection of America's European policies.

Highly sensitive as well to the trends in German public opinion that emerged in the late 1980s, which attested to the very favorable image Mikhail S. Gorbachev had obtained in Germany, Bonn took a generally cautious stand on arms control matters. In a stance that was directed as much against Bonn's allies as against its opponents, the German government argued for an arms control negotiating framework that would deal simultaneously rather than consecutively with strategic nuclear arms, battlefield nuclear weapons, conventional forces, and chemical weapons, hoping to enlarge its diplomatic leverage by linking issues where it had some influence (such as conventional troop levels) with those where it had little (such as strategic nuclear weapons).[29]

In the late 1980s this issue mainly took the form of which arms control forum should be given precedence: the larger framework of the CSCE or the smaller one of MBFR. The outcome of the East-West Conference on Disarmament (CDE) in Stockholm, although not spectacular, seemed to indicate that the larger CSCE framework (which encompassed Europe from the Atlantic to the Urals) held a larger promise for European arms control arrangement than the narrower MBFR framework, within which the two alliances had for more than a decade dragged their feet in endless and largely fruitless deliberations.[30] At the meeting of NATO foreign ministers in June 1987 in Reykjavík it was decided to connect the CSCE forum, which comprised thirty-five nations, with the smaller MBFR forum in an attempt to deal more constructively with future conventional arms talks. The foreign ministers noted that they were "agreed that the future security negotiations should take place within the framework of the CSCE process, with the conventional stability negotiations retaining autonomy as regards subject matter, participations and procedures," and that they "took the decisions necessary . . . to press ahead with its work on the draft mandates to be tabled at the CSCE meeting and in the Conventional Stability mandate talks currently taking place in Vienna."[31]

This carefully qualified statement (especially with respect to retaining autonomy over subject matter and participation) masked a fundamental disagreement between the United States and some of its West European allies. Whereas many Europeans saw in the CSCE framework large opportunities for progress in East-West arms control, the United States retained its generally skeptical view of the CSCE process and used the CSCE forum primarily to score propaganda points against the Soviet Union on human rights issues and related topics. What was fundamentally at issue was the question of an all-European security compact, which the Soviet Union had favored for decades (and revived in summer 1988) and the United States had resisted all along, seeing in it a Soviet attempt to weaken the Western alliance and encourage a sense of neutralism in Europe. In other words, the United States continued to perceive in a pan-European security arrangement a threat to its traditional policy of double containment. As always, arms control arrangements signified political arrangements. But in the 1980s the prospect of involving all of Europe (including the "neutrals" in the East-West contest) in a postwar European settlement held powerful attractions to those Europeans who wanted to see the division of their continent at least attenuated if not overcome. They believed that an all-European security compact based on East-West arms control would in the long run pave the way for an all-European political concert—a long-range calculation made more urgent if the American military commitment to Europe were to weaken in the future. One American commentator noted:

> It may be 10 years or 50, but US troops will leave Europe someday, and our direct influence there will inevitably lessen. How this happens is the essential question. Will it be gradually, through a careful process involving both parts of Europe, including the Soviet Union, in constructive arrangements to replace the artificial, bifurcated postwar stability with a more pan-European but democratic system in which the US plays an important role, or suddenly, through intra-NATO crisis and a fit of irrationality? CSCE is part of a lengthy transition. In its Western-oriented value system and guarantees for American involvement, it should be a model for rational efforts to construct 21st Century Europe; it may even provide part of the institutional framework. The alternative is that if US insensitivity is a major contributor to CSCE's breakdown, the second scenario will gain plausibility.[32]

The Strategic Defense Initiative, German Security Interests, and German-American Relations

In the United States the debate over SDI, which followed President Reagan's announcement in March 1983 of plans for a strategic defense shield for America, was largely focused on its technological feasibility, its consequences for arms control arrangements with the Soviet Union, and its potential for protecting the territorial security of the United States in the remainder of this century and beyond.[33]

But the administration's intention to shift from strategic deterrence to strategic defense also raised fundamental questions about the form, content, and viability of the historic transatlantic security compact. The implied abolition of the principle of strategic deterrence, which had for decades served American diplomacy in dealing with both opponents and allies, signaled in a compressed formulation a total reversal of long-standing precepts of American strategy.[34] Irrespective of whether an American defense shield would ever be deployed, the intentions reflected in the idea of SDI symbolized a new attitude in Washington toward both America's opponents and its friends, and carried with them a profound meaning for the Atlantic community and the German-American security connection.

Such a drastic reversal of the traditional U.S. strategic posture could of course not be effected by mere proclamation. Its implementation was retarded not only by technological and fiscal obstacles but by the powerful political, economic, institutional, and bureaucratic constituencies that the principle of deterrence had obtained over the decades in the United States and abroad. The implementation of a strategic defense shield would mean that NATO strategy and its subsidiary targeting doctrines would have to be revamped, force postures and procurement priorities readjusted, intraservice rivalries in the United States given a new complexion—to mention just a few of the factors that slowed down such a fundamental change in U.S. strategy, making it incremental rather than revolutionary. Also, future American presidents may deemphasize SDI or future American legislators starve it with leaner appropriations. In the late 1980s SDI was a political doctrine far from being a strategic reality.

Even so, SDI reoriented as a political symbol the diplomatic discourse between the United States and the Soviet Union and between the United States and its European allies. Although SDI existed only as a futuristic technological blueprint it nonetheless reflected a political program that existed then and there. In this respect, it did not matter whether SDI would become a physical reality in the future; its political ramifications and underlying strategic calculations lent it a diplomatic reality in the present. For the alliance, SDI (or Star Wars, as it was popularly known) turned into a super-issue, condensing a number of sub-issues with long and troublesome histories of their own into a critical mass of nuclear-strategic and political problems.[35]

The West Europeans' and West Germans' response to the idea of strategic defense was also influenced by the ideological and political ambience of the Reagan administration. And in this respect the Reagan administration had already created in its first term what one might call a reassurance gap, incurring with Western Europe a policy deficit in both style and substance. Its harsh Cold War rhetoric, its disarray on strategic matters, its patent lack of interest in arms control, the ideological bent of its foreign policy—all these factors and many more handicapped the administration in articulating a drastic reversal of America's postwar strategic posture. Perhaps no administration or president could have pulled this off successfully, but Reagan's, having aroused deep suspicions about its ultimate strategic intentions and deep apprehensions about its diplomatic circumspection, appeared especially ill suited to the task.[36]

The American idea of converting strategic deterrence to strategic defense profoundly disquieted the Federal Republic. From the German perspective, deterrence has always conveyed the reassuring intent to prevent the outbreak of hostilities; defense has always meant that deterrence has failed and hostilities have broken out, presumably involving the German people and German territory. Over the decades, deterrence came to signify for the Germans an antiwar or at least a prewar military posture; defense signified a wartime posture and the ultimate calamity. Even though its doctrinal purity and political plausibility had suffered over the decades, extended deterrence was an indispensable myth of the alliance embodying the fiction that the allies were sharing benefits and risks in equal measure. The perceived effect of SDI on the question of "differentiated security" was a main reason why the defense experts of the Bonn government—most prominently Defense Minister Manfred Wörner and the chief of his planning staff, Hans Rühle—strongly opposed SDI when it was first announced, recanting only later with a set of reasons not nearly as persuasive as their initial objections.[37] The traditional German aversion to singularity, along with the fear that SDI would ultimately lead to American unilateralism, were at the core of Bonn's uneasiness about a defense-dominated American strategy.

The Reagan administration sought to reassure the Germans by arguing that SDI would make America invulnerable, thereby strengthening the American nuclear commitment to the alliance. But the question of whether a defensive shield above America would tend to decouple or strengthen the American nuclear connection to Western Europe allowed of no conclusive answer. The strategic and technological facts permitted totally opposite conclusions (as was the case in the Eurostrategic debate): should the territory and people of the United States become inviolable, it might help couple the United States to the defense of Europe, but it might also encourage a more distant association with Europe, raising the old issue of whether a nuclear war might be limited to Europe.[38]

Nor were the Germans reassured by Washington's argument that an extended "transition period" would cushion the change from an offensive nuclear strategy to a defensive one. A long transition would merely compound the Federal Republic's old security problem of the diminished credibility of the American nuclear commitment with the new problem of feasibility, complicating NATO's strategy of preplanned escalation (what German planners call "*vorbedachte Eskalation*") and unraveling the carefully crafted and intricate web of NATO's contingency planning and targeting doctrines.[39] All these were predicated on the assumption of mutual assured destruction and would have to be revised under conditions of mutual assured security between the United States and the Soviet Union. This was yet another reason why the West Europeans distrusted the tortuous and implausible argument with which Washington sought to square the circle: that strategic defense would guarantee the continuing viability of extended deterrence at the same time as sharing SDI technology with the Soviet Union would render the opponent invulnerable as well.

Generally, the Reagan administration's defense of SDI was weakened by the conflicting arguments and assumptions that its spokesmen presented to the public. The administration was itself divided as to feasibility, timing, technology sharing, and strategic purpose, and in the years following the president's announcement in 1983 its sweeping goals of providing total security for the American people were scaled back to more modest levels. At the end of the Reagan administration, the general disarray that afflicted its arms control and security policies also undermined its rationale for a strategic defense shield for the United States.

Nonetheless, the Kohl government was dutiful in its public support for the American program. After the strong opposition voiced by government spokesmen in the earlier stages of the SDI idea, Bonn avoided airing its concerns in public, took refuge in the alleged economic benefits of technology sharing that would accrue to the Federal Republic, extended lukewarm support to a West European regional defense shield, and generally sidestepped the complicated issues and serious dislocations of its own security interests that would follow from the implementation of an SDI program.[40] Chancellor Kohl had gained office in 1982 at least in part with the promise of improved German-American relations, and for political as well as temperamental reasons he did not wish to burden his relations with the American administration, although he was being urged even from within his own cabinet to press German interests more assertively.[41] The German government hoped that the problem of SDI would ultimately disappear. But the SDI debate in Germany followed closely on the heels of the Eurostrategic debate, ran parallel to the double-zero controversy, and placed an additional burden on German-American relations at a time when the objectively different security interests of the United States and the Federal Republic had already created frictions. The SDI program caused a serious domestic rift in both countries, and both governments were themselves divided: that of the United States in trying to find a coherent rationale for the purposes of SDI, that of Germany in trying to express its reservations in a way that would not burden German-American relations and the cohesion of the center-right coalition in Bonn.

The SDI debate of the mid- and late 1980s also touched on the role of conventional weapons in Europe, raising (as always) conflicting political and military considerations. On the one hand, the prospect of American invulnerability, unrealistic as it may have been, diverted attention from what NATO considered its serious shortcomings in the area of conventional capabilities and undermined public support for efforts to redress them. On the other, there was wide agreement among strategic analysts that a strategic defense shield (were it deployed) and a concurrent drastic reduction in Soviet and American strategic offensive systems (were it achieved) would if anything require a reemphasis on conventional defense in Europe. Although many advocates of a conventional buildup of NATO forces in Europe viewed Moscow as engaging in an unrelieved quest for military superiority, analysts with a more benign assessment of the Soviet threat also pointed to the advantages for Western Europe of returning to the "basics" of European security: the defense of territory. A number of influential Western analysts, anticipating American disengagement from Europe and fearing the collapse of NATO under the weight of its unresolved issues, called for a sweeping reorganization of NATO's organizational structure and a reshaping of its strategy that would face squarely the implications for West European security of nuclear parity between the United States and the Soviet Union. Among other suggestions, such as dropping NATO's long-standing option of first use of nuclear weapons,[42] some urged a turning away from nuclear deterrence toward conventional deterrence, because this would compel Europeans to rely more on themselves and less on the United States and relegate nuclear weapons to a less obtrusive and more reassuring role. For example, Michael Howard argued, "The necessity for nuclear countermeasures should be fully and publicly explained, but they should be put in the context of the fundamental task which only non-nuclear forces can effectively carry out—*the defense of territory*. Nuclear deterrence needs to be subordinated to this primary task of territorial defense, and not vice versa" (italics in original).[43]

But a return to the basics of territorial defense and conventional deterrence would raise troublesome questions for the Federal Republic's security posture. In the first place, the burdens of reemphasizing conventional defense would devolve primarily on the Federal Republic, which would find it difficult to shoulder them—fiscal, demographic, and domestic political considerations would stand in the way. Other NATO partners were unlikely to rely on the deterrent functions of conventional forces and to incur the costs connected with such an emphasis. Although many Germans welcomed an intensified Franco-German security partnership,[44] France and Britain were not about to finance a larger conventional force, which would enforce an even more distinct and visible division of labor between the role of the West European nuclear powers and the conventional-force responsibilities of the Federal Republic. Moreover, many Germans have traditionally opposed the denuclearization of Central Europe and (rationally or not) favored a low nuclear threshold, so that their country would not be overrun and destroyed with conventional weapons. But the nuclear threshold would clearly be raised by the improvement of territorial defense capabilities, especially with modernized, "smart" weapons or the attack-oriented AirLand Battle doctrine of the U.S. Army (which would allow interdiction in the attackers' territory and deny them a sanctuary). This raising of the nuclear threshold was one of the avowed purposes of the improvement in conventional defenses, which also brought to the fore the troublesome political and moral question of a defense strategy that envisaged the destruction of the German Democratic Republic and East European countries.[45] (See chapter 1.)

Above all, the discussion about territorial defense reopened the fundamental question of the nature of the security threat that the Federal Republic faces in the remainder of this century. The requirement of deterring a conventional attack on the territory of West Germany, although basic, is probably the least likely contingency, given the nature of the European political order and the general diminution of territorial issues in the industrialized parts of the world. The political pressures that the Warsaw Pact might exert through its military and strategic posture, which have been the central concern of both the Federal Republic and its West European allies, are perhaps less easily averted with conventional preparations and the modernization of NATO's conventional capabilities, unless they are also backed by a joint West European nuclear commitment to the defense of the Federal Republic.

Strategic Defense, American Unilateralism, and the European Political Order
Irrespective of whether the United States would ever implement a strategic defense shield in whole or in part, its underlying aspirations reflected a trend in American strategic thinking that would survive even if a defense-dominated nuclear strategy were scrapped because of political, financial, or arms control considerations.

From the perspective of the Reagan administration, the protection of the American people and American territory was held hostage to the distasteful principle of mutual assured destruction and its twin principle, deterrence. Both principles required the consent of the opponent, which was obtained because of the opponent's own vulnerability. For the Reagan administration, the core purpose of SDI was to guarantee the protection of the United States without the consent of anyone.[46] Seen from the American viewpoint, faith in central deterrence—that is, deterrence of an attack on the United States itself—could be maintained or restored in one of three ways: by the restoration of American strategic superiority, an American withdrawal from its commitments to the alliance (a disavowal of the principle of extended deterrence), or a political accommodation with the opponent: "The effort to regain strategic superiority, or some semblance thereof, and a policy of withdrawal are two radically different ways to attempt a restoration of faith in deterrence. Either way may be pursued largely independent of the will and desire of the Soviet Union. This is one of their undoubted attractions and is to be sharply contrasted with the third course, détente, which is evidently dependent on the cooperation of the Soviet government. The attraction of détente, on the other hand, is that it is easier to pursue than strategic superiority while less likely to result in the sacrifice that withdrawal probably entails."[47]

Clearly, each of these three options carried with it not only distinct implications for the military strategy and arms control policies of the United States, but raised fundamental questions about the geopolitical stance of the United States and the future of the German-American security compact.

It is in this context that the idea of a strategic defense umbrella obtained its central geopolitical significance. The Reagan administration's quest for SDI, and the thinking associated with it, lent themselves to a twofold purpose. A strategic defense shield would advance both of the geopolitical options for restoring faith in central deterrence that some perceive to be "radically different": strategic superiority and withdrawal from the obligations of extended deterrence.[48] It would enable future American administrations to pursue both options simultaneously, widening the range of American diplomacy and allowing a shift in geopolitical priorities. This was a major reason why at the end of the Reagan administration SDI retained a powerful and stubbornly persistent political constituency. The options of obtaining strategic superiority and of disengaging from Europe may be very different, but they need not be politically contradictory. A strategic defense shield would provide for their concurrent implementation, allowing future American administrations to hold such geopolitical options in abeyance, as suspended decisions that could be activated in the years to come.

During the Reagan administration the attraction of gaining superiority over the opponent as well as independence from allies coalesced into complementary impulses, fed by powerful resentments toward the Soviet Union and equally powerful frustrations with American allies.[49] These impulses may weaken in succeeding American administrations, but they may also grow stronger. For what could have a larger appeal to the American people and many of their leaders than a geopolitical strategy that would make the United States safe as well as independent, superior in competing with the adversary in the only area in which the adversary could claim to be a superpower, and liberated from the complications and risks of managing entangling alliances? Consciously or not, the American hopes associated with SDI reflected both aspirations in equal measure, making them mutually supportive in their strategic, political, and emotional logic.[50]

Moreover, the Reagan administration's emphasis on a revitalized maritime strategy and a more pronounced Pacific orientation of American diplomacy pointed in the same geostrategic direction, augmenting the opportunities for American superiority and unilateralism that a defense-dominated nuclear strategy would provide.[51] The combination of

American unilateralism, Pacific orientation, and an assertive maritime strategy is sustained by a long historical lineage and deep emotional suasion. Traditionally, Americans who prefer a more distant association with Europe (for political, psychological, or even theological reasons) have often urged a closer involvement of the United States in the Pacific and a corresponding reliance on a maritime global strategy.[52]

The unilateralist potential of a strategic defense shield, and the attitudes that created for it a devoted political constituency in the United States, clearly called into question not only the principle of strategic deterrence but also the principle of containment, signifying a fragmentation of the postwar complementarity among the elements of double containment and of deterrence and reassurance.[53] For if containment has meant anything in the postwar diplomacy of the United States, it has meant and required a deep and continuing American engagement in the affairs of Europe.[54] A weakening of this involvement, coupled with the erosion of deterrence and reassurance, would lead to the unraveling of the historic American geostrategy that checked the Soviet Union at the same time as it enveloped the Federal Republic in Western integrative structures. This would in effect press future German governments to seek alternative anchor points for the Federal Republic's central security interests, a risky and distasteful prospect for their neighbors and themselves, and a total reversal of the intentions that informed America's postwar policy of containment.[55] In pushing for SDI so insistently and making it the centerpiece of its arms control and security policies, the Reagan administration accelerated (perhaps unintentionally and most likely unnecessarily) a rethinking in Western Europe about the viability of the transatlantic security connection that also implied a rethinking about the future applicability of America's postwar policy of political containment.

In the Reagan administration, political and strategic intentions seemed pointed in opposite directions. On the one hand, planning for a strategic defense shield laid the groundwork for a decidedly unilateralist potential for American diplomacy, which was viewed with concern abroad. On the other hand, the Reagan administration gave no indication that it wanted to embrace the qualifications of the principle of containment that its military strategy program entailed, let alone refute the principle. Having rejected détente throughout most of its time in office, the Reagan administration also rejected the opportunity to restore a measure of complementarity to the historic twin principles of America's European policies, containment and deterrence. Political imperatives suggesting continuing engagement in Europe and elsewhere seemed to be colliding with military-strategic imperatives, suggesting a measure of disengagement. How were political proximity and strategic distance to be reconciled?

Were an American inclination toward unilateralism to meet with a growing European inclination toward independence or neutralism (in other words, European unilateralism) the alliance would be eaten away from both directions, for the Europeans and especially the Germans were in the grip of a similar set of contradictory calculations and sentiments. Committed to European détente and seeing it endangered by a confrontational American diplomacy toward the Soviet Union, they argued for the divisibility of détente. Dependent on the security commitment of their transatlantic partner, they argued simultaneously for the indivisibility of deterrence. The trends toward American unilateralism and the trend toward European neutralism were fed by the same sources.[56]

I I

The Partition of Germany and Europe

Every mistake is in a sense the product of all the mistakes that have gone before it, from which fact it derives a sort of cosmic forgiveness; and at the same time every mistake is in a sense the determinant of all the mistakes of the future, from which it derives a sort of cosmic unforgiveableness.

—GEORGE F. KENNAN

For centuries, amid the conflagrations that shaped their common and separate destinies, the powers of Continental Europe could agree on one thing only: the need to prevent the unification of Europe under one of their own, to which they would have to relinquish their individual sovereignty. Spain, France, Germany—all were defeated by grand coalitions formed against them on the Continent, coalitions that were invariably successful because they always obtained invincible support from the maritime powers to the west or from the Great Eurasian power to the east. The European balance of power, when threatened from within by hegemony that the Europeans themselves could not contain, was redressed from the outside and brought back into equilibrium. As Ludwig Dehio wrote: "Just as the crystals in a geode face inward towards each other, so the members of our family of states turned their energies inward and against each other, never outward in mutual solidarity, for it was the powers outside, nurtured by European discord, who guaranteed the European system. . . . For the rise of England, and of America behind her, to world power, and the corresponding rise of Russia on the other side, were the price that our continent had to pay for preserving the freedom of individual sovereign states and of its whole system of the balance of power."[1]

On their part, the great powers "on the wings of Europe," conscious to what extent their own interests and security required a functioning European balance, were prepared to preserve it and to intervene when the Continental European powers could not maintain it against one of their own. The United States, as it replaced a weakening Britain in the role of balancer in the twentieth century, came to recognize this geopolitical imperative reluctantly and acted on it only intermittently, as when it entered the First World War and then withdrew again to its domestic preoccupations. In the nineteenth century Britain had protected American interests at the same time as its own, while America saw its manifest destiny in westward expansion and splendid isolation, feeling exempt from the tainted maxims of power politics that it identified with the jaded and amoral proclivities of an outmoded European cabinet diplomacy. And yet as it entered the twentieth century, American diplomacy was compelled to respond to the inescapable challenges of the balance of power, in Europe as well as in the Far East, even as it denied their validity and called for the permanent abolition of power politics, couching the purposes of American foreign policy in the language of international law and morality.

The geopolitical interests of the United States were thus in conflict with those of Germany. After its unification in 1871, Germany had become the predominant European power, with aspirations that soon reached beyond the confines of the Continent, and with energies that could not be restrained by Continental coalitions alone, even when augmented by the maritime power of Britain. Having restored the European balance by decisively intervening in the First World War, America withdrew into isolationism, abandoning the task of helping to pacify Europe and leaving a resentful and only temporarily weakened Germany to become again the dominant European power. After the Second World War, which had exhausted the victorious as well as the vanquished European powers, the United States was again confronted with an unbalanced European system of states: this time unhinged by the Soviet Union, which had an army in the middle of Europe and historical interests requiring a European political order that would once and for all stifle security threats to Russia.

What had been the historic balancing powers on the wings of Europe met in 1945 at the center stage of the Continent, and were soon locked in the protracted and inconclusive conflict that has shaped the international order of the second half of this century. Perceiving an expansionist Soviet empire in Europe and elsewhere, the United States responded with a global strategy of containment that embodied the commitment to maintain for the foreseeable future a countervailing American sphere of influence in Europe and Asia. Although this commitment became quickly justified in ideological terms, its central rationale was in fact geostrategic, and as the policy of containment applied to the Continent it reflected the perennial American interest in a European political equilibrium.[2]

But amid the virulent discords that became known as the Cold War, the two opposing superpowers retained a common interest in preventing the reestablishment of a new hegemonic European power. Even as they competed with one another in the postwar decade for a preeminent position in Europe, which inevitably meant competing over who would decide the future of Germany, both superpowers were determined that no third power should regain a hegemonic position on the Continent.

By the mid-1950s it had become apparent to both superpowers that they could deny one another supremacy and that they would have to share a duopolistic European order and respect one another's sphere of influence. Even before the end of the Second World War, it had become quite clear to the United States and its most trusted ally, Britain, that they would have to divide control over Europe and Germany with the Soviet Union, in effect dividing with Stalin their countries' victory over Hitler. Although some rethinking took place in Washington between the last days of the Second World War and the onset of the Cold War over the future status of Germany, the Russian dominion over most of Eastern Europe and parts of Central Europe quickly became a historical fait accompli, sustained by Soviet military might and political control.[3]

America's and Russia's common interest in a stable European order was soon enlarged by the inescapable recognition that the survival of each was linked by the developing nuclear stalemate. Along with a new international economic system, created and dominated by the United States, the European political balance and the global nuclear balance became the central structures of the postwar international order. From the ruins of the old European system of states the transatlantic and Eurasian balancers created a dualistic European order that they themselves dominated, dividing Europe with their adjoining spheres of influence. Superior in their military technology and determined to strengthen their security, the new superpowers created massive nuclear arsenals that imposed their own restraints, augmenting those that stemmed from the European political equilibrium.

As the political center of gravity shifted away from Europe toward the Euramerican and Eurasian superpowers, Europe itself, weak but potentially strong, became a future balancer in the East-West contest, which signified a fundamental reversal of the traditional geopolitical roles. The collapse of the old European system of states and its replacement by a global superpower duopoly moved the role of the balancer away from the edges of Europe to the Continent itself. As for defeated Germany, seemingly weakened beyond restoration, its former enemies were less fearful that it could again disturb the global order directly, than that it might in the future unbalance the regional European order by throwing its weight either with the West or with the East, and hence affect the global balance of power indirectly. At least potentially, Germany replaced Britain in its traditional role as the arbiter of the European equilibrium, a role which neither superpower was ready to concede to the Germans.[4]

It was a role that France was also determined to deny the Germans. If anything France laid claim to the role itself, especially during the years

when General de Gaulle charted an independent course for French foreign policy. The West Germans in any case vigorously denied any such
ambitions, embraced with apparent conviction the strictures placed on
their diplomacy through international conventions, and constantly reaffirmed their unswerving loyalty to the West. Even so, Franco-German
relations in the postwar era were characterized by a persistent and energetic rivalry that underlay many of the issues contested between Bonn
and Paris, even though it was sublimated in the integrative economic and
political arrangements of Western Europe and masked by periodic declarations of mutual amity. Fundamentally, France had never become reconciled to the increase of German power that resulted from the unification
of Germany in 1871. When the perennial German threat to French interests and security became compounded during the Cold War by the Soviet
threat, French diplomacy aimed to contain both a renascent West Germany and an immensely powerful Soviet Union—a French version of
double containment for which French resources proved insufficient.
Moreover, although French and American policies were aimed at the
same targets, they required a different diplomatic thrust. As the Federal
Republic became the indispensable partner of America's own policy of
double containment, German diplomatic leverage vis-à-vis France grew;
and the major instrument with which American statecraft checked the
Soviet Union and Germany—integrative military, economic, and political institutions—restrained France as well, depriving it of diplomatic
maneuverability. Caught between America's dominance of the Western
alliance and the double threat posed by the Soviet Union and Germany,
the French effort at double containment led to contradictory and largely
irreconcilable policies that fractured postwar French diplomacy. America's European policies contained not only Russia and Germany but also
France.[5]

For these reasons and of course others, the division of Germany and
of Europe has remained the most palpable legacy of the Second World
War. For the Germans it meant the bifurcation of their postwar political
and socioeconomic development, raising the insistent question of what
would ultimately prove more enduring: their longer common history
since 1871, or their shorter, separate one since 1945.[6] For Europe it has
provided stability and peace, even as it led to frustrations and tensions.
For the superpowers, who sustained it with increasingly conservative
European policies, it advanced fundamental geostrategic purposes and
provided a relatively clear-cut and tolerable boundary between their
empires in Europe, permitting them to project their rivalries onto other
areas of the world. The Iron Curtain, which divided Europe as well as
Germany, became the line of demarcation between the Cold War blocs
and the forward line of defense for Washington's policy of containment—
a policy that envisaged only a long-range resolution of the division of

Europe, whereas its implementation sharpened it in the short run and middle run.[7]

In light of these considerations it is not surprising that from the beginning of the Cold War a major source of conflict was the shape of the European political and economic order and the place that should be assigned to Germany within it. The division of Germany had its origin in the disagreements among the four occupying powers that controlled Germany in the postwar years, and the partition was institutionalized in 1949 with the establishment of the Federal Republic of Germany and the German Democratic Republic. Both German states owe their existence to the tensions that divided the Soviet Union and the Western powers. Finding it impossible to rule Germany together and determined to deny each other control over all of it, the Cold War antagonists established German client states in their zones of occupation and later incorporated them in their respective alliances and spheres of influence. As a result of the Cold War the historic "German question," which had agitated Europe since the nineteenth century, became a bipolar, global contest between the powers on the wings of Europe even as it retained its traditional Continental dimension, that of containing a too powerful Germany. It was ultimately the interplay between its global and European dimensions—at times complementary, at other times contradictory—that lent to the German question its special dynamics and compounded significance.

One should not ascribe inevitable outcomes to historical events (practice retrospective prophecy, as it were) simply because their consequences appear so logical that one cannot conceive of plausible alternatives. But the postwar division of Europe and Germany, on the basis of which the superpowers sought to deny one another the control of all of Europe, reflects a compelling geostrategic logic if not an inescapable historical necessity. Again the powers at the wings of Europe settled the Continent's balance of power, this time through partition and durable spheres of influence. For the first time in modern history the Germans in the West became aligned with the great insular power across the Atlantic, while the Germans in the East became attached to the great Eurasian power in the East.

There emerged a striking similarity in the positions that West Germany and East Germany began to occupy in their respective alliances: each is the most important and loyal member of its alliance, and each superpower is determined to maintain and delineate its sphere of influence in retaining the allegiance of its German ally.[8] Over the decades, the status of the two German states in their respective alliances and the nature of their relations with one another have remained the central concern of the European policy of the United States and the Soviet Union, as well as of their allies. Any significant change in this status and in the relationship between the two Germanies signals to all parties concerned a significant change in the European and global balance of power. At the border between the German states, the American and Soviet empires meet in their starkest form, and any development that portends an alteration of the status quo or an excessive degree of cooperation between the two German states is viewed with caution if not with suspicion.

All this has led to a deeply paradoxical development in postwar Europe. Europeans are aware that the sources of the Cold War are deeply embedded in contending political, geopolitical, and ideological systems, and that the division of Europe can be overcome only gradually, if at all. But deeply rooted as well are the historical memories and contemporary impulses that seek to overcome the divisive consequences of the Cold War, which are sharpened by the recognition that the fall of Nazi Germany liberated Western Europe but delivered Eastern Europe to Soviet subjugation. Many Europeans on both sides of the divide consider the partition of their Continent unnatural, a constant source of tension, and potentially explosive. Although East Europeans and East Germans are not uncritical of the political and economic systems of the West, they are nonetheless restive after half a century of confinement to their geographical and political space.[9] In Western Europe too there is growing resentment of the political perversity that has divided the Continent and severed historical bonds which, although they were not always amicable, nonetheless attest to a common cultural provenance.[10]

But although many Europeans chafe under the partition of their continent, they regard the division of Germany as a much less urgent matter. They view with apprehension the prospect of a reunited Germany, which might once again become the predominant Continental power, and they appreciate the sentiment expressed by François Mauriac—that he loved Germany so much he was glad there were two of them—and reportedly shared by East Germany's leader, Erich Honecker.[11]

As a consequence, the attitudes of West Europeans and East Europeans toward the shape of a desirable European order have for decades been ambivalent or contradictory. On the one hand, there is widespread recognition that the division of Europe can be bridged only if the division of Germany is at least attenuated, and that the reuniting of Europe requires some measure of accommodation between the Federal Republic and the German Democratic Republic, perhaps falling short of reunification but culminating in some form of stable and perhaps internationally guaranteed confederation.

But there is also concern that a more fundamental reconciliation between the two Germanies could form a critical mass of energies and aspirations that would overwhelm the Continent and again unbalance the existing European equilibrium. The fear remains that the Germans, if reunited, would again embark on their historic *Sonderweg*—their "special path" through modern European history, which skirted the major routes of Europe's political, intellectual, and ideological developments and led the Germans after 1933 to inflict such tragic consequences on others and on themselves. Europe retains the painful, historical memories of how the Germans, burdened by their belated political unification, retarded *embourgeoisement*, and rapidly accelerating nationalism, were from the nineteenth century poised at the center of Europe, increasingly powerful and yet incapable of making a full and secure political, intellectual, and ultimately moral commitment to the norms of Western civilization.[12]

The West Germans have also come to recognize that the partition of their country can be ameliorated only in the context of a wider settlement of the European political order, and that the meaning of "national unity," which their Basic Law commits them to advance, lies less in territorial reunification and the restoration of a unified *Nationalstaat* than in intra-German amity, the peaceful coexistence of the two German states, and the preservation of a sense of nationhood.[13] The West Germans realized from the beginning that historical experience and contemporary calculations of national interests fed deep reservations on the part of their allies as well as of their opponents, which stood in the way of obtaining their backing for the cause of German unity. Although the West European partners and the transatlantic ally of the Federal Republic are politically and in some cases legally committed to extend this backing, successive governments in Bonn have arrived at the painful recognition that this commitment is limited to verbal proclamations and diplomatic maneuvers.

Even the nature of the verbal support changed over the decades, along with changes in East-West relations and in the way the Germans themselves defined the nature of the German question. In the 1950s Bonn in effect called for reunification on the basis of absorbing East Germany and refused to accept the postwar border arrangements in the East. This policy obtained for Bonn the largest measure of verbal support from its allies (and especially from the United States), perhaps because it was so patently unrealistic that one would not have to worry about the possibility that it might succeed.

In the 1960s the Germans had given up real hope for reunification and phrased their Eastern policies primarily in legal terms, using juridical formulas as a rearguard action to obstruct or retard East-West accommodation, arms control, and the legitimization of the status quo. Burdened by the accumulated weight of entrenched diplomatic positions and slowed on the domestic political scene by the holding action of the Right, Bonn's Eastern policy lost the support of Bonn's allies and led to renewed charges from the East that the political leadership in West Germany was incorrigibly revanchist. Bonn dissipated its diplomatic energies with sterile legalisms and halfhearted overtures to the East, determined to keep the German Democratic Republic ostracized and deny it the international legitimization it sought so insistently.

In the 1970s Bonn's Ostpolitik revitalized German diplomacy and became the centerpiece of détente, although it was viewed at least in its early stages with a good deal of suspicion in Western capitals. Building on tentative revisions that had begun in the 1960s, Ostpolitik entailed a reformulation of the German question, placing it fully in a European context and transforming it from an issue of legal rights and the enlargement of territory into an issue of human rights and the enlargement of intra-German contacts. With the collapse of détente in the late 1970s and the general deterioration of Soviet-American relations during Reagan's presidency, both German states undertook efforts to shield their mutually profitable mini-détente from the larger context of Soviet-American disagreements that beclouded relations between East and West in the 1980s.

5

Reunification and the European Political Order: The Alliance Consensus of the 1950s

Wir tragen alle die nationale Einheit im Herzen, aber für den rechnenden Politiker kommt zuerst das Notwendige und dann das Wünschenswerte, also zuerst der Ausbau des Hauses und dann dessen Erweiterung.
—OTTO VON BISMARCK, 1868

After the Third Reich has abused and thrown away our unity by denying freedom, unity must be subordinated to the superior and wider aim of freedom, for today a demand for unity surely has an anachronistic flavor about it. No political watchword can be translated into a new situation without carrying with it traces of the soil in which it grew previously.
—LUDWIG DEHIO, 1953

Of all German foreign policy goals, the aim of reunifying Germany has proven the most intractable and elusive. Even its later and less ambitious formulation—achieving an intensified relationship and an engaged coexistence with East Germany—has met with resistance and setbacks, yielding only inconclusive and tenuous results.

At the end of the Second World War and the beginning of the Cold War (in retrospect the conflagrations of the former seem to have merged almost imperceptibly into the confrontations of the latter) the gradual division of Germany and of Europe took on an almost inevitable quality. When the two German states were established in 1949 the obstacles to reuniting them were already formidable. The Germans' commitment to work for German unity, which is enshrined in the Federal Republic's Basic Law, must have appeared to them as not much more than a declara-

141

tion of hope that they could reverse the political developments of the early 1950s, which deepened the division of their country with each new step in East-West diplomacy. These developments were indeed momentous. They shaped the European state system for the remainder of this century and solidified the partition of Germany until it became for all practical purposes irrevocable when both German states were fully integrated in their respective alliances in 1955.

Throughout the 1950s the Western powers and Bonn were reasonably certain that a united and democratic Germany would side with the West. They insisted that East Germany hold free elections before an all-German government were formed, and that such a government later enjoy freedom of action, including the possibility of membership in the Western alliance. The West basically held up to the Soviet Union the prospect that not only West Germany but a unified Germany would become absorbed in the Western alliance, and this at a time when the East German uprising of 1953 demonstrated to the Soviet Union that its hold on East Germany depended on the presence of Soviet tanks and that it could expect no gains from elections.[1] The Western powers in effect suggested that a united Germany should in the future have more diplomatic flexibility than they were willing to grant the Federal Republic at present, a fatuous diplomatic stance that merely masked the demand that a united Germany would have to be part of the Western alliance. The West was asking the Soviet Union to stake its control over East Germany and Eastern Europe, its geostrategic position on the Continent, and the Soviet fruits of victory in the Second World War on the outcome of elections which were a foregone conclusion for the West and most likely for the Soviet Union as well.[2]

Soviet proposals for unification were equally unrealistic. The Soviet Union continually advocated neutralizing a united Germany and forming an all-German government in which East and West Germany would be represented equally. Accepting such proposals would have prevented the rearmament of West Germany and precluded the restoration of the Federal Republic's legal sovereignty, and it would have jeopardized the viability of the West's military and economic alliances by excluding Germany from them. In short, Moscow's proposals threatened the foundations of Washington's double-containment policy and Bonn's own sense of self-containment, which propelled it toward permanent attachment to the West. The Western powers and especially the United States, with the concurrence of the Federal Republic, had made the political, economic and military integration of West Germany the centerpiece of their European policies (which were in the early fifties not yet fully implemented), and any Soviet moves that would have stood in their way were sharply rejected by the West. The Soviet Union expected the West to accept a power vacuum in the heart of Europe, which would have provided many opportunities for Soviet manipulations and interference, at a time when the West was laying the groundwork for a transatlantic security compact and West European integration, and when drawing a clear line between East and West in Europe seemed to hold the most promise for Western efforts at containment.

Not surprisingly, no satisfactory formula could be found that would accommodate the conflicting interests of the parties involved. The positions and arguments advanced by both sides were fundamentally irreconcilable, and lent an increasingly unreal and propagandistic quality to verbal exchanges between East and West on the German question. Power calculations allowed neither side to go beyond repeating its own interpretation of what constituted an equitable solution to the German problem. Neither the United States nor the Soviet Union could support the creation of a unified Germany that would be genuinely free to conduct its external affairs and thus act as a potential balancer in the East-West conflict. The first choice of each side—to draw a united Germany into its own orbit under effective supervision—could be successfully vetoed by the other side, given the realities of the global and regional balances of power. On the other hand, for each side to secure the allegiance and power potential of the part of Germany it already controlled promised to increase substantially its strength in the East-West confrontation. The stakes were high and involved not only the two Germanies but the cohesion of the two alliances and the viability of their military and economic planning.[3] The very importance of the issue thus precluded solving the German question by striking a "global deal" between East and West at another front of the Cold War struggle (such as by rearranging the Asian balance of power with the help of Communist China), even though this possibility was frequently alluded to in German political circles.[4]

During the 1950s (and especially after West Germany was integrated in NATO and East Germany in the Warsaw Pact), both superpowers grew into their role as guarantors of Europe's stability, accepted their respective spheres of influence, and appeared increasingly prepared to stabilize them with policies that posed no fundamental threat to the incipient status quo and the equilibrium of the postwar European state system.

This arrangement represented a fundamental geostrategic compromise between the United States and the Soviet Union, obtaining important gains for both. The Soviet Union solidified its power position in Europe, which was no longer threatened after 1955, and subsequently began a twenty-year diplomatic campaign to legitimize it. The United States succeeded in its efforts at double containment, keeping the Soviet Union within the boundaries of influence that the Soviet army had secured in Central Europe at the end of the Second World War, and tying a cooperative Bonn government to integrative transatlantic and West European institutions. American policies toward the Soviet Union and Germany were complementary, effectively checking the Soviet empire at its European periphery, and gaining in the process the concurrence of the West German government and most West Germans, who endorsed these policies in the elections of 1953 and 1957.[5]

Turning toward the West, Facing toward the East:
The Contradictions of Bonn's Germany Policy

In light of these forbidding diplomatic circumstances, no one then or now could deny or underestimate the weight of necessity, the burden of acquiescence that was placed on the German government in these early years when the Federal Republic had neither the power nor the authority to conduct its own foreign policy. This is especially so with respect to Germany's reunification, which even the Western powers could not have resolved for the Germans, assuming they had wanted to.

But it was not only the East-West fissures produced by the Cold War and the conflicting interests of the superpowers that deepened the partition of Germany. Bonn's own sense of priorities (the product of both necessity and choice) and the nature of the goal itself obstructed Germany's reunification. From the beginning of the Federal Republic, the goal of national unity and the goal of joining the Western alliance as an equal led to a series of contradictions and paradoxes, subtle in their origins but far-reaching in their consequences.

The question of German unity was from the outset surrounded with juridical and political considerations that led Bonn in later years to resort to increasingly convoluted legal and procedural arguments in advancing its Eastern policies. The German architects of the Basic Law, conscious of their historical roles and protective of their historical reputations,[6] did not want to be held responsible for assenting however indirectly to the partition of their country. Toward that end, they claimed for the new state only a provisional and incomplete status and chose to regard it as a transitory stage on the way to German reunification—a view and commitment reflected in the Basic Law itself.[7] This meant that the new state was obliged to question its own permanence so as not to obstruct juridically or politically the path toward its own completion, the reunification of the divided nation. Even the term *Basic Law* was chosen to indicate that a final German constitution could not be drafted until all Germans were free to approve it.

At the same time, however, Bonn pressed for the restoration of sovereignty, which once achieved unavoidably sharpened the division of Germany. This was especially so because sovereignty was purchased by means of the tight integration of West Germany in the Western military, political, and economic alliances, all of which necessarily deepened the division of Germany and Europe, aggravated East-West rivalries, and burdened the relationship between the Federal Republic and the German

Democratic Republic. The realization that their own diplomatic efforts in the West contributed to the partition of their country could not help but create misgivings among Germans toward a Western policy that they favored on intrinsic grounds.

There was a further paradox: in an important sense, Bonn did not even consider the Federal Republic a new state. Although the Adenauer government wished to demonstrate the moral distance that separated the new political order from the horrors of the Nazi regime, it felt compelled to assert a legal continuity with Hitler's Reich so as to buttress the claim that it was the legitimate spokesman for all Germans, in the East as well as the West, and that the Federal Republic could legitimately seek to restore the German borders of 1937.[8] In other words, the juridical status that the Germans crafted for the Federal Republic was continuous with respect to the past, provisional with respect to the future.

The status of successor that the Federal Republic claimed for itself had at least one positive consequence: the West German government, in contrast to its counterpart in the East, accepted the moral and financial responsibilities of paying restitution to victims of the Nazi regime and thus contributed to the moral rehabilitation of the German people.[9] But Bonn's claim that it spoke for all Germans, and its associated claim for the reunification of Germany within the borders of 1937, stamped the government at least from the perspective of the East (and especially Poland) as a revisionist force that sought to change the territorial and political status quo in Central and Eastern Europe.

When successive German governments applied their increasingly tortured legal arguments to the German question, especially in the 1960s, they burdened the entire range of German diplomacy. The legal language in which Bonn couched its Eastern policies became a source of irritation and impatience in the West and a source of apprehension and hostility in the East. A fine line divided Bonn's insistence on democratic principles and national self-determination from obdurate legalism, its demand for justice from self-righteousness, and its determination to protect German interests from insensitive obstinacy. Making legal claims on the other Germany and expressing juridical reservations about the existing border arrangements was not well suited to German diplomacy in a part of Europe that had suffered so much from the lawlessness of the Germans a few years earlier. Bonn's insistence on the provisional nature of postwar border arrangements, correct as it may have been in terms of international law and the contractual arrangements among the victors of the Second World War, was a severe political handicap. The Germans were not always mindful of the psychological fact that the oppressed have a longer memory than the oppressor.

There was also an uneasy relationship between West Germans and East Germans. Many West Germans felt that their compatriots in the East had merely exchanged one dictatorship with another and that a sharp distinction should therefore be drawn between the East German people, who deserved compassion and liberation, and their government, which deserved condemnation and opposition. But referring to the German Democratic Republic as "the zone" or "so-called GDR," or putting "GDR" in condemning quotation marks (which remained the editorial policy of the Springer press for decades), expressed a disdain toward the East German regime that could not always be limited to the government alone and that spilled over into a somewhat patronizing attitude toward the people. Also, applying the term *Mitteldeutschland* to East Germany implied future border revisions and evoked in Eastern Europe an understandable sense of apprehension, fueling the suspicion that influential political circles in the Federal Republic were determined to reverse the postwar European territorial status quo and reclaim German territory that had become part of Poland.[10]

The Cold War itself imposed psychological contradictions on the West Germans. On the one hand, it brought about and sealed the partition of their country; on the other, it accelerated their economic reconstruction and political rehabilitation. In subtle ways, it even seemed to advance their moral rehabilitation. As the Communist East succeeded Nazi Germany as the primary threat to Western values and interests, the ideological dimensions of the Cold War became for many Germans an unacknowledged but psychologically satisfying moral diversion. Anti-Bolshevism served to displace or relativize German guilt, allowed the Germans to focus on the present evils of the Soviets rather than the past evils of the Nazis, and provided an "integration ideology" for the new political system.[11] The Germans saw themselves as partners in a common Western effort to contain the Soviet threat (this view was not discouraged in the West, especially not in the United States), and they grasped the opportunity to demonstrate their adherence to the West and thus share in the political and moral respectability that this association extended to them. Many Germans squarely faced their individual and collective guilt, but there were also many who saw in the political crimes and repressions of the East a belated justification of their own acquiescence in the Nazi regime and of their unremitting hostility to communism.

Throughout Adenauer's tenure as chancellor, the brittle quality of Bonn's Eastern policy was also the consequence of diplomatic distance and the chancellor's political temperament. Although the chancellor was constantly involved with the Western leaders during the intricate and protracted negotiations that made Germany a member of the Western alliance, he had little contact with Eastern leaders. The German government's political agenda in the West was intricate and congested; its diplomatic calendar in the East was plain and uncluttered. Even though the Soviet Union was a constant and towering presence in Adenauer's thinking, his personal temperament, life experiences, and innermost values and political reflexes did not permit him to pursue a more flexible Eastern policy. Adenauer's Eastern policies were characterized by a deep and unrelieved hostility toward communism and by his conviction that the Soviet Union was embarked on world conquest, which might in Europe take the form of armed aggression.[12]

The differences between Bonn's Western policies and its Eastern policies stemmed not only from the differing opportunities of implementing them and from differing degrees of diplomatic involvement, but from the fundamentally different character of Bonn's aspirations in the West and in the East. This had a profound effect on the Germans themselves. Bonn's Western policies, skillfully advanced by Konrad Adenauer, evoked among Germans a different emotional, psychological, and political response than those directed toward the East. Westpolitik brought them allies, a measure of rehabilitation and respectability, and a level of prosperity unprecedented in German history, permitting them also a sense of forgetful historical ease and the prospect of political and economic normalcy.

But the Germans' policies in the East, torn between the desire for reconciliation and the resentments caused by the division of Germany, the loss of people and territory, and the suffering of millions of Germans who had fled or been expelled from the East, brought them face to face with their troubled past and with the painful recognition that the partition and dismemberment of their country were the retributions exacted by history for the outrages committed by the Nazi regime. The Germans were constantly made aware that they were paying the costs of having lost the Second World War in the East, not in the West.[13] Often it seemed as if the Germans and their government sought in the West a lasting peace but in the East merely an armistice.

There was yet another serious disability inherent in Bonn's Eastern policy, which distinguished it from Bonn's Western policy. The success of Adenauer's Westpolitik in the 1950s was in large measure attributable to Bonn's readiness to abjure territorial claims if necessary—the issue of the Saar is a case in point.[14] Bonn realized that its integrative Westpolitik was part of a larger political and economic trend in postwar Western Europe, in which territorial issues were diminishing in importance. Bonn's diplomatic concepts of integration and equality were thus eminently suited to the political and economic temper of the time, lending them a certain "modern" character. This contrasted positively with the more old-fashioned view of the European political order entertained in France, and it attuned Bonn's policies to those of the United States, obtaining significant diplomatic leverage for the Federal Republic.

Bonn's Ostpolitik, on the other hand, was at its core a policy that reflected territorial aspirations and was necessarily couched in territorial as well as legal and political terms.[15] Bonn refused to recognize or officially deal with the East German government, arguing that because it was not freely elected Bonn had the duty and the right of "sole representation" of all Germans, including those in East Germany. The two German states were, so to speak, founded against one another, and each sought to establish its own legitimacy by denying it to the other.[16] Bonn also refused to recognize the Oder-Neisse frontier as the permanent border between Poland and Germany. After the East German government and all the other members of the East bloc had recognized Poland's claim on the Oder-Neisse territories and East Prussia (1950), Bonn adamantly refused to regard the territorial status quo in that area as anything but provisional.[17] Aside from the legal merits of the question (which rested on the Potsdam Agreement's provision that no permanent revision of Germany's border could take place before a final all-German peace treaty), the Adenauer government intended to preserve its concession as a trump card to be played at a time when the larger question of Germany's unification would be on a comprehensive diplomatic agenda. But the legalistic rigidity of Bonn's position and the territorial connotations of its reunification policies precluded a more dynamic Eastern policy and enabled Moscow to strengthen its hold over its East European allies, especially Poland, by being the protector of the status quo.

By calling in effect for the incorporation of East Germany into West Germany and for border revisions in the East, Bonn denied the validity of existing political arrangements in Eastern and Central Europe and sought to reverse the territorial consequences for Germany of the Second World War. In addition to conflicting with fundamental political interests of the Soviet Union and its allies (and those of Bonn's allies as well), this policy lent a certain anachronistic flavor to Bonn's diplomacy. This stood in sharp contrast to the modernity of Bonn's Western diplomacy, which accepted and exploited the logic of political and economic interdependence and recognized the diminishing relevance of territorial considerations.[18] It is also true, however, that the Federal Republic could not itself escape the burdens of its special geographical position at the dividing line of Europe and its emplacement at the forefront of the Western alliance. Inevitably, the territorial dimensions of Germany's security policies (which led to rearmament and integration into the West) reinforced the territorial connotations of its policies in the East, making for a politically damaging combination that severely burdened Bonn's Eastern diplomacy.

The Federal Republic's location on the dividing line of Europe also compelled it to face two distinct European political and economic systems. Both Western and Eastern Europe were being rapidly integrated into the spheres of influence of the superpowers, but the Western sphere was energized by the dynamics of a modern global economic order, which was presided over by the United States as the hegemonic economic power and in which there was a considerable sharing of benefits. By contrast, East Germany and Eastern Europe were shackled to a superpower beset by economic problems and isolated from the dynamics of the global economy. The allies of the Soviet Union were mired in economic stagnation, and they shared with their Soviet partner problems rather than benefits.* Geographically, the two Germanies remained at the epicenter of European politics, but in the global contest between the superpowers they were relegated to the perimeter of two opposing empires.[19] Bonn's policies were aimed in both directions, seeking integration in the West along with German reunification in the East, and the government found it impossible to craft a diplomacy that could have straddled the imperial divide and served this dual purpose.

The contradictions between Bonn's Ostpolitik and Westpolitik left their imprint on all German foreign policy goals and burdened the entire range of German diplomacy. Behind every issue that Bonn negotiated in the West stood the obtrusive reality of Germany's division, constantly forcing the German government to appraise the results of its Western policies with a view toward their consequences in the East. Bonn's aspirations and policies became an uneasy mix of conflicting attitudes about international politics and the meaning of the "national" interest, embracing a territorial mode of thinking in one context and rejecting it in another, looking forward and backward in history at the same time, being both in and out of tune with fundamental political, economic, and psychological developments in the postwar European order.

*This economic asymmetry led the West Germans quite early to formulate economic policies that would help bridge the division of Germany and not impose a stringent economic partition on top of the existing political and military ones. Although intra-German trade was beneficial for both sides (though much more so for the East Germans), it was from the beginning guided more by political considerations than economic or monetary ones, especially on the part of Bonn. Given the special relationship between the German states, the trading relations were inevitably special as well. The conduct of inter-German trade required recourse to convoluted financial and rhetorical fictions, such as "accounting units" to overcome the nominal equivalence of the Western D-Mark and Eastern D-Mark, and labeling imports and exports "deliveries" and "purchases" so that Bonn could avoid the appearance of recognizing the East German government. Bonn obtained a special status for inter-German trade within GATT, arranged for special EEC dispensations for inter-German trade that in effect gave East Germany quasi-membership in the customs union of the Community, and facilitated trade over the years with "swing" credit arrangements that eased the GDR's monetary difficulties. See Robert Dean, *West German Trade with the East: The Political Dimension* (New York: Praeger, 1974); Reinhold Biskup, *Deutschlands offene Handelsgrenze. Die DDR als Nutzniesser des EWG-Protokolls über den innerdeutschen Handel* (Berlin: Ullstein, 1976); Heinrich End, *Zweimal deutsche Aussenpolitik. Internationale Dimensionen des innerdeutschen Konflikts, 1949–1972* (Cologne: Verlag Wissenschaft und Politik, 1973); Claus-Dieter Ehlermann et al., *Handelspartner DDR. Innerdeutsche Wirtschaftsbeziehungen* (Baden-Baden: Nomos, 1975).

In their separate and compounded significance, all these reasons lent a quality to Bonn's diplomacy in the East totally different from that in the West. Throughout the 1950s and into the 1960s, the same attitudes and calculations that endowed Bonn's diplomacy in the West with dynamism and a sense of the possible led, when directed toward the East, to paralysis and an almost eerie infatuation with the implausible. Both dimensions of Bonn's diplomacy were held together by the same logic, one being the consequence of the other. The Eastern aspect of Bonn's Germany policy, oriented toward Moscow and its allies, was passive and static because it was derivative, an appendage of Bonn's policy toward Washington. Devoid of a political imagination and diplomatic energy of its own, it consisted almost entirely of negative elements.

The dilemmas that afflicted Bonn's Eastern policies made it difficult for Adenauer's government to articulate and defend a Germany policy that could claim some semblance of plausibility, much less hold out the likelihood of success. The patent contradictions between striving for the unity of the Western alliance and for the unity of Germany forced upon German conservatives (who were indefatigable in professing their devotion to both) a more or less permanent political *Lebenslüge* with which they denied to others and most likely to themselves that these goals were irreconcilable. It required recourse to a shaky and ultimately unconvincing rationale (it turned into a mere rationalization) to sustain the government's argument that it was genuinely committed to the cause of German unity and that its policy of integration into the West not only allowed a future resolution of the German question but would actually lay the groundwork for it.

Bonn's rationale basically consisted of two connected premises, superficially convincing in their reliance on Realpolitik but resting on highly questionable assumptions: the need to secure the Western powers' support for German reunification and Bonn's intention to obtain it by increasing German leverage within the alliance; and Bonn's purported expectation that in the course of time the power of the West (and by implication the power of the Federal Republic within the West) would increase sufficiently to induce the Soviet Union to settle the German question on terms acceptable to Bonn.

Although both premises appeared compelling in their political logic, their underlying assumptions proved unrealistic. Western support was secured on paper only, and even then with restrictions that made it for all practical purposes useless. And the assumption that the balance of power would shift in favor of the West, so implausible that it is questionable whether Adenauer himself believed it, was quickly repudiated by military-strategic developments and the solidification of the European status quo, which followed from the inclusion of the two German states in their respective alliances.

Securing Western Support for German Reunification:
Abjuring German Neutrality

In turning to the West for support on the German question, the Germans were not swayed by any illusions. Bonn realized that powerful historical memories and political considerations stood in the way of obtaining the support, and that the Western powers would view the prospect of a unified Germany with apprehension, especially if such a Germany were not securely attached to the West. It was therefore not unrealistic for Bonn to argue that the first and irreducible requirement of its reunification strategy was to increase the influence of the Federal Republic and ensure that the West would not treat the German question as a secondary issue that could conceivably be traded off in an overall settlement of the Cold War—for Adenauer a *cauchemar de détente* as recurring as had been Bismarck's *cauchemar des coalitions*.[20] Germany's political weakness and dependent juridical status demanded increasing political leverage and the restoration of sovereignty. The Federal Republic needed to become indispensable to the West.

But this unexceptionable premise of Bonn's reunification policy led to fundamental contradictions. In the first place, it was clear to Bonn from the beginning that in contrast to other West German foreign policy goals, such as security, or political and economic recovery within the framework of the Western alliance, the unification of Germany required at least the acquiescence of both Cold War blocs, if not their direct sponsorship, and that the key to the German question lay in that respect in Moscow.[21] But it was also incontrovertible that Bonn's staunch pro-Western policies, which sustained Washington's strategy of containment, could not possibly have made unification acceptable to Moscow. The more Bonn's diplomacy succeeded in the West, the less likely it became that it could succeed in the East. Bonn's readiness to rearm and join the Western alliance enhanced Germany's position in the West, but it also sharpened the division of Europe and Germany and exacerbated the conditions that made unification difficult in the first place. The calculations that purportedly informed Bonn's reunification policy appeared unconvincing because they rested on a circular and self-defeating argument: the more Bonn succeeded in increasing its leverage in the Western alliance (which tended to be when East-West tensions ran highest), the less could Moscow be expected to risk allowing East Germany to slip away from the Soviet sphere of influence.

Moreover, enhancing German leverage in the Western alliance required that Bonn abstain from a dynamic Eastern policy and not engage Moscow, the indispensable partner of such a policy, in a constructive diplomatic dialogue. The Western powers would have viewed German overtures to the Soviet Union with misgivings and suspicions and could have checked them not only on political but on legal grounds. In the early

1950s the Federal Republic was not yet a sovereign state (indeed, with respect to German unity, the residual rights of the Four Powers precluded it from ever fully becoming one), and the Western Allies held ultimate veto power over Bonn's foreign policy.[22] If Bonn had approached Moscow on the German question, it would have jeopardized the entire treaty structure that was to restore sovereignty to the Federal Republic. This would have undermined the power base from which Adenauer expected at some future date to deal with the Soviet Union (and with the Western Allies), not to speak of the consequences for Bonn's plans to integrate West Germany in the Western alliance and the political risks that Bonn would have incurred had the Western powers suspected the German government of seeking an accommodation with the Soviet Union.

An equally debilitating factor in Bonn's unification policy that fundamentally called into question Bonn's basic premise of gaining Western support was the ambivalent and politically vacuous nature of that support, which set preconditions for uniting Germany that no one could have expected the Soviet Union to meet. Although the Western powers pledged to support German unification in the Paris Agreements of 1954 (the Germans refer to them as the "Germany Treaty"), this commitment was made reluctantly, and hedged in ways that effectively meant that the Western powers would abide by it only after it had become impossible to implement.

In the first place, the Western powers defined "reunification" more narrowly than did Bonn: for them reunification meant the bringing together of the Federal Republic, the GDR, and Berlin, and not the restoration of Germany within the borders of 1937. Even more important, the wording of the Western commitment left no doubt that a reunified Germany would have to be part of the West.[23] In other words, a central condition for obtaining the West's support for reunification was that a reunited Germany be within the Western sphere of influence—that it would in effect be an enlarged Federal Republic, bound by the same contractual obligations that tied the Federal Republic to the Atlantic alliance and West European institutions.

No one could have expected the Soviet Union to assent to such a stipulation. As it was, the Western plans for rearming West Germany, and the concurrent diplomatic projects of restoring sovereignty to the Federal Republic and making it part of the Western alliance, caused great anxiety in Moscow, and the Soviet Union and its allies in the East bloc undertook a series of diplomatic moves to forestall them. After the outbreak of the Korean War and the resulting plans for rearming the Federal Republic, the East bloc's foreign ministers met in Prague in fall 1950 and spelled out a number of preconditions for negotiating with the West on German reunification: no rearmament of West Germany, no reconstruction of West Germany's military-industrial potential, the conclusion of a peace treaty and withdrawal of occupation forces, and an all-German government established on the basis of equal representation for East and West Germany.[24]

After NATO's conference in Lisbon in February 1952 and a few months before the signing of the treaty for the European Defense Community (EDC), the Soviet Union launched a major campaign in March 1952 to disrupt the Western alliance and keep the Federal Republic from joining it by stirring up popular opposition to German rearmament in Germany, France, and Britain. In the famous note of March 10, the Soviet Union called for neutralizing Germany and withdrawing the occupation forces, including those of the Soviet Union, and dropped its previous demand that American bases be scrapped as a Western concession. Crucial paragraphs provided that "the existence of organizations inimical to democracy and to the maintenance of peace must not be permitted on the territory of Germany," and that Germany be obliged "not to enter into any kind of coalition or military alliance directed against any power which took part, with its armed forces, in the war against Germany."[25] In a subsequent note, the Soviet Union threatened that there would be "new difficulties" for reunification if West Germany joined the EDC.

On March 25 the Western powers replied to the Soviet Union that the all-German government the Soviets had suggested as the basis for negotiating a peace treaty would have to be established through free elections in East and West Germany. The Western note, which closely reflected Adenauer's own thinking, rejected detailed discussions on a peace treaty until conditions had been created for free elections, and until a freely elected all-German government had been established. It also questioned the Soviet note's reference to the German frontiers determined by the Potsdam Agreement and stressed that no definitive German frontiers were as yet established. As for the limitations on a German government's freedom to join alliances, the West argued that "the all-German government should be free both before and after the conclusion of a peace treaty to enter into associations compatible with the principles and purposes of the United Nations."[26]

To the Western powers and Bonn, Moscow's plan appeared to be at best a strategem to disrupt the Western alliance, at worst a design to extend Soviet control over all of Germany. The Soviet proposals were fraught with risks and uncertainties and could have caused an important shift in the power balance of the Cold War. The treaty establishing the EDC and restoring West German sovereignty was about to be signed, and the NATO strategy and conventional force goals formulated at the Lisbon Conference one month earlier made a German contribution to the Western defense effort appear indispensable. Further, at this time Washington's policy of containment was expected to benefit most from a "forward strategy" and a clear-cut political and military line with which to confront the Eastern bloc unequivocally. The Western powers had to weigh the uncertain and risky prospect of a neutralized Germany against the certainty of a Western increment of power at a crucial stage in the Cold War. By 1952 the Western powers and the German chancellor were determined not to permit any interruption or delay in their plan to integrate the Federal Republic in the Western alliance. In fall 1952 George F. Kennan noted in his diary: "Our [decision makers] were basing their entire hopes on the ratification of the German contractuals and the European Defense Community, and they were unwilling to contemplate at any time within the foreseeable future, under any conceivable agreement with the Russians, the withdrawal of United States forces from Germany. . . . Our stand meant in effect no agreement with Russia at all and the indefinite continuance of the split of Germany and Europe."[27]

Between 1952 and the ratification of the Paris Agreements of 1954, East-West diplomacy continued to evolve around the issue of German neutrality.[28] After Stalin's death in 1953, there was another flurry of diplomatic activity on the German question between East and West, and speculation (especially in later years) that some of those contending to succeed Stalin might have been ready to make major concessions on the German question.[29] When the four foreign ministers met in Berlin in February 1954, Anthony Eden presented the first version of his "Eden Plan for German Reunification in Freedom," which called for free elections as the prerequisite for reunification, but also proposed a European collective security system designed to allay Soviet fears of a united, non-neutralized Germany. The Soviet Union again insisted that elections would have to be arranged through negotiations between East and West Germany and countered the Eden Plan by proposing the almost complete withdrawal of occupation troops from a neutralized Germany, the safety of which would be guaranteed by a European security pact. The Soviet Union was willing to concede that NATO need not be dissolved as a prerequisite for such an arrangement, although the United States was specifically excluded from the proposed European security treaty.[30]

The crucial difference between the two proposals was again whether a united Germany would be free to join the Western alliance. But by 1954 the rearming of Germany had become even more urgent to the West. There was no chance that the Western powers (or for that matter Bonn) would have reconsidered their plans for tying the Federal Republic to the Western alliance. The demise of the EDC and the decision to have Germany join NATO as an alternative had intensified Western efforts to obtain a German military contribution, and the decision to deploy tactical nuclear weapons in Europe made it appear urgent that German rearmament proceed on course: the role of the German Bundeswehr had increased in importance by becoming an essential element of the West's nuclear deterrence strategy in Europe. The changing East-West military balance, resulting primarily from the explosion of a thermonuclear device in the Soviet Union and the development of a long-range bomber, finally left "no hope whatever that Western forces could be withdrawn from West Germany, for then the only deterrent to a lightning occupation of the whole country by the still overwhelmingly superior Russian forces would be an American threat of all-out war, whose credibility, always somewhat ambiguous for moral and political reasons, was now beginning to be further undermined by Soviet technical advances."[31]

In January 1955, shortly after NATO decided to deploy tactical nuclear weapons in Europe and a few months before the Federal Republic formally joined NATO, the Soviet Union intimated that international supervision of free elections might be feasible after all if the two German governments could reach an agreement. In response, Chancellor Adenauer stressed that the Western allies' pledge to support reunification depended on German acceptance of the provisions of the Paris Agreements and characterized the new Soviet proposals as a tactical diversion, arguing that the Soviet Union could readily sabotage free elections because the way they would be conducted required agreement by both Germanies and the Four Powers. Further, the Soviet plan would mean neutralizing a unified Germany that would be deprived of effective Western protection, while allowing Soviet intervention in internal German affairs whenever the Soviets chose to interpret German policies as not proceeding along "peace-loving and democratic" lines.

Bonn argued that the Soviet Union was not offering unification in exchange for the scrapping of the Paris Agreements, but a series of preliminaries that could be withdrawn at any time. Adenauer explained that he was not actually following a "policy of strength," which would be ridiculous with only twelve German divisions, and reiterated that West European integration was the precondition for effective negotiations on reunification.[32] In a final attempt to dissuade Bonn from joining NATO, the Soviet Union repeated in February 1955 that the Paris Agreements would become the chief obstacle to a settlement of the German question and make German reunification "impossible for a long time to come." On the other hand, rejecting the Agreements would make it "possible to hold free, all-German elections this year with the aim of reestablishing Germany's unity on a peaceful and democratic basis."[33]

In the eyes of many of Adenauer's critics, now as well as then, rejecting the Soviet proposals signified a careless or even cynical failure to explore the last opportunities for unification.[34] But for Adenauer the central issue was that of German neutrality, which for him was totally unnegotiable. Adenauer constantly feared that Germany would break loose from the Western moorings to which he was attaching it (it amounted to a political obsession), and that under his successors German diplomacy could return to play a seesaw *Schaukelpolitik* between East and West.[35] Adenauer's distrust of the political maturity and circumspection of his fellow Germans was so deep that he wanted German diplomacy irrevocably embedded in the alliance.[36] The possibility of a neutralist and drifting Germany in the heart of Europe raised for Adenauer (and of course others) the specter of a repetition, or perpetuation, of Germany's historic *Sonderweg*—its singular and autonomous path through European history, which had brought such misfortunes to Germany's neighbors and to the Germans themselves. Adenauer was determined to obviate such future calamities. But he was also aware that in seeking to prevent Germany from embarking in the future upon a neutral and independent diplomatic course in Europe, he aimed for a reversal of truly historic proportions that might not take hold unless it were enforced by restraining Germany through international commitments and integrative institutions.[37]

Adenauer's fear of German neutralism was compounded by his fear that Germany might become diplomatically isolated, either by its own choice or by the default of others. Until the end of his life Adenauer entertained deep suspicions that the United States would ultimately prove an unreliable ally and disengage from Europe (perhaps meeting a neutralist Germany halfway),[38] and strike a deal with the Soviet Union that would leave Germany adrift in Europe.[39] This was a primary reason why he sought an irrevocable German attachment to France and sealed it with the Franco-German "reassurance" treaty of 1963: after all, France had no choice but to remain on the Continent and could be counted on to keep a watchful eye on Germany.[40]

It was essentially for the same reason—preventing German neutralism—that integration into the West was for Adenauer a lorica to ward off political evil: it was the political pendant to his abhorrence of neutrality, and the Western diplomatic corollary to his Eastern policies. Where others, and especially the SPD opposition in Bonn, perceived fundamental contradictions between his Western and his Eastern policies, the chancellor saw in his unqualified attachment to the West the logical complement to his refusal to consider neutrality in the East. Integration into the West meant a secure foundation for the future of German diplomacy, the irreducible base for a constructive role for Germany in the European state system. For Adenauer neutrality was an exorbitant price for unification; shelving unification was a fair price for West integration. This unshakable conviction of the correctness of his priorities and values circumscribed for Adenauer the meaning of Germany's "self-containment"—a restraint imposed by choice as well as necessity—and explains the intellectual clarity and singlemindedness of his foreign policy. For Adenauer, what was possible was at the same time desirable.[41] "One of Adenauer's basic convictions was that Germany needed to be securely anchored in Western Europe. To protect the Germans from themselves, he considered it necessary that Germany be irrevocably integrated in a European community so as to remove the objective possibility that it might once again leave in its domestic politics the path of a state of law and democratic liberties."[42]

Adenauer's clear-cut choice between the diplomatic antipodes of neutrality and integration explains other aspects of Adenauer's policies as well: his assent to rearmament, his devotion to Franco-German reconciliation, his preference for a "little Europe" as an integrative construct (for a larger one would tend to dissipate institutional restraints), his insistence on German equality in the alliance, and his unswerving support of America's double-containment policy. It was in the large correspondence of beliefs, policies, and political reflexes between the team of Eisenhower and Dulles and the German chancellor that one must look for the deepest sources of the German-American amity and mutual trust that characterized the 1950s.[43]

Adenauer expected something in return. When Bonn pledged as part of the Western treaty package of 1952–54 to support faithfully its treaty obligations, forswear the use of force in seeking unification, and develop a united Germany along peaceful and democratic lines, it had from the German viewpoint entered into a solemn and binding legal compact with its allies (especially the United States). In return for rearming and committing themselves totally to the West, the Germans felt entitled to the Western powers' support for an Eastern policy that would safeguard German interests. When Bonn began to feel by the late fifties and even more so in the early sixties that these interests were no longer sufficiently appreciated in Washington, the German-American diplomatic accord began to erode.

As for the question of whether Adenauer prevented German reunification (that is, whether last opportunities for resolving the German question were irretrievably lost by Adenauer's disdain for Soviet proposals) perhaps a fair judgment would be that in the early and mid-1950s the issue of German reunification was already moot, although it remained important in East-West diplomacy. Whatever may have been the degree of Adenauer's commitment to German unity (given his sense of priorities and the adverse international circumstances it could not have been very great), it is improbable that he destroyed realistic chances for unification. France was opposed in principle; the United States, determined to rearm Germany and implement its double-containment policy, could have restrained a more dynamic Germany policy; and the Soviet Union's major purpose in calling for German neutrality was to prevent the rearmament of West Germany.[44] Most likely the Eastern side provided no real opportunity to obtain German reunification, and most likely the Western allies would have prevented the Germans from seizing it had it been real. But this must remain a matter of historical conjecture, because at several crucial junctures Adenauer showed little interest in exploring Soviet intentions and testing the sincerity of Soviet proposals.

By the mid-1950s it had become clear that although the central tenet of Adenauer's reunification policy was proved correct (that Washington and Moscow held the key to the German question and that reunification required the consent of both), the German government had found it impossible to formulate and advance a solution acceptable to both super-powers. None of this is to say that unification on terms acceptable to Bonn could necessarily have been achieved if the Federal Republic had *not* aligned itself with the West. The Soviet Union could have sabotaged unification at any juncture in the diplomatic sequence that the Kremlin proposed for bringing it about. Nonetheless, had the circumstances re-mained the same, Bonn could not have hoped to improve chances for reunification by pursuing a policy of integration with the West.

Negotiating from a Basis of Strength?

The policymakers of the Federal Republic, especially Konrad Ade-nauer, claimed to be fully aware of this, arguing that their long-range calculations anticipated a point where circumstances would be more propitious and that Bonn's unification policies (as well as those of the Western allies) were designed to bring about such circumstances as quickly as possible. The second major premise of Bonn's official unifica-tion policy was in effect that with the passage of time the balance of power between the two Cold War blocs would shift in favor of the West, thus allowing negotiations "on the basis of strength" that would induce the Soviet Union to settle the German question on Western terms.

Again Bonn's official pronouncements sought to reassure the German public with arguments about the West's willingness to support reunifica-tion that were highly questionable. Although the Western powers sup-ported Bonn's rigid stand vis-à-vis the Soviet bloc, they showed no great enthusiasm or determination in furthering the cause of German unity. Whatever may have been their deepest political *arrières-pensées* on the German question, both Cold War camps considered it politic to give at least verbal support to German aspirations for unification. This obliged the Western powers to buttress Bonn's public claims that there would be a satisfactory settlement of the German question once the Western power position had improved. As Robert Osgood has noted, this was a highly disingenuous Western diplomacy:

> As for entering into negotiations to end the division of Germany and Europe, all spokesmen of the Truman and Eisenhower administra-tions officially looked forward to a negotiated removal of what [George F.] Kennan called the "great political and military cramp" in the center of Europe, but they professed to believe that this would come about when the West achieved such a powerful political and

military posture and when a prospering democratic West Germany exerted such an irresistible "attractive power" that the Soviet government would have no alternative but to accept unification on the basis of Germany's freedom to join NATO. By this formula they paid the verbal price for West Germany's willing collaboration with NATO and perpetuated a delusion, which served, in effect, as a justification for keeping Germany divided.[45]

Even if Bonn and the Western allies had in fact expected a favorable shift in the East-West balance of power (which is improbable considering the Pentagon's pessimistic contingency planning in the early and mid-1950s) such expectations were dashed by the Soviet Union's acquisition of nuclear capabilities. A Western policy of rollback and liberation of Eastern Europe (the campaign slogans with which the Eisenhower administration had entered office), or even of strong pressure on the Kremlin, became inconceivable in light of the retaliatory power the Soviet Union was developing, which was demonstrated by events in East Germany in 1953 and Hungary in 1956.[46] Adenauer's "policy of strength," either illusory or fatuous to begin with, had lost all semblance of plausibility when the developing nuclear standoff between East and West was soon reflected in an standoff on the German question. More than ever before could either side deny the other control of both Germanies.

But the restraints imposed by the changing military-strategic balance, although important, were not really the crux of the matter. More important was a shift in the political balance. The inclusion of the two German states in their respective alliances connoted an emerging European political equilibrium rather than an increase in Western military strength. When the Federal Republic joined NATO and the German Democratic Republic joined the Warsaw Pact, the European political order became more stable and the volatile and nervous diplomatic activities of the early 1950s settled down to a quiescent political balance in Europe. Although it may be an exaggeration to say that "the Geneva Summit Conference of 1955 in fact marked the end of the Cold War in Germany,"[47] it did conclude five years of East-West maneuvering, during which the line of demarcation through Germany had become increasingly solid and uncontested. Moscow's attempts to deny the Western alliance the increase of power expected of a West German military contribution had failed: the Federal Republic was fully committed to a Western course and was becoming an integral part of the economic, military, and political institutions of the West. But the failure of Moscow's Germany policy could not be converted into a success for Bonn's Germany policy. Neither had Germany's influence on the German question increased in the alliance, nor had the Western powers achieved the superiority of power vis-à-vis the Soviet Union that was purportedly central to Adenauer's policy.

On the contrary, the absolute and relative strength of the Soviet

Union had increased substantially, and the Cold War balance of power was moving toward an equilibrating deadlock of which the existing state of affairs in Central Europe was one manifestation. The Soviet Union, having failed to prevent German membership in NATO, began to accept the status quo in Central Europe and turned to other Cold War fronts, especially in the Middle East and Africa. Instead of becoming more conciliatory with the passing of time on the German question, the Russians' attitudes stiffened in exactly the way they themselves had predicted. The Soviet Union shifted to a policy of "two Germanies," which meant that Moscow sought to gain international recognition for the GDR, and which found its most specific and immediate expression in the Kremlin's readiness to establish diplomatic relations with Bonn in 1955.

For Bonn this posed a dilemma. Establishing relations with Moscow tended to underline the division of Germany and in fact lent it a certain de jure recognition. The German Foreign Office entertained serious reservations about such a step, and the Western powers were notably unenthusiastic.[48] But the German chancellor knew he could not block diplomatic channels of such importance for the German question, even if this step lent cogency to Moscow's contention that in fact two equal and sovereign German states had come into being. By 1955 Nikita Krushchev and other Soviet leaders began to stress that the unification of such differently developing societies as those of East Germany and West Germany could not possibly take place at the expense of East Germany, and during Adenauer's visit to Moscow late in 1955 Krushchev said he was no longer interested even in bringing up the question of West Germany's withdrawal from the Western alliance.[49] The Soviet Union was apparently convinced that the status quo was tolerable, that it would ultimately gain international recognition, and that time was working for Soviet interests, as was reflected in Krushchev's remark to Adenauer that "the wind is not blowing in our face." Although Adenauer obtained the release of German prisoners of war remaining in the Soviet Union—an important humanitarian and emotional issue in Germany—the Russian-German summit in Moscow proved a total failure as far as the German question was concerned.*

Clearly, Adenauer's hope to deal with the Soviet Union from a posi-

*The establishment of diplomatic relations between Bonn and Moscow provided the immediate occasion for the formulation of Bonn's so-called Hallstein Doctrine in December 1955. To buttress the West German claim to sole representation of all Germans, which appeared weakened by the formal accreditation that both German states now had in Moscow, Bonn developed a legal and diplomatic formula providing that the Federal Republic would withhold or withdraw diplomatic recognition from governments that recognized the East German regime—except the Soviet Union. On the basis of this doctrine, Bonn broke diplomatic relations with Yugoslavia in 1957, when Marshal Tito formally recognized the German Democratic Republic.

tion of strength had not materialized by 1955. Equally important, not even the Western orientation of Bonn's reunification policy had succeeded. To be sure, the improved status of the Federal Republic had become acknowledged both legally and politically. The German government had become formally entitled to conduct (within certain limits) its own foreign policy; the Western powers had reaffirmed their pledge to support the unification of Germany diplomatically; and the plans to create a European Economic Community soon allowed the Germans to flex their economic muscle in an integrated, multilateral context.

But none of these diplomatic achievements, which were of a high order considering the Federal Republic's starting point in 1949, could be converted into growing German influence on the German question or induce the Western powers to energize their Germany diplomacy. On the contrary, the United States increasingly appreciated the benefits that derived for Western diplomacy from a stable if divided Europe, it was aware of the risks involved in seeking to overturn it, and the accession of West Germany to NATO removed the urgency of the German issue and rendered it dormant. The willingness of the Soviet Union after 1955 to seek a stabilization of the European status quo was reciprocated on the Western side. In East-West diplomacy, the idea of a general settlement of the European question was being replaced by the idea of seeking a more easily obtainable and perhaps equally satisfying political settlement on the basis of a divided Germany and Europe.[50] The development of Soviet nuclear capabilities, coupled with a less aggressive Soviet political posture in Europe, led to a serious reappraisal by the West of the potentially volatile political situation in Central Europe and to a corresponding inclination to "defuse" the Cold War in general and the German question in particular. Even as the superpowers jockeyed for diplomatic advantage on the Continent, the partition of Europe became for them a kind of geostrategic repose, a sanctuary of relative stability from which to pursue their rivalries in less settled arenas of the Cold War. In Europe both sides were poised in watchful proximity and always ready to grasp tactical advantages, but also deeply afraid of fundamental change. John Lukacs wrote decades later: "We may regret, in retrospect, the unwillingness of John Foster Dulles and President Eisenhower to explore the possibilities of a broad rearrangement of Soviet-American relations, including those of a reciprocal disengagement from certain positions of Europe. In 1955 the Austrian State Treaty showed the existence of such possibilities. Yet in 1956, during and after the Hungarian uprising, a turning point in the Cold War came: [later] Khrushchev and his colleagues realized that his predecessors' fears were unfounded; the United States was not interested in changing the division of Europe."[51]

Not only the United States and the Soviet Union lost interest in changing the European status quo. The German question also lost some of its urgency in Europe. It was precisely the integration of the two German states in their alliances, and the means of control that these alliances provided, that brought a reassuring sense of stability to Europe, accompanied by a growing relief that the perennially troublesome German issue had found at least for the interim an acceptable solution. Far from rekindling interest in German reunification, the Federal Republic's accession to the Western alliance turned into a political palliative for its partners in the alliance. Western Europe was preoccupied with economic reconstruction and the political problems attending the formation of the European Economic Community, which led to a redirection of political and economic energies and a corresponding readiness to accept the division of Europe as inevitable and not amenable to change in the foreseeable future. On both sides of the European divide, the feeling took hold that it was easier to deal with the reality of two Germanies than the potentiality of one, especially because both were restrained institutionally, and because one could even count on one's Cold War opponent as a partner in the common enterprise of defusing the German problem.

All this meant that Bonn's hope to deal with the Soviet Union from a basis of strength had become illusory, not only because of the development of Soviet nuclear capabilities but because Soviet readiness to respect the status quo in Europe evoked a similar readiness in the West.[52] The Western dimension of Bonn's reunification policy was eroding for the very reason that Bonn had claimed would strengthen it: Germany's accession to the Western alliance. Germany's turning to the West, which Adenauer had claimed would secure Western support for unification, diminished Western interest in the German question, and the gradual shift from Cold War to coexistence tended to diminish rather than increase the influence of Germany within the Western alliance.[53]

But there was a large irony in this. Although neither premise of Adenauer's Germany policy had withstood the test of political realities (Bonn's influence on the German question within the alliance had not grown stronger, the Soviet Union had not grown weaker) Adenauer had succeeded in his overriding political purpose: German neutrality was averted and the Federal Republic securely anchored to the West. What had failed was not Adenauer's policy, but the public rationale with which he had defended it.

The developing nuclear stalemate and Moscow's European policies, which were oriented toward the status quo, led to gradual but significant changes in Western policy, especially in the area of European security arrangements. In the early 1950s the Western powers had demanded that the unification of Germany precede the creation of a European security system and that arms control measures, which inevitably would affect the political configuration, be postponed until some resolution of the German problem had been effected. This began to change in the mid- and late 1950s. Prime Minister Anthony Eden of Britain spoke of the German question and European security arrangements as "twin problems," and there was a noticeable shift from viewing the solution of the German question as a precondition for security arrangements to the attitude that these were parallel desiderata without any specific priority.[54]

These developments, which raised serious apprehensions in Bonn, were underlined after 1955 by Moscow's Germany policy. After West Germany's accession to NATO, the Soviet Union persistently tried to solidify further the *political* line of division in Central Europe (reflecting the Soviet interest in legitimizing the territorial status quo) and at the same time to blur the East-West *military* boundary running through Germany (reflecting the Soviet interest in complicating NATO's defense strategy and weakening the West's posture of nuclear deterrence). Both purposes underlay Soviet proposals for military disengagement and Soviet pressures on Berlin.

Disengagement: Another Lost Opportunity?

The disengagement proposals advanced by the Soviet Union and its allies centered on arms control measures such as a nuclear-free zone in Central Europe and a thinning out of conventional troop levels on both sides. They invariably provided that the status quo—the division of Germany—would be the basis for an arms control agreement between the superpowers, and they envisaged the participation of West and East Germany as equal partners. Thus acceptance of the proposals would have led to a de facto recognition of the GDR, as well as a weakening of the West's military presence at the periphery of the Soviet bloc. In particular, these proposals threatened the deployment of American nuclear weapons in Central Europe and also threatened Bonn's gradually developing interest in gaining a voice in nuclear decision making, and these were undoubtedly the reasons why disengagement proposals multiplied rapidly in both Eastern and Western Europe. Nuclear disengagement (in later years called the denuclearization of Europe) was unacceptable to the Germans on both military and political grounds. Disengagement would have undermined NATO's "forward strategy," which Bonn sought to strengthen to make nuclear deterrence more convincing, and brought the GDR a step closer to international recognition and legitimacy. For the United States also, a nuclear-free corridor in Central Europe was totally unacceptable on military and political grounds, and the reception accorded in Washington and Bonn to the most prominent of Western disengagement proposals, advanced by George Kennan in 1957, bespeaks how the Eisenhower administration and the Adenauer government saw their central security interests and European policies threatened if military disengagement were effected in Central Europe.[55]

Bonn's suspicions of Moscow's motives appeared the more justified because the Soviet proposals were never specifically linked with the question of unification but seemed primarily designed to disrupt NATO, foreclose the deployment of U.S. nuclear weapons in Europe, and deny the Federal Republic a share in controlling nuclear arms. All Soviet proposals started with the assumption that two German states existed and that they would participate in negotiations as equals. Acceptance of even the initial stages of the Soviet plans would have implied Western recognition of East Germany, which could then have sabotaged all further progress toward unification. Adenauer also distrusted Western proposals for East-West security arrangements, such as the Herter Plan, which linked reunification with arms control and a European security system, because he suspected that they stemmed not so much from a desire to see Germany reunified as from the need to diminish East-West tensions and explore all possibilities for arms control. Adenauer considered these proposals unwise even though it was unlikely that the Soviet Union would accept them, because once they were presented as concessions they would become the basis for further Soviet demands at the next stage of East-West discussions. From Bonn's perspective, these proposals implied a willingness to water down the Western position and would lead to a gradual de jure recognition of the German status quo.

For Bonn, linking progress on arms control and security questions with progress on the German question cut both ways. On the one hand, the Germans perceived the linkage to be in their interest and insisted on retaining it; on the other, they did not want to be viewed as having obstructed arms control. More important, they feared that Washington's interest in the German question had eroded so much that German insistence on linking it to arms control would simply allow the Western powers formally to trade off aspects of the German question for progress on arms control.[56] The American side described itself as perplexed by this German shift of emphasis, and John Foster Dulles was quoted as saying that he seemed more committed to Germany's reunification than was the German chancellor.[57]

Bonn's attitude on disengagement highlighted a fundamental paradox of the unification issue. Bipolarities of interest, tension, and power were not conducive to unification: this was the lesson of the period before 1955. But the developing nuclear standoff between the United States and the Soviet Union and the concurrent loosening of the two Cold War blocs in the late 1950s seemed no more likely to bring unification. For Bonn, any lessening of tensions or intimations of Western flexibility raised the prospect that conciliatory arrangements between the two superpowers might be made bilaterally and at the expense of the German question. This was the fundamental dilemma for Bonn's unification policy: without an abating of East-West tensions neither side could afford to allow unification on the opponent's terms, yet an accommodation between East and West made it likely that the German status quo would get not only a tacit but a legal blessing. The German question became afflicted with a series of connected paradoxes: unity required détente, détente required recognizing the military and political balance on the global and European levels, but this balance rested in turn on the division of Germany and Europe.

On the surface it would seem that fissures in the two Cold War alliances would have enhanced Bonn's chances to pursue an active unification diplomacy. The enforced relaxation of Moscow's control over its Eastern European satellites and the emerging Sino-Soviet dispute seemed to provide openings for Western probing, and the conflicts within the Western alliance helped make the Federal Republic a pivot, the support of which was solicited by both Washington and Paris. There was no lack of advisers and critics in Bonn and elsewhere who urged Adenauer to adopt a more flexible and imaginative Eastern policy to take advantage of the fragmentation of the Soviet monolith, and who suggested a more dynamic policy toward East European countries and a less rigid stand on the Hallstein Doctrine and the Oder-Neisse border. Long-range considerations clearly required that the Germans themselves take some initiative on unification and that Bonn modify its adamant Eastern policy and establish political and diplomatic contacts with the East European countries with national interests directly affected by the German question.

But the major unification efforts made by the Adenauer government after 1955 were not really directed toward bringing about unification on terms acceptable to Bonn—for that there was little hope—and Bonn concentrated its diplomatic efforts on the problem of preventing the legitimization of the status quo in Central Europe. This change of emphasis had important implications for Bonn's Germany policy within the Western alliance, for it meant that the primary function of the Western powers on the German question was to deny the Soviet Union and East Germany a legitimization of the existing state of affairs.

On this issue the fissures in the Western alliance held conflicting implications for Bonn's Germany policy. With tensions growing between Washington and Paris (especially after Charles de Gaulle returned to power), the West German government was placed in the difficult position of taking sides in Franco-American disagreements, explicitly as well as implicitly. This complicated Bonn's entire diplomatic agenda and in particular its unification policy. Although de Gaulle had recognized the Oder-Neisse border in 1959, Bonn hoped that France would help deny legitimacy to the status quo and the East German regime. This was borne out by French support of Adenauer's tough stand on the recurring crises in Berlin, during which the United States and Great Britain were much more conciliatory toward the Soviet Union. Further, many decision makers in Bonn were convinced that in the long run the unity of Europe would be the key to the German question, and that for this reason alone the support of France was indispensable. But there was considerable and widespread doubt about French willingness to work enthusiastically for unification itself and a suspicion, in Walter Lippmann's words, that "the hard line France takes about Berlin and the Soviet Union is founded . . . on a basic French national determination not to have to live with a large united Germany. At bottom the hard policy is directed not against the Russians but against those Germans who want to make an opening to the East."[58]

On the other hand, although Bonn may still have entertained hopes that the United States would in principle be less hostile to the idea of German unity if it could be accomplished on Western terms, it was Washington (along with London) that seemed willing to show more flexibility on procedural issues tending to legitimize the existing state of affairs in Europe, as events in Berlin soon demonstrated. In other words, the tensions between the two aspects of the German question—unification itself, and preventing the legitimization of the status quo—were underscored both by the centrifugal tendencies in the Eastern bloc and by the fissures in the Western alliance. Short-run efforts to prevent the legal and political solidification of the status quo were in conflict with long-range planning for unification.[59]

Toward the end of the 1950s Bonn's Germany policy was characterized by an almost desperate sense of suspicion (directed toward the West as well as the East), a growing fear of diplomatic isolation, and a realistic premonition of things to come. Hans Buchheim noted: "More and more the question 'how do we get closer to reunification' turned into the problem 'how can we prevent that the partition of Germany obtains a seal of approval' [or] 'what must we do to keep the German question open until chances for its satisfactory solution reappear.' "[60]

The Remaining Political Ambiguity: Berlin

In 1958, a decade after the Berlin Blockade and the Allied airlift, West Berlin again became the focal point of the Cold War in Europe.[61] Since 1949 Berlin had been the last vestige of the Four Powers' responsibility for all-German affairs. The Allied military and West German political presence in the western part of the city had constantly irritated the East German regime and the Soviet Union. Because the Soviet Union wanted to freeze and legitimize the political status quo in Central Europe, the isolated city presented Moscow with tempting opportunities to extract from the West de facto recognition of East Germany. The Soviets hoped to use Berlin to force the Western powers and the West Germans to deal directly with East Germany. Berlin was a logical tool for such purposes because its political and legal status was not beyond challenge and because the access routes from the Federal Republic to West Berlin were the most vulnerable point of the Western defense perimeter. The Soviets enjoyed local superiority of power, and could apply pressure and engineer provocations with fine gradations.

In December 1958 the Soviet Union proposed to the Western powers that negotiations be undertaken with a view toward giving West Berlin the status of a demilitarized free city. In case agreement could not be reached within six months, the Soviet Union threatened to transfer its rights regarding access to Berlin to the GDR. This confronted the Western powers with the prospect that they would have to deal directly with the East Germans on these matters, extending de facto recognition to them at the same time as their own rights would be abrogated.

These Soviet moves posed a serious threat to what Bonn perceived as its vital interests. The establishment of a free city, perhaps under some form of supervision by the United Nations and independent of both East Germany and West Germany, would have destroyed an important element of the Four Powers' responsibility for all-German questions. Equally important, it would have severed the already tenuous political and constitutional link between West Berlin and West Germany. As reflected in the special provisions for West Berlin in the Federal Republic's constitution, the Western powers had never been enthusiastic about a too specific and visible integration of West Berlin into the Federal Republic, primarily because they wanted to preserve the legal status of Berlin under the Four Power Agreement. Although there was a de jure separation of West Berlin from the Federal Republic, there was a de facto economic, political, and symbolic connection at least as strong and visible as that between East Berlin and East Germany, which Bonn was determined to preserve. The creation of an isolated, miniature state of West Berlin would have shut out the Western powers and excluded the political influence of the Federal Republic as well. A major political ambiguity hindering the Soviet policy of two Germanies would have been clarified and resolved in Moscow's favor.

Khrushchev's ultimatum on Berlin posed a quandary to the West, for West German interests were not the same as those of the three Western Allied powers. Bonn had an equal interest in securing the status of Berlin and in securing it in a way not detrimental to the larger issue of German reunification. But the Western powers and the United States in particular were much more concerned with their status in Berlin than with the ramifications on the broader German question, realizing that their stance on Berlin would be judged by world public opinion on both political and moral grounds, that their international prestige was on the line, and that their continuing rights to deal with all-German questions were most visibly expressed in the joint Allied control of the city.

This realization forced on Bonn an intricate set of calculations. The

Germans could expect that the United States, faced with the unpalatable prospect of either dealing with the GDR or risking a major confrontation with the Soviet Union, would make concessions on legitimizing the partition of Germany in return for obtaining a reaffirmation of the American status in Berlin. At the same time, because so much was at stake for the United States on the Berlin side of the equation, the German chancellor saw no need to ease the Americans' problem if this would require German concessions on the reunification issue: Washington had no choice but to be tough on the Berlin question, but it had the choice of being soft on the German one.

Adenauer decided to eliminate the linkage between the two issues. Realizing that world opinion would be with the Germans on the Berlin question but not on the unification question, and determined to prevent or at least complicate an East-West deal on the German one, Adenauer demanded from Washington that these issues be dealt with separately.[62] The American secretary of state in turn floated the idea in public that one might deal with the East Germans as "agents" of the Soviets, and he told the German ambassador in private that even though the United States would risk armed conflict to defend Berlin, such a response would have to be triggered by a clearly aggressive action on the part of the Soviet Union, not by a Western refusal to accept East German modalities on Western access to Berlin. Public opinion would not accept going to war over such "formalities."[63] But formalities were the crux of the matter for the Germans. As Hans Buchheim noted:

> [Dulles] was of course right, but he circumvented . . . the core of the problem, namely the consequences of this type of crisis management for subsequent developments on the German question. In the present circumstances, it was precisely formalities which were of decisive significance for the German question. After all, the Soviet Union had no reason to uncover its flank with an aggressive action and provide the U.S. with a cause to risk armed conflict. On the contrary, she was in the comfortable position of being able to handle formalities quite peacefully—i.e., push the control practices by officials of the GDR so far that no Western tricks of interpretation could portray them as . . . [anything else except] . . . the exercise of state authority by the GDR. With that, the Soviet Union would have achieved the real aim that caused her to initiate the crisis: significant progress toward the de facto recognition of the GDR.[64]

During the next three years the Berlin question was bandied back and forth at East-West conferences in Geneva, Camp David, Paris, and Vienna. The United States and Britain were apparently willing to come to some sort of terms with the Soviets, perhaps on the basis of a "symbolic" reduction of Western forces, but Adenauer and de Gaulle followed a much more intransigent line.

The issue came to a head in 1961.[65] In the intervening three years, refugees had poured into West Berlin from East Germany in increasing numbers, drawing needed manpower from the shaky East German economy and posing embarrassing political problems. By July 1961 the number of refugees entering West Berlin had reached ten thousand a week, and at a meeting of leaders of the East Bloc in Moscow at the end of the month the decision was made to stop this flow by erecting a wall. On August 13 the East German People's Police and the National People's Army occupied East Berlin and began to block transit between East and West Berlin. This step not only closed the last door between East and West Germany but also destroyed the last symbol of the unity of Germany and Berlin. The Soviets had in fact achieved a tightening and clarification of the political line running through Germany. By "delegating" their rights in East Berlin to the East German government, they had for all practical purposes concluded the separate peace treaty with which they had threatened the West for so long. The division of Germany was complete.

6

Toward Diplomatic Isolation:
Bonn and the German Question in the 1960s

No matter how quickly, by what way or by what means we may attain re-unification—we shall never lose sight of this aim for one moment. A Federal Government which ceased to realize every day anew that this aim takes priority before all others would fail in its duty and responsibility to the German people and to later history.

—LUDWIG ERHARD, 1965

The Germany policy of the Adenauer era, aimed at reunification and an all-German peace treaty, had arrived at a dead end at the beginning of the 1960s. It threatened to isolate us within the Western alliance, even though one could not expect of it tangible progress toward German unity in the foreseeable future.

—WILHELM G. GREWE

The Berlin Wall not only symbolized the completion of Germany's partition, and therefore also the utter failure of Bonn's Germany policy, but was a signal of the changing political climate that surrounded the German question in the West.[1] An important element in this political climate was the change of leadership in Washington. Although there had already developed abrasions between Bonn and Washington during the last years of the Eisenhower administration (especially after Christian Herter succeeded John Foster Dulles as secretary of state), the change of leadership in Washington brought a significantly different atmosphere to German-American relations. When the new atmosphere also brought with it new policies, Bonn and Washington began to drift apart.

A Changing German-American Relationship:
The Erosion of Double Containment

When the Kennedy administration responded to the building of the wall in a way that was from Bonn's perspective insufficiently firm, it signified for the German government as well as for the SPD opposition that Washington had lost interest in the German question. The building of the wall was a traumatic event for the Germans. Willy Brandt, then lord mayor of Berlin, later claimed that the inadequacy of the Western response led him to think about a new German Ostpolitik,[2] and the resulting disappointments, suspicions, and recriminations burdened the entire range of German-American relations.[3] Chancellor Adenauer had all along feared a softening of the Western position on the German question, worrying in particular that the two superpowers would arrive at an accommodation at the expense of German interests (this premonition was perhaps the most insistent in that it could not be expressed openly), and he was hardly reassured by what he considered a waffling American response during the Berlin crisis of 1961. The events of summer 1961 mark the beginning of a decade in which the Germans' suspicions of their transatlantic partner turned into open disagreements.

Substantive disagreements on the German question, on security issues, on arms control, and on alliance policy were sharpened by personality conflicts. In the early 1960s German and American leaders were separated by differences of age, diplomatic style, public careers, and ultimately life experiences, and the cordiality and mutual trust that had cemented German-American relations during the Eisenhower years gave way to a crisp and more distant diplomatic intercourse. The aging German chancellor found it difficult to adjust to changing political circumstances at home and abroad, and his deep anxieties about the reliability of American diplomacy seemed confirmed by what he perceived as unwarranted American flexibility in dealing with the Soviet Union in general and the German question in particular.

But differences of opinion, style of governance, and political temperament were only the surface manifestations of much deeper problems that had their origins in the late 1950s but were obscured by the continuity provided by the personalities of the Eisenhower administration. Whatever the consequences may have been for the cause of German unification, during the 1950s there was a general German-American accord, incomplete but fundamental, on how to deal with the Soviet Union, Eastern Europe, and East Germany. In the 1960s this congruence of attitudes between Bonn and Washington diminished drastically. In the 1950s it had been in the interest of the Western powers to encourage the Germans in their tough and uncompromising stand toward the East; in the 1960s this stand was becoming an impediment to a more flexible

Western policy toward Moscow. In neither case was the real question that of supporting German unity. The real question was how to persuade the Germans to adjust their own Eastern policies to those of the United States and, when the Cold War turned into a phase of coexistence, to the changing circumstances of East-West diplomacy. Persuading the Germans had proven relatively easy in the 1950s; it proved very difficult in the 1960s.

The basic problem was not of course that the Kennedy administration or later the Johnson administration would have wanted the Federal Republic to loosen its ties to the West: Washington's fundamental interest in double containment remained firm. But the growing recognition in Washington that the nuclear balance of terror required a circumspect American diplomacy toward the Soviet Union also demanded that potential crises in Europe be defused, and that such constructive items on the East-West diplomatic agenda as arms control should replace such intractable issues as German unification.[4] The United States and the Soviet Union developed a common interest to stabilize the European state system (by accommodation rather than by confrontation), which was augmented, especially after the Cuban missile crisis, by their mutual vulnerability to nuclear destruction.[5]

America's central geostrategic interest in a stable European equilibrium of power—under American hegemony if possible, under an American-Soviet condominium if necessary—reemerged with powerful clarity by the 1960s. Increasingly it became apparent that official Washington and influential members of the American foreign policy establishment were counting on the continuance of the existing postwar European order, because Germany's division, its central stabilizing feature, was seen as benefiting Europeans in both alliances, having redressed the imbalance of the European power configuration that had resulted from Germany's unification in 1871. Based on the maxims of classical Realpolitik, this view in effect credited both the United States and the Soviet Union with having solved Europe's old problem of how to contain an excessively powerful Germany, and assigned to the superpowers the continuing right and obligation to be the guarantors of the European status quo and the guardians of their respective spheres of influence. Even as the Soviet Union remained an opponent, it became in Europe a geostrategic partner of the United States.[6]

Washington's conviction that a stable European equilibrium was a vital American geostrategic interest was more easily acted on in the 1950s, when the stark confrontations of the Cold War sharpened the division of Europe and Germany and inevitably drew the Federal Republic closer to the West. In the 1960s, when both NATO and the Warsaw Pact lost cohesion and the Cold War yielded to coexistence, matters became more complicated. It was precisely the division of Germany that helped stabilize the European status quo, but Bonn was most adamant in insisting that this status quo be denied recognition and legitimization. Faced with a changing military balance and a changing European political order, the Kennedy and Johnson administrations were in effect redefining America's containment policy toward the Soviet Union. But Bonn strongly opposed the policy changes that accompanied Washington's new approach to the East-West conflict: a strong interest in arms control, a qualification of the American nuclear commitment to Europe, acceptance of the European status quo, and a shift of American diplomatic energies to the Third World arena of the East-West conflict. What Washington perceived as necessary adjustments of entrenched and outmoded Cold War positions, Bonn perceived as the selling out of vital German interests. America's double-containment policy was faltering because Washington's Soviet and German policies were no longer congruent. The redefinition of Washington's containment policy toward the Soviet Union also required a redefinition of its twin component, Washington's containment policy toward the Federal Republic. When Washington attempted to fashion such a redefinition, the Germans rejected it.

As a consequence of the developing incongruence between the Soviet and German components of Washington's double-containment policy, there arose a deep insincerity in German-American relations. The United States remained officially committed to support German unification and to regard Bonn as the only legitimate spokesman for all of Germany. To have done otherwise would have amounted to a public abrogation of the solemn transatlantic compact of the Paris Agreements, when Bonn traded its assent to rearmament for the restoration of sovereignty and for the American pledge to support German unification. Bonn and Washington did not fully trust one another, but neither side felt free to bring out in the open the underlying conflict of interests and intentions. Bonn in particular feared the consequences for both foreign and domestic policy: at stake was a central premise of Germany's pro-Western integration policy, and the justifications with which Adenauer had defended it against his domestic opponents. The American president viewed Bonn's pro-Gaullist inclinations with deep misgivings, perceiving a danger for the cohesion of NATO and the European pillar of his two-pillar Grand Design for the alliance. But his own actions were contributing to these inclinations. The German chancellor felt obliged to turn to France to obviate German diplomatic isolation if the United States should disengage from Europe, even as he also feared that France might itself embark on a diplomatic course detrimental to German interests. The German side could not bring itself to express openly its deepest conviction—that both the United States and the Soviet Union preferred the continued division of Germany—and shied away from admitting that carefully crafted contractual commitments among allies were devoid of political substance. The American side was in turn equally reluctant to admit to its lack of interest in German unification, although it expressed it indirectly.[7]

Especially unpalatable to Bonn was the implied convergence of Soviet and American interests on the German question. Even worse, and for the West Germans almost unthinkable, was the unavoidable corollary that East Germany, which persistently sought to stabilize the European status quo, was sharing this interest with both superpowers. The rigidity of Bonn's Eastern diplomacy was maneuvering the Federal Republic into a position where its allies, although nominally supportive of its unification strategy, were sharing basic political interests with its opponents, including the odious regime in East Berlin that Bonn continued to ostracize. Although many influential German leaders, especially on the conservative side of the political spectrum, prided themselves on their tough realism in dealing with the Soviet Union, they found it much more difficult to apply the same realism in dealing with their transatlantic partner. On the question of German reunification, many Germans tended to give Americans a bit more credit and the Russians a bit more blame than they deserved. Illusions refused to die. Whereas Bonn's ambassador to NATO saw in NATO the hegemonic instrument of the United States, which he judged totally uninterested in the German question (see chapter 1, note 25), Bonn's ambassador to London confided to his diary in 1965 that "NATO is much more than a purely technical military alliance. NATO is for us the guarantee that member states—above all, the United States—lend the Federal Republic the political support which it needs so urgently in the contest over reunification."[8]

During the Kennedy years almost every diplomatic encounter between Bonn and Washington on the German question turned into an occasion for mutual reproach. Bonn found it extremely difficult to obtain what it considered the necessary backing for its Germany policy, and Washington in turn viewed German recalcitrance with increasing impatience and concern.

German displeasure and American annoyance became most glaring when Bonn increasingly took recourse to legal arguments in pressing its case in Washington (primarily through its ambassador, the former law professor and Adenauer's long-time confidant Wilhelm Grewe), eliciting from President Kennedy a mixture of boredom and irritation.[9] In these years there was a great temptation for Bonn to extend to its dealings with the West the same legalistic diplomacy with which it approached the East—a rearguard action that could not stem the tide of events. It is essential to realize that Bonn's "diplomacy by law" was directed as much against its partners as against its opponents. Toward the end of his chancellorship Adenauer's suspicions were so sweeping, encompassing his allies in the West as well as his opponents in the East, that they amounted to an "all-horizons" diplomacy of distrust, similar to de Gaulle's all-horizons policy of nuclear deterrence.

But it would be too simple to blame a legalistic German cast of mind for Bonn's tendency to translate politics into law and to safeguard political interests by relying on the legal instruments of treaties, formal interpretations of treaty provisions, addenda, explanations of intent, *Junktims*, *ex nunc* and *ex tunc* invalidations, and so forth. The complexities of these legal arguments more often than not reflected the complexities of the political issues that were being addressed or settled. There were very practical reasons why the Germans were determined to nail down political arrangements in detailed legal provisions. When it came to questions pertaining to Germany's reunification, the Germans were suspicious of the West as well as of the East. The legal codifications of political understandings that Bonn reached with the Western allies on the German question were an important safeguard of German interests, and Bonn was determined to preserve them. Such considerations necessarily put Bonn on a collision course with a president eager to move beyond the entrenched positions of the Eisenhower-Dulles era, impatient with legal doctrine, and weary of listening to reiterations of Bonn's orthodox views on the Cold War in general and the German question in particular.*

It is not difficult to understand the president's exasperation with Bonn's legal remonstrations, but neither is it difficult to appreciate the Germans' consternation when they saw legal arguments, which for them incorporated carefully negotiated, fundamental understandings between allies, treated as tiresome and mostly irrelevant digressions. The Germans perceived in Washington's new attitude a weakening of America's commitment to support Bonn on the German question (including that of Berlin), thus confirming Adenauer's deep suspicions. The Americans viewed Bonn's obstinacy as an irritating obstacle to a more flexible American global policy and as an indication that the Germans were

*For the Germans, domestic considerations also played a role. In the 1950s, when the governments led by the CDU/CSU joined the various political, economic, and military institutions of the Western alliance, the Social Democrats constantly attacked the policy because of its adverse effects on the prospects for Germany's reunification, and subjected it to judicial review. Later, when Willy Brandt launched Ostpolitik, the CDU/CSU opposition accused the government of not obtaining sufficient concessions from the East and also turned to the courts for clarification and redress. German leaders were sensitive to current criticism and future historical judgment, and aware of the risk of having their foreign policy subjected to domestic judicial review. They sought to demonstrate through their careful attention to legal considerations that they were equally circumspect with respect to safeguarding German political interests. All parties aimed to protect their political fortunes and historical reputations by careful attention to legal matters.

incapable of adjusting to the new realities of the 1960s, which required moving from the direct confrontations of the Cold War toward the more ambiguous contests of coexistence.

The Changing Political Content and Diplomatic Shape of the German Question

As the European territorial status quo obtained de facto recognition even as the Western powers still denied it de jure legitimization, it became obvious that a resolution of the German question, if feasible at all, could not possibly result from territorial rearrangements or a merging of the two German states. The basis on which the Western powers had made their commitment to support reunification—absorbing East Germany into West Germany and absorbing a united Germany into the Western alliance—had by the 1960s become even more unrealistic than it had been a decade earlier. If Bonn wanted to keep in step with events and trends in Europe and avoid diplomatic isolation, it needed to redefine the meaning of German unity, stripping it of territorial connotations, transforming it into a question of intra-German rapprochement, and adjusting it to the changing dynamics of the European state system.

As the political content of the German question changed in the eyes of most American and European statesmen (except in Bonn), so did its diplomatic and geographic shape. In the 1960s the issue of German unification was at the same time narrowing and broadening, threatening from two directions what Bonn perceived to be its vital interests and making it even more difficult for Bonn to keep pace with the changing political dynamics of the East-West context of the German question. Unable to reconcile and adjust to the simultaneous contraction and expansion of the German question, Bonn was drifting into diplomatic isolation.

The German question was narrowing in the sense that the Western Allies, and especially the United States, became interested primarily in safeguarding their status in Berlin. On the Western diplomatic agenda the German question had for all practical purposes shrunk to the issue of how the Western presence in Berlin and unimpeded access to the divided city could be politically strengthened and juridically solidified. For the Western Allies, Berlin was where their national interests and international prestige remained closely and visibly engaged. Although President Kennedy never claimed to be a Berliner (he said it was a source of pride to be *able* to say "Ich bin ein Berliner"), there was no question that the United States, France, and Britain perceived their status in Berlin to be of great symbolic and diplomatic significance. It had become the residue of their interest in the German question, which was no longer demonstrated in any other significant way, and it underlined the continuing, residual rights of the Four Powers for matters pertaining to all of Germany. Had it not been for Berlin, these rights would have been condemned to atrophy for lack of day-to-day application and relevance. By clinging to their rights in Berlin, the Western powers were safeguarding their rights in a future general settlement of the German question and of the European political order.

At the same time, the issue of German unification was broadening. There was a growing recognition that a solution or even attenuation of Germany's division could take place only within the wider context of the European state system, that the partition of Germany and partition of Europe were intertwined in a convoluted political and historical dialectic, inseparable and yet distinct, and that the future of Germany could no longer be decided on the basis of a quadripartite agreement among the victors of the Second World War but required a multipartite European settlement of the Cold War. Whereas in the 1950s the issue of German reunification had been embedded in a variety of Eastern proposals and Western counterproposals that remained at least partly focused on Germany (such as German peace treaties and the issue of German neutrality), in the 1960s the German question became part of proposals for pan-European security arrangements. The context and the content of the German question were changing as the German question was becoming absorbed in the larger area of European security arrangements. Even though American and West German diplomacy distrusted Soviet proposals for a pan-European security system, primarily because such a system would have undermined the European pillar of Washington's Grand Design and unraveled NATO, the idea of seeking for European security policies a broader framework that would augment or even transcend the two security alliances was beginning to take hold in Western Europe. The German question was becoming Europeanized.[10]

The Western powers contributed not only to the trend that narrowed the German question to Berlin, but also to the trend that broadened it to Europe. In effect, they favored recognition of the Oder-Neisse border, openly characterized the aim of German unification as a distant goal and not the topic of a realistic foreign policy, and were not averse to a somewhat improved relationship between the two Germanies: "In its basic outlines, American, British, and French ideas anticipated intellectually what would . . . later become Brandt's new Ostpolitik. . . . But the time was not yet ripe [and] Bonn offered tough and tenacious resistance."[11]

Movement with a Policy of "Little Steps"

Bonn found it difficult to energize its Eastern policies because it could accept only one element of the changing East-West relationship in the 1960s—the growing importance of Eastern Europe—and because its political and legal inhibitions prevented it from addressing even that recognition in an adequate and constructive way.

The basic problem with Bonn's Germany policy in the early and

mid-1960s was that it could not cope adequately with the political transformation of the German question and the concurrent narrowing and
broadening of its diplomatic geography. It was not so much that German
thinking in and out of government suffered from a depleted imagination,
for many advisers in Bonn called for a more dynamic approach to the
East. But the official German political position was frozen in its legal logic
and stern in its moral repudiation of the East (especially East Germany),
and any significant change in this position would have been checked by
powerful domestic political constituencies that repudiated a more flexible German diplomacy. The apparent need to develop a more constructive attitude toward East Germany and to recognize the territorial
status quo in Europe would have entailed a rethinking from which the
West German governments of the 1960s and especially their conservative
supporters shied away, almost as if they felt compelled to withhold from
themselves its distasteful implications and consequences. The ineradicable conviction that dealing with the repugnant regime in East Germany
in any formal way would be morally reprehensible and politically and
legally deleterious lent to German diplomacy a grim and sturdy determination.

To be sure, the Germans were themselves aware that changing political circumstances required of them new exertions in the cause of German
unity. By 1963, when Ludwig Erhard became chancellor, dissatisfaction
with the stagnation of Bonn's Eastern policies had become widespread in
West Germany. In the late 1950s Adenauer himself, disappointed by the
patent lack of interest of the West, had entertained rather novel ideas on
the German question,[12] and during the last years of his government his
second foreign minister, Gerhard Schröder, had initiated steps to gradually normalize relations with Eastern Europe. These new approaches
toward Eastern Europe became the central element of Erhard's Eastern
policies (Schröder remained foreign minister in his cabinet), and were
based on the recognition that the rigid dualism of the Cold War had given
way to a more polycentric European political order and that Bonn could
no longer afford to ignore the states of Eastern Europe.[13]

Whereas Adenauer had seen the key to the German question in
Moscow and had been very cautious not to arouse Soviet suspicions by
engaging East European capitals bilaterally, Schröder was convinced that
an "opening to the East" was the precondition for a more dynamic
Germany policy. This more flexible approach, which sought closer economic, political, and diplomatic relations with Eastern Europe and led to
the establishment of German trade missions in Warsaw, Budapest, Sofia,
and Bucharest, was intended to complement French and American efforts to develop better relations with Eastern Europe and reflected the
belief that the countries of Eastern Europe had gained more flexibility in

pursuing their own interests.* In spring 1964 Schröder said: "I believe
that there are indications that in some East European countries there is
growing understanding for the German problem and that their judgment
is more independent than it has been in the past. It appears to me that our
desire for true relaxation of tensions is meeting with more understanding
in those countries than with the Soviet government for the time being.
Let us not underrate this trend, for the voice of those states is beginning
to carry more weight."[14]

But the obstacles to Bonn's policy of movement were formidable, no
less so because some of them were self-imposed. Even though trade
missions were established in Eastern Europe, Bonn remained unwilling
to make compromises that would have weakened its position on the
Oder-Neisse border or the legal claims of the Hallstein Doctrine. Bonn's
"desire for true relaxation of tensions" was expressed only in reassur-
ances about Bonn's good intentions, but did not extend to scrapping its
refusal to accept the existing borders in Europe. Bonn seemed unaware
that mere declarations of good intentions meant little in Eastern Europe
when coupled with demands for territorial revision, backed up by West
Germany's increasing economic and military power. If anything, Bonn's
insistence on the provisional character of Europe's postwar borders gave
the Soviet Union a convenient rationale for maintaining its hold on
Eastern Europe as the guarantor of the territorial status quo, and the
unresolved German question helped contain centrifugal pressures in the
Soviet bloc because it symbolized an important common interest of the
East bloc countries.

By clinging to the territoriality of the German question, Bonn was

*Here again, Bonn sought to use its economic capacities for foreign policy purposes.
The anticipated economic benefits for West Germany were not that significant (although
German trade with the East grew substantially in the mid- and late 1960s), but they were
important to Eastern Europe and served Bonn as surrogate diplomatic channels and as a
substitute for the outright diplomatic recognition that Bonn could not extend because of the
inhibitions of the Hallstein Doctrine. In subsequent years West Germany's trade with
Eastern Europe (and the Soviet Union) remained an important political mode of communication and increased in intrinsic importance as well. Although hampered by East-West
trade embargos and restrictions on technology transfers (which led to periodic abrasions
between Bonn and Washington), the West Germans generally remained firm in maintaining
Germany's historic trade relations with the East. See Heiner Ernst, *Der Osthandel. Eine
politische Waffe?* (Stuttgart: J. Fink, 1964); Michael Kreile, *Osthandel und Ostpolitik* (Baden-
Baden: Nomos, 1978); Rolf Krengel, *Die Bedeutung des Ost-West Handels für die Ost-West
Beziehungen* (Göttingen: Vanderhoeck & Ruprecht, 1967); Hermann Clement and Petra
Pissula, *Die Wirtschaftsbeziehungen zwischen der BRD und der Sowjetunion. Entwicklung, Bestim-
mungsfaktoren und Perspektive* (Hamburg: Weltarchiv, 1976); Matthias Schmitt, "Ökono-
mische Perspektiven in der Ostpolitik," *Aussenpolitik* 22, no. 4 (1971): 193–208; Angela Stent,
From Embargo to Ostpolitik: The Political Economy of West German-Soviet Relations, 1955–1980
(Cambridge: Cambridge University Press, 1981).

fundamentally at odds with developments in Europe. Although many Europeans welcomed some diplomatic flexibility in maneuvering between the two superpowers, most everyone understood that whatever room for maneuver was available could not possibly entail a rearrangement of the borders in Europe. On the contrary, it was precisely the general acceptance in both parts of Europe of the territorial status quo that was the irreducible precondition for political change—as de Gaulle had acknowledged when he recognized the Oder-Neisse frontier in 1959 before he launched his diplomatic campaigns in the East. By refusing to accept this precondition, Bonn undercut from the beginning its initiatives in Eastern Europe and condemned them to political irrelevance. Again it was East Berlin, not Bonn, that was more closely attuned to what the changing East-West context required (and portended) with respect to the German question.

Bonn's refusal to sanction the European status quo was of course connected with its determination to deny recognition to the East German regime and isolate it in the Eastern bloc—an explicit intention of Bonn's "policy of movement." But this was yet another fundamental miscalculation. The East European governments, which after all owed East Germany support and were highly sensitive to the policy guidelines set forth by the Kremlin, could hardly be expected to endorse Bonn's attempt to ostracize the East German regime. The diplomatic influence of the GDR within the Eastern bloc was increasing (as was symbolized by the Soviet-East German Friendship Treaty of 1964), and the possibility that Bonn's policy could create dissension among the countries of Eastern Europe or drive a wedge between them and the Soviet Union was dismissed by Schröder himself, when he suggested that such an attempt would presumably not only fail but place an even heavier burden on German-Soviet relations.[15] Although Bonn was willing to trade and talk with the countries of Eastern Europe, the Erhard government, constrained as it was by ingrained habits of thought and by conservative elements within the ruling CDU/CSU, could not develop a more positive attitude toward East Germany. Through this failure, Bonn denied itself the opportunity to pursue its Eastern policy on all three levels: vis-à-vis Moscow, Eastern Europe, and East Berlin.[16] By excluding East Germany (and to some extent even Moscow) from its more innovative diplomacy, Bonn constricted its diplomatic effort to Eastern Europe at the same time as it doomed that effort by withholding the major concession that could have impressed East European countries, the recognition of the territorial status quo in Europe.

Both on the grounds of refusing to deal with East Germany and on those of refusing to face squarely the reality of the status quo, Bonn was out of step with the trends of the European state system in the 1960s. At a time when polycentric developments were loosening the two alliances, when much of Europe was in diplomatic flux, and when France and Rumania became the symbols of a new and independent diplomacy, the frozen hostility between the two German states seemed like a solid and steady bracket that counteracted the centrifugal forces of Europe and the two alliances. The partition of Germany and the military balance seemed to be the most solid structures of the East-West contest. As Pierre Hassner noted at the time, "The German problem is the most rigidly stable element of the European picture. It is not the German problem which is again on the move, it is everything else in Europe which seems to be moving, and it is the German partition which, if only by its links with the presence of Soviet and American troops, constitutes not only the exception but also the limits of this movement."[17]

It may well be that the East Germans would not have been receptive to more accommodating West German overtures. They were at most interested only in some vague form of "confederation," and by 1965 the East German government had apparently stopped trying to obtain tacit recognition through increased contacts with the Federal Republic and had imposed considerably more stringent conditions on negotiations with Bonn (such as prior recognition).[18] This was exemplified in the abortive "speakers exchange program" of 1966, which had been initially suggested by the East Germans to foster a dialogue between prominent West German leaders of the SPD and East German speakers from the SED, and to air opposing views on the German question in both parts of Germany. Although the East Germans had agreed to a preliminary program, they later changed their minds, apparently because they did not want to enable effective West German speakers to address the East German people.[19]

Even so, the Erhard government might profitably have ceased seeking to isolate the East German regime, if only to put it on the defensive. Even a partial modification of Bonn's policy appeared risky, however. Because Bonn's diplomacy toward the Soviet bloc held together with logical (although self-defeating) juridical consistency, compromising one part would have compromised the whole, and scrapping one of its essential tenets would have caused the collapse of Bonn's entire legal-political reunification strategy and perhaps entailed a revision of its other foreign policy programs as well. A dynamic diplomatic offensive in Eastern Europe would have required recognition of the Oder-Neisse border and the renunciation of the Hallstein Doctrine. This would have undermined both the Four Powers' responsibility for all-German affairs (not because the Western powers supported Bonn's claim to the borders of 1937, but because Bonn argued that Germany's definitive borders could not be settled before a final peace conference), and Bonn's claim to sole representation of all Germans. This in turn would have destroyed the rationale for ostracizing the East German regime. In toto, these changes would have signaled a major reversal of Bonn's long-standing Germany policy, with important repercussions for Bonn's overall foreign policy program.

Neither Erhard's political temperament nor his quickly diminishing political fortunes allowed such a drastic reversal to take place. In spring 1966 Bonn renewed its efforts to reassure Eastern Europe of Germany's constructive attitude by promulgating a "peace note," which set forth proposals that were in effect watered-down versions of proposals initially made by Warsaw Pact countries.[20] These proposals did not offer important concessions on military-strategic matters before political solutions, nor did they change Bonn's determination to isolate East Germany diplomatically, deny it legal recognition, and insist on the provisional nature of Germany's eastern borders.

In any case, Erhard's compromise proposals came too late as far as the Soviet Union was concerned. During Khrushchev's later years the Soviet Union had initiated a more accommodating approach to Bonn (though it was short-lived) and proposed a nonaggression pact between NATO and the Warsaw Pact, thus implicitly including the United States and Canada in an arrangement for European arms control.[21] By contrast, Brezhnev's and Kosygin's proposal of the mid-1960s (as enunciated in the Bucharest declaration of July 1966) made no mention of nonaggression pacts and envisaged the dissolution of the two alliances and hence the elimination of the American presence from Europe.[22] During the 1960s the Soviet Union's European policies also were trying to adjust to the changing European political order and did not exhibit a clear-cut pattern, and Soviet diplomacy between the Cuban missile crisis and the 1968 Czech crisis was, as William Hyland characterized it, "an amorphous blur" that eluded a definitive analytical summary.[23] Faced with conflict within the Warsaw Pact over reforming the alliance and pressured by East Germany and Poland to apply a hard line toward Bonn, the Kremlin reiterated a series of tough demands: no German access to nuclear weapons, no change in the present frontiers in Europe, and recognition of the East German regime.

Bonn's Eastern Policies and Franco-German Relations

Bonn's revised reunification policy was deficient not only because of its misdirected and ineffective diplomatic thrust in the East, but also because Erhard and Schröder could not establish a working relationship with de Gaulle. Adenauer's central assumption that Moscow and Washington held the key to the German question continued to be valid in the 1960s but required some modification, because the loosening of the Western alliance and the Soviet bloc had increased the importance of France for resolving the German question. Even though Bonn did not manage to act on it, many Germans began to realize that reunification could be accomplished only in the context of a larger European settlement, and that in this context France was as important a partner for Germany's "opening to the East" as was the United States.

Generally, the fragmentation of the two Cold War blocs had increased the importance for German reunification of the secondary powers in both Western and Eastern Europe. There was a feeling in Bonn that neither Washington nor London had a program for reunification or a deep interest in it, and that both were geopolitically too detached to provide much long-range assistance for the cause of German unity. This was coupled with the feeling that, in the words of George Liska, "West Germany has no real substitute for France; only France can legitimize the German interest in reunification and in politically and otherwise unprovocative military rehabilitation in the eyes of the less forgiving smaller nations of Western and Central-Eastern Europe. She has, moreover, no apparent substitute for a strong France. Only such a France can combine diplomatic firmness with diplomatic flexibility in regard to the Soviet Union; the firmness is guaranteed and the flexibility is circumscribed by France's own need for West Germany if she is to have the respect of the Eastern as well as the Western super-power."[24]

This line of argument appeared especially plausible to the "Gaullists" in Bonn in light of the Johnson administration's growing involvement in Vietnam, which not only diminished Washington's stature in Europe but also seemed to reflect a redirection of American geostrategic preoccupations. Yet de Gaulle's determination to exclude the United States from a "Europe from the Atlantic to the Urals" was unacceptable to Bonn, not only because of security concerns but because the Germans suspected that de Gaulle's real interest in resolving the German question stemmed precisely from his desire to speed American withdrawal, to remove a main legitimization for the superpowers' presence in Europe, and to overcome a major obstacle to a more independent French foreign policy.[25]

In short, the debilitating problem that had plagued Bonn during the last years of the Adenauer regime—the need to choose between Washington and Paris on almost every important item on Bonn's foreign policy agenda—became even more pronounced during the Erhard years, when the centrifugal tendencies within the Eastern and Western alliances increased the leverage of France. In opting for the United States on most issues that divided Washington and Paris, Erhard also opted for a fundamentally static and conservative European policy, because Washington found the status quo in Europe entirely acceptable (as did Moscow). France, on the other hand, was fully committed to a dynamic foreign policy intended to exploit the changes taking place in Western and Eastern Europe, and de Gaulle might have supported some form of German-German arrangement in the restraining context of a Franco-Soviet security system.

One central feature of the West European state system in the 1960s, which reverberated into every aspect of East-West relations and Bonn's foreign policies, was that France and Germany pursued Eastern policies that were not only opposed but isolated. Neither Paris nor Bonn could obtain genuine support for its Eastern policies, in the West or in the East. Like the American government, de Gaulle was in effect revising France's own double-containment policy, which had since the beginning of the Cold War sought to solve the fundamental dilemma of French postwar foreign policy: reconciling the "goals of 1944" against Germany with the "goals of 1947" against the Soviet Union.[26] But the way de Gaulle sought to implement this policy in the 1960s, by carving out a third way between the superpowers and calling for a Europe from the Atlantic to the Urals, was for different reasons unacceptable to the United States, Britain, the Federal Republic, and ultimately the Soviet Union.

In the first place, de Gaulle's dynamic Eastern policies, which required maximum diplomatic mobility, had highly divisive and self-isolating consequences for his Western policies: French diplomacy threatened Washington's transatlantic Grand Design, led to the weakening of NATO, excluded Britain from the Common Market, called into question the future of West European integration, and met with Bonn's opposition on all counts. Second, the splendid isolation that de Gaulle achieved in the West could not be converted into a genuinely effective policy in the East. While the Soviet Union may have welcomed de Gaulle's role as a "spoiler" in the West, it was less enthusiastic about seeing him play that role in the East. In fact, de Gaulle's dynamic foreign policy was fully appreciated only in Eastern Europe, where it came to an end with the Soviet invasion of Czechoslovakia in 1968. "The determination of the superpowers to maintain the status quo in Europe, and the acceptance or acquiescence of the European countries (satisfied, resigned, or coerced, as the case was) in the international structure in which they lived . . . were too much for de Gaulle's farreaching and diverse attempts to change things. This was clear from 1963 on, however well de Gaulle's theater convinced many—to their horror or delight—of the contrary."[27]

Germany, which was pursuing frozen Eastern policies and equally static Western policies that were at least in part their consequence (such as the retardation of arms control), was similarly moving toward diplomatic positions that found little support in either the West or the East. Rather than isolate East Berlin, Bonn was isolating itself.[28] Although fundamentally different, both French and German policies toward the East were ultimately condemned to failure. It was symptomatic of what ailed Franco-German relations in the 1960s that the two major Western European powers, although themselves isolated on many of their most cherished foreign policy goals, could not find common ground for a genuinely supportive and constructive partnership. Fundamental considerations of "high" politics stood in the way, which also doomed the prospects for a more highly integrated Western Europe. What emerged was an involuted conflict between France and Germany, with both sides seeking a reconfiguration of the European political order, and with both sides ultimately thwarted by the durability of Europe's partition and the superpowers' intention to support it.

In their rivalry with the French, the Germans were at some disadvantage.[29] An essential element of de Gaulle's reorientation of French foreign policy was a loosening of ties with the Western alliance (especially the United States) and a corresponding readiness to establish closer contacts with the Soviet Union and Eastern Europe. Each new Gaullist success in Eastern Europe increased suspicions in Bonn that de Gaulle intended to place German reunification policy under French tutelage (with France acting as a broker rather than as Bonn's partner), or, even worse, that de Gaulle was toying with the idea of returning to his postwar plan for a Franco-Soviet understanding.[30] In 1964 de Gaulle warmly celebrated the twentieth anniversary of the Franco-Soviet alliance, extended seven-year credits to Moscow through a new trade agreement, and generally exhibited great cordiality toward the Soviet Union and East European countries. In his press conference of February 4, 1965, de Gaulle pointedly noted that German reunification was a European problem that would have to be settled largely by Germany's neighbors, implying that Germany as well as the United States would play a secondary role in the settlement. Both dimensions of French foreign policy—loosening ties with the West, creating ties with the East—were highlighted by de Gaulle's decision to withdraw from NATO in 1966 and by his state visits to the Soviet Union in 1966 and Poland in 1967. The principle of "détente, entente, cooperation" that de Gaulle held out to the Soviet Union and the East bloc countries implied exclusion of the United States from a European settlement, and this intention was unacceptable to Bonn. The shift toward a Franco-Soviet accommodation had a profound impact on Franco-German relations not only because it called into question a long-standing premise of Bonn's reunification policy (that Bonn would as much as possible support French Atlantic policy and European policy if France would support Bonn's Eastern policy), but because it also served notice to Bonn that de Gaulle intended to exploit fully the new international circumstances, at Germany's expense if necessary.[31]

West Germany, on the other hand, had little diplomatic maneuverability. Bonn's close alignment with the United States curtailed diplomatic initiatives, the Germans were handicapped in seeking a rapprochement in the East by the historical burdens of the past as well as by the rigidity of their policies of the present, and the distant relations between Bonn and Moscow deprived Bonn of effective access to the center of Soviet bloc power in the Kremlin. "It was . . . more logical to attempt, as de Gaulle did, to encourage separatism in Eastern Europe and *at the same time* cultivate good relations with the Soviet Union than it was to attempt, as the Federal Government did, to encourage separatism in Eastern Europe and yet oppose any extension of the Soviet-American détente as inimical to German interests. De Gaulle could appear to exploit the Soviet-American relationship, and thus seemed to be anti-American; the Federal Government frequently appeared to oppose it, and thus seemed to be anti-Russian" (italics in original).[32]

Little Steps toward East Germany: The Ostpolitik of the Grand Coalition

The Grand Coalition government of Christian Democrats and Social Democrats, which replaced the Erhard government late in 1966, had its origin in an economic crisis that led to a political crisis, and it was not well suited for revitalizing Bonn's foreign policies.[33] Only rarely did the Grand Coalition speak with one voice, and the foreign policy checks and balances that were built into the Grand Coalition not only diluted specific policy measures but fostered an attrition of governmental accountability.[34] Even so, there was some hope that the new government could overcome the impasse of Bonn's reunification policy and avoid as much as possible the damaging consequences of making choices between Washington and Paris. Generally, Chancellor Kiesinger and Foreign Minister Brandt were committed to a more imaginative foreign policy and a more assertive stance vis-à-vis the United States, and they hoped to harmonize Bonn's transatlantic and West European policies.[35] Erhard had been forced to resign at least in part because of his irresolute diplomacy, which had been widely criticized for contributing to the deterioration of Franco-German relations and for failing to further the cause of German unity.

Moreover, the SPD had for many years pressed for a more open-minded and innovative reunification policy, and favored contact with East German officials. Their presence in the government clearly meant that they intended to put some of their ideas into practice. Kiesinger and Brandt were determined to move beyond the Erhard government's hesitant foreign policy revisions and to attune German policy to the changing circumstances of the 1960s. The Grand Coalition's explicit declarations that Bonn would welcome an improvement in East-West relations even if it were not preceded by progress on the German question thus constituted a significant modification of policy. This was also reflected in Bonn's willingness to discuss arms control measures and other East-West agreements even if they were not directly linked to the issue of reunification.

The new departure in Bonn's Eastern policy was soon given verbal and symbolic expression.[36] In widely reported speeches, Kiesinger declared no longer valid the Munich Agreement of 1938 (in which Czechoslovakia ceded territory to Germany), which eased Bonn's relations with Czechoslovakia;[37] he expressed Bonn's desire for a fundamental reconciliation with Poland and intimated that even though Bonn could not relinquish its legal claim to sole representation of the German people, it was prepared to accept the East German government de facto and would not object to a European renunciation-of-force agreement that both Germanies would sign. In response to Walter Ulbricht's new year's message of 1967, in which he spelled out a number of stringent preconditions for a confederation of the two German states (among others that relations be normalized, Bonn renounce nuclear control in any form, an agreement be reached that West Berlin would develop into an autonomous territory, existing borders be recognized, and armaments be mutually reduced), Bonn made numerous suggestions, including fewer restrictions on travel, expanded trade and credit arrangements and other economic projects, cultural and news-media exchanges, coordination of communication networks, and linkage of energy markets.

Although East Berlin's response was largely negative, there followed an unprecedented exchange of letters and other communications between Chancellor Kiesinger and Willi Stoph, head of the East German cabinet, which was notable not so much for its content—both sides reiterated their familiar positions—as for the semiofficial status it lent to intra-German contacts. It was a significant achievement of the Grand Coalition to have made this opening to East Berlin, considering in addition the coalition's diverse domestic political constituency on the German question. It represented the recognition that Bonn's Germany policy was condemned to stagnation if it would not proceed on all three levels (toward East Germany as well as toward Eastern Europe and the Soviet Union), and it provided a basis of continuity for Germany's new Ostpolitik when Willy Brandt became chancellor in 1969.[38]

Bonn's efforts to establish closer relations with Moscow and East Berlin were largely failures: the Kremlin persisted in a generally negative attitude,[39] and in 1968 the East Germans put new pressures on the access routes to West Berlin, imposing stringent passport and visa requirements. But the initial responses in some East European capitals were more encouraging. The most visible result of the Grand Coalition's initiative in Eastern Europe was the opening of diplomatic relations with Rumania in January 1967 (which had been initiated during the Erhard administration), the establishment of a trade mission in Prague in August 1967, and the resumption of diplomatic relations with Yugoslavia in early 1968. Although Kiesinger used the occasion of the German-Rumanian agreement to reemphasize Bonn's claim to sole representation of the German people, it was clear that the claim and its diplomatic corollary, the Hallstein Doctrine, were in effect being shelved.

It would indeed have been difficult to maintain that the Hallstein

Doctrine was in full effect when two German states, each speaking for its own territory and population, were fully accredited in Bucharest and Belgrade as well as in Moscow. Even so, the Grand Coalition, under pressure from conservative elements in the CDU/CSU, sought to maintain the legal shadow if not the political substance of the doctrine. To exempt the East European countries from its applicability Bonn now reinterpreted the Hallstein Doctrine, saying it should not apply to countries that had no free choice in the matter of recognizing the East German regime because of their imposed membership in the Soviet bloc. This so-called "birthmark" theory could of course not cover Yugoslavia, for Tito had recognized the Ulbricht regime in 1957 on his own volition. Before allowing Belgrade a dispensation from the birthmark theory, Bonn was careful to make sure that this further watering down of an already watered-down version of the Hallstein Doctrine would not trigger a mass recognition of East Germany by Third World countries.[40]

But now that Bonn was opening up lines of communication with Eastern Europe, it was the East German government that resorted to contractual formulas to constrain Bonn's diplomatic offensive. After Bonn had established diplomatic relations with Rumania, the East Germans formulated a "Hallstein Doctrine" of their own (later known as the "Ulbricht Doctrine"), insisting that no socialist country open diplomatic relations with the Federal Republic until Bonn was ready to recognize East Germany, accept the existing borders in Europe, renounce any nuclear role, and recognize West Berlin as a separate political unit.

When the East Germans presented this proposal to the Warsaw Conference of Foreign Ministers in February 1967, it did not gain official endorsement, primarily because of Rumanian objections. But during spring 1967 the East German formula was at least partly accepted and formalized through a series of bilateral agreements with Poland, Czechoslovakia, Hungary, and Bulgaria, in which these countries called for normalizing relations between the two German states, a security guarantee among neighboring states, and the defeat of "militarism and neo-Nazism" in West Germany. The signatories also stressed the permanence of present borders and characterized West Berlin as a separate or even independent unit. East Germany had already succeeded in incorporating its demands in the Bucharest declaration of the Warsaw Pact countries in July 1966, but they were not specifically connected with the issue of the recognition of the Federal Republic by East European countries.[41] These contractual obligations were buttressed by the Karlovy Vary Conference of European Communist Parties in April 1967, which generally endorsed the East German demands even though it did not, as some members suggested, formulate an injunction that would have prevented Eastern European states from establishing diplomatic relations with Bonn unless the West German government fully recognized East Germany. The conference issued a communiqué that endorsed East Germany's stand on border questions and nuclear matters, however, and called on West Germany to drop its claim to sole representation of the German people as a precondition for normalizing relations with Eastern Europe.[42]

In effect, the East bloc countries had formed a contractual "iron triangle" based on friendship and mutual assistance treaties, consisting of the GDR, Poland, and Czechoslovakia, later to include Hungary and Bulgaria. East Germany, which until then was connected only to Moscow with a friendship treaty, had now obtained a multilateral commitment supporting its position on the Germany and Berlin questions. The Grand Coalition's Ostpolitik produced the opposite result from the one intended: East Germany was not being isolated but integrated, the Warsaw Pact's position on the German question was not loosening but tightening, the difficulties of addressing the German question had increased and not decreased.[43]

As was the case during the Erhard administration, Bonn's difficulties in charting a more dynamic approach to Eastern Europe resulted not only from East German countermeasures and the Kremlin's resistance but also from its own political and conceptual inhibitions. Some of these inhibitions were unavoidable. Clearly, Bonn's Eastern policy could not be as flexible and consistent as France's, because no German government could have matched de Gaulle's disavowal of NATO or his disdain of the United States, even if it had wanted to. Other handicaps were largely self-imposed. Although the new government made hesitant efforts to move beyond the entrenched Cold War positions of its predecessors, and although long-established central tenets of Bonn's foreign policy were modified, the Grand Coalition (especially its more conservative members and supporters) did not entirely stop trying or hoping to extract concessions from the Soviet bloc in return for a more accommodating West German stand on West Berlin, the nuclear nonproliferation treaty, the recognition of East Germany, or the Oder-Neisse border.

The Oder-Neisse issue is a case in point. On the question of the German-Polish frontier, Bonn's position had been ambivalent and inconsistent all along. In spite of Schröder's efforts to normalize relations with Eastern Europe, the Erhard administration had persisted in arguing that a final settlement of Germany's Eastern borders must be preceded by the establishment of an all-German government, holding out to Poland the unacceptable prospect of having to deal with a united Germany on a vital question. Not surprisingly, the Polish government and the Kremlin pictured East Germany as the indispensable bulwark for maintaining Polish security vis-à-vis West Germany, and castigated Bonn for harboring revanchist designs. East European attitudes on the Oder-Neisse frontier and other issues stemmed from what these countries and the Soviet Union perceived to be genuine national interests; in fact, they symbolized the partial convergence of communist and national interests, which frequently characterized the foreign policies of East European countries toward the Federal Republic and were cemented by Bonn's inflexible Eastern policies. As long as Bonn's policy was based on the claim that a final settlement of Germany's frontiers rested with the Four Powers, there was at least some rationale for questioning their permanence (although the Western powers had never committed themselves to support reestablishment of the German borders of 1937). When this claim was augmented by the assumption that reunification required a fundamental German rapprochement with Eastern Europe, an obstinate West German position on the Oder-Neisse question became even more damaging to the prospects for reunification and more at odds with the basic strategy for realizing it than had been the case during the Adenauer period.

Influential policymakers in Bonn realized that reunification and frontier revision were incompatible goals, especially in the context of the Grand Coalition's more flexible Eastern policy. In his inaugural statement, Chancellor Kiesinger made no mention of Bonn's traditional demand for the "borders of 1937," and he implied that Bonn would accept the Oder-Neisse frontier as the eastern border of a united Germany. The issue of whether to recognize the Oder-Neisse border strained the Grand Coalition from the beginning. It was brought out in the open in spring 1968, when Foreign Minister Brandt, speaking not in his official capacity but as the leader of the Social Democrats, defied the long-time policy of the Christian Democrats and called for "recognition and respect" of the Oder-Neisse border, until a peace treaty would settle the issue definitively.[44]

The questionable rationale behind Bonn's attempt to trade juridical concessions for diplomatic and political gains was also exemplified by Bonn's equivocations about the Nuclear Nonproliferation Treaty. Eastern European capitals could hardly be expected to accept calmly a nuclear decision-making role for Bonn: distrust of German intentions ran high, and a West German role in nuclear decision making would have significantly altered the Central European balance of power, for a similar role for East European countries within the Soviet bloc was only a remote possibility. It is however doubtful whether Bonn's tacit offer to withdraw the implicit threat of gaining a nuclear voice could have succeeded in converting East European apprehensions into the conciliatory attitudes Bonn wished to foster. Considering the burden of Germany's past actions in Eastern Europe, the use of veiled threats was a psychologically inept way to dispel suspicions and to create a climate of opinion favorable to reunification. Although the Grand Coalition's attitude toward the nonproliferation treaty was much more realistic than that of the Erhard government (Willy Brandt's attitude was especially so), influential decision makers, including cabinet members, persisted in opposing the non-proliferation treaty purely in terms of power politics, making it difficult for the government as a whole to dissociate itself from the implied threat of this position.

The Reversals of August 1968

Even before the Soviet invasion of Czechoslovakia in August 1968, the Grand Coalition's diplomatic initiatives in Eastern Europe had been largely arrested. All the same, the invasion had major implications for Bonn's Eastern policies. In the first place, the failure of the liberal experiment in Czechoslovakia undermined some major assumptions of Bonn's long-range unification strategy. The events of summer 1968 made clear that the Soviet Union and some of its allies would not tolerate a weakening of the bloc's forward position in Central Europe and that the Soviet Union was determined to uphold its sphere of influence even if this required the use of force. This may not have come as a large surprise to many Western statesmen, but it did bring into focus the conflicting perceptions of the West and the Soviet Union on the meaning and extent of coexistence and détente in the 1960s.[45] For Bonn, the significance of the invasion lay less in its impact on the question of German unity itself—even before August 1968 the prospects were remote—than in the feeling of frustration and resignation it engendered in Germany.[46] What appeared to have been a rational, temperate, and at least superficially plausible Germany policy seemed to have been invalidated by events that further cemented the division of Europe and gave political encouragement to those in the Federal Republic who had opposed Bonn's more flexible course to begin with.

This is not to say that the Grand Coalition's "opening to the East" was ill conceived. There was considerable moral and political merit in Bonn's willingness to pursue reconciliation with Eastern Europe in the hope that increased contacts would lead to an eventual solution of the German question, or at the very least facilitate the rehabilitation of Germany in Eastern Europe. In any case, it was difficult to conceive of any feasible diplomatic alternative that would not have condemned the Federal Republic to an increasingly outmoded, static, and intransigent role in the flexible interplay between East and West that characterized the 1960s. Nonetheless, after the invasion Bonn was faced with a significantly different situation. There remained little reason to expect that meeting Soviet demands would advance the cause of German unity, because it now seemed likely that East European developments favorable to reunification would be met by the Soviets with a physical "veto," whereas Bonn's acquiescence in Soviet demands would further undermine the familiar foundations of its Eastern policy and arouse domestic criticism.

There was also a subtle but direct and important connection between

Bonn's new Eastern policy and the events of August 1968. Even though Moscow was not adverse to a bilateral accommodation between Washington and Moscow, the Kremlin strongly opposed having its allies pursue dynamic and independent policies of coexistence with the Western powers at the periphery of the Soviet bloc. A multilateral policy of relaxation might upset the bilateral foundations for a Soviet-American understanding by erasing the clear delineation between the two spheres of influence in Central Europe. For strategic and political reasons, the Soviet Union needed to retain the triangle formed by East Berlin, Warsaw, and Prague, which anchored Moscow's "forward" policy in Europe. By making the establishment of closer ties with West Germany a divisive issue in the Soviet bloc, the smaller successes of Bonn's Ostpolitik in Eastern Europe helped start a chain of events that led to a larger failure. Moscow might have continued to tolerate the growing economic and political contacts between Bonn and Prague if by mid-1968 Czechoslovakian liberalization had not threatened the Communist Party's continued control, creating the risk that Prague might reorient its foreign policy along with its domestic political order. Because Bonn's Eastern policy was instrumental in establishing a conducive international setting within which Prague could extend the liberalization of its domestic policy to foreign policy, the Kremlin's clamp-down on Czechoslovakia simultaneously dealt Bonn's Eastern policy a decisive blow.[47] This was especially serious in that the Eastern bloc cited as part of its justification for intervening in Czechoslovakia the massive West German credits and favorable trade terms that Bonn had extended to Prague—an accusation that was echoed in France and led to an acrimonious exchange between Chancellor Kiesinger and General de Gaulle.[48] Moscow and Paris were blaming Bonn for what had happened in Prague.

The "freezing" of the East European political arena that resulted from the Soviet invasion reemphasized for Bonn the importance of the other two major arenas—Moscow and East Berlin. The invasion demonstrated unequivically that the key to a rearranged European order lay in Moscow, and that Bonn's diplomacy needed to shift its priorities if it expected to influence the rearrangement. The GDR's diplomatic influence in the Eastern bloc increased after the invasion;[49] and "where in the past Bonn saw the most favorable prospects in courting East Europe first, the USSR second, and East Germany third, if at all, after August [1968] the USSR emerged clearly as the overwhelmingly dominant bargaining partner and even East Germany gained in stature after a fashion. This meant that [Bonn needed to] think more seriously than ever before about what [had] hitherto been deemed impermissible concessions, on the GDR, on the frontiers, and on nuclear weapons."[50] All this greatly complicated Bonn's policy at a time when the three-level approach had just been put into tentative operation with a more conciliatory attitude toward East Berlin.

After years of frustration with a static and apparently hopeless reunification program, a more dynamic German policy in Eastern Europe had provided a constructive outlet for West German political energies, especially because Bonn could make use of its economic potential, which it had long sought to convert into a political asset.[51]

The freezing of the East European arena not only compelled Bonn to redirect its diplomatic efforts toward Moscow and East Berlin, but also diminished the importance for German reunification of Germany's neighbors, notably France. The events of August 1968 marked the arrest of the polycentric developments in Europe of the 1960s, reintroduced a polarization of the European political order, and in the process incapacitated German and French Ostpolitik. On the other hand, American policy toward the Soviet Union was hardly affected. Much like the Soviet Union, the United States had no interest in revising the European status quo; and Washington's interest in reducing Soviet-American tensions and in reaching an arms control arrangement with the Soviet Union was so compelling that a few weeks after the invasion Washington resumed talks with Moscow. It was more apparent than ever that the United States and the Soviet Union had tacitly agreed to respect one another's spheres of influence and thus were not about to redraw them.[52]

Perhaps most important, the Soviet invasion demonstrated to Bonn that it needed to improve its relations with East Berlin. But the burdens of the past lay heavily on the Kiesinger government. During the years of Adenauer and Erhard, East Germany had been nothing more than an object of Bonn's policy, especially when Bonn explicitly sought to isolate the East German government from its partners in the Warsaw Pact and from its own people. By denying the German Democratic Republic formal recognition, Bonn in effect imposed harsher conditions for normalizing relations with East Germany than it did on East European capitals. (This punitive double standard was in a sense reemphasized by the Grand Coalition's revision of the Hallstein Doctrine, because the revision weakened Bonn's claim to sole representation of all Germans but did not lead to a reversal of Bonn's nonrecognition policy.)[53] Moreover, to the extent that Bonn justified its hard line toward East Germany by stressing the Four Powers' continuing legal and political responsibility for all-German affairs, it weakened its own case by taking independent initiatives on the German question. Bonn was torn between conflicting considerations. Its entire Eastern policy was clearly based on the political premise that a Four Power settlement was not politically feasible in the foreseeable future and that the Western powers had not pressed Bonn's claims hard enough. But its legal premise necessarily remained focused on the Four Powers' continuing responsibility for all-German affairs and the Western Allies' contractual obligations to aid Bonn in achieving unification. Political realism clashed with juridical formalism.

By the late 1960s it had become incontrovertible that a forward-looking Germany policy demanded that Bonn view East Germany as a potential partner and not only as an opponent, and that German unity ultimately depended on the willingness of both German states to arrive at a mutually acceptable modus vivendi. There was a widespread desire in West Germany to establish closer contacts with the East German people and encourage an internal liberalization of the East German regime; and there was also the recognition that the contradictions between the punitive and conciliatory aspects of Bonn's policies toward East Berlin could be only superficially reconciled with the argument that the former was directed toward East Germany's regime and the latter toward its people. The East German regime was not entirely unsuccessful in gaining support for the sweeping economic, social, and political transformations it had made since 1949; and it was highly doubtful that given a free choice, the people of East Germany would have wished simply to adopt the institutional, political, and socioeconomic system of the Federal Republic. Unpopular as the East German regime may have been in certain respects, one could not deny its economic and social achievements, with which many East Germans could identify precisely because they had made them possible with their own labors and sacrifices. This made it psychologically hazardous for outsiders (especially the affluent West Germans) to denigrate the regime too indiscriminately.[54]

It was the recognition of these developments as much as the desire for a more flexible reunification policy that had led the Grand Coalition to reexamine Bonn's policy toward East Germany. But aside from the opposition that Bonn encountered in East Germany and the Soviet bloc, Bonn most likely had added to its difficulties with the East Germans by conducting its reunification policy over the years in a style that could not help but grate on the political sensitivities of East German decision makers. In terms of Realpolitik, it made little difference that East Germany's leadership fully deserved to have its sensitivities violated: its conduct within East Germany and along the border had over the years provided ample justification for ostracizing it. But there was a special psychological edge to the relationship between the two Germanies, and even the Grand Coalition's principle of "acceptance without recognition" was not sufficiently positive to cut through the long-accumulated layers of ill will.[55] It required a more fundamental and sweeping acceptance of the weight of historical necessity that was pressing down on Bonn's Eastern policies. Almost a quarter-century after the end of the Second World War, it required that Bonn face the East with the same realism with which Adenauer and his successors had dealt with the West during the first two decades of the Federal Republic. It required a new Ostpolitik.

7

A New Ostpolitik for the 1970s and 1980s

If one wants to dismantle the boundary markers of Europe one must cease trying to move them.

—WILLY BRANDT, 1970

A free-wheeling, powerful Germany trying to maneuver between East and West, whatever its ideology, posed the classic challenge to the equilibrium of Europe, for whichever side Germany favored would emerge as predominant. . . . We were determined to spare no effort to mute the latent incompatibility between Germany's national aims and its Atlantic and European ties.

—HENRY KISSINGER

Soon after the SPD-FDP coalition government of Willy Brandt and Walter Scheel took office in October 1969, it became clear that the new government intended to pursue a highly dynamic policy toward the East. Although the election of 1969 had not been fought over foreign policy issues (economics and educational reform were most prominent), a new Ostpolitik was the primary political purpose that brought the Social Democrats and Free Democrats together in a coalition.[1]

The new Ostpolitik that Bonn initiated in the late 1960s and early 1970s extends with a remarkable continuity into the 1980s. Although controversial both at home and abroad at its inception, the Eastern policies put forward by the new government have become the mainstay of Bonn's Germany policy, basically unaffected by the changes of government that brought to the chancellorship Helmut Schmidt in 1974 and Helmut Kohl in 1982. The Schmidt government reaffirmed the major outlines of the Ostpolitik it had inherited (although its most dramatic

195

results had by then been achieved); the much-touted political "turning point" claimed by the Kohl government upon entering office specifically excluded Ostpolitik, where the new chancellor announced the intention to proceed with continuity; and adherence to Ostpolitik was a precondition for the FDP's becoming a partner in the center-right coalition of 1982.[2] There have been modifications in nuance, emphasis, and rhetoric, as well as changes in the international political environment and diplomatic climate in which Bonn's Ostpolitik needed to proceed, but there has been no fundamental redirection of Bonn's own policies. During the last two decades Bonn's Ostpolitik has obtained a similar measure of legitimacy, on the domestic as well as foreign political scene, as that which became attached to German Westpolitik during the first two decades of the Federal Republic. Basically, Bonn's Ostpolitik proved durable because at its inception it reflected policies whose time had come, because it served fundamental interests of the Federal Republic, and because there emerged no reasonable alternative to it in the future.

Change and Continuity: Matching Ostpolitik and Westpolitik

For reasons of history, geography, and the question of German unity, the aspirations reflected in the Western policies of détente of the 1960s were especially pertinent to the Federal Republic. Bonn hoped that by attuning its diplomacy to the dynamics of détente it could keep pace with major political developments in Europe and retain German leverage in the various political, strategic, and economic issues contested between the Atlantic alliance and the Warsaw Pact. Bonn's Ostpolitik, which spanned all these issues and reached across the two alliances, was thus an important element in the interest calculations of both sides, not because Bonn acted as a "balancer" between East and West (this was neither intended nor possible) but because Willy Brandt's Ostpolitik was the sine qua non for an accommodation in Central Europe.[3]

The ideas behind Bonn's new Ostpolitik were not new. By the late 1960s it had become apparent that the German question had become Europeanized, and that it needed to be transformed from an issue that implied the enlargement of territory into an issue of enlarging human contacts between the German people and of improved relations between the two German governments. The Europeanization and deterritorialization of the German question were inevitably connected: both were the consequence of the changing international environment surrounding the German question. Bonn's new Ostpolitik therefore envisaged a "European peace order," a European context in which the Germans would achieve not reunification (the term was for all practical purposes dropped by the new government) but a solution to the German question through a gradual process of "change through rapprochement," which would in turn lead to a regulated coexistence (*geregeltes Nebeneinander*) in Europe.

Bonn hoped that this new European order would establish in the long run a peaceful context for solving the German question by providing a pluralistic political order that would respect ideological and other diversities and deemphasize the territorial base of the European state system. Although the Brandt government no longer spoke of unifying the two Germanies, it fully subscribed to George F. Kennan's remark, made many years before, that "if Germany had to be united, then she must be a part of something larger than herself. A united Germany could be tolerable only as an integral part of a united Europe."[4]

The Brandt government was determined to render complementary what had been conflicting elements of Bonn's previous Eastern policies, and to combine them into a logically and politically consistent package: to accept the reality of the GDR and lend it some measure of juridical legitimacy with the principle of "two German states within one German nation," to accept the Europeanization and deterritorialization of the German question and along with it the legitimization of the general European territorial status quo, and to approach the Soviet Union and Eastern Europe with a diplomacy that conveyed accommodation and rapprochement rather than threats to the existing border arrangements in Central and Eastern Europe. This meant above all that Brandt was willing to renounce a central diplomatic principle of the Adenauer years, which had already deteriorated throughout the 1960s—that progress on the German question would have to precede a fundamental rapprochement with the East—and was ready to replace it with the reverse principle that a further deepening of the split between East and West Germany could be averted only on the basis of such a rapprochement. The Brandt government was willing to do its part in legitimizing the territorial status quo in Central Europe, and bring West German foreign policy in line with the explicit demands of the Eastern countries and the implicit expectations of its Western allies.

Chancellor Brandt was convinced that the time had come to reach an accommodation with the East—twenty-five years after the end of the Second World War and fifteen years after the Adenauer government had reached a formal reconciliation with the West in the Paris Treaties of 1954—and move beyond the stale confrontations of the past and instill a new sense of realism into Bonn's foreign policy. Brandt believed that for moral as well as political reasons West Germany should face up to the consequences of the Second World War and the Cold War, and adjust the style as well as the content of its foreign policy to the realities of the 1970s. Bonn's new Ostpolitik was intended to put together a coherent political agenda in the East that was characterized by the same degree of political logic, clarity of purpose, and conciliatory intent that had characterized Adenauer's Western diplomacy in the 1950s. The sense of the possible, the necessary, and the inevitable that had given Konrad Adenauer's

policies of the fifties their compelling dynamic were in the 1970s personified by Willy Brandt and exemplified in the Eastern policies he pursued.[5]

There was a deeper symmetry as well. At the core of Adenauer's
integration policies in the West had been the eagerness to transcend the
outmoded preoccupations with national borders and the divisive policies
and emotions that had traditionally accompanied them and brought such
misfortunes to Europe. The historical logic and moral suasion of Adenauer's Western policies had their source in his determination to make
territorial issues disappear in Western Europe and create an integrated
state system in which national boundaries would lose their political,
economic, and emotional significance. At the core of Willy Brandt's Eastern policies was a similar intent, carried forward by a similar political and
moral determination: based not on the illusion that the political, economic, and ideological circumstances of Eastern Europe or East Germany
would in the foreseeable future permit a process of East-West "integration"—that seemed unlikely—but on the recognition that entertaining
territorial aspirations in the East was as politically outmoded and morally
questionable as in the West. Brandt was determined to convey to the
East, which had suffered at German hands perhaps more than the West,
the same measure of political accommodation and moral sensitivity that
Adenauer had extended to the West. By the early 1970s Bonn's Eastern
policies began to match on political as well as moral grounds its Western
policies, which had become the foundation of the Federal Republic's
foreign policy.[6]

East-West Détente and Ostpolitik

The new Ostpolitik did not drift away from these foundations, but
rather reaffirmed and augmented them, making them the irreducible
base for Bonn's new initiatives in the East. Bonn was careful to stress the
continuity of West German foreign policy vis-à-vis the Western alliance as
well as the East, and made clear that it had no intention of loosening its
ties to the West. Bonn was fully aware that its dealings with the Soviet
Union and Eastern Europe would be dangerous and self-defeating without the backing of the Western allies; and on such issues as the status of
West Berlin, the United States, Britain, and France were of necessity
directly and formally involved. Because the Brandt government made a
satisfactory resolution of the Berlin question the precondition to any West
German accommodation with the East, the symbolic and practical involvement of the Western powers in Bonn's Ostpolitik was assured.

Throughout its negotiations with the East, Bonn took great pains to
keep its allies informed, not only to avoid the impression that Germany
might by toying with a neutralist policy between East and West, but
because Bonn was genuinely convinced that it could succeed in its approach to the East only with the support of the West. Willy Brandt and

the new minister of defense, Helmut Schmidt, stressed the antecedents rather than the new departures of Bonn's Ostpolitik and how it augmented the general détente policy of the West. They made repeated assurances that West Germany would not become a "floating kidney" or "wanderer between the two worlds," and reiterated their commitment to NATO, the Paris Treaties of 1954, and their own constitution.[7] In short, Bonn vehemently denied that Ostpolitik meant a movement toward neutrality.

The extraordinarily defensive nature of these justifications pointed to the sensitivity and reservations with which the Western powers responded to Bonn's initiatives in the East. For even though Bonn's Ostpolitik followed rather than preceded other dynamic Western approaches to the East, the initial response to Ostpolitik of their partners demonstrated to the Germans that their own approach called for a delicate balance of movement and restraint.[8] Especially in Washington and Paris, there remained the deep-seated suspicion that by recognizing the status quo in Europe the German government hoped to change it, and indeed this was the Germans' intention.[9] For Bonn, however, changing the status quo did not mean changing territorial arrangements but transforming the political confrontations of Europe into more amicable relations. Even so, Bonn's allies were aware that underneath Bonn's acceptance of the status quo lay longer-range calculations and deeper aspirations that they found disquieting and ultimately threatening.[10] Bonn's protestations to the contrary notwithstanding, Ostpolitik contained at least the seeds of future German neutralism, irrespective of the intentions of the current German government. Washington was clearly concerned about the continuing viability of its postwar double-containment policy, and some of its original architects (such as Dean Acheson) were among the most vociferous critics of Bonn's Ostpolitik, seeing in it a dangerous and alarming departure from Bonn's past diplomatic practice of conducting its Eastern policies under American tutelage.

But the Nixon administration faced a somewhat paradoxical situation. German willingness to accept the status quo and a less confrontational modus vivendi in Europe helped cement and stabilize the territorial and political realities of the European state system; and the Germans seemed ready to offer their official and long-overdue assent to Washington's own policy of recognizing the legitimacy of the East-West boundaries of Europe and the political realities they circumscribed. Throughout the 1960s the Germans had been accused of not keeping pace with developments and obstructing or retarding the solution of important East-West issues (such as arms control) because of their determination to deny legitimacy to East Germany and the existing European border arrangements. By accepting and encouraging a redefinition of the German question and turning it from an essentially territorial issue into an issue of enlarged human contacts, Bonn offered an unobjectionable political and moral rationale for its Eastern policies. It was difficult for the Western powers to find plausible public reasons for opposing Bonn's initiatives in the East, and equally difficult to obstruct them politically unless Washington resorted to such crude diplomatic instruments as asserting the continuing right of the Western powers to deal with matters pertaining to all-German affairs. Henry Kissinger alluded to this possibility in his memoirs, phrasing the matter quite delicately, however, in his use of the term *tools*: "Whatever the [Soviet] strategy, its purpose was to divide the Alliance and isolate us. But we were not without recourse. The Federal Republic did not have the bargaining tools to conduct its *Ostpolitik* on a purely national basis—and our other allies could not do without our security umbrella. On Berlin the negotiating strength of the two sides was too unequal; with the city isolated and East Germany occupied, the Federal Republic needed the support of its allies."[11]

The reactions to Bonn's Ostpolitik in the West demonstrated how carefully the Germans needed to balance diplomatic innovation with diplomatic tradition. Too little readiness to support East-West accommodation had in the past brought charges of obstructionism (especially when Bonn dragged its feet on arms control); too much enthusiasm for détente raised fears that Bonn would weaken its ties to the West to create better prospects for German unity. The suspicion that the Federal Republic was an actual or potential revisionist European power, prepared to unhinge the status quo for the sake of German unity if given the opportunity, was close to the surface of many of the political, military-strategic, and economic issues that were contested between Bonn and other capitals. The pace and direction of Bonn's Ostpolitik required careful calibration so as to mesh them with the involuted double dynamics that surrounded the German question: its broader East-West dimension involving the two superpowers, and its narrower (but older) dimension involving Germany's neighbors.

These dual dimensions assured as well the centrality of Bonn's Ostpolitik in the diplomatic calculations of the Soviet Union. Since its establishment the Federal Republic had in effect been involved in two distinct conflicts with the Soviet Union: the general East-West conflict, and a more specific German-Soviet conflict over the division of Germany and the issue of German borders. So long as the Federal Republic persisted in pressing forward its narrower conflict, it could not accept without severe reservations the general détente policies that its Western allies began to pursue in the 1960s. This was a major reason why Bonn had drifted into diplomatic isolation and burdened its diplomacy in other important areas: its Western alliance policies, relations to the developing nations in Africa and Asia, and even European integration. A major purpose of the new Ostpolitik was to get out of that corner.[12] Both alliances were preoccupied with détente, as was reflected by American, British, and French policies and NATO's acceptance of Soviet nuclear-strategic equality, as well as by the Soviet shift from the Bucharest proposal of July 1966, which called for a European security system aimed at dissolving the Atlantic alliance, to the much more modest Budapest proposal of March 1969, which did not question the participation of the alliance and its members in a European security arrangement. By the late 1960s it had become clear to the Soviet Union that a policy aimed at disintegrating NATO could not succeed, but that a policy aimed at stabilizing and legitimizing the European status quo could obtain the consent of the Federal Republic, the indispensable partner in this large diplomatic enterprise.

From Moscow's perspective, the developments of the early 1970s were of a magnitude perhaps unparalleled in postwar Soviet diplomacy. The Soviet Union had all along aspired to be a superpower equal to the United States, an aspiration that lacked plausibility except in two important areas: the Soviet Union had achieved nuclear parity, and it headed (like the United States) a powerful military-political alliance. The codification of nuclear parity in SALT I and the legitimization of the Soviet sphere of influence in Eastern Europe must have appeared to Leonid Brezhnev not only as the crowning point of his career but of Soviet postwar diplomacy.[13] In return, the Soviet Union was prepared to recognize the status quo of West Berlin and its ties with the Federal Republic, and not impede access to it. It was an arrangement based on the mutual recognition of existing realities.

But the Soviet Union saw something even larger in the partial codification of the East-West military balance, which led to SALT I and ultimately SALT II, and in the partial codification of the European status quo, which led to the Helsinki accords of 1975. For Moscow, equality with the United States in military matters and in the shared status of presiding over alliances became the foundation and symbol for Soviet equality with the United States in political matters. The Soviet Union wanted to be acknowledged as a global superpower, an aspiration that reflected not merely a quest for gaining advantages in the East-West contest but a deep-seated Soviet need for self-assurance and international recognition of Soviet achievements. One cannot understand the Soviet sources of conduct in foreign affairs in the 1970s (and perhaps in the 1980s) without recognizing this mix of self-doubt and self-assertiveness, the grudging recognition of Western economic and technological superiority, that are at the core of the collective Soviet political personality. But in seeking to realize its ambitions, the Soviet Union pursued a global policy for which its means proved insufficient, primarily in economic and monetary terms but also in diplomatic and ideological terms. (For example, what the Third World needed the most—a restructuring of global economic and monetary regimes—the Soviet Union could provide the least.) One reason for the waning Soviet interest in détente in later years was the realization that the West was unwilling to extend to the Soviet Union such a sweeping recognition, especially because Moscow's claim for superpower status could be sustained only in the area of military power and in the increasingly shaky foundations of its empire in Eastern Europe.

In all these Soviet hopes and calculations Bonn's Ostpolitik played a crucial role. Without Bonn's willingness to normalize relations and recognize the status quo, the Soviet Union's intention to have its European sphere of influence legitimized by an East-West European peace conference would have been deprived of its political centerpiece and diplomatic substance. After all, it was the West Germans who had persistently fought the recognition of the status quo, seeing in it a juridical seal of approval of the division of Germany. It was Bonn's readiness to recognize the existing realities in Central and Eastern Europe that attached real meaning to the convening of the Conference on Security and Cooperation in Europe (CSCE), which was the capstone of a twenty-year Soviet effort to gain legitimacy for Moscow's sphere of influence in Eastern and Central Europe and which amounted politically and symbolically to a belated European peace treaty.[14]

The centrality of Bonn's Ostpolitik for Soviet diplomacy significantly altered the triangular relationship among the Federal Republic, the Soviet Union, and France, and permitted Bonn to redress the political imbalance that had developed in the Franco-German relationship of the 1960s. Charles de Gaulle's vision of a Europe from the Atlantic to the Urals had been rooted in the assumption that the Kremlin's leadership would see sufficient advantages in a gradual loosening of the two military blocs in Europe, even if this required relaxing Soviet power in Eastern Europe. But it is difficult to see how the Soviet Union could have perceived the situation in the same way: Moscow was interested in solidifying the status quo, not changing it. On the other hand, Germany's Ostpolitik of the early seventies offered what the Soviets wanted most: recognition of the German Democratic Republic, the Oder-Neisse border, and the overall territorial and political status quo in Eastern and Central Europe. German Ostpolitik solidified the status quo, whereas French Ostpolitik had threatened it.

The Eastern Treaty Package

The specific manifestations of Bonn's Ostpolitik were the treaties signed by the Federal Republic and the Soviet Union in August 1970 and by the Federal Republic and Poland in December 1970.[15] These were followed by the Quadripartite Agreement on Berlin in 1971, the Basic Treaty between the two German states in 1972, and the West German-Czechoslovakian Treaty in 1973.

The German-Soviet Treaty, which was signed after intense and highly intricate negotiations, centered on mutual renunciation of the use of force and on West Germany's declaration that it had no territorial claims against any country and undertook to "regard today and in future the frontiers of all States in Europe as inviolable . . . including the Oder-Neisse line . . . and the frontier between the Federal Republic of Germany and the German Democratic Republic." Because the treaty in effect acknowledged the territorial and political consequences of the Second World War, Chancellor Brandt was no doubt correct in saying that "nothing is lost with this treaty that was not gambled away long ago." For Bonn the real significance of the treaty lay not in its specific provisions (considering that the use of force in German-Soviet dealings was highly unlikely), but in its symbolic and political impact. It paved the way for Bonn to turn to Eastern Europe and East Germany with the implied approval of the Soviet Union, and it permitted Bonn to participate actively in the détente policies of the 1970s. Both Moscow and Bonn viewed the treaty as an essential element in their overall foreign policy framework and as a symbol of reconciliation. Ostpolitik and the Moscow treaty became an important ingredient in an intricate set of dealings between and within the two alliances, cutting across several kinds of issues and strung together by a series of preconditions, "pre-payments," and quid pro quos, in which all parties involved sought to maximize their gains while hedging against possible losses.

Although the treaty's central terms signified Bonn's acceptance of the status quo, this acceptance was somewhat hedged. In a "Letter of German Unity" signed by Foreign Minister Walter Scheel and attached to the treaty at Bonn's insistence, the West German government reserved the right to "work for a state of peace in Europe in which the German nation will recover its unity in free self-determination." The treaty was hedged in another way, which was politically more practical and immediate. When Chancellor Brandt signed it in August 1970, he tied its ratification by the Bundestag to a successful resolution of the Berlin problem, which meant first a satisfactory general agreement among the Four Powers, and second a subsequent, subsidiary, inter-German agreement settling the issue of access to Berlin through East Germany and providing improved visiting privileges in East Germany for West Berliners. The Brandt government felt that in return for West Germany's acceptance of the general status quo in Europe, the Soviet Union should accept the status quo in Berlin: that is, reaffirm the continuing rights and responsibilities of the Western powers and the political presence of West Germany that had developed over the past two decades.

The Soviet Union attached great importance to the treaty as the first step toward the convening of the CSCE, for which the Kremlin was pushing insistently to legitimize the European territorial and political status quo, reduce American influence in Europe in an atmosphere of détente, intensify economic and technological contacts with Western Europe, and concentrate on domestic issues and the China problem. The United States, however, was unenthusiastic about the CSCE, because Washington feared it could be turned into a big propaganda advantage for the Soviet Union and accomplish little in terms of settling outstanding disputes. As a precondition for agreeing to CSCE, the Nixon administration demanded progress in the negotiations on strategic arms limitation, on conventional force reductions, and on the status of West Berlin.[16] West Germany in turn agreed to support actively the CSCE in a declaration of intent attached to the German-Soviet treaty (the so-called "Bahr paper," named after Egon Bahr, Bonn's chief negotiator with Moscow). When Chancellor Brandt visited General Secretary Leonid Brezhnev in September 1971, he pledged to "accelerate" efforts to arrange a security conference, and Brezhnev in turn implied that the Soviets were willing to accede to Western demands that any reductions of military forces in Europe would have to be genuinely balanced and mutual.

In addition to its intrinsic importance, the treaty between Bonn and Moscow set the stage for the treaty between the Federal Republic and Poland. The latter treaty contained provisions similar to those of the former, and again the actual legal terms were less significant than the political, psychological, and moral ramifications of the document. The treaty was negotiated during more than nine months of hard bargaining, and its terms provided essentially for West Germany's acceptance of the Oder-Neisse border (it states that the line formed by the Oder and Neisse rivers represents Poland's Western border with East Germany), for full diplomatic relations between the two countries, and for the renunciation of force in their dealings with one another. In a separate accord, Poland agreed to issue exit permits to a limited number of ethnic Germans living in Poland so that they could be reunited with their families in West Germany.

Although some of the formulations of the treaty were identical with those of the treaty negotiated with Moscow, there were some major symbolic and political differences. Bonn's treaty with Moscow was essentially a renunciation-of-force treaty with sections affirming the inviolability of frontiers, and the wording of its specific provisions did not fully satisfy Moscow's partners in Warsaw, East Berlin, and Prague. Bonn's treaty with Poland carried a somewhat different emphasis. It was essentially a frontier settlement treaty with renunciation-of-force provisions, directed toward normalizing relations between the two countries, and addressed more specifically to the historical and moral dimensions of German-Polish relations: Willy Brandt said on signing the treaty in December 1970, "My government accepts the results of history."[17] These differences in emphasis and formulation not only reflected a somewhat different sense of priorities on the part of Moscow and Poland, but indicated a shift in the Warsaw Pact from a multilateral pact diplomacy coordinated in Moscow to a more independent, bilateral diplomatic style, dictated in part by the reluctance of the West to participate in the CSCE.[18]

From the beginning, Bonn faced great difficulties in augmenting its Ostpolitik with a dynamic Deutschlandpolitik toward East Germany. Although Bonn was prepared to make major concessions, as demonstrated by Brandt's policy declaration of October 1969, negotiations between East Germany and West Germany proved the most troublesome element in Bonn's Eastern policy. The major source of these difficulties was that Bonn's new approach to East Germany, although innovative and flexible, stopped short of meeting major East German demands. During the first year of the Brandt government it gradually became clear that the new government was willing to accommodate East Berlin in several important respects: (1) to accept the reality of the German Democratic Republic as a state and deal with it on the basis of full equality; (2) to renounce implicitly previous West German claims that only the Federal Republic could legitimately speak for all Germans; (3) to treat the frontier between East and West Germany as an inviolable political-legal border rather than a "demarcation line"; (4) to negotiate a treaty with East Berlin regulating the relations between the East and West German states; and (5) to refrain from interfering in East Germany's trade and cultural exchanges with the Third World.

This policy stopped short, however, of according full recognition to the German Democratic Republic and accepting it as a second state of Germany in international law, which is in essence what the East German government demanded. In the face of this demand, the Brandt government played down the concepts of "reunification" and "self-determination" but maintained and reemphasized the idea of one German nation (also embodied in the original East German constitution).[19] Bonn insisted that the relations between East and West Germany could not be the same as those between "foreign" states, and that a treaty between the two would have to reflect a "coexistence" type of special relationship (*ein Nebeneinander*), which could perhaps arrest the growing divergence between their social and political structures, normalize relations between them, and from there proceed to cooperation (*Miteinander*).[20] The Brandt government reemphasized the continuing responsibility of the Four Powers and pointed out that it could not in any case legitimize of its own accord the permanent division of Germany. (Of course, Bonn's stress on the Four Powers' residual rights and responsibilities was also necessary for a more direct political purpose, that of obtaining a satisfactory Berlin agreement in the face of East German opposition.) Moreover, the Brandt government made clear that it continued to prefer that allied and Third World countries not extend formal recognition to East Germany, although it was understood in Bonn that an increasing number of countries would in fact do so, especially in the Third World.[21]

When the two German chiefs of government met in spring 1970 at their highly publicized summit conferences in Erfurt, East Germany, and Kassel, West Germany, the concrete results were meager and the discussions did not go much beyond the reiteration by both sides of their respective views. Even so, at Kassel, Chancellor Brandt implicitly offered to his East German counterpart, Prime Minister Willi Stoph, that East Germany as well as West Germany could become a member of the United Nations, an idea followed up during the treaty negotiations between Bonn and Moscow when it was stated explicitly that West Germany and the Soviet Union would actively promote membership in the United Nations of both German states.[22] The meetings were also of great symbolic importance in that the Federal Republic in effect recognized the GDR as an equal negotiating partner.[23] Both sides played a game of wait-and-see, however, realizing that the final outcome of their negotiations would be strongly affected by the larger context of East-West relations.

The key that unlocked the frozen intra-German negotiations and provided an accelerating impetus for them was the Four Power agreement on the status of Berlin, signed in September 1971.[24] After almost seventeen months of intricate and highly technical negotiations, the four signatories agreed that "irrespective of the difference in legal views, the situation . . . shall not be changed unilaterally," and although the three Western powers acknowledged that West Berlin was not a constituent part of West Germany (a view they had held all along in any event), the Soviet Union in turn acknowledged that the ties between West Germany and West Berlin could be maintained and developed. In essence, the Berlin Agreement provided a Soviet guarantee of unimpeded access from West Germany to West Berlin, gave West Berliners the right to visit East Germany and East Berlin, and allowed West Berlin to retain its ties to the Federal Republic (including the right of West Berliners to travel on West German passports). The Soviet Union in turn obtained assurances that Bonn would not conduct presidential elections and other constitutional business in West Berlin. In other words, the Soviet Union no longer maintained that West Berlin was part of East Germany or a separate entity, and renounced the corollary claim that the East Germans had the right to control the access to Berlin enjoyed by the citizens of West Germany and the three Western powers. From the Western perspective, the legal and political status of West Berlin had become solidified.[25]

No doubt the Four Power accord on Berlin represented something of a diplomatic setback for East Germany, for the GDR had to acknowledge the legitimacy of West German and Western involvement in West Berlin as well as the Soviet Union's continuing responsibilities in East Germany. Bonn was in a favorable position vis-à-vis the East German government, because it made a Berlin settlement the precondition for ratifying the Moscow and Warsaw pacts, which the Soviet Union viewed as an essential first step toward the multilateral legitimizing of the European status quo that it expected to gain from a European security conference. The subsequent negotiations between East and West Germany over the supplementary agreement and implementing arrangements were accordingly tense and difficult, even though in early May 1971 the hard-line East German leader Walter Ulbricht had been replaced by the somewhat more flexible Erich Honecker, a change of leadership that may have been encouraged by Moscow to assure a successful outcome for the Berlin negotiations. After protracted and highly intricate negotiations, agreement was finally reached in December 1971 on the subsidiary, technical arrangements for transit traffic of civilian persons and goods.[26] This intra-German agreement provided for normalized access to West Berlin from West Germany, an exchange of small enclaves between West Berlin and surrounding East Germany, and improved visiting privileges for West Berliners in East Germany (from which most had been barred since 1952) and East Berlin (from which most had been barred since 1966).

The settlement of the Berlin question was symptomatic of the shift in priorities that characterized the détente policies followed by East and West in the 1970s. For the Soviet Union, the Four Power and intra-German agreements on Berlin facilitated the stabilization of the postwar European status quo and its multilateral legitimization in an all-European conference. For the Western powers, the Quadripartite Agreement on Berlin was an essential component of the entire treaty package that Bonn negotiated with the East. It reiterated and symbolized the continuing rights and responsibilities of the Four Powers over all-German affairs and demonstrated how large an influence the victors of the Second World War retained in supervising the diplomacy of both West and East Germany and therefore in shaping the general contours of the European political order. For the two German states, the Berlin agreement was of central importance as well. The divided city symbolized the emotional intensity and human costs of the East-West conflict; and the first formal accord between the Federal Republic and the GDR reflected the need for both Germanies to respond to large-scale trends toward détente in both the Western and the Eastern alliances.

Although the East German government would clearly have preferred to hold out for more favorable terms on the Berlin issue and by all accounts felt heavily pressured by the Soviet Union, the outcome of the Berlin negotiations did not necessarily reflect a lessening of East German influence in Moscow.[27] East Germany obtained the Soviet Union's continued support for a clear-cut separation of the two Germanies, strengthened its status as an important partner of the Soviet Union in matters of European policy, and shared with the Kremlin the overriding interest of stabilizing the status quo in Central Europe.[28] The Quadripartite Agreement in fact legitimized the role of both the Federal Republic and the GDR in the everyday management of Berlin. Although the Four Powers maintained control over issues of security and status, the two German states obtained competence over subsidiary problems that might arise in the context of the agreement. In this way Berlin was actually turned over to a six-power regime, leading to its partial "Germanization."[29]

It was not until after the Quadripartite Agreement was completed that inter-German relations achieved larger results.[30] Negotiations on the so-called Basic Treaty between the two German states had officially been under way from June to November 1972, with neither side changing its bargaining position significantly. The East German government was holding out for recognition as a sovereign state under international law, whereas the Federal Republic maintained that there existed two German states in one nation, which required that the relations between the two German states remain "special." But there was some urgency to conclude these negotiations. The United States had given its assent to the CSCE process (and the first round of negotiations was to begin in November), and both Washington and Moscow wanted to see the intra-German Basic Treaty completed by this date. This interest was shared by Chancellor Brandt, who had called an early election for November that was widely viewed as a plebiscite on Bonn's Ostpolitik. The Basic Treaty was initialed shortly before the election (the results of which amounted to an endorsement of Bonn's Eastern policies), ratified by the Bundestag in May 1973, and entered into force in June after ratification by the GDR's Volkskammer.[31]

In the end, the Basic Treaty included a number of topics on which the two German states agreed to disagree.[32] Each goverment recognized the equality, boundaries, and territorial integrity of the other, while at the same time making no clear reference to the "sovereignty" of the states, nor to Germany as one nation. Also, the two Germanies agreed to exchange permanent representatives instead of ambassadors—a compromise between the conflicting views held in Bonn and East Berlin of the "statehood" of East Germany. The rights of the Four Powers vis-à-vis Germany were upheld, the issue of citizenship remained unsettled, and the West German government qualified its claim to represent all Germans.[33] According to some, the treaty "formally left the door open for future steps in support of the reunification imperative and allowed Bonn a flexible inner-German policy through its very ambiguity."[34]

A similarly satisfying ambiguity characterized the conclusion of the West German-Czechoslavakian Treaty. Although official negotiations on a treaty did not begin until May 1973, Bonn had held several rounds of talks with Prague since 1970 to arrive at a compromise that would satisfy Prague's demand for an ex tunc renunciation by Bonn of the Munich

Agreement, declaring it invalid from the beginning, and Bonn's preference for an ex nunc renunciation, which amounted to a declaration of subsequent invalidity. The final treaty states that the Munich Agreement was "void as stated in this treaty," but it kept intact the legal safeguards that Bonn had insisted on retaining.[35] The treaty, which was signed in December 1973, also enabled Bonn to resume diplomatic relations with Hungary and Bulgaria, who had insisted on prior settlement of the issues dividing Bonn and Prague.

The momentum of West Germany's Ostpolitik was by and large arrested on the completion of the Eastern treaty package with the Soviet Union, Poland, Czechoslavakia, and the German Democratic Republic, and the Four Power Agreement on Berlin, all of which were capped by the Helsinki Conference. Intra-German relations in particular did not show the results that Bonn would have hoped to achieve. East Berlin insisted on a policy of *Abgrenzung*, limiting intra-German contacts to questions in which the East Germans were primarily interested (such as intensified economic and technological relations), to the exclusion of others that would have signaled an improvement of the political climate. Moreover, the East Germans' preference for delimiting their relations with Bonn corresponded to Moscow's changing view of the general nature of the German question. Once Bonn had accepted the general status quo in Europe, Moscow's interest shifted to preventing a close relationship between the two German states, which might pose a threat to the internal cohesion and stability of the Warsaw Pact. If the Soviet Union could have had its way, détente would have remained a limited and essentially static condition of European politics.[36]

Consolidating Ostpolitik in the West: Helmut Schmidt

When Helmut Schmidt took over from Chancellor Brandt in May 1974, the intensive phase of Germany's Ostpolitik had ended and a period of uneasy consolidation begun. Almost from the beginning of Schmidt's administration, urgent domestic economic and fiscal problems required attention—problems related to the general malaise of the Western economies, the energy crisis, and a variety of other issues that directed Bonn's focus more toward the West than the East. Although dictated by international and domestic developments, this shift in West Germany's concerns was enhanced by differences in personality and political outlook between the new chancellor and the old. Whereas Willy Brandt was more of a visionary and had other traits that made him probably the ideal chancellor for initiating and orchestrating Germany's Ostpolitik, Helmut Schmidt was a much more pragmatic politician, more inclined by temperament, training, and political experience to deal with practical issues such as economic, monetary, and military-strategic matters—in short, precisely those issues of Westpolitik that were moving toward the center of Bonn's attention. Schmidt was more interested in general East-West détente, especially when it was fundamentally threatened in the late 1970s, than in the specifics of intra-German détente, the management of which generally devolved on his foreign minister, Hans-Dietrich Genscher.

This is not to say that Bonn's relations with the East were neglected. In 1976 Helmut Schmidt entered into an agreement with Poland that allowed 120,000 ethnic Germans to emigrate in exchange for $95 million in trade credits and pension settlements, and Bonn negotiated a new transportation agreement with East Germany easing access to West Berlin. During the mid-1970s a number of political, economic, and human rights issues were the subject of continuing discussions held by Bonn with East Berlin, Moscow, and the East European capitals. But it was obvious that a period of consolidation and retrenchment had begun and that the most dramatic and fundamental aspects of Ostpolitik had been concluded. This period of consolidation was not an easy one, but reflected a mix of satisfactions and disappointments. One problem was the continuing strain between the two Germanies. Both sides were constantly jockeying for positions that would underline and reinforce their respective understandings of the agreements between them. As Bonn and East Berlin tested the legal parameters of the Basic Treaty for their elasticity and possibilities for interpretation, intra-German political, economic, and psychological arrangements were thrown into a state of flux. The relationship between the two sides remained tense and ambivalent, cooperative in some respects but also charged with suspicion and conflict.[37]

Although Bonn's Ostpolitik had lost its most dynamic and dramatic dimensions, it nonetheless had important reverberations for the entire range of German diplomacy, because it left Bonn with a generally solidified international position. The Schmidt government could deal both with its partners and with its opponents from a position of increased strength and flexibility, because it had inherited from its predecessor a significantly improved diplomatic base: territorial issues and their attendant sources of distrust in the East had been largely removed, there was a continuing and more constructive dialogue with the Warsaw Pact that held some promise of overcoming the burdens of the past, and there had come about a closer matching of the twin components of German security policy, defense and détente, putting real substance in the Germans' interpretation of the meaning of NATO's Harmel Report. The Western powers had obtained what amounted to a Soviet endorsement of the permanent involvement of the United States and Canada in the security system of Europe, and they had managed to achieve a remarkably well coordinated position in the multilateral political process of the CSCE. Bonn had adjusted its own diplomatic position to the general climate of

Western expectations of détente, and there had come about a general invigoration of Bonn's diplomacy in the West and the East, in large part the result of Bonn's having shed the constraints of its Eastern policies of the 1960s. In subtle but profoundly important ways, Bonn's new Ostpolitik obtained for German diplomacy as much impact in the West as it had in the East.[38]

The Demise of East-West Détente and the Rise of German Mini-détente

The most significant international change that affected Bonn's new Ostpolitik was the deterioration of East-West détente; and it may be useful to entertain some more general reflections on the nature of East-West détente in the 1970s before turning to its impact on Bonn's Eastern policies and in particular on its Germany policy.

The devolution of détente was perhaps preprogrammed in its origins. The politics of détente are, like all politics, governed by the balance of power, and the East-West détente of the 1970s could have been expected to succeed only if this fundamental premise had not been called into question. Both sides would have had to be convinced that it was mutually advantageous to stabilize and perhaps institutionalize existing power relationships, and both would have had to remain confident that in the process of implementing this understanding the power relationship would not be altered to the disadvantage of one side, especially not through the deliberate policy of the other. A successful policy of détente required a policy of mutual restraint, based on a mutually acceptable constellation of power and influence.

In the world of the 1970s, only a limited number of East-West power relationships and interest calculations could meet those conditions, the stabilization of the European status quo and the partial stabilization of the strategic military balance being the most prominent. These two fundamental components of East-West détente were mutually reinforcing and led to CSCE and SALT I.[39] Most other aspects of the East-West competition and of the Soviet-American balance of power were too uncertain, ambiguous, unbalanced, and dynamic to permit even a preliminary rapprochement and its codification. As a consequence, détente necessarily entailed a mix of conflict and cooperation: a readiness to show restraint in some areas and exercise the freedom to compete and enhance one's power in others, a willingness to draft an acceptable code of conduct on some issues and not on others, an inclination to freeze the status quo in some competitive situations and to accept possible changes in others. In other words, détente incorporated both a static and a dynamic dimension, with the clear implication that a codification of understandings would be possible only in the static component and not in the dynamic. Détente implied a readiness to leave aside the impossible to be able to attempt the possible.

In light of their central importance for the implementation and continuance of East-West détente, arms control and the stabilization of the European status quo should have been shielded from disturbances in three essential ways. First, détente should have been considered divisible and protected from sources of corrosion or breakup in such areas as the Third World.[40] Second, there was the danger that setbacks in one central component would overlap into the other. Third, there was the possibility that contradictory developments would weaken from within each of the central components and hence endanger the foundations on which East-West accommodation rested. The reason for the increasing corrosion of détente in the late 1970s and early 1980s was in large measure that none of these three requirements could be met successfully, which ultimately burdened not only East-West relations but also intraalliance relations.

With respect to the first requirement, the divisibility of détente, Moscow's human rights transgressions and its moves in Angola, Ethiopia, Yemen, and most dramatically Afghanistan aroused such disappointment and indignation in Washington that the very concept of détente was shunned in the domestic political discourse of the United States. The United States linked the core elements of détente to other issues and insisted on the indivisibility of détente. The Soviet Union experienced similar disappointments.[41] It suffered a major decline of influence in the Middle East, Indonesia, and China and among the communist parties of Western Europe; there was a general decline in the appeal of the Soviet "model" in an increasingly diversified world; the Soviet Union was ultimately denied the status of a superpower equal to the United States, which had been a major aim of its diplomacy; and it did not obtain sufficient economic benefits from the West to help ease its chronic economic problems.* Linked with issues that had no direct bearing on arms

---

*West German trade with the East, notably the GDR, doubled during the 1970s, and the proportion of West German trade accounted for by Eastern Europe and the Soviet Union rose from 6 to 8 percent, reaching its peak by the mid-1970s. By the early 1980s German exports to the Soviet Union were at the same level in real terms as in the mid-1970s, and the huge indebtedness of Eastern Europe in the late 1970s was a check both on Western bankers and on East European planners. The transfer of technology from the West to the East remained a sensitive issue between the United States and Western Europe, and became especially troublesome for German-American relations when the Federal Republic entered into a mutually advantageous natural gas pipeline deal with the Soviet Union. The questions of energy dependence, technology transfers, and credit arrangements were seen by all participants not only in terms of their economic impact (although this was important) but also in terms of their political significance. The Federal Republic's trade and monetary relations with East Germany, Eastern Europe, and the Soviet Union remained delimited by the structural restraints of highly different economic systems and the inescapable realities of the terms of trade and comparative advantage and by the political parameters that surrounded East-West relations. For a well-balanced German view of these economic and political dimensions see Otto Wolff von Amerongen, "East-West Trade and the Two Ger-

control and the stabilization of the European status quo, East-West détente was insufficiently shielded from turbulence. Whereas the Soviet
Union saw détente as "compartmentalized competition," Washington
attached to it preconditions through linkage.

The second requirement of détente, the need to avoid setbacks of one
component spilling over into the other, could not be met either. President
Carter felt obliged to shelve the SALT II treaty, and his successor's distaste
for arms control and East-West deténte throughout most of his two
administrations deprived European regional détente of a supportive political atmosphere.

Finally, the third requirement of détente, guarding against the possibility that fractious dynamics would develop within each component,
proved equally problematic. The international legitimization of its sphere
of influence in Eastern Europe that the Soviet Union had obtained at
Helsinki was being undermined from within, which ultimately led to the
imposition of martial law in Poland. At the same time as the Soviet
empire in Eastern Europe obtained some measure of recognition from the
outside, it could not arrest corrosion on the inside. Moreover, the remarkably well coordinated Western position during the Helsinki conference and follow-up conferences exacted a considerable price from the
Soviet Union on human rights and related matters.[42] Equally debilitating, the arms control element, which had been an essential foundation of
the détente process of the 1970s, began to atrophy during the Reagan
administration.

In short, in the decade and a half following the initiation of East-West
détente in the early 1970s, the political preconditions that would have
assured its continuing viability corroded for a variety of interlocking
reasons, in both domestic and foreign policy, East and West.

The deteriorating international context inevitably affected the prospects for continuing intra-German détente.[43] Tentative, incomplete, and
contentious to begin with, intra-German détente was deprived of a supportive East-West diplomatic bracket that could have held it together. The
more remarkable was the attempt on the part of both German states to
shield their mutually profitable mini-rapprochement from the inclement
international atmosphere that began to surround it. This did not happen
right away, nor did it happen for congruent reasons. The central issue
between the two German states remained. East Germany wanted to be

manys," in *West Germany, East Germany and the German Question* (Washington: American
Institute for Contemporary German Studies, 1986), pp. 23–31. See also Michael Kreile,
Osthandel und Ostpolitik (Baden-Baden: Nomos, 1978); Claudia Wörmann, *Der Osthandel der
Bundesrepublik. Politische Rahmenbedingungen und ökonomische Bedeutung* (Frankfurt am Main:
Campus, 1982). For additional literature on the issues of German trade with the East see the
notes to the introduction to part III.

recognized and treated by West Germany in legal, diplomatic, and political respects as a foreign state like any other.[44] West Germany, on the other hand, although it acknowledged the existence of two independent German states on German soil, persisted in arguing that the relationship between them was special, and that the common historical provenance of the German nation precluded on political, legal, and ultimately moral grounds that one German state treat the other as if it were a foreign country.

Even so, both German states managed to protect their bilateral relations to a significant extent from renewed East-West tensions. In effect, they managed to render détente at least in part divisible and practiced "selective détente," a possibility that had worried Henry Kissinger in the early stages of Bonn's Ostpolitik in the 1970s.[45] The invasion of Afghanistan did not unduly burden intra-German relations, and although a planned visit between Chancellor Schmidt and General Secretary Erich Honecker was postponed, both sides managed to protect their relationship with small, incremental steps that were important to them.[46] Bonn's Ostpolitik continued to produce results: greater freedom to travel for East and West Germans, facilitating long-interrupted meetings of families and friends; assured and eased access to Berlin;[47] intensified cultural and scientific contacts and exchange of information; cooperation on environmental issues such as industrial pollution; expanded trade; and a variety of subsidiary arrangements that tended to ease the barriers between the Germans on either side of the European divide. The importance for Bonn of improved intra-German relations was also demonstrated in the Federal Republic's reaction to the imposition of martial law in Poland in 1981 (which took place when Chancellor Schmidt was visiting General Secretary Honecker in East Germany). Schmidt's reaction, governed by his intention to keep relations with Eastern Europe open and not to punish the Polish people with economic sanctions, was considered highly inadequate by the Western allies (especially the United States) and led to charges that the Germans were insensitive to the human aspects of the Polish crisis.[48]

When Helmut Kohl succeeded Helmut Schmidt as chancellor in 1982, he did not bring about a redirection of German Ostpolitik. In his first government declaration he was careful to proclaim his intention to adhere to the modus vivendi with the East embodied in Bonn's Eastern treaty package, which had been negotiated a decade earlier and which his own party had denounced so vehemently. Bonn's relations with Moscow suffered however from the general cooling of East-West relations during the Reagan administration and from Bonn's determination to implement NATO's double-track decision (leading to intermittent, acrimonious diplomatic exchanges between Bonn and Moscow).[49] But during his visits to Moscow for the funerals of Yuri Andropov and Konstantin Chernenko, the German chancellor acquainted himself with the person and views of Erich Honecker, and there were unmistakable signs that both German leaders were anxious to shield intra-German relations from East-West tensions and not let the deteriorating international climate interrupt the intra-German dialogue that had been established in the previous years. Amid Soviet charges that Bonn was again embarked on a revanchist course in Europe, Honecker spoke of "damage limitation" and the continuing need to sustain the inter-German dialogue. The East Germans seemed to be discovering their long-rejected German historical lineage and began to show a new and ideologically ambivalent appreciation of such German historical figures as Martin Luther, Frederick the Great, and Otto von Bismarck; the West Germans were similarly engaged in a somewhat nostalgic reinterpretation of Germany's common historical provenance and a corresponding willingness to look on East Germany with a less jaundiced and hostile attitude. As Richard Löwenthal noted at the time, "It would be entirely mistaken to see this move toward rapprochement in the context of past hopes for reunification in a national state, let alone of dreams of pan-Germanism. . . . Rather, what has created the striking sense of common political interest between two German states of very different political structures and ideologies has been, first, the revival of a sense of common nationhood during the period of détente, and second, the rising sense that they face a common threat as détente has given way to confrontation between the superpowers."[50]

If anything, Bonn's new government seemed prepared to nurture intra-German relations with more dramatic measures and symbolic gestures than those of the routine relations of the Schmidt years, and pointed with pride and satisfaction to the progress being made in the Germans' own mini-détente. In 1983 Franz-Josef Strauss, head of the CSU, helped to arrange a five-year credit for the GDR amounting to one billion D-Marks (and in January 1988 capped his own Ostpolitik with a visit to Moscow), and in 1985 trade agreements with East Germany were further enlarged and psychologically augmented with a growing number of visiting arrangements. In the first half of the 1980s the number of visitors in both directions increased substantially, and 1985 marked the resumption of youth group exchanges that had been cut off in 1983.[51] Negotiations on an environmental agreement were also resumed, leading to concrete proposals for controlling pollution. In 1986, after years of negotiations, a cultural agreement was signed that allowed for cultural exchanges and cooperative broadcasts. Most dramatically, Erich Honecker visited the Federal Republic in fall 1987 (after delays due to the deleterious climate of East-West relations and Moscow's displeasure with Bonn's policies on security issues) in circumstances that amounted to those of a state visit and that allowed only one interpretation: the German Democratic Republic had at last succeeded in its thirty-year quest for legitimacy and achieved its aim of being recognized as the political and diplomatic equal of the Federal Republic.[52]

Important as these events were in their symbolic and practical implications, one could hardly describe inter-German relations of the 1980s as characterized by mutual amity. Even so, these relations appeared sufficiently cooperative to other European powers, most prominently France, to bring to the surface again deeply held suspicions. Above all there was the fear, present throughout the postwar era, that the Germans were incorrigibly afflicted with neutralist tendencies and engaged in an inter-German rapprochement that could ultimately go beyond merely mending relations, cementing these relations in ways that threatened Germany's neighbors.[53]

These anxieties and suspicions were fed by developments that had less to do with the results of intra-German détente, which were not all that spectacular, than with developments within the Western alliance. In particular, the diplomatic inadequacies of the Reagan administration indirectly contributed to these anxieties. There is no need to lay every malaise of the Atlantic alliance and Western Europe at the doorstep of Washington; the Europeans themselves contributed to it as much as anyone else. But problems were bound to be raised by Washington's sterile East-West diplomacy and its disquieting arms control policies, which were excessively indifferent in the first Reagan administration and excessively sweeping in the second. These problems were particularly severe in Germany, which was more directly affected by either excess than other European NATO members. As a consequence, those Germans who found the Reagan administration's security and Soviet policies especially worrisome were encouraged in their view that they should find a more constructive relationship on their own with the East, including the GDR.

The political rhetoric of the Reagan administrations added to these concerns. The more the United States escalated its verbal assaults on the Soviet Union to levels of stridency recalling the Cold War, the more it produced in Europe and especially in Germany the opposite reaction: American bellicosity and European pacifism were interdependent. Moreover, the demise of détente and the reemergence of the security debate in the Federal Republic in the 1980s demonstrated again the inevitable interrelatedness of security issues and the German question. Both the deployment of INF forces and the decision to withdraw them caused consternation in the Federal Republic (the former on the Left, the latter on the Right), bringing to the surface the SPD's latent distrust of the United States, but also raising the traditional anxieties of the Right that the United States could not be relied on to safeguard German security interests whenever Soviet-American relations or American domestic politics demanded otherwise.[54]

Given the historic connections in the Federal Republic between the politics of arms and Ostpolitik, it was inevitable that criticism of Washington's security policies would overlap into German attitudes on how to deal with the East. As always in the history of the Federal Republic, "the problem of nuclear dependence [was] entangled with the problem of how to confront or accommodate the adversary. Anxieties about American nuclear protection feed anxieties about American relations with the U.S.S.R.: Will the United States sacrifice defense of its allies in order to diminish the risks of confrontation with the U.S.S.R. (a common apprehension in Europe during the origins of détente in the late 1960s), or will it jeopardize the benefits of détente in an effort to strengthen its confrontation (the more recent concern following the decline of détente in the late 1970s)?"[55] This combination of factors—enlarged contact between the two Germanies and disenchantment with Washington's security policies—lent a special dynamic to the Federal Republic's foreign policies in the 1980s and thus magnified the suspicions about a new German Sonderweg among Bonn's allies in Western Europe.[56]

A New German Sonderweg?

The fears of Germany's neighbors that a new German Sonderweg was again being charted or might already have been embarked on were deepened by the revival of the idea of Germany's *Mittellage*: its central geographic and historic position in Europe, from which it was displaced by the Cold War and the partition of Europe and of itself, putting each German state on the periphery of a contending empire.[57] In the 1980s the concept of *Mitteleuropa* regained a new and perhaps premature and exaggerated prominence, and the associations evoked by it—undoing Yalta, lifting Central Europe from the grasp of the superpowers, pushing the Soviet Union and the United States back toward the wings of Europe, where they had been poised before the Second World War—inevitably renewed as well the question of what role Germany would play at the center of a reconstituted and less dichotomous European political order.[58] Timothy Garton Ash wrote in 1986: "Central Europe is back. For three decades after 1945 nobody spoke of Central Europe in the present tense. . . . The post-Yalta order dictated a strict and single dichotomy. Western Europe implicitly accepted this dichotomy by subsuming under the label 'Eastern Europe' all those parts of historic Central, East Central, and Southeastern Europe which after 1945 came under Soviet dominion. The EEC completed the semantic trick by arrogating to itself the unqualified title 'Europe.'"[59] This is true enough. One might add, however, that conservative circles in the Federal Republic, by continuing to refer to the GDR as *Mitteldeutschland*, resorted to a semantic trick of their own, with the opposite intention: denying the legitimacy of the GDR and laying claim to the lost territories east of the GDR. Semantic promise and semantic threat: how close and conflicting they remained in Europe!

But just as the question of German reunification was transformed from one of enlarging territory to one of enlarging human contacts, so were the meaning and the implications of the German Sonderweg and Germany's *Mittellage* in Europe. From the beginning of the 1980s both Germanies claimed and accepted a special responsibility that devolved on the Germans because of their geographic and historical location in the center of Europe. In 1981 the West German historian Rudolf von Thadden coined for intra-German relations the term *community of responsibility* (*Verantwortungsgemeinschaft*), and in 1983 East Germany's chief, Erich Honecker, alluding to the impending deployment of new nuclear weapons in the Federal Republic and the Soviet threat to reciprocate with increased deployments in the GDR and Czechoslovakia, spoke of a "coalition of reason" that should govern the relationship between the two Germanies. Generally there developed a feeling among the Germans in both states that they shared a special responsibility for maintaining a peaceful European order, that no war should ever again have its origin in Germany, and that for better or worse there persisted for the German nation a common historical genealogy.[60]

But there was also a sense that a general improvement of East-West relations remained the indispensable precondition for maintaining or enlarging a constructive intra-German relationship. This became especially pertinent when East-West relations were cooling during the Reagan administration, and when both Germanies were insistently reminded that their own special détente was ultimately delimited by the general climate of East-West relations. In 1984 Germany's president, Richard von Weizsäcker, used the term *Sonderweg* when he said: "It is unthinkable to bring about a situation of détente in Central Europe when the overall East-West climate has arrived at a low point. Therefore it is in the interest of intra-German relations not to undertake an ill-suited attempt to embark in this respect on a special path. At bottom we always arrive at the same recognition: we are part of a larger East-West climate."[61]

But it was precisely the cooling of the East-West political climate in the 1980s that highlighted the singularity of inter-German détente and raised anxieties among the Germans' neighbors, who had become accustomed to and reassured by the special abrasions that had characterized the relationship between the two German states. Whereas in the 1960s everything in Europe seemed to be in diplomatic motion except intra-German relations, in the 1980s this situation was reversed. Against a generally stagnant backdrop of East-West détente, intra-German détente was characterized by its own dynamic, and the two German states appeared ready to intensify and energize their bilateral relationship while everything around it became frozen as a consequence of the general deterioration of East-West relations.[62] Whereas in the 1960s the Germans were out of step with East-West developments because they moved too hesitantly in accepting the political and territorial realities of the postwar European political order, in the 1980s they were out of step because they seemed to be moving too energetically. Each cadence produced problems for the Federal Republic, causing either impatience or suspicion. As always in the postwar period, Bonn's diplomacy suffered when it failed to match its own rhythm of involvement in inter-German relations with the deeper rhythm of general East-West relations.

III

The Political Economy of the Federal Republic

Whenever economic, financial, territorial, or military policies are under discussion in international affairs, it is necessary to distinguish between say, economic policies that are undertaken for their own sake and economic policies that are instruments of political policy—a policy, that is, whose economic purpose is but the means to the end of controlling the policies of another nation.

—HANS J. MORGENTHAU

For years our economic policy has been at the same time our foreign policy.
—HELMUT SCHMIDT, 1975

By any measure the economic history of the Federal Republic is a success story. In the course of four decades the Germans, literally having risen from the ashes of their cities, turned starvation into abundance, worthless tender into a sought-after international currency, hard-currency shortages into tremendous monetary reserves, a crippled industry into the largest export economy of the world.

But the political dimensions of the story are equally remarkable. West Germany's political economy is the product of the political circumstances of postwar Europe, and its early development was strongly influenced by the East-West conflict and by the guidelines issued by the postwar economic superpower, the United States.[1] The rapid economic reconstruction of the Federal Republic in the 1950s was made possible by propitious foreign and domestic political circumstances; and economic recovery in turn laid the foundation for a viable domestic political order, obtained solid support for the pro-Western policies of the Adenauer government, and enlarged the international influence and prestige of the Federal Republic. Like its security arrangements, the Federal Republic's postwar economic order was shaped by external factors, and its early history is inseparable from such major German foreign policy events as rearmament and the restoration of sovereignty.

In later years as well, security and economics remained intertwined, as when the United States, beset by monetary and economic problems, pressed the Germans to pay for their security dependence on America, or when the Germans in turn applied their economic prowess to support their Eastern and Western diplomacy. The Federal Republic's economy carries a large political import not only because it was shaped by political dimensions and circumstances, but also because successive German governments consistently used economic and monetary instruments to further their political intentions, both domestic and foreign.

The metaphor that depicts West Germany as an economic giant and political dwarf is unfortunate and misleading. Whatever its stature may be, the Federal Republic defines and pursues its interests in ways that do not allow for a sharp distinction between politics and economics. Over the decades West Germany's growing political influence was grounded on and consistently sustained by economic and monetary power. As a consequence, the connections between the Germans' economic capacity and their foreign policy goals in the East and West have drawn considerable attention, and the Federal Republic's partners are inclined to evaluate German economic and monetary strength in political terms rather than purely economic terms. The huge foreign reserve holdings of the Federal Republic, the D-Mark's preeminence in the European Monetary System (EMS) and its growing reserve role in the global system, the Germans' trade with the East, and their special loan arrangements with East Germany are hardly ever assessed in strictly economic or monetary terms. They are generally scrutinized with a view toward their underlying political purposes and consequences.[2]

This is the more so because over the decades the Germans have become more assured in voicing their views on what they consider an appropriate German role in the European, transatlantic, and global configurations of power, and because they have frequently couched these views in the vernacular of economic diplomacy. On the whole, they have not voiced their opinions stridently or sought to implement them heavy-handedly. Even so, their real or imagined aspirations have occasioned suspicion as well as confidence, criticism as well as approbation.

The Germans' habit of expressing at least some of their political intentions in the language of economics goes back to the postwar years. Faced with the destruction of their cities and their economy, and confronted with the horrors of the Nazi regime and the resulting international condemnation, the Germans viewed the idea of work as much more than the means to economic reconstruction. Economic exertion became the path to political and moral rehabilitation; economic success became an instrument of individual and collective self-projection, a measure that calibrated for the Germans their deliverance from ostracism and the restoration of their self-esteem.

In later years too, the West Germans welcomed the opportunity to translate political demands, which might still have been suspect because of Germany's past, into more respectable economic demands. Politics continually quoted economics. This compensated the Germans for their handicap of being unable to couch political aims in military-strategic language, as Charles de Gaulle had managed to do so dramatically with the French nuclear force de frappe and the politically motivated doctrines for its possible uses. As an alternative, the Germans began to view economics as the continuation of politics by other means, and they fashioned for themselves a diplomatic vocabulary that was suitable for that purpose. Practical necessities and psychological satisfactions went hand in hand.

But as the economic and monetary power of the Federal Republic increased over the decades, and as monetary and trade problems began to dominate the political agenda in Western Europe and the transatlantic alliance, economic issues themselves became more contentious and more clearly charged with political meaning. Economic language inevitably became less neutral and more likely to be interpreted and understood as an expression of power politics.

There was another reason why the articulation of German interests became more complicated. Bonn's diplomacy had always been highly effective in the multilateral setting of international organizations (in contrast to France, which derived the vitality of its foreign policy from unilateralism) and had frequently succeeded in turning international cooperation to national advantage. This circumstance had the added benefit that Bonn could express German aspirations in the language of Europe and the Atlantic alliance rather than in terms of discredited German national interests. The Germans could nurture the attitude (perhaps an illusion) that being a good German was the same as being a good Atlanticist or a good Europeanist.

This began to change when the Atlantic and West European alliances increasingly diverged in purpose and corroded from within, and when the Federal Republic gained a role of leadership in the European Community. Hard choices had to be made between allies, Bonn's opportunities to advance national interests in the name of general international cooperation were becoming less ample, and the legitimizing ecumenical language in which German purposes could be expressed in the past became less convincing in the new circumstances. This was a delicate matter, because other European powers, especially France, were highly sensitive to the Federal Republic's translation of economic power into political leverage. As the opinions of the Federal Republic gained more weight, the Germans had to become mindful that authority, although more than advice, is less than a command.

From the perspective of its partners, the Federal Republic's suspicious economic activities included German trade and monetary relations with the East, especially when they involved projects that the United States perceived to be detrimental to Western security interests and conducive to creating an undesirable German dependency on Soviet energy (such as trading German pipelines for Soviet gas).[3] Indeed, all Bonn governments from the beginning have used economic policy for political purposes when dealing with the East, and especially East Germany. The punitive intent of this policy was reflected in the way Bonn used financial inducements in the late 1950s and throughout the 1960s to enforce its Hallstein Doctrine in Third World countries, demanding that they with-hold diplomatic recognition from the German Democratic Republic in return for West German foreign aid. But Bonn also pursued a more accommodating intent with its Eastern economic policies. This was re-flected in the special GATT arrangements on which Bonn insisted at Torquai in 1951 so as not to ostracize East Germany, in the EEC's dispensa-tions for inter-German trade that Bonn obtained in 1957, which in effect gave East Germany quasi-membership in the customs union of the Com-munity, and in many other economic and monetary ventures, such as the long-standing "swing" credit arrangements that have considerably eased the GDR's monetary difficulties over the years. Economic and monetary relations between the two Germanies have always been of a special kind and cannot be viewed in normal terms of trade and money. The regular trade flows between the two is much more significant for the GDR than it is for the Federal Republic, and the resource transfers from the Federal Republic to the GDR are reciprocated primarily with political goods, such as the easing of travel restrictions and other humanitarian benefits.[4]

German trade policies toward Eastern Europe and the Soviet Union were also explicitly designed to bridge on the economic level the deep political and military-strategic divisions between the two Europes and the two Germanies, and to foster transactions that would convey a coop-erative intent amid the chronic abrasions of the East-West conflict. The politics of German-Russian trade can be traced back to the 1920s,[5] and that it became good business as well as good politics for the West Ger-mans to trade with the East (especially in the 1960s, when trade ex-panded considerably) should not obscure the reality that the initial steps were motivated more by politics than by economics. The volume and nature of East-West trade continues to be guided on both sides by politi-cal as well as economic considerations.[6]

The view of the Federal Republic as an economic giant was not un-challenged in Germany, irrespective of what political leverage derived from that stature.[7] In the 1970s and 1980s, when Americans suggested an economic axis between Washington and Bonn to ease the American trade deficit or obtain a stronger or weaker dollar, or when they called for the German economy to act as a locomotive and pull the industrialized world from economic stagnation, the Germans reacted cautiously.[8] Highly placed persons in government and business responded with self-depre-cation, appealingly modest in tone and supported by statistics attesting to the vulnerability of the German economy to global economic distur-bances. But economic performance must in any case be assessed from a longer perspective and in relative terms. Compared with its European partner-competitors, the Federal Republic has obtained the status of primus inter pares, if not that of an *économie dominante*, and the structural characteristics of the German economy would seem to indicate that temporary difficulties can be overcome with appropriate policies, despite growing concern with the adverse economic impact of demographic changes (a declining and aging population) and with the "technology gap" between key sectors of German industry and those of the United States and Japan.[9]

Those outside of Germany who have argued that the Federal Republic converts economic power into political power have generally expressed their argument in two different versions, each with a significantly different view of the past and different policy implications for the present and future. The first version suggests that a more dynamic political-economic role was thrust upon the Germans by force of circumstance, that their economic power increased largely through inadvertence, in a fit of work-oriented absentmindedness,[10] and that they should in any event shoulder the political responsibilities of an economic superpower. The second version perceives a conscious and perhaps sinister German effort to accelerate the translation of economic power into political power, with the intention of realigning regional and global balances of power to make them more congenial to German national interests.[11] In other words, the first version suggests that the Germans did not know what they were doing; the second alleges that they knew only too well.

Both these views are deficient. They are misleading in their assessment of the past and hence flawed as guidelines for the future; they confuse targets of opportunity with targets of design; they blur the difference between the style and substance of economic diplomacy; and above all, they fail to recognize that the dynamics of the German political economy stem from purposes that are simultaneously political and economic, domestic and foreign, amenable as well as resistant to governmental direction.[12] The increment of the Federal Republic's economic and political influence has come about by opportunity as well as by design: the Germans have become stronger in absolute terms on the basis of their own conscious efforts, stronger in relative terms by the default of others. A properly balanced analysis of Germany's political economy and of its policy implications for Germany's partners and opponents must begin with the realization that the distinctions between politics and economics, and between domestic and foreign policy, have from the beginning been more fluid in the Federal Republic than in most other countries. The historical record reveals a remarkable continuity in the way the Germans have used economic policy for political purposes, both foreign and domestic, and suggests that its present and future uses are better understood with an appreciation of its role in the past.

The continuity of the Federal Republic's economic and monetary policies was enforced by powerful domestic constituencies, which obliged successive German governments to obey a relatively strict code of economic conduct. In the course of four decades the Federal Republic acquired its own economic way of life and a singular economic persona, which like so much else in the postwar history of Germany was the product of both external and internal circumstance. The Germans of the postwar generation soon embraced and passed on to later generations a system of economic convictions, fed by historical memories and contemporary experience, that became so pervasive in its daily impact that it should be accorded its own term: economic culture.[13] Protected by custom as well as by law, economic culture reflects the way a society channels individual ambition and the process of economic acquisition, the way it defines its own type of economic and social success. Over the years the Federal Republic's economic culture merged with its political culture and social norms, congealing into a powerful set of conventions that accompanied the Germans' economic life from the routines of the workplace to the policies of the German government and Bundesbank.[14] It shaped attitudes on saving and expenditure, the relationship between management and the worker, budgetary and fiscal policies, the expanse of the social security net, and a variety of other types of economic behavior and inclinations, all of which are ultimately reflected in the whole array of technical economic indicators.

Aside from the stress on a stern work ethic, which many saw as diminishing in the Germany of the 1980s,[15] this set of economic conventions has always centered on domestic monetary stability and the determination to protect it from domestic and foreign encroachment. The German D-Mark became the symbol of German probity, industriousness, economic success, and ultimately political responsibility.[16] There developed among the Germans a deep conviction that society should be spared the enforced redistribution of income that results from inflation (and deflation), that the equilibrium of money was a precondition for the equilibrium of society, and that price stability ("neutral" money) meant equitable economics and therefore fair politics.

Throughout Germany's postwar economic history runs a persistent theme: the Germans' stubborn determination to retain a measure of economic and monetary independence, the freedom to organize their national economic life according to the principles and values they cherish, even as they exploit the opportunities and accept the obligations of their participation in an interdependent global economy and an integrated regional West European economy. For decades the Germans have made strenuous efforts to protect their economic culture, their national

economic self-definition, against the powerful forces of global interdependence and regional integration. Although the Federal Republic
early on embraced the notions of the open economy and of integration
and interdependence, the Germans' system of economic beliefs became
quickly infused with a self-protective element. At the same time as they
opened to the outside world their markets for goods and money, they
sought to retain the capacity to shape their own economic way of life,
urging others to emulate the German model or else meet with German
disapproval. When disturbing monetary intrusions began to press in on
the Germans, they cast an ever-watchful eye on partners whose economic policies they distrusted, and they looked energetically for instruments to shield from external threats Germany's price stability and its
symbol, the D-Mark. Increasingly, the Germans resented that international inflation (especially in the late 1960s and throughout the 1970s)
turned into an unauthorized social arbiter that distorted the distribution
of international income.

The location of the German political economy in a regional as well as a
global context, enveloped both by economic integration and by economic
interdependence, exerted on the Germans a conflicting pull that became
the distinguishing feature of the Federal Republic's economic opportunities and problems. In contrast to Japan, West Germany entered the
postwar global economy through an intervening set of regional economic
institutions. Surrounded by a West European common market (which is
based on a customs union and absorbs one-half of Germany's exports), a
significant portion of German economic energies were directed toward a
regional economic system in which the Germans soon predominated,
and which served them as a welcome cushion against the vagaries of the
world trading system. The European Monetary System (EMS) similarly
provided the Germans with a more manageable regional arrangement on
which to fall back, while their monetary policies were also guided by
national and global considerations.

Regionalism is a fundamental feature of the Federal Republic's political economy, which touched every aspect of Germany's domestic and
foreign policies. It meant among other things that the conflict between
global interdependence and national "autonomy" was further complicated for the members of the European Common Market by the restraints
and obligations imposed by regional integration, setting up contradictory
relationships among all three precepts. In addition to seeking a politically
acceptable equilibrium among full employment, price stability, and balanced external accounts (the classical Keynesian "magic triangle") the
Federal Republic's political economy developed amid the conflicting political norms and economic requirements of global interdependence, regional integration, and national self-assertion. This confronted the Ger-

mans with intricate economic and monetary problems and demanded of them a complicated set of calculations, a series of economic triangulations with constantly tilting baselines and shifting angles.[17]

At the same time, these enforced triangulations of German economic and monetary policies held huge advantages for the Federal Republic. Globalism and regionalism could be played off against one another, creating a two-way compensatory and cushioning effect for the Federal Republic's national economy. Although each contained its own restraints and obligations, they also held out the opportunity of hedging and equilibrating, spreading risks, and enlarging Germany's economic and political leverage.[18]

The Federal Republic's political economy developed in relatively distinct phases. If one applies a somewhat relaxed chronology, there emerges an early period from roughly the currency reform of 1948 to the free convertibility of the D-Mark and the creation of the European Economic Community in the late 1950s. This is a period of the German "economic miracle," a decade characterized by a remarkable congruence of German and American attitudes on a desirable international economic order and on the importance of the Federal Republic's participation in the fledgling institutions of West European integration.

In the 1960s this congruence gradually disappeared primarily as a consequence of monetary disagreements, further adding to the problems of Bonn's foreign policies: the German-American security compact was under increasing stress, the United States demanded monetary compensation for its military presence in the Federal Republic, Bonn felt increasingly isolated in its Eastern policies, and the German-French political compact was strained because of fundamentally different views of West European institutions and of the transatlantic alliance.

In the 1970s, as the Federal Republic matured into a major economic power and became increasingly confident of its economic prowess and the political leverage it provided, the global and regional economic systems were again rearranged and created new circumstances for Germany's diplomacy, setting the stage for the complex economic and political problems that arose in the 1980s.

8

Political and Economic Reconstruction: The Formative 1950s

The supply of men's needs came to depend on more foreign sources, as men began to import for themselves what they lacked, and to export what they had in superabundance; and in this way the use of money currency was inevitably instituted. The reason for this institution of a currency was that all the naturally necessary commodities were not easily portable; and men therefore agreed, for the purpose of their exchanges, to give and receive some commodity which itself belonged to the category of useful things and possessed the advantage of being easily handled for the purpose of getting the necessities of life.

—ARISTOTLE, *Politics*

The political problems posed by trade stem in large measure from the mercantilistic instinct which seems to be inbred in human beings. The economist insists that the purpose of production is consumption, and of work, expenditure. People tend to believe that within a domestic economy: There is often no difficulty in inducing people to spend well up to their incomes. In international dealings, however, intuition tells most men that it is better to export than to import. The advice may be based on an innate propensity to miserliness, that is, to accumulate gold—if not for psychic satisfaction, then for power or strength.

—CHARLES P. KINDLEBERGER

For a fuller understanding of the formative period of the Federal Republic, the years 1949 to 1955, it is essential to realize that political recovery and economic reconstruction were closely connected.[1] The new Bonn government under Chancellor Konrad Adenauer had only a limited and revocable measure of authority over domestic and foreign policy, and the road toward the restoration of sovereignty (which took place in 1955, even though it was hedged in important respects) is the same road that led to the phenomenal economic reconstruction that the Germans achieved by the mid-fifties.

The Road to Political Recovery

The new German state established by the three Western occupation powers in 1949 was endowed with its own constitutional document, the Basic Law. But it was also governed by the provisions of the Occupation Statute, which imposed stringent limitations on the German government and reserved crucially important matters to the control of the former occupation authorities: foreign affairs and foreign trade, disarmament and demilitarization, reparations, control of the Ruhr basin, displaced persons and refugees, the protection, prestige, and security of Allied soldiers and their dependents, respect for the Basic Law and the constitutions of the Länder, and control of German prisoners sentenced by Allied courts. Further, the Allied powers reserved for themselves the right to reassume full authority if this appeared necessary for reasons of security or the continuance of democratic government.

The Allied High Commission, which succeeded the military governors of the occupation regime, for all practical purpose controlled the Federal Republic's foreign affairs and was also invested with the power to regulate or at least supervise domestic political and economic developments. The politics and economics of the newly established Federal Republic were under joint German-Allied management, with the Western allies retaining for themselves the ultimate legal and political authority. In its early years the Federal Republic had neither the power nor legitimacy to conduct its own foreign policy. Both West and East Germany were products of the Cold War. "The two German states are not regimes that created foreign policies, but foreign policies that created political regimes."[2]

The Western powers were determined to lead the Germans toward the domestic freedoms of a democratic political order, but they were equally determined that the new republic be restrained in its foreign policy.[3] This determination matched that of Chancellor Adenauer, who also saw in the Federal Republic an untested political experiment, and believed that the content and direction of the Federal Republic's sociopolitical order, sustained by complementary economic principles, should be shaped by a close, permanent attachment to the cultural and ethical values of the Western democracies.[4] Adenauer abhorred the idea of German neutrality (irrespective of whether Germany would be united or not), and he did everything in his power to obviate that possibility in the future.[5]

All these goals necessarily required a fundamental and lasting recon-

ciliation with France and the United States. They also required the restoration of legal sovereignty, so that the Federal Republic could join West
European and transatlantic alliances as an equal, with freely given consent. The sovereignty for which Adenauer aimed was thus of a rather
special kind: once obtained, it would be immediately "dissipated" (*auf-
heben* would be the perfect Hegelian term) within treaties that bound
Germany to the West. Many aspects of the sovereignty that was returned
to the Germans were immediately "frozen" in the international organizations that the Federal Republic joined. Integration and equality rather
than the quest for sovereign independence became the central precepts
of the Federal Republic's Western policies. In any case sovereign independence had lost much of its meaning in the postwar European order.[6]
In contrast to Adenauer's Eastern policy, his Western policy was attuned
to the developing transnational and interdependent trend of postwar
international politics and economics, conciliatory in its political and
moral attitudes, and characterized by a keen and virtually unerring sense
of the possible.

As the Federal Republic turned more and more toward the West, the
restoration of sovereignty became a less critical concession for the Allies.
Adenauer's European policy became the symbol of Bonn's willingness to
be tied to the West rather than to pursue a neutralist policy between East
and West. At the same time, Bonn's stubborn agitation for political and
economic concessions prompted the Allies to accelerate the creation of
integrative political and economic structures that could bind the Federal
Republic to the Western alliance. To check the Germans, formal international conventions became a necessity. The fear (especially in Paris) that
Germany's political and economic recovery might proceed along national
lines, unencumbered by international restraints, made integrative arrangements seem imperative. At least they would help control Germany's resurgence, and at best they might enlist for French purposes
Germany's political and economic potential, thus buttressing the French
position vis-à-vis the Anglo-American powers. The creation of an integrated postwar Western Europe provided the framework for Germany's
political reconstruction. The European Community, the Federal Republic—and NATO—were made for one another.

But even though the French, prodded by self-interest and the United
States, supported the German government's principle of integration,
they were hesitant to accept its twin component, the principle of equality.
France consistently sought to curtail the Germans' influence in international organizations and to deny them equal status, whereas the United
States constantly pushed for a solution that would be acceptable to the
Germans and bring them into the Western alliance as soon as possible. At
bottom, the French were worried about what they considered a fundamental asymmetry in the postwar European balance of power, a concern

that de Gaulle articulated as early as September 1945 when he noted that "Germany was amputated in the East but not in the West. The current of German vitality is thus turned westwards. One day German aggressiveness might well face westwards too. There must therefore be in the West a settlement counterbalancing that in the East."[7]

In fall 1951 the Western powers agreed that in return for Germany's rearmament, the Occupation Statute would be replaced by a treaty restoring sovereignty, and that West Germany would become an equal member of the European Coal and Steel Community (ECSC). Because these so-called Bonn Conventions were to take effect at the same time as the treaty for the European Defense Community (EDC), Germany's progress toward political recovery seemed arrested when the French National Assembly voted down the EDC treaty in August 1954. In fact, the Allies anticipated many of the provisions of the conventions, and already acted in accordance with them as much as possible in their dealings with Bonn.

In any case, NATO and the enlarged Brussels Treaty Organization (renamed the Western European Union) quickly supplied an alternative contractual framework within which to restore German sovereignty. The Paris Agreements of October 1954 included essentially the same provisions as the Bonn Conventions of 1952, and indeed from the German viewpoint contained some improvements.[8] In addition to the restrictions placed on German armaments, the three Western powers retained their rights regarding German reunification, a final German peace treaty, and Berlin. The political connections that throughout had linked a number of German foreign policy issues were most poignantly reflected in the legal interlocking of the components of the Paris Agreements, signed in conjunction on October 23, 1954: the protocol for terminating the occupation regime, the official invitation to Germany to join NATO and the Brussels Pact, the Saar Agreement, and the Status of Forces Convention (the last of which retained certain rights for the Western Allies). On the day the Paris Agreements took effect, May 5, 1955, the Federal Republic became a sovereign state. Ten years after the end of the Second World War, the Federal Republic had become an integral part of the Western alliance.

The Road to Economic Reconstruction

These compelling international circumstances, which had such a profound effect on the Federal Republic's remarkably speedy political recovery, were equally instrumental in easing the way toward German economic recovery.

Few will deny the Germans of the postwar generation the credit they deserve for their prudent economic policies, the remarkable energy they applied to reconstruct their country and its economy, and the mixture of ingenuity and labor with which they sought to elevate their depressed standard of living and at the same time work their way back to a measure of international respectability and moral rehabilitation. But it is equally true that these efforts would have been less successful or at least greatly retarded had it not been for highly favorable international circumstances. The rapid and sturdy economic reconstruction of the new republic required external connivance as well as internal energy.

Even in its early stages, the Cold War had a profound impact on the future course of Germany's political economy. Because the four occupying powers could not agree on a joint economic program for occupied Germany,[9] American economic policies left an imprint on the Western zones of occupation even before the establishment of the Federal Republic. The economic reconstruction program advanced by the American and British occupation authorities before 1949 guided the West German economy in a direction that, although not totally irreversible, would have proven costly and disruptive had it been redirected fundamentally.[10] In addition to supporting currency reform and channeling counterpart funds into critical sectors of the economy, Allied economic policy made its most important and lasting impact on the German economy by stressing the need for free markets and liberalized trade. Also, as Charles S. Maier has pointed out, the economic dimension of German-American relations "was fundamental in the postwar years because German political institutions had been devastated. Production promised a surrogate for politics at a point when West Germany was not entrusted with politics. Indeed, the American model was attractive because Germans felt Americans had substituted economic rationality and administration for many of the areas that seemed to be governed in the Old World by political ideology."[11]

Postwar European trade was heavily restricted by bilateral payments agreements, which were the result of dollar and gold shortages and the nonconvertibility of European currencies. Intra-European trade practically amounted to a sophisticated form of international barter. The Joint Export and Import Agency (JEIA), which was under the control of the Anglo-American occupation authorities and in full charge of export and import dealings in the American and British zones of occupation, was determined to make "Bizonia" an example of trade-and-payments liberalization to be emulated by the rest of Europe.[12] At first, the stringent policies followed by JEIA hurt German exports and forced JEIA to backtrack to a series of bilateral trade-and-payments agreements, but ultimately they contributed substantially to the competitiveness of the German economy after the establishment of the Federal Republic and the creation of the Coal and Steel Community and the European Common Market.[13]

Initially, JEIA's policies were intended to complement the Allied program for the decartelization and decentralization of the German economy; they were energized and politically transformed by the Marshall

Plan. In addition to providing outright grants of commodities, the Marshall Plan was also an important source for favorable loans, operating on a counterpart-funds principle: money realized from the sale of American goods was paid into a German capital fund, which in turn granted loans on favorable terms that could be applied toward the reconstruction of the German economy. Most important, the Marshall Plan was intended by Washington to bring about European recovery not only through the massive injection of American aid but by pushing the Europeans to accept the long-range liberalization of European trade-and-payments policies.[14] Herein lies the long-range political and economic significance of the Marshall Plan, which obtained for the United States enormous diplomatic leverage in postwar Europe, especially Germany.[15] The United States exercised "patronal leadership" and issued guidelines that prevented the West Europeans from dealing with their economic and monetary problems bilaterally.[16] Instead they forced them to treat common problems in common ways, especially within the institutional arrangements of the European Payments Union and the Organization for European Economic Cooperation (OEEC).[17] By enforcing multilateral solutions for trade and monetary problems, curtailing the centrifugal forces of nationalism (political, monetary, and economic), and engendering attitudes supportive of West European integration, the Marshall Plan laid the foundations for currency convertibility and the integrative economic structures of the 1950s.[18]

All this was especially welcome to the Germans. They shared the benefits of American largesse with the rest of Western Europe, important for psychological as well as practical reasons, and the political suppositions of the Marshall Plan (that Western Europe had a common fate and that the United States intended to be involved in it) implied to the Germans that they would be permitted to participate in the political and economic reconstruction of Europe. The general internationalism of the Marshall Plan (later reflected in the principles of West European integration) was a substitute ideology for many Germans, especially of the younger generation, who could cling to it amid the disillusionments created by the Nazi regime.

After the Federal Republic was established in 1949, East-West tensions continued to provide an incentive for the Western powers, especially the United States, to assist the Germans in their quest for economic recovery, if only to lay the economic and social foundations for their political and military integration in the Western alliance and to ensure the success of a capitalist economic order in Western Europe.[19] After the outbreak of the Korean War and the decision to rearm Germany, the Western powers gradually lifted their controls over production in key industries, and in 1955 the Agreement on Industrial Controls, an adjunct to the treaty structure that restored West German sovereignty, officially abolished the remaining economic controls.

The step-by-step removal of Allied controls in the early 1950s was highly important, because it opened up production bottlenecks that had impeded economic recovery since the late 1940s. At the same time, Allied controls over production also had some beneficial effects. Curtailment of production, coupled with the conservative economic policy of Ludwig Erhard, the minister of economics, created a surplus capacity in the German economy that helped check inflationary trends and made German exports highly competitive in international markets. Between 1952 and 1954 exports and the gross national product continued to rise rapidly, and by the end of 1954 the gold and foreign-exchange reserves of the Federal Republic amounted to more than $2.5 billion.

Large population movements also contributed to the economic growth of the Federal Republic. In the 1940s and 1950s millions of refugees and expellees from Germany's former Eastern territories and the GDR fled to West Germany. This contributed at first to the economic difficulties of the densely populated area of the Federal Republic, but later helped to support economic growth. The newcomers brought with them a strong incentive to rebuild their economic fortunes, and the pent-up demand for consumer goods and housing exerted a strong economic push that extended into the 1960s.

Another important factor was that during the first two decades of the Federal Republic economic growth was sustained by a nearly complete industrial peace. In the early 1950s the German labor movement was more interested in matters of industrial management, especially the question of codetermination, than in wage issues, and trade unions (although close to the SPD opposition) generally followed a wage policy that encouraged the development and use of industrial capacity as a way of reaching full employment.[20] Also, aggregate demand did not require the stimulus of large wage increases, because of the long pent-up domestic demand for consumer goods.

Even so, the early 1950s were difficult years for the Federal Republic's economic reconstruction, requiring of the Germans hard work as well as prudent economic policies. Insufficient investment retarded economic growth, and unemployment rose to more than 10 percent of the labor force. Bonn was determined to sustain confidence in the monetary system, which had undergone a most drastic cure in the currency reform of 1948, for it feared that inflation and high export prices would have disastrous economic and psychological consequences. Also, inflation would have made it difficult for the Federal Republic to overcome its balance-of-payments deficit with increased exports and therefore to implement its commitment to liberalizing internal and external trade.

This situation seemed to call for a tight monetary and fiscal policy, and whenever possible a balanced budget. In view of the high level of unemployment, such a conservative policy was at times difficult to follow and hard to defend politically, for it lent credence to the SPD's argument that the government was insensitive to the social costs of a market economy. But it had a very beneficial effect on German exports, which became highly competitive as a result of stable prices, domestic underconsumption caused by unemployment, and the need to replace destroyed industrial plants and production facilities with modern technology (and the innovative socioeconomic attitudes that were required to make it successful).[21] Producers were forced to concentrate on export markets; satisfactory exports in turn allowed a general if gradual liberalization of import restrictions. Liberalization of external trade complemented what Bonn was trying to achieve by relaxing control on domestic markets. "By freeing other European countries' exports to Germany [liberalization] encouraged reciprocal concessions and became a stimulus to exports. By exposing the German domestic market to foreign competition, it stimulated competition at home. Although the freeing of her foreign trade created some tense situations and one or two minor upsets, it became the keynote to Germany's policy."[22]

Economic Interdependence and Political Containment

The international monetary and trade regimes established by the Bretton Woods monetary system of 1944 and the General Agreement on Tariffs and Trade (GATT) in 1947 were essentially a creation of the United States.[23]

The Bretton Woods monetary system was based on a fixed dollar-gold parity, fixed exchange rates among major currrencies, which would be changed only in case of fundamental disequilibrium and then only with the authorization of the International Monetary Fund (IMF), and the free convertibility of currencies. The General Agreement on Tariffs and Trade was at bottom a multilateral commitment to adhere to free trade, based on reciprocity, nondiscrimination, and the most-favored-nation principle, which meant that all members were to keep trade restriction to a minimum and avoid preferential treatment of trading partners. In effect, the commitment made by governments in the GATT arrangement not to impede the flow of trade matched the commitment of the Bretton Woods monetary system not to impede the flow of payments.[24] Together, these two commitments were the core of the liberalized global economic system the United States intended to establish in the postwar era. Although their implementation was in some cases delayed until the late 1950s (as with the free convertibility of currencies) or only imperfectly realized (as with the aim of free trade), they nonetheless provided the basis for liberalized trade and monetary regimes congenial to American economic and political interests.

Aside from urging its West European allies to accelerate the creation of a liberalized trading regime, in the 1950s Washington attached much importance to its policy with respect to the balance of payments, not only because of the inherent importance of monetary transactions, but also because this policy had no regional, geographical limitations and reflected a global direction and extent.

The architects of the Bretton Woods agreement and the free-trade principles of GATT had looked backward as well as forward.[25] The only two countries that really mattered at Bretton Woods, the United States and Britain, had vivid memories of the depression years of the 1930s, when the breakdown of international rules had permitted national governments to harm themselves and their economic partners through competitive devaluations and import restrictions to achieve what was considered a basic economic objective, balanced bilateral trade. Because the conduct of the war had given many governments a large measure of control over their economies, it appeared the easier to extend these rules to the postwar period and apply them to a multilateral construct, in a sense replacing domestic control with international conventions.

After the Second World War the United States found itself in the role of central banker for the world, with the dollar the principle reserve currency and Washington providing liquidity for the postwar economic reconstruction of Europe and Japan through large American balance-of-payments deficits. During the "dollar shortage," from the end of the Second World War until the late 1950s, the United States was in effect exempt from balance-of-payments restraints, allowing it to pursue foreign policy objectives irrespective of their effect on the American payments position. Although a payments balance or imbalance is by definition a mutual relationship, the American status as the world's banker permitted Washington to pursue unilateral balance-of-payments policies by issuing dollars in accordance with its own sense of monetary, economic, and political priorities rather than those of its partners.[26]

Above all, Washington's central interest in establishing global trading and monetary regimes lay in retaining for itself a highly privileged position, which offered the United States a large measure of autonomy in dealing with its domestic economic and monetary priorities but required America's allies to accept restraints on their own economic policies. Opened to the flow of goods, services, and money that percolate through liberalized global trading and monetary regimes, the governments of the weaker powers were to a large extent denied the opportunities to act as gatekeepers between domestic and foreign economic and monetary processes. The welfare benefits of an interdependent global economic order were obtained at the expense of national economic independence and the political autonomy of organizing economic life according to national preferences. Multilateral interdependence became the central feature of the postwar economic order, defined by the norms and rules of liberalized international monetary and trading regimes and sustained by the unchallengeable hegemony of the United States.

But America's partners saw little reason to challenge American hegemony, quite aside from their lacking the power to do so. The arrangement held attractions for everyone: the United States obtained political leverage abroad and economic flexibility at home, its partners obtained the means to earn and finance their postwar economic reconstruction. Perhaps most important, the fixed exchange rates of the Bretton Woods monetary system, established on the basis of political as much as economic considerations, provided the Federal Republic (and Japan) with undervalued currencies and thus with the opportunity to finance their economic reconstruction through highly competitive exports.[27]

In these early years the burdens that were ultimately placed on the industrialized countries as a consequence of liberalized trade and monetary regimes were still relatively light. Dollars were scarce and in demand, and postwar European and Japanese economic reconstruction were significantly advanced by the liquidity provided by American balance-of-payments deficits. The United States, aside from arranging for export-favorable exchange rates for its trading partners, extended trade advantages to the Europeans, and the Europeans were not yet questioning American monetary privileges until the free convertibility of currencies in the late 1950s signaled that the Bretton Woods system was being implemented in earnest. Only then did it become clear "how the American position of power enabled it to pursue both domestic objectives (recovery from recession) and other foreign policy objectives (those related to containment) without the restraints imposed by external accounts. The Europeans, by contrast, had to tailor domestic policy to life in the international economy. Those who did so most successfully, such as West Germany and to a lesser extent France, began to show considerable economic promise compared to those who did not, such as Great Britain."[28]

Indeed, the American foreign policy objectives relating to containment were an important reason why the potential for transatlantic economic discord was still checked in the early 1950s. With the onset of the Cold War and the intense East-West confrontations of the early 1950s (especially the Korean War), the liberalizing trade and monetary regimes created by the United States obtained an even larger purpose: they were soon perceived as a central instrument of the policy of containment. American economic and monetary capacity, important in its own right, became a core element of the overarching political strategy of containing the Soviet Union in Europe and the Far East at the same time as it laid the foundations for the postwar reconstruction of the global economy.[29] An open global economic order, sustained by the unimpeded flow of goods, services, and capital across national boundaries, was intended to serve America's strategic interests as well as its economic interests. The Western containment effort against the Soviet Union was to be based on the solid economic foundations of a viable world trading and monetary system.[30] Political containment, strategic deterrence, and economic predominance became the interlocking components of America's postwar European policy.

Initially conceived as a global "open door" for the United States, the tensions of the Cold War gradually contracted these international economic regimes over the decades to the trilateral relationships among the United States, Western Europe, and Japan, with the Communist economic and monetary bloc continuing in a subordinate, regional role. As the Cold War intensified, the United States became determined to deny the Soviet Union and its East European allies the economic benefits of the new international economic order. When the East bloc countries did not take part in the Marshall Plan, after the Berlin blockade of 1948 the United States initiated mandatory export licensing controls, withdrew most-favored-nation treatment from all communist states and drew up a list of "strategic" goods that could not be exported to the Communist bloc. The exclusion of the Soviet Union and its allies did not prove a serious disadvantage for the development of the postwar economic order. It removed what would have been an obstacle to the integration of West European economies, eased the future implementation of America's global monetary and trade strategy, and underpinned the American political containment effort in Europe and Asia.[31]

The Economic Miracle and German-American Partnership

The inherent tensions between the multilateral norms of international economic interdependence and the national economic norms of member states could be papered over relatively easily in the postwar period. The United States was strong and its partners weak and dependent, and in the case of the Federal Republic the United States could apply not only economic leverage but the additional political clout that came with its special juridical status, first as an occupying power and then between 1949 and 1955 as the most powerful member of the Allied High Commission.

But this clout was not really necessary. As in several other important instances, the German-American economic relationship in these years was characterized not by the imposition of the hegemonic power's will on a weaker and resisting partner, but by the active consent of Bonn to a course of action that it itself favored. Although opposed by the German Social Democrats (who feared the restoration of international capitalism), from the perspective of the German government the obligations involved in participating in an open economic order did not appear too onerous, making for an agreeable combination of choice and necessity. It is essential to realize that the much-touted German economic miracle took place in circumstances and during a time when the ground rules of the transatlantic, West European, and West German economic orders were sufficiently complementary to obtain large benefits for the principal participants, in politics as well as economics.[32]

In contrast with later, problematic decades, the 1950s were a period when German and American economic principles were complementary and, equally important, when the meshing of international and West German domestic economic principles was sustained by the whole range of German policies toward the West. The achievement of economic recovery was complemented and underpinned by Bonn's policy on political recovery, and by extension its policy on security and rearmament. Each element of Germany's Western diplomacy was supported by adjacent elements, making for an amalgam of policies and attitudes that was held together by a powerful political, economic, and moral logic in both foreign and domestic policy. All this had a bearing on later difficulties, because many Germans came to believe that the rules of the game had been changed on them in economic as well as military-strategic and political matters, and that German interests were no longer sufficiently appreciated and accommodated in Washington. Also foreshadowed in those early years is the basic dilemma that soon beset the Federal Republic's goal of monetary and economic stability: the more it succeeded within Germany, the more it created tensions and conflicts with the outside world. Current success already contained future problems; the generally harmonious relationship with the economic superpower already carried the potential for future conflict.[33]

For the United States too, this was a relatively tranquil period in German-American relations, not yet beclouded by the multitude of problems and tensions of later years.[34] American diplomacy in the postwar period acted with a large measure of circumspection and foresight, in that it channeled the energies of the Germans and Japanese toward economic prosperity and political rehabilitation and eased their way toward participation in a postwar international economic order in which they soon had an increasing degree of power and responsibility.[35] The United States was generally mindful that the arrangements made or envisaged for world trade and monetary relations would in the long run have to serve not only American interests but also those of other countries—a realization that became increasingly difficult to implement in later decades.[36] The circumspection and foresight of American diplomacy during the 1950s assured the solidification of the American influence in Western Europe and in West Germany, and thus assured as well the viability of Washington's double-containment policy. In contrast to their East German compatriots, the West Germans became persuaded that their superpower protector not only provided them with security but showed them the way toward political, economic, and perhaps moral rehabilitation. Military victories are always harsh on the vanquished. But American military victory over Germany at the end of the Second World

War was soon followed by a more gentle and leisurely conquest, accomplished by economic inducements, political prodding, and diplomatic persuasion.

Whatever the precise mix of purposes that motivated American diplomacy—enlightened self-interest, hegemonic aspirations, altruism, the need to enlist the Germans as allies against the Soviet Union—the fact remains that in these years the foundations were laid for a remarkably stable German-American relationship that obtained in both countries a solid base of domestic political support. The infiltration of Western Europe by the transatlantic hegemonic power, accomplished through the benevolent and irresistible invasions of the American economy and the American way of life, established for the United States a sphere of influence every bit as pervasive as the one that the Red Army secured for the Soviet Union in Eastern Europe.

The Germans in turn saw large economic and political benefits in opening their economy to the global economy,[37] and they quickly developed a rather distinct notion of how to deal with the implications of having an "open" economic order. From its inception, the political economy of the Federal Republic was shaped by so-called neoliberalism and a strong commitment to a stable currency. These preferences were reflected in the principles of the "social market economy" and embodied in the person of Economics Minister Ludwig Erhard. The concept of the social market economy was based on a sharp distinction between the economic order (*Wirtschaftsordnung*), which was the responsibility of the state, and the economic process (*Wirtschaftsablauf*), which was left to market forces.[38] To protect free markets from the distortions that monopolies and inflation inflict on them, the Germans created an anticartel office endowed with strict legal powers, and a central bank (first the Bank Deutscher Länder and from 1957 the Deutsche Bundesbank) with a large measure of autonomy from the Bonn government to ensure that the goal of monetary stability would not be compromised by political pressures. The German central bank was intended to be the guardian of a stable D-Mark.

The Germans disavowed from the beginning any economic principles that would have been tainted by economic nationalism. Erhard was not looking toward the government to implement the economic "national interest," whatever that might be, but preferred to rely on the equilibrating forces of open international and domestic markets. For Erhard national economic autonomy was as outdated a concept as national political sovereignty was for Adenauer. Adenauer deeply mistrusted the political maturity of his fellow Germans and quite readily ceded traditional aspects of national sovereignty to integrative West European structures, to tie the Germans permanently to the West and obviate any future German neutralism. Erhard mistrusted in equal measure the influence of politics on the economic process and was happy to cede traditional aspects of national economic autonomy and to open the German economy to the influence of global markets.

On the surface it would seem that these two sets of attitudes, personified by the chancellor and his minister of economics, were complementary and mutually reinforcing. But they were so only to the degree that both men detested national solutions to political and economic problems. Beyond that, the implications of their policies were quite different and indeed conflicting. Adenauer's readiness to abjure the political principle of national sovereignty pushed him almost inevitably toward West European integration: there were no global or all-European institutional alternatives to which aspects of German sovereignty could have been surrendered. Erhard's readiness to renounce national economic autonomy pushed him toward economic globalism and away from economic regionalism, which he disliked not only because of its limited size but because of its potential for the political direction of economic and monetary policies.[39]

The differences between Adenauer and Erhard were emblematic of two profoundly different views of what setting was desirable for the Federal Republic's economic and political exertions. It was ironic that these divergent perceptions were personified by the two leading political figures of the Christian Democratic Party, the current and future chancellors, but they had a long lineage in German history and left a deep imprint on postwar German foreign policy. They amounted in effect to a split between a fundamentally West European orientation in German foreign policy and diplomacy and a fundamentally Atlanticist orientation, which necessarily widened when the United States and Western Europe began to drift apart in the 1960s. As it turned out, both German views and their underlying aspirations were ultimately compromised. So of course was the SPD's preference, international socialism, which ran counter to the free-market orientation of the postwar international economic structures led by the United States.

Implied in Erhard's support of global interdependence and an open German economy was the expectation that the market forces percolating through the global system would in fact be beneficial and equitable, and above all guided by a sense of responsibility on the part of the system's major architect and guarantor, the United States. It implied in particular that the guarantor of the system would itself exercise political restraint in domestic and foreign matters and generally abstain from the political direction of the economic and monetary *process* at the same time as it guaranteed the formal and informal institutions of the international economic and monetary *order*. In short, there was the premise that the international economic system presided over by the United States would by and large complement and sustain the German economic system favored by Erhard.

Already by the mid-1950s the question arose as to whether or not the

D-Mark should be revalued to safeguard internal monetary stability, primarily because there was already the danger (which intensified in the 1960s) that Germany's considerable current account surpluses might "import" the inflationary trends of other countries. The German monetary system was strongly susceptible to the forces of the international monetary system (among others, the monetary policies of the United States), the rules of which obliged the Germans to intervene in monetary markets whenever the D-Mark deviated from its fixed parity and in doing so disrupted their domestic monetary policies. But German export industries fought revaluation, and when it occurred in 1961 it came too late to check an inflationary upsurge in the Federal Republic, which in effect raised German inflation to the prevailing international level.

From the beginning, Ludwig Erhard could apply his economic principles most easily in the area of external policies, and the Germans developed a lasting commitment to export surpluses, seeing in them the basis for technological advancement and high employment. As a consequence, there developed a hidden neomercantilist core at the Federal Republic's economic system:

> West Germany's liberalism developed into a highly successful, although subtle, mercantilism. Not in the primitive sense that the government subsidized exports and impeded imports, which, for ideological reasons, it neither wanted to do nor, for lack of administrative means, could do. It developed of itself . . . because growing portions of the West German gross national product were absorbed abroad rather than at home, which was easily accomplished owing to price and cost advantages. The Federal Republic didn't need to develop full employment policies, growth policies or other economic programs. She received everything she needed through her markets—which became increasingly foreign markets—without having to fear dependencies or pressures for integration.[40]

By the mid-1950s Erhard and his supporters in industry and commerce felt a growing sense of urgency in reaching for secure access to global markets and averting the pressures for regional economic integration. The German and European proponents of West European economic integration were pressing hard for the establishment of a European Economic Community (and later managed to accelerate its implementation), and the German minister of economics was determined to open the German economy to the world market before it would be enveloped by the restraints of West European economic integration.

The Politics and Economics of European Integration
    There existed from the outset a contradiction between global interdependence and regional integration. A common market, which eliminates customs barriers among its members and creates a common customs

barrier toward outsiders, is almost by definition a violation of the principle of global trade liberalization. But the conflicting economic principles of West European integration and transatlantic interdependence were bridged by fundamental political considerations. In the postwar period the United States consistently encouraged European economic integration, built around a common market, because it considered the potential economic cost to the United States to be far outweighed by the political benefits.[41] Washington encouraged West European integration as a means of overcoming traditional European antagonisms and fears of German revival, and it subordinated narrow American economic interests to the larger purposes of American foreign policy, especially in the area of national security.

In pursuing its central foreign policy goal of containing the Soviet Union and the Federal Republic, the United States applied all the instruments of foreign economic policy—commercial policy, foreign-investment policy, foreign-aid policy, and balance-of-payments policy—frequently sacrificing trade and monetary interests for the overriding purpose of implementing and sustaining its national security goals.[42] The integration of Western Europe became, along with NATO, the keystone of Washington's double-containment policy in Europe. Europe's unification was required not so much for economic reconstruction as for dealing with the German problem.[43]

From the German perspective, political considerations were also paramount. The disagreements that divided Adenauer and Erhard on this issue reached beyond economics into political fundamentals. At bottom, Adenauer was not very much interested in either economic or security issues. He appreciated their intrinsic importance but consistently subsumed them to political priorities. For Adenauer and his Europeanist supporters, the creation of a viable, integrated West European economic order was an indispensable element of their diplomatic program, and for this large and overriding political purpose, the establishment of the European Coal and Steel Community and later of the European Economic Community was of crucial importance.

The future partners of the Federal Republic in the Community were also guided by large political calculations. In May 1950 the French foreign minister, Robert Schuman, acted on advice given by Jean Monnet and others in proposing a common market for coal and steel that would include France, the Federal Republic, the Benelux countries, and Italy.[44] Aside from its inherent importance for the future European order, this proposal could be attributed to at least two aspects of the Cold War. In the first place, the rearmament of the Federal Republic seemed inevitable, and France was determined before agreeing to it to create at least a rudimentary international body for supervising Germany: international arrangements for regulating the production and marketing of coal and steel looked like an effective check on the war potential of Germany. Second, France was acutely conscious that German influence within the Western alliance was increasing, because the Western defense arrangement needed the Federal Republic. The Ruhr industrial complex was still under the control of the International Ruhr Authority, which had been created by the occupation powers, but French policymakers were afraid that the growing influence of Germany might lead to the scrapping of Allied restraints. To preclude national German control over the industry of the Ruhr basin, France proposed the ECSC.

Moreover, the French and especially Schuman feared the prospect of unbridled economic competition between Germany and France, and sought to curtail it with integrative arrangements:

> [In 1949] France's Jean Monnet, honored later as the principal architect of the European common market and community, faced the problem of excess German energy and production. Monnet's starting point was the same as Robert Schuman's, except that Monnet harbored deep forebodings about stimulating Germany to look eastward. Momentarily that might ease competition [between France and Germany], but ultimately it would mean an end to hopes for trade liberalization and, more threateningly, "the re-establishment of prewar cartels"; perhaps, eastward outlets for German expansion, a prelude to political agreements; and France back in the old rut of limited, protected production.[45]

For the Federal Republic the establishment of the ECSC meant the abolition of the International Ruhr Authority, held out hope for an amicable solution of the Saar issue, and represented a significant advance toward the restoration of German sovereignty, because the ECSC replaced an Allied instrument of control with an international organization in which the Federal Republic was an equal. This promised gains both for the legal aspect of political recovery and for Adenauer's larger aspiration: a fundamental reconciliation with France in the context of a Western European community.

The establishment of the ECSC exemplifies the kind of mixed legal, political, and economic advances that Bonn made through its policy of reconciliation and cooperation with the West. Bonn did not gain traditional forms of political sovereignty or economic autonomy but equality in an integrative international organization. West Germany won economic benefits as well. The Schuman Plan removed the steel-production bottlenecks that had hampered economic reconstruction and in effect reinstated the coordination of coal and steel management, which had been outlawed by the Allies and from which German industrialists expected great benefits. The lifting of Allied coal and steel controls was also crucial because it freed basic raw materials at a time when their shortage seriously retarded economic reconstruction. Finally, participation as an equal in an important international organization was for the German government and the German people a symbol of their emergence from the dark years of the postwar period. Economic and psychological benefits merged in a powerful political combination, strengthening Chancellor Adenauer's hand in both foreign and domestic politics.

The complementarity of the political and economic aspects of Bonn's recovery goal was further exemplified by the European Economic Community, established in 1957 through the Treaty of Rome. After two years of negotiations, the six countries already joined in the ECSC—West Germany, France, Italy, and the Benelux countries—agreed to form in stages a common market for industrial and agricultural products by eliminating customs barriers and import quotas among the Six and establishing a common external tariff.[46] They also agreed to coordinate social policy and to create a European Atomic Community (Euratom), with the understanding that there would ultimately be a single administrative body for the ECSC, Euratom, and the EEC. French and Belgian overseas territories gained an associated status, and a joint development fund was established to help finance investments in these territories. Special provisions were made for intra-German trade, which in effect obtained for the German Democratic Republic the status of an "associated" member.[47]

At the core of the Community was an economic compact between the Federal Republic and France that became the basis for their economic cooperation in the Community: the Germans obtained an enlarged market for their industrial products, the French for their agricultural products. But this arrangement had ambiguous economic and technological consequences for France: it propelled German export industries into modern, technology-oriented economies of scale, whereas in France it slowed the modernization of industry by subsidizing the agricultural sector. It forced the Germans to look forward and outward, and induced the French to look backward and inward.[48] Although Adenauer himself assessed the value of the Common Market primarily in political terms, the long-range economic benefits for Germany were substantial. By 1957 the West German economic miracle was well under way (indeed, it would have been inappropriate to continue talking of the goal of economic "recovery"), and on the whole West German industry was well equipped to operate within and exploit the economies of scale made available by the EEC.

During the mid-1950s the Federal Republic further reduced tariffs and other import restrictions, but continued to show a considerable balance-of-payments surplus, especially with the countries of the European Payments Union. Domestic demand was restrained by a tighter monetary policy, and it was mainly the increasing foreign demand that kept the economy in full swing. Even though seasonal employment fluctuated significantly, unemployment was no longer a problem, and the Germans initiated a campaign to attract foreign labor, primarily in the agricultural and construction sectors. The budget continued to show a healthy surplus, in part because the funds allotted for the establishment of the Bundeswehr were not yet called on. Although imports from the dollar area rose faster than exports, goods and services supplied to American troops more than equalized the dollar-area import deficits. There was no serious inflationary trend, although the government felt obliged to admonish business and labor to exercise restraint on profit margins and wage demands.[49]

These generally favorable economic conditions, which also prevailed in other countries of the Six, began to level off somewhat by 1957. This was the major reason why the Rome treaties for the Common Market had been drafted in some haste and with a feeling of urgency: they were to be safely executed before adverse economic conditions in the member states brought on second thoughts about dropping traditional protectionist devices.[50] During 1958 and 1959 the German economy again showed high growth rates, although different sectors of the industry were developing unevenly. Coal mining in particular suffered from reduced demand and high inventories, and Bonn felt it necessary to restrict coal imports from the ECSC.[51] Steel production also fell somewhat, and this aggravated the structural malaise of the coal-mining industry. But exports in general remained high, and during the first half of 1960 they showed an increase of 21 percent over the comparable period in the preceding year, with a particularly marked increase in exports to Germany's Common Market partners. Imports rose 25 percent, and import restrictions were further liberalized.[52]

Toward an Imperfect Union

The political aspirations reflected in the Treaty of Rome, which specifically acknowledged that its signatories intended the Common Market to be the next phase in building a united Europe, gave rise to the hope among Europeanists that crucial and perhaps painful economic measures would be assessed by the participants in light of the larger promise of political union. After attempts to unite Europe militarily with the European Defense Community had failed, economic integration was now expected to pave the way to political union, and Adenauer's goal of merging the Federal Republic into a united Western Europe seemed to have proceeded one step further.

But there were serious disabilities built into the structures of European integration. The idea of a West European common market alone was a revolutionary development in the tortuous history of Europe, not to speak of the political aspirations that were connected with it. Historical memories and hard-headed practical considerations of the day inhibited a supranational authority and bureaucracy from promulgating and implementing policies that heretofore had been the prerogative of the nation-state. Some supporters of European cooperation believed in a confederal approach, which would retain the principle of national sovereignty and strictly limit the authority of the Community. Others preferred a federalist approach that would intensify integration, either by political decisions taken at the top, or propelled by segmental cooperation that would prove so profitable for all parties that it might spill over and precipitate a more complete form of economic and political union. These diverging views of the European Community checked its progress from the very beginning, leading to a permanent conflict between the political alternatives of federalism and confederalism.[53]

In retrospect, it should not be surprising that the Treaty of Rome could have been only a preliminary, uncertain, and hesitant step toward economic and political union. From its inception, forces of convergence and divergence worked on the Community at the same time.[54] A powerful impulse toward convergence stemmed from historical experience. Within the span of one generation, Europe had torn itself apart in two wars, and the promise of international amity reflected in the Treaty of Rome held a powerful sway over such eminent Europeanists as Robert Schuman, Jean Monnet, Alcide de Gasperi, and Konrad Adenauer. The idea of Europe also had great attractions for the younger generation, serving especially for the Germans as a substitute ideology after the disasters of the Nazi regime and the unattractive tenets of Communism.

Practical economic and commercial considerations were equally important. A strong impulse toward convergence stemmed from the similar nature of many problems facing the political economies of the Six in the 1950s, and from the recognition that these problems could be best ameliorated in a cooperative endeavor—an impulse strongly encouraged by the United States. But the Treaty of Rome aimed for more than cooperation. It spelled out steps toward economic and political integration and created the institutions to implement them. This meant in effect that a variety of national economic policies, such as those relating to trade and money, fiscal matters, income and growth, wages and labor, and the budget, would have to be sufficiently complementary that the economic core of the Community, a customs union, would not be fractured.

And here historical experience was a brake and a source of divergence. In the course of their national histories, the Community members had developed very different and long-standing practices and attitudes about how to shape their national political economies. Each had developed its own economic culture. There were important differences among the Six on the division of labor between state and society, the mix of public, semipublic, and private structures, relationships between interest groups and bureaucracies, uses of taxation, sensitivity to inflation and unemployment, attitudes on economic growth, and the preoccupation with national security, to mention only a few examples. The members' domestic political and economic institutions were quite divergent, as were their explicit and implicit codes defining the appropriate role of government in the economy and society. Also different were their attitudes about the extent to which their governments should act as gatekeepers, protecting their economies against outside pressures and interference to retain a measure of autonomy in an interdependent world.

The obstacles to policy coordination stemmed not only from conflicting interests, but from differences in national styles of problem solving and decision making. Although the economic problems in different countries of the Community were similar, they were not identical and there were different ways of approaching them. In each country powerful juridical, political, and ideological traditions had developed that circumscribed the proper role of government in the economy and society—to use a single phrase for a highly complex reality. These traditions and their institutional manifestations (for example, unitary or federal systems of government) differed across national boundaries. Also, in each country there were entrenched administrative practices that were unique and resisted international coordination. Although the bureaucratic instinct may be universal and timeless, it could not be stripped totally of its local historical and institutional context. Although governments everywhere were pressured to solve economic and social problems, their impulses and capacities to act were energized and inhibited in different ways. Moreover, in each country opinion was divided on the appropriate size and function of the Community, and there was uncertainty how regional markets and institutions would affect the economic interests of various sectors of the economy. The constant redistribution of income that takes place in national economies through governmental policies needed to be reevaluated in a larger context, especially because the redistribution was bound to be skewed by such measures as the Community's Common Agricultural Policy (CAP) and the price-support system connected with it.[55]

An additional source of divergence was rooted in the different foreign policy considerations of EEC members. From the outset, the coordination of national policies (not to speak of integration) was impeded not only by internal, domestic obstacles but also because each member of the European Community had distinctly different relationships with the United States, the Soviet Union and Eastern Europe, and regions such as the Middle East and Africa.[56] France and Belgium saw in the Community a way to revitalize their colonial policies (a prospect to which the Germans strongly objected), and the Federal Republic obtained special arrangements for its trade with East Germany, so as not to erect an economic border in addition to the already existing political, diplomatic, and military dividing borders that stemmed from the membership of the two Germanies in their respective alliances.

History, geography, and a preoccupation with German unity made the Federal Republic a special member of the Community, just as they had made it a special member of NATO. The political dynamics of the European Community were such that economic issues, although important in their own right and insistently pressed forward by calculations of national interest, were more often than not informed by fundamental foreign policy considerations. Integrative spillover effects did indeed take place as the industrial, commercial, and agricultural interests in the member states began to experience the economic benefits of the Community's larger markets. But these considerations of low politics were effectively checked by the considerations of high politics in the area of national security and other aspects of foreign policy, which had contributed to the demise of the European Defense Community.

These differences not only made it impossible for the Community members to agree on a common foreign policy, but also made it difficult to fashion a coordinated response to the technical monetary and trade issues that confronted the Community from the outside. A major weakness of the Treaty of Rome was the failure to provide the Community with effective instruments in monetary policy. This was not surprising, because the coordination of monetary policies, let alone the creation of a common currency, presupposes a degree of cooperation among states that seemed difficult to achieve in the 1950s and indeed continued to elude governments in the 1980s. When the European Payments Union expired on January 1, 1958, it left the new European Community without cooperative monetary arrangements such as automatic support payments, a common numeraire, or other guidelines for monetary cooperation. The partial currency coordination that had been achieved in the EPU evaporated, and currency policy was in effect returned to the auspices of national governments.

This suited Ludwig Erhard, who preferred a more global orientation for the German economy, whereas Chancellor Adenauer would have preferred a stronger regional authority. But in the absence of coordinating monetary arrangements, the primary task of providing strength and momentum for West European integration fell upon the customs union and the common agricultural policy, and they ultimately proved to be an insufficient regional counterweight to the global pull of monetary flows that came with the convertibility of currencies in the late 1950s.

The lack of an effective monetary authority turned out to be a most serious shortcoming. When monetary forces from the outside (primarily the United States) exerted different pressures on Community currencies (especially the D-Mark and the French franc), the Community had no effective ways of dealing with them, leading to acrimonious disagreements that threatened the intricate price-support and variable levy systems of the CAP. At the very time when the Community launched its historic experiment of a common market and the promise of further integration connected with it, the last missing piece of the Bretton Woods monetary system, free convertibility of currencies, was put in place, soon to overwhelm the regionalism of trade with the globalism of money.

As a consequence of all these developments, the institutions of the Community were from their inception weakened or retarded from two directions simultaneously. One set of disharmonies and centrifugal pressures came from inside the Community itself, the result of the competing national economic and political interests of the member states. Another set of tensions pulled on the Community from the outside, reflecting the irresistible intrusions of global money and the diverging foreign policy interests of the member states on such matters as the East-West conflict, the transatlantic alliance, and national security policies.

The political and economic processes that were about to be pressed through the Community's untested institutions were thus characterized by a fundamental paradox. Although the political economies of Western Europe had become in major respects more alike, owing in part to the governments' need to satisfy the demands of their electorates, their parallel development did not impel them toward more highly integrated institutions but at best toward more coordination of national policies. Domestic as well as foreign policy calculations made the advancement or intensification of integration unacceptable to some governments of the Community and important segments of their domestic political constituencies, leaving policy coordination as the only alternative. Coordination became the substitute for integration.

In light of these political and institutional disabilities, and the international and national cross-pressures that were at work on the untested institutions of West European integration, it was to be expected that major obstacles would from the outset check the progress toward economic and political union.

9

European Integration and the German-American Connection: The Corrosive 1960s

Inflation is fraud perpetrated on the people.

—KARL BLESSING

The major political problems arising from international capital movements concern not their manipulation, stimulation, or restraint for purposes of foreign policy, but the embarrassment they create within the normal pursuit of domestic ends.

—CHARLES P. KINDLEBERGER

The political and economic compromises embodied in the Treaty of Rome masked at least for the time being serious disagreements among the signatories over the ultimate power and purposes of the Community's institutions. This issue was closely connected during the early 1960s with the question of the Community's enlargement: disagreements over the membership of the Community reflected differences over the political and economic purposes of the Community. In turn, differences over the size and authority of the Community became tied to disagreements over the shape of the European political order, the transatlantic security compact, the East-West conflict, and the best way to deal with the monetary problems of the mid- and late 1960s.

The Issue of Enlargement

The early momentum toward enlargement, which ultimately led in the 1980s to a doubling of the EEC's original membership, ran parallel to

254

the remarkable success of the common market. The economic benefits and advantages that the Community offered its members, including a wider market and enlarged trade, impressive growth in the gross national product, and rapidly rising standards of living, made it an attractive economic example even to those who were less than enthusiastic about its political implications and who found its integrative principles easily resistible. The Community exerted a powerful economic pull even on those unwilling or unable to join.

Bonn was of two minds on the question of enlargement. The Europeanists, Adenauer and his closest advisers, feared that premature enlargement would weaken the integrative potential of the Community from the outset and strain Franco-German relations. They were right on both counts, which explains their dilemma and frustration in dealing with France, which wanted the Community to be both small and politically weak. The Atlanticists, Erhard and his supporters in industry and commerce, would have felt more comfortable had the German economy not been enclosed by a common external tariff, and they feared that unquestioning support of a "little Europe" would strain German-American relations. Perhaps one could say that for the Europeanists politics dominated economics, whereas for the Atlanticists economics dominated politics.

In Bonn, questions about the appropriate size of the EEC frequently took the form of technical economic arguments, which were forcefully articulated within the government by Erhard. On the whole, the German economy seemed well equipped to operate within economies of scale such as those of the EEC, especially with respect to industrial products, which found a larger market through the customs union. The major trouble spot was agriculture, having been traditionally shielded from foreign competition through direct and indirect subsidies. German industrialists saw large advantages in a European common market, but they were also confident that they could do very well in global markets, integrated or not, leading them to warn of the dangers that might arise from the economic and political separatism of the Six. In particular, German industrialists were concerned that the EEC's common external tariff would raise German tariffs and thus impede trade with countries outside the Community, a serious matter in that many German manufacturers (especially in machinery, manufactured goods, and chemicals) exported more of their products to countries outside the EEC than to the members of the Common Market. These concerns mainly took the form of suggestions that Britain be given membership in the EEC, and that this membership be made as easy and inviting as possible.

German trade unionists and their supporters in the opposition SPD were troubled as well, fearing that economic integration would strengthen the hand of European industrialists by providing them with an enlarged, consolidated power base. All these reservations about a common market might have been lessened had there been a free-trade-area agreement with those European countries not ready to join the Six. But this possibility was strongly opposed by many French agricultural and industrial interests, who saw the primary benefit of joining the Common Market in the protection it offered from outside competition. Although there was some expectation that the Community's agricultural price levels would ultimately approximate world prices, this proved illusory from the outset, and remained so with some exceptions during subsequent decades.[1]

For the Federal Republic, political considerations were much more important than economic ones. The Adenauer government had insisted all along that it favored a broader EEC membership and would especially welcome the inclusion of Britain, even though Britain's own political and economic misgivings made its accession unlikely in the foreseeable future. Moreover, General de Gaulle, who had returned to power in 1958, was known to be highly critical and suspicious of British and American influence in the realm of the Six, where he aspired to a leading role for France. Although Adenauer continued to stress that Bonn did not oppose extending an open-ended invitation to European countries, new developments soon threw grave doubts on his determination to enlarge the Common Market.

Great Britain, having failed in its attempt to organize a free trade area comprising seventeen nations (this divided the Six for a long time), agreed with Norway, Sweden, Denmark, Austria, Switzerland, and Portugal to form the European Free Trade Association (EFTA), effective in May 1960. During fall and winter 1958 there were intricate negotiations on whether to allow an expansion of the Common Market to accommodate the proposed free trade area, and if so under what conditions. Adenauer, and especially Erhard, made repeated attempts to mediate between London's proposal for a free trade area (which Erhard favored) and de Gaulle's insistence that the EEC be kept pure by excluding Britain, a country with dubious "European" credentials. De Gaulle feared that Britain would evade EEC provisions from the beginning by seeking to maintain its close economic ties with the Commonwealth and its close political and military ties with the United States. Although Adenauer and de Gaulle had quickly established a remarkable rapport, Franco-German tensions were already developing, which foreshadowed the dilemma that confronted Bonn in 1963 when de Gaulle vetoed British accession to the EEC.[2]

Despite the uneasiness in important industrial and commercial circles in West Germany about the impending economic split of noncommunist Europe, and a good deal of opposition in Bonn to Adenauer's Gaullist orientation, the chancellor's overriding concern with Franco-German reconciliation and a Western European union finally led him to throw his support behind de Gaulle. Such political considerations as the need to cement Franco-German reconciliation and avoid diplomatic isolation on the German question took precedence over other considerations.[3] Soon after, de Gaulle reciprocated by endorsing Adenauer's determined stand on the developing Berlin crisis of November 1958, during which the Anglo-American powers showed a much more conciliatory attitude and flexibility than did Bonn and Paris. The requirements of Bonn's Eastern policies were, perhaps inevitably, reaching into Bonn's attitudes on European integration.[4]

The issue of enlargement was of course of interest to the United States as well. When Britain led the negotiations for the creation of EFTA in summer 1959, it apparently hoped for the support of the United States. But in the fall Washington advised London against establishing EFTA on the grounds that doing so would create further difficulties for the American balance of payments, which was already precarious. The United States continued to support the EEC, however, which also complicated American economic policy, for the express reason that the Common Market served fundamental political purposes, such as encouraging close cooperation between France and the Federal Republic and sustaining the Cold War effort in Europe. At the same time, Washington urged American and Canadian participation in an organization that would succeed the OEEC, later established as the OECD, in which the newly affluent European nations would share the burden of aiding underdeveloped countries and impose fewer obstacles on American attempts to remedy difficulties with its payments position.[5] It was no secret that the primary purpose in finally establishing EFTA was to pressure the EEC into acceding to a larger free-trade arrangement in Europe. Although the United States did not favor establishing yet another economic group for this purpose, the idea of a wider economic area was welcomed in Washington. An economic split of capitalist Europe would be avoided, and American and Canadian membership in the OECD would help lay the economic foundations of what would later be called Washington's political "grand design" for the Atlantic community.

The prospect of an intensified transatlantic economic order sponsored by the United States was anathema to both de Gaulle and Professor Walter Hallstein, a close adviser to Adenauer and the president of the Common Market Commission. This was perhaps the only time they were agreed on a matter of importance, and even then for totally different reasons.

Hallstein was a convinced Europeanist determined to strengthen the institutions of the Community. He feared that pressures for wider membership would dilute from the outset the integrative provisions of the Treaty of Rome, and he therefore floated a plan that would accelerate their implementation. One thrust of the Hallstein Plan was aimed at the Federal Republic. The Germans had made important unilateral tariff reductions during summer 1957 (they now stood 20 to 25 percent below the base rate of January 1957). This step was strongly favored by Ludwig Erhard, who did not of course share Hallstein's devotion to a "little Europe" economic and political construct. These cuts would have allowed the Federal Republic to make almost no additional tariff reductions within the EEC until the end of 1961, and from a practical as well as a psychological point of view, the Federal Republic would not yet have fully experienced the reciprocal nature of EEC obligations. Because the Common Market and EFTA had both scheduled tariff reductions for July 1960, Germany's early unilateral reduction would also have strengthened EFTA's hand in negotiating with other Common Market countries. Germany would have suffered the least and could have remained on the sidelines. Hence in March 1960 Hallstein suggested accelerating the implementation of Common Market goals by doubling the reduction in customs duties of 10 percent planned for July, and by imposing the common external tariff that had not been scheduled until January 1, 1962.[6]

Hallstein's proposal was intended not only to anchor the Federal Republic's commitment to the Community and strengthen the position of the EEC vis-à-vis EFTA, but to prevent a possible dilution of EEC provisions by potential applicants, especially Britain. The acceleration plan would strengthen the economic foundations of the EEC and in that respect support French policy. The plan also favored French political objectives, and may have originated in the economic section of the French foreign ministry.[7] The United States expressed approval of the acceleration plan, but pressed again for a "reconstituted OEEC" that would include the United States and Canada.[8]

> By a master stroke of diplomacy, Professor Hallstein and the Quay d'Orsay were able to adopt a totally new strategy. . . . The balance of payments of the United States was just beginning to give serious concern. The Americans were therefore all the more reluctant to countenance any new larger areas that would discriminate against them. The move to convertibility, in December 1958, played right into their hands, for with the dissolution of the European Payments Union, the larger Europe of the fifteen or eighteen could be argued to have lost its economic relevance. The whole problem could thus be placed into an Atlantic framework: and there the United States could be relied upon to support the Community for political reasons, and to oppose British schemes for economic reasons.[9]

But the Hallstein Plan also underlined de Gaulle's fundamental dilemma in balancing the conflicting ramifications of enlarging the Community and giving it more power. Both supporters and opponents of enlargement perceived it as weakening the integrative potential of the

Community, a reason why de Gaulle should have supported it. But enlargement also meant an Anglo-American foothold within the Community, with large political and economic consequences, which is why de Gaulle could not support it. Throughout the 1960s the keynote of French European policy was to keep these conflicting diplomatic purposes in balance, to keep the Community small as well as politically weak, and by and large this strategy succeeded. In effect, de Gaulle inherited the European policies of Jean Monnet, Robert Schuman, and Guy Mollet but turned them into French policies, extracting every possible advantage for the French economy from the Common Market at the same time as he reduced it to a technical organization, arresting its integrative potential.

Britain's hopes of inducing the EEC to consent to a wider European economic community had clearly faded by 1961. Early in the year Britain began to show an interest in forming a commercial link with the Six, and proposed a "harmonized" common tariff between the Six and Britain, with the proviso that Britain would not be required to apply the common tariff to its six EFTA partners and the Commonwealth states. Agricultural products were to be excluded from the arrangement entirely. By mid-year, however, London applied for full membership, realizing that de Gaulle would oppose an association limited to industrial goods and that Britain would have little to fear from the political evolution of the Community in light of de Gaulle's rather contemptuous attitude toward supranational institutions. The most pressing reasons for Britain's decision were the hope that it could deal more successfully with its serious economic problems, and the opposition to the creation of EFTA of the new administration in Washington, which strongly urged British membership in the EEC.[10]

The American and British expectations that the EEC could be turned from a little Europe into a less exclusive organization reinforced de Gaulle's already substantial and deep-seated misgivings. The Labour party's swing against the Common Market, a bracing plebiscite in France that supported de Gaulle, the increasingly tense negotiations at the Common Market's headquarters in Brussels, and, perhaps most important, the signing of the Anglo-American Nassau Agreement contributed to the stiffening of the French position on British accession.

The timing of this important event was almost unbelievably maladroit. De Gaulle suspected that a decision with such fundamental ramifications must have been considered by both sides for a considerable time, which suggested lack of candor if not outright duplicity on Harold Macmillan's part during his recent conferences with de Gaulle. The Nassau agreement also meant that the British nuclear deterrent now depended specifically on the United States technologically as well as politically, and this at a time when Britain was expected to cast its lot wholeheartedly with the European cause. The dowry of nuclear capabilities and secrets that Britain might have presented to its future partners in the Common Market was now indefinitely committed to Washington and NATO, and British political inclinations still seemed primarily Atlantic rather than European.

Whatever de Gaulle's primary reason may have been for excluding Britain from the EEC, it is clear that the conflicts that developed between the Anglo-American powers and France during the late 1950s and early 1960s immensely complicated Adenauer's task of integrating Germany in a Western European community. Though Germany could hardly afford to weaken its military and political ties with the United States, de Gaulle, the indispensable partner for Adenauer's European policy, was determined to shut out Anglo-American influence in Europe (especially among the Six), and consistently sought to enlist Bonn's support in this effort. Moreover, it was becoming obvious that de Gaulle's concept of Europe was significantly at odds with that of Adenauer. Although both preferred a little Europe, de Gaulle opposed genuinely integrative measures that would curtail the national independence of member states, and he apparently expected his European partners to help buttress France's position in world politics by providing economic and political support. Surely de Gaulle found it easy to assent to Adenauer's deepest diplomatic purpose—to tie his fellow Germans securely to the West—but he feared German economic and political dynamism and the prospect that France would be outvoted in the Community. Although de Gaulle sought to contain Germany in Europe, he shied away from supporting the requisite integrative institutions: they would have contained France as well.

Matters were further complicated by the new character that West Germany's goal of political recovery had taken on after Bonn gained legal equality. Even before the restoration of sovereignty in 1955, there had existed considerable tensions between the legal and political aspects of recovery, because the legal aspect, equality, generally had to be pursued with the support of the United States (and a more reluctant Great Britain) in the face of French opposition, whereas the political aspect, German membership in a Western European community, clearly required France's sympathetic understanding. By and large these tensions posed no insuperable obstacles to Bonn, however: the Atlantic alliance was still cohesive, and Bonn had the leverage provided by the issue of German rearmament.

The situation was quite different in the late 1950s and early 1960s. Once the legal aspect of the recovery goal had been largely resolved with the restoration of sovereignty, the remaining political aspect was subjected to severe cross-pressures, because the disagreements between the United States and France were splitting the Western alliance. Moreover, Bonn's Atlanticist security policy no longer complemented its recovery policy, for the latter necessarily became focused on France—in part because France held the key to the Western European community, in part because the United States had run out of sovereignty payoffs for Bonn. In addition, Adenauer was obliged to turn to Paris for support of Bonn's Eastern policy, because the United States and Britain appeared eager to reach an accommodation with the Soviet Union, most likely on the basis of the status quo in Germany.

By early 1963 the choices confronting Adenauer allowed little equivocation in siding with France or the Anglo-American powers. In fall 1962 de Gaulle and Adenauer had drafted a Franco-German friendship treaty that provided for regular meetings between French and German officials, required consultations between the two governments on all important questions of foreign policy, and envisaged cooperative efforts in defense matters, agricultural policy, industrial development, and cultural exchange programs. Before January 1963 it was still possible for Bonn to equivocate about the tug-of-war between France and the Anglo-American powers. Although Adenauer stood firmly behind Hallstein's acceleration proposals, Bonn also agreed to make substantial contributions to the West's foreign aid programs and to coordinate its bilateral aid programs in Latin America with the Alliance for Progress.[11] In addition, Bonn sought to ease the American balance-of-payments problem by repaying debts in advance and taking measures to return American capital to the United States, and made compensatory gestures to Britain, agreeing to prepay debts, increase German purchases of British armaments, and liberalize drawing rights on D-Mark deposits with the International Monetary Fund.

Although it contained no explicit provisions of great importance and although some of his advisers cautioned him about its implications,[12] the treaty symbolized for Adenauer the reconciliation between France and Germany, the core of his European policy. A few days before Adenauer was to arrive in Paris for the official signing of the treaty, de Gaulle held his famous press conference of January 14, 1963, and announced the French decision to exclude Britain from the EEC. Most likely, not even Adenauer's intervention on behalf of Britain could have induced de Gaulle to reconsider. In any case, a determined stand by Bonn on the question of British accession would have meant that the friendship treaty might fall by the wayside or become meaningless at its inception.

For de Gaulle proper timing was crucial. Adenauer was a lame-duck chancellor whose successor could not be expected to show equal understanding toward de Gaulle's ambitions in Western Europe. In fact, because of his unswervingly pro-French policy, Adenauer had become increasingly isolated both at home and abroad. His relations with the Kennedy administration were burdened by disagreements over American policy toward the Soviet Union, and his relations with London had been strained for some time owing to his support of French interests and his suspicions that Britain aimed for a Cold War détente by supporting the disengagement of the two alliances in Central Europe. At home, Adenauer's foreign policy and increasingly authoritarian style of governing had split his own party and cabinet and were drawing sharp criticism from many quarters. By this time there were in effect two German foreign policies, not one. The first was Adenauer's, which resulted in the Franco-German friendship treaty and allowed de Gaulle to blackball Britain's membership in the EEC with Germany's implicit acquiescence. The second was that preferred by Economics Minister Erhard and Foreign Minister Schröder, who advocated a more flexible course and tended to support the Anglo-American position not only on matters pertaining to the Common Market and the Atlantic alliance but also on a less rigid Eastern policy.[13]

The Issue of Community Institutions

When Ludwig Erhard succeeded Konrad Adenauer in fall 1963, the policy differences between France and Germany had reached a critical juncture. Since the Algerian ceasefire in spring 1962, de Gaulle had solidified his domestic and international position, presided over a significant recovery of the French economy, and was beginning to implement his overall foreign policy more forcefully. Yet practically every item on this agenda opposed German foreign policy, at a time when the new chancellor in Bonn was much less sympathetic to French projects than Adenauer had been. This was not merely a question of personalities. Toward the end of the Adenauer administration, Bonn and Paris already had serious disagreements, which stemmed primarily from Adenauer's Atlanticist security policy. These disagreements were generally balanced, however, by Adenauer's support of de Gaulle on other issues, such as his European policy, with which Adenauer could at least partially identify on intrinsic grounds. Because Erhard and the other Atlanticists in Bonn did not share de Gaulle's concept of a European order (or for that matter Adenauer's), the balance between agreements and disagreements all but disappeared from Franco-German relations during the Erhard administration.[14]

A major difficulty with Franco-German relations during the 1960s was that each side had such a tightly structured and fully enunciated foreign policy program, with all components logically and politically interlocked. Compromise on a single component became difficult, because it would have threatened either in reality or in perception the construct as a whole. For example, Franco-German disagreements over NATO and the size and nature of the EEC were closely related to both sides' overall foreign policy conceptions. De Gaulle had all along opposed enlargement of the Community's membership, and especially the inclusion of Britain, fearing that it would undermine the political and economic cohesion of the Six and allow the United States to strengthen its influence in Europe by proxy through London. This policy was in direct conflict with the preferences of the Atlanticists in Bonn, who wanted a larger membership for precisely the reasons that de Gaulle objected to it. For years Erhard and Schröder had favored a larger framework for European cooperation than that of the Six (for economic and military reasons as well as political and cultural ones), and they had consistently argued that this larger European enterprise should be part of an Atlantic partnership with the United States. Thus while de Gaulle was opposing practically every facet of American foreign policy—NATO, the MLF, the Nassau agreement, the test ban treaty, Vietnam—Erhard was aligning Bonn with Washington's positions. Paris and Bonn pursued policies based on fundamentally different conceptions of a desirable European and transatlantic order, and the more de Gaulle widened the gap between American and French foreign policy the more he forced Erhard to declare himself in favor of Washington.

The dilemma that these circumstances posed for Bonn's policy became glaring during the "NATO crisis" of 1966, which highlighted the serious conflict between French and German foreign policy conceptions: Bonn, convinced of the continuing need for a unified transatlantic deterrence posture in Europe, consistently sought to strengthen NATO and the American presence in Europe, which meant aligning Bonn with Washington and against Paris on a matter de Gaulle regarded as crucially important.

Connected with all these issues and in itself a major source of tensions between Bonn and Paris was the future of the Common Market, and in a larger context the political future of Europe. From the beginning of the European integration movement, it was intended that the integrative economic structures of the Coal and Steel Community, Common Market, and Euratom pave the way for political integration, and that the executive authorities of these organizations be transformed into genuinely supranational governing bodies, responsive to policies made in a strengthened European Parliament rather than those promulgated by the national representatives in the Council of Ministers. Although de Gaulle opposed any development that would undermine national sovereignty, there were no serious disagreements among the Six about the future of the Community's institutions so long as each member had a veto in the Council of Ministers. Beginning with the third stage of the Treaty of Rome in 1966, however, majority voting in the council was to be adopted, and proponents of political integration hoped that this would mark the transformation of the Common Market from a loose confederation of states into a supranational political union. The most that de Gaulle was willing to concede, however, was institutionalized, regular consultations among the governments of the Six, similar to the bilateral consultations found in the Franco-German cooperation treaty.

This attitude contrasted sharply with that of Erhard, who called for establishing an EEC political authority with limited but specific powers, and proposed that specific legislative powers be delegated to the European Parliament and that the Common Market have its own financial resources. Erhard's attitude was something of a surprise, for he had been notably unenthusiastic in the past about political and economic integrative structures limited to the Six. He changed his mind partly because he wished to avoid narrowing Germany's European policy to a bilateral arrangement between Bonn and Paris. As the chances for British membership in the EEC diminished and it became clear that de Gaulle viewed West Germany primarily as an object of his foreign policy rather than as his partner, Erhard began to consider German interests best served by strengthening the political and economic cohesion of the Six as well as their future integrative potential, rather than holding out for the uncertain prospect of an enlarged Community.[15]

Not surprisingly, when Franco-German disagreements about political fundamentals were further aggravated by disagreements about economic specifics, a major crisis hit the Common Market. After protracted negotiations, the EEC partners had reached preliminary agreement on a common policy for beef and dairy products in 1963. During 1964 the EEC's major concern was to reach a conclusive agreement on agriculture and especially on a common cereal price, to match in the agricultural sector the internal tariff reductions already achieved in the industrial goods sector. This required Franco-German agreement on a compromise formula that would balance German concessions on agriculture, strongly opposed by agricultural interests in the Federal Republic, against French concessions on a common external tariff for EEC, which were of great importance to German industrial interests. This issue was finally settled when Germany accepted a uniform EEC cereal price (which involved paying heavy subsidies to German farmers), and France agreed to a considerably shortened "exception list" of products that would not be affected by the common, across-the-board cuts in EEC tariffs to be negotiated in the Kennedy Round.

The Kennedy Round of tariff negotiations had its origin in the Trade Expansion Act of 1962, which authorized the President to negotiate within the context of the General Agreement on Tariffs and Trade (GATT) reciprocal tariff cuts on a wide range of commodity categories rather than commodity by commodity, as under the preceding Reciprocal Trade Agreements program. The Trade Expansion Act was a direct response to the establishment of the Common Market, for the anticipated common external tariff of the Six made it seem desirable to achieve across-the-board reductions on tariffs in the United States as well as Europe. West Germany was especially eager to see the Kennedy Round brought to a successful conclusion because of the benefits that would accrue to German industrial interests, and Bonn was willing to make considerable sacrifices to France on agricultural issues within the Common Market to gain French approval for significant tariff cuts during the GATT negotiations. After complex and at times acrimonious bargaining, the fifty-three members of GATT agreed in 1967 to reduce tariffs over five years by an average of 37 to 38 percent (the goal had been 50 percent), primarily on industrial items.[16]

The very resolution of the tariff issue, however, led indirectly to the Common Market crisis of summer 1965. As part of their deliberations on agricultural questions, the Six had made provisional arrangements in 1962 for the operations and funding of an agricultural fund to subsidize exports, which would help EEC agricultural goods compete on the lower-priced world market and compensate EEC farm interests for their loss of markets within the EEC. Aside from technicalities, the major political issue became the proposal by the Common Market Commission for the fund's operation, which would have endowed the Community with a supranational budgetary authority independent of the members' national control. By allowing the European Parliament to dispose of the anticipated revenues, it would have been transformed from an ineffectual debating forum into a legislature with limited but genuine fiscal powers.

As expected, de Gaulle's reaction was wholly negative. The French government was not only opposed to the substantive provisions of the proposal but deeply annoyed because it had been publicized in the European Parliament without prior submission to the national governments.[17] When the issue of agricultural financing became aggravated by disagreement over the timing for abolishing industrial tariffs and establishing a common agricultural market, the French staged a walkout in early July 1965, recalling their representatives to the Community organs and the Council of Ministers.

The consequences of the French boycott were far-reaching and resulted in a decisive setback for the supranational potential of the Community. Although the issue of agricultural financing was resolved in May 1966, almost a year after the walkout, in the interim de Gaulle had reexamined the supranational potential of the Treaty of Rome. As a result, he set up three conditions for continued French participation in the EEC: that the EEC members agree on agricultural financing, that the Commission renounce its supranational ambitions, and that the majority-voting provisions in the Treaty of Rome be deleted. In January 1966 the foreign ministers of the Six reached a compromise on de Gaulle's conditions. They agreed to retain the principle of majority voting, but the French made clear that they would reserve a veto power when important French interests were threatened. Although the Commission's formal powers of initiative remained essentially intact, its independence was significantly curtailed through the stipulation that the Commission consult with the member governments before making important policy proposals.

Bonn's reaction to these economic and political developments was mixed. There was relief that the Common Market was once again operative (although German farmers felt that their interests had been slighted), and that the EEC had agreed to stand united during the Kennedy Round. But the Common Market crisis also demonstrated that the members were deeply divided on the future political course of the Community.

Although de Gaulle's tenacious insistence on a final settlement of agricultural issues had advanced the economic cause of the EEC by ensuring that there would be a common market for industry and agriculture by July 1968, his inflexible opposition to supranational principles set back decisively the political and psychological cause of the European Community. De Gaulle's timing was no coincidence. By 1965 the focus of the Common Market was shifting from removing trade barriers within a customs union to the more ambitious project of adopting common commercial and monetary policies in an economic union—functions traditionally reserved for national governments. If this tentative spillover effect had been allowed to go unchecked, the freedom of national governments to shape their economic, monetary, and social policies would have been curtailed, with far-reaching repercussions in the two areas where de Gaulle wanted maximum flexibility: foreign policy and defense. This was the real issue underlying the Common Market crisis. The high politics of military-strategic issues (such as the Multilateral Nuclear Force), the nature of Franco-German relations, and the implications of Common Market institutions for the transatlantic and European political order were reaching into the low politics of agricultural support payments and other mundane economic matters. Miriam Camps noted at the time:

> By 1965 it was completely clear that the Five, and particularly the Germans, would not accept French views on defense. . . . The real lesson of the cereals prices "victory" at the end of 1964 was not that the Germans yielded to the French on this point or had put loyalty to the community above the interests of the German farmer, but that they had stuck to the MLF and were conceding on what they considered to be a far less important issue. The steam may have gone out of the MLF by the spring of 1965, but presumably one of the reasons why the United States felt that it could let the steam out was that it had, by then, few doubts as to where German loyalties lay if they were ever forced to choose between the United States and France. Nor had General de Gaulle.[18]

By the mid-1960s de Gaulle's foreign policy program had largely succeeded for the time being. He had revitalized French diplomacy and French Eastern policy, undermined the cohesion of the Atlantic alliance by leaving NATO and pressing the United States on monetary matters, managed to keep the EEC both small and weak, and not totally alienated his German partners in Bonn. Indeed in November 1966, when the CDU/CSU party caucus nominated Kurt Georg Kiesinger to succeed Ludwig Erhard as chancellor, the future of French-German relations was a major consideration. Kiesinger was acceptable to the party's Atlanticists (though they would have preferred Foreign Minister Schröder) as well as to its Gaullists (who were divided in their preference for other candidates), so he was a natural compromise candidate. Kiesinger was a known Francophile who had consistently supported European integration, and his tenure as minister-president of Baden-Württemberg since 1958 had allowed him to refrain from taking controversial positions on foreign policy questions. Bonn's attempt to maintain a balance between Atlanticists and Gaullists was also reflected in the makeup of the Grand Coalition cabinet that Kiesinger put together with the Socialists: Strauss became minister of finance, and Schröder shifted from foreign affairs (where he had consistently opposed de Gaulle) to defense to make room for the SPD's Willy Brandt. Brandt was known to favor a more positive and imaginative policy toward France, and his party had bent to political necessity and come to support the Western-oriented security and integration policies it had fought so insistently in the 1950s.

With Kiesinger as chancellor and Brandt in the foreign ministry, the style of Franco-German relations initially took a turn for the better. Both men were determined to restore a more harmonious political climate (Kiesinger spoke of "an absolute reanimation" of the Franco-German treaty of 1963) and during the first half of 1967 there was a marked improvement in Franco-German relations, sustained primarily by Bonn's evident desire for accommodation and cooperation. Kiesinger postponed his first visit to Washington until he had had a second conference with de Gaulle and refused to intervene on Britain's behalf when London renewed its application for EEC membership (it was again rejected).[19] Perhaps most important, he relented in the face of insistent French pressure and agreed to the removal of Walter Hallstein as the head of the EEC Commission.[20]

In spite of these German concessions, however, the substantive disagreements between France and German proved as pronounced and intractable as they had been during the Erhard administration. Although Bonn and Paris managed to agree on the continued stationing of French troops in Germany (a legal and political issue stemming from the French decision in 1966 to withdraw from NATO), other issues large and small remained unresolved. Bonn continued to support the Atlantic alliance (even though the Grand Coalition was more assertive vis-à-vis Washington than Erhard had been), to favor the admission of Britain and the Scandinavian countries to the Common Market, and to resist French efforts to make Bonn renounce access to control of nuclear weapons. In addition, the Soviet occupation of Czechoslovakia in August 1968 led to serious Franco-German disagreements: de Gaulle echoed the Soviet argument that the Federal Republic was to blame for the invasion because its aggressive economic policy and great economic power would have exerted an irresistible drawing power on an independent Czechoslovakia, and Kiesinger remonstrated that de Gaulle's encouragement of centrifugal tendencies in the Soviet bloc had caused more trouble than had any German policies.[21]

The Crisis of the French Franc and the Issue of Revaluation

Amid these serious disagreements over political fundamentals came the crisis of the French franc, which turned into a crisis of Franco-German relations and ultimately led to a serious rethinking about the need of establishing monetary institutions for the Community.

The Franco-German monetary crisis of October 1968 had a particularly damaging effect on relations between Paris and Bonn, because it followed a series of corrosive disagreements over almost every important aspect of German and French foreign policy, and pitted French interests directly against German interests in a contest of will that aroused strong emotions on both sides.

Like many monetary crises, the crisis of the franc had its origin in a balance-of-payments deficit. For a number of years the French economy had suffered from moderate inflationary pressures (and low growth rates), which increased greatly during summer 1968 after the French government arranged for generous settlements with the labor unions to end a series of crippling strikes.[22] These wage increases, averaging 13 percent, coupled with an expansionary monetary policy designed to facilitate recovery and stimulate economic growth, led to inflation and a deterioration of the balance of trade. The resulting payments deficit created a crisis of confidence in the franc, which was further aggravated as speculators sold francs for D-Marks: between June and November, France lost more than $4.5 billion in reserves, and during November alone West Germany acquired $2 billion in such speculative funds, with a sizable portion coming from France.

That speculators sold francs for D-Marks (rather than for dollars, for example) was an indication of why the crisis of the franc became a crisis in Franco-German relations. The franc deteriorated rapidly despite efforts to prop it up with internationally negotiated swap arrangements, and at the same time the D-Mark strengthened. During 1968 the German economy was recovering from a recession caused by stringent anti-inflationary measures, and the German wage and price level had been stabilized as a result of the reduced demand for goods and services. Consequently, German export prices were highly competitive, leading to a massive trade surplus which, along with the inflow of capital and a low inflation rate, made the D-Mark one of the strongest currencies in the foreign exchange markets. These factors created the expectation that the Federal Republic, which already held a huge surplus of foreign currency reserves, would revalue the D-Mark as it had in 1961 during similar circumstances. This expectation encouraged speculators to sell francs for D-Marks, thus further depressing the market value of the franc and increasing the value of the D-Mark. In short, the weak franc and strong D-Mark were feeding on each other.*

When the finance ministers of the OECD's ten leading financial powers met in Bonn in November 1968 to resolve the monetary crisis, the French and German positions were diametrically opposed. De Gaulle, who had characterized the possibility of devaluing the franc as "the worst of absurdities," instructed his finance minister, François-Xavier Ortoli, to push for a revaluation of the D-Mark. This position was supported by the United States and Britain; the Germans were adamantly opposed, arguing that revaluation would raise their export prices and could lead to loss of foreign markets and domestic recession, and Chancellor Kiesinger had already committed himself on nationwide television not to permit the revaluation of the D-Mark during his tenure.

Both sides viewed the immediate economic issue as inextricably tied to fundamental political questions.[23] De Gaulle clearly intended to impose his will on Bonn again and to extract concessions that would leave unimpaired France's prestige and political and economic maneuverability. The Germans felt that their prosperity was well earned: they were industrious, exercised self-discipline in resisting inflationary trends, and had made substantial outlays for modern and efficient capital equipment. They worried about "imported" inflation,† and believed they were being asked to pay the price for the inflation in France. The Germans were especially annoyed because they attributed inflationary pressures in France to the exorbitant costs of such Gaullist trimmings of power as the

---

*This was possible because the Bretton Woods monetary regime was unable to adjust to international differences in price levels and economic activity, except within the relatively narrow "trading bands" of currency exchange rate fluctuations. When the market price of a currency moved above or below the trading bands, which were the limits set by the International Monetary Fund (IMF) for day-to-day fluctuations of currency values, a country's central bank was required to sell or buy sufficient quantities of its currency until the currency price reverted to the parity level on currency exchange markets.

†"Imported inflation" had been a problem since the late 1950s, when German balance-of-payments surpluses were becoming a source of inflation and the Bundesbank had to choose between allowing inflation and agreeing to revaluation vis-à-vis countries with higher inflation rates. The problem became aggravated with free convertibility: a restrictive German monetary policy intended to curb inflation actually attracted capital and thus became self-defeating. This led the German government and central bank in March 1961 to revalue the D-Mark from 4.20 to the dollar to 4.00. With this step the Germans formally acknowledged their determination to give "internal price stability primacy over unconditional exchange-rate stability." See Otmar Emminger, *Verteidigung der* DM. *Plädoyer für stabiles Geld* (Frankfurt am Main: Fritz Knapp, 1980), p. 30. See also the remarks by Karl Blessing, then president of the Bundesbank, in *Der Spiegel* 18, no. 27 (1964): 28.

force de frappe, which in turn were being used by de Gaulle to impose his foreign policy conceptions on Bonn.[24]

Although de Gaulle's manipulations during the gold and pound sterling crisis of November 1967 had gravely endangered the fixed parity of gold, dollar, and pound, the United States and Britain were highly sympathetic to the French plight one year later, because they also suffered from balance-of-payments difficulties. Also, a French decision not to devalue the franc was expected to work to Britain's advantage at least in the short run, because it would keep French products from gaining a competitive edge over British exports and avert immediate danger to the pound. Washington had long favored a moderate revaluation of the D-Mark. On the other hand, Italy, the Netherlands, and Belgium leaned toward the German position, because the existing parities among the D-Mark, lira, guilder, and Belgian franc were relatively realistic, and because these countries would have suffered from a revaluation of the D-Mark.

After a series of acrimonious sessions the German view prevailed on the central issue, that of revaluation. Although the D-Mark was not revalued, a quasi-revaluation of 4 percent was effected with selective border adjustments, lowering the price of imports with rebates and raising the price of German exports with border levies. The finance ministers also agreed to make available to France $2 billion in credits.[25] These agreements were not contingent on French devaluation, but it was widely assumed that the French had little choice but to devalue the franc by 10 to 15 percent. It therefore came as a surprise when de Gaulle made a terse announcement that the franc would not be devalued, which was soon followed by another announcement spelling out a tough domestic deflationary program to help correct domestic economic difficulties and keep the franc afloat.

Most likely, de Gaulle's decision was influenced by the humiliating circumstances in which the devaluation would have been carried out, and by his resentment of the way the strength of the German currency was being translated into political power. The irritations that had been building up on both sides during years of controversy clearly made the outcome of the currency confrontation a question of national prestige, and lent to the crisis a psychological significance. The political ramifications were large. Aside from incurring intangible political costs, de Gaulle's decision required postponement of some of his most cherished ambitions, such as developing intercontinental ballistic missiles, equipping the French army with tactical nuclear weapons, and completing the H-bomb testing program in the Pacific.[26] Moreover, the domestic austerity measures initiated by the French government—price and wage freezes, spending cuts, an increase in the value-added tax to reduce consumption, currency exchange controls, and several others—were politically controversial and threatening to France's precarious domestic tranquility, which had just recently been restored. Indeed, these factors contributed to the retirement of de Gaulle in April 1969.

The Germans also paid a price for their political "victory." In the first place, there was by no means unanimous agreement in West Germany that the government's refusal to revalue the D-Mark was based on sound economic reasoning. Because the taxation of exports and subsidy for imports applied only to manufactured goods (it excluded services, agricultural products, and capital transactions), the burden of the government's decision was placed primarily on export-sensitive sectors of the economy without much benefit accruing to the German consumer, and the government was accused of sacrificing the interests of German export industries for the purpose of German foreign policy. It was also argued that the across-the-board adjustments that accompany revaluation would have been more efficient as well as more equitable, because they would not have required the services of the bureaucracy's fiscal apparatus. As it was, most monetary experts viewed the taxation of exports as at best a stopgap, which by leaving open other options for the future was intended to strengthen the government's hand during negotiations on more fundamental reforms of the international monetary system.[27]

Moreover, the Germans' demonstration of economic power caused a good deal of resentment and created a community of interest among France, Britain, and the United States, because all three countries suffered from balance-of-payments difficulties that would have been eased by revaluing the D-Mark and because de Gaulle's decision not to devalue the franc provided a welcome breathing spell for the ailing pound and dollar. Thus Bonn found itself in the uncomfortable and unusual position of being opposed by its three major allies simultaneously, a position even more awkward than having to choose sides between Washington and Paris.

Most damaging of course was the blow dealt to Franco-German relations. In taking uncompromising and psychologically charged stands on the revaluation issue, both sides showed a lack of imagination and circumspection. The Germans, deeply aware of the disparity between their economic power and their political influence and frustrated by it, found in the currency crisis an irresistible opportunity to demonstrate to their allies and to themselves the importance of Bonn in Western councils. De Gaulle, who had consistently nourished German frustrations by brusquely treating Bonn as at best the junior partner of the Franco-German entente, approached the crisis with his usual arrogance, taking it as a matter of course that rules of reciprocity were suspended in favor of France.

The resignation of General de Gaulle in spring 1969 quite naturally led to speculation about the future of Franco-German relations. The official response in Bonn was cautiously optimistic, but both the German government (which faced an election in September) and the new French government under Georges Pompidou (which was preoccupied with the tasks of transition) clearly preferred to postpone major initiatives until the fall. The major exception to this was the surprise announcement in early August that the French government had decided to devalue the franc by 12.5 percent.

The French decision followed a new "crisis of the franc" in early May, which was the direct result of de Gaulle's resignation and followed roughly the same pattern as the crisis of November 1968. During the crisis of May 1969 Bonn renewed its pledge not to revalue the mark (a decision that a government spokesman called "final, unequivocal, and for eternity"), but in contrast to November 1968 there was relatively little international agitation and acrimony, and the repercussions of Bonn's stubborn determination were felt largely in domestic politics, leading to serious disagreements between the coalition partners over the direction of German monetary policies. The French devaluation, however, again raised intricate issues between Paris and Bonn, largely because of its effect on the Community's farm pricing system. The solution that was finally accepted suspended uniform support levels for farm products and "isolated" the French agricultural market for twenty-eight months, raising French farm prices only gradually.[28]

It was precisely the chronic problems stemming from the Community's common agricultural policy and its intricate pricing mechanism that compelled the Community to consider expanding its functions into the area of common monetary management. Although the Community's agricultural market was shielded by import duties from cheaper world agricultural products, its Community price level (expressed in units of account) was not protected from exchange-rate fluctuations within the Community. Each parity adjustment among Community currencies skewed the pricing system of the CAP arrangement, working to either the advantage or the disadvantage of producers and consumers in one country or another, requiring complicated negotiations on compensatory payments within the Community. (This was unpalatable on political grounds as well. There was a good deal of criticism of the CAP on intrinsic grounds, and the periodic crises of the pricing system constantly called attention to the issue of the CAP itself.) In the absence of a genuine monetary unit, the green agricultural "dollar"—the numeraire for the common agricultural price level—was much too weak to cement divergent European currency values. In no case could it be expected to provide a monetary shield against monetary pressures from without the Community. The global pull of the international monetary system, flush with U.S. dollars, exerted an irresistible but differential pull on EEC currencies. In the absence of a genuine monetary authority the customs union, the CAP, and the green dollar proved insufficiently strong to provide monetary cohesion.

Not only the differential pull of outside monetary forces made it difficult for Community currencies to remain within an acceptable range of fluctuations. Developments within the Community also threatened the stability of exchange rates. As always in the history of the Community, external impediments to coordination were more than matched by internal ones. Members of the EEC pursued different economic policies, which along with other economic and political factors affected the market values of their currencies. But these differences in market values could not readily be reflected with incremental adjustments of par values, given the principle of more-or-less fixed exchange rates of the Bretton Woods monetary system. The system was too rigid to accommodate smoothly to the day-by-day pressures exerted by monetary forces. As a result, pressures for adjustment erupted in periodic monetary crises.

The Inadequacies of Community Institutions

Underneath the constant economic tensions and political abrasions occasioned by the Community's agricultural financing system lay much more fundamental problems. The periodic contortions of the CAP's pricing system were merely a technical symptom reflecting the lack of coordination among economic policies, the political inadequacies of the Community's institutions, and the economic inequities that arose from the complex interplay of global, regional, and national monetary systems.

A major reason for the differing economic policies of the Community's members was that by the mid- and late 1960s important economic, political, social, demographic, psychological, and generational changes were taking place in Europe.

During the years preceding and following the Common Market crisis of 1965, the political and economic dynamics of European integration were in effect arrested. Decisions that had been made a decade earlier had been implemented (indeed accelerated), whereas others were held in abeyance. But the economic success of the Common Market had been extraordinary. During the ten years since they had joined in their common enterprise, trade expansion among the Six had grown phenomenally, their prosperity reached unprecedented levels, and the customs union and a common agricultural market based on the unity of agricultural prices had been installed. Europe had become more self-assured, a postwar generation was reaching maturity, and the dramatic economic changes brought on by the Common Market had turned into the daily routines of economic and social life.

In the 1950s the major impetus toward creating a European Community had come from economic scarcity and political necessity. But in the 1960s the members' economic policies and the Community's institutions were required to shift from managing economic reconstruction to managing prosperity and economic well-being. This proved in many ways more difficult than managing scarcity, and the Community became in part a victim of its own success. In member countries the focus of political life shifted to issues that attend socioeconomic affluence: enlarging the social security net, improving the conditions of the workplace, safeguarding a life style oriented toward consumption—in short, they shifted to what has been called the revolution of rising entitlements. These developments increased public spending, which in many member states was not financed through increased taxation or production and therefore led to high inflation.

These socioeconomic and political developments made it very difficult for the Community to achieve a coordinated economic policy, let alone a common economic policy. Because the integrative potential of the Community had been checked by the events of the mid-1960s, its institutions could not solve or even properly address the modern socioeconomic and sociopolitical issues that were emerging, leaving this task to be performed more or less adequately by the national governments. This amounted to a retreat to the domain of national politics at a time when global and regional issues called for a multilateral and coordinated response. The problems experienced by the Community's members were globally and regionally interdependent, but the attempts to solve them were nationally directed. Among other negative consequences, the seeming irrelevance and increasing bureaucratization of Community institutions led to disappointment among the younger European generation, a certain *Europamüdigkeit*, and the stagnation of integrative political dynamics weakened the Community even in the area where success had already been achieved, that of the customs union and the agricultural pricing system.[29]

In failing to address common problems with a common response, all parties were at fault. The governments of Western Europe were primarily guided by domestic political considerations; they pursued divergent foreign policies and were at odds over security issues; and they appeared ready to revert to a more national perspective on problem solving (perhaps following their deepest inclinations), now that the immediate and inescapable pressures of postwar economic reconstruction had been relieved. The institutions of the Community could in any case not be expected to grow beyond the limits of competence and authority that the members governments had drawn for them. In many respects, the cause of European unity never recovered from the failure of the Community's member governments to respond to the challenges of the 1960s and grasp the opportunities for institutional growth that they represented.

The Decline of the Transatlantic Compact and the Global Monetary System

The difficulties created in the 1960s for German economic and foreign policies by the Community's discord were aggravated by the tensions that had developed between the principles of Germany's economic order

and those of the global monetary regime. The deep and robust complementarities that characterized German-American economic relations in
the 1950s began to weaken in the 1960s. The tensions among the norms of
global interdependence, regional integration, and national autonomy
were becoming increasingly visible and troublesome.

From its inception, the Bretton Woods system was expected to restrain inflation (indeed, it was feared that it might have a debilitating
deflationary effect), and it was assumed that its fixed exchange rates
would need to be adjusted only occasionally.[30] From the time of de jure
convertibility of currencies until the mid-1960s, the system was in fact
relatively stable, and formal adjustment of exchange rate in consultation
with the IMF in cases of "fundamental disequilibrium" was used only
rarely among major currencies. But underneath this outward stability the
par-value arrangement increasingly turned into a machinery for generat-
ing and transmitting inflation, threatening the Federal Republic's goal of
domestic monetary stability.

Ironically, the monetary system worked best when not yet fully implemented. The Bretton Woods system, led by the United States, in effect
began its decline at the very time when it had reached its full implementation with the free convertibility of currencies in the late 1950s, for it was
the unimpeded outflow of dollars and the obligations of central banks to
accept it on the basis of fixed exchange rates that ultimately strained the
system beyond its breaking point.[31] By the mid-1960s the monetary
system had become distended with an increasing amount of dollars, and
the par-value provisions of the system could not adjust gradually enough
to the divergent internal economic developments and policies of its major
participants, which affected the market value of their currencies and
strained their fixed par values.[32] As the differences in economic performance among nations became severe in terms of inflation, growth and
unemployment rates, and fiscal and budgetary policies, the global monetary system proved insufficiently supple to respond incrementally and
therefore erupted in periodic crises. Monetary market forces could exert
themselves only within the narrow limits that had been established on
the basis of what were primarily political decisions. Superimposed on the
varying dynamics of national economies was a fixed-rate international
monetary system that was inelastic and essentially static.

In the first half of the 1960s the only major country with a surplus that
achieved relative monetary stability was the Federal Republic; the only
major country with a deficit that achieved relative monetary stability was
the United States. But America posed problems of an even more serious
nature for the international monetary system and Germany. The principles of fixed exchange rates and convertibility of the Bretton Woods
system not only allowed the inflation of one country to be transmitted to
another country, they also generated inflationary effects through non-

inflationary structural payments deficits, such as those that the United States incurred in the early and mid-1960s. Although the United States did not yet suffer from excessive inflation (this came later in the 1960s), it was nonetheless exporting inflation because of massive capital outflows and the gradual structural deterioration of the American trade balance. In the 1960s a huge dollar outflow from the United States created excessive liquidity in European capital markets for a variety of reasons: an over-valued dollar, military expenditures abroad, the waning competitiveness of American products, fiscal and budgetary policies, foreign investment opportunities, and the temptation to jump over the EEC tariff barriers with American money rather than American goods.

The reasons that pushed American money abroad were the concrete manifestations of a deeper reality and reflected a fundamental rearrangement of the postwar international economic order. The phenomenal success of the European and Japanese reconstruction also signified that the economic relationship between the United States and the other industrialized countries was becoming more normal, that the unusual circumstances of the postwar era were coming to an end. The structural deterioration of the American balance of trade and balance of payments vis-à-vis Western Europe and Japan was the actual as well as the symbolic event of that readjustment, putting pressure on both the trade and the monetary regimes established in the postwar period.[33]

This structural readjustment, this trilateral spreading of prosperity and economic power among the United States, Western Europe, and Japan, was precisely what placed the most fundamental strain on the global monetary system, perhaps because the system had been designed for hegemonic leadership and could function best in the hierarchical economic and political order of the postwar period.[34] Much as the Community's stagnating institutions were unable to address the issues of the 1960s and essentially for the same reasons (a lack of political foresight and will), the world monetary system led by the United States found it too difficult to respond to the requirements of managing affluence in the 1960s, although it had dealt successfully with the requirements of scarcity in the 1950s. The full implementation of Bretton Woods through free convertibility of currencies eased the international redistribution of income, distorted as that redistribution remained so long as fixed exchange rates stayed in effect. To put it a different way, in the 1960s attempts at managing differential inflation rates among national economies proved difficult enough; managing an underlying and fundamental international redistribution of income in a smooth way proved impossible. In 1973 Otmar Emminger described the structural adjustment of prosperity in the 1960s as follows:

> This post-war adjustment implied, inter alia, that over time the large
> discrepancy between the income levels of the U.S. and other coun-

tries had to be progressively reduced. To give an illustrative example: the income per capita in Germany at the beginning of the fifties was only about ⅓ of that of the United States, and in 1960 was still only 44 percent. By 1973 it has risen to 85 percent of the American level, and to over 90 percent if the most recent exchange rates were to be applied. . . . Even with complete cost and price stability in the United States, if Europe and Japan had wanted to maintain their fixed dollar parities they would have had to accept an inflationary upward adjustment of their income and price levels. . . . This structural adjustment, or normalization, process presented much greater problems to the system of fixed parities than the conventional problem of inflation differentials.[35]

The chronic American balance-of-payments deficit reflected a fundamental disequilibrium that Washington was unable or unwilling to redress. As the U.S. Federal Reserve resisted repatriation of overseas dollars in exchange for gold, Europeans grew impatient of accumulating them and surrendering tangible assets to American interests in exchange for paper money that increasingly lacked reserve backing.[36] Massive capital outflows and after the mid-1960s the costs of Vietnam and the Johnson administration's Great Society programs (financed with government debt) produced a dollar glut on the market, which countries with strong currencies were committed to absorb and which could not be redeemed for gold because of the declining American gold stock.[37] America's partners began to feel that the United States was abusing its privilege of seigniorage. More extreme European critics, such as Jacques Rueff, saw the Federal Reserve as running a "paper mill," a "perfect inflation machine";[38] others considered the excessive accumulation of dollars in Europe a "reverse Marshall Plan."[39] Yet the dollar was protected against devaluation by its privileged position within the rigid international monetary system, a position that the Europeans felt should not absolve America of balance-of-payments discipline.

Generally, the Europeans felt that the major source of these problems lay across the Atlantic. Unlike the Americans, they believed that the central issue between the United States and Western Europe was money rather than trade, especially because the United States enjoyed a consistently favorable balance of trade with the Community. In the European view, the United States was acting irresponsibly and selfishly in not taking steps to remedy its chronic balance-of-payments problems (although Washington did make efforts to stem capital outflows) and in shifting a major part of the resulting adjustment burden onto its European partners. American deficits, which had been seen as a blessing in the 1950s, were now perceived to be the major burden placed on the West European economies.[40]

Of course Washington also had economic complaints. The United

States argued that Europeans had too conservative an attitude toward long-term credit and investment and that the allegiance to gold of some European central banks smacked of economic atavism in an age of complex postindustrial economics. Washington also resented trade discrimination by the EEC and accused the Community of violating GATT and betraying the principle of Atlantic free trade. Indeed, the GATT regime was also slackening. Although the Kennedy Round of tariff reductions (1962–67) had led to substantial cuts, other trade restrictions were growing, in many instances escaping from GATT's supervision and sanctions. The sources of Washington's displeasure with EEC practices were manifold, but focused largely on the Community's protectionist agricultural policy and its preferential trade agreements with an increasing number of countries.[41]

The resulting breakdown of the monetary and trade consensus had a devastating impact on the unity of the alliance. The mutual satisfactions that characterized the economic relationships of the 1950s gave way to the strains of the 1960s, which placed a particularly heavy burden on German-American relations.

The Federal Republic as Odd Man Out

The economic and monetary developments of the 1960s put a double strain on German monetary policy, one originating in the European Community, the other in the global system led by the United States. Although the principles of global interdependence and regional integration had been implemented only partly in the real world of money and trade, their impact on Germany's domestic monetary management was becoming increasingly visible, seriously burdening the Federal Republic's relations with its West European partners and its transatlantic ally.

When large discrepancies developed between Germany's consistently low inflation and the higher inflation of other members of the global monetary system, or when structural deficits of other countries exported inflationary pressure, the Federal Republic became the odd man out, with the D-Mark becoming the target of heavy speculative pressure. Obliged to provide D-Marks at fixed rates, the German Bundesbank was forced to absorb a large amount of dollars and other currencies, which created excessive liquidity within Germany. Although not immune to inflationary trends, the relatively conservative economic policies of the Federal Republic contrasted significantly with those of other EEC countries, and the Germans wanted their EEC partners to agree to a genuine and durable harmonization of their economic, regional, and sectoral policies.[42] This was to be done not on the basis of the highest inflation rate, but according to the degree of stability acceptable to the Federal Republic. In 1969 the president of the Bundesbank complained:

After trying for years to obtain a better coordination of economic and monetary policy—both in the narrower context of the EEC and the larger one of OECD—we must admit to ourselves that our conceptions of the primacy of monetary stability are not shared in equal measure by other countries. Even in those countries where monetary stability occupies a similarly high place on the scale of economic-political goals, the preconditions for retaining stability are mostly not as propitious as in the Federal Republic.[43]

"Imported" inflation was indeed a problem, especially in light of the Germans' sensitivity to the debasing of their currency. Capital inflows either constantly pushed the D-Mark toward appreciation or created excessive domestic liquidity.[44] Indeed, under the Bretton Woods regime of exchange rates, Germany was left with only two major remedies for its persistent balance-of-payments surplus: inflation and revaluation. Revaluation posed its own problems (which I have discussed in connection with the crisis of the French franc), and induced inflation, which was urged on the Germans in a study issued in 1967 by the OECD, was unacceptable for even more fundamental reasons.[45]

After experiencing disastrous inflation in 1923 and 1948, the Germans were understandably reluctant to promote inflation, especially because they felt they were being asked to underwrite what they regarded as undisciplined monetary practices by other governments. A German government with an encouraging or even permissive attitude toward inflation would have courted disaster at the polls and risked being shunned for violating the central tenet of Germany's economic culture.[46] In other words, the sacrosanct principle of the German domestic monetary system, a low inflation rate, was violated by the prevailing inflationary trend of the international monetary system. Inevitably, this burdened German-American relations because the expansionary monetary trend was basically set by the United States.

The Germans faced an insolvable dilemma. On the one hand, they continued to enjoy the benefits of an undervalued and thus export-boosting D-Mark—the result of fixed exchange rates that had the added attraction of providing predictable export-import pricing. The Germans were becoming prosperous under the auspices of the international monetary system, accumulated large foreign currency reserves through substantial and chronic balance-of-payments surpluses, and gradually developed an attitude about their economic prowess amounting to a form of "export nationalism."[47] On the other hand, the fixed-parity and free-convertibility principles of the Bretton Woods regime provided no effective safeguards against imported inflation and constantly threatened domestic price stability, the central principle of Germany's economic culture. Capital inflows, which bloated the domestic monetary supply,

generated heavy inflationary pressures in the Federal Republic and reduced the effectiveness of Germany's countercyclical fiscal and monetary
policies. In fact, the D-Mark was rapidly becoming the "counterpart
currency" of the dollar. For decades to come a strong D-Mark went hand
in hand with a weak dollar (and vice versa); rarely did the currencies rise
or fall together. Throughout the 1960s and early 1970s huge monetary
movements, either speculative or propelled by other factors, forced the
German central bank to create new money without leading to a corresponding contraction of the money supply in the major originating
country, the United States. This monetary and political asymmetry, characteristic of fixed-exchange-rate systems with obligatory currency interventions, became a major cause of world inflation.[48]

From the German perspective, the adjustment process of the Bretton
Woods system appeared cumbersome, and above all placed the major
burden of dealing with inflation on surplus countries rather than deficit
countries. Indeed, as early as 1964 the IMF noted in its annual report that
"international adjustment through changes in relative costs and prices
typically involves more upward adjustment in surplus countries than
downward adjustment in deficit countries."[49] Although the Germans
accepted the obligations of global interdependence and regional integration, they also wished to retain a measure of national independence on
issues that they regarded as vital for their economic welfare. In essence,
Bretton Woods had become anathema to the Federal Republic's domestic
economic principles.

But the Germans shied away from the responsibility of bringing down
Bretton Woods; indeed they helped support it. The myth that Bretton
Woods still worked could be sustained only because the German Bundesbank committed itself in 1967 not to convert dollars into gold (in effect it
had already stopped doing so in 1964), and otherwise refrained from
shaking the regime, as the French did with great relish.[50] The United
States in turn was induced by its monetary problems to apply strong
pressures on Europe to carry a larger burden of NATO's defense costs.
These pressures were necessarily pointed directly at the Federal Republic: the Germans were prosperous, and their security depended on
the United States. What had developed was a German-American relationship of mutual dependence. The United States supplied the Germans
with security benefits (which Washington considered a major source of
its balance-of-payments problem), and insisted on repayment in the form
of military offset payments, military purchases in the United States, and
other burden-sharing arrangements within NATO. The Germans opposed
such highly visible and politically charged payments (offset arrangements were finally terminated in 1976), arguing that their constant support of the global monetary system amounted to a massive if indirect
subsidy of the American monetary position.[51]

But even though West Germany made greater efforts in the 1960s and early 1970s than any other country to cushion the monetary system against constant onslaughts of the dollar, in effect helping to postpone the demise of Bretton Woods, differences between Bonn and Washington over monetary matters were serious and fundamentally irreconcilable, for they stemmed from opposing views of what constituted responsible monetary practices. For the United States, the export of money became the key feature of its international economic posture, ultimately leading to fundamental and long-lasting dislocations of its domestic economy. For Germany, the exportation of goods and the importation of money (and with it the importation of inflationary pressures) became the key feature of its political economy in the 1960s and early 1970s. The Germans paid for their domestic success of price stability with foreign policy problems.

The frequent German complaints about imported inflation were also the metaphor of deeper and unspoken dissatisfactions, masking political resentments and diplomatic frustrations. France insisted on Germany's support for the Common Agricultural Policy because the policy was the keystone of the Franco-German compact made when the two countries entered the Community framework, and the Germans felt they were the paymasters of Europe, absorbing the inflation rates caused by others and helping them support military and political ventures that were in some instances, as in the case of France, directed against the Germans themselves. As for the United States, the Germans felt called on to underwrite American policies even though they questioned the wisdom of these policies. They felt obliged to sustain them with D-Marks and political support because of their security dependence on the United States and their economic dependence on transatlantic and global markets.

It is essential to realize that the economic and monetary problems of the 1960s occurred at a time when successive governments in Bonn felt that their foreign policy goals were insufficiently understood and supported both in Washington and in Paris. In the 1960s Bonn's security policy was shaken by doctrinal and political shifts within NATO and the unpalatable political implications of East-West arms control negotiations, and its Eastern policy was in effect threatened with diplomatic isolation, as it constantly limped behind the more dynamic policies of its partners. The Germans' frustrations and grievances in the area of economic and monetary issues take on their full meaning only when placed in the context of other issues of central importance to them. In certain respects, the Germans transferred their complaints and disillusionments from one policy area to another.

10

The Enlargement of the Community and New Monetary Regimes: The Turbulent 1970s

> Looking back over the past ten years, one cannot but call it a turbulent decade. Apart from political turmoil—from Vietnam and Watergate to Iran and Afghanistan—it brought us to the breakdown of the dollar-based system of fixed exchange rates, two oil price explosions, the worst recession and the most stubborn inflation in the postwar period.
>
> —OTMAR EMMINGER, 1980

> All goods must be measured by some one thing. Now this unit is really demand, which brings and holds all goods together . . . but money has become, by virtue of convention, a sort of representative of demand. That is why it has the name it bears [nomisma]: it exists by law or convention [nomos], and not by nature; and we have the power of changing or cancelling its value. . . . Money suffers the same vicissitudes as goods: its value is not always constant; but it is steadier than the values of goods. That is why all goods must be priced in money; for then there will always be the possibility of exchange and with it of association between man and man.
>
> —ARISTOTLE, Ethics

The enumeration of German concerns that concluded the last chapter is also a suitable beginning for a consideration of the Federal Republic's reaction to the economic and monetary events of the 1970s, from a somewhat different perspective.

This different perspective emerges in the first instance from the somewhat different view on these matters of the new German government that came into office in October 1969. The new government in Bonn, under the SPD's Willy Brandt as chancellor and the FDP's Walter Scheel as vice chancellor and foreign minister, was determined to establish as quickly and convincingly as possible its Europeanist and Atlanticist credentials.

This seemed essential for at least three reasons. First, for almost two decades the SPD had opposed practically every important component of Bonn's foreign policies. To be sure, in the early 1960s the SPD after a painful internal process of adjustment had come to accept the main features of Bonn's security policies. But it had remained opposed to the narrow West European confines of the EEC and become a major voice of anti-Gaullist sentiment in the Federal Republic, echoing in that respect the Atlanticist wing of the CDU. Second, Willy Brandt was the first Social Democratic chancellor since the years of the Weimar Republic, and he and his party needed to demonstrate the SPD's capacity to govern responsibly after years as the opposition, especially in the area of foreign policy. Finally, the new government was determined to revitalize Bonn's stagnant Eastern policies (indeed, this was the political base of the coalition between the Social Democrats and the Free Democrats), and its preoccupation with the East required it to secure its diplomatic connections in the West in Washington, Paris, London, and Brussels.

The political configuration in other important capitals had changed as well. Georges Pompidou had replaced Charles de Gaulle as president of France, bringing a more nuanced Gaullism to French foreign policy; the British had arrived at a more convincingly constructive attitude toward the Common Market; and in both Washington and Moscow a new type and style of leadership were seeking to modify some basic tenets of postwar American and Soviet foreign policy. In particular, the United States began to rethink its trading and monetary policies and the transatlantic economic compact it had fashioned in the postwar era. It was a time of change, signifying a departure from the stagnant and timeworn diplomatic positions of the mid- and late 1960s.

By the late 1960s it had become clear in Europe that the mutually connected issues of the Community's size, its measure of institutional authority, and the erosion of the Bretton Woods monetary system required new initiatives. There was much controversy over the nature of these initiatives even as there was uncertainty about what forms they should take, where they would lead, and what their ultimate consequences would be. The postwar economic, strategic, and political order was coming to an end—in fact it had come to an end, its demise barely masked by the absence of clear-cut and compelling alternatives. Old economic and political structures were visibly eroding; new ones were only dimly visible and in any case marked by their own infirmities.

Community Enlargement and Monetary Union

In early December 1969 the EEC chiefs of government met at The Hague for an EEC summit, which dealt with the issues of enlarging the Community, the need to intensify economic and monetary union, and the supranational potential of the Community's institutions. At the summit in The Hague, the Six also agreed on a plan drafted by a committee led by Etienne Davignon of Belgium, which called for the EEC foreign ministers to meet twice a year (with lower-level officials to meet more frequently) in an attempt to arrive at a "European" foreign policy. At the first meeting in Munich in November 1970, the foreign ministers commissioned policy papers on a European Security Conference and the Middle East, which were considered at the second meeting, in Paris in May 1971. The report on the security conference was readily approved, but the Community's "peace plan" for the Middle East (which Israel viewed as pro-Arab) raised a good deal of controversy.

The French position on British entry had softened somewhat since de Gaulle's resignation. The French felt the need of Britain as a counterweight to an economically powerful and politically more assertive Germany,[1] and they expected Britain to buy a large amount of agricultural products from France once it was deprived of its privileged arrangements with the members of the Commonwealth. But President Pompidou was nonetheless determined to exact a stiff price for consenting to the EEC's enlargement. Above all he wanted an agreement to establish final financial regulations covering trade in agricultural goods, as well as measures that would enlarge the Community's activities in other fields, such as monetary, fiscal, industrial, and energy policies. Although the other five nations had no intrinsic objections to harmonizing the policies in these fields, they did not wish to have these issues interfere with the larger political question of Britain's entry. The French, on the other hand, insisted on a common position by the Six toward Britain on as many outstanding issues as possible, for they were convinced that their partners had in the past used France's rejection of Britain's entry as an excuse to play down their own reservations about enlarging the Community. In any event, France consented to early negotiations for British entry as soon as the Six concluded new EEC accords on farm financing and monetary policy—the overriding French interests.

The EEC summit provided the new German chancellor with a welcome opportunity to demonstrate his interest in European questions, but it also raised some troublesome political and economic issues for Bonn. The chancellor, his foreign minister, and their respective parties had long been committed to advancing the cause of British entry into the Common Market. The Brandt government also expected economic benefits from British membership and, more important, believed that it would provide added backing for its own Ostpolitik. Both Paris and Bonn looked toward

London for economic gain and political support, both perceived in London a suitable partner for their foreign policy aims, and both came by and large to be disappointed. Britain, a latecomer to the Community, was uneasy with the need to coordinate national policies to which the Six had become accustomed, and it remained a curiously detached European power, preoccupied with its chronic economic problems, determined to retain its postimperial insularity, and retaining the psychological attitude of the perennial balancer even as it lacked the power to act as one.[2]

At the summit in The Hague of 1969, Willy Brandt energetically pressed for British entry in the EEC and supported the idea of a European "monetary personality." With respect to the latter, Bonn's new government was much less enthusiastic about the implications of the common monetary policy advocated by the French. This issue was hedged for the time being. After the summit, the EEC's foreign ministers and ministers of finance and agriculture met in Brussels to guide the Common Market from its "transitional period" into its final and irrevocable stage, which according to the Treaty of Rome was to take effect on January 1, 1970. Two major problems were being negotiated: the financing of a common farm policy and the related issue of reinforcing the European Parliament's budgetary powers, thus giving the Common Market independent financial resources. On farm financing, agreement was reached to continue the existing practice of drawing on direct national contributions as well as farm import levies, and to begin turning over to the Community all tariffs on industrial imports (and a proportion of revenues collected through indirect taxation in the member states). Beginning in 1971, half the yield of food-import levies and industrial tariffs would go to the Community, and the proportion was to increase to 100 percent by 1975. France consented to a rather insignificant expansion of the European Parliament's power by giving it the final say from January 1, 1975, in elaborating the Community's budget, and by granting it limited powers to increase indirect taxes to help defray administrative costs.

As a response in part to external challenges and in part to internal dynamics, during 1970 and 1971 the Community launched several new programs, all of which had important implications for German foreign policy and the Common Market's relations with the United States: the Community established a common commercial policy, increased further the number of its preferential trade agreements, began negotiations for enlargement with Britain, Denmark, Norway, and Ireland, and set up a timetable toward establishing a monetary union under the so-called "Werner Plan" (named after Pierre Werner, the prime minister and finance minister of Luxembourg).

To take measure of the meaning and importance of the Werner Plan one must consider again the background of the global monetary system and the Federal Republic's reaction to it in the late 1960s.

In reaching toward a West European par-value system, the Europeans were in effect moving toward a regional Bretton Woods system (to be capped perhaps by a single currency for the Community) at the same time as the global Bretton Woods system was gradually edging toward floating exchange rates. During the period between the late 1960s and 1973 (the year the fixed-rate Bretton Woods system was replaced with floating rates), an embryonic West European monetary system was turning to a more regional fixed-rate arrangement. The dynamics of the global monetary system and the West European, regional monetary system were heading in opposite directions: the global system was moving toward floating rates, the regional system sought to retain and institutionalize fixed rates.

For the Federal Republic this posed intricate problems, because the overriding monetary interest of Germany, domestic price stability, now needed to be pursued amid the impending structural changes of the global and regional monetary systems. The Germans were eager to be relieved of their Bretton Woods obligations, which had threatened their domestic objective of monetary stability, but they could not escape from a similar set of burdens in a regional context. Although the rules of the game were changing, Bonn and the central bank in Frankfurt continued to experience the conflicting pull of global and regional monetary systems on domestic objectives and price stability. Of course the burdens of the regional constraints were mitigated by the ability of the West Germans to export price stability along with goods. As the strongest regional currency, the D-Mark could be used to impose monetary discipline on Western Europe without sacrificing the competitiveness of German goods.[3]

There was a powerful and seductive rationale behind the idea of the Werner Plan. Of the major industrial centers of the world—the United States, Japan, and Western Europe—only Europe did not have the benefit of a single currency, and many Europeans saw in the establishment of a monetary union the crowning achievement of economic integration, which would for all practical purposes approximate political integration. Others viewed it primarily as a shield against the disruptive dollar and a solution to the nagging problem of the CAP's financing system. Everyone was agreed on the commercial advantages of trading with more predictable exchange rates, even if they were to fall short of merging into a single currency and a full monetary union.[4]

The decision to create a single-currency area for the Common Market was, along with the decision for enlargement, the most momentous event since the establishment of the Community. But it was hedged in major respects and there was nothing irrevocable about it. Primarily at the insistence of the Federal Republic, the Werner Plan provided for several stages, the implementation of each to be conditional on progress in coordinating economic, budgetary, and fiscal policies. In effect, the

Germans made only a preliminary and revocable commitment, which could be annulled if the first stage of the economic and monetary union (the narrowing of margins and mutual financial assistance) did not lead after four years to the second stage of the plan.

The major reason for the German insistence to link monetary and economic union was that the various EEC members disagreed sharply over the institutional oversight of monetary support arrangements, and that their motives for seeking monetary union were at least in part contradictory. All six members of the Community wanted a system of regional exchange rates that would guard the Common Market against outside inflationary trends and disturbing capital transactions (especially from the United States), and that would provide an alternative to the dollar and pound sterling as a reserve currency. There was little agreement within the Community on how to accomplish this, however, and there was even less consensus on the economic and political purposes that were to be served by the Werner Plan.

Had the plan been fully implemented it would have required the harmonization of a wide variety of monetary and fiscal policies that were still the prerogative of national governments, and the Germans were unwilling to underwrite and finance the economic policies of their partners unless they conformed to German economic preferences and met Bonn's exacting standards of monetary stability and restraint. The French wanted a common currency policy to guard against the powerful influence of the dollar in European economic and monetary affairs, and they anticipated benefits from the currency assistance program as well as from the narrowing of the wide currency trading bands that undermined the Community's common farm policy, of which France was the chief beneficiary. The German government pushed for central institutions to put teeth in the economic guidelines and monetary and fiscal targets called for by the Werner Plan, believing that unless the Community could enforce economic and budgetary discipline on its members, West Germany would be obliged as the richest Common Market member to bail out economically weaker and perhaps fiscally more profligate EEC partners. In Europe two contending schools of thought were developing. The "monetarists" (primarily France and Belgium) believed that such monetary measures as joint floating and pooling of monetary reserves should determine the dynamics and development of an EEC economic and monetary union: monetary union first, policy harmonization later. The "economists" (primarily the Federal Republic and the Netherlands) insisted that binding stabilization programs and the coordination of national economic policies precede the linking of exchange rates and the pooling of monetary resources: economic harmonization first, monetary union later. Italy and Luxembourg were on the sidelines, arguing the compromise position of "parallel development."[5]

The disagreement between Germany and France stemmed at bottom

from the conflicting political priorities of their national political economies, which required different monetary policies. The Federal Republic
was approaching the status of an economic superpower (soon there was
talk in Washington of a German-American economic "bigemony"), and
the Germans were primarily interested in economic consolidation, and of
course in domestic monetary stability. The French had fallen behind and
felt the need to energize their economy with dynamic and expansionary
growth policies, even if they resulted in inflationary pressures.[6] Both
sought to turn the provisions of the Werner Plan to their own advantage
and to impose their own views on the economic and political development in the Community.[7] Fundamental political and economic considerations prevented agreement on what the purpose and meaning of a
monetary union ought to be, except for the negative reason that it might
provide an escape from U.S. monetary policy. But the Community's
failure to achieve a consensus on harmonizing economic policies also
deprived it of the opportunity to deepen its integration, which became
even more urgent with the Community's impending enlargement. Inevitably, this failure also made it much more difficult to arrive at a common
foreign and defense policy, then as well as later.

Two schools of thought reemerged in the Federal Republic as well,
making Bonn's attitude on the Werner Plan ambivalent from the beginning. The old disagreements between the political regionalists and the
Liberal economic globalists, which had divided governments led by the
CDU in the 1950s and 1960s, reappeared in the government led by the SPD.
Like Adenauer, Brandt gave precedence to a regional political solution,
and at the conference in The Hague of December 1969 he supported the
idea of a "European currency personality." Karl Schiller, Brandt's fellow
Social Democrat and the government's economics minister, followed in
the footsteps of Ludwig Erhard and with the support of the Bundesbank
sought to retain for Germany as much monetary control as possible: the
Germans were agreed that price stability was their overriding objective,
but were less certain whether the regional framework was the appropriate context in which to achieve it.[8] The carefully hedged stages of the
Werner Plan reflected this ambivalence between political and economic
considerations. But the Werner Plan failed to get off the ground in any
event (it was reanimated a few years later in the less ambitious provisions
of the "currency snake"), because the Europeans could not agree on how
to deal with the dollar. In May 1971 the Germans floated the D-Mark
independently, but this was merely another indication that they could
not sufficiently reconcile their economic and political differences within
the EEC.

Even the French had second thoughts. Pompidou was quickly fright-
ened off by the supranational implications of the Werner Plan and hoped
for support from the British, who were expected to belong to the EEC

between 1973 and 1975 (when the crucial negotiations over supranational monetary arrangements would be implemented). On May 24, 1971, after his conference with President Pompidou, Prime Minister Edward Heath told the House of Commons:

> We agreed that the identity of the national states should be preserved within the framework of the growing Community. This means, of course, that while the European Commission has provided and will in the future continue to provide a valuable contribution, the Ministerial Council should also in the future remain the forum in which important decisions are taken, and that the process of harmonization will not receive preference over decisive national interests. We agreed that the maintenance and strengthening of the structure of cooperation in such a Community requires that all decisions should in practice be taken unanimously if the vital interests of one or several Members are at stake.[9]

The likelihood of British membership had a bearing on the issue in yet another way. There was some hope that London's worldwide financial relations could make the Community a leading financial center of the world. The Six had enough resources to instill a new vitality in British financial markets, and sufficient monetary clout to stave off the periodic speculative pressures exerted on the pound sterling in currency markets. France insisted, however, that Britain not join the Community unless it terminated the reserve role of sterling. The French opposed continuation of the privileged access to London's capital market enjoyed by the developed sterling-area countries,[10] because from it London would gain advantages not available to other EEC countries in financial, insurance, and trading transactions. The French also feared that the EEC would be burdened with Britain's financial obligations, for there had been periodic speculative runs on the pound, and investors were holding more than $10 billion in British pounds and treasury securities (while Britain's own gold and currency reserves were only about one-third of that). Perhaps most important, the French entertained the unrealistic hope that Paris could become the financial center of the Common Market, and therefore sought to start the competition on a roughly equal footing.

The role of sterling was a central if unofficial issue during the negotiations over British entry that began in spring 1971. It was widely understood that after Britain's application had twice been rejected in the preceding decade a third failure would be the last, and there was much relief when a two-day summit in Paris between Prime Minister Heath and President Pompidou in May opened the way for enlarging the Community to include Britain and the other applicant states, Ireland, Denmark, and Norway. During the meeting Heath agreed to phase out sterling as a reserve currency, and in June the final negotiations on British entry were completed in Luxembourg. They provided that Britain would join in January 1973 and would set aside in stages its tariffs against other Community members by 1977. The other EEC members were to proceed in the same way with their own tariffs against British goods, which were generally lower to begin with. In November the British Parliament consented to British entry by an unexpectedly wide margin (356 to 244), and although detailed enabling legislation was still required, British accession had for all practical purposes been accomplished. In January 1972 Britain and the other applicants formally joined in a treaty enlarging the Community to ten members, which included a "fiscal act" consisting of special agreements and declarations and a special protocol pertaining to the role of the pound sterling in the new enlarged market. (Norway, the fourth prospective new member of the EEC, never joined. Norway's Socialist prime minister, Trygve Bratteli, favored membership and signed the treaty of accession in January 1972, but a referendum in September 1972 organized by the succeeding Conservative government resulted in a narrow majority against Norway's membership.)

The Monetary Crisis of 1971 and the Smithsonian Agreement

In addition to its internal disputes, the Community faced serious external problems (especially with the United States), which came to a crucial stage during 1971 and 1972. As always, they aggravated tensions within the EEC.

The sources of Washington's displeasure with EEC practices were manifold but focused largely on three related areas: the Community's preferential trade agreements with an increasing number of countries (notably in the Mediterranean) which violated the most-favored-nation principle;[11] the Community's protectionist common agricultural policy; and the unloading of the Common Market's high agricultural surpluses (encouraged by high, subsidized EEC price levels) on traditional U.S. markets, especially in the Far East and North Africa. Moreover, the United States feared that these detriments to American trade would become even more formidable when Britain and the other applicants joined the Common Market and EFTA's remaining members might gain associated status.[12]

Spokesmen for the Common Market objected in turn to American quotas on many important commodities, and especially criticized the American Selling Price (ASP) system, which levied duties on benzenoid chemicals not on the price of the import but on their domestic prices in the United States. Above all, the Europeans felt that the central issue between the United States and the Common Market was monetary rather than commercial. In the European view, the United States was acting irresponsibly in not taking drastic steps to remedy its balance-of-payments problems and in shifting a major part of the burdensome consequences onto its European allies and trading partners. The United States had been running deficits for most of the last two decades, and the countries in dollar surplus were for all practical purposes no longer even demanding American gold for American dollars.

In the 1970s the dollar came under serious pressure, which in turn rendered the D-Mark an even more desirable object of speculation. Washington had abused the dollar's reserve role for years, and the United States now faced serious short-term payments difficulties. Between 1965 and 1970 Washington had financed budgetary deficits with excessive monetary expansion, the Federal Reserve had pursued an erratic stop-and-go policy, and in 1970 the United States ran a deficit of $10.7 billion to foreign central banks. International money markets became convinced that the dollar was overvalued, and speculation against it increased. Persistent dollar crises between 1969 and summer 1971 involved massive capital movements and sustained runs on American reserve assets, mainly gold. During 1970 the lowering of American interest rates and a strong speculative outflow of dollars from the United States led to an even larger influx of dollars into Europe, and in 1971 the United States experienced its first trading deficit since 1893. During the first quarter of 1971 the American trade deficit totaled $5 billion, and when the U.S. Federal Reserve massively increased the money supply in January 1971 to July 1971 the resulting outflow of short-term funds undermined the remaining confidence in the dollar and persuaded international markets that the dollar's devaluation had become inevitable and imminent.[13]

Faced with the prospect of losing its remaining gold reserves as other governments converted dollars into gold, President Nixon in August 1971 unilaterally suspended the dollar's convertibility to gold and imposed a 10 percent surcharge on certain imports.[14] These actions, which effectively ended a key feature of the Bretton Woods arrangement (the principle of fixed exchange rates remained intact for the time being), set in motion a series of events with political and economic consequences that were far-reaching, if hard to foresee in their specific effects.

When President Nixon ended the convertibility of dollars into gold and imposed the 10 percent surcharge on imports, he insisted that the United States would not devalue the dollar. Instead, Washington wanted other countries, especially the Common Market countries and Japan, to revalue and thus increase the cost of their exports. (The 10 percent import surtax was intended to provide leverage for Washington's negotiations with Japan and Europe.) The American position was basically that the dollar's problems stemmed from the protectionist and unfair trade and exchange-rate policies of other countries, and their unwillingness to share adequately in their own defense and in other burdens that the United States had shouldered for many years.

Beginning in the 1960s and throughout the 1970s the close connections between security and economic policies in the German-American relationship became increasingly problematical. At the core of the problem was the question of whether common military-strategic goals within the alliance, the very commonality of which was being called into question, could also engender common economic interests (a view pressed by the United States), or whether economic problems should be treated separately from issues of security (a view held by West European and German governments). As the disagreements on this issue became sharper, and as the issue of burden sharing narrowed to the costs of maintaining U.S. troops in Europe, it necessarily pointed specifically to the Federal Republic. At the same time, there was a much larger dimension to the issue. Throughout the postwar period the United States had sought to preserve American hegemony in the military-strategic context of NATO. As the American balance-of-payments position weakened and American gold reserves were drained, Washington used a highly assertive burden-sharing policy to ease the monetary pressures, urging the Europeans to make larger financial contributions and shoulder larger political and economic burdens. This comprehensive view of burden sharing created an increasingly problematic and abrasive linkage between security issues and economic issues.[15]

In September 1971, after preliminary negotiations were under way between the United States and the other countries of the Group of Ten, Secretary of the Treasury John Connally, Jr., made clear that the United States wanted not only a substantial realignment of exchange rates but also support for its military-strategic expenditures and foreign aid programs.

To the Europeans, it seemed preposterous that they should adjust their currency parities and make other concessions to absorb a huge amount of American goods and services, simply to allow the United States to continue its investments abroad and prop up American military-strategic commitments around the world. America's allies felt that they were already helping indirectly to finance the Vietnam War (during the 1960s America's net balance-of-payments deficit on military expenditures amounted to $32 billion) while the United States was buying up European industrial plants with money that European countries were lending either directly or indirectly. The French in particular were concerned that the United States was buying up real assets with inflated dollars, and that many economic decisions affecting important sectors of European economies were taken in the United States.

But other EEC countries also turned away attempts by American companies to acquire additional subsidiaries in Europe.[16] The Europeans argued that they had already helped considerably: the Germans had floated the D-Mark in May 1971, which caused a good deal of domestic political difficulty; EEC countries had helped sustain the two-tier gold market system; and they (especially the Germans) had not demanded repayment of debts, accepting a huge amount of U.S. Treasury bills while the United States refused to devalue the dollar or curb inflation. EEC members urged the United States to devalue the dollar; Washington argued that the dollar was overvalued only against the currencies of a dozen or so countries, notably Japan, Canada, and the countries of Western Europe, and that a dollar devaluation would strengthen the dollar against all other currencies to the disadvantage of developing nations (an argument that the Europeans viewed as somewhat hypocritical in light of the import levy of 10 percent across the board). Throughout the 1960s the United States had resisted the necessity of adjusting the dollar price of gold: "This change, when finally undertaken, was forced by foreign monetary authorities, especially those in Great Britain and France. Changing the price of gold was much more than a U.S. problem. All countries with large gold holdings were involved, for the change redistributed wealth among nations."[17]

All parties agreed that in addition to the short-term problem caused by the monetary crisis, there was a need to reform the world monetary system itself. Fears were widespread that unless the differences between the United States and Europe and Japan could be ironed out speedily, amicably, and fundamentally, retaliatory protectionism between trading areas would result, contracting world trade and causing a disastrous reversal of the postwar trend toward relatively liberalized trade and investment policies. At the very least, the uncertainty over exchange rates and international trade arrangements could be expected to dampen long-term economic planning and increase the dangers of world recession.

But the Europeans found it difficult to speak with a single voice. For although the Community's commitment to a monetary union and common currency was fundamentally at odds with the American desire for freely floating exchange rates, differences among EEC members (especially between France and Germany) made it difficult for the Community to articulate a common position. France opposed an appreciation of the franc vis-à-vis the dollar, and the Germans had already increased the value of the D-Mark by floating it in May 1971. France adopted a dual exchange rate (a "commercial" franc rate for foreign trade and a "financial" franc rate for all other transactions), but Bonn deplored dual markets and other ways of controlling exchange rates, preferring a free market solution such as the floating of the D-Mark.

The economic and monetary disagreements between France and Germany, which were aggravated by the personal disputes between their finance ministers Valéry Giscard d'Estaing and Karl Schiller, were also tied to larger and conflicting political purposes.[18] The German government wanted to shield German-American relations from the increasingly acrimonious disputes between the United States and Europe, fearing adverse consequences for its Ostpolitik and the related matter of the continued American military presence in Europe.[19] The Germans were therefore much more willing than the French to accommodate Washington, which tempted Washington into a clumsy attempt to undermine the Europeans' bargaining position by holding out the possibility of bilateral negotiations between Washington and Bonn.

At the same time, the "concerted" European float against the dollar advocated by Karl Schiller would have enhanced Germany's economic and political position in the Community. By narrowing the fluctuations among EEC currencies and shaping them into a more coherent monetary "unit," the strongest (the D-Mark) would inevitably push the others up to higher values against the dollar and attenuate upward pressures on the D-Mark, protecting the competitiveness of German exports in Europe. This would have had deflationary consequences in all EEC countries, a welcome effect from the German point of view but something the other countries were less willing to accept. In short, the partial harmonization of EEC exchange rates against the dollar would have tended to give the D-Mark a central place among EEC currencies, which France found unpalatable for political as well as economic reasons.

The French therefore advocated a large revaluation of the D-Mark in addition to the substantial upward revaluation that had already taken place since May, and opposed a devaluation of the franc. (Although France did not favor a concerted float, wider trading margins were also unacceptable. They would have disturbed the Community's agricultural financing system and allowed the D-Mark and other currencies to drift down, thus putting an end to the franc's advantageous undervaluation.) These issues were ultimately resolved in a compromise. But they again demonstrated that the economic and monetary interests of France and Germany were divergent and that these differences strongly affected the political positions of both nations on European integration.

In concurrence with the Franco-German discussions, acrimonious negotiations were taking place between the United States and Western Europe. Washington was pressing for an upward revaluation of European currencies, specific and fundamental measures to lower barriers against American exports, and higher contributions to American military expenditures. The Europeans sought a devaluation of the dollar and a lifting of the import surcharge. While these negotiations were being held at various conferences of the International Monetary Fund (IMF), the Organization for Economic Cooperation and Development (OECD), the Group of Ten, and the General Agreement on Tariffs and Trade (GATT), the Europeans employed a variety of measures to keep their currencies from rising too high, including intervention in monetary markets, adjustment of interest rates, and exchange controls. But these measures were coordinated inadequately if at all, because conflicting political and economic calculations of the various European countries precluded a common position.

The protracted Euro-American monetary talks were finally brought to an end in December 1971 in Washington, when President Nixon agreed to drop the import surcharge and devalue the dollar by 8.6 percent against the price of gold, or 7.9 percent against foreign currencies. (Although this was accomplished by increasing the price of gold from $35 an ounce to $38 an ounce, it did not mean that the U.S. Treasury would henceforth be willing to supply gold at the new price.) All in all, the formal devaluation of the dollar and the upward revaluation of foreign currencies decreased the value of the dollar by about 10 to 12 percent. Against the dollar the German D-Mark went up 13.5 percent and the French franc and British pound 8.6 percent.

Nixon's characterization of the accord of December 1971 as "the most significant monetary agreement in the history of the world" was something of an overstatement. The Smithsonian Agreement turned out to be only a provisional settlement of the world's monetary problems. It left unresolved such important issues as the convertibility of the dollar balances held by central banks, the roles of gold, dollars, and Special Drawing Rights in a new international monetary system,* the problem of short-term capital flows, and the touchy issue of negotiating trading arrangements involving the United States, the European Community, and Japan. In effect the events of 1971 allowed continued American monetary expansion for a few years by shifting most adjustment measures to America's trading partners, but they also put renewed pressures on the new parities established with the Smithsonian Agreement of December 1971. After 1971 the world revolved around an unalloyed dollar standard, until the standard itself crumbled in 1973 with the generalized float of the dollar and the concerted float of stronger EC currencies. But Washington refused to redeem American reserve assets for foreign-held dollars, abstained from intervening in the foreign exchange markets to support the new dollar parity, and shifted the risk of holding dollars as reserve assets to its trading partners by scrapping exchange rate guarantees, which it had extended in the past with swap networks and Roosa bonds.[20]

In the 1970s American policies allowed the dollar to decline, to shift adjustment pressures to other countries, induce them to underwrite perpetually imbalanced budgets, and increase the competitiveness of American exports—only to reverse the procedure in the 1980s on the

*Special Drawing Rights (SDRS) are a reserve asset created by the International Monetary Fund in 1969, made up of prescribed quotas of financial contributions remitted by IMF members.

basis of an overvalued dollar. Throughout, domestic economic consider-ations took precedence over foreign policy consequences: "Looking at government policy over five administrations helps reveal a number of themes which, if not invisible in shorter perspective, are more sharply apparent in the longer stretch. Most obvious is the close connection between domestic and foreign economic policy. In retrospect, a good part of American foreign economic policy seems the attempt to make an international system out of the consequences of the economic policies pursued at home. . . . By the end of the seventies, [a] loss of direction, combined with nostalgia for outworn hegemonic formulas, pointed to-ward increasing conflict between American policy and the realities of a more plural world."[21]

In Germany the arrangements of December 1971 were generally well received. There was relief that the international monetary system had at least been patched up if not fundamentally reformed, and that the Com-munity's attempts to establish a monetary union could proceed after having been interrupted by the floating of the D-Mark in May 1971. But troublesome issues remained in the wake of the Smithsonian conference. The realignment of currencies again complicated the Community's agri-cultural financing system (as had the unilateral floating of the D-Mark in May 1971), and required price adjustments through levies and subsidies so that prices could remain constant in terms of national currencies. Nor were the difficulties between the United States and the Community resolved in any thoroughgoing way. The dollar did not regain sufficient strength, which kept up pressure on the D-Mark and created new uncer-tainties about future monetary developments, and the dollar's noncon-vertibility remained a problem, with Washington putting off any sweep-ing solution and the Europeans remaining eager to obtain other reserve assets for the dollar balances they had accumulated.

Most disturbing perhaps was the continuing American pressure to revise the EEC's farm support program. A basic change in the farm pro-gram would have shaken the Community's very foundations because the central compact made between France and Germany in the mid-fifties would have been undone (the French had accepted industrial free trade in return for agricultural free trade, supplemented by a generous agricul-tural support system), and it would have been hazardous in domestic politics given the political power of the German and French agricultural lobbies. Acquiescence in Washington's demands would have meant dis-mantling the agricultural basis of European integration and an important element of its domestic political support, without which there could be no hope of monetary, economic, or political union.

With respect to monetary union, although the fully integrative inten-tions of the Werner Plan were in effect abandoned, the Community did move through the European "currency snake" toward a more stringently coordinated monetary arrangement. In 1972, after the Smithsonian Agreement, the EEC Commission and EEC finance ministers decided to launch a new attempt at narrowing currency margins within the EEC.[22] At that time, currencies could in an extreme case fluctuate by as much as 9 percent, which was considered too large a margin for effective monetary coordination. It was therefore agreed to narrow the permissible difference between EC exchange rates to plus or minus 2.25 percent. This "snake" arrangement was to be constrained within the "tunnel" of the range of fluctuation permitted the dollar by the Smithsonian Agreement, which was plus or minus 4.5 percent. The basic purposes of the snake arrangement were generally the same as those of its abortive predecessor, the Werner Plan, and its successor, the European Monetary System of the late 1970s (although not nearly as ambitious): to provide for national economic discipline, to create regional monetary stability amid global monetary disturbances, and to extend integration into the monetary area.

But the snake-in-the-tunnel arrangement rested on shaky premises, both within and without the Community. The snake relied on an elaborate set of central bank interventions to keep an EEC member within the 2.25 percent range, primarily by buying or selling one's national currency, using the dollar only to sustain the joint float against the dollar. This obliged EEC central banks to buy the weaker EEC currencies (to be repurchased by the weaker members later), amounting to a short-term credit arrangement. There was the perennial difficulty of harmonizing the divergent economic and financial situations of the member states. Like other integrative monetary arrangements, the snake entailed a transnational redistribution of income, transferring financial resources from the prosperous to the weak and obliging the weak, at the insistence of the strong, to follow domestic policies that would make their currencies more robust. France, Britain, and Italy found it onerous to fulfill the attending obligations and therefore left the snake (in the case of France to return later, only to leave again), or insisted on special dispensations of the rules. In effect only five of the nine EEC members remained part of the snake, which was itself quickly transformed into a D-Mark zone. By the mid-1970s EEC countries were for all practical purposes split into two monetary groups, a situation hardly conducive to the Community's monetary, economic, or political cohesion—especially since non-Community European nations were pegging their own currencies on the D-Mark.

In 1975 the German Bundesbank complained again about what the Germans saw as the basic problem of the snake arrangement: "The European system of narrowed margins has proved to be more vulnerable than had widely been assumed. Recent events have confirmed that fixed exchange rate relationships, even if they apply only to a limited region, cannot be defended in the longer run unless they are supported by parallel trends among all participants in prices, costs, and balances of payments."[23] With respect to outside support, there could of course be a tunnel only for as long as the dollar had a fixed exchange rate. But the weakness of the dollar kept the snake at the upper limits of the tunnel from the beginning and ultimately led in spring 1973 to the collapse of the tunnel itself.[24] The generalized float of the dollar in effect marked the demise of the Bretton Woods system.[25]

All things considered, from the German perspective the system of floating exchange rates in effect from 1973 was better suited to cope with the monetary strains than was the fixed-rate system it replaced. The generalized float of the dollar and the transition to a regime of floating exchange rates returned a measure of monetary autonomy to the Bundesbank in that it allowed a nationally directed monetary policy.[26] As a former chief of the Bundesbank noted, this amounted to a Copernican revolution in the international monetary system: "Exchange rate stability was no longer decreed from outside, but achieved and sustained by inside stability. . . . Domestic economic stability [became] recognized as the basic precondition for stable foreign economic relations, which corresponds to an old German concern."[27] This concern was price stability. Floating exchange rates also implied that the value of a national currency would reflect the level of price stability and that it would become more difficult to import, or export, inflation.

But fluctuations of exchange rates turned out to be much more erratic than had been expected. Because inflation rates among industrial countries ranged between 5 and 20 percent, it was not surprising that nominal exchange rates would also change. But they rarely changed by the right amount to offset differentials in inflation. They overshot in both directions for long periods, causing real exchange rates to vary considerably. Moreover, floating exchange rates affected trade negotiations between the United States and the EC, for sharp movements in exchange rates distorted or neutralized trade concessions, minimizing or canceling their real effects.[28] The fluctuations in the relationship of D-Mark to dollar were particularly pronounced. After the beginning of generalized floating in 1973, there was between 1973 and 1978 a steady and strong appreciation of the D-Mark, then a rapid decline between January 1980 and August 1981 that brought the price of the dollar in D-Marks to 2.57, only about 10 percent below the level of late March 1973. There were shorter, three- to six-month cycles as well, and there were of course daily fluctuations in the range of 1 to 3 percent.[29]

In 1974, when Helmut Schmidt took over the chancellorship from Willy Brandt, economic problems had come to the foreground on Germany's foreign policy agenda. Compared with the economic malaise of many West European countries and the United States, the condition of West Germany stood out in general as an example of economic and monetary strength. Although real GNP growth was modest, exports were booming, unemployment and inflation were among the lowest in the OECD area, and the German economy had weathered the oil price shock of 1973–74 without fundamental distortions. Even so, Bonn faced difficulties. In fall 1975, when the EEC Council of Ministers took up the Community's budget for 1976, Germany found itself outvoted in supporting a substantially larger cut in agricultural supports than the other countries viewed as desirable. Bonn did not resort to its right of veto, but spokesmen made it clear that Germany did not intend to be placed repeatedly in such an isolated position.

As far as Bonn was concerned, the fundamental issue was the Community's unsound fiscal policy with regard to regional aid and social funds, assistance to nonassociated developing countries, and above all the common agricultural policy. The Schmidt government took a much tougher stand than had any previous German government on the issues of fiscal responsibility and reform of the Community's entrenched bureaucracies. Bonn made it clear that it would agree to monetary demands by EEC members only if they would seek to solve the larger structural problems of the Community. This was clearly a reflection of the personal convictions of the new chancellor. Although Schmidt was willing to be a "good European," and in particular to support measures that could lead to monetary union, he also demanded that fellow EEC members make reforms in return for Germany's heavy financial contributions to the Common Market. But Bonn was persuaded that criticism of the Community was justified by France's decision to leave the European single-currency area (although Germany offered to underwrite with substantial loans the costs to France), Italy's imposition of import controls (in spite of massive German financial assistance), the uncoordinated Community response to the energy crises, Britain's waffling over some aspects of its commitment to the EEC, and several other, smaller issues. Correctly or not, the Germans felt that the monetary plight of some EEC countries was due in large part to economic improvidence and political irresponsibility, and that the sense of drift in the Community could be overcome only by political leadership that faced up to the challenges of the future and was more resistant to the day-by-day pressures of political expediency.[30]

From the Snake to the European Monetary System

The new global and regional monetary systems that emerged in the 1970s, subjected to centrifugal pressures, were also endangered from their inception by worldwide financial developments. As national authorities in Europe, Japan, and the United States compensated with inflationary economic policies for the transfer of economic wealth from the industrialized North to the oil-producing nations that was implied by the rise in oil prices, the West German fears of global or imported inflation were revived and realized. The initial problem with the oil price rise in 1973–74 was the fear that there would be insufficient liquidity to finance the oil import bills of the major industrial countries. The rise created a short-lived dollar shortage that ended the downward pressure on the dollar. A secondary concern of the West Germans in particular was that industrialized nations would compensate for the loss of purchasing power caused by the oil price rise with inflationary fiscal and monetary policies.

The result was an uncontrolled and uncontrollable expansion of global liquidity. Neither national central banks nor international monetary organizations were able to cope with massive shifts of capital, which escaped governmental control and which were accelerated by a rapid multiplier effect through currency markets open twenty-four hours a day around the world. The price of national currencies was set by capital flows responding to political developments rather than economic fundamentals such as trade balances, national growth rates, gross domestic investment, and other objective indicators of national economic strength. Monetary factors and capital flows began to overwhelm the real economy, and a wide gap opened between the goods market (the production sector of the economy) and the capital market (the financial sector). Calling for joint German-American monetary arrangements to help narrow the gap, the Bundesbank's chief said: "What the Bundesbank would like to achieve over the *medium term* is to let the exchange rate of the D-Mark move by and large in line with the differences in inflation rates between West Germany and a weighted average of other major countries. This would mean that we would, in relation to our industrial partner countries, neither import nor export inflation via the exchange rate. This goal is not easy to achieve because in the short run *other influences can exert a more powerful effect on exchange rates than inflation differentials*" (italics in original).[31] Although the exchange rate is perhaps the most important price in an economy, at this time it seemed on the way to becoming the only price that mattered. These monetary and political developments led to unanticipated and wide currency fluctuations, which distorted trade balances, magnified the hazards of lending and borrowing, impeded transnational economic coordination, and undermined regional attempts at monetary integration.

On these uncertain and shifting grounds, the Federal Republic and France joined forces to plan yet another integrative monetary construct—a development aided by the close friendship between Valéry Giscard d'Estaing and Helmut Schmidt. In summer 1978 Germany and France launched a major new initiative toward a European Monetary System (EMS), in a renewed attempt to coordinate more closely the currencies and economies of the EEC members. At this time the currency snake, in which the EEC currencies were held to a narrow range of fluctuation, had lost much of its meaning because it had shrunk to a D-Mark zone: this consisted of countries (including nonmembers of the EEC) that could afford to have their currencies rise with the D-Mark, or that were helped by the Germans to do so.

The idea of a revived European monetary union was first floated in October 1977 by Roy Jenkins (a former Labour chancellor of the exchequer and home minister, and at the time the president of the EC Commission), but it could not have got off the ground without the close political and personal rapport between President Giscard d'Estaing and Chancellor Schmidt. Both were determined to revitalize European monetary coordination and create a protective shield against global monetary disturbances.

The European Monetary System, not joined by Britain and allowing Italy certain dispensations, entailed highly complex intervention mechanisms to stabilize intra-European exchange rates. At its core was a European currency unit (ECU), a composite monetary basket that would serve the EMS settlement process as a numeraire, reserve asset, and means of settlement; it was modeled after the Special Drawing Rights of the International Monetary Fund. Although the EMS was primarily a mechanism for fixed exchange rates rather than a monetary union, there was the expectation that the ECU would ultimately become a common currency for the Community and a major reserve asset along with the dollar and SDRs.[32] Changes in central rates required the consent of all participants (an important difference from the "snake" arrangement), and the use of the ECU as the fixed numeraire for the central rates was intended to assure that a change in the ECU central rate of one currency would also modify the rates of other currencies. This amounted to the creation of a parity grid, which was of particular importance to the Germans who wanted multiple and simultaneous intervention obligations that made adjustments the joint responsibility of surplus and deficit countries. The EMS was to provide credit support for members (EEC members would put one-fifth of their reserves into a common fund) and the plan envisaged at a later stage the operation of a European Monetary Fund, supplemental to the IMF, with credit facilities geared to regional European needs, and having the potential to become a rudimentary European central bank.

In short, the key features of the EMS were a set of rules limiting exchange-rate movements between EEC currencies, a joint unit of account, a complex system of intervening in the exchange markets, and a system of credit facilities to aid EMS countries experiencing balance-of-payments difficulties. It represented a move toward an exchange rate union rather than the full blown monetary union announced at the summit in The Hague in 1969.[33]

This joint Franco-German initiative reflected larger political and monetary considerations. Chancellor Schmidt's European proclivities, which were genuine but restrained by his sense of realism,[34] were encouraged by his close political and personal collaboration with President Giscard d'Estaing and by the need to protect the D-Mark and the overall European monetary market from Washington's passive dollar policy, a task that the snake had performed inadequately. To the extent that the EMS was designed as a dollar shield, it was the regional complement of broader efforts at creating a new monetary order. By embedding the D-Mark in a regional system of fixed exchange rate, the EMS dispersed throughout the system the monetary liabilities and political uncertainties inherent in a single-currency, nationally denominated numeraire, which the D-Mark would otherwise have borne directly and solely. Even though in a parity grid the stronger currency remains the most attractive, it was to be expected that the attractiveness of the D-Mark as an object of speculation would be spread over the wider ECU currency portfolio.[35] The EMS represented at bottom an attempt to denationalize reserve holdings, a function that Special Drawing Rights performed on the global level only to a limited extent.

This did not mean that the EMS carried with it a deliberate anti-American bias. The trend toward diversifying international reserves led the D-Mark to occupy a modest but for the Germans uncomfortably large role in the evolving international monetary system. In fact this development intensified German-American cooperation, as the Germans attempted to contain the D-Mark's reserve role, the Americans began to stabilize the dollar, and both tried to prevent the "easy money" available on the Eurocurrency markets from circumventing their domestic minimum reserve requirements. When the Carter administration began its dollar stabilization program in 1978, it reversed at least for a time the American practice of placing most adjustment obligations on allies and trading partners, which had begun with the turbulence of the 1960s and was renewed with Washington's disconnection of the dollar-gold parity. The weakening of the dollar, the attending danger that OPEC countries would begin to shun it, the accelerating inflation in the United States, and the Europeans' resolve to protect themselves with the EMS compelled the United States to replace its dollar policy of benign neglect with one of animated concern. The resulting closer cooperation between the Federal Reserve and other major central banks resembled the situation of the 1960s, except that Washington's monetary and political clout diminished in the 1970s and 1980s, and the ground rules of the game had been revised considerably. The D-Mark had become the main counterpart currency to the dollar, making it the chief intervention currency for the dollar and the chief reserve currency of the United States (a role it was to share increasingly with the Japanese yen).[36]

Even so, the general enfeeblement of American leadership that Schmidt saw embodied in the Carter administration had an important bearing on the creation of the EMS. In the early years of the Carter administration the dollar fell steeply against the D-Mark, yen, and other currencies. The Europeans and Japanese believed that the United States was consciously talking down the dollar in an effort to redress the American payments deficit by cheapening American exports and increasing the price of imports. The dollar's steep decline deepened divisions within the Atlantic economy that were partially smoothed over by the Carter administration's dollar support program, which pledged American intervention in the foreign exchange markets to support the dollar, financed by the issuance of foreign currency securities, the so-called Carter bonds.[37] The infirmities of American diplomacy and the volatility of the dollar, forcing the West Germans to sustain the conflicting shocks of hot and cold monetary *Wechselbäder*,[38] seemed to require a coordinated European political alternative, of which the EMS was the monetary manifestation. The EMS was seen as a step toward monetary stability in Europe, and as a coordinating instrument that could provide an alternative to the Community's political integration, place its impending enlargement on a more solid regional monetary foundation, underline the urgency of CAP reforms, and lend credence to the Europeans' claim that they intended to put their own house in order.

Yet the Bundesbank remained wary of any solution to the problems of Europe or the dollar that incurred an obligation to support a fixed rate of exchange for the D-Mark. This was particularly true in 1978, when inflation rates varied from 3 to 12 percent within the EMS countries. The Bundesbank enjoyed the relative autonomy it had obtained since the generalized float of the dollar in 1973 and was not eager to surrender it to a European endeavor that had the potential to mire West Germany in an *Inflationsgemeinschaft* rather than the anticipated and publicly stated objective of a *Stabilitätsgemeinschaft*. Unlike the French, the Bundesbank believed that economic policies should be harmonized before exchange rates, and that "stable exchange rates should be seen mainly as symptoms and indicators of stable—and harmonious—underlying trends in the various member countries."[39] This had been the German position since the Werner report, but the exigencies of politics had overwhelmed the logic of economics.

The EMS was a symbolic as well as a practical step toward a more self-assertive Europe, an attempt only partly successful. It must again be noted that the EMS, like other monetary arrangements based on pegged rates, can function only if the participants recognize the need for harmonizing monetary and fiscal policies and if they agree on a commonly acceptable set of economic targets. In other words, the EMS faced the challenge of sustaining fixed exchange rates while the participants' economies remained out of step—a task over which the Bretton Woods regime stumbled, and for which the EC currency snake had proved too weak.

The managers of the dominant currency in the EMS, the D-Mark, obtained a variety of measures to enforce some degree of discipline on their partners. Although the D-Mark was not a true world trading currency (relatively little trade with third countries was in D-Marks, even though that role was growing), the component of world trade factored in D-Marks was twice the size of those of the sterling and French franc, which was of some consequence to the Germans because of their growing and diversified commercial interests in the Third World. Whether or not one views the EMS as a disguised German currency area—some argue that a par-value system requires a hegemonic or dominant currency—the dominant role of the D-Mark in the system enlarged the Federal Republic's monetary leverage and hence its political leverage. This was a delicate matter (and remains one), for some Europeans were concerned that in the EMS regime the German Bundesbank would reduce other European central banks to satellites and play the same stage-managing role that the U.S. Federal Reserve played before the collapse of the Bretton Woods system.[40]

Although some Europeans feared the potentially dominant role of the Bundesbank in the EMS, the German central bank was initially very skeptical if not outright hostile toward the entire idea. To be sure, German interest in the EMS coincided with the regime's two primary objectives: stable exchange rates and stable domestic prices. The idea of an EMS was propelled forward by the currency chaos of 1978, and was created expressly to develop a zone of monetary stability in the Community and implicitly to shield Europe from Washington's policy of benign neglect toward the dollar. But the coordination of economic activities presaged by the EMS was a mixed blessing for the Federal Republic. In general, the increased reserve currency role of the D-Mark made the Federal Republic's internal monetary management potentially more difficult,[41] and the political compromises underlying monetary coordination required the narrowing of contrasting national positions. Weaker European countries were called on to attain the level of economic and monetary performance demanded by the stronger ones, but the stronger ones were obliged in turn to adjust their own interests and expectations to the political and economic realities of the entire Community, and this was a prospect that the Bundesbank, the stern guardian of German economic mores, viewed with some apprehension. Indeed, the Bundesbank's chief, Otmar Emminger, threatened that the bank might not intervene in capital markets to maintain EMS parities if doing so would mean losing control over the domestic monetary supply, pointing with satisfaction to the demise of Bretton Woods, which had enabled the Germans to use monetary-supply policy as an instrument of domestic economic management. The Bundesbank was not about to relinquish the instrument or have it dulled by onerous obligations to intervene on behalf of sliding EMS parities.

But the Germans claimed to have no inclination to translate monetary strength into political leverage, and gave little indication that they sought to do so.[42] Chancellor Schmidt was acutely sensitive to the political connotations of Germany's monetary power. He clearly saw the risks of having Germany appear to be pursuing national interests and political leverage too assertively. Schmidt did not want to see the D-Mark play too large a role as a clearly identifiable reserve currency because of the possible negative implications, politically, psychologically, and monetarily. As in many other instances, the Germans preferred a European institutional context for implementing their national policies, shying away from purely national justifications and trying to avoid the perception that they were striving for national independence of action or heavy-handed political influence. The close relationship between the German chancellor and the French president was extremely helpful in this regard.

As always, intra-European tensions tended to burden German relations with the United States, which were uneasy during Schmidt's chancellorship for several reasons. Schmidt opposed Secretary of State Henry Kissinger's tough attitude on Eurocommunism, viewing it as nervous and short-sighted; the Middle East war in 1973 and the energy crisis caused irritation between Washington and Bonn; and the offset agreements through which Germany had purchased American weaponry and U.S. bonds to finance the stationing of American troops were for all practical purposes scrapped. During the early days of the Carter administration problems between Washington and Bonn were aggravated by the issues of human rights, the export of nuclear technology by Germany to Brazil,[43] the neutron bomb, Washington's failure to support the dollar in international markets, and the American demand that Germany help the world economy through a more dynamic fiscal program. Despite sustained American support of the dollar and a current account surplus of $3.7 billion in 1980, the oil price rise of 1979–80, the fall of the Shah and the hostage crisis in Iran, the invasion of Afghanistan, and entrenched inflationary expectations had the cumulative effect of undermining further international confidence in the dollar and American leadership of the Atlantic economy.

It would be inaccurate to describe these policy differences as a "crisis" in German-American relations. Nonetheless, Bonn's policies and attitudes were signals that the Germans believed their economic and monetary power carried with it a sense of responsibility (Germany's monetary reserves were the largest in the world, twice those of the United States). This was reflected in an intensive German diplomatic effort sustained by development aid in the Third World, and in general in a more assertive foreign policy. By and large, this was not done heavy-handedly. From Bonn's point of view, the Germans were propping up the United States as well as the European Community: they were asked to support the French farmers as well as the American dollar, to underwrite Italy's attempt to overcome economic and political disarray, to finance the lion's share of the EEC nuclear research program as well as American defense costs in Europe, and to continue to subsidize the Community's regional development programs. At the same time, the Germans saw themselves being asked to undermine the very basis of their economic well-being through what they considered ill-advised economic and monetary policies. In short, they felt that the "equalizing" measures suggested to them were a leveling down to a lower common denominator, when they believed that the process should be the reverse: that Germany's partners should make stronger efforts to match the Federal Republic's economic and monetary performance.

But the Germans could hardly afford to allow a weakening of the European base of their foreign policies. Fundamentally, the shift of American policies toward Europe and the EEC in the 1970s, which was initiated by the Nixon administration and carried through by Gerald Ford and Jimmy Carter, signaled the abrogation of the postwar transatlantic economic compact. The essence of this compact was that the United States, based on its hegemonic and monetary position, would be willing to make economic sacrifices in return for political privileges.[44] By the late 1960s and early 1970s both sides pushed for altering the framework within which the postwar political and economic arrangements had been made. The growing strength of Europe and Japan made the Bretton Woods arrangement seem obsolete, and the United States, rather than allow vast foreign dollar holdings to curtail its domestic economic autonomy, abandoned Bretton Woods for its own reasons.[45] In effect, the world monetary crises of the early 1970s heralded a long overdue reorganization of the world monetary system and revolved essentially around the economic, strategic, and political role of the United States in world affairs and what part of this role the European allies were willing and able to continue financing.[46] By the late 1970s the changes in the basic postwar understanding between the United States and·Germany concerning security policies and arms control, monetary policies, and East-West détente had led to a significant erosion of the German-American partnership, inducing Bonn to intensify its European ties and seek an even closer Franco-German partnership.[47]

11

The Politics and Economics of the 1980s: Germany, the Stagnation of European Integration, and the Decline of American Hegemony

A word of warning: when discussing the rise and fall of empires, it is well to mark closely their rate of growth, avoiding the temptation to telescope time and discover too early signs of greatness in a state which we know will one day be great, or to predict too early the collapse of an empire which we know will one day cease to be. The life-span of empires cannot be plotted by events, only by careful diagnosis and auscultation—and as in medicine there is always room for error.

—FERNAND BRAUDEL

At all times, an old world is collapsing and a new world arising; we have better eyes for the collapse than the rise, for the old one is the world we know.

—JOHN UPDIKE

As it took office, the Reagan administration was burdened with the economic legacy of the Carter administration—a low growth rate, an inflation rate of 12.5 percent, an unemployment rate of 7.5 percent, and a discount rate of 13 percent—and was determined to restore America's economic health and what it considered America's inadequate military strength. The revitalization of American economic and military power, to be accomplished with a painless mix of tax cuts and economic growth, was the centerpiece of Ronald Reagan's election campaign and the core of the administration's political agenda.

The new administration's economic strategy focused on the need to reduce inflation with a contractionary monetary policy and with supply-side fiscal measures which by cutting taxes and social welfare expenditures would stimulate growth, enlarge the tax base, and reduce unemployment and budget deficits. Ultimately, the Reagan administration found it impossible to square the economic circle, and it managed to live up to its promise in two areas only: after a severe recession in the early 1980s the American economy enjoyed a continuous six-year expansion, and the U.S. Federal Reserve managed to stanch inflation and inflationary expectations. In most other respects, the worrisome economic trends of the 1970s became aggravated: massive budget and trade deficits, financed by borrowing at home and abroad, transformed the United States from a net creditor nation to a net debtor for the first time since before the First World War; by the end of the Reagan administration the national debt was estimated to have grown from $1 trillion to $3 trillion; Federal debt equaled 41 percent of gross national product in 1987 compared with 26 percent in 1980; in the early 1980s, unemployment reached its highest level since the Depression, although it dropped to tolerable levels by the end of the decade; and massive trade deficits (about $150 billion in 1988) led to growing foreign debt and dependence on a huge inflow of foreign capital, raising questions about the structural competitiveness of the American economy and stimulating protectionist pressures in the American Congress.[1]

Although the economic and monetary difficulties of the United States were of long standing, the Reagan administration's method of addressing them was novel and reflected a fundamentally different political and ideological approach to economic problem solving.[2] In the postwar period the American political discourse about the sources and consequences of budgetary deficits was characterized by a significant measure of consensus. Countercyclical Federal deficits had become more or less acceptable, and both parties in Congress as well as in the White House had relied on Keynesian remedies to aid economic recovery.[3]

The Reagan administration broke the postwar consensus for a number of reasons: trends in economic thinking and ideological inclinations, the role assigned to tax reduction as an instrument of supply-side policy without compensatory reduction of spending, and uncertainty about what level of unemployment should trigger countermeasures. Above all, the administration stressed the importance of the Federal Reserve's monetary policy as the primary tool in macroeconomic management. This appeared both desirable and necessary, for domestic as well as foreign political and economic reasons. The novel economic program of the Reagan administration raised a good deal of criticism (even in the president's own party), and from the perspective of the White House the frequency, speed, and flexibility with which the control of domestic liquidity and interest rates could be applied by a sympathetic Federal Reserve contrasted favorably with the slow and politically cumbersome budgetary process of the Congress.[4] Propelled forward by practical as well as ideological reasons, monetary policy appeared a more attractive and supple instrument than fiscal policy.

This inclination was reinforced by the floating exchange rate mechanisms of the global monetary system: the domestic economic proclivities of the United States were encouraged by international circumstances. The shift from fixed exchange rates of the Bretton Woods monetary regime to floating rates in the early 1970s required the United States to use different methods for implementing its basic strategy of retaining domestic economic autonomy: different rules of the game required different policies. Floating exchange rates, and the growing ease and volume with which private funds moved across national boundaries in pursuit of higher returns and investment opportunities, made monetary policy the supreme instrument to affect national and international economic activity and investment incentives and disincentives. The appreciation or depreciation of the dollar, engineered in large part by the money-supply and interest-rate policies of the Federal Reserve, created a powerful tool for managing the national economy, compared with which fiscal and budgetary policy lost some of its attractions and importance. Also weakening were the forces of the "production" economy relative to those of the "capital" economy. As Otmar Emminger noted when the dollar was moving toward its peak of the mid-1980s, "What for every other currency would be a cause of weakness—huge budget and trade deficits—seemed to drive the dollar higher and higher. . . . There can be no doubt that the overriding influence on the exchange rate of the dollar is *capital flows*, which have completely overwhelmed the influences of trade and current account balances" (italics in original).[5] This made the dollar rate highly unpredictable because it responded less to the tangibles of trade flows and the realities of the factors of production than to the variety of motivations that propel diverse capital flows.

The implementation of the administration's economic policy reflected a novel combination of what Helmut Schmidt called super-Keynesian deficit fiscal behavior and super-contractionary monetary behavior,[6] signifying a marked departure from conventional techniques of postwar Keynesian demand management. The administration viewed budgetary policy as an instrument of aggregate supply rather than as an instrument for dealing with aggregate demand, and in the process aggravated the problem of "crowding out": private savings were absorbed to fund the federal debt and service its interest charges and diverted from financing industrial modernization, improvements to the infrastructure, research and education, and similar investments in the future. What developed was "a bizarre and extreme mix of easy fiscal and tight monetary policies unprecedented in our history. Compared to the feasible alternative, tighter budgets, and easier money, their mix resulted in a lot of crowding out, partly at the expense of domestic investment mostly in the form of mammoth import surpluses, depleting our nation's net claims on the rest of the world, and making the US a net debtor. . . . We were caught in a vicious spiral: deficits, more debt, more interest charges, bigger deficits, higher interest rates, more crowding out, and so on."[7]

Monetary Policy and Economic Alliance Management

Initially, the money-supply and high-interest-rate policy of the Reagan administration was aimed at reducing the high level of inflation and the inflationary expectations embedded in the American economy. This intention was warmly greeted by American allies. The Germans in particular saw in Washington's strategy of economic revival the confirmation of their own economic proclivities. Although they were uneasy with the slick logic of Reaganomics, the Germans believed that Washington's monetary policy held out the hope that the corrosive effects of inflation on the international monetary system would be checked, and that a more supportive psychological environment and specific economic incentives would persuade Germany's partners to adopt macroeconomic policies oriented toward stability. At least in principle, the Germans also welcomed the administration's decision to intervene in the foreign exchange market only to reduce the volatility of exchange rates. Although Washington favored governmental abstinence in the economy at least in part on ideological grounds, reflecting a faith that the market would find the equilibrium price of the dollar, it was also guided by practical considerations, such as the realization that uncoordinated intervention policies would prove ineffective and the hope that price stability in the United States would of itself calm foreign exchange markets. When the Reagan administration announced its view that the greatest contribution the United States or any other country could make to world development was to "pursue sound economic policies at home," it seemed to embrace the central maxim of the Federal Republic's economic culture.[8]

But high American interest rates were soon pressed in the service of what America's partners saw as the less commendable purpose of substituting for American budgetary discipline. Supply-side fiscal measures failed to create sufficient economic growth and tax revenues, and the political difficulty of making deep cuts in social welfare programs to pay for the military buildup began to undermine the Reagan administration's economic strategy. American monetary and interest-rate policies were turned into props to support American domestic overconsumption and military overextension by attracting foreign capital to compensate for low domestic savings and by providing the financial sustenance for chronic budget and trade deficits. High interest rates and capital inflows pushed up the value of the dollar, which Washington chose to interpret as a vote of confidence in American economic leadership and policies, and in effect abetted domestic overconsumption of foreign goods and the deindustrialization of the American economy.[9]

Between 1980 and 1982 American real interest rates rose from almost zero to 8 percent, which brought down inflation and helped finance the budget deficit but also increased unemployment and contributed to a global recession. The administration's reliance on a contractionary monetary policy as the chief instrument of economic management, complemented by a burgeoning budget deficit, drew sharp criticism in Europe because it forced real interest rates to be higher in Europe than they would have been otherwise, impeded economic recovery, overvalued the dollar, and increased the Third World's debt burdens. The dramatic appreciation of the dollar between 1981 and its peak in 1985 was not sustained by American intervention in the foreign exchange markets but by the high level of real interest rates in the United States, the rate differential between American and European capital markets, and the attraction of the United States as a safe haven for capital. Although the long-range prospects of the American economy began to look better after the economic upturn of 1983, American economic strength, high interest rates, and European weaknesses (including deep-rooted structural problems in some countries' aging manufacturing sector, labor market rigidities, and regulatory burdens) combined to create a serious overvaluation of the dollar.

When the Europeans began to complain about high American interest rates, they were presented with the somewhat disingenuous argument that U.S. interest rates were not the highest among the industrialized powers, that they did not represent American policy, and that no linkage existed in any case between large budget deficits, high interest rates, and volatile exchange rates. The Europeans and particularly the Germans were not persuaded. Without mentioning the United States by name, in 1981 the German finance minister criticized those nations that "relied to a large extent on monetary measures in order to fight inflation," calling instead for a broader-based approach that would comprise mutually supportive instruments and policies, above all the reduction of budgetary deficits. The Germans began to attribute to American economic policies their own economic problems of the early 1980s: zero growth, rising unemployment, a current account deficit, and a weak D-Mark.[10]

Although German complaints about American economic policies mainly took the form of technical arguments about interest-rate policy and the perennial problem for the Germans of retaining control over their domestic monetary policy,[11] at bottom the Germans opposed American policy for its purported selfishness and lack of leadership. At the IMF meeting of October 1982, the German finance minister, Manfred Lahnstein, called for reducing the American budget deficit as a step toward normalizing interest rates and stressed the need for international cooperation in the economic field, which had been agreed on at the economic summit in Versailles of June 1982 and was to be reiterated at Williamsburg in May 1983.[12] Lahnstein noted that medium-sized countries such as the Federal Republic had reached the limits of what they could accomplish on their own, that cooperation required shared responsibilities and benefits, and that the United States, as the world's largest economy and leading reserve center, would need to shoulder special responsibility.[13]

The Germans believed that American fiscal and monetary policies were dominated by purely domestic economic and political considerations (despite the commitment made by the Carter administration at the summit in 1978 in Bonn to take into account the effect of American policies on others), and that the United States sought to sustain its economic well-being and military-strategic preoccupations not by its own exertions but by borrowing from the rest of the world. In essence the Germans argued that American budget deficits were caused by inadequate taxes and a bloated military budget, and financed by attractive interest rates as a compensating measure for low domestic savings. The United States was seen as living beyond its means. In addition, the Germans feared that volatile exchange rates and a poor economic performance in the Federal Republic and elsewhere would generate protectionist sentiments and threaten the openness of international trade.[14] Following their long-standing position, the Germans emphasized the need for free trade, condemned the proliferation of voluntary bilateral export restraint agreements, and argued that it was the responsibility of the United States, Western Europe, and Japan to keep the international trading system open. In particular, they were concerned that there could develop in the future a system of sectoral protectionism and a general trend toward transforming the competition of goods into a neomercantilist "policy competition," leading to the establishment of "policy cartels."[15]

Unlike earlier American presidents, Ronald Reagan was disinclined to show deference to Chancellor Schmidt's experience and expertise, as were his advisers. The chancellor's own views, barely masked while he was in office and later expressed in a form unrestrained by diplomatic niceties, amounted to a scathing condemnation of American fiscal and monetary policies and an equally robust critique of American foreign policy in general: "The size of the United States, its vitality and dynamic energy, the fact that it has a genuine common market (rather than one in name only) consisting of 235 million people, with a single currency and a single legal tax system, and, finally, its superior military strength mean that, given the state of the Western world in the mid 1980s, the leadership role can be assumed only by the United States. However, the United

States is not prepared to lead. Instead, isolationist, America-centered, hegemonial, and internationalist tendencies vie for supremacy."[16]

Schmidt's successor, Helmut Kohl, and the new center-right coalition over which he presided, in essence entertained the same misgivings about American economic policy although they expressed them less forcefully. The new government and the new opposition agreed that the American budget deficit and high interest rates slowed German economic recovery by draining Europe of capital, and in so doing set limits to required structural industrial modernization in Germany, complicated efforts to reduce German unemployment, and generated massive American trade deficits and protectionist pressures in the American Congress. Although an undervalued D-Mark boosted German exports, structural unemployment in the Federal Republic remained high, and German monetary policy became subservient to the task of maintaining external balance rather than the need to reduce unemployment, stimulate the economy with lower interest rates, and assure price stability. The Germans basically argued that America's economic strategy induced an unearned and unjustifiable international redistribution of assets, similar in its intended effect to what had taken place in the later stages of the Bretton Woods monetary system, dissimilar in that the new international monetary arrangements required different American policies to accomplish the same purpose.

The dollar began a steep decline during the second Reagan administration owing to slower growth in the United States, a narrowing of inflation and interest rate differentials among the industrialized powers, and a massive American trade and budget deficit. Fundamentally, there was a growing realization that the dollar was overvalued. At the economic summit in Bonn of May 1985, the agenda was dominated by the threat of American protectionism, acrimony over the high level of American interest rates, and the volatility of foreign exchange rates. The heads of state agreed to take measures that would correct persistent economic imbalances, stem protectionism, and improve the stability of the world monetary system. Toward that end the participants pledged to follow policies furthering noninflationary economic growth and adopted a specific policy program meeting the needs of the international economy. The United States agreed to implement "rapid and appreciable cuts in expenditure and a substantial reduction in the budget," the Federal Republic pledged more flexible economic policies and a more fluid labor market, and to reduce the public sector of the economy, the budget deficit, and taxes, and the Japanese promised to liberalize their capital market, internationalize the yen to precipitate a rise in its value, and facilitate access to the Japanese market. There was general agreement to make foreign exchange markets more stable. The push toward increased intervention in the foreign exchange market was not popular in the Federal Republic, however. Finance Minister Gerhard Stoltenberg stated point-blank in a debate in the Bundestag that there was no alternative to a system of flexible exchange rates, even though he acknowledged the need to reduce their volatility and to effect better coordination and surveillance.[17]

Throughout the mid-1980s the Germans expressed reservations about American economic management and insisted that the problems experienced by the United States were the result of its huge and apparently permanent budget deficits, aggravated by growing private and corporate debt. Beginning with the meeting of the Group of Five at the Plaza in September 1985, which produced agreement among the United States, Germany, Japan, Britain, and France that the dollar was overvalued, the American treasury followed a policy of devaluing the dollar, hoping to cut the trade deficit, obviate protectionist trends in the U.S. Congress, and obtain monetary support from Japan and Germany. Indeed, the dollar fell sharply from its peak in February 1985, and the Germans and Japanese began to resist a further depreciation of the dollar: Bonn in particular feared that a cheaper dollar would generate domestic inflation and have a negative effect on German exports. The Europeans began to argue that the United States had not fulfilled its part of the bargain (to bring down the budget deficit), and they resented Washington's attempt to put the burden of adjustment on its partners, pressuring them to reflate their economies and reduce their competitiveness by condoning an appreciation of their currencies.

But the Germans refused to be pressed into a new role of locomotive, which had weakened their economy during the Carter years.[18] Chancellor Kohl and Finance Minister Stoltenberg argued that the German economy was growing fast enough, and that Germany's high unemployment (about 9 percent) was structural and not cyclical and could be reduced only through greater mobility of labor and flexibility of capital. In addition, the German Bundesbank resisted American pressures to adopt a more expansionary monetary policy, arguing that the money supply was growing too fast as it was. Although they did not express themselves officially in this way, the Germans essentially argued that the United States postponed economic reform through the importation of foreign capital, and that Bonn was unwilling to finance American overconsumption at the cost of German economic and monetary stability. Although the Germans were highly sensitive to the political consequences of German-American economic problems, they were reluctant to energize the transatlantic economy, unless the United States reduced its deficit by cutting government spending or raising taxes.

The decline of the dollar that began in March 1985 and accelerated after the meeting at the Plaza leveled off in 1987. But an overvalued D-Mark, the result of an 80 percent appreciation since 1985, put new pressures on the dollar, which were aggravated by the failure of the

Japanese-American accord of early 1987 to stabilize the dollar-yen exchange rate. In February 1987 the finance ministers and central bank governors of the Group of Six met at the Louvre and announced that "their currencies were now within ranges broadly consistent with underlying economic fundamentals . . . [and that] further substantial exchange rate shifts among their currencies could damage growth and adjustment prospects in their countries." They also expressed their determination to "cooperate clearly to foster stability of exchange rates around current levels."[19] The meeting at the Louvre established common ground among the participants that "excessive volatility in exchange rates could jeopardize, instead of speed, the process by further impairing prospects for investment and growth in surplus countries." But it also established a consensus that confidence in the dollar depended on prudent fiscal policies as well as monetary policies,[20] and there was some concern that even if volatility could be eliminated in the exchange market it would show up elsewhere—all of which was for the Germans yet further confirmation of their view that sound domestic economic policies rather than extensive market intervention were the proper way to address international monetary problems.

At the Louvre, the countries committed themselves not only to maintaining the current levels of their exchange rates (although never made public, the exchange rate target agreed on was in the range of 1.80 to 1.90 D-Marks to the dollar), but also to assuring that their underlying economies would justify the rates. The United States again promised to lower the Federal budget deficit, and Japan and Germany promised to accelerate their economies.[21] But the understanding stood on shaky ground to begin with and was further weakened when Washington chided the Germans in fall 1987 for not lowering their interest rates sufficiently, and when the stock market's plunge in October put renewed strains on the world economy. French and British spokesmen joined Washington in urging the Federal Republic to assume expansionary fiscal and monetary policies, and as always the Germans resisted. Confronted with the argument that Germany's inflation rate of 1 percent, sluggish growth rate, and 8.4 percent unemployment rate were sufficient reasons for stimulating the German economy, Economics Minister Martin Bangemann responded, "We cannot accept it when someone tells us we have done things wrong when quite clearly we have achieved things."[22] By late 1987 the Louvre understanding was in effect suspended when all major parties ceased their monetary interventions in support of the dollar and when the United States began to view a falling dollar as a lesser evil than climbing interest rates. Indeed, there was speculation that Bonn's refusal to stimulate the economy or hold down interest rates had caused Washington to revert to its previous policy of allowing the dollar to fall in an attempt to reduce the American trade deficit. Washington and Bonn again disagreed on what constituted responsible monetary and fiscal practices.

When President Reagan admonished the Germans and Japanese in fall 1987 to energize their domestic economies and thus ease the American balance-of-trade burdens (a remedial connection they consistently denied), it was merely a further demonstration that the American side viewed the Germans' preoccupation with monetary stability and fiscal responsibility as an obstinate and irrational economic idée fixe, detrimental to American national economic interests and the health of the global economy at large. For the German side, American demands were yet another example of how the administration refused to raise taxes and attempted to pass on to America's economic partners the burden of American profligacy. In particular, the Germans shied away from the obligation to prop up exchange rates with massive interventions, fearing adverse consequences for Germany's price stability and for the probity of the Bundesbank. The Bundesbank's chief, Karl Otto Pöhl, noted that "Huge trade imbalances and strong divergencies in . . . economic, fiscal and monetary policy still exist. In these circumstances, overambitious commitments to peg certain exchange rate levels or target zones run the risk not only of clashing with domestic monetary objectives but of collapsing when the markets test them. Central banks and governments can easily lose their credibility in such a process. Therefore, it is less ambitious but more realistic to concentrate on managing the existing system pragmatically and flexibly."[23]

The Stagnation of European Integration

From its inception, a primary objective of the EMS was to achieve closer monetary cooperation among the Community members in the hope that this would energize the flagging dynamics of European integration, lend urgency to the task of coordinating economic policies, create a zone of monetary stability in Europe, and help stabilize global and regional exchange and monetary relations. But these hopes were only partly realized, and even then in a sense for the wrong reasons. As it turned out, the EMS addressed only marginally the need to arrive at common economic programs among the member states, and Britain was conspicuous by its absence. The major source of stable exchange rates within the EMS was less the harmonization of economic policies and the convergence of economic performance (although a gradual convergence became visible in the mid- and late 1980s) than the weakness of the D-Mark vis-à-vis the dollar, which eased tensions between the D-Mark and its European partner currencies. For better or worse, the fortunes of the D-Mark and the stability of the EMS central rates remained dependent on extra-European factors, primarily the strength or weakness of the dollar, rather than on intra-European harmonization of economic policies.[24] Most of the EMS currency alignments that took place between 1979 and 1988 occurred before 1983, when there was a significant widening of inflation rate differentials. From March 1983 to April 1986, when the dollar was strong, the EMS managed to foster a zone of monetary stability (interrupted only by a devaluation of the lire in July 1985), obtaining the most stable three-year period since the generalized float of the dollar in 1973:

> Ever since the inception of the EMS the dollar-DM relationship has exerted a decisive influence on its working. For long periods the appreciation of the U.S. currency created pressures outside the system that fostered the cohesion of the participating currencies. The period of calm in the EMS continued, notwithstanding the inflation differentials between the member countries, until early 1981, when the *Bundesbank* took restrictive measures to counter the high dollar interest rates. . . . German attempts to pursue an "active" policy vis-à-vis the dollar created new tensions in the EMS, leading to general realignments in June 1982 and March 1983. From then until July 1985, when the lira was devalued as a precautionary move, was the longest period of calm in the EMS. This can be attributed to the persistent strength of the dollar and the corresponding weakness of the DM, which damped the tensions in the system.[25]

The reversal of this situation after 1985–86, when the dollar lost considerable strength, did not fracture the existing EMS arrangement, but it put renewed strains on its operation and increased Britain's reluctance to join it. From the German perspective, however, the EMS continued to serve important functions even though the Bundesbank was not eager to see it advanced toward a genuinely integrated common-currency area before West European economic policies were coordinated effectively. The Germans were acutely aware that the troublesome fluctuations of the dollar exchange rate were the result primarily of capital flows (rather than trade flows), propelled by a variety of motivations of a political and psychological nature that overwhelmed the influence of trade and current account balances. In the EMS, on the other hand, mutual payments relations were determined more by the large volume of trade and service transactions among the members than by capital transactions. This provided an important source of monetary stability for the Germans, for their exports to the Community amounted to more than 50 percent of their total exports, and to almost 70 percent if one also counted their exports to EFTA countries (such as Norway, Finland, Iceland, Sweden, Austria, and Switzerland), many of which pegged their exchange rates to the D-Mark. The Germans' monetary policies were embedded in a "mixed" global-regional monetary system, providing them with a cushion in either direction, which was a major reason why they were not eager to tie together the dollar, yen, and EMS blocs: doing so would have diminished the monetary flexibility and the opportunities for hedging that they preferred.[26]

Even so, the stability of the EMS rested ultimately on the coordination of European economic policies, which was as difficult to achieve in the 1980s as it had been before.[27] President François Mitterrand (who succeeded Giscard d'Estaing in 1981), Prime Minister Margaret Thatcher, and Chancellor Helmut Schmidt followed significantly divergent economic policies, which posed severe difficulties for France's adherence to EMS guidelines and which kept Britain out of the EMS arrangement entirely.[28] Matters were further complicated by the enlargement of the Community, which introduced even larger differences among the economic systems and policies of the membership. In fact, enlargement could be accomplished only on the basis of a two-tier monetary membership in the Community, the tiers to consist of those who managed to adhere to the exchange rate mechanism and the intervention obligation, and those whose currencies made up the ECU basket, the numeraire of the nascent European money.[29] This arrangement was in some respects similar to that of the currency snake, the participants in which were drawn from members as well as nonmembers of the Community.[30] In 1984 Chancellor Helmut Kohl openly implied the need for two types of membership in the EEC, which would allow members to proceed with different speeds and integrative intensity, leading to an *Europe à deux vitesses*.

The second enlargement of the Community, which brought into the Community Greece (1981) and Spain and Portugal (1986), immensely complicated the coordination of economic and monetary policies and brought about a de facto dual membership. As the Community expanded to twelve members, it increased in heterogeneity, and the possibilities for deeper integration became even more remote. Through its southern expansion the Community was joined by countries that required regional support programs and faced serious problems of modernization, and the accession of which seemed attractive to the older members more on political than on economic grounds. The doubling of its membership since the Treaty of Rome was a mixed blessing for the Community. For most Europeans, enlargement meant (as it had all along) that the potential for integration had weakened and that quantity increased at the expense of quality. Indeed some Europeanists suspected that those who had called for enlarged size were not eager to see enlarged integration. When the Community's leaders met in Brussels for their semiannual summit in summer 1987 and in Copenhagen in November, the Community was in effect divided into two camps, making it impossible for them to agree on reforms of the budget or of farm policy issues, which had escaped solution even when the membership was less heterogeneous.[31]

Even the modest reform of the Treaty of Rome effected in the late

1980s, new voting rules, tended to reinforce North-South differences. Unable to veto Community projects on their own, members now needed to form alliances among the like-minded. The European Commission hoped to bridge regional imbalances and obtain more "cohesion" in the Community through increased spending on the South (plus Northern Ireland), and it found itself on a collision course with the richer members who wanted a more disciplined budget. As always, the automatic subsidies paid to the Community farmers was a central issue. (In 1987 the rising cost of these subsidies outstripped the Community's income by more than $5 billion, an amount somewhat lower in 1988.) Although France, supported by members like Italy, Greece, Spain, and Portugal, was ready to increase spending on farm policy and other Community programs, the northern countries, led by West Germany and the United Kingdom, sought to reduce expenditures. But whereas Britain wanted cuts in farm spending, Bonn's coalition government wanted to retain the subsidies paid to Germany's farmers.

When the Community decided in 1988 to proceed with its plan to establish a true common market by the end of 1992, it set itself a goal that many observers considered unrealistic.[32] The anticipated leveling of prices across Europe was expected to tempt Western Europe to build protective walls against the United States and Japan to encourage the reindustrialization and technological modernization of Europe, setting in motion retaliatory measures; the called-for harmonization of value-added taxes (or at least the narrowing of their disparities) was seen as a curtailing of the national prerogatives of taxation and a further erosion of jealously guarded aspects of national sovereignty; the European Commission, traditionally sluggish, was required to pass several hundred separate pieces of enabling legislation; and the unresolved issue of the Community's farm support program, which consumed two-thirds of the Community's budget and kept agricultural prices far above world levels, demanded settlement before those who tended to support it (primarily France and the Federal Republic) would compromise on the broader single-market issues with those who opposed it (primarily Britain and the Netherlands). The implementation of a genuinely barrier-free common market by 1992 required above all the coordination of a variety of economic policies, which had proven beyond the political capacities of the Community in the past and posed a constant threat to the cohesion and operation of the European Monetary System.

Although the prospect of creating a single, borderless market was greeted with a good deal of excitement in Europe and found wide support in Germany, the indispensable element for such a market to succeed—monetary union—was viewed with less enthusiasm. At the EC summit in Hannover in summer 1988, Prime Minister Thatcher opposed even the creation of a study commission to examine the role of a future

European central bank (without which monetary union could not be implemented); and the German government was notably cautious. Neither Chancellor Kohl nor Finance Minister Gerhard Stoltenberg endorsed the idea of a central bank (although Foreign Minister Hans-Dietrich Genscher supported it), cautioning that the creation of such an institution (and the currency union) were long-term goals and that the Federal Republic would insist on specific safeguards. Not surprisingly, the Bundesbank was even less supportive. In an internal policy paper the Bundesbank spelled out some of the exacting conditions that would have to be met before it would accede to a central European bank, the general thrust of which reiterated the long-standing German position that economic policies would need to be coordinated before a monetary union could succeed, and clearly implied that Community members would need to toe the German line on monetary matters. One member of the Bundesbank directorate argued that political union should precede monetary union, and noted pointedly that while Germany was unified in 1871, the German Reichsbank was not established until five years later.[33]

Aside from their inherent economic and political difficulties, the coordination of economic policies and the harmonization of prices and taxes were as always complicated by the disparate general foreign policies of the major members. Although in the late 1980s the French and Germans were conservative with respect to allowing drastic or rapid reforms of the Community's agricultural subsidy system, they were somewhat more venturesome on military issues, aiming for some degree of Franco-German collaboration and perhaps even a modification of NATO institutions. Britain, on the other hand, although more innovative in finding ways to stanch the constant financial drain of the support-price system, shunned the EMS and remained conservative with respect to NATO structures and their practical and symbolic meaning for continuing a special British-American relationship. For reasons of domestic and foreign policy it remained highly questionable whether the Community could coordinate its divergent economic policies and enable its institutions to foster imaginative and effective leadership.[34]

The failure of the Community to respond to the economic and political challenges of the 1980s was in essence a failure to come to terms with the contradictions of a modern state system that was itself a mixture of the old and new. In the postwar period there developed a complex set of relationships within and across national boundaries, usually described as economic interdependence, in which societal demands were pressed forward through formal as well as informal channels, governmental as well as private organizations, national as well as international and supranational institutions. But global interdependence and regional integration (which is in effect an intensive and institutionalized form of interdependence) required a supportive political context. The international state system needed to be sufficiently stable, predictable, and permissive for economic interdependence to take hold (this precondition the United States implemented after the Second World War), and national economic and political systems needed to be sufficiently open to accept the intrusions of economic interdependence and the curtailment of national autonomy that resulted from them.

A powerful impulse toward cooperation in the Community stemmed from the similar demands that citizens of member states made on their governments and the similar means that governments had of directing domestic and foreign economic processes: trade and monetary policy, fiscal policy, income policy, wage policy, labor policy, taxation policy. Similar challenges were tackled with similar policy instruments: "The final result of this process tended to be a situation in which the economic activities of all economic units [within the state] were coordinated, while the largest and most influential economic unit in the system, the state, influenced the total process to a certain extent but never fully controlled it. Geographic proximity, intensive business and cultural relations and firmly established trading and capital links also contributed to the similarities of economic institutions and economic policy objectives in the industrial countries with managed market economies."[35]

But there were also important dissimilarities among such important members as Germany, France, and Britain in the division of labor between state and society, the mix of public, semipublic, and private structures, the relationships between interest groups and bureaucracies, the uses of taxation, sensitivity to inflation and unemployment, attitudes on economic growth, and the preoccupation with national security, to mention only a few examples. Their domestic political and economic structures were quite divergent, as were the explicit and implicit codes that define the appropriate role of government in the economy and society.[36]

Moreover, politics retained for national dispositions a large area of autonomy and independence, especially in the area of security issues and the high politics of fundamental foreign policy questions. Even in the area of welfare politics, national governments retained ample discretion in establishing their own hierarchy of social and economic values and in selecting the mix of policies they believed best suited to its implementation. Governments retained a large say in deciding which ways and to what extent they would shield themselves from the intrusions of global interdependence and regional integration. Although they could not escape interdependence without incurring heavy costs, governments could qualify their acquiescence or resistance in different ways and in different degrees, and their choice was shaped as much by internal historical, institutional, political, and ideological orthodoxies as by the force of external circumstance.

Rational calculations of interest were supported by emotional and psychological factors. Although economic interdependence called into question the meaning of the national interest and narrowed the opportunities for national self-identification, nationalism could thrive in the context of interdependence, and interdependence could survive competing nationalisms.[37] Even as it became deficient in providing for their welfare and security, the nation-state retained the primary allegiance of its citizens, who continued to look toward it for their material and perhaps even spiritual satisfactions. In this respect not much had changed since 1953, when Hajo Holborn wrote, "There is danger that the plain citizens of the European countries may not see the wood of unity for the trees of alphabetical letter-agencies. Their loyalties cannot be lured away from the customary national governments to novel institutions which savor of impersonal technocracy."[38]

For all these reasons and others, the similarities of national objectives were not sufficiently compelling to accelerate integration.* Instead, the conflicting forces of convergence and divergence combined in the uneasy compromise of coordination. Although the Community achieved some progress,[39] this progress was inadequate when measured against the technological, economic, military-strategic, and ultimately political challenges that confronted Western Europe in the 1980s and beyond. To be sure, the EEC currency snake and its more substantial successor, the European Monetary System, represented a step toward a more tightly integrated West European monetary regime. But even though the difficulties occasioned by the dollar because of its excessive strength or its excessive weakness provided added incentives for fashioning a coordinated European monetary policy, they did not lead to full monetary integration.[40] A common European currency would amount to de facto political union, because its creation would require the important prerogatives remaining with national governments in economic, monetary, social, fiscal, and foreign policies to be given over to supranational institutions. Again, coordination rather than integration appeared to be more acceptable, especially because the foreign policies and security interests of major Community members were divergent. For practical reasons as well as psychological reasons, for considerations of security as well as of welfare, West European integration remained incomplete. This was so even though intensified European integration might provide a more effective check on the political energies of the Federal Republic, which

*There was also the fundamental issue of political accountability. If national governments were to turn over to the Community an increasing amount of their social legislation (including perhaps taxation), the EEC's political institutions, most notably the European Parliament, would need to be strengthened to ensure democratic governance. Moreover, in countries with complicated systems of federation, such as the Federal Republic, laws and policies promulgated by the Community would ultimately have a large effect on the internal constitutional arrangements of member states.

was a major reason why the Community was launched in the first place.[41]

In other words, the politics of the European Community, like those of the industrialized world in general, remained a mix of traditional and novel elements, reflecting a dialectic of independence and interdependence. Interdependence was sustained because in seeking to meet the demands pressed upon them by their electorates, governments were compelled to turn outward to satisfy them. These interest calculations did not allow the disintegration of interdependence toward a more fragmented, disconnected, or nationally oriented economic system, but neither did they propel it toward more integration and supranationality.[42] Interdependence, and the coordination of policies and concordance of norms required for its operation, was a halfway house between integration and disintegration.[43] It was the prototypical phenomenon of a state system in transition.

The Decline of American Hegemony

At the end of the Second World War and at the beginning of the Cold War the United States dominated the international monetary and trading regimes it had created, conducted its diplomacy with foresight and imagination, stood at the peak of international prestige, and had an invulnerable nuclear force that guaranteed America's security and that of its allies. Over the years there came about a relative decline of American power that was as remarkable as its rise.[44] By the 1980s the United States was sharing its predominant economic position with Western Europe and Japan, had fought one war in Asia to a stalemate and lost another, was compelled to acknowledge the Soviet Union as its equal in nuclear-strategic capabilities, and had suffered a decline in political influence because of the mismanagement of foreign and domestic affairs.

A major reason for the weakening of American diplomacy was the imbalance between American ambitions and resources that developed in the 1960s, a disjuncture of ends and means that the United States did not manage to redress sufficiently in the 1970s and 1980s.[45] The economic and political costs of the Vietnam War and the Great Society fostered deep dislocations of the American economy, and Washington's attempt to press American allies into underwriting policies they found costly and misguided undermined America's security alliances and strained the monetary regime the United States had created in 1944, until it collapsed in the early 1970s. In the 1970s, under the impact of rising energy costs and worldwide stagflation, neither the American nor the international economy could provide the continued growth required to satisfy the persisting political demands in the industrialized world for large-scale social expenditures. The result was an enforced redistribution of income on the global, regional, and national levels, marked by the political tensions and conflicts that accompany a "zero-sum" competition over limited resources.[46] In the 1980s the American economy became further burdened by fundamental structural problems and shortsighted policies, the consequences of which were only temporarily postponed and could be attenuated if at all only through renewed American leadership abroad and reconstituted economic strength at home.

In conducting its postwar contest with the Soviet Union, the United States became (like its geostrategic rival) increasingly mired in an outmoded "military-territorial" international state system, unable or unwilling to adjust to the competitive economics and ambiguous politics of a more modern trading state system that it had itself created in the postwar decade.[47] It seemed set on an atavistic path, preoccupied with the ambitions that drove the traditional military-territorial state system, losing sight of the larger issues and real stakes of the Cold War, straining its resources with the illusory goal of nuclear superiority and territorial invulnerability, and losing in the process the support of allies and the capacity to compete economically.[48] The United States waged the East-West contest on a playing field tilted in favor of the opponent, aiming for a victory in the Cold War on terms that might have been significant in an older state system but that had lost much of their relevance in a modern one. In relative terms, the United States was weakening in areas of power that were increasing in importance.[49]

The decline of American hegemony abroad also weakened the foundations of the American empire at home. The management of a permanent Cold War economy and a permanent social service economy not only overtaxed resources but bloated the military budget, distorted the economy and the direction of technological research and development, diminished the competitiveness of American goods, and condoned a debtor mentality in every sector of American public and private life. Americans were slow to learn that economic interdependence is a two-way street, that the American economic and monetary system had become as open as that of its major partners, that their cherished postwar position of domestic economic autonomy was eroding, and that the costs of diminishing American power would ultimately be felt economically as well as psychologically.

But Americans found it difficult to turn the tide. The availability of foreign credits temporarily postponed the realization that the United States would have to deal with its chronic trade deficit (especially because its status as a net debtor had shrunk its net earnings on foreign investment), and that it would have to come to terms with the dislocating effects stemming from the long periods of an overvalued dollar.[50] The only possible solution, higher productivity with a lower standard of living, would have required all contending economic forces in America to accept responsibility for having brought about these dislocations, and this recognition would have pointed to a silent complicity between the

American government and the American economy, the former having incurred huge budget deficits, the latter huge trade deficits.[51] The reformulation of America's economic diplomacy and the restoration of economic and political "solvency" was for this reason even more difficult to accomplish than the rethinking required because of the eroding American power base abroad.[52] For it was in the area of economics, the day-to-day redistribution of benefits and burdens, that postwar American political and social habits had become most deeply embedded, resisting fundamental change and slowing the restoration of a broad and durable consensus on American foreign policy.

The Erosion of American Consensus on Foreign Policy
    The decline of American power engendered deeply felt disappointments and frustrations among the American people and policy makers and created sharp divisions over the ends and means of American foreign policy. This cleavage required bridging before American diplomacy could regain vitality and purpose abroad and a political base at home.
    No one would pretend to offer in a few pages more than the most tentative and preliminary speculations on a subject of such magnitude, complexity, and controversy as the domestic sources of American foreign policy in the second half of this century, and how they were translated into institutional processes, bureaucratic policy making, and American diplomacy. And yet there is a compelling need for the United States and its partners to reflect on the connections between American foreign and domestic policies, for what is at stake are the domestic political, economic, and psychological foundations that have sustained America's European policies over the decades, with fundamental implications for German-American relations.
    It is a truism that the Atlantic alliance and in particular its German-American backbone can ultimately be only as secure and viable as its domestic foundations.* This holds true especially for the United States, the alliance's superpower. In a sense America's foreign policy agenda constitutes the diplomatic equivalent of a dominant international reserve currency: its strengths and weaknesses begin at home, but its reach and effect radiate abroad, affecting every aspect of American foreign relations, whether adversary or cooperative. With the corrosion of American power, the corrosion of the consensus on American foreign policy is at the core of the growing uneasiness of America's allies with the shifts of U.S. diplomacy.
    It should not be surprising that America's people, policy makers, and

_____
*There is also the more specific consideration that lack of domestic consensus on foreign policy in member countries multiplies the likelihood that the governments in power, not representing a national consensus but a domestically disputed foreign policy program, may meet their obverse view on foreign policy matters in the governments of other alliance members. A Right orientation in one country may meet with a Left orientation in another.

ultimately entire political process responded to the decline of American power with a perplexed consternation and with deep frustrations directed toward both American allies and opponents. Like Henry Luce, many Americans had expected that the end of the Second World War would inaugurate "the American century" and that the United States would "assume the leadership of the world," a status earned by an irresistible and lofty combination of American strength and virtue. But at the same time as the United States reached the capacity and (with some reluctance) the determination to implement a Pax Americana, it saw itself challenged by the Soviet Union, in a contest that proved remarkably protracted and inconclusive. In the course of the four postwar decades the East-West conflict gradually demonstrated the ambiguities of power and morality, beclouded the clarity of America's national purpose, confused the calibrations of American gains and losses, overtaxed the resiliency of American institutions, and increasingly weakened the domestic base on which the postwar structure of American foreign policy had rested.

From the inception of Washington's grand strategy of containing the Soviet Union, the American debate over its wisdom and feasibility had turned in large measure on the question of whether it could be sustained domestically.[53] But in fact the Truman and Eisenhower administrations managed to place postwar American diplomacy in a generally supportive domestic political context.[54] Aside from couching the challenge of containing the Soviet Union in ideologically rewarding terms, this was accomplished by augmenting American policies abroad with suitably appealing policies at home, creating a bipartisan consensus that encompassed the major elements of foreign and domestic policies.

This was made possible by two connected historical trends: the parallel and mutually reinforcing development of the United States into a world power and into a modern social welfare state. In the postwar period each development sustained the other; internal and external calculations of interest became meshed in a compelling dialectic of power and purpose that laid the foundations of the American empire. In the 1940s and 1950s, as the economic programs and social aspirations of the New Deal gained broad bipartisan domestic support and political legitimacy (reflected in the centrist socioeconomic program of the Eisenhower administrations), the United States simultaneously created international economic and monetary regimes that not only helped advance America's economic interests and security requirements abroad but also promoted economic prosperity and political stability at home. The economic exertions of the Second World War had reenergized the flagging American economy of the late 1930s, and the postwar international order created by the United States proved beneficial to the American economy at the same time as it eased European and Asian reconstruction and established the economic base for the political containment and military-strategic deterrence of the Soviet Union. The requirements of American welfare and of American security were complementary, and they were implemented with policies that obtained the support of American allies at the same time as they secured the bipartisan domestic consensus on which American foreign policy could rest.[55]

But the overextension of American resources over the following decades dissipated the large complementarities that had characterized American domestic and foreign policies in the 1940s and 1950s. Fundamental economic dislocations at home and the corrosion of American power abroad were accompanied by deep divisions in the American electorate on both domestic and foreign policy and a corresponding inability of American institutions to deal with them effectively.[56] American liberals (there is no effective American Left) remained committed to supporting essential social welfare programs and perceived a growing and costly trend toward militarizing American diplomacy, which they viewed as debilitating on intrinsic grounds and drawing away scarce resources from domestic needs. Conservatives opposed the growing costs and objectives of domestic program that they considered misguided, but at the same time supported the growth of American military power, generally finding it difficult to accept that an adversary relationship with the Soviet Union in the nuclear age required accommodation as well as confrontation.[57] Basically, both liberals and conservatives resisted the tolerance of ambiguity and the patient exertions required in conducting a responsible and effective foreign policy and remained susceptible to the historical temptations of American diplomacy, withdrawal and overextension.

On the European side of the Atlantic alliance, these developments were viewed with growing concern. As early as the late 1940s and the 1950s Europeans had worried about what they perceived to be a historically unsteady American diplomatic temperament both in the long run and in the short run, which might revert American policies from global engagement to hemispheric isolation—a concern that was voiced by such European statesmen as Charles de Gaulle, Konrad Adenauer, Anthony Eden, and Georges Pompidou. There was the nagging fear that America would retreat again to the transatlantic wing of Europe, whereas its great rival to the east would by geographic inevitability as much as by political choice remain proximately poised, half in the wing, half on center stage.*

This fundamental concern grew both among European governments

---

*In 1953 Ludwig Dehio wrote of the efforts to create West European integration: "But America, the leader of the Anglo-Saxon powers, regards herself merely as the midwife at the birth of this new unification. As soon as it develops its own life and existence, she will be content to withdraw, though of course with the intention of maintaining the desired balance from the distance of her island continent purely by means of sea and air power, just as England had been able to do for centuries with the European balance of power." *Germany and World Politics in the Twentieth Century* (New York: W. W. Norton, 1967), p. 130.

and among their publics when they witnessed shorter-term vacillations of American diplomacy stemming from changes of American administration or even disagreements within the same administration. European statesmen generally refrained from expressing such concerns in public, in part so as not to burden even further the cohesion of the alliance, in part because to do so would have amounted to a fundamental criticism not only of American diplomacy but also of America's political institutions and political life. But such concerns underlay many of the specific issues that were contested in the alliance.

The Germans in particular grew uneasy about the uncertainties of the American domestic political process because they realized that what was happening inside America would at some point necessarily be projected outward as well.[58] For the Federal Republic the domestic political developments in the United States were of central importance—second only to its own.

IV

Foreign Policy and Domestic Politics

The contest over foreign policy is at the same time the contest over internal policy and the social content of the political order: Foreign policy sets the limits to the possibilities of our economic and social policy.

—KURT SCHUMACHER

When the Federal Republic was established, its future political direction and the constitutional framework that was to guide it were as much the consequence of external circumstance as of internal choice, if not more so.[1] Everyone was aware that powerful and most likely irresistible outside forces were reaching into the untested domestic political system, that the range of domestic and foreign policy options was narrow, and that the opportunities for genuine self-assertion were severely limited. The Germans knew that the Western powers' containment policy toward the Soviet Union encompassed them as well.

The West Germans' attitudes and policies toward the postwar European order were inevitably shaped by the complex and contradictory emotions evoked by the essential features of postwar German history: defeat, deliverance, and division. Defeat meant unconditional surrender, international condemnation, and the destruction of country, people, and self-image. But it also brought deliverance from the totalitarian yoke of the Nazi regime and raised the hope that the path toward a democratic political order would also lead to economic reconstruction and perhaps moral rehabilitation. Theodor Heuss, the first president of the Federal Republic, spoke of May 8, 1945, as a deeply paradoxical day, when "we were at once delivered and destroyed." But deliverance also led to the loss and division of German territory and German people, a consequence of Germany's defeat in the Second World War and of the collapse of the wartime alliance that quickly turned into the Cold War. Defeat, deliverance, division: a triangle of cause and effect that contained a stern historical and moral logic and for the Germans a deeply ambivalent feeling about the new European political order.

Their circumstance of physical and psychological need often forced from the Germans a response to public issues at once sharply focused, as in the heated dispute over rearmament, and evasively turned inward and withdrawn, as when it reflected deeply held private hopes, resentments, and anxieties. For the postwar Germans politics was both a specific and a general engagement, with an open and public agenda as well as a hidden and private one. The realm of politics contained for the Germans deeply troubling questions about themselves and their history, about what in that history was a source of pride or shame, about what should be saved and cherished or cast away and disowned. Although the Germans were tempted to erase history and abdicate politics, often succumbing to a resigned spirit of "without me," there was no impregnable inner sanctuary that could have provided safe refuge from politics. History and politics were everywhere.

The inescapable weight of politics in the Germans' daily life stemmed not only from the past but also from the present. Domestic politics were inextricably tied to foreign policy developments. Within the constraints imposed on them, the government led by the CDU/CSU and the major voice of opposition, the SPD, contested issues that were simultaneously foreign and domestic: they and all other parties realized that the outcome of foreign policy issues would have a large and perhaps decisive influence over what kind of political, economic, and social order would ultimately be established in Germany. The struggle over foreign policy was at the same time a struggle over the content and direction of domestic policy. The meshing of domestic and foreign policies became the essence of West Germany's political culture.

Formulated as abstractions, the major foreign policy goals of security, political and economic recovery, and reunification were not contested—most everyone wanted to see them achieved. But the apparent incompatibility between pursuing an energetic, pro-Western security and recovery policy and simultaneously advancing the cause of German unity led to sharp conflicts over the priority that should be assigned to West German foreign policy goals, and hence also over the priorities of the political and social values that the contending parties hoped to instill in the new republic.

As a consequence, the sharply polarized East-West contest of the 1950s was reflected in a strikingly similar way in the Federal Republic's domestic political contest. This was not because the government and the opposition were divided along pro-Western or pro-Soviet lines or because they were not equally committed to a democratic political order, but because it quickly became apparent that West Germany's foreign policy goals in the West and in the East were incompatible and most likely mutually exclusive. As it became incontrovertible that Bonn's alignment with the Western powers secured political and economic recovery but failed to advance unification, the issue of foreign policy priorities became crucial. So long as the opposition perceived acceptable alternatives (real or imagined) to the government's foreign policy program, consensus was impossible.

It would be well to recognize that the divisions that existed among political parties and other political groupings also existed within individuals, and that these more personal contradictions, ambivalent perhaps and shifting, carried over into the arena of public discourse. It would be a mistake to see firm distinctions of policy preferences between one party or another without also noting the inner conflicts that beset the individual, forced to establish a private sense of priorities before expressing it as a vote or other public act and before seeing it more or less adequately reflected in the foreign policy programs of political parties.[2] This inner sense of the complexity of political issues may be one reason why the Federal Republic quickly obtained a remarkably stable democratic order. Rather than laying responsibility and blame for foreign policy failures on a system of government, the individual was compelled to experience existentially the costs and benefits that were attached to Bonn's diplomacy.

The history of the domestic political contest over Bonn's foreign policy is the history of a "great compromise" between the Left and Right, which attests to the capacity of the major German parties to bend to necessity, to the Germans' psychological resiliency and adherence to democratic ground rules and constitutional principles, and to the remarkable stability of the Federal Republic's political order. This compromise, slowly forged over the decades, was effectively imposed by the shifting political, military-strategic, and economic realities of the European and global state system. The constraints of necessity always weighed heavily on all aspects of German diplomacy, especially in the formative years of the Federal Republic. They inevitably favored those contestants on the domestic political scene who were attuned to what was possible, and whose own sense of priorities corresponded more closely to the opportunities and strictures of the international political environment than did that of their opponents.[3]

More than anything else, it was this force of circumstance that in the course of four decades narrowed the gap between the major contending forces over foreign policy in German domestic politics. It required both Left and Right to adjust their respective Western and Eastern policies to changing international circumstances, to move toward a political middle ground, and to legitimize the gradual convergence of their foreign policy programs. Ultimately, both bowed to reality and recognized that they could not reverse the political facts that their respective foreign policy programs had helped create on the international and domestic political scene.

It was a necessity to which Left and Right yielded only with the utmost reluctance. During their first decade in power, the Christian Democrats were much closer than their opponents to the current of historical events and trends, securing for themselves a wide and solid domestic political base: an absolute majority in the elections of 1957 (which amounted to an endorsement of Bonn's Western policies) and in later years a powerful voice in governing the Federal Republic. Abetted by propitious international circumstances, the governments led by the CDU/CSU that held power after 1949 succeeded in implementing central elements of their Western-oriented foreign policy program, creating practically irreversible international commitments and domestic socio-economic circumstances that compelled the Social Democrats either to revise their foreign policy agenda and assent to the major principles of Germany's economic order, or else remain a permanently crippled political minority. After opposing them for a decade, by the late 1950s and early 1960s the SPD was in effect endorsing the transatlantic security policy and integrative European policy of the CDU/CSU. For the Social Democrats this was an initially painful process that began in the mid-1950s and culminated in the formation of the Grand Coalition government in 1966, in which the SPD's Willy Brandt became vice chancellor and foreign minister.

During the 1970s it was the Social Democrats and their coalition partners, the FDP, who were more closely attuned to changing global and regional political circumstances. In the 1960s the CDU's hesitant attempts to energize its stagnant Eastern policies and adjust its Western policies to a changing alliance had proven insufficient to keep Bonn from drifting into diplomatic isolation, from which the Federal Republic was rescued in the late 1960s and early 1970s by the Eastern policies of the SPD-FDP coalition government. The elections of 1972 amounted to an endorsement of the new Ostpolitik, and it was now the Christian Democrats' turn, first in the role of opposition and then after their return to power in 1982, to revise their preferred foreign policy agenda and adjust it to changing international and domestic political circumstances.[4] From the mid-1970s throughout the 1980s the CDU/CSU was forced to accept the major premises of the Ostpolitik which the SPD had initiated. This process of adjustment had begun with the CDU's own Eastern policy of "little steps" in the mid-1960s, and culminated in 1987 when Chancellor Helmut Kohl received East Germany's chief, Erich Honecker, in Bonn during what was in everything but name a formal state visit.

A compromise is not a consensus. It is the product of necessity and not choice, the acceptance of what is perceived to be second best. The specific modalities of the Federal Republic's foreign policies, the preferred priority of conflicting foreign policy goals, the inherent tensions between Germany's attachment to the West and its aspirations in the East—these and many other issues remained intensely contested in the

1980s and provoked a spirited dialogue between government and opposition. Although the great compromise between Left and Right was the basis in the 1980s for the general orientation of German politics, there remained a wide range of foreign policy issues that divided government and opposition (as well as contending factions within political parties), and there persisted a vigorous debate over the present and future course of German diplomacy.

But the terms of discourse were changed—the parameters of what constituted the political center on foreign policy matters were rearranged. In the course of four decades, diametric opposition was replaced by a middle position, bracketed and sustained by the great compromise. The long, slow movement toward the center, first from the Left and then from the Right, had by the 1980s led the Germans toward a political middle ground in which the center was no longer the crossing point of two extremes but a provisional agreement on the major outlines of the Federal Republic's foreign policies. It entailed as well a broad consensus on the major outlines of Germany's economic policies, which in contrast to the early years of the Federal Republic no longer allowed a fundamental redirection with respect either to the domestic dimension or to the foreign dimension.

Although the great compromise, imposed from outside, had moved the major political parties and their constituencies toward the middle of the political spectrum, there seemed few opportunities to convert the middle position at home to a centrist diplomacy abroad. The basic tensions that beset German foreign policies for decades were unresolved, above all the conflict between integration in the West and German unity in the East. That the German Left and Right learned to face these contradictions from a centrist perspective attests to the adaptability and maturity of Germany's political process, but the contradictions remained and could not be overcome merely by a shifting German point of view.[5]

The gradual convergence on foreign policy in domestic policy proceeded in two phases.[6] The first begins in 1949 and extends through the years of the Grand Coalition (1966–69), two decades during which intense confrontation gradually gave way to partial consensus (a burden of adjustment that fell primarily on the Social Democrats) and produced by the mid-1960s a convoluted and tentative reconfiguration of positions, which was symbolized by the willingness of both major parties (the CDU/CSU and the SPD) to enter into a formal coalition in 1966. During the second phase, extending from 1969 to the 1980s and covering the chancellorships of Willy Brandt, Helmut Schmidt, and Helmut Kohl, the Federal Republic's Ostpolitik gained full domestic political legitimacy—a process of adjustment that fell primarily on the CDU/CSU and compelled it to accept the major outlines of Willy Brandt's reformulation of Bonn's Eastern policies.

Concurrent with these developments (and partly their result), there came about a gradual redefinition of the German-American partnership. The Germans and West Europeans, their self-esteem bolstered by economic prosperity and the belief in their superior cultural provenance, began to take a more critical measure of their transatlantic partner—an attitude reciprocated on the other side of the Atlantic. Although accelerated by disputes over specific foreign policy matters and the general infirmity of American policies, this reorientation of European attitudes had larger and more intractable causes that allowed of no diplomatic remedies. The widening gap between America and Europe was ultimately the result of differing historical experiences, social values, and national temperaments. Whatever their historical origins may have been, these conflicting inclinations underlay (deeply as well as subcutaneously) many of the concrete political controversies that threatened the present and future cohesion of the Atlantic alliance.

12

From Dissent to Convolution, 1949–69: The Left Moves toward the Center

Germany's Social Democratic Party recognizes that the European and Atlantic treaty systems, of which the Federal Republic is a part, are the basis and framework for all German efforts in foreign and reunification policy.
—HERBERT WEHNER, 1960

In the formative phase of the Federal Republic, between its establishment in 1949 and the restoration of sovereignty and its membership in NATO in 1955, it was above all Chancellor Konrad Adenauer who personified the confluence of necessity and choice that characterized Bonn's foreign policy. Even the severely limited options available to the German government were attractive to Adenauer, because they allowed him to pursue foreign and domestic policies that corresponded to his own and intrinsic preferences. Adenauer's overall vision of a desirable political order for Western Europe and the Federal Republic could be realized even though Bonn had little room for diplomatic maneuver on the international scene. Although not all elements of the heterogeneously constituted CDU/CSU shared in equal measure Adenauer's overriding commitment to a little Europe with a Catholic orientation, his acquiescence in German rearmament, and his unyielding rejection of German neutrality,[1] the German chancellor, who was also the foreign minister in the early years of the Federal Republic and maintained effective control of his party, soon emerged as the towering influence in shaping Bonn's foreign policy.[2]

The Free Democrats, who became the most important coalition partner of the CDU/CSU for almost two decades, were backed by business interests who favored economic Liberalism and by middle-class voters who resented the Catholic tinge of the CDU and its Bavarian sister party, the CSU. They wanted Germany to play a more independent role between East and West than Adenauer's integrative Western policies would allow and were not nearly as committed to his little Europe policy as were many of the Christian Democrats. The FDP favored a wider framework for European political and economic cooperation and generally pressed more vigorously for reunification than did the CDU/CSU. The party aimed to make itself a third force in foreign and domestic policies, an attempt that it managed to sustain by modifying its own programmatic preferences in the decades to come. Small but vigorous, the FDP sought for itself the same position in German politics that it sought for Germany in European politics. But the FDP's emphasis on Realpolitik and Germany's national interest, coupled with the nationalistic sentiment of some groups in the party, posed no serious obstacles to its support of Adenauer's barter with the Western powers of rearmament for sovereignty.[3] The government's pro-Western policy could command a solid parliamentary majority.

The opposition's foreign policy priorities were almost exactly the reverse of Adenauer's. For a number of reasons the Social Democrats gave their highest priority to unification rather than integration into the West. At least initially, the Social Democrats' program for a new socioeconomic and political order in Germany was Marxist-reformist and had pronounced antibourgeois and anticlerical overtones. They did not want the Federal Republic joined to the capitalist, conservative transatlantic and West European alliances, feared the power of international cartels in an economically integrated Europe, and felt a much closer affinity with the sociopolitical and cultural attributes of Britain and the Scandinavian countries, where political and socioeconomic life had been significantly shaped by socialist parties. They would have preferred that the Federal Republic's political and diplomatic commitments to the West be held in abeyance, keeping open the option of future reunification and retaining the possibility of lifting Germany from the Cold War grasp of a dualistic European order.

Moreover, the division of Germany had weakened the SPD considerably by cutting the party off from areas in which it had received strong electoral support during the Weimar Republic. The SPD's commitment to reunification stemmed from political and ideological reasons, but was reinforced by the need to solidify and extend the power base of the party. The geographical space of a truncated Germany was too narrow to support the political program with which the Social Democrats wanted to rebuild German society; and the geographical space of Western Europe was too confining to support that program internationally. Whereas the Christian Democrats and especially Adenauer himself could turn abroad to such basically sympathetic figures as Robert Schuman, Jean Monnet,

Alcide de Gasperi, and of course Dwight D. Eisenhower and John Foster Dulles, the German Social Democrats were by and large deprived of such international support for their own domestic and foreign policy program.

Although the Social Democrats had no intrinsic objections to Adenauer's policy of reconciliation with the West, they also believed that the specific commitments resulting from the policy—rearmament, German membership in the Western alliance, and the establishment of conservative domestic socioeconomic principles—were detrimental to German unity and to the implementation of the social order they preferred. The Social Democrats were also emphasizing their devotion to an ill-defined German "national interest" because they did not want to be accused again of a self-abnegating internationalism, as had happened in the Weimar Republic. But the SPD's "nationalist" orientation placed the party in a doubly awkward position. Its own traditions had always stressed the international dimensions of the class struggle; and the political and psychological ambience of the Federal Republic was in the postwar years suffused by a sweeping internationalism, in large part a compensatory reaction to the stifling geographic confinement and political isolation that had followed in the wake of the Second World War.

As a consequence of their preferred order of foreign policy priorities, the Social Democrats were much more willing than the government to test Soviet unification proposals (such as the notes of March 1952 and disengagement plans), and they frequently accused the government of dragging its feet on unification, letting opportunities for profitable negotiations pass by, and lacking initiative, flexibility, and foresight. Above all the opposition was convinced that the German question could be resolved only by keeping diplomatic distance between the Cold War blocs, and that this would require accommodation not only in the West but also in the East. At the core of the foreign policy dispute between government and opposition was their irreconcilable disagreement over Germany's present and future role in the European state system. Adenauer abhorred neutrality; the Social Democrats could have accepted it, provided that it were accompanied by a genuinely democratic domestic political order.

Because all the government's foreign policies were inextricably interlocked, the opposition was led to a sweeping condemnation of the entire range of Bonn's pro-Western policies. The Social Democrats fought membership in the European Defense Community, the Coal and Steel Community,[4] and NATO, developed a deep and abiding aversion to America's double-containment policy and accused Adenauer of being its willing instrument, and acquiesced only reluctantly and with grave reservations in plans for the European Common Market. But it was precisely the internal consistency of the government's foreign policy agenda, and above all the linkage of rearmament and sovereignty that was its core, that prevented the SPD from gaining widespread and effective support for its equally consistent foreign policy agenda. For although most West Germans wanted reunification and were not eager to rearm, they were also aware that Adenauer's foreign policy advanced economic reconstruction and political rehabilitation, and that continued success depended on German participation in the Western alliance. Because rearmament was a key element in the government's foreign policy, the opposition attacked it vehemently. The SPD objected to rearmament on four major grounds: it would damage the prospects for reunification by aligning West Germany with one of the Cold War camps, would increase world tensions and antagonize the Soviet Union without substantially improving Western defense, could prove disruptive to the fledgling German democracy by bringing to the fore the militarist elements and other objectionable remnants of the old order, and would envelop Germany in a conservative Western European union that could split noncommunist Europe. But the opposition to rearmament was dispersed—in the trade unions, churches, and among intellectuals and university students—and it had a difficult time coordinating its demands forcefully.

In essence, the SPD advanced a foreign policy program that had little chance of success internationally and that went against the grain of postwar German politics and the political temper of many German voters. The practical and immediate requirements of economic reconstruction, the desire of an adequate standard of living after years of deprivation, the gains promised by the government's Western policy—in short, the widespread recognition that Adenauer's policy showed the way to stability, recovery, and international respectability—made opposition to rearmament an essentially emotional response that had to face a daily test against expediency and the hope for "normalcy."[5]

Moreover, in contrast to the prompt economic and political benefits that resulted from the government's pro-Western policies, the question of unification became increasingly abstract and hypothetical. The distant nature of the goal stemmed not only from the obvious risks and obstacles of implementing a unification policy diplomatically but also from the problem of relating the goal to more immediately relevant and concrete issues of the day. West Germans were constantly being asked to choose between unification and political and economic reconstruction. Even if a large part of the population had been willing to pursue unification determinedly, the daily realities of political and economic life would have stood in the way.[6] Aside from the forbidding international circumstances, the cause of unification underwent constant attrition on the domestic political scene.[7]

The problems that Bonn faced in advancing reunification internationally were thus strikingly reflected domestically. The Western orientation of Adenauer's unification policies gained the support of powerful German interest groups and a large part of the electorate because these policies also yielded immediate and extensive economic and political benefits. In contrast, the Social Democrats' strategy for achieving re-unification—avoiding integration into the West and testing the possibili-ties for accommodation with the Soviet Union on the basis of a neu-tralized united Germany—implied risks and posed uncertainties, and because it was opposed by the Western powers could not have yielded payoffs for the Federal Republic in terms of sovereignty and economic reconstruction.

The FDP deliberately attempted to bridge these two conflicting strat-egies for reunification by pursuing a basically pro-West line, but always made clear that the party was ready to explore openings to the East that appeared to advance reunification.[8] The FDP's attempts to occupy the center were however undercut domestically by both Right and Left, especially the Christian Democrats, who appealed to a wide group of supporters with the prospect of political and economic normalcy. Impor-tant as its center position was, the FDP needed to retain a distinct political profile, balancing its socioeconomic preferences, which inclined it to-ward the Christian Democrats, against its foreign policy preferences, which inclined it toward the Social Democrats. This was a position of risk as well as opportunity for the Free Democrats, in which they remained for decades.

Whereas rearmament turned into a key domestic issue because it gave the government the political lever needed to advance Adenauer's foreign policy program in the West, political recovery was an intensely contested issue because it represented the specific values that the contending par-ties wished to instill in the new republic. The choice of a route to political recovery was the choice of a direction for Germany's society and econ-omy; the pursuit of political recovery in international diplomacy was regarded as having a long-range effect on the future domestic order. For all parties the crux of the matter was always the question of how to exercise the limited rights of sovereignty that were being restored to the Federal Republic. Because these rights were not at disposition for any purpose other than that of tying Germany to the West, they inevitably helped implement the Christian Democrats' political and economic pro-gram but obstructed that of the Social Democrats. Whereas the interests of the Western powers obviously complemented Adenauer's plans for joining Germany to a West European community, they were necessarily adverse to the SPD's call for mobility of action, which might lead to reunification, and also to the SPD's long-range plans for Germany's do-mestic order. For Adenauer necessity was combined with virtue. For the Social Democrats, the international barter that restored sovereignty in exchange for rearmament was objectionable on most grounds.

From Polarization to Partial Compromise: The Left Moves toward the Center
By 1955, after Germany had joined NATO and the developing West European institutions, the drastic incompatibility of security, recovery,

and democratic freedoms on the one hand and unification on the other had become moot. It was also becoming obvious that unification on terms other than those proposed by the Soviet Union was not likely. Gradually these incontestable realities freed the Social Democrats from their preoccupation with unification and allowed them to assess other foreign policy issues on their own merits and with more detachment. This process of adjustment was aided by the SPD's internal changes (bringing to the top such leaders as Fritz Erler, Herbert Wehner, and Willy Brandt) and its willingness to scrap its quasi-Marxist domestic political program.[9] There emerged a reformist wing within the SPD (mostly SPD parliamentarians), who were determined to change the SPD's orientation and image from a doctrinaire instrument of the class struggle into a broad-based party that would appeal to a wider constituency and demonstrate to the electorate that the party was capable of constructive participation in the governance of the Federal Republic. The SPD party program arrived at in 1959 in Bad Godesberg further extended the party's readiness for political accommodation into the sphere of domestic socioeconomic issues, accepting in effect the CDU's principles of the social market economy.[10] By the late 1950s the points of agreement among the major political parties and interest groups increased, accelerated by the growing strength of the more flexible elements in the SPD, the CDU/CSU, and the FDP and by a gradual lessening of the ideological nature of the Federal Republic's political process.

After the election of fall 1957, which was widely regarded as a popular endorsement of Adenauer's foreign policies, the SPD renewed its efforts to stir up popular opposition to having American nuclear weapons deployed on German territory,[11] and in 1959 the party presented another detailed Germany Plan, which advocated step-by-step military disengagement and gradual political and economic integration of the two Germanies. This plan offered a concession that not even the Social Democrats had proposed before—withdrawal of foreign troops from West and East Germany without prior agreement on unification—and it embraced the Soviet idea of a "confederated" Germany by proposing the establishment of all-German institutions in which Bonn and East Berlin would be represented equally. The issue of free elections in each part of Germany was left to the last of the integration plan's three stages.[12]

But even this accommodating proposal was rejected by the Soviet bloc, and a year after its introduction the Social Democrats themselves considered it a thing of the past. The Social Democrats' utter disappointment with the Soviet reaction to their Germany plan for disengagement led them to readjust their entire foreign policy program. The building of the Berlin Wall in 1961 was a traumatic event that accelerated the SPD's specific acceptance of the political realities and contractual commitments that Adenauer's integrative Western policy had established, and by the early 1960s the party made them the irreducible premise of its own foreign policy program. During the election campaign of 1961 the SPD began to endorse most aspects of the CDU's Western alliance policy, and Willy Brandt, mayor of West Berlin and the SPD's candidate for chancellor, admitted that the security of West Germany rather than unification had become the primary issue.

With this announcement the great reversal of the SPD's policy priorities was explicitly acknowledged.[13] By 1963 the SPD regarded itself as the true champion of NATO, urging Adenauer to resist de Gaulle's disruptive NATO policies. The SPD began to support a full-fledged German defense effort within the Western alliance and offered suggestions for enhancing its deterrence posture. The party even supported Washington's doctrine of flexibility, agreeing with its premise that extended deterrence was diminishing in credibility and that the Western alliance needed additional conventional forces.[14] Whereas the Adenauer government was critical of Washington's flexible response strategy and began to question some of NATO's military planning, the Social Democrats were moving toward the American position. It was not so much that they were fully persuaded by the American military-strategic rationale as they feared de Gaulle would persuade Adenauer to place Germany's security under the protection of France's nuclear umbrella rather than America's. At a time when Adenauer began to criticize the revamping of American strategic doctrine, his most vociferous critics began to endorse his earlier, unqualified support of NATO.

The FDP's commitment to unification was subject to the same pressures. During the election campaign of 1961 the Free Democrats still called for a more "independent" foreign policy and asserted that the Germans themselves, rather than the Four Powers, were ultimately responsible for reunification. As late as the beginning of 1962 the FDP proposed that Bonn hold exploratory talks on its own with the Soviet Union, and some elements of the party flirted with the prospect of a bilateral German-Soviet understanding. But shortly afterward the FDP's chief, Erich Mende, declared that the party had reconsidered its foreign policy stand and was now opposed to Germany's neutrality and disengagement proposals for Central Europe. The FDP renounced its suggestions for bilateral discussions with the Soviet Union and instead emphasized the need to encourage liberalization of the East German regime to better the lot of the East German people.[15]

These changes in the Social Democrats' and Free Democrats' attitude toward disengagement and NATO were accompanied by their combined opposition to the government's European policy. De Gaulle had agreed to support Adenauer's hard line toward the Soviet bloc if Adenauer would support de Gaulle's little Europe policy, restricting membership in the Common Market. The SPD opposed both positions. Still hoping that polycentric trends within the Soviet bloc might aid reunification, the Social Democrats favored a much more flexible policy toward the Soviet Union and Eastern Europe, supported Washington's readiness to seek East-West détente, and were highly critical of de Gaulle's attempts to restrict the membership of the Common Market and gain a position of leadership among the Six. Although still in opposition, the SPD was moving toward foreign policy positions more closely attuned to the realities of the East-West contest and intra-alliance developments than were those of the government.[16]

Even the SPD's misgivings about the European Community helped push the party toward the center of the political spectrum. The SPD's objections to a small Europe of the Six were shared in important German political and economic circles (influential elements in the CDU, the Free Democrats, industry and banking); and that they were shared by the United States as well simply added to the ironic position in which the Social Democrats found themselves. Although not based on congruent reasons, the preference of this heterogeneous group for a larger Common Market complemented its support of NATO and its opposition to de Gaulle's design for a Western European construct under French hegemony and a European nuclear protectorate led by France. These divergent groups were much less willing than Adenauer to make allowances for de Gaulle's foreign policy, which was disrupting the Western alliance and which they perceived to be contrary to Germany's political, economic, and military-strategic interests. On political as well as economic and military-strategic grounds, the German Atlanticists had common objectives: to admit Britain to the Common Market and thwart de Gaulle's design for a European order under French leadership, to embark on a more flexible and imaginative Eastern policy, to pursue a security policy based on close cooperation with NATO and the United States, and not least to seek a change of regime in Bonn. On this basis the Social Democrats, the Free Democrats, and the liberal wing of the CDU established a partial, tenuous, implicit, but nonetheless important consensus. Agreement or disagreement on foreign policy began to reach across party lines, setting the stage for the intricate realignments of the mid-1960s.

Most fundamentally, the impulses for the political realignments in Bonn came from changes in the international context of Bonn's foreign policies. The blurring of previously polarized domestic positions on political-economic as well as military-strategic issues stemmed in part from the apparent hopelessness of the unification issue and from the gradual fragmentation of the Western alliance. As it became necessary to choose between Washington and Paris, long-standing tensions within the governing coalitions and the CDU could no longer be contained. Given the sensitivity of the West German political process to external influences, the disagreements between the United States and France not only created serious problems for Bonn's foreign policy but also undermined Adenauer's domestic support on foreign policy issues, even within his own party.

The attrition of support for Adenauer's foreign policy program was accelerated by an erosion of his personal authority.[17] The Free Democrats made a good showing in the elections of 1961 at the expense of the CDU/CSU, for the Social Democrats had also gained, and insisted that they would rejoin the governing coalition only if Adenauer agreed to step down as chancellor by 1963. The coalition formed in 1961 by the CDU/CSU and FDP, precarious to begin with, collapsed after one year;[18] and although the FDP was finally persuaded to rejoin a reshuffled cabinet, the internal cohesion of the coalition and of the CDU/CSU had been shaken fundamentally. Adenauer was a lame-duck chancellor unable even to prevent the chancellorship from going to Ludwig Erhard, whom he had opposed and openly humiliated all along, warning that he was insufficiently astute in international affairs and lacking in political acumen, vision, and experience.[19]

Convolutions at the Center, 1963–69

The partial and tentative consensus that had emerged on foreign policy matters was symbolized in the person of the new chancellor. Ludwig Erhard was the very embodiment of Germany's successful quest for normalcy. He was the patron saint of the "economic miracle," he represented the pro-Atlantic consensus that reached across Bonn's political spectrum (manifested in staunch support of NATO and of a wider membership in the Common Market), and he seemed to favor a less doctrinaire, more flexible policy toward the Soviet Union and Eastern Europe. On the surface it would seem as if this rudimentary consensus would have provided Bonn with a long-sought opportunity to face foreign policy issues with resolution and on a secure foundation of domestic support. But it soon became apparent that the international environment was as intrusive and fractious as it had been before, and that external events continued to raise controversy in Bonn.

The biggest obstacles to effective policymaking were the widening conflict between the United States and France, and Bonn's irresolute diplomacy toward the East. As it became clear that Erhard was inclined by preference and induced by circumstances to support Washington rather than Paris, the consensus that had been in the making proved insufficiently broad and deep. A polarization of political viewpoints soon developed, but in contrast to the disagreements that differentiated the parties in the fifties, the debate between the Gaullists and the Atlanticists reached within party lines as well as across them, with the majority party, the CDU/CSU, containing strong advocates on both sides. The "consensus" did not rest on a solid inner core of undisputed foreign policy preferences or on a cohesive domestic political base. It revolved around refracted foreign and domestic policies and was supported by dispersed political and economic constituencies. Bipolar confrontation had given way to fragmentation. The domestic political configuration in the Federal Republic on foreign policy remained a mirror of the European political order.

At the core of the Gaullists' disagreement with the Atlanticists was a considerable disenchantment with the United States. The Gaullists believed Washington was insufficiently firm, ready to make deals with the Soviet Union over the heads of Europe and Germany, and that de Gaulle's plans for Europe held out much greater promise for resolving German foreign policy problems. The German Gaullists were sympathetic to France's attempts to fashion a more independent role for Europe in world politics, based on close Franco-German cooperation and sustained by the economic and military potential of the Common Market. Not surprisingly, they were unenthusiastic about the prospect of British membership in the EEC, and gave only perfunctory support to the government's policies for enlarging the Common Market.

The rapid deterioration of Franco-German relations, Erhard's lack of success in Washington, and Bonn's more flexible Eastern policy aggravated these tensions within the CDU/CSU. The Gaullists opposed Erhard not only because of what they viewed as his misguided anti-Gaullism and naive pro-Atlantic policy, but also because of the government's more conciliatory Eastern policy, which they regarded as similarly lacking in realism and determination. The Gaullists were much more closely identified by conviction as well as past association with the orthodox Cold War position of the Adenauer years, and they generally followed a hard-line policy toward East Germany and Eastern Europe, opposing any modification of the Hallstein Doctrine and the official government position on the Oder-Neisse border (bringing them out of line with de Gaulle, who had recognized the Oder-Neisse frontier in 1959).

While Chancellor Erhard and Foreign Minister Schröder were attacked by the Gaullists within their own party for making a dangerous "opening to the East," they were chided by their coalition partners, the FDP, for not making the opening wide enough. Although the Free Democrats favored the government's Common Market policy, their commitment to a dynamic reunification policy led them to attack their coalition partners' hesitant gestures toward Eastern Europe much more stridently than did the SPD opposition.[20] In fact, the Social Democrats were by now stressing "bipartisanship" in foreign affairs. The SPD was determined to eradicate in the voters' minds the idea that the party was less security-conscious or pro-NATO than the CDU/CSU, and generally refused to be drawn into the controversy between Atlanticists and Gaullists, arguing that Bonn should try not to incur the enmity of either Washington or Paris.

The lines between government and opposition were blurred. The CDU/CSU (and to some extent also the FDP) played the role not only of party in power but also of unofficial opposition on some major foreign policy issues, while the official opposition, the SPD, shared several of the government's policy preferences and tried to straddle the fence on the issues that divided the majority party. The resulting ambiguity of party images was most likely of considerable help to the CDU/CSU in the lackluster election campaign of 1965, for Erhard proved a formidable vote getter, and the party almost regained the absolute majority it had lost in 1961. In contrast to previous years, in 1965 a vote for the CDU/CSU expressed ambivalence about foreign policy and could be interpreted as a refusal to choose either a pro-Atlantic or a pro-Gaullist position. Although the traditional coalition arrangement between the CDU/CSU and the FDP was reestablished after the election, this was widely viewed as an interim solution. Erhard's ineffectiveness as a chancellor and his loss of prestige were already so debilitating that at the very moment of the electoral triumph of the CDU/CSU, to which he contributed substantially, rivals within his own party were making plans to topple him.

The jockeying for position in Bonn led to a convoluted interplay between domestic and foreign policy considerations, leading to a diffuse and amorphous political situation. In their determination ultimately to wrest power from Erhard and preclude Schröder from succeeding him, the Gaullists rather than the Atlanticists flirted with the prospect of a Grand Coalition with the Social Democrats, even though the foreign policy conceptions of the SPD were much closer to Erhard's and Schröder's line on Atlantic policy and to the FDP's on Eastern policy, and hence in conflict with the preferences of the Gaullists. By contrast, Erhard, Schröder, and others feared that a Grand Coalition with the Social Democrats, although relatively acceptable to them from the viewpoint of foreign policy matters, would lead to the absorption of their power in a conglomerate "national front." Nor could the FDP be expected to welcome the prospect of a Grand Coalition or for that matter of an all-party coalition. The FDP constantly feared that it would fall below the 5 percent of the vote required for representation in the Bundestag and was threatened with exclusion by proposed changes in the electoral law; it needed to maintain its image as a third party and the leverage it provided. All this contrasted with the situation prevailing in the 1950s, when the line dividing government from opposition was sharp, when foreign policy preferences generally complemented domestic policy preferences and power calculations, and when these disparate positions were articulated by specific parties in relatively clear-cut confrontations.

The intricate patterns of alignment and opposition in the 1960s, in which domestic and foreign policy considerations coalesced, were in a sense doubly involuted. In the first place, the unpleasant necessity of supporting either Washington or Paris led to a polarization of views that bore some similarities to the polarization of the 1950s. But the constituency of one view, Atlanticism, was dispersed over a wide political spectrum and not concentrated in a single political party. Advocates of the opposing view, the Gaullists, were situated primarily in one party, but groups within the CDU/CSU were also the major spokesmen for Atlanticism. The lines between tradition and innovation on domestic policy, between party positions on foreign policy issues, and between domestic and foreign policy were becoming blurred. The political process lacked transparency and accountability.

There was yet another convolution of views, also imposed from the outside. For even though the conflict between the United States and France was genuine, the positions of the Atlanticists and Gaullists in Bonn were not truly aligned with the positions of Washington and Paris. The domestic alignments on foreign policy issues in Bonn were forming around alternatives that had no real counterparts in international diplomacy. The foreign policy interests of the Federal Republic, whether interpreted by the Atlanticists or by the Gaullists, no longer corresponded with those of the United States or France:

> The "Gaullists," while eager to move closer to Paris, did not at all see eye to eye with President de Gaulle's Eastern European policies and were rather frightened by his visions of a Greater Europe embracing the Communist East. The "Atlanticists" were lured by the dream of German participation in nuclear defense and of a kind of "special relationship" between the United States and the Federal Republic, even long after it had become clear that Washington had dropped the MLF concept and was as interested as de Gaulle himself in furthering an understanding with the Soviet Union and with Moscow's Eastern European allies. To a large extent, the controversy between these schools of opinion was something like a tragi-comedy of errors: the German clients of France and America still fought out battles which their foreign friends had already abandoned.[21]

The complexities of this situation and the inherent difficulty of dealing with them would have proven a substantial challenge for any chancellor. Erhard, handicapped by a divided party and coalition as well as by the deterioration of his personal influence, was rapidly losing his grip on power in Bonn. His insecure political position severely hampered the government in addressing domestic and international problems. In foreign affairs, where skillful manipulation and a judicious balancing of conflicting courses of action was required, Erhard's diplomacy seemed to consist almost entirely of pro-Atlantic gestures and occasional Gaullist rhetoric, sustained primarily by goodwill and personal bonhomie. He had failed to persuade the Johnson administration to come around to the German viewpoint on the MLF, Franco-German relations were at their lowest point since the establishment of the Federal Republic, and the government's halfhearted overtures to Eastern Europe had brought only meager results, merely annoying the right wing of the CDU/CSU without impressing the Free Democrats or Social Democrats.

On domestic issues, things were not going much better. For the first time since the launching of the economic miracle, a serious recession hit West Germany, causing unemployment and aggravating budgetary and fiscal problems. Increases in tax revenues, which were necessary to continue financing generous social programs, did not materialize. Erhard alienated many of his supporters through his inept handling of economic and budgetary matters, in which he was supposed to be an expert, and even his vote-getting abilities were diminishing when he sought to apply them in state elections.[22] The chancellor's days in office were clearly numbered, and in December 1966 the Christian Democrats and Social Democrats joined forces in a national coalition government, which gave them an overwhelming majority in the Bundestag.

The extensive deliberations and negotiations that preceded the formation of the new government, during which all parties considered joining every possible coalition arrangement, demonstrated the growing pragmatism and lessening ideological nature of the political process, exemplified by the willingness to adjust party policy to gain political advantage.[23] This is not to say that substantive political questions in domestic and foreign affairs did not figure prominently in the parties' deliberations. In fact, the major justification for the Grand Coalition was that a joint effort by the two major parties could lead to a resolution of major political problems that were confronting Germany: Bonn's foreign policy was in complete disarray, the attrition of governmental authority and feeling of political drift under Erhard had led to widespread demands for stronger leadership, there was a serious economic and budgetary crisis, and several crucial constitutional issues not only required a two-thirds majority in the Bundestag, but also called for a measure of bipartisanship and a willingness to share political responsibility.

With respect to foreign policy, the Grand Coalition's major and most general endeavor was to enlarge Germany's diplomatic flexibility and instill a measure of realism. Even during the Erhard government, there had been a clear and widespread sense in the Federal Republic that the general principles that had guided German foreign policy during its formative years under Adenauer, and that had been formulated in a Cold War setting, were inapplicable in a setting of East-West coexistence. A responsible "national front" government seemed to offer the chance of a reappraisal of Bonn's foreign policies, and there was considerable hope in the Federal Republic that a more dynamic and effective diplomacy could be launched by the new leaders, all of whom had in one way or another been dissatisfied with Erhard's conduct of foreign policy. It looked as if new opportunities were present, and in its early statements the Grand Coalition promised to exploit them. Several months after the formation of the Grand Coalition, Theo Sommer wrote: "The German scene has changed beyond recognition. After years of drift and indecision, a new sense of vigor and purpose permeates Bonn . . . [and] only now is there a government that can face the uncertainties of the future with the comforting feeling that its home base is intact. Probably it took the Grand Coalition to provide a reliable parliamentary majority for any policy of innovation and to produce a new style of leadership: relaxed though determined, self-confident but not arrogant, matter-of-fact but imaginative."

But international and domestic factors combined to make it difficult to move toward the resolution of outstanding foreign policy problems, and two years later Sommer complained: "Even the election on September 28 [1969] will not change the way the political deck is stacked these days and the way the players have devised their strategy. Presumably Kiesinger will be the next chancellor again, and the next coalition will again hoist the black-red [CDU/CSU-SPD] banner. One should not be fooled, however: this is neither a question of [election] percentages, nor a question of personalities, it is simply a question of lack of will for change. One must note this with regret, because any other coalition would be better for state and society than the present one."[24]

In a sense, the Grand Coalition was the premature symbol of the fundamental rapprochement between Left and Right that was slowly developing underneath the surface of the political landscape and that emerged in the 1970s. But it was torn by conflicting views on domestic politics and could not work effectively on foreign policy because of internal checks and balances. The institutional responsibility for the conduct of foreign affairs was blurred—Kiesinger, as chancellor, had the constitutional right to determine the general direction of policy, whereas Brandt, in the foreign office, was clearly the innovator in foreign policymaking. Even before the Soviet invasion of Czechoslovakia the Grand Coalition was working at cross-purposes, with the more conservative CDU/CSU elements acting as a constant brake on the SPD's more innovative elements. There was a clash over international monetary policy and the nonproliferation treaty,[25] and the invasion of Czechoslovakia, from which neither the innovators nor the conservatives could derive any comfort, tended to strengthen the position of the conservatives. It seemed to confirm their argument that the reformists, with no guarantees from the Soviets, were undermining the consistency and legitimacy of the orthodox German viewpoint in the face of an unreconstructed Soviet imperialism.

Although Chancellor Kiesinger had contributed to Bonn's new initiatives (for example by communicating directly and semiofficially with the

East German Prime Minister, Willi Stoph) he was temperamentally less venturesome than the SPD, and he was kept in check by the more conservative elements within his party. In March 1968 he felt obliged to dissociate himself specifically from Willy Brandt's call at the SPD party conference for "recognition and respect" of the Oder-Neisse border. Even so, the Grand Coalition managed to enlarge the dimensions of Germany's Ostpolitik, primarily by its willingness to deal with the GDR; and it prepared the way for its subsequent intensification when Willy Brandt became chancellor.

Considering how divided it was on how to address them, the Grand Coalition also coped relatively successfully with the recurring international monetary crises of the 1960s and the domestic economic recession of 1966–67. But this could not be accomplished without placing a heavy stress on the coalition's cohesion. During the international conference on currency problems in Bonn in November 1968, the foreign policy conservatives (most notably Finance Minister Franz-Josef Strauss) and the reformist-liberals (represented by the SPD's economics minister, Karl Schiller) still acted in concert to hold an inflexible line against the revaluation of the D-Mark urged by France, the United States, and Britain. To be sure, Schiller and Strauss were motivated by different political and economic considerations. Schiller feared that revaluation would retard his pump-priming economic program, with which he had guided the German economy out of the recession of 1966–67; Strauss opposed it because it would have burdened the budget and (perhaps more important) because he viewed the currency confrontation with France as an opportunity to demonstrate the diplomatic assertiveness that he felt had been lacking in Bonn's foreign policy for a long time.

The Schiller-Strauss partnership was in any case short-lived. When the question of revaluation resurfaced in spring 1969, it turned into the most explosive issue of the election year and for all practical purposes split the Grand Coalition. This was somewhat ironic in that the new wave of speculative money that rushed into Germany in May 1969 brought with it relatively little new international pressure to revalue the D-Mark. The pressure came from inside the Federal Republic. To stem the inflow of capital, the cabinet decided after a stormy session not to revalue, overriding the Bundesbank, a majority of academic economists, and most important, Economics Minister Karl Schiller. The foreign and domestic economic ramifications of the issue were highly intricate, and not nearly as clear-cut as the opposing sides portrayed them. But the very complexity of the issue encouraged its oversimplification in the public debate, in which the Social Democrats accused the Christian Democrats of abetting inflation, and the Christian Democrats charged their opponents with politically motivated manipulation of the exchange rate. The proponents as well as the opponents of the government's decision were very much aware of its political and psychological impact, especially in an election year. The opponents of revaluation—they ultimately included Chancellor Kiesinger himself, who had consulted with industrialists and financiers—doubted that Germany's unilateral floating of the D-Mark would provide for a lasting stabilization of German monetary policies, which were undercut by the trends of the Bretton Woods monetary system; and they were of course aware that export-sensitive industrial interests (which tended to support the CDU/CSU and FDP) opposed revaluation, as did farm interests that stood to lose by it unless compensated with additional subsidies. The advocates of revaluation, most prominently Schiller and the Bundesbank, felt that stopgap measures had proven insufficient to correct the persisting current account surpluses and that the D-Mark would have to be shielded from inflationary trends abroad: the Federal Republic's first economics minister from the ranks of the SPD came to the defense of monetary stability, protecting the probity of the D-Mark and gaining for his party the legitimacy it needed in economic and monetary affairs.

The line between the two sides in the controversy was finally drawn pretty much along party lines, with the Free Democrats castigating both sides for their public squabbling and politicking over a serious economic issue. All parties not only had their eyes on the forthcoming election, but sought to protect the fundamental socioeconomic goals of their political constituencies. The CDU/CSU conservatives and moderates were responsive to the interests of their traditional supporters among farmers, big business, and small entrepreneurs. Schiller, who was not unpopular with big industry after his economic revitalization program helped push up profits in 1968, nonetheless supported his party's commitment to lower-income groups and small savers; and the Social Democrats wanted wage earners to share more fully in Germany's prosperity through higher wages without having industrial employers annul these wage gains through rising prices. Stabilizing the D-Mark and subjecting German industrial and commercial interests to more intense international competition, which was expected to follow from a D-Mark revaluation, would serve that goal as well as slow the economic boom. When the Grand Coalition decided one day after the election of September 1969 to allow the D-Mark to float toward revaluation, this was in effect a decision forced on the caretaker cabinet. It was taken to forestall a new international monetary crisis, and in anticipation of a formal revaluation by the Social Democrats who were expected to become the senior partner in a new coalition government.

The fractured positions on Ostpolitik, security policies, and monetary policies that characterized the Grand Coalition were symptomatic of the continuing sensitivity of the Federal Republic's domestic political process to outside influences.[26] The Social Democratic Left continued to move into the mainstream of German politics, but the convolutions at the center made it difficult to define what constituted a centrist position. By the late 1960s the leadership of the major political parties was not faced with a groundswell of opposing viewpoints on foreign policy but rather with a general disorientation and malleability. The German public had become increasingly frustrated with the impasse of German foreign policy, and seemed willing to examine alternatives. Yet the political parties found it difficult to formulate plausible foreign policy options. This made for a significant difference between the early 1950s and late 1960s: the sharply dualistic European order during the height of the Cold War had lent itself easily (perhaps too easily) to formulate equally sharply defined and conflicting responses; by the late 1960s the international restraints on Bonn's policies (although still intrusive) were less clear-cut, resisted polarization, and thus demanded a less focused response.

The domestic political scene in the Federal Republic had become more convoluted as well, reinforcing the convolution on foreign policy questions. As always, external and internal dimensions of the Federal Republic's political process were closely intermeshed, even though it was not always easy to establish a precise cause-and-effect connection in their mutual dynamics. In the 1960s the political management of their economic prosperity proved as difficult for the Germans as the management of their economic reconstruction in the 1950s—not dissimilar in that respect from the difficulties the European Economic Community experienced in intensifying integration. Affluence brought with it a certain hedonistic utilitarianism; the general attrition of political ideologies in the Europe of the 1960s encouraged political parties to become more pragmatic in their platforms and policies; and in the German case the electoral system promoted appeals to the middle-of-the-road majority by penalizing political parties that had narrow programs and small constituencies.

Neither the Erhard administration nor the Grand Coalition managed to translate the evolving political and socioeconomic pragmatism into effective foreign policy making or genuinely innovative domestic reforms. Instead, the absence of effective leadership, the crisis of political imagination in a setting of de-ideologized prosperity, and a certain aversion (especially among the young) to the political expediency exemplified by the Grand Coalition led to a countertrend: on the Right, the short-lived appeal of the National Democratic Party approached voters with an essentially traditional, conservative nationalism that had neo-Nazi overtones; and the loosely organized extreme Left formed an "extraparliamentary" opposition, arguing that the SPD's submergence in the German political establishment had deprived the political process of an opposition party worthy of the name, and that the premises of German foreign and domestic policies should be radically reexamined.

It was to the credit of the Grand Coalition that it dealt with these complex and ambivalent political and socioeconomic circumstances in a way that preserved political stability; ironically, it may have helped that political accountability during these years was refracted and opaque. The Grand Coalition managed to contain domestic turbulences—teach-ins, sit-ins, and so on—that resulted from the Left's dissatisfactions with the established order in the 1960s; and this helped the SPD demonstrate that it could govern responsibly, especially in foreign and economic policy, where Foreign Minister Willy Brandt and Economics Minister Karl Schiller obtained wide visibility and approbation internationally as well as domestically. Ineffective as it was in policymaking, the Grand Coalition fit the political temper of the time and fulfilled a stabilizing role in both foreign policy and domestic policy. It was a government of transition, reflecting a society in transition.

As was to be expected, in the election year of 1969 programmatic differences within the Grand Coalition were heightened as the CDU/CSU, the SPD, and of course the small opposition party, the FDP, sharpened their political profiles for the campaign. But the peculiar calculations that had brought the coalition partners together in the first place made them mute their public controversy. Neither party wanted a full and open break, because both anticipated that the election results might force them to continue their programmatically unnatural and politically uneasy partnership. As it turned out, what emerged from the election of September 1969 was a coalition of an entirely different makeup, with an entirely different program, and with entirely different problems.

13

Convergence at the Center, 1969–89: Party Politics, German-American Relations, and the Euro-American Partnership

The Eastern treaties are a historical fact, which must be accepted as such and with which we must live; and the policies that led to them were, if not in every single respect, mostly inescapable.

—WILHELM GREWE, 1987

What is new about the current situation is that America is being doubted not by its traditional critics but by its older friends.

—HENRY KISSINGER, 1987

Consensus is possible. . . . Despite all the differences in our histories and our cultures, we all act on the basis of what are, in principle, the same fundamental values. We all believe that the dignity of human individuals must be inviolable. . . . Our governments can do justice to their responsibilities only by acting, not by adopting tactical communiqués formulated to appeal to public opinion in their own countries.

—HELMUT SCHMIDT, 1985

The coalition government of Social Democrats and Free Democrats that was established on the basis of the election of September 1969 rested on a slim majority in the Bundestag. Even more important, the members of the new government, under the SPD's Willy Brandt as chancellor and the FDP's Walter Scheel as vice chancellor and foreign minister, did not see eye to eye on a number of important issues. Although the Social Democrats and Free Democrats had common ground on foreign policy issues (above all in their determination to make new approaches to the East and enlarge the Common Market), they were much farther apart on domestic

355

issues, especially in economic and social policy, where the Free Democrats were closer to the Christian Democrats than to their new coalition
partners.[1] As always, the iron rule of the Federal Republic's coalition
politics applied: a center-left coalition (SPD-FDP) must shield itself from
the divisive effects of domestic issues, a center-right coalition (CDU/CSU-
FDP) from those of foreign policy issues.

The inherent tensions between the SPD and the FDP on economic
issues and its tenuous majority in the Bundestag pushed the new government to emphasize foreign policy, where its base of agreement seemed
most secure and where its major interest lay. But the government's
parliamentary majority was threatened by defectors who could not go
along with the revisions of Bonn's Ostpolitik, and the new government
faced a determined and powerful opposition. The Christian Democrats,
out of office for the first time in the history of the Federal Republic and
bitter because they were denied a voice in the government even though
they had drawn the most votes in the election, were eager to act as
vigilant, exacting, and vociferous critics of the new coalition, in the hope
of toppling it as soon as possible.[2]

From the beginning the coalition's Ostpolitik drew the opposition's
most intense fire.[3] The Christian Democrats argued that Bonn's Eastern
policy (especially as reflected in the provisions of the Moscow and Warsaw treaties, and in the inter-German accord on Berlin) would allow the
Soviet Union to solidify and legitimize its influence in Eastern Europe
and East Germany without making adequate concessions to the West,
and that it would work to the detriment of long-range German and
Western European security interests, weakening the Western defense
effort and bringing about a reduced American commitment to Europe.[4]
Entrenched Cold War positions were at stake, and their defenders were
determined not to yield. Opposition spokesmen set an exacting array of
preconditions for accepting the Eastern treaties, and the right wing of the
opposition, especially the CSU's chief, Franz-Josef Strauss, suggested in
effect that Brandt's Eastern policy was selling out German interests. The
CDU/CSU opposition of the early 1970s was attacking the government with
the same charges that the SPD had lodged against Adenauer twenty years
earlier. In the 1950s the government was accused by the Social Democrats
of selling out German interests in the West; in the 1970s it was accused by
the Christian Democrats of selling them out in the East.

In spring 1972 the controversy over the government's Ostpolitik
reached a critical point, in part because the Moscow and Warsaw treaties
were going through preliminary debates in the Bundestag, in part because the parliamentary support of the SPD-FDP coalition had become
so precarious that the survival of the government was threatened. Although these two factors were related, the difficulties of the government
stemmed from causes that went beyond its Ostpolitik. At the height of

the coalition's crisis over Ostpolitik, quarrels continued within the government over tax reform and related issues. The political consequences of the government's inability to solve economic problems, especially inflation, were particularly serious, for the controversy over Ostpolitik prevented the coalition from falling back to a safe position on foreign policy matters. The inner contradictions of the coalition on socioeconomic matters prevented it from acting decisively on domestic issues, and its fundamental raison d'être, foreign policy, rested on the narrowest of margins in the Bundestag and was forcefully attacked by the opposition.

But the intense controversy over the ratification of the Moscow and Warsaw treaties—most CDU/CSU members abstained from voting—could not hide the irreversibility of Bonn's Ostpolitik. The intricate connections between the government's Eastern policy and a variety of other issues of great importance to both East and West (such as the Helsinki Conference, the SALT talks, mutual and balanced force reductions, and general East-West détente) meant that a collapse of Ostpolitik would have serious repercussions not only among Bonn's opponents in the East but also among its allies in the West, not to speak of the consequences for the Allied and inter-German accord on Berlin. The Christian Democrats realized that if they were to bring down the treaty structure of Bonn's Ostpolitik, they would shoulder the responsibility for having obstructed the central foreign policy goal of both the East and the West. The CDU/CSU opposition found it as difficult in the 1970s to offer a realistic alternative to the government's foreign policy program as had the SPD opposition twenty years earlier. The obtrusive realities of the international context were as powerful and inescapable in the 1970s as they had been in the 1950s.

Toward the Grand Compromise: The Right Moves toward the Center
The election of 1972 (in which the SPD-FDP coalition won a comfortable majority, with the SPD gaining for the first time more votes than the CDU/CSU), was widely interpreted as an endorsement of the government's Ostpolitik. The election results of 1972 were in effect the practical and symbolic pendant of the election results of 1957, which had amounted to an endorsement of Adenauer's Westpolitik. Not even the opposition could overlook the implication that the German electorate wished to clarify the issue by giving the architects of Ostpolitik a clear signal of approval. Just as in the late 1950s foreign and domestic circumstances had compelled the Social Democrats to initiate a rethinking of their own positions on the Western policies of the CDU/CSU and accept the treaty package that resulted from them, so were the Christian Democrats obliged in the mid-1970s to begin their own reevaluation of Bonn's Eastern treaties and accept the domestic political endorsement they obtained. Although German conservatives sought legal redress to weaken the

political impact of Bonn's inter-German accord with East Berlin, the political, psychological, and moral foundations of Bonn's new Ostpolitik were laid, both at home and abroad. By 1974, when Willy Brandt resigned over the discovery that his personal assistant was an East German spy (his authority had already been undercut for other reasons), the foreign and domestic dynamics of Ostpolitik had become virtually irreversible. The large outlines of Bonn's Eastern policies could not be fundamentally altered by Brandt's successors, Helmut Schmidt and Helmut Kohl, who carried them forward into the 1980s.

The continuing coalition of SPD and FDP, led by Helmut Schmidt as chancellor and the FDP's Hans-Dietrich Genscher as foreign minister, soon became preoccupied with domestic and international economic problems. Of course Ostpolitik and especially the relations between West and East Germany were not neglected by either government or opposition, but a significant shift of priorities was taking place. In the years before and after the elections of 1976 (which after a lackluster campaign characterized by internal dissension in the CDU/CSU returned the coalition government to power), economic and social questions began to come to the fore. Bonn became preoccupied with reducing unemployment and public borrowing, reforming the pension and health systems, and shielding Germany's economy from the international recession and the monetary problems that threatened the Federal Republic's prosperity and price stability. Ostpolitik was in a state of stagnation; Westpolitik demanded vigorous attention.

The emerging prominence of economic issues, in which both domestic and international dimensions were inextricable, put a severe strain on the cohesion of the coalition: the need to address urgent economic and social issues pressed against the neuralgic point of the SPD's and FDP's partnership. From the 1970s and into the 1980s, the left wing of the SPD became increasingly critical of what it viewed as an excessively centrist orientation of the party's leadership, accusing it in effect of political opportunism and of obliging the Free Democrats with an unwarranted and exaggerated accommodation of the FDP's preferences on socioeconomic programs. For substantive reasons as well as personal ones, these divisive grievances became more troublesome after Helmut Schmidt replaced Willy Brandt. The dynamics of Ostpolitik had run their course, the Free Democrats were gaining an even larger voice in shaping the coalition's socioeconomic policies, and Schmidt, at the right wing of the party on domestic and foreign policy, presented a more inviting target for the Left's discontent than had Willy Brandt. As a result, on several key issues of socioeconomic policy, arms control and nuclear energy policy, and on NATO's double-track decision on INF deployment, Schmidt was closer to the SPD's coalition partners and even the opposition than to the left wing of his own party.[5]

The centrist position that Schmidt managed to occupy in German politics was a source of strength in the electorate at large (some said the Germans would have liked a CDU government under Helmut Schmidt), but became a source of contention within his own party and weakened his hand in the coalition politics of the government. From the mid-1970s the Federal Republic seemed to move in a more conservative political direction (in large part in reaction to the more radical excesses of the late 1960s),[6] and the "inner reforms" advocated by Willy Brandt (for the implementation of which his Ostpolitik left little time or political energy) were for all practical purposes dropped by Helmut Schmidt. In some major respects, the change of leadership from Brandt to Schmidt was more of a turning point in German politics than the later change from Schmidt to Kohl.[7]

The opposition found it difficult, however, to formulate plausible domestic and foreign policy alternatives. Chancellor Schmidt's crisp style of governing, his articulate presentation of the many international economic, monetary, and military-strategic problems facing the Federal Republic, and his own broad experience in addressing them made him a difficult target for the opposition's attempts to dislodge the government.[8] The CDU/CSU further weakened its chances of success by selecting the CSU's chief, Franz-Josef Strauss, as its candidate for chancellor in 1980, personalizing the election campaign with a highly controversial figure and thus underlining the lack of serious programmatic differences between them and the government.[9] But the government's success at the polls (greater for the FDP, which had gained, than for the SPD, which had remained stable) could not be converted into a more cohesive coalition. Although the election campaign and results had confirmed the chancellor's personal popularity, they also pointed up the tensions within the SPD. Almost from the beginning of the coalition of 1980 the Free Democrats, bolstered by their own electoral success and the growing international reputation of their foreign minister, yielded to their periodic need to establish a clear programmatic profile and seemed ready to cast about for a new coalition partner.[10]

Although there were no fundamental disagreements on foreign policy within the government itself, the FDP and the left wing of the SPD were clearly pulling the coalition in opposing directions, with the chancellor trying to straddle an increasingly uncomfortable center position. NATO's double-track decision, with which the chancellor was so closely identified, was most strongly opposed within his own party;[11] the left wing of the SPD felt strong sympathy with the Greens (a new party that first obtained representation in the Bundestag in 1983), especially in their opposition to nuclear energy, their attempt to restore a somewhat arcadian quality to modern society, and their strongly neutralist foreign policy, which was tinged with anti-Americanism. The left wing of the SPD and trade union leaders complained that the government's socioeconomic program contained no new social reforms and too many concessions to the FDP, and the weakening economic and financial situation of the Federal Republic, which reflected the deteriorating international economic situation and was aggravated by inflation, imposed an increasingly divisive zero-sum burden on the financing of the government's domestic programs. When the Free Democrats abandoned the coalition over budgetary and fiscal measures in fall 1982, taking up the chancellor on his repeated threats of resignation, it was merely the last in a series of disputes that had weakened the coalition beyond repair. The partnership between the SPD and FDP had become timeworn and fatigued, suffering from programmatic differences, party politics, and personal abrasions and growing distrust among cabinet members. The coalition could not be salvaged, even though it was generally agreed on the major outlines of Bonn's foreign policies. The FDP turned to the CDU/CSU, forming with it a center-right coalition government.

Helmut Kohl, the new chancellor, and Hans-Dietrich Genscher, still the foreign minister, were quick to express their intention of providing continuity in German foreign policy. The new government reiterated the Federal Republic's support for NATO's double-track decision (while the SPD's half-hearted support became even more ambivalent and conditional now that the party was in opposition), and Chancellor Kohl was determined to create a more harmonious diplomatic climate with the United States, having blamed his predecessor for the deterioration of German-American relations and a failure to check neutralist tendencies within his party. The Free Democrats took a more guarded view of American policies than their coalition partner, and maintained it throughout the 1980s. They approached Washington's SDI program with great caution, shied away from an association with the strident Cold War rhetoric of the Reagan administration, and intensified their European and Third World policies. They also saw in Defense Minister Manfred Wörner's apparently unqualified endorsement of the Pentagon's plans for NATO and the Federal Republic a threat to the remnants of East-West détente. The Free Democrats clearly sought to maintain a centrist position on foreign policy, which, in the center-right government's political constellation, meant a pulling to the left; and they were determined to check the rightist security policies of the CDU/CSU and the maverick diplomacy of their arch foe, Franz-Josef Strauss, whose frustration over not having been offered a sufficiently prestigious cabinet post in Bonn periodically tempted him to conduct his own foreign policy from the minister-president's chancellory in Munich.

With respect to Bonn's Ostpolitik, and especially its inter-German component, the new center-right coalition followed a course of continuity, imposed by necessity as well as choice. The continuation of

Ostpolitik had been a precondition for the FDP's joining the new coalition (some prominent FDP members had opposed the change to begin with), and many Christian Democrats were as determined as were the Free Democrats and Social Democrats to salvage the mini-détente between the two Germanies amid the general cooling of East-West relations. The CDU/CSU had learned to adjust to Bonn's Ostpolitik with relative equanimity (in 1983 Franz-Josef Strauss arranged for a most generous loan package for East Germany), and although there remained differences of nuance, style, and rhetoric, the major lines of Eastern policy were not seriously altered by the Kohl government, which was affirmed in office in the elections of 1983 and 1987.

If one looks at the election results of 1983 primarily in terms of its results—a revitalized CDU/CSU, a weakened SPD, a restored FDP, and the presence of the new Greens—there emerges a striking similarity to the political configuration of the 1950s. But this is misleading for a number of reasons, especially in the area of foreign policy. Although the implementation of NATO's double-track decision with the deployment of Pershing II and cruise missiles was an important and emotionally charged foreign policy issue, it was far overshadowed by economic problems (high unemployment, inflation, budget deficits) and environmental issues.[12] The real losers were the Social Democrats (making their worst showing since 1961 with 38 percent of the vote), but they were hurt more by internal dissension, the inability to put together a coherent party platform, and a weak candidate for chancellor (Hans-Jochen Vogel having replaced an embittered Helmut Schmidt) than by their waffling over the NATO double-track decision.[13] Bonn's Ostpolitik was in any case not a campaign issue. It had by then become largely immune to serious domestic political challenge and obtained what amounted to political institutionalization in the Federal Republic.[14] Along with Bonn's abiding interest in arms control, Ostpolitik and a concomitant determination to rescue intra-German détente from the deteriorating general climate of East-West relations remained mainstays of Bonn's foreign policy program and of its domestic political base—in part because of their intrinsic benefits (increased and intensified contacts between the two Germanies), which gathered strong support across the entire political spectrum, in part because there was no viable alternative. Just as the SPD had been handicapped in the 1950s by failing to come up with a plausible alternative to Adenauer's Westpolitik, so the CDU/CSU found it impossible in the 1980s to fashion a realistic alternative to the Ostpolitik initiated by the SPD and FDP. In both cases, the exigencies of the international political environment had obtained broad domestic support for the exertions of Bonn's diplomacy.[15]

Even so, although the substance of Bonn's foreign policy was carried over from the 1970s and remained largely untouched in the 1980s, unaffected by the lackluster election campaign of 1987, the rhetoric and

political atmosphere surrounding it were different. This applied especially to Bonn's Eastern policies. Ostpolitik did not hold the same meaning for everyone, and a candid public debate over its ultimate purposes
would have revealed that the broad agreement on current policy
stemmed primarily from the narrow range within which it could be
implemented at present. It did not necessarily imply agreement on where
it should lead in the future. The external restraints on current policy
muted potential internal disagreement over future developments. Not
surprisingly, there remained significant political, temperamental, and
psychological differences that distinguished all parties from one another.
Their strongest political convictions on the nature of the Soviet threat, the
value of the German-American security connection, the implications of
arms control, and the proper approach to a wide range of domestic
socioeconomic issues continued to evoke from the major parties disparate
reflexes that were rooted in deeply held views of what domestic and
foreign policy was all about.[16] Under the surface of the public political
discourse were stubbornly held attitudes and mutual resentments on all
parts of the political spectrum (no less powerful for being often masked),
and these affected the nuance and style of the parties as they approached
issues on which they may have had some substantive agreement.

The conservatives of the CDU/CSU stuck to some of their traditional
Cold War positions, and remained sensitive to political constituencies
that favored a more assertive and less conciliatory Eastern policy (such as
expellee organizations). They remained convinced that the Social Democrats (especially their left wing) were somehow dissolute in their approach to foreign and domestic politics, neither entirely responsible nor
fully respectable, and altogether too soft in dealing with the Soviet Union
and national security. In particular, the Right continued to suspect the
Left of harboring darker aspirations, above all with respect to loosening
the Federal Republic's moorings to the West and mapping a neutralist
path for Germany in a reconstituted European political order.[17] The Left
reciprocated with its own reservations. The Social Democrats remained
deeply averse to their opponents' political preferences in both foreign
and domestic policy. They opposed what they perceived as the Right's
incorrigibly bellicose views of the East-West contest and its reflexive pro-
American inclinations, and they saw in the conservatives' economic policies an insensitive approach to social issues and a belated attempt at
restorative conservatism, authoritarian in spirit and always ready to
grant the state a large interventionist role on issues of law and order
while proclaiming at the same time the need to protect the economy from
the encroachments of socialist state-planning. Although tempered by the
overwhelming middle-of-the-road orientation of German politics, the
terms *Left* and *Right* and the political positions associated with them had
by no means lost their meaning in the politics of the Federal Republic in
the 1980s.

Amid these Left-Right tensions the Free Democrats managed to retain political leverage, not only because of their traditional Liberal philosophy, protective of free enterprise as well as individual liberties, or because their centrist foreign policy position had required of them less painful adjustments than those imposed first on the Social Democrats in the 1950s and 1960s and on the CDU/CSU in the 1970s. They had become an important balancer and power broker in the party system because it had become doubtful whether either German Social Democracy or Christian Democracy could gain an electoral majority in the political landscape of the Federal Republic of the 1980s.[18] With the Left and Right apparently lacking foreign or domestic policy programs sufficiently persuasive to command majority support, the centrist position of the FDP, although always threatened from either direction, seemed at least for the time being secure, and the party was careful to keep itself *koalitionsfähig* (acceptable as a coalition partner) for a future center-left or center-right coalition. Indeed, in the elections of 1987 (which after a campaign dominated by socioeconomic, fiscal, and budgetary issues reaffirmed the coalition in power), the Free Democrats and Greens returned to the Bundestag with a comfortable and reassuring margin of safety.

The party consensus on the major outlines of German Ostpolitik solidified in the 1980s, which obscured the differing hopes and reservations that all parties may have entertained about its ultimate purpose and direction. The parties had moved toward a centrist position that contained no long-range centrist Eastern policy or an incontrovertible mandate for German diplomacy. Except for the determination to sustain German Ostpolitik with the patient and persistent application of small and incremental steps (not much else seemed possible), there existed no logically compelling or politically feasible diplomatic agenda that could have overcome the continuing dichotomy between the Federal Republic's integration in the West and its desire to attenuate the separation from the other German state in the East.[19] Bonn's diplomatic efforts remained delimited by the international context that surrounded the German question, and they were checked as well by the wary distance imposed by East Germany. As always in the history of the Federal Republic, its inner responses in the 1980s corresponded to the outer circumstances of its diplomacy: polarized in the 1950s, refracted and convoluted in the 1960s, convergent in the 1970s, unfocused in the 1980s. The "great compromise" that had emerged over the decades on the major outlines of German foreign policy continued to be enforced in the 1980s by the limits placed on German diplomacy.

Pressures on German-American Relations

In the 1980s the most divisive issues that agitated the foreign policy discourse in Germany and threatened the great compromise came not from the East but from the West. The disputes among the major German parties over the appropriate German response to arms control and to security issues in general stemmed at bottom from the divisive nature of these issues in the Western alliance. The controversy over the government's determination to deploy intermediate-range and cruise missiles, the disagreements within and without the coalition over the missiles' removal in the wake of the double-zero INF accord of 1987–88, the need to adjust to the erratic arms control policies of the Reagan administration, the question of how to face the political and military challenges of a post-INF Europe—these contentious issues were brought to the Federal Republic primarily as a result of problems within the alliance.

As the Reagan administration burdened the cohesion of the alliance with highly questionable security and arms control policies, the general concerns in Western Europe about the quality of American leadership became especially pronounced in the Federal Republic. Many West Germans, although convinced that their security interests and general commitment to the West required their continuing support of NATO, began to reconsider the political burdens and risks that this support entailed. The Federal Republic's security dependence on the United States, and the diplomatic dependence that accompanied it, were being reexamined. Considering the widespread disenchantment in Europe with American diplomacy, and that the disenchantment began to encompass what Europeans considered the vagaries of American domestic politics, it should not be surprising that it found expression in shrill tones as well as measured tones, especially on the German Left. More important, however, the Germans' unease was not limited to the extremes of the political spectrum but had also settled at the political center. The views of the peace movement, of the heterogeneously constituted Greens (whose political platform included concerns that were nuclear as well as environmental, practical as well as metaphysical), and even of the left wing of the SPD were probably less important in their long-range political impact than were the subtly changing attitudes at the center.[20] As Henry Kissinger pointed out in 1987, "What is new about the current situation is that America is being doubted not by its traditional critics but by its older friends."[21]

Symptomatic of these doubts among America's older friends was the response in Germany to the plans for modernizing NATO's tactical nuclear weapons on German soil.[22] Primarily at issue was the modernization of the aging 88 Lance missiles (deployed mainly in Germany), because their short range and small yield made them especially suitable for use on a relatively narrow battlefield such as the two German states. In 1988 CSU chief Franz-Josef Strauss predicted in public that the Bundestag would oppose the modernization of Lance missiles; and prominent CDU members (including Chancellor Kohl and the chairman of the CDU/CSU caucus in the Bundestag, Alfred Dregger) repeatedly voiced their fears that the modernization of short-range missiles would singularize the Federal Republic as the potential battlefield in a nuclear war.[23] Dregger strongly welcomed a proposal made by East Germany's leader, Erich Honecker, for negotiations aimed at reducing battlefield weapons, and castigated Washington's insensitivity to German security concerns: first in arranging for the double-zero accord, then in pressing for the modernization of nuclear weapons that were of use primarily on German territory. Considering the pro-American credentials of such prominent German conservatives, they could hardly be accused of harboring neutralist tendencies. Opposition in Germany to the new missiles ranged across the entire political spectrum, prompting the Social Democrats to speak of the emergence of a "new consensus" on foreign and defense policy.

The United States was insistent that NATO's short-range nuclear weapons be modernized, making it an issue of loyalty to the alliance. Defense Secretary Frank C. Carlucci went so far as to suggest that the United States might withdraw its troops from Germany if Bonn banned nuclear weapons from German territory, and ranking American legislators argued that the decision to modernize was made before the INF accord and reflected NATO requirements that had become even more pressing afterward. If the decision to modernize were not implemented, there would come about a "structural disarmament" of NATO, because the Warsaw Pact had also deployed 1,400 comparable short-range missiles on its territory, mostly in the German Democratic Republic.

The political effect in Germany was devastating, and the Bonn government took recourse to delay and public silence. At a time when Soviet diplomacy had taken a more sophisticated and conciliatory turn, the United States again appeared incorrigibly obsessed with nuclear arms, unremitting in its determination to maintain and augment its nuclear presence in the Federal Republic. Inevitably, German dissatisfactions spread, below the surface as well as openly, from issues of security to issues of Ostpolitik: security issues, and especially arms control matters, were as always connected to the Federal Republic's Eastern policies. Alliance problems and security matters overlapped into the area of Germany's Ostpolitik. The perennial German dilemma of striking a judicious balance between loyalty to the alliance and security interests on the one hand, and a commitment and determination to keep alive détente and an active Eastern policy on the other, was sharpened less as a consequence of Soviet diplomatic maneuvers than as a consequence of intra-alliance disagreements. The consensus on foreign policy embodied in the great compromise was more susceptible to intrusions from the West than to incursions from the East—either when it was called into question on such issues as the double-track decision of 1979 and the double-zero accord of 1987–88, or when it was reaffirmed by the widespread opposition to the modernization of short-range nuclear weapons.

The conflicting pulls of Bonn's security interests and détente interests put a severe strain on German-American relations and the domestic foundations that sustained them. The cohesion of the German-American political compact was stressed both from the outside and from the inside. Objective differences of interests in politics, military-strategic matters, and economics were accompanied by subjective national differences in how to respond to them. In some major respects, the domestic developments on foreign policy issues were moving in opposite directions in Germany and the United States.[24] Whereas the Germans had managed to reach a centrist position on the foreign policy spectrum, unfocused and potentially unstable as that position may have been, the United States had moved away from a significant measure of consensus in the 1950s toward a pronounced polarization in the 1980s. Among other reasons, such as the economic and political pressures that rent the bipartisan base of American foreign policy (see chapter 11), this trend was accelerated because many American policymakers clung to the belief that American diplomacy retained a large measure of flexibility. Americans perceived large foreign policy options; the Germans perceived none. The diplomatic antipodes of overextension and withdrawal, each deeply rooted in American history and each successful in attracting contemporary partisans, appeared (accurately or not) to many Americans as genuine choices. American attitudes on East-West détente remained wedded to the idea, encouraged by the rhetoric and diplomatic stance of the Reagan administration, that the United States could select from among Soviet policies that were either accommodating or bellicose, even as it should have become clear that domestic socioeconomic and political constraints placed severe limits on both superpowers' foreign policy options.[25]

The Germans, on the other hand, perceived no real foreign policy options and were continually required to hold in abeyance decisions that would have amounted to a genuine choice from among conflicting possibilities. Changing objective conditions in German-American relations, including shifts in the global and regional balances of power, conflicting security interests and diverging views on what constituted acceptable monetary practices, and differing perceptions of the nature of the Soviet threat and the political and strategic purposes of NATO, were aggravated by significantly different views of what range of foreign policy alternatives was available to Washington and Bonn. Although these differing views may have been justified on objective grounds—America after all remained a superpower, with a Pacific reach as well as an Atlantic reach—they further added to the dissatisfactions that characterized German-American relations in the 1980s.

With respect to security issues and arms control, or more broadly with respect to the nature and purpose of the East-West conflict, it became increasingly clear that there was no longer agreement over the nature and intensity of the Soviet threat. In part these differing assessments no doubt derived from the differing views provided by a global and by a regional geostrategic perspective. Washington saw itself challenged by Moscow everywhere and on everything; the Germans took a narrower and more limited view of the Soviet threat. Many Germans did not share the perception of many Americans that the United States was in all major respects different from the Soviet Union, and they tended to see Soviet foreign policy as opportunistic and historically determined rather than innately predatory and driven by the ideological aim of world conquest.

But there also were reasons for the differing views of the Soviet threat that could not be explained by global and regional perspectives alone and that stemmed from deeper domestic sources rooted in cultural and ideological predispositions, in differing institutional and bureaucratic memories, and ultimately in different historical experiences and geopolitical instincts.

Imperial Decline versus National Renewal

In addition to disagreements over arms control issues and the appropriate way of dealing with the Soviet Union, German-American relations increasingly suffered from a slow but steady erosion in the area of economics.

The decline of America's economic hegemony and the economic renewal of Germany (and the corresponding growth of the Germans' political self-confidence) could not help but raise as well larger questions about the changing nature of the German-American partnership, for it was in the area of economics and the social attitudes that attend it that German-American disputes had some of their deepest roots. It did not help matters psychologically or politically that Germany and Japan, perhaps in part as a result of having lost the Second World War, seemed to have surpassed the United States in their ability to respond to the challenges and opportunities that accompanied the interdependent monetary and trading systems of the postwar era. The shift toward the economic elements of power allowed the Federal Republic to translate its economic vitality into political leverage, and although the Germans periodically complained that they were called on to pay subsidies of one sort or another and to act as the paymaster of Europe, the relative shift from military elements of influence to economic ones benefited them. Generally speaking, the German political economy and the German political system adjusted smoothly to the inevitable complications and uncertainties attending the transformation of the international balance of power and its component elements, making for a sharp contrast with the dilatory and inadequate American response to these transformations. It was ultimately the disparity in economic performance (and in the underlying social forces) that pointed the two partners in different directions. Where America seemed to have failed, Germany seemed to have succeeded.

As was the case in all other industrialized countries, the Federal

Republic needed to balance the often conflicting desiderata and implementing policies of the "magic triangle": balance-of-payments equilibrium, domestic price stability, and optimal employment. But for external and internal reasons the Federal Republic managed to deal more successfully than most of its economic partners with macroeconomic issues and the perennial problem of external equilibrium versus internal equilibrium to which John Maynard Keynes had pointed so insistently since the 1920s.

This was never easy. Domestic price stability was constantly threatened by the forces of global interdependence and regional integration. From 1952 a persisting balance-of-payments surplus complicated domestic monetary management, and by the mid-fifties the concept of "imported" inflation dominated the policy discussions in Germany about how the domestic price level could best be shielded against external inflationary influences. Moreover, the currency convertibility achieved in the late 1950s undermined the bite of domestic credit and interest-rate policy, allowing lenders and borrowers to circumvent it internationally. With the divergent inflation rates of countries and the intervention obligations of Bretton Woods, this made the goal of domestic price stability very difficult to obtain, and the 1970s and 1980s brought new challenges in the form of oil price shocks, a new international monetary regime, the European Monetary System, the enlargement of the Community, and the continuing differences between German and American monetary policies and their underlying economic inclinations.

Nonetheless, the Germans succeeded with appropriate policies in containing the external pressures that threatened to disrupt their primary domestic economic and monetary objectives. By and large, they managed to shield their economic culture from outside encroachments, even as their own economic policies exploited as well as resisted the imperatives of global interdependence and regional integration. Although the European Community posed its own problems for the Federal Republic's macroeconomic management, it also presented an economic counterpoise to the global trading and monetary system and offered the Germans a politically more secure and economically more manageable form of regionalism. The Germans' pro-European proclivities were sustained by the powerful forces of economic self-interest. The dynamics of the global economy and the regional economy could be played off against one another, retaining for the Germans not a measure of economic autonomy (a misleading and atavistic term) but a measure of discretion in shaping their preferred domestic economic program. Penetrated by outside forces as their economy and society had been from the beginning, the Germans nonetheless managed to sustain their own economic culture.

This had a profound impact on Germany's domestic politics, solidifying the centrist orientation of German political culture from which political parties could deviate only at the peril of losing electoral support. It was ultimately the correspondence between their economic and political culture that allowed the Germans to deal with the challenges of modernity and its psychological and political dislocations in ways that proved politically and socioeconomically less disruptive than in most other industrial countries. The "neocorporatist" model of tripartite bargaining by the state, employers, and trade unions (introduced in the late 1960s in response to the first large-scale postwar recession), although not entirely successful, nonetheless ameliorated the conflictual politics of distribution that arose from a stagnant economy.[26] With some exceptions, Germany's labor-management relations were characterized by a mutuality of interests and shared responsibility, which contributed importantly to the maintenance of industrial peace.[27] Also, except in its early years and during the structural unemployment of the 1980s, West Germany found itself experiencing overemployment. But the inflationary consequences resulting from it were relatively moderate (in fact, were less than in other countries), for the economy was helped by a general cooperation between unions and management and by appropriately circumspect monetary policies.[28]

In all this, monetary stability played a crucial role. The Germans managed to avert as much as possible the enforced redistribution of income caused by inflation and the skewed economic and hazardous political consequences that attend it. In guiding their economic development on a path that assured continuing prosperity and safeguarded the principles they wished to have govern their economic life, the Germans also managed to distribute economic benefits in ways that resulted in incremental social change and political stability. Their extensive social security net and entitlement programs rested on historical tradition and commanded wide and unchallengeable political support; and the quality of their educational system and its diminishing class bias encouraged a gradual process of socialization.

Equally important, in turning to an economic life dominated by exports, the Germans also fashioned a historic reversal of their traditionally inner-directed economic impulses, providing yet another sharp contrast with America's inability to project outward its economic energies. The real German economic miracle "is that none of the politicians or economists of that time, neither on the German nor the allied side, foresaw that the partial state regenerated in West Germany was condemned to the burden of export. . . . Germany could only handle the double problem of substitution for lost domestic markets and the absorption of the newly added population to normal employment if it established itself in the expanding world market. This meant a complete break with the history and development of the old Reich and the Weimar Republic, both of which had drawn their economic growth impulses from the domestic, not the foreign market."[29] The Germans' need and determination to have their exports remain competitive in international markets had a large impact on their domestic economic, labor, and social policies, and served as yet another link between their domestic and foreign policies. Externally, economic prowess energized German foreign policy; internally, prosperity acted as a political sedative.[30] In no small measure, it was this sense of inner equity and renewal that eased the Germans' painful process of accepting the severe limitations placed from the outside on the Federal Republic's foreign policies.

Because of all these interlocking developments, which span four decades and reach into every aspect of the Germans' public and private lives, the nature of the problems affecting German-American relations is not clearly illuminated by the much-touted concept of the so-called successor generation, which basically rests on the premise that the location of the transatlantic political fault line is a function of shifts of age.[31] This confuses cause and effect, and obscures the deeper and larger reasons why Germany and America are drifting apart. It is true that Germans under the age of forty have no personal recollections of American diplomacy in the postwar period and of the remarkable rapport that developed between American and German policymakers in the late 1940s and throughout the 1950s. The generation of Germans that reached political awareness in the past three decades is informed by a significantly different image of the United States. Vietnam, Watergate and the Iran-contra affair, American sponsorship of oligarchic regimes, and a variety of other questionable attitudes and practices have raised general concern about the nature of American politics and created a much less benevolent image of the United States than the one projected in earlier decades.[32]

But changing German perceptions of the United States were not primarily the result of subjective change in successive generations (if this were the case, transatlantic problems would go away if only one could arrest the process of aging) but rather of objective conditions.[33] Beyond the question of image, appearance, and the inevitable value changes that are associated with "generation gaps," there came about a new reality. As the international balance of power began to shift significantly in the 1970s and 1980s, it became apparent that across a wide array of economic, monetary, military-strategic, and political issues German and American interests simply were no longer as congruent as they had been in earlier decades, and that American diplomacy found it increasingly difficult to cope with the decline of American power and resorted to policies that presented to the world the darker side of America. The cleft that began to divide America and Germany stemmed not from the discontinuities of successive political generations. Its deepest and ultimately irremediable cause lay in the differences of the two countries' societies and the public and private values that are embedded in them. While the partnership between Americans and Germans rested on the common ground of devotion to a democratic political order, their dissimilar socioeconomic conventions inevitably inclined them toward divergent political values, in domestic policy as well as in foreign policy.

German reservations about the transatlantic compact, which transcended the boundaries of age and political persuasion, were shared in Western Europe generally. Over the decades many Europeans became apprehensive about what they considered America's mismanagement of domestic and foreign affairs, increasingly concerned over what they viewed as the erratic and unpredictable shifts in American diplomacy. With their own increasing self-assurance they developed a more guarded view of their transatlantic partner.[34] A deeply rooted cultural European arrogance toward the United States, dormant in the postwar years when Europe survived through American largesse, reemerged and led to a somewhat disdainful European attitude toward what it perceived as America's economic, political, and cultural inferiority.[35]

The Europeans' unease was reciprocated on the American side by an equally deep sense of frustration and disappointment, fueled by a growing resentment of European and especially German policies that went beyond and ran deeper than the normal disagreements of a working alliance. Americans resented the growing burden of military expenditures and believed them to be shared inequitably with the alliance; they tired of European reservations about the wisdom and direction of American diplomacy and believed that their own exertions for a common cause were insufficiently appreciated on the other side of the Atlantic. American and West European disappointments fed on one another, accelerating in an interplay of frustrations and leading to a more guarded relationship.

Americans found it difficult to understand that the Europeans' reservations about the United States did not for that reason move them closer to Moscow or make them unreliable alliance partners, "neutralist" or "anti-American." The changing European perception of the United States, although increasingly critical of American diplomacy and the domestic pressures that direct it, did not necessarily imply a compensatory European or German sympathy for the Soviet Union, although this became more likely with the skillful diplomacy of Mikhail S. Gorbachev.[36] American allies expect more of the United States than from the Soviet Union and, after all, Americans expect them to expect more.[37] The pejorative metaphor of "equidistance," with its connotation that the Europeans' apprehensions about American diplomacy placed them at one corner of an equilateral political and moral triangle, can be supported only if one holds a zero-sum view of the East-West political contest, where one's loss is the other's immediate and inevitable gain.[38] But it did mean that the Europeans' confidence in American leadership needed to be continually earned in the day-to-day conduct of American diplomacy. It needed to be earned as well in the conduct of American domestic policy, for many Europeans increasingly connected their view of Washington's foreign policy with their assessment of the political process in the United States. Their long-run expectations about the political reliability and circumspection of their transatlantic partner evolved as much from their perception of America's future domestic political order as from their perception of current American diplomacy. And here a certain European equidistance in the East-West contest did emerge: the conviction took root in Europe that the disabilities of either superpower, although fundamentally different, were both detrimental to European interests, and that neither America or Soviet Russia could be entrusted with the fate of Europe.

There is a broad and deep reservoir of goodwill toward the United States in the Federal Republic that stretches across the incremental and porous boundaries of age, socioeconomic status, and political awareness.[39] But the translation of that goodwill into the practical policies that ultimately determine the nature of German-American relations does not proceed automatically. It requires circumspection and nurture on both sides of the Atlantic, especially on issues that are centrally important for either party. It would also require a larger understanding of the concurrent tides of imperial decline and national renewal that have carried America and Germany into a new state system, burdening their relations politically, economically, and psychologically, and complicating the task of transforming their partnership so that it can meet present and future challenges.

Epilogue

Deutschland, ein unendlicher Prolog . . .

—CARL ZUCKMAYER

The military-strategic, political, and economic developments of the last decades, although important in their own right, were only the surface manifestations of deeper historical trends in the postwar era. For underneath the technical disputes about military strategy and economics, and underlying the conflicts that corroded the transatlantic compact and slowed the progress of West European integration, there was a powerful current of socioeconomic, political, and psychological forces, which exerted a steady pull on the governments of Western Europe and the United States. These forces were the combined result of the changing nature of the state and the new ways in which states interact in the modern state system. They go to the roots of the perennial preoccupations of the state: welfare and security.[1]

At the risk of oversimplifying an immensely complex and at times contradictory development, one may suggest that two distinct forces act on modern governments, and through them on contemporary international politics: one enhances governmental power, another curtails it. Powerful historical forces in the postwar era have modified the role of the modern state, broadening its capacity to shape events in some respects, narrowing it in others.

On the one hand, the welfare demands of its citizens have pushed the modern state toward a peak of power and activity unprecedented in its tortuous history. Whatever a country's political institutions, economic arrangements, and ideological preferences may be, remedies for the

373

economic and social problems of the individual are sought in public policy and collective action. This has changed the meaning of national welfare and the ways it is advanced. Above all, it has required a growing political sensitivity to the revolution of rising expectations or, as Daniel Bell has called it in a sharper term, the "revolution of rising entitlement."[2] Modern governments have become increasingly responsive to the welfare demands of their electorates and feel obliged to undertake the responsibility for meeting them. The improvement of the material well-being of its citizens through state intervention has become a central purpose of state activity. Satisfying the rising claims of its citizens has become a major source of the state's legitimacy and of a government's continuance in office. In varying degrees, politics rather than the market has become in many countries the primary arena for the redistribution of income, status, and other public satisfactions. Politics extends everywhere into wider areas, touching on aspects of public and private life that in the past escaped governmental scrutiny as well as solicitude. The modern state has become pervasive in its activities, assertive of its prerogatives and responsibilities, and powerful in what it can give, take, or withhold.

On the other hand, although the power of the state is increasingly obtrusive and dominant in its domestic context, it has become compromised in new ways in its international context. In the first place, the requirements of national welfare can be met only by wide-ranging commercial, monetary, and technological interactions on the international level, which demand economic coordination and political accommodation. To meet their responsibilities for mass social and economic welfare, modern governments are compelled to deal with one another in ways that, although not lacking in conflict and competition, nonetheless demand cooperation and a willingness to condone restraints on state behavior and sovereign prerogatives. The interdependence of modern economics and the realization that welfare can no longer be achieved or even circumscribed in national terms have eroded the privileged political position and institutional autonomy of the nation-state. Internal state power is sustained by external cooperation.

Second, the interdependence of welfare is powerfully augmented in the modern state system by the interdependence of security. The dangers of the nuclear age and its multiple balances of terror have irreversibly penetrated the former impermeability of the traditional nation-state, the territorial foundations of its claims to sovereignty and to the allegiance of its citizens, and the classical diplomacy with which it sought to manipulate its external space.[3] Even though nationalism has retained its emotive force, the interdependence of security and welfare in the postwar era has eaten away at the territoriality of states and at the attitudes, aspirations, and policies that have traditionally been attached to it. In Europe especially, there developed a heightened consciousness that international security was indivisible, that there were in the industrialized world no conceivable political stakes that would warrant recourse to arms, and that the interdependence among nations stemmed not only from enlightened economic self-interest but also from their shared vulnerability and collective insecurity.

This trend was reinforced as the traditional security concerns of preserving territorial integrity against outside intrusions began to diminsh relative to economic issues. Although security issues are a matter of national survival in the nuclear age and in that sense unsurpassed in importance, a shift of emphasis became noticeable in the postwar decades, away from the unrelieved and threatening immediacy of military-strategic issues and toward a primacy of economic issues. As a consequence, such measures of power as military capacity were becoming less immediately applicable in the industrialized part of the world. Given appropriate circumstances, economic power turned out to be a much more supple, subtle instrument of diplomacy than military power. This is not to say that military power became unimportant, or that it did not translate into political leverage. But the relative weight of the traditional central concerns of the state, security and welfare, began to shift, or, as reflected in the term "economic security," began to merge. Many governments and their citizens, especially in Western Europe, came to see their interests protected as much through the political and economic balance of power as through the military balance of power, and there was a growing aversion to the militarization of East-West diplomacy and the mode of thinking associated with it.[4]

The emerging state system in Europe and the world at large is a peculiar amalgam of the past and present, moving toward an uncertain future. It is multidimensional, contradictory, and in transition. It is infused with the forces of economic and technological modernity and the social values that attend them, but also beset by historical memories, aspirations, and attitudes that are obsolescent and yet resilient, bending to atavistic inclinations.

The three major strata of the modern state system—the territorial-geopolitical, the nuclear-strategic, and the economic-interdependent—reflect an uneasy mix of conflicting and complementary elements, making for a strained dialectic of tradition and innovation. Although deeply shaped by the inescapable realities of nuclear arms and modern economics, which transcend national boundaries and seem impervious to the territorial imperative, there are still territorial compulsions and stubbornly nationalist ways of dealing with international conflict and cooperation. Even as they contend with the politics of postindustrial societies, the economics of internationalism, and the fear of nuclear annihilation, these remnants of the past culminate in policies that remain territorially based and nationally directed and that cling to an exaggerated reliance on military power and a misplaced confidence in the military balance.

There persists furthermore an inescapable territoriality of a wider and deeper significance. Although technology has shrunk the world, geostrategic location remains a powerful force in contemporary international politics. In large measure, a country's national interests and diplomatic inclinations are still determined by how it is situated in its political space. West Germany and Western Europe are tied to the postwar Euro-American state system, which although bound together by security needs, trade, money, and values is nonetheless disconnected by the Atlantic and counterpoised by the Pacific. This allows the distant alliance superpower to redirect its interests and energies toward its Western shore, or to respond to the world with its traditional and cherished choice of withdrawal and abstention. East Germany and Eastern Europe, on the other hand, remain linked to the Eurasian superpower, which has historical tides of involvement in Europe that are deep and steady, being less a matter of choice than of immutable geostrategic proximity.[5]

All these factors and many more created new restraints and opportunities for the conduct of foreign policy. Many military and economic issues contested between East and West and within the West were essentially political issues couched in technical terms. Negotiations over such technical questions as arms control, trade agreements, monetary reform, and technology transfers were not only attempts at problem solving, but also reexaminations of the sources and purpose of power in the last third of the century. The constellations of power and influence on the three major strata of world politics were being rearranged at the same time as the relative importance of the three levels themselves was shifting. A new definition of power was under way.

By and large, the emerging modern state system enhanced the security position, economic vitality, political stability, and diplomatic leverage of the Federal Republic. The Germans met the challenges of the modern social welfare state more successfully than many other industrialized countries; they struck a judicious balance between their security requirements and welfare requirements and financed them with prudent fiscal and budgetary policies; and in the course of four decades they became habituated to the "openness" of their society, economy, and polity to the security intrusions of the nuclear age and the welfare intrusions of the modern economic age. They had stripped as much as possible the territorial connotations from their Eastern policies, and the shift of emphasis from the military-strategic elements of power to economic elements tilted the global and regional balance of power in a direction favorable to them. They came to terms with the various interdependencies of the modern state system.

Moreover, the general historical trend toward growing openness and vulnerability in modern societies and economies produced a certain leveling effect, from which the Germans profited in relative terms. Perhaps more than their membership in international institutions, it was their success in adjusting to the conditions of the modern state system that gave the Germans the measure of equality and integration that they had sought so insistently in the transatlantic and West European alliances. In the European Community, where the Germans obtained an ample share of equality, there was inadequate integration; in NATO, which checked the Germans through deep integration (embodied in America's dominance of German security policies), there was not enough equality. For the Germans, their postwar diplomatic precepts of equality and integration, the basis of their attachment to the West, became skewed and disconnected, the first being satisfied in an institutional context lacking sufficient integration, the second embodied in an institutional context lacking sufficient equality.

By the late 1980s the accumulated weight of German power, unguided by any clear sense of direction, was pressing against transatlantic and West European institutions that were themselves in flux and that may yet prove inadequate to guiding the European political order toward the new century. The combined inadequacy of the transatlantic and West European political compacts—one eroding, the other stagnant, drifting apart in what Claude Cheysson has called "progressive divorce"—raised the danger that the Federal Republic would embark on a European policy insufficiently enveloped and sustained by its traditional institutional contexts. As the historic postwar constraints on German foreign policy changed, whether and how these institutions could continue to provide a supportive and mutually acceptable framework for the energies of German diplomacy came into question. Neither NATO nor the Community seemed to keep pace with the political, strategic, and economic transformations of the 1980s, each continuing to rely on the other to serve the increasingly outmoded function of containing the Federal Republic while containing the Soviet Union.[6]

Measured against German aspirations of the 1950s, the fading of the transatlantic and European compacts and the thwarting of Bonn's reunification efforts would have to be considered major foreign policy failures. But it was precisely the absence of Atlantic unity, European unity, and German unity that increased the political leverage of the Federal Republic, making it the object of the West's economic expectations and political anxieties and the East's inducements and pressures. In the 1980s the question arose of how to apply this leverage, and toward what purpose, at a time when German foreign policy goals were becoming less dramatic than in the past and the familiar guidelines of German foreign policy more ambiguous—even as Bonn's security interests remained tied to America and its diplomatic room for maneuver remained delimited by the general climate of East-West relations and the continuing dualism of the European state system.

The emerging European state system poses a special challenge to the United States and the resiliency of the historic transatlantic compact, for what is at stake is America's historic postwar European policy of double containment. If the United States hopes to keep in step with the evolution of the European order and influence it constructively and farsightedly, there must come about a redefinition of double containment with respect both to its Soviet dimension and to its German dimension. American diplomacy cannot succeed in Europe if it cannot restore a viable balance and indeed a new complementarity between America's Soviet policy and its Germany policy. If America were to fail in reshaping the twin precepts that guided its postwar European policies, it should not expect to retain its diplomatic leverage in Europe. This is the most insistent lesson of the past, and it applies with renewed force and urgency to the present and future. Unless the United States manages to deal with the growing contradictions of double containment and avoids the dual perils of confrontational diplomacy and unilateralism, it will be difficult to persuade allies in Europe (and for that matter opponents in the Kremlin) that American diplomacy reflects a mature consideration of common and conflicting interests.

This requires in the first instance a rethinking of American policy toward the Soviet Union. Even before Mikhail S. Gorbachev came to power there was a compelling need for the United States to pursue a policy of détente with the Soviet Union, not unconditionally but energetically, and based on a realistic calibration of Soviet and American strengths and weaknesses and an equally sober assessment of long-range American and Soviet geostrategic interests.[7] The task, made more urgent by Gorbachev's accession, demands above all a redefinition in Washington of its discord with the Soviet Union, which would recognize the diminished diplomatic utility and political relevance of nuclear arms, stem the erosion of American economic power, and address the East-West conflict at its political and geostrategic sources.[8] The United States must regain the sense that the origins of the Cold War lay not in the physical threat to territorially or otherwise narrowly defined American security interests but in the political challenge to broadly interpreted American geostrategic interests, which included the creation of spheres of influence and the making and keeping of allies. What is at stake in the East-West dispute cannot be won in a bilateral zero-sum contest with the opponent; it is won among America's partners, whose continued confidence in American diplomacy is itself the stake.

Redefining the East-West contest with those terms in mind would if anything point to Soviet weaknesses rather than Soviet strengths, and accrue in the long run to the West's advantage. In might help avert the growing danger that American allies perceive Soviet-American tensions more and more as a dualistic, imperial contest over power, from which their own interests would tempt them to withdraw, rather than a vigorous competition over socioeconomic values, political purpose, and the direction of a new state system, in which they would be determined contenders.[9] A revitalized American policy of détente would reflect at its core a more measured policy of containment, in effect the continuation of containment by other means, and take into account that the major threat to American interests lies not in an imbalance of power between America and its opponents but in an imbalance between American power and American commitments.

In the second instance, a rethinking is required of the traditional complementary component of America's Soviet containment policy, the containment of the Federal Republic. This demands above all that Washington treat the Federal Republic as a full-fledged partner and elevate the German-American relationship to the full measure of maturity that it deserves. It is time to shed attitudes that regard the Federal Republic as a junior partner whose own central security interests can be slighted almost at will (as the double-zero arms control controversy demonstrated in the late 1980s) at the same time as Washington expects Bonn to help ease the consequences of America's mismanaged economy and irresponsible fiscal and budgetary policies. There must come about a thorough revision of Washington's postwar policy of containing the Federal Republic that corresponds more closely to the new realities of the German-American relationship and is stripped of any connotations of American tutelage. This would ease the singularity of the Federal Republic in the Western alliance and the German frustrations resulting from it, and would therefore address the roots of what ails relations between Bonn and Washington.

In essence, there needs to come about a relaxation of tensions between the United States and the Federal Republic, a "détente" between partners. Both with respect to the Soviet Union and with respect to Germany, the United States must undertake to transform America's postwar policy of double containment and turn it into a policy of double détente. It is true that "the overriding reality is that Western Europe—and, most importantly, West Germany—is as committed to the détente that has grown up since the late 1960s as it is to the alliance,"[10] but it is precisely this state of affairs that makes it imperative for American diplomacy to show a more circumspect and conciliatory disposition, refrain from habitually opposing a pan-European security framework and intensified East-West trade, and arrive at a new meshing of its Soviet policies and Germany policies. The United States should support and help guide the creation of an all-European security compact, which could first augment and later supplant the postwar Cold War alliances, transforming and thereby fulfilling their historic task of providing a stable and mutually acceptable framework for the energies and legitimate interests of the two German states.[11]

In the third instance, Washington needs to rethink the historic connection between political containment and strategic deterrence with a view toward creating a new complementarity between double détente (if it can be effected) and deterrence and reassurance. Transforming America's double-containment policy into a double-détente policy also demands a reconfiguration of the multiple dimensions that have always connected containment and deterrence in America's European policies. Political purpose must again be implemented with a supportive transatlantic American security policy. Here the United States would have to come to terms with a troublesome but not insoluble paradox: on the one hand, nuclear weapons are ill-suited for managing the alliance, especially when nuclear issues become divisive, and they are much too terrifying to be a symbol of the alliance's cohesion; on the other, the nuclear bond between the United States and the Federal Republic remains important for both sides. German governments continue to place a high value on the nuclear presence of the United States in Europe, and although they want the nuclear balance in Europe checked with arms control agreements they do not want to see it abolished. The Soviet Union is close, America is distant, and any arms control agreements that underline this fundamental geostrategic asymmetry are bound to have negative political repercussions.

On their part, the United States and Western Europe continue to regard Germany's acceptance of American nuclear weapons as the "corset" that ties the Federal Republic to the West. If Washington could divest itself of the nuclearization of its foreign policy (which it should in any event because of its debilitating effects and diminishing utility in the East-West contest), it could restore a measure of reassurance and enhance for the Germans the acceptability and desirability of the American nuclear presence in Europe. Germans have always judged America's reliability more in terms of its diplomacy than in terms of its military prowess, and a sensitive American security policy could go a long way toward attenuating the security problems that have beset German-American relations. For Washington, the proper order of priority should be not deterrence and reassurance but rather reassurance and deterrence. Only in this way can there come about a mutually tolerable reconnection of political and strategic purpose, a complementary meshing of America's European policies, and a new congruence of reassurance and deterrence with double détente.

This is especially true for American arms control policies, which have always signified the close connection between politics and strategy. Unless the United States transforms its arms control policies with a view toward meeting basic German interests, there is the danger that the Soviet Union may profit doubly from the exigencies of the postwar nuclear age: first, in reaping diplomatic advantage from having gained nuclear parity with the United States, and second, in reaping diplomatic advantage from the scaling down of nuclear weapons. The task facing American diplomacy is to make certain that the build-down of nuclear arms (and not only the build-up) can be turned to the diplomatic advantage of the West, and that the disposition of weapons strengthens rather than weakens the alliance.

NATO, which has long suffered from the disjuncture of politics and strategy, must reconnect them and develop a political and strategic posture sensitive to the changing political circumstances in Europe and adequate to meeting the challenges of the coming decade. So much of Western diplomacy has been predicated in the past on the size of the Soviet military establishment and on Soviet diplomatic intransigence that it threatens to succumb to Soviet diplomatic dexterity during the Gorbachev years. But it would be difficult for the Soviet Union to displace America from Europe, unless the United States displaced itself through inept diplomacy. Should there come about a new phase of détente, the United States would remain an indispensable partner for Europe: in arranging for the reduction of nuclear and conventional arms, in avoiding the militarization of space, in seeking long-range resolution of regional conflicts, in erecting a common "European house."

Finally, what is required of the United States is a fundamental rethinking of the uses to which economic diplomacy can and cannot be put in furthering American strategic interests.[12] The need to arrive at a reconfiguration and new meshing of the postwar American strategies of double containment and of deterrence and reassurance applies with equal cogency to the diplomatic application of American economic power. The growing imbalance between American power and American commitments, which stems in large part from the relative weakening of America's postwar economic hegemony and the privileges that were attached to it, calls for a full, painful recognition of the deleterious consequences of having stripped American foreign policy of a sound economic and monetary base. For many years after the Second World War, economic power was for the United States an indispensable augmentation of the political concept of containment and the strategic concept of deterrence. The reformulation of America's political and strategic policies requires a concurrent reformulation of America's economic and monetary policies, which would reestablish a sound economic base at home and create a pluralistic economic order abroad going beyond the intermittent bilateral "special relationships" that the United States preferred after the war—

first with Britain, then with the Federal Republic, later with Japan.[13] For it is ultimately the triple disjuncture of containment, deterrence, and economic diplomacy that has undermined the foundations of the American empire at home and abroad and that demands with critical urgency a reorientation of how the United States can deal effectively with the challenges of the 1990s and beyond.

From the European perspective, the basis for revitalizing American power and purpose must be laid at home. What is required in the United States and would obtain wholehearted endorsement in much of Europe is a disconnection of views on each side of the political aisle: on the conservative side, a commendable appreciation of the limits of government intervention in the American economy has been coupled with an overreliance on the utility of military power; on the liberal side, an appreciation of the limits of military power has been coupled with an overly relaxed view of economic and monetary responsibilities. A reconfiguration of America's political culture is needed, in which an enlightened, responsible economic conservatism is decoupled from an infatuation with arms and joined with a stance on military-strategic matters that realizes their marginality for American diplomacy. Without such a reconfiguration, Europeans may reassess the long-term costs and benefits of their partnership with the United States and begin to question the value of its continuance.

For the West European neighbors of Germany and especially France it is not sufficient to indulge in the reiteration of historic suspicions, understandable as they may be. These suspicions must be converted into more constructive attitudes and imaginative policies, which go beyond the symbols of joint military brigades, maneuvers, councils, and declarations of amity. Joint policies are also required, with a view toward reviving the idea of a West European defense community, sustained by sufficient conventional forces to obtain their own convincing deterrent effect, backed by a Franco-German nuclear condominium, and cemented by joint commitments that render indivisible the defense of Western Europe. In the long run, it will not suffice for France to keep supporting an American nuclear presence in Europe (always with the proviso that it be in the Federal Republic and not in France), to express concern about the Germans' more qualified support of NATO's nuclear presence and their purported neutralist tendencies while at the same time pointing to the satisfying lack of domestic opposition to French nuclear policies, and to leave the Germans in the dark about French defense concepts, trying to assuage them with hesitant and ambivalent declarations about the mutuality of security concerns.[14]

France will need to decide what it fears more: the full incorporation of the Federal Republic in a revitalized, militarily and economically inte-

grated Western Europe, with the attendant risk that Germany may dominate it and with the burdensome commitment that would follow if France
extended its nuclear deterrence to Germany; or the prospect that the
Federal Republic will be tempted, *faute de mieux*, to make independent
security arrangements, either by reaching for nuclear capabilities of its
own (even the unthinkable must be thought) or through a more accommodating posture toward the East.[15] Like the United States, France will
need to rethink its own postwar policy of double containment and convert it to a policy of double détente, with a view toward narrowing the
wary distance that has separated Franco-German attitudes and policies,
protestations to the contrary notwithstanding. Britain and the smaller
West European powers should engage in some rethinking as well, especially when they claim to see in a closer Franco-German security accord a
threat of a joint Franco-German hegemony in Western Europe.[16]

In other words, what is called for within the Western alliance is the
conversion of multiple sets of containment policies, American as well as
West European,[17] into equally complicated but ultimately more promising sets of détente policies sustained by plausible security arrangements
and a supportive economic base. One may well ask whether these transformations of attitudes and policies can obtain the necessary diplomatic
energy and domestic political support in Washington and West European
capitals that their implementation would demand.[18] It would require a
high level of leadership on both sides of the Atlantic to balance the
conflicting impulses of Europe and America and to fashion a concerted
statecraft sensitive to the complexities and ambiguities that result from
them.

The world of the 1980s is more complex than that of the 1950s. The
American architects of the postwar transatlantic compact exhibited an
almost patrician sense of the geometry of power, measured and self-
assured, confident of American power and purpose, and yet watchful of
opponents who might challenge them. Their West European counterparts were equally circumspect and forward-looking, their own clarity of
purpose sharpened by their weakness and lack of alternatives. In the
1980s and 1990s these postwar roles and the intellectual preparations and
diplomatic exertions they demand are reversed. American statesmen will
need to craft policies that move within the constraints of the relative
decline of American power; European statesmen will need to fashion
policies that deal responsibly with the increment of European power. The
contest over the future shape of the European political order will be won
by those who have a clearer view than others of the present and future
dynamics of European and global politics and who can translate this
recognition into effective policies sustainable at home as well as abroad.

But there was little evidence in the late 1980s that Western Europe
could rise to the occasion. The Community appeared to have abdicated

leadership along with having abandoned the hopes for political union that accompanied its origins, and its institutions, inadequate as agents of change and yet powerfully entrenched, seemed ill suited as instruments for the political renewal of Europe. Uncertain whether they could implement their announced goal of creating a genuine single market by the end of 1992, the nations of Western Europe were characterized by a peculiar mix of attributes: both fecund and sclerotic, modern and atavistic, they were unable to decide which economic, social, and security policies to adjust and coordinate to concentrate their political and economic energies in a common cause, and which policies they wanted to pursue independently so as to retain their cherished cultural diversity and historic autonomy. There is in the making a semi-Gaullist Europe, replete with the psychological attitudes and historical aspirations that urge a separate European path between the two nuclear superpowers, but devoid of a plausible political vision that could chart it and lacking still a unified economic base that could sustain it.[19]

The European Community has a larger population than the Soviet Union, a gross national product more than twice that of the Soviet Union, and a superior technological and industrial base. In view of this superiority the West Europeans must ask whether they truly regard themselves as so lacking in common purpose and strength that they cannot establish on their own a sufficiently credible joint deterrent, nuclear and conventional, to safeguard their fundamental security interests, augmenting if not replacing an increasingly shaky American commitment to their defense. This question is the more insistent if Europeans really believe that America would rather avenge than protect them and that Washington's grand strategy values them primarily as a forward bastion of American security interests that can be traded away in a conflict to purchase American time with European space. If the West Europeans cannot arrive at a self-assuring answer to this question, then they should indeed continue to accept the American diplomatic tutelage they resent and the American nuclear protection they distrust. In that case they should do so not grudgingly and with endless complaints but willingly and openly, as do those who recognize and accept their lack of resolve and are ready to pay the price in loss of power, purpose, and prestige.

For their part, the Germans require a supportive transatlantic and West European context for their exertions. They should not be induced to embark on a European policy of their own, however indirectly or inadvertently. Nor is there any real indication that they wish to do so. They remain committed to their diplomatic precepts of integration and equality, which have guided their Western policies since the beginning of the Federal Republic, but they also believe that a more substantial meaning would have to be instilled in them, an acknowledgment in real political terms of the prominent status they have earned in the alliance.[20] There would be no surer and more damaging way to revive a feeling of "exceptionalism" among the Germans than to lead them to surmise that their special status in the alliance is a perpetual and irreducible condition of membership. They have always been highly sensitive to their singularity within the alliance in political as well as military-strategic matters, and it would not be inappropriate to say that a Sonderweg was imposed on them within the alliance from the beginning. The singularity of their historic position in Europe is burdensome enough without being compounded by their continuing singularity in the alliance.

To be sure, these two reasons for Germany's singularity are historically and politically related and cannot be separated by diplomatic fiat. But they can be ameliorated by a Western diplomacy that recognizes changing conditions in Europe and is sensitive to changing political conditions in the Federal Republic.[21] Whatever the Germans' "special path" through the new European order may turn out to be, it is a road that proceeds through a political landscape drastically different from those of the past. The world has changed, Europe has changed, and the Germans have changed. If the frustrations engendered by the Germans' Sonderweg in the alliance are to be prevented from spilling over into the more worrisome connotations evoked by their historic Sonderweg in Europe, Western diplomacy must aim for a new European concert that reaffirms, reinvigorates, but also transcends the traditional West European and transatlantic institutions that initially bound the Federal Republic to the West. The two Germanies still appear solidly divided, and Europe still suffers from what George F. Kennan called its "great cramp": its frozen position astride the rim of the two empires. But it is precisely the prospect that this cramp may relax and in the process reopen the German question that has become a troubling issue for the United States, the Federal Republic's neighbors, and ultimately the Germans themselves.

There needs to come about a European state system that does not force the Germans to avoid or postpone all major choices from among a constructive Ostpolitik, European integration, and a continued German-American security connection. In the past the Germans have had so little political leeway and diplomatic maneuverability in choosing among conflicting foreign policies that an exercise in political imagination appeared futile, irresponsible, or both. It would be beneficial for the emerging European order if this could change. For what is ultimately at risk for the West is the Germans' own sense of self-containment, their heritage of the Adenauer years, which over the decades has laid such solid foundations for the Germans' attachment to the West and their rejection of neutralist alternatives. In turn, the Germans themselves must resist the temptation to affirm their political identity through reflexive opposition or unques-

tioning allegiance to American policies. But Americans must realize that
the Federal Republic has become a regional superpower and that even an
ally cannot determine the interests of its partner on the partner's behalf.

For the Germans, self-containment would not have to mean permanent self-abnegation, were it sustained by an alliance that revitalized the
principles of equality and integration. With the necessary changes in the
Western powers' policy of double containment, the Germans' sense of
self-containment should undergo a change of meaning as well. The
Germans should accept the exceptional responsibilities that their special
historical lineage and geographical location have imposed on them, not
with the incandescence of ideology or the freezing arrogance of power,
but with the moderating skepticism of the intellect and in the warming
light of reason and self-interest. These responsibilities cannot lie in the
abdication of Germany's power—too much of it has already been accrued
to be ignored—but neither can they lie in the abdication of purpose, for
too much is at stake for America, for Europe, and for Germany.

Notes

Epigraph. Horace, *Satires, Epistles and Ars Poetica*, with an English trans. by H. Rushton Fairclough (London: William Heinemann, 1926), pp. 324–325.

1. For an example of such a collective effort see the monumental six-volume history of the Federal Republic by Karl Dietrich Bracher et al., eds., *Geschichte der Bundesrepublik Deutschland* (Stuttgart and Mannheim: Deutsche Verlags-Anstalt and F. A. Brockhaus, 1981–87). The individual volumes are: Theodor Eschenburg, *Jahre der Besatzung, 1945–1949*; Hans-Peter Schwarz, *Die Ära Adenauer, 1949–1957*; Schwarz, *Die Ära Adenauer, 1957–1963*; Klaus Hildebrand, *Von Erhard zur Grossen Koalition, 1963–1969*; Karl Dietrich Bracher, Wolfgang Jäger, and Werner Link, *Republik im Wandel, 1969–1974. Die Ära Brandt*; and Wolfgang Jäger and Werner Link, *Republik im Wandel, 1974–1982. Die Ära Schmidt.*

2. Even the question of whether the Federal Republic should be accorded its own historiographic identity is charged with political meaning. In their brief but reflective introduction to the *Geschichte der Bundesrepublik Deutschland*, the editor-historians write: "No matter how firmly it resisted, the Federal Republic has obtained a history, which should be told. The older [Germans], who have lived it, as well as the younger ones who have inherited it, should learn how the historical ground on which they stand is constituted. . . . The history of a state does not begin only when it perceives itself as such. It begins with the founding of the state, no matter how reluctantly that was effected." Even so the editors note, with a tone of caution if not apology, that the writing of such a history should not in itself be construed as deepening the division of Germany. They explain as follows their historiographic procedure, above all its gradually narrowing focus on the Federal Republic itself rather than on both German states: "This is not a political decision. The historian's task is not to determine whether a divided country should be rejoined but to describe and explain what was. And it is a fact that the Federal Republic went its own way." Foreword of the editors in Eschenburg, *Jahre der Besatzung*, pp. 7–8.

On the obligation of contemporary German historiography to be relevant to

public discourse see Joachim C. Fest, "Noch einmal: Abschied von der Geschich-
te: Polemische Überlegungen zur Entfremdung von Geschichtswissenschaft und
Öffentlichkeit," in *Aufgehobene Vergangenheit. Porträts und Betrachtungen* (Stuttgart:
Deutsche Verlags-Anstalt, 1981), pp. 239–261; Thomas Nipperdey, *Nachdenken
über die deutsche Geschichte. Essays* (Munich: C. H. Beck, 1986); Hermann Graml
and Klaus-Dietmar Henke, eds., *Nach Hitler. Der schwierige Umgang mit unserer
Geschichte. Beiträge von Martin Broszat* (Munich: R. Oldenbourg, 1987); Werner
Weidenfeld, ed., *Geschichtsbewusstsein der Deutschen. Materalien zur Spurensuche
einer Nation* (Cologne: Verlag Wissenschaft und Politik, 1987).

The treatment of Germany's division in East German historiography is
sketched in Wolfgang Seiffert, "Das Konzept der 'sozialistischen Nation' als
Faktor der innerdeutschen Politik," in Klaus Lange, ed., *Aspekte der deutschen
Frage* (Herford: Busse-Seewald, 1986), pp. 289–305. See also Andreas Dorpalen,
German History in Marxist Perspective: The East German Approach (London: I. B.
Tauris, 1986).

In describing the relations between the two German states, I have used the
terms "inter-German" and "intra-German" and not "inner-German," which remains the preferred term of the West German government. Also, I have followed
the established American practice of referring to the Federal Republic as West
Germany and the German Democratic Republic as East Germany, which is
frowned on by Germans who believe they must sustain their claim on the
territories lost to Poland by reserving for them the term *Ostdeutschland*. German
sensitivities on this issue remain raw. For example, in reviewing Ann L. Phillips,
Soviet Policy toward East Germany Reconsidered: The Postwar Decade (New York and
Westport, Conn.: Greenwood, 1986), Wolfgang Pfeiler felt obliged to chide Phillips for using the term "East Germany" in the title of her book! See *German Studies
Review* 10, no. 3 (October 1987): 622–623.

On the political and linguistic issues attached to the term *Germany* see Karl
Römer, "Was ist Deutschland?" *Deutschland Archiv* 8, no. 8 (1975): 856–866; Helmut Berschin, *"Deutschland"—ein Name im Wandel. Die deutsche Frage im Spiegel der
Sprache* (Munich and Vienna: Olzog, 1979); Berschin, "Wie heisst das Land der
Deutschen? Zur sprachpolitischen Bewertung des Namens 'Deutschland' und
der Namen der beiden deutschen Staaten," *Deutschland Archiv* 13, no. 1 (1980):
61–77; Wolfgang Bergsdorf, *Herrschaft und Sprache. Studie zur politischen Terminologie der Bundesrepublik Deutschland* (Pfullingen: Neske, 1983).

3. See for example Wolfram F. Hanrieder, "Compatibility and Consensus: A
Proposal for the Conceptual Linkage of External and Internal Dimensions of
Foreign Policy," *American Political Science Review* 61, no. 4 (December 1967): 971–
982; Hanrieder, "International and Comparative Politics: Toward a Synthesis?"
World Politics 20, no. 3 (April 1968): 480–493; Introduction to Wolfram F. Hanrieder, ed., *Comparative Foreign Policy: Theoretical Essays* (New York: David McKay,
1971).

4. As Alfred North Whitehead has written, "Each mode of consideration is a
sort of searchlight elucidating some of the facts and retreating the remainder into
an omitted background." Of course, one historian's background is the other's
center stage, and in that sense theory consists as much of what is not said as of
what is. Whether we theorize by elucidation or by omission, we tend to load the
evidence and skew the meaning of the historical record, or at least the emphasis.

See F. M. Cornford, *The Unwritten Philosophy* (Cambridge and New York: Cambridge University Press, 1967), esp. pp. 1–2; Hans-Georg Gadamer, *Wahrheit und Methode* (Tübingen: J. C. B. Mohr-Paul Siebeck, 1960); Robert G. Collingwood, *The Idea of History* (Oxford: Clarendon Press, 1946), p. xii; William James, *Pragmatism* (New York: Longmans, Green, 1907), pp. 7–8; Stuart Hampshire, "Philosophy and Fantasy," *New York Review of Books*, September 26, 1968, pp. 51–53, esp. p. 52.

5. Wolfram F. Hanrieder, "Dissolving International Politics: Reflections on the Nation-State," *American Political Science Review* 72, no. 4 (December 1978): 1276–1287; Hanrieder, "The International System: Bipolar or Multibloc?" *Journal of Conflict Resolution* 9, no. 3 (September 1965): 299–308; Richard Rosecrance, *The Rise of the Trading State: Commerce and Conquest in the Modern World* (New York: Basic Books, 1986); Paul Kennedy, *The Rise and Fall of the Great Powers: Economic Change and Military Conflict from 1500 to 2000* (New York: Random House, 1987); Walter L. Bühl, *Das Ende der amerikanisch-sowjetischen Hegemonie? Internationale Politik im Fünften Kondratieffschen Übergang* (Munich: Olzog, 1986).

6. John H. Herz, *International Politics in the Atomic Age* (New York: Columbia University Press, 1959); Anthony Giddens, *A Contemporary Critique of Historical Materialism*, vol. 2, *The Nation-State and Violence* (Berkeley: University of California Press, 1987).

7. I am of course thinking here of the concept of *conjuncture*, which "requires the historian to compare the various trends discernible in the different variables . . . and on this basis to construct a dynamic model." E. LeRoy Ladurie, *The Territory of the Historian* (Chicago: University of Chicago Press, 1979), p. 26. See also Fernand Braudel, *The Mediterranean and the Mediterranean World in the Age of Philip II* (New York: Harper & Row, 1972), vol. 2, esp. pp. 892–900; Max Weber, *Gesammelte politische Schriften* (Tübingen: J. C. B. Mohr, 1968), 3d ed., pp. 170–171.

8. The reader interested in historiographic issues will have realized that I am attempting to translate concerns of method into concerns of form. As Leon Edel points out in speaking of his work as a biographer, it is precisely in the area of form (and not of course in the area of facts) that we are permitted imagination and a large measure of analytical freedom. See Leon Edel, Preface to *Henry James, the Master: 1901–1916* (Philadelphia: Lippincott, 1972). See also Hayden V. White, *The Content of the Form: Narrative Discourse and Historical Representation* (Baltimore: Johns Hopkins University Press, 1987); Walter Benjamin, *Reflections* (New York: Harcourt Brace Jovanovich, 1978), pp. 223, 236. If one were to compare my earlier books on West German foreign policy with the present one, differences in form would become apparent. See Wolfram F. Hanrieder, *West German Foreign Policy, 1949–1963: International Pressure and Domestic Response* (Stanford: Stanford University Press, 1967), esp. pp. 1–10, 228–245; Hanrieder, *The Stable Crisis: Two Decades of German Foreign Policy* (New York: Harper & Row, 1970); Hanrieder, *Fragmente der Macht. Die Aussenpolitik der Bundesrepublik* (Munich: Piper, 1981), esp. pp. 9–14.

Generally speaking, historians choose either a vertical or a horizontal mode of analysis. Some historians prefer a vertical sequence of analysis (succession in time) to demonstrate that the events and structures of one period, say a century, can be understood only by referring to a previous one. This orientation, which exemplifies what is sometimes called the narrative tradition in historiography, interprets history as a linear sequence of significant human actions, presses events into a chronological order, and traces connections that are primarily successive in character—a tendency reinforced by the knowledge that the historian already has of the outcome of the events being analyzed, unless one is dealing with contemporary issues.

Other historians prefer a horizontal temporal spread (simultaneity in time) to stress the interconnectedness among various aspects of the same stage of historical development and explain the relationships among such factors as organized violence, economic activity, legal structures, moral imperatives, aesthetic sensibilities, and a variety of other manifestations of the social order. Although it cannot of course totally ignore matters that are sequential, this orientation represents a mode of analysis fundamentally different from that offered by the first. Maurice Mandelbaum, for example, has argued that "the task of the historian is not one of tracing a series of links in a temporal chain; rather, it is his task to analyze a complex pattern of change into the factors which served to make it precisely what it was. The relationship which I therefore take to be fundamental in historiography is . . . a relationship of part to whole, not a relationship of antecedent to consequent." "A Note on History as Narrative," *History and Theory* 6, no. 3 (1967): 413–419; the quotation is from pp. 417–418. See also Daniel Lerner, ed., *Parts and Wholes* (New York: Free Press of Glencoe, 1963); George Kubler, *The Shape of Time: Remarks on the History of Things* (New Haven and London: Yale University Press, 1962); Fernand Braudel, *On History* (Chicago: University of Chicago Press, 1980); Reinhart Koselleck, *Vergangene Zukunft. Zur Semantik geschichtlicher Zeiten* (Frankfurt am Main: Suhrkamp, 1979), especially pt. 3; Paul Ricoeur, *Temps et Récit* (Paris: Editions du Seuil, 1983); W. von Leyden, "History and the Concept of Relative Time," *History and Theory* 2, no. 3 (1963): 418–419; Wolfram F. Hanrieder, "Crises and Evolutionary Change in International Politics," *Polity* 16, no. 2 (Winter 1983): 329–342; Norman Jacobson, "Causality and Time in Political Process: A Speculation," *American Political Science Review* 58, no. 1 (March 1964): 15–22.

9. For a theoretical discussion of the issue see Friedrich Meinecke, *Die Idee der Staatsräson in der neueren Geschichte*, ed. Walther Hofer (Munich: R. Oldenbourg, 1957); Siegfried Kracauer, *History. The Last Things Before the Last* (New York: Oxford University Press, 1969), esp. chap. 5. For a demonstration of the close connection between foreign and domestic policies in the Federal Republic see Hanrieder, *Stable Crisis*, chap. 4.

10. Kurt Schumacher, "Die Staatsgewalt geht von den Besatzungsmächten aus" (SPD pamphlet, n.d. [probably 1948]).

11. In his first government declaration (September 20, 1949), Chancellor Konrad Adenauer noted: "Lacking among the Federal ministries is a foreign ministry. . . . But although we do not have a foreign ministry, this does not mean that we abjure all activity in this area. The paradox of our situation is precisely that even though the foreign relations of Germany are handled by the Allied High Commission, each and every activity of the Federal government or the Federal parliament in the domestic affairs of Germany somehow also entails a foreign connection." Auswärtiges Amt, *Die Auswärtige Politik der Bundesrepublik Deutschland* (Cologne: Verlag Wissenschaft und Politik, 1972), p. 148.

12. Ernst-Otto Czempiel, "Der Primat der Auswärtigen Politik. Kritische Würdigung einer Staatsmaxime," *Politische Vierteljahresschrift* 4, no. 3 (September 1963): 266–287.

13. Hajo Holborn, *Inter Nationes Prize, 1969* (Bonn-Bad Godesberg: Inter Nationes, 1969), p. 21.

INTRODUCTION AND OVERVIEW

Epigraph. W. H. Auden, *The Dyer's Hand and Other Essays* (New York: Random House, 1948), p. 5.

INTRODUCTION TO PART I

Epigraph. Carl von Clausewitz, *On War*, ed. and trans. Michael Howard and Peter Paret (Princeton: Princeton University Press, 1976), p. 605.

1. On the origins of central and extended deterrence see Bernard Brodie, "The Development of Nuclear Strategy," in Wolfram F. Hanrieder, ed., *Arms Control and Security: Current Issues* (Boulder: Westview, 1979), pp. 19–37; Bernard Brodie, *Strategy in the Missile Age* (Princeton: Princeton University Press, 1965); Alastair Buchan, ed., *Problems of Modern Strategy* (New York: Praeger, 1970); Robert E. Osgood, *NATO: The Entangling Alliance* (Chicago: University of Chicago Press, 1962); Morton Halperin, *Defense Strategies for the Seventies* (Boston: Little, Brown, 1971); Lawrence Freedman, *The Evolution of Nuclear Strategy* (New York: St. Martin's, 1981); Glenn H. Snyder, *Deterrence and Defense* (Princeton: Princeton University Press, 1961); George F. Kennan, *Russia, the Atom and the West* (New York: Harper & Bros., 1957); Samuel P. Huntington, *The Common Defense: Strategic Programs in National Politics* (New York: Columbia University Press, 1969); William W. Kaufmann, *The McNamara Strategy* (New York: Harper & Row, 1964). On the connection between containment and deterrence see John Lewis Gaddis, *Strategies of Containment: A Critical Appraisal of Postwar American National Security Policy* (New York: Oxford University Press, 1982). On the general principles of deterrence see Frank C. Zagare, *The Dynamics of Deterrence* (Chicago: University of Chicago Press, 1987). See also Jane E. Stromseth, *The Origins of Flexible Response: NATO's Debate over Strategy in the 1960s* (New York: St. Martin's, 1988).

A historical overview of extended deterrence is presented in Anthony H. Cordesman, "Deterrence in the 1980s: American Strategic Forces and Extended Deterrence," in Robert Nurick, ed., *Nuclear Weapons and European Security* (New York: St. Martin's for the International Institute for Strategic Studies, 1984), pp. 721–22; Aaron L. Friedberg, "A History of U.S. Strategic 'Doctrine,' 1945 to 1980," *Journal of Strategic Studies* 3, no. 3 (December 1980): 37–71; Henry Rowen, "The Evolution of Strategic Nuclear Doctrine," in Laurence Martin, ed., *Strategic Thought in the Nuclear Age* (London: Heinemann, 1979).

2. See Michael Howard, "Reassurance and Deterrence: Western Defense in the 1980s," *Foreign Affairs* 61, no. 2 (Winter 1982–83): 309–324.

3. See Earl C. Ravenal, *NATO: The Tides of Discontent*, University of California Institute of International Affairs, Policy Papers in International Affairs, no. 23 (Berkeley, 1985), esp. p. 12. As Britain's former Defense Minister Denis Healy put it, "A one percent chance of a U.S. nuclear retaliatory strike would be enough to deter the Russians but a 99 percent chance might not be sufficient to reassure the Europeans." Quoted in Jane M. O. Sharp, "Nuclear Weapons and Alliance Cohesion," *Bulletin of the Atomic Scientists* 38, no. 6 (June 1982): 34.

4. See Pierre Hassner, "Recurrent Stresses, Resilient Structures," in Robert

W. Tucker and Linda Wrigley, eds., *The Atlantic Alliance and Its Critics* (New York: Praeger, 1983), pp. 61–94, esp. p. 85.

5. For a discussion of the disjuncture between political purpose and strategic preparations in the Reagan administration see Barry R. Posen and Stephen W. Van Evera, "Reagan Administration Defense Policy: Departure from Containment," in Kenneth A. Oye, Robert J. Lieber, and Donald Rothchild, eds., *Eagle Resurgent? The Reagan Era in American Foreign Policy* (Boston: Little, Brown, 1987), pp. 75–114.

6. Jonathan Dean, "Military Security in Europe," *Foreign Affairs* 66, no. 1 (Fall 1987): 22–40; Dean, *Watershed in Europe: Dismantling the East-West Military Confrontation* (Lexington, Mass.: Lexington Books, 1987); Joseph Joffe, *The Limited Partnership: Europe, the United States, and the Burdens of Alliance* (Cambridge, Mass.: Ballinger, 1987).

CHAPTER 1: *Security for Germany, Security from Germany*

Epigraph. Herbert Blankenhorn, *Verständnis und Verständigung. Blätter eines politischen Tagebuchs, 1949 bis 1979* (Frankfurt am Main: Propyläen, 1980), p. 356.

1. Dean Acheson, *The Struggle for a Free Europe* (New York: W. W. Norton, 1971), p. 125. Perhaps the Germans were themselves reaching for that entanglement. As William Pfaff has observed, "Having abdicated politics, and even cultural autonomy in the immediate postwar years, when nearly everything German seemed discredited, West Germany willed its dependence upon the United States." Quoted in Stephen F. Szabo, "Skepticism toward American Leadership: The New Generation in Germany," *Transatlantic Perspectives*, no. 7 (Washington: December 1982): 10–12; the quotation appears on p. 10.

2. Robert E. Osgood, NATO: *The Entangling Alliance* (Chicago: University of Chicago Press, 1962), p. 30.

3. Hans-Gert Pöttering, *Adenauers Sicherheitspolitik, 1956–63. Ein Beitrag zum deutsch-amerikanischen Verhältnis* (Düsseldorf: Droste, 1975); Annelise Poppinga, *Konrad Adenauer. Geschichtsverständnis, Weltanschauung und politische Praxis* (Stuttgart: Deutsche Verlags-Anstalt, 1975); Roland G. Foerster et al., *Von der Kapitulation bis zum Plevenplan. Anfänge westdeutscher Sicherheitspolitik, 1945–1956*, ed. Militärgeschichtliches Forschungsamt, vol. 1 (Munich: R. Oldenbourg, 1982).

4. Edgar McInnis, Richard Hiscocks, and Robert Spencer, *The Shaping of Postwar Germany* (New York: Praeger, 1960), p. 133. See also Blankenhorn, *Verständnis und Verständigung*, p. 175.

5. *New York Times*, December 10, 1949, pp. 1–2.

6. Viewed from the distance of the 1980s, the plan for an integrated European army seems only of marginal importance, especially because it did not come to fruition. But the failure to establish a unified European army had serious long-range consequences. It deprived the dynamics of West European economic integration of a supportive security component, precluded a possible spillover from economic and military integration into the area of a common foreign policy, permitted France in the 1960s to leave the integrated command of NATO without remaining bound to an effective subsidiary European defense structure, and deprived the Europeans of developing an institutional alternative to NATO. On the demise of the EDC see Raymond Aron and Daniel Lerner, *France Defeats the EDC*

(New York: Praeger, 1957); Edgar S. Furniss, Jr., *France: Troubled Ally* (New York: Praeger, 1960); Paul Noack, *Das Scheitern der Europäischen Verteidigungsgemeinschaft. Entscheidungsprozesse vor und nach dem 30. August 1954* (Düsseldorf: Droste, 1977). For a new look based on newly available documents see Rolf Steininger, "Das Scheitern der EVG und der Beitritt der Bundesrepublik zur NATO," *Aus Politik und Zeitgeschichte*, suppl. to *Das Parlament*, B 17/85 (1985), pp. 3–18. For security reasons Bonn preferred membership in NATO; for advancing Western European integration Bonn favored the EDC. See Hans-Erich Volkmann and Walter Schwengler, *Die Europäische Verteidigungsgemeinschaft. Stand und Probleme der Forschung*, vol. 7, Militärgeschichte seit 1945 (Boppard: Harald Boldt, 1985).

7. Hans Buchheim, *Deutschlandpolitik, 1949–1972. Der politisch-diplomatische Prozess* (Stuttgart: Deutsche Verlags-Anstalt, 1984), p. 49. For an early argument for German membership in NATO see Chatham House Study Group, *Atlantic Alliance: NATO's Role in the Free World* (London: Royal Institute of International Affairs, 1952).

8. Osgood, *NATO: The Entangling Alliance*, p. 115.

9. Alastair Buchan and Philip Windsor, *Arms and Stability in Europe* (New York: Praeger, 1963), esp. p. 38; Hans Speier, *German Rearmament and Atomic War* (Evanston, Ill.: Row, Peterson, 1957); Malcolm W. Hoag, "Rationalizing NATO Strategy," *World Politics* 17, no. 1 (October 1964): 121–142; Catherine McArdle Kelleher, *Germany and the Politics of Nuclear Weapons* (New York: Columbia University Press, 1975), esp. chaps. 2, 3. As early as spring 1951, a study by the Pentagon had argued that the tactical use of nuclear weapons would be more effective in Europe and Asia than strategic bombing. See David C. Elliot, *Project Vista: An early Study of Nuclear Weapons in Europe* (Santa Monica: California Seminar on International Security and Foreign Policy, discussion paper no. 108, August 1987). War games conducted by the Seventh Army in Europe had already demonstrated in 1952 that a tactical nuclear war would require more manpower than a conventional one. See Alain C. Enthoven and Wayne K. Smith, *How Much Is Enough?* (New York: Harper & Row, 1971); and Bernard Brodie, *Escalation and the Nuclear Option* (Princeton: Princeton University Press, 1966), p. 12.

10. See Wolfram F. Hanrieder, *The Stable Crisis: Two Decades of German Foreign Policy* (New York: Harper & Row, 1970), chap. 1.

11. Speier, *German Rearmament*, p. 210.

12. Actually Bonn was not formally asked to participate in the deployment of IRBMs. In December 1957 NATO agreed to establish a nuclear stockpile, and in 1958 Bonn announced its intention to accept pilotless cruise missiles that could carry nuclear warheads and about three hundred Nike-Ajax air defense missiles, both under dual key arrangements with the United States. Gordon A. Craig, "Germany and NATO: The Rearmament Debate, 1950–1958," in Klaus Knorr, ed., *NATO and American Security* (Princeton: Princeton University Press, 1959), pp. 236–259; David N. Schwartz, *NATO's Nuclear Dilemmas* (Washington: Brookings Institution, 1983), pp. 70–72.

13. See Osgood, *NATO: The Entangling Alliance*, p. 255; Wilfrid L. Kohl, *French Nuclear Diplomacy* (Princeton: Princeton University Press, 1971), pp. 54–61; Kelleher, *Germany and the Politics of Nuclear Weapons*, pp. 149–153.

14. Richard Neustadt, *Alliance Politics* (New York: Columbia University Press, 1970), esp. pp. 30–55.

15. William B. Bader, "Nuclear Weapons Sharing and the German Problem," *Foreign Affairs* 44, no. 4 (July 1966): 693–700, esp. pp. 693–694.

16. Arthur Schlesinger, referring to Secretary McNamara's use of the term *interdependence* in his speech in Ann Arbor of June 1962, notes that this "mellifluous" term was "misleading because what McNamara meant at bottom was precisely the *dependence* of western security on a nuclear deterrent under American control" (italics in original). Arthur Schlesinger, Jr., *A Thousand Days: John F. Kennedy in the White House* (Boston: Houghton Mifflin, 1965), p. 776.

17. Ibid., pp. 780–787.

18. Wilhelm G. Grewe, then German ambassador to the United States, presents a full account of German motives and the tensions that the MLF produced for German-American relations. But he plays down German intentions to use the MLF (and later Bonn's opposition to the Nonproliferation Treaty) to gain leverage for Bonn's Eastern policy, a point of considerable importance to his chief, Foreign Minister Gerhard Schröder, and to Kai-Uwe von Hassel, the minister of defense. See Wilhelm G. Grewe, *Rückblenden, 1976–1951* (Frankfurt am Main: Propyläen, 1979), pp. 616–629, 691–693. For a more detailed analysis of the various stages of German support for the MLF, and disappointment with it, see Kelleher, *Germany and the Politics of Nuclear Weapons*, chapters 9, 10. For the connections between Bonn's Eastern policy and the nonproliferation treaty see chapter 3. For a discussion of American motives see Schlesinger, *A Thousand Days*; George W. Ball, *The Past Has Another Pattern* (New York: W. W. Norton, 1982), esp. pp. 262, 266–267, 269–270; Theodore C. Sorensen, *Kennedy* (New York: Harper & Row, 1965), esp. pp. 567–570, 572–573.

19. This was more appearance than reality. President Johnson and Chancellor Erhard reportedly had signed an agreement in June 1964 that by January 1965 at the latest, the MLF agreement was to be executed by the powers willing to accede to it, with the implication that this arrangement could conceivably be limited to the United States and Germany. In the light of the objections voiced against it by other members of NATO, the Soviet Union, and American officials (including the disarmament negotiator at Geneva), it is unlikely that this possibility was very seriously considered by the president. See *Der Spiegel* 18, no. 42 (1964): 33–34.

20. Cost sharing for American troops stationed in Germany had been a point of contention for a number of years, because Washington wanted the Germans to continue easing the deficit in the American balance of payments through arms purchases in the United States, whereas the Germans insisted that they already had an adequate stock of military equipment. (During 1961–64 West Germany purchased $2.5 billion worth of American arms and munitions.) The issue aroused a good deal of annoyance on both sides, with the Americans threatening troop withdrawals and one German commentator suggesting that Secretary McNamara "appears to many as a tireless arms merchant with shockingly high-pressure sales techniques." Theo Sommer, "Bonn Changes Course," *Foreign Affairs* 45, no. 3 (April 1967): 477–491; the quotation appears on p. 483. During the early months of the Grand Coalition in spring 1967 a compromise was reached that called for German-American monetary cooperation rather than for continuing German weapons purchases to offset the dollar cost of American troops. The new approach provided that Germany would not convert into gold the dollars

earned from American military spending in Germany (the central bank of West Germany in any case followed a general policy of not cashing in dollars for gold) and that Germany would purchase medium-term securities in the United States, thus relieving the American balance-of-payments position. See Gregory F. Treverton, *The Dollar Drain and American Forces in Germany: Managing the Political Economics of Alliance* (Athens: Ohio University Press, 1978); Elke Thiel, *Dollar-Dominanz, Lastenteilung und amerikanische Truppenpräsenz in Europa. Zur Frage kritischer Verknüpfungen währungs- und stationierungspolitischer Zielsetzungen in den deutsch-amerikanischen Beziehungen* (Baden-Baden: Nomos, 1979). See also Horst Mendershausen, *Troop Stationing in Germany: Value and Cost* (Santa Monica: RAND Corp. memorandum RM-5881-PR, December 1968); Mendershausen, "West Germany's Defense Problem," *Current History* 54, no. 321 (May 1968): 268–274. For a more recent look at the issue see Klaus Knorr, "Burden-Sharing in NATO: Aspects of U.S. Policy," *Orbis* 29, no. 3 (Fall 1985): 517–536.

21. Initially, before the signing of the Franco-German friendship treaty of January 1963, de Gaulle had indicated to Adenauer that he had no objections to German participation although the MLF was of no interest to France. Later, however, de Gaulle was strongly opposed to German participation, most likely because of his disappointment over the meager results emerging from the friendship treaty and because he feared that the MLF might actually be implemented. See Grewe, *Rückblenden*, p. 619.

22. In addition to de Gaulle's increasingly vehement objections to Bonn's interest in the MLF, the new British Labour government that came into office in October 1964 strongly opposed the German government, with Prime Minister Harold Wilson declaring in Parliament his agreement with Moscow that there should not be more fingers on the nuclear trigger (November 23, 1964).

23. Kelleher, *Germany and the Politics of Nuclear Weapons*, p. 277.

24. Grewe, *Rückblenden*, p. 684.

25. Ibid., p. 791. In this confidential memorandum, Grewe went on to quote from a commentary in the *New York Times* (November 6–7, 1965) to the effect that official circles in Washington believed that "the U.S. has used NATO to assure its participation in European diplomacy to contain traditional European rivalries and to preserve a powerful influence over the direction of West German policies." Grewe, *Rückblenden*, p. 790. A few years later, in May 1968, Grewe again expressed his concerns about NATO to a small group of high-level German political figures (including Chancellor Kiesinger) and NATO ambassadors: "The alliance is in a phase in which it fulfills its defense functions only in a reduced measure, in which its . . . functions in East-West relations are not noticeable, but in which its control function over the German partner has moved more strongly into the foreground" (p. 797).

26. Ibid., pp. 629–633.

27. See the interview with Foreign Minister Gerhard Schröder repr. in *Europa-Archiv* 20, no. 15 (1965), sec. D, pp. 384ff.

28. The establishment of the NPG was also connected to the French decision to leave NATO. The French had signaled their intention to withdraw in early summer 1965, when they canceled their participation in the NATO staff exercise Fallex 66. In response to the cancellation, Secretary McNamara proposed the establishment of a four- or five-member NATO "select committee" for nuclear planning (which

later became the NATO Nuclear Planning Group), the intended function of which was at least in part to overcome French obstructionism within the alliance and integrate the French force de frappe with NATO strategy. France declined to participate in either committee. For discussions of the background see Edgar S. Furniss, Jr., "De Gaulle's France and NATO: An Interpretation," *International Organization* 15, no. 3 (1969): 349–365; Elliot R. Goodman, "De Gaulle's NATO Policy in Perspective," *Orbis* 10, no. 3 (1966): 911–929.

29. De Gaulle had himself tried for several years to convert the Germans to a European security system under French leadership, but the implied exclusion of NATO and the United States found little support in Bonn, for military as well as political reasons. (For example, in 1964 de Gaulle was reported to have asked the Erhard government for a German financial contribution to the force de frappe so that the program could be completed by 1970, while insisting on sole French control.) The whole question was raised again as part of the Christopher Soames affair of February 1969, which marked a low point in British-French relations. Soames, the British ambassador to France, had reported to his government a conversation with de Gaulle during which the general had suggested new British-French approaches to European questions, such as replacing the Common Market with a wider and looser economic and political organization of Western European nations, with an inner directorate (consisting of Britain, France, Germany, and Italy) that would also form the nucleus of a European defense system to replace NATO. When the British disclosed the substance of the conversation to their allies in the Western European Union, French spokesmen denied that the conversation had been accurately reported.

30. For a description of the NPG and its functioning see Richard E. Shearer, "Consulting in NATO on Nuclear Policy," *NATO Review* 27, no. 5 (October 1979): 25–28; Paul Edward Buteux, *The Politics of Nuclear Consultation in NATO, 1965–1980: The Experience of the Nuclear Planning Group* (New York: Cambridge University Press, 1983); Thomas C. Wiegele, "Nuclear Consultation Processes in NATO," *Orbis* 16, no. 2 (Summer 1972): 462–487; Arthur Hockaday, "Nuclear Management in NATO," *NATO Letter*, May 1967; Harlan Cleveland, *NATO: The Transatlantic Bargain* (New York: Harper & Row, 1970), pp. 54–65. For German views see Kurt Birrenbach, *Meine Sondermissionen. Rückblick auf zwei Jahrzehnte bundesdeutscher Aussenpolitik* (Düsseldorf and Vienna: Econ, 1984), pp. 222–225; Wilfried Hofmann, "Die Beteiligung der Bundesrepublik Deutschland an den Entscheidungsprozessen der NATO," in Deutsche Gesellschaft für Auswärtige Politik, *Regionale Verflechtung der Bundesrepublik Deutschland. Empirische Analysen und theoretische Probleme* (Munich and Vienna: R. Oldenbourg, 1973); Dieter Mahncke, *Nukleare Mitwirkung. Die Bundesrepublik Deutschland in der Atlantischen Allianz, 1954–1970* (Berlin: de Gruyter, 1972).

31. Justin Galen [pseud.], "NATO's Theater Nuclear Dilemma: A New Set of Crucial Choices," *Armed Forces Journal International* 116, no. 5 (January 1979): 16–23; the quotation is from p. 20.

32. See David Schwartz, *NATO's Nuclear Dilemmas* (Washington: Brookings Institution, 1983); Paul Bracken, *The Command and Control of Nuclear Forces* (New Haven and London: Yale University Press, 1983); Richard Ned Lebow, *Nuclear Crisis Management: A Dangerous Illusion* (Ithaca: Cornell University Press, 1987). See also the discussion of Robert McNamara's speech in Athens in Desmond Ball,

Can War Be Controlled? Adelphi Paper no. 169 (London: International Institute for Strategic Studies, 1981).

33. The terms of the strategic discourse, increasingly couched in technical jargon, were also shaped by the enormous productivity of the American defense intelligentsia. An elaborately angular and stately architecture of scientific strategic thought was erected on the elliptic and shifting grounds of political purpose. Uncertain, unprovable, and often unexamined political assumptions were translated into the misleading certainties of the numbers that calibrate the East-West military balance and into the shaky rationality that governs the logic of nuclear and conventional war scenarios. See Fred Kaplan, *The Wizards of Armageddon* (New York: Simon & Schuster, 1983); Gregg Herken, *Counsels of War* (New York: Oxford University Press, 1987, expanded ed.); Arthur Herzog, *The War-Peace Establishment* (New York: Harper & Row, 1965), esp. chap. 2; Lawrence Freedman, *The Evolution of Nuclear Strategy* (New York: St. Martin's, 1981), esp. chap. 12; Paul Dickson, *Think Tanks* (New York: Atheneum, 1972); Roman Kolkowicz, "The Strange Career of the Defense Intellectuals," *Orbis* 31, no. 2 (Summer 1987): 179–192.

34. John Lewis Gaddis, *Strategies of Containment: A Critical Appraisal of Postwar American National Security Policy* (New York: Oxford University Press, 1982). See also Jerome H. Kahan, *Security in the Nuclear Age: Developing U.S. Strategic Arms Policy* (Washington: Brookings Institution, 1975).

35. Harmel Report on "The Future Tasks of the Alliance" (December 1967), in "Report of the Council," *Texts of Final Communiqués, 1949–1974* (Brussels: NATO Information Service, n.d.), pp. 198–202.

36. One needs, however, to take into account the difference between the "declaratory doctrine" and the "actual use doctrine" which, for the United States, was embodied in the U.S. Single Integrated Operational Plane (SIOP) after 1962. Desmond Ball and Jeffrey Richelson, eds., *Strategic Nuclear Targeting* (Ithaca: Cornell University Press, 1986), esp. chaps. 1–3. See also Desmond Ball, *Targeting for Strategic Deterrence*, Adelphi Paper no. 185 (London: International Institute for Strategic Studies, 1983); Freedman, *Evolution of Nuclear Strategy*.

37. Franz-Josef Strauss, *The Grand Design: A European Solution to German Reunification* (New York: Praeger, 1966), p. 50.

38. *White Paper 1970 on the Security of the Federal Republic of Germany and on the State of the German Federal Armed Forces* (Bonn: Federal Ministry of Defense, 1970), p. 33.

39. As Uwe Nerlich pointed out, "Despite the fact that the differences of opinion on strategy questions between Washington and Bonn reached a peak in the years 1961 and 1962, there was a good deal of complementarity during that phase with respect to the development of armed forces. Under the impact of the 1961 Berlin crisis, the Federal Republic extended military service time from 12 to 18 months and agreed to raise troop levels from 350,000 to 500,000 men, while the United States raised its nuclear strength in Europe by 60 per cent. . . . It is a remarkable paradox that the strategic conceptions of Bonn and Washington became extremely opposed in 1961–62 when their defense policies became more complementary while there was a good deal of correspondence between Bonn and Paris on strategic conceptions when their defense policies had more and more ceased to serve common interests." See Uwe Nerlich, "Die nuklearen

Dilemmas der Bundesrepublik Deutschland," *Europa-Archiv* 20, no. 17 (1965): 637–652; the quotation appears on p. 641. See also James L. Richardson, *Germany and the Atlantic Alliance* (Cambridge: Harvard University Press, 1966), pp. 39–62.

40. "Nuclear issues . . . tend to be most prominent in the Alliance when confidence in political cohesion is weakest, and they will be most sensitive for that country which must fear most for its security from a decline in American involvement—the Federal Republic. All nuclear disputes in . . . alliance history, from the MLF to the neutron bomb and TNF, have also been disputes about the specific role of West Germany in the Alliance and about German-American relations." Gregory Treverton, "Nuclear Weapons in Europe," in Robert Nurick, ed., *Nuclear Weapons and European Security* (New York: St. Martin's for the International Institute of Strategic Studies, 1984), pp. 38–71; the quotation is from p. 59.

41. Wolfram F. Hanrieder and Graeme P. Auton, *The Foreign Policies of West Germany, France and Britain* (Englewood Cliffs, N.J.: Prentice-Hall, 1980), esp. pp. 108ff.

42. This also applied to the recurring suggestions, controversial within the Federal Republic as well, to enlarge the geographical area of NATO's security concerns for purposes of safeguarding energy supplies (especially in the Middle East and Persian Gulf region), so as to match a broader definition of security with a broader commitment to maintain it.

43. Kelleher, *Germany and the Politics of Nuclear Weapons*, esp. p. 271.

44. The Germans distinguished between two versions of what in English is called "forward defense": *Vorneverteidigung* and *Vorwärtsverteidigung*. The former is a defense posture that engages the enemy as early and as close to the German border as possible; the latter carries with it a more dynamic meaning inasmuch as it suggests that a basically defensive posture can nonetheless carry hostilities onto enemy territory once an attack has taken place. In 1967 Foreign Minister Gerhard Schröder issued instructions that the term *forward strategy* be translated as Vorneverteidigung, to avoid misunderstandings because of the more aggressive implications of the term *Vorwärtsverteidigung*. See Grewe, *Rückblenden*, p. 687.

Actually, during most of NATO's life "forward defense" had never been much more than a palliative slogan. When first enunciated by General Eisenhower in 1951 it meant the fallback of NATO troops to the Rhine; only by 1963 was NATO sufficiently prepared to implement its first-line defense plan on West Germany's borders with the Soviet bloc. Even then, shortage of troops and lack of space for maneuver threw serious doubts on the efficacy of the principle of forward defense. (See *Der Spiegel* 20, no. 33 (1966): 30–39, esp. the interview with General Kielmansegg, then commander of NATO's central sector.)

The *White Paper* issued by the German Ministry of Defense in 1979 notes that "for the Federal Republic of Germany there can be no alternative to forward defense: in view of her geostrategic situation, her population density near the border of the Warsaw Pact, and the structuring of her economy, any conceptual model of defense involving the surrender of territory is unacceptable. . . . Such a concept of operations would not be in accordance with the mission to preserve the integrity of our territory. The presence close to the border of our own and allied forces in German territory demonstrates effectively to the Warsaw Pact the Alliance's deterrence and defense capabilities." *The White Paper, 1979: The Security of the Federal Republic of Germany and the State of the German Federal Armed Forces*

(Bonn: Federal Ministry of Defense, 1979), p. 126. See also Samuel P. Huntington, "Conventional Deterrence and Conventional Retaliation in Europe," *International Security* 8, no. 3 (Winter 1983–84): 32–56; Richard K. Betts, "Conventional Deterrence: Predictive Uncertainty and Policy Confidence," *World Politics* 37, no. 2 (January 1985): 153–179.

45. From the beginning of the rearmament debate the Germans were highly sensitive to this issue. For example, the implications of the decision in 1954 by NATO to deploy tactical nuclear weapons met with considerable resistance on the part of some German military planners. The cause célèbre of Colonel Bogislav von Bonin is an instructive example. In the early 1950s Bonin, chief of planning in the newly established Blank Office (the predecessor to the German Defense Ministry), strongly criticized the adequacy of NATO planning for the defense of West Germany and in particular argued for the forward deployment of German contingents near the East German border. Bonin's planning in effect called for a national German defense strategy, and the attendant political implications made it seem desirable to relieve him of his planning functions in 1953. In summer 1954 he proposed deploying a German force of about 150,000 volunteers along the West German border in defensive "blocking units" at a depth of about fifty kilometers. This was to be an all-German force, operating separately from NATO contingents, which would have been pulled back behind the Rhine. Bonin's plan, based primarily on the contingency of a Soviet attack with tanks, was officially rejected by the Blank Office both because it contravened NATO planning and because it was considered militarily inadequate; further, it seemed to emphasize the division of Germany by drawing a clear-cut military boundary between East Germany and West Germany. See Speier, *German Rearmament*, pp. 75–82. The memorandum by Bonin "Rearmament and Defense Planning," which is actually about rearmament and reunification, is reprinted in Klaus von Schubert, ed., *Sicherheitspolitik der Bundesrepublik Deutschland. Dokumentation 1945–1977*, vol. 2 (Bonn: Bundeszentrale für politische Bildung, 1978), pp. 110–114. For a fuller account of the Bonin affair and the ensuing domestic discussion in the Federal Republic see Wolfram F. Hanrieder, *West German Foreign Policy, 1949–1963: International Pressure and Domestic Response* (Stanford: Stanford University Press, 1967), pp. 110–112.

46. Furniss, "De Gaulle's France and NATO: An Interpretation"; Goodman, "De Gaulle's NATO Policy in Perspective."

47. See Kenneth Hunt, *NATO without France: The Military Implications*, Adelphi Paper no. 32 (London: International Institute for Strategic Studies, 1966); Carl H. Amme, Jr., *NATO without France: A Strategic Appraisal* (Stanford: Hoover Institution on War, Revolution and Peace, 1967).

48. Bernard Brodie, "How Not to Lead an Alliance," *Reporter*, March 9, 1967, p. 23. The statement was made by Under Secretary George Ball on April 10, 1966. See also my comments on President Carter's PRM-10 of 1977 (chapter 2).

49. Charles Burton Marshall, Foreword to Amme, *NATO without France*, p. ix. For a full discussion of the political purposes of French nuclear diplomacy see Hanrieder and Auton, *Foreign Policies*, chap. 5.

50. In later years the importance of French nuclear weapons to nuclear strategy increased. See David S. Yost, *France's Deterrent Posture and Security in Europe*, pt. 1, *Capabilities and Doctrine*; pt. 2, *Strategic and Arms Control Implications*,

Adelphi Papers nos. 194, 195 (London: International Institute for Strategic Studies, 1984–85); Yost, *France and Conventional Defense in Central Europe* (Marina Del Rey, Calif.: European American Institute for Security Research, 1984).

51. See Klaus Hildebrand, "Zur Problematik der deutsch-französischen Beziehungen in den sechziger Jahren des 20. Jahrhunderts," in Henning Köhler, ed., *Deutschland und der Westen. Vorträge and Diskussionsbeiträge des Symposions zu Ehren von Gordon A. Craig* (Berlin: Colloquium, 1984), pp. 169–184, esp. pp. 177–180.

52. Paul Frank, formerly state secretary in the German foreign ministry, made this remark in 1982. Quoted by Peter Bender, "Fest im Westen—Brücke zum Osten," *Die Zeit*, February 17, 1984, p. 3.

53. In 1987 U.S. Army personnel in West Germany (excluding Berlin) totaled about 204,000, while the U.S. Air Force maintained 41,000 troops and 328 combat aircraft in the Federal Republic. See *The Military Balance, 1986–1987* (London: International Institute for Strategic Studies, 1986), pp. 28–29.

54. The potential for these instabilities and the necessity for Soviet-American cooperation in minimizing them are discussed in David Calleo, *The Atlantic Fantasy: The U.S., NATO, and Europe* (Baltimore: Johns Hopkins University Press, 1970).

55. As U.S. Sen. Sam Nunn argued many years later: "If the allies really want, or will continue to settle for, a nuclear tripwire, then I believe the U.S. should recognize this at some point and adjust our own military commitment and our defense priorities. We can provide for a nuclear tripwire—or even what some would call an extended tripwire—with far fewer conventional forces and personnel than the U.S. currently has stationed in NATO." *Congressional Record*, 98th Cong., 2d sess., June 18, 1984, sec. S, p. 7453.

56. John J. Mearsheimer, *Conventional Deterrence* (Ithaca: Cornell University Press, 1983), p. 165.

57. William W. Kaufmann, "Nonnuclear Deterrence," in John D. Steinbruner and Leon V. Sigal, eds., *Alliance Security: NATO and the No-First-Use Question* (Washington: Brookings Institution, 1983), pp. 43–90; *Discriminate Deterrence: Report of the Commission on Integrated Long-Term Strategy* (Washington: GPO, 1988).

58. It may well be that in the future innovations in conventional strategy will be jeopardized by congressionally mandated budget cuts and the Soviet-American INF accord of 1987–88, which will require the elimination of many cruise missiles and theater ballistic missiles that might otherwise have carried conventional warheads in conjunction with these strategies.

59. McGeorge Bundy, "The Future of Strategic Deterrence," *Survival* 21, no. 6 (November-December 1979): 268–272; the quotation appears on p. 271. Helmut Schmidt, *A Grand Strategy for the West: The Anachronism of National Strategies in an Interdependent World* (New Haven and London: Yale University Press, 1985), p. 27.

60. George Liska, "From Containment to Concert," *Foreign Policy*, no. 62 (Spring 1986): 3–23; the quotation is from p. 15. See also Colin S. Gray, "Keeping the Soviets Landlocked: Geostrategy for a Maritime America," *National Interest*, no. 4 (Summer 1986): 24–36; esp. p. 30, where the author writes, "The Soviet-American rivalry, geostrategically, is a contest between states that have enormous difficulty exerting direct military pressure on one another."

61. There was a certain asymmetry in the superpowers' use of nuclear diplomacy for managing their alliances. Because of the different nature of the West

German-American and East German-Soviet security compacts and of the two alliances in general, Washington's nuclear diplomacy toward the alliance obtained more leverage than Moscow's. At the same time, however, arms control negotiations over Eurostrategic weapons obtained for Moscow an indirect voice in Western deliberations within the alliance.

62. See Christoph Bertram, "Political Implications of the Theater Nuclear Balance," in Barry M. Blechman, ed., *Rethinking the U.S. Strategic Posture* (Cambridge, Mass.: Ballinger, 1982), pp. 102–128, esp. p. 107; on the question of public support for a nuclear strategy see Michael Howard, "Forgotten Dimensions of Strategy," *Foreign Affairs* 57, no. 5 (Summer 1979): 975–986; Gregory Flynn and Hans Rattinger, eds., *The Public and Atlantic Defense* (Totowa, N.J.: Rowman & Allanheld, 1985).

63. Treverton, "Nuclear Weapons in Europe," pp. 38–71; the quotation appears on p. 58. See also Gregory F. Traverton, *Making the Alliance Work: The United States and Western Europe* (Ithaca: Cornell University Press, 1985).

64. François Duchene, "SALT, die Ostpolitik und die Liquidierung des Kalten Krieges," *Europa-Archiv* 25 (1970): 639–653, esp. p. 649.

65. Jonathan Dean, "How to Lose Germany," *Foreign Policy*, no. 55 (Summer 1984): 54–72; Dean, *Watershed in Europe: Dismantling the East-West Military Confrontation* (Lexington, Mass.: Lexington Books, 1987).

66. Helga Haftendorn, *Security and Détente: Conflicting Priorities in German Foreign Policy* (New York: Praeger, 1985). This does not necessarily mean that German interests do not continue to be served by NATO's framework. As Pierre Lellouche has pointed out, West Germany's long-term strategy of obtaining German unity may well require the continuation of NATO: "What this strategy implies . . . is that West Germany's fundamental interests are to keep both the NATO alliance in its present form, not only as the 'safety net' of its security but also as the foundation of its overture to the East, and its *Ostpolitik* toward Moscow and the GDR. . . . West Germany has been trying quite successfully in recent years to have the rest of Europe share its national interests, by rallying the smaller European countries, but also France as well, to the cause of European détente. In effect, the West German game is to turn *deutsche Ostpolitik* into *europäische Ostpolitik*, thereby isolating the United States within NATO on the central question of East-West relations. . . . A recent and notable element of this West German effort is the Genscher plan, which aims at opening European discussions on security policy within the EEC framework (including arms control of course, but excluding purely military questions, which are left to NATO)." "Does NATO Have a Future?" in Robert W. Tucker and Linda Wrigley, eds., *The Atlantic Alliance and Its Critics* (New York: Praeger, 1983), pp. 129–154; the quotation appears on pp. 146–147.

67. Yost, *France and Conventional Defense*, esp. pp. 29–47, 87–103.

68. Robert E. Osgood, *American and European Approaches to East-West Relations*, Occasional Papers in International Affairs (Washington: Johns Hopkins Foreign Policy Institute, 1982), p. 1 (italics in original).

CHAPTER 2: *The Devolution of Extended Deterrence*

Epigraphs. Henry Kissinger's remark is from his speech in Brussels (September 1, 1979) "NATO: The Next Thirty Years," which is reprinted in *Survival* 21, no. 6 (November-December 1979): 264–268; the quotation appears on pp. 265–266. The quotation from Helmut Schmidt appears in "If the Missiles Go, Peace May Stay," *New York Times*, April 29, 1987, p. 31.

1. A. W. DePorte, *Europe between the Superpowers: The Enduring Balance* (New Haven and London: Yale University Press, 1979), p. 168.

2. This principle of "mutual assurance" between adversaries, as Robert E. Osgood calls it, requires that neither side will initiate nuclear war. But this undermines the confidence of one's allies in extended deterrence: "Clearly, the search for means to assure the adversary that one will *not* strike first tends to undermine the credibility of active nuclear deterrence, which depends upon convincing the adversary that one *will* strike first" (italics in original). *NATO: The Entangling Alliance* (Chicago: University of Chicago Press, 1962), p. 189. See also Michael Howard, "Reassurance and Deterrence: Western Defense in the 1980s," *Foreign Affairs* 61, no. 2 (Winter 1982–83): 309–324. For a more technical discussion of the essential criteria for a credible deterrence strategy see Anthony H. Cordesman, "Deterrence in the 1980s: American Strategic Forces and Extended Deterrence," in Robert Nurick, ed., *Nuclear Weapons and European Security* (New York: St. Martin's for the International Institute of Strategic Studies, 1984), pp. 72–122, esp. pp. 74–77.

3. Anthony H. Cordesman notes, however, "In strictly military terms, the U.S. does not require strategic superiority. The increase in U.S. strategic warhead numbers to over 9,000, combined with the capabilities of U.S. and Allied theatre nuclear forces, creates a situation where the U.S. can credibly strike large numbers of Warsaw Pact targets using only a relatively few strategic systems. Large numbers of survivable warheads are desirable, however, to minimize any Soviet incentive to launch limited counterforce attacks, or to strike the U.S. in some other limited way. Further, perceptions regarding relative superiority have an undeniable political and deterrent effect." "Deterrence in the 1980s," p. 75. See also McGeorge Bundy, "To Cap the Volcano," *Foreign Affairs* 48, no. 1 (October 1969): 1–20, esp. pp. 17–18.

4. Earl C. Ravenal, *NATO: The Tides of Discontent*, University of California Institute of International Affairs, Policy Papers in International Affairs, no. 23 (Berkeley, 1985), p. 12. See also n. 3 to Introduction, above.

5. Roger Hilsman, "NATO: The Developing Strategic Context," in Klaus Knorr, ed., *NATO and American Security* (Princeton: Princeton University Press, 1959), pp. 11–36, esp. pp. 14–16.

6. Lord Ismay, *NATO: The First Five Years* (Utrecht: Bosch, 1955), p. 47.

7. Alastair Buchan and Philip Windsor, *Arms and Stability in Europe* (New York: Praeger, 1963), p. 34. Even so, Eisenhower's commitment to the use of nuclear weapons, tactical or strategic, was not nearly as "automatic" as was implied. Part of the subsequent difficulties with the Euro-American strategic relationship was an early European misreading of the New Look and of massive retaliation. See Lawrence Freedman, *The Evolution of Nuclear Strategy* (New York: St. Martin's, 1981), esp. chaps. 4–6.

8. Acheson notes that in November 1949 he pointed out to the SPD's leader, Kurt Schumacher, that "an attempt by the Social Democratic Party to curry favor with the voters or the Russians by baiting the occupation would be given short shrift." Dean Acheson, *The Struggle for a Free Europe* (New York: W. W. Norton, 1971), p. 95.

9. Ibid., p. 188.

10. This line of argument persisted into the 1980s, offering yet another example of the striking continuity of German security concerns. Justin Galen (the pen name of a former senior civilian official in the Department of Defense) wrote in 1979: "Any attempt to improve NATO's conventional forces without correcting its growing problems in nuclear capability . . . could cause deep European distrust of the U.S. and European fear of U.S. 'decoupling' of its strategic forces. . . . The LTDP [Long-Term Defense Program] has come to symbolize the question in many European minds of how much conventional defense is safe for Europe. . . . Our allies have begun to ask whether the Americans may be increasing NATO's conventional component in order to be able to fight a more protracted conventional war, in an attempt to make Europe a self-contained area of conflict." "NATO's Theater Nuclear Dilemma: A New Set of Crucial Choices," *Armed Forces Journal International* 116, no. 5 (January 1979): 16–23; the quotation appears on pp. 16–17.

11. See the discussion of the Bonin case in chap. 1, n. 45.

12. For the rationale see Henry A. Kissinger, *Nuclear Weapons and Foreign Policy* (New York: Harper & Bros., 1957), pp. 190–194; for the retraction see *The Necessity for Choice* (New York: Harper & Bros., 1961), pp. 81–86.

13. David Alan Rosenberg, "The Origins of Overkill: Nuclear Weapons and American Strategy," in Norman A. Graebner, ed., *The National Security: Its Theory and Practice, 1945–1960* (New York: Oxford University Press, 1986), p. 146. Even before the outbreak of the Korean War, in spring 1950, a special task force in Washington had prepared a study, submitted to the National Security Council as NSC-68, that was in effect a geopolitical assessment of the American position in the postwar world. Among a number of projections of American security requirements, NSC-68 estimated that the Soviet Union would by the mid-fifties obtain a considerable nuclear capability, raising the question of what Western defense efforts would be required once a nuclear stalemate had developed. In effect, NSC-68 already cast doubt on the future viability of extended deterrence and called for establishing large conventional forces on the Continent. See "NSC-68: A Report to the National Security Council," *Naval War College Review* 27, no. 3 (May-June 1975): 51–108; Samuel F. Wells, Jr., "Sounding the Tocsin: NSC-68 and the Soviet Threat," *International Security* 4, no. 2 (Fall 1979): 116–158; Paul Y. Hammond, "NSC-68: Prologue to Rearmament," in Warner A. Schilling, Paul Y. Hammond, and Glenn H. Snyder, *Strategy, Politics and Defense Budgets* (New York: Columbia University Press, 1962), pp. 267–378; Lawrence W. Martin, "The American Decision to Re-arm Germany," in Harold Stein, ed., *American Civil-Military Decisions* (Birmingham: University of Alabama Press, 1963), pp. 643–665.

14. "Firebreaks are an imperative of our security in an era of nuclear parity, but they impair alliance cohesion. This is more than a simple antithesis; it has the aspect of a paradox, since the enhancement of any level of military recourse can be regarded alternatively as a link to higher levels of escalation and as a self-contained effort. Improved conventional defense can postpone nuclear escalation and widen the firebreak between conventional war and nuclear war. On the other hand, earlier resort to discrete and controlled tactical nuclear weapons invokes the specter of limiting even a nuclear war to European territory, creating yet another firebreak, this one between theater and total nuclear war." Ravenal, *NATO: The Tides of Discontent*, pp. 15–16.

15. See Charles N. Marshall, "Détente: Effects on the Alliance"; Alfons Dalma, "The Risks of a Détente Policy to Central Europe"; and James E. King, Jr., "Toward Stability in Central Europe," all in Arnold Wolfers, ed., *Changing East-West Relations and the Unity of the West* (Baltimore: Johns Hopkins University Press, 1964), pp. 17–54, 93–124, 125–170.

16. *New York Times*, December 12, 15, and 18, 1962, pp. 3, 1, and 4; Coral Bell, *The Debatable Alliance* (New York: Oxford University Press, 1964), p. 91.

17. Raymond Aron, *The Great Debate* (Garden City, N.Y.: Doubleday, 1965), p. 79.

18. Actually the concept of graduated deterrence was put forth by the Eisenhower administration in the late 1950s, in an acknowledgment that it was no longer credible to threaten the Soviet Union with strategic war in case of localized, conventional attacks. Graduated deterrence in effect was a doctrine of "limited nuclear war," raising the threshold for the implementation of massive strategic retaliation and threatening instead the use of tactical nuclear weapons against military targets in a local theater. See Richard Smoke, *National Security and the Nuclear Dilemma: An Introduction to the American Experience* (Reading, Mass.: Addison-Wesley, 1984) p. 88. Smoke also points to the strong similarity between the principles of flexible response and NSC-68 (drafted in 1950), noting that "it is not much of an exaggeration to say that Flexible Response represented the same philosophy as NSC-68, brought up to date" (pp. 89–90). See also Richard Smoke and Alexander George, *Deterrence in American Foreign Policy: Theory and Practice* (New York: Columbia University Press, 1974), pp. 40–45.

19. Henry A. Kissinger, "The Unresolved Problems of European Defense," *Foreign Affairs* 40, no. 4 (July 1962): 515–541; the quotation appears on p. 520.

20. Buchan and Windsor, *Arms and Stability in Europe*, p. 12.

21. Cordesman, "Deterrence in the 1980s," p. 82.

22. Ibid., p. 83.

23. For a full account see Michael MccGwire, *Military Objectives in Soviet Foreign Policy* (Washington: Brookings Institution, 1987), esp. chaps. 2, 3.

24. In 1983 George Kennan wrote, "The fact is that there are today, in this threatened world of ours, no windows of vulnerability that could be opened or closed. We are vulnerable—totally vulnerable. There is no way that could be changed. It is today precisely to the *intentions* of the potential opponent, not to his *capabilities* (or ours), that we must look for our salvation" (italics in original). "Zero Options," *New York Review of Books*, May 12, 1983, p. 3. Henry Kissinger made a similar point when he complained, with respect to bureaucratic establishments, that "technical issues enjoy more careful attention, and receive more sophisticated treatment, than political ones. . . . Things are done because one knows how to do them and not because one ought to do them. . . . Pragmatism, at least in its generally accepted form, is more concerned with method than with judgment; or rather it seeks to reduce judgment to methodology and value to knowledge." "Domestic Structure and Foreign Policy," in Wolfram F. Hanrieder, ed., *Comparative Foreign Policy: Theoretical Essays* (New York: David McKay, 1971), p. 35. For the importance in arms control of assessing political intentions see the contributions to Barry M. Blechman, ed., *Preventing Nuclear War: A Realistic Approach* (Bloomington: Indiana University Press, 1985).

25. On the difficulties of calibrating the superpowers' military balance in

Europe see Alois Riklin, "Audiatur et altera pars. Dreifache militärpolitische Lagebeurteilung," *Aus Politik und Zeitgeschichte,* suppl. to *Das Parlament,* B 3/81 (1981): 3–22; Wolfram F. Hanrieder and Larry V. Buel, eds., *Words and Arms: A Dictionary of Security and Defense Terms, with Supplementary Data* (Boulder: Westview, 1979), esp. chap. 7, "NATO/Warsaw Pact Military Balance: How to Make the Balance Look Good/Bad." See also the lecture given by Michael Howard at the Royal United Services Institute on January 16, 1986, published in the *Journal of the Royal United Services Institute for Defence Studies* 131, no. 2 (June 1986): 3–10.

26. See Günther Schmid, *Entscheidung in Bonn: Die Entstehung der Ost- und Deutschlandpolitik, 1969–1970* (Cologne: Verlag Wissenschaft und Politik, 1979).

27. "The Nixon-Ford years saw the most substantial reductions in American military capabilities relative to those of the Soviet Union in the entire postwar period. Washington deployed only two new strategic weapons systems during that period—the Minuteman III MIRVed ICBM, and the Poseidon SLBM—while the Russians made operational eight new or updated ICBMS, two new SLBMS, and the Backfire bomber, capable, by some estimates, of reaching American targets. . . . Adjusting for inflation, American defense outlays actually declined at an annual rate of 4.5 percent between 1970 and 1975; corresponding estimates for the Soviet Union show an annual increase of around 3 percent." John Lewis Gaddis, *Strategies of Containment: A Critical Appraisal of Postwar American Security Policy* (New York: Oxford University Press, 1982), pp. 320–321. See also Werner Kaltefleiter, "Europe and the Nixon Doctrine: A German Point of View," *Orbis* 17, no. 1 (Spring 1973): 75–94.

28. Pierre Hassner, "Recurrent Stresses, Resilient Structures," in Robert W. Tucker and Linda Wrigley, eds., *The Atlantic Alliance and Its Critics* (New York: Praeger, 1983), pp. 61–94, esp. p. 61.

29. Actually, the first instance of American counterforce strategy occurred during the Kennedy administration. Once the new administration had discovered that there was no "missile gap," Secretary of Defense Robert S. McNamara assessed the position of the United States as being so superior that Washington would not have to rely on massive retaliation and therefore shifted briefly to a declared counterforce strategy, with targeting plans that avoided Soviet cities. As a consequence, "The first three years of the 1960s can thus be described as the zenith of extended deterrence—at least in the sense that the US could have put the SIOP [Single Integrated Operational Plan] and NATO Nuclear Strike Plan (NSP) into operation to defend Europe with near impunity." Cordesman, "Deterrence in the 1980s," p. 78. In 1975 Schlesinger argued that "the threat of mutual annihilation limits the range of hostile actions which can be deterred by strategic forces and places more emphasis on the deterrent roles of theater nuclear and conventional forces." James Schlesinger, *The Theater Nuclear Force Posture in Europe,* quoted in North Atlantic Assembly, *Conventional Defense in Europe: A Comprehensive Evaluation* (Brussels: North Atlantic Assembly, 1985), p. 35 n. A year later, in his *Annual Defense Department Report,* Schlesinger contended that "in an age of essential nuclear parity, few of us would be happy with a concept for the defense of Western Europe that was heavily dependent on an early recourse to nuclear weapons. Most of us would agree, once having looked at the facts, that a nonnuclear defense of Western Europe is feasible." *Annual Defense Department Report, FY 1976 and FY 1977* (Washington: GPO, 1975), sec. I, pp. 17–19.

Driving the point home more bluntly, Deputy Secretary of Defense David Packard had told a European audience in 1973 that "with the present nuclear balance, the United States would not use its nuclear force against the Soviet Union short of a direct threat to the survival of the United States." Quoted in Raymond E. Burrell, *Strategic Nuclear Parity and NATO Defense Posture* (Washington: National Defense University Research Directorate, 1978), pp. 15–16. This of course left open to interpretation the precise definition of a "direct threat to the survival of the United States," just as it left unmentioned the possibility of using nuclear weapons short of an attack on Soviet territory.

30. For the background see Desmond Ball, *Déjà Vu: The Return to Counterforce in the Nixon Administration* (Santa Monica: California Seminar on Arms Control and Foreign Policy, 1974); Lynn Davis, *Limited Nuclear Options: Deterrence and the New American Doctrine*, Adelphi Paper no. 121 (London: International Institute for Strategic Studies, 1976); Alfred Goldberg, *A Brief Survey of the Evolution of Ideas About Counterforce* (Santa Monica: RAND Corp. memorandum RM-5431-PR, October 1967); Henry S. Rowen, "Formulating Strategic Doctrine," in Commission on the Organization of the Government for the Conduct of Foreign Policy, vol. 4, app. K, *Adequacy of Current Organization: Defense and Arms Control* (Washington: GPO, 1975), p. 222; Benjamin S. Lambeth, "Selective Nuclear Operations and Soviet Strategy," in Johan J. Holst and Uwe Nerlich, eds., *Beyond Nuclear Deterrence* (New York: Crane Russak, 1977); Fritz Ermarth, "Contrasts in American and Soviet Strategic Thought," *International Security* 3, no. 2 (Fall 1978): 138–155.

31. Department of Defense, *Report of the Secretary of Defense James R. Schlesinger to the Congress on the FY 1975 Defense Budget and the FY 1975–1979 Defense Program, March 4, 1974* (Washington: GPO, 1974), p. 38. There was, however, some question as to whether this comprehensive principle of choosing targets was compatible with the McNamara doctrine. See Thomas C. Schelling, "What Went Wrong with Arms Control?" *Foreign Affairs* 64, no. 2 (Winter 1985–86): 219–233, esp. pp. 229–230.

32. Richard M. Nixon, *United States Foreign Policy for the 1970s: A Report to the Congress*, vol. 1 (Washington: GPO, 1970), pp. 54–55.

33. U.S. Congress, *U.S.-U.S.S.R. Strategic Policies*, Hearings before the Subcommittee on Arms Control, International Law and Organization, Senate Committee on Foreign Relations, 93d Cong., 2d Sess., March 1974 (Washington: GPO, 1974), p. 8.

34. *White Paper, 1975–76: The Security of the Federal Republic of Germany and the Development of the Federal Armed Forces* (Bonn: Federal Ministry of Defense, 1976), p. 21.

35. Here too there may have been some distinction between declaratory doctrine and actual use planning. The SIOP and the release guidelines for theater nuclear weapons were probably not very different from those that preceded them. See Desmond Ball, *Targeting for Strategic Deterrence*, Adelphi Paper no. 185 (London: International Institute for Strategic Studies, 1983).

36. William C. Cromwell, *The Eurogroup and NATO* (Lexington, Mass.: D. C. Heath, 1974), p. 30. It is questionable whether in practical terms regionally differentiated deterrence would be feasible. See Paul Bracken, *The Command and Control of Nuclear Forces* (New Haven and London: Yale University Press, 1983).

37. The unrealistic nature of American theorizing about limited nuclear war

in Europe is pointed out in Bracken, *Command and Control*; Bruce G. Blair, *Strategic Command and Control: Redefining the Nuclear Threat* (Washington: Brookings Institution, 1985). See also Albert Wohlstetter and Richard Brody, "Continuing Control as a Requirement of Deterring"; and Paul Bracken, "War Termination," both in Ashton B. Carter, John D. Steinbruner, and Charles A. Zraket, eds., *Managing Nuclear Operations* (Washington: Brookings Institution, 1987), pp. 142–196, 197–214.

This view might be shared by the Soviet Union. "The problem does not seem to lie with the *credibility* of extended deterrence, which is likely to be continuously reinforced by Soviet intelligence as the U.S. improves her capabilities, plans and exercising. It seems instead to lie in the lack of any clear Soviet belief that the West can manage such conflicts with skill and restraint, and in the Soviet perception that NATO currently has a mix of forces whose vulnerability and limited command-and-control capabilities have sufficient first-strike characteristics to create a strong Soviet incentive to launch large-scale disabling strikes in an initial attack, or to pre-empt at the first rough indicators that NATO may be bringing its forces to readiness" (italics in original). Cordesman, "Deterrence in the 1980s," p. 112.

38. See Sherri L. Wassermann, *The Neutron Bomb Controversy: A Study in Alliance Politics* (New York: Praeger, 1983); Alex A. Vardamis, "German-American Military Fissures," *Foreign Policy*, no. 34 (Spring 1979): 87–106; Lothar Ruehl, "Die Nichtentscheidung über die 'Neutronenwaffe,'" *Europa-Archiv* 34, no. 5 (1979): 137–150. For a full account from the German perspective see Hubertus Hoffmann, *Die Atompartner Washington-Bonn und die Modernisierung der taktischen Kernwaffen. Vorgeschichte und Management der Neutronenwaffe und des Doppelbeschlusses der NATO* (Koblenz: Bernard & Graefe, 1986). See also David S. Yost and Thomas C. Glad, "West German Party Politics and Theater Nuclear Modernization since 1977," *Armed Forces and Society* 8, no. 4 (Summer 1982): 525–560.

39. The controversy over PRM-10, a top-secret review of America's global military strategy prepared during Carter's administration, began with a column by Rowland Evans and Robert Novak in the *Washington Post* that described details of a meeting by the Senior Coordination Council (SCC) meeting of the National Security Council on July 28–29, 1977, where certain aspects of PRM-10 were allegedly discussed pertaining to American strategy to counter an invasion of Western Europe by the Warsaw Pact. According to Evans and Novak, National Security Adviser Zbigniew Brzezinski told the group, "It is not possible in the current political environment to gain support in the United States for procurement of the conventional forces required to assure that NATO could maintain territorial integrity if deterrence fails. Therefore, we should adopt a 'stalemate' strategy. That is, a strategy of falling back and leaving the Soviets to face the political consequences of their aggression."

That fallback, according to PRM-10, would be to the Weser and Lech rivers in West Germany, resulting in the loss of approximately one-third of the Federal Republic's territory—including the cities of Hamburg and Munich. Evans and Novak reported that no disagreement was voiced by the group, but that it was noted there would be "hell to pay" if the Germans ever found out. The administration immediately denied the report, though President Carter made no statement personally. This inaction only underscored already worsening tensions in the alliance regarding America's commitment to the defense of Europe, particularly that of the Federal Republic. A senior military officer reportedly stated that "the President should have said something." See Rowland Evans and Robert Novak, "Conceding Defeat in Europe," *Washington Post*, August 3, 1977, sec. A, p. 19; Edward Walsh, "'Pullback' Policy in Europe Denied," *Washington Post*, August 4, 1977, sec. A, p. 12; Michael Getler, "Bonn Is Disturbed over Report of U.S. 'Pullback Policy,'" *Washington Post*, August 5, 1977, sec. A, p. 16. See also David N. Schwartz, *NATO's Nuclear Dilemmas* (Washington: Brookings Institution, 1983), pp. 213–214.

Referring to the flap over PRM-10 of August 1977, Earl C. Ravenal writes, "This was nothing new; the controversy over depth of defense is as old as Germany's accession to NATO in the mid-1950s. For strategic reasons NATO should defend in depth, but for political reasons it must defend forward. The larger point is that all of Europe is America's field of maneuver, its expendable trade for time and safety. But one ally's depth is another's country." *NATO: The Tides of Discontent*, p. 13.

40. See the epigraph to this chapter.

41. McGeorge Bundy et al., "Nuclear Weapons and the Atlantic Alliance," *Foreign Affairs* 60, no. 4 (Spring 1982): 753–768. See also Gert Krell et al., "The No-First-Use Question in West Germany," in John D. Steinbruner and Leon V. Sigal, *Alliance Security: NATO and the No-First-Use Question* (Washington: Brookings Institution, 1983), chap. 8; Jonathan Dean, "Beyond First Use," *Foreign Policy*, no. 48 (Fall 1982): 37–53.

42. For a cogent German response, which reaffirmed the political and strategic importance of "first use," primarily because it presents the opponent with uncertainty about the Western response, see Karl Kaiser et al., "Nuclear Weapons and the Preservation of Peace," *Foreign Affairs* 60, no. 5 (Summer 1982): 1157–1170. See also Krell et al., "The No-First-Use Question in West Germany"; Jonathan Dean, "Beyond First Use," *Foreign Policy* 48 (Fall 1982): 37–53.

Some Germans believed that a declaration of no first use would leave them with the worst of both worlds: decision makers might believe that such a declaration would be credible (which would make conventional war more likely), whereas the continuing existence of nuclear weapons would imply their use in spite of declaratory policies. See John J. Mearsheimer, "Nuclear Weapons and Deterrence in Europe," *International Security* 9, no. 3 (Winter 1984–85): 19–46.

43. Ravenal, *NATO: The Tides of Discontent*. See also Colin S. Gray and Keith Payne, "Victory is Possible," *Foreign Policy*, no. 39 (Summer 1980): 14–27; Colin S. Gray, "Presidential Directive 59: Flawed but Useful," *Parameters* 1, no. 1 (March 1981): 28–57; Edward N. Luttwak, "The Problems of Extending Deterrence," *The Future of Strategic Deterrence*, Adelphi Paper no. 160, pt. 1 (London: International Institute for Strategic Studies, 1980): pp. 31–37. See also Graeme P. Auton, "Ballistic Missile Defense and NATO," in Wolfram F. Hanrieder, ed., *Global Peace and Security: Trends and Challenges* (Boulder: Westview, 1987), pp. 190–218.

44. Ravenal, *NATO: The Tides of Discontent*, p. 26.

45. See Michael Mandelbaum, *The Nuclear Revolution* (New York: Cambridge University Press, 1981), esp. chap. 6; Glenn Snyder, "The Security Dilemma in Alliance Politics," *World Politics* 36, no. 4 (July 1984): 461–495.

German security concerns were agitated again in the early part of 1988 with the publication of *Discriminate Deterrence*, the report issued by the Commission on Integrated Long-Term Strategy (Washington: GPO, 1988). The report implied that

American strategy had been too "Eurocentric" in the past and should emphasize a wider range of contingencies, and, most worrisome from the German point of view, stated that "the alliance should threaten to use nuclear weapons not as a link to a wider and more devastating war—although the risk of further escalation would still be there—but mainly as an instrument for denying success to the invading Soviet forces." The report also reiterated the theme of Henry Kissinger's speech in 1979 in Brussels (he himself served on the commission), that "to help our allies . . . we cannot rely on threats expected to provoke our own annihilation if carried out." Although the report contained nothing the Germans would not have suspected in any case, it raised a big fuss in the Federal Republic, especially among German conservatives. See Josef Joffe, "Germany: Anti-Americanism on the Right," *Wall Street Journal*, February 10, 1988, p. 21. For a discussion of the implicit similarities between *Discriminate Deterrence* and the Soviet study *Strategic Stability Under the Conditions of Radical Nuclear Arms Reductions* (1987) see Wolfram F. Hanrieder, "Implications for Western Security and the German-American Compact," in Sanford Lakoff, ed., *Beyond* START? *A Soviet Report with Commentaries*, University of California Institute on Global Conflict and Cooperation, Policy Paper no. 7 (San Diego, 1988), pp. 54–61.

46. See Seweryn Bialer, *The Soviet Paradox: External Expansion, Internal Decline* (New York: Alfred A. Knopf, 1987), esp. chaps. 3, 4, 7.

47. Henry Kissinger, *The White House Years* (Boston: Little, Brown, 1979), p. 382.

CHAPTER 3: *The Political Dimensions of Arms Control*

Epigraphs. Carl von Clausewitz, *On War*, ed. and trans. Michael Howard and Peter Paret (Princeton: Princeton University Press, 1976), p. 604; Strobe Talbott, "Of All People: Pursuing the Paramount Impulse," *Time*, October 20, 1986, p. 16.

1. This view of arms control, which firmly places its possibilities and limits in a political context, seems to me more appropriate than to link arms control merely to strategy, as does Hedley Bull. See his "Arms Control: A Stocktaking and Prospectus," in Alastair Buchan, ed., *Problems of Modern Strategy* (New York: Praeger, 1970), pp. 139–158, esp. pp. 140–142. See also Thomas C. Schelling and Morton H. Halperin, *Strategy and Arms Control* (New York: Twentieth Century Fund, 1961), p. 2. For some early assessments of arms control see Donald G. Brennan, ed., *Arms Control, Disarmament, and National Security* (New York: George Braziller, 1961); Hedley Bull, *The Control of the Arms Race* (London: Bradbury Agnew, 1961). See also Herbert F. York, "U.S.-Soviet Negotiations and the Arms Race: A Historical Review," in Wolfram F. Hanrieder, ed., *Technology, Strategy, and Arms Control* (Boulder: Westview, 1986); David Holloway, *The Soviet Union and the Arms Race* (New Haven and London: Yale University Press, 1983); Coit D. Blacker, *Reluctant Warriors: The United States, the Soviet Union, and Arms Control* (New York: W. H. Freeman, 1987); Raymond L. Garthoff, *Détente and Confrontation: American-Soviet Relations from Nixon to Reagan* (Washington: Brookings Institution, 1985); William G. Hyland, *Mortal Rivals: Superpower Relations from Nixon to Reagan* (New York: Random House, 1987).

2. Strobe Talbott, "Of All People: Pursuing the Paramount Impulse," *Time*, October 20, 1986, p. 16.

3. See Wolfram F. Hanrieder, "Arms Control and the European Political

Order: Compatibilities and Incompatibilities between the United States and Western Europe," *Bulletin of Peace Proposals* (Oslo) 16, no. 3 (1985): 291–301; see also the articles in the same issue by Thomas Risse-Kappen, Eckhard Lübkemeier, and Steven E. Miller. For a more recent account of arms control issues and the Federal Republic see the contributions in Wolfram F. Hanrieder, ed., *Arms Control, the FRG and the Future of East-West Relations* (Boulder: Westview, 1987).

4. The best interpretive account remains Robert E. Osgood's *NATO: The Entangling Alliance* (Chicago: University of Chicago Press, 1962), esp. chap. 10. See also Michael Howard, *Disengagement in Europe* (Baltimore: Penguin, 1958); Eugene Hinterhoff, *Disengagement* (London: Stevens & Sons, 1959), in which the complete texts of the Eden Plan and the Rapacki plans are among the appendices. George F. Kennan's well-known BBC-Reith Lectures, in which he called for withdrawal of American and Soviet forces from Europe in conjunction with the reunification of Germany, are reprinted in his *Russia, the Atom, and the West* (New York: Harper & Bros., 1958). See also Kennan, "Disengagement Revisited," *Foreign Affairs* 37, no. 2 (January 1959): 187–210; and Kennan's *Memoirs*, vol. 2, *1950–1963* (Boston: Little, Brown, 1972), chap. 13. Already in 1949, when he was the head of the Policy Planning Staff of the Department of State, Kennan had considered various plans in which Allied and Soviet troops would withdraw from their respective zones to enclaves on the eastern and western borders of Germany. Gen. Omar Bradley, chairman of the Joint Chiefs of Staff, strongly objected. See Dean Acheson, *The Struggle for a Free Europe* (New York: W. W. Norton, 1971), p. 70.

For the German perspective see Helga Haftendorn, *Security and Détente: Conflicting Priorities in German Foreign Policy* (New York: Praeger, 1985), esp. pp. 44–47, 60–64; Konrad Adenauer, *Erinnerungen*, vol. 2, *1953–1955* (Stuttgart: Deutsche Verlags-Anstalt), pp. 441ff; Wilhelm G. Grewe, "Containment, Disengagement and What Next?" *Western World* 14 (1958): 19ff. For the domestic political repercussions in West Germany see Wolfram F. Hanrieder, *West German Foreign Policy, 1949–1963: International Pressure and Domestic Response* (Stanford: Stanford University Press, 1967), esp. pp. 202–205; Anselm Doering-Manteuffel, *Die Bundesrepublik Deutschland in der Ära Adenauer* (Darmstadt: Wissenschaftliche Buchgesellschaft, 1983), p. 96.

5. *New York Times*, June 2, 1982, p. 1. In the 1970s also, the idea of nuclear-free zones in Europe remained the topic of discussion. See Wolfgang Heisenberg, "Nuklearwaffenfreie Zonen als Gegenstand der internationalen Rüstungskontrolldiplomatie," *Europa-Archiv* 31, no. 13 (1976): 445–452; William Epstein, "Nuclear Free Zones," *Scientific American* 232, no. 4 (1975): 18–33.

6. For Chancellor Adenauer, arms control issues were also important as an issue of status. Adenauer's Westpolitik aimed to achieve for West Germany an equal status with Britain and France, which would have been impossible with a Central European security regime guaranteed by the major powers. In 1959 Adenauer is reported to have said that as long as he lived he would know how to prevent an arms control zone in Central Europe. See Hans-Peter Schwarz, "Adenauer und Russland," in Friedrich Kroneck and Thomas Oppermann, eds., *Im Dienste Deutschlands und des Rechtes. Festschrift für Wilhelm G. Grewe* (Baden-Baden: Nomos, 1981), pp. 365–389, esp. p. 388.

7. Alastair Buchan and Philip Windsor, *Arms and Stability in Europe* (New

York: Praeger, 1963), p. 43; see also Donald Watt, "Germany," in Evan Luard, ed., *The Cold War: A Re-appraisal* (New York: Praeger, 1964), pp. 118–119.

8. *Deutschland im Wiederaufbau, 1956* (Bonn: Presse- und Informationsamt der Bundesregierung, 1957), pp. 47–48.

9. See Hans Buchheim, *Deutschlandpolitik, 1949–1972: Der politisch-diplomatische Prozess* (Stuttgart: Deutsche Verlags-Anstalt, 1984), pp. 83–87, esp. p. 87; for an account of the interview with Hearst see *Frankfurter Allgemeine Zeitung*, April 28, 1958.

10. George F. Kennan, *Memoirs*, vol. 2, *1950–1963* (Boston: Little, Brown, 1972), p. 260.

11. See among others the Warsaw Pact's proposals from the meetings in Prague (October 1969) and Budapest (March 1969), the "Karlovy Vary Declaration," and the "Bucharest Declaration" of the Warsaw Pact Political Committee. See also I. Orlik and V. Rasmerov, "European Security and Relations between the Two Systems," *International Affairs* (Moscow) 13, no. 5 (May 1967): 3–8, 14; Jaroslav Sedivy, "European Co-operation, European Security," *Literarni Noviny* 16 (February 25, 1967): 1, 5, trans. in *Czechoslovak Press Survey* (Munich: RFE Research, 1967); Centre d'Etudes de Politique Etrangère, "Modèles de sécurité européenne," *Politique Etrangère* 32, no. 6 (1967): 519–541; *Statement on Defence Estimates, 1967* (London: HMSO, 1967), p. 4; Curt Gasteyger, *Europe in the Seventies*, Adelphi Paper no. 37 (London: International Institute for Strategic Studies, 1967); Erik Blumenfeld, "Wege zu einer europäischen Friedensordnung," *Europa-Archiv* 22, no. 3 (1967): 95–104. For a later German contribution see the study sponsored by the German Foreign Policy Association, "Alternativen für Europa: Modelle möglicher Entwicklungen in den siebziger Jahren," *Europa-Archiv* 23, no. 23 (1968): 851–864.

12. For a full discussion see Pierre Hassner, *Change and Security in Europe*, pt. 1, *The Background*, Adelphi Paper no. 45 (London: International Institute for Strategic Studies, 1968).

13. See Georg R. Bluhm, *Détente and Military Relaxation in Europe*, Adelphi Paper no. 40 (London: International Institute for Strategic Studies, 1967); Karl E. Birnbaum, "Das westliche Bündnis und die europäische Sicherheit," *Europa-Archiv* 23, no. 7 (1968): 225–234.

14. See Gerhard Wettig, "Die europäische Sicherheit in der Politik des Ostblocks 1966," *Osteuropa* 17, nos. 2–3 (1967): 93–113, esp. pp. 106–111; Philip E. Mosely, "The United States and the East-West Détente: The Range of Choice," *Journal of International Affairs* 22, no. 1 (1968): 5–15.

15. *New York Times*, July 4 and 27, 1963, p. 1.

16. See Philip Windsor, *Germany and the Management of Détente* (New York: Praeger for the Institute for Strategic Studies, 1971), pp. 139–140.

17. Hassner, *Change and Security*, p. 4.

18. Theo Sommer, "Bonn Changes Course," *Foreign Affairs* 45, no. 3 (April 1967): 477–491. See also his "Objectives of Germany," in Alastair Buchan, ed., *A World of Nuclear Powers?* (Englewood Cliffs, N.J.: Prentice-Hall, 1966), pp. 39–54.

19. There were other objections to the treaty. The Germans argued that the treaty would hamper European scientists and engineers in their work on the peaceful applications of atomic energy, thus favoring the military nuclear powers in commercial competition for building nuclear power plants, that certain inspec-

tion features of the treaty would engender industrial espionage, and that the treaty would impede European integration by undermining the importance and past achievements of Euratom. None of these objections, however, was as serious and fundamental as those that stemmed from the political and military-strategic implications that the treaty's provisions held for Bonn's overall foreign policy.

20. In January 1965 a "secret" report was submitted to President Johnson by a special panel led by Roswell L. Gilpatric, a former deputy secretary of defense, which reportedly urged the President to drop the MLF so that work could progress on a nonproliferation treaty; in July, William C. Foster (then the head of the State Department's disarmament agency and later the chief negotiator for the United States at the negotiations over the NPT in Geneva) spelled out in some detail the American rationale for making the NPT the centerpiece of Washington's global strategy and Soviet policy. William C. Foster, "New Directions in Arms Control and Disarmament," *Foreign Affairs* 43, no. 4 (July 1965): 587–601, esp. pp. 596, 600. For the German perspective see Kurt Birrenbach, *Meine Sondermissionen* (Düsseldorf and Vienna: Econ, 1984), chap. 3, pp. 176–122.

21. *New York Times*, July 13, 1965, p. 8.

22. When Averell Harriman was sent to Bonn in summer 1965 to give assurances that the United States would not sell out West German interests to obtain a nonproliferation treaty, sources in Washington emphasized that this was a general commitment and specifically excluded the demand that the Soviet Union undertake concrete steps leading to the reunification of Germany. The sources were quoted as saying that the United States was "not willing to complicate its undertaking toward a major achievement in arms control by tying it to one of the world's most intractable political problems." See Arthur J. Olsen, *New York Times*, July 25, 1965, sec. 1, p. 2; on Harriman's own views see Margarita Mathiopoulos, "The American President Seen through German Eyes: Continuity and Change from the Adenauer to the Kohl Era," *Presidential Studies Quarterly* 15, no. 4 (Fall 1985): pp. 673–706, esp. pp. 686–688, based on materials from the Harriman Archives.

23. Mason Willrich, "SALT I: An Appraisal," in Mason Willrich and John B. Rhinelander, eds., *SALT: The Moscow Agreements and Beyond* (London: Free Press, 1974); the quotation appears on p. 261.

24. *Christian Science Monitor*, March 8, 1966, p. 2.

25. "Commentator's Corner," *Pravda*, March 12, 1968, p. 5.

26. Hassner, *Change and Security*, ⊦. 20.

27. See Willy Brandt, *Aussenpolitik, Deutschlandpolitik, Europapolitik* (Berlin: Berlin Verlag, 1968), esp. p. 97. For the summary of a speech with a similar theme by Chancellor Kiesinger see *Europa-Archiv* 22, no. 18 (1967): 683–684.

28. Lothar Ruehl, *Machtpolitik und Friedensstrategie* (Hamburg: Hoffmann und Campe, 1974).

29. See Brandt, *Aussenpolitik*, p. 88; Interview with Chancellor Kiesinger, *Der Spiegel* 31, no. 13 (1967): 42–53. See also *New York Times*, March 30, 1967, p. 17; Franz Horner, "Der Atomsperrvertrag: Politischer Idealismus oder Realismus?" *Politische Studien* 18, no. 176 (November-December 1967): 691–704.

30. See Harlan Cleveland, "NATO after the Invasion," *Foreign Affairs* 47, no. 2 (January 1969): 251–265; Ludwig Nau, "Neue militärische Überlegungen in der

Bundesrepublik," *Frankfurter Hefte* 23, no. 11 (1968): 743–746; and Robert Ranger, "NATO's Reaction to Czechoslovakia: The Strategy of Ambiguous Response," *World Today* 25, no. 1 (January 1969): 19–26. The invasion also added to the doubts about the political and military value of the French force de frappe or a similarly structured European nuclear force. See Claude Delmas, "L'Affaire Tchèchoslovaquie et la logique nucléaire," *Revue Politique et Parlementaire* 70, no. 791 (September 1968): 5–8.

31. Wilhelm G. Grewe, *Rückblenden, 1976–1951* (Frankfurt am Main: Propyläen, 1979), pp. 700, 702–703; see also p. 689.

32. See J. P. Ruina and M. Gell-Mann, "Ballistic Missile Defense and the Arms Race," *Proceedings of the Fourteenth Pugwash Conference on Science and World Affairs* (London: Central Office, Pugwash Conference on Science and World Affairs, 1964), pp. 232–235; Richard L. Garwin and Hans A. Bethe, "Antiballistic Missile Systems," *Scientific American* 218, no. 3 (March 1968): 21–31; Herbert York, *Race to Oblivion* (New York: Simon & Schuster, 1970). In September 1967 Secretary McNamara argued in a speech in San Francisco: "Now let me come to the issue that has received so much attention recently: the question of whether or not we should deploy an ABM system against the Soviet nuclear threat. To begin with, this is not in any sense a new issue. We have had both the technical possibility and the strategic desirability of an American ABM deployment under constant review since the late 1950s. While we have substantially improved our technology in the field, it is important to understand that none of the systems at the present or foreseeable state of the art would provide an impenetrable shield over the United States. Were such a shield possible, we would certainly want it—and we would certainly build it. At this point, let me dispose of an objection that is totally irrelevant to this issue. It has been alleged that we are opposed to deploying a large-scale ABM system because it would carry the heavy price tag of $40 billion. Let me make it very clear that the $40 billion is not the issue. If we could build and deploy a genuinely impenetrable shield over the United States, we would be willing to spend not $40 billion, but any reasonable multiple of that amount that was necessary." For the full text of the speech see *Department of State Bulletin* 57, no. 1476 (1967): 443–451; the quotation is from pp. 447–448. See also Laurence W. Martin, "Ballistic Missile Defense and Europe," *Bulletin of the Atomic Scientists* 23, no. 5 (May 1967): 42–46; Louis Morton, "The Anti-ballistic Missile: Some Political and Strategic Considerations," *Virginia Quarterly Review* 42, no. 1 (Winter 1966): 28–42.

33. See J. I. Coffey, "Soviet ABM Policy: The Implications for the West," *International Affairs* 45, no. 2 (April 1969): 205–222; Coffey, "Strategic Superiority, Deterrence and Arms Control," *Orbis* 13, no. 4 (Winter 1970): 991–1007. On the Soviet incentives for limiting ballistic missile defenses (BMD) see Michael Mcc-Gwire, *Military Objectives in Soviet Foreign Policy* (Washington: Brookings Institution, 1987).

At the summit in Glassboro, New Jersey, in 1967, when President Johnson and Defense Secretary McNamara met with Alexei Kosygin, the American side could not persuade the Russians to give up their lead in ABM systems. See Raymond L. Garthoff, "SALT and the Soviet Military," *Problems of Communism* 24, no. 1 (January-February, 1975): 22.

34. In the debate in 1967–70 over the deployment of an American ABM system

there was relatively little discussion, outside a circle of strategic experts, of the technical, strategic merits or the technological feasibility of a ballistic missile defense. There was the more general fear that the United States would isolate itself politically and psychologically from Europe and move toward the strategy and diplomacy of a "Fortress America." On grounds of pure military strategy, the implications of freezing ABM systems allowed diametrically opposed interpretations. Although one could argue that the ABM treaty helped couple the United States to Europe because it kept America as vulnerable as Europe, one could also suggest that SALT I made "European governments feel more dependent on America and hence more vulnerable." See Ian Smart, "Perspectives from Europe," in Willrich and Rhinelander, SALT, pp. 185–208, esp. p. 187; John Newhouse, Cold Dawn: The Story of SALT (New York: Holt, Rinehart and Winston, 1973), p. 271.

35. Article 6 of the treaty, included at the insistence of nonnuclear powers, obliges the nuclear powers to pursue in good faith negotiations to curb the nuclear arms race, and clearly was intended to impose some parity of obligations on the nuclear haves and the nuclear have-nots.

36. During summer 1969, when both superpowers were preparing to negotiate some kind of agreement on slowing down the strategic weapons race, the joint communiqué issued by President Nixon and Chancellor Kiesinger after their meeting in Washington in August said that they believed progress in the arms limitation talks was "interrelated with a climate favorable for dealing with long-existing European problems."

37. Pierre Hassner, "Europe: Old Conflicts, New Rules," Orbis 17, no. 3 (Fall 1973): 895–912; the quotation is from p. 903.

38. Strictly speaking, MAD depended not only on proscribing heavy ABM systems, but also on the character and ways of deploying offensive weapons. Soviet strategists were reluctant to accept the legitimacy of MAD as such. See Robbin F. Laird's account in France, the Soviet Union and the Nuclear Weapons Issue (Boulder: Westview, 1985).

39. This specificity also applied to the Quadripartite Agreement on Berlin, as Henry Kissinger noted in his memoirs: "Berlin exceeded even SALT in its intricacy and esoteric jargon . . . the negotiation was encrusted by years of haggling over legalisms. There was scarcely any topic, from the exact form of a stamp on a pass to the legal status of the entire city, that had not been squabbled over with the Soviets in the 1950s and 1960s." White House Years (Boston: Little, Brown, 1979), p. 823. See also Seymour M. Hersh, The Price of Power: Kissinger in the Nixon White House (New York: Simon & Schuster, 1983), pp. 418ff; Alan B. Sherr, "The Languages of Arms Control," Bulletin of the Atomic Scientists 31, no. 11 (November 1975): 23–29.

40. Herbert Blankenhorn, Verständnis und Verständigung (Frankfurt am Main: Propyläen, 1980), pp. 558–559. The fundamentally opposed perceptions of Washington and Bonn on a desirable European political order that are reflected in this remark are truly ironic. Despite Blankenhorn's suggestion that the superpowers were not "urgently interested in a solution of European issues," they were in fact quite interested, except that their solution entailed solidifying the status quo rather than keeping it in flux, as was the German position in the 1960s.

41. See John G. Keliher, The Negotiations on Mutual and Balanced Force Reductions. The Search for Arms Control in Central Europe (New York: Pergamon, n.d.).

42. See John N. Yochelson, "MFR: West European and American Perspectives," in Wolfram F. Hanrieder, ed., *The United States and Western Europe: Political, Economic and Strategic Perspectives* (Cambridge, Mass.: Winthrop, 1974), pp. 251–281.

43. Wilhelm Grewe notes that the initial Western proposals for mutual balanced force reductions (put forth at Reykjavík in 1968) were aimed primarily at the Federal Republic. Wilhelm G. Grewe, *Die deutsche Frage in der Ost-West Spannung. Zeitgeschichtliche Kontroversen der achtziger Jahre* (Herford: Busse-Seewald, 1987), p. 18. See also *Strategic Survey, 1970* (London: International Institute for Strategic Studies, 1971), esp. p. 22.

44. MBFR was not sustained on the American side by well-thought-out concepts but seen as a device to check congressional efforts to reduce U.S. troop levels in Europe and as a countermove to proposals by the Eastern bloc for a European security conference. John N. Yochelson, "MBFR: The Search for an American Approach," *Orbis* 17, no. 1 (Spring 1973): 155–175.

45. For a discussion of the German viewpoint on MBFR see Helga Haftendorn, *Abrüstungs- und Entspannungspolitik zwischen Sicherheitsbefriedigung und Friedenssicherung. Zur Aussenpolitik der BRD, 1955–1973* (Düsseldorf: Bertelsmann, 1974), esp. pp. 239–294. See also Uwe Nerlich, "Die Rolle beiderseitiger Truppenverminderungen in der europäischen Sicherheitspolitik," *Europa-Archiv* 27, no. 5 (March 5, 1972): 161–168.

46. For a discussion of the connection between MBFR and the CSCE see Paul Noack, *Die Aussenpolitik der Bundesrepublik Deutschland*, 2d ed. (Stuttgart: W. Kohlhammer, 1972), pp. 150–159. See also Harmel Report on "The Future Tasks of the Alliance" (December 1967), in "Report of the Council," *Texts of Final Communiqués, 1949–1974* (Brussels: NATO Information Service, n.d.), pp. 198–202.

47. Grewe, *Rückblenden*, p. 674.

48. On the background of the West European and German attitudes before and during the SALT I negotiations see Ian Smart, "Perspectives from Europe". See also François de Rose, "The Future of SALT and Western Security in Europe," *Foreign Affairs* 57, no. 5 (Summer 1979): 1065–1074, esp. p. 1065.

49. Christopher J. Makins, "Bringing in the Allies," *Foreign Policy*, no. 35 (Summer 1979): 91–108, esp. p. 96.

50. The link between SALT II and SALT III was opposed by the French, who feared that limitations on Eurostrategic weapons would affect the validity of the NATO doctrine to protect France's neighbors and cause continuous difficulties between the United States and Europe. See de Rose, "Future of SALT"; Pierre Lellouche, "French Defense Policy," in Edwin H. Fedder, ed., *Defense Politics of the Atlantic Alliance* (New York: Praeger, 1980), pp. 31–47, esp. p. 41. Lellouche, pointing to the objections to SALT II voiced by most French security analysts, writes: "Essentially, SALT II is seen as reflecting a central strategic balance that is progressively shifting in favor of the Soviet Union. Even if this evolution is not perceived as directly affecting United States security . . . these changes are seen above all as adversely affecting the credibility of the U.S. guarantee to Europe" (p. 41).

51. Makins, "Bringing in the Allies," p. 92.

52. "An Interview with Helmut Schmidt," *Time*, June 11, 1979, pp. 39–40.

53. Manfred Wörner, "SALT II: A European Perspective," *Strategic Review* 7, no. 3 (Summer 1979): 10.

54. Josef Joffe, "Why Germans Support SALT," *Survival* 21, no. 5 (September-October 1979): 209–212.

55. U.S. Senate, Committee on Foreign Relations, *The SALT II Treaty: Hearings,* pt. 3, p. 92.

56. *Department of State Bulletin* 66, no. 1722 (Washington: GPO, 1972): 892–893.

57. Many Europeans shared the view expressed by McGeorge Bundy in 1969: "The strength of the American guarantee will be neither increased nor decreased by acceptance of parity, and the level of American commitment in Europe is not a proper topic for bargaining in the SALT talks. It was never the American superiority in nuclear weapons that was decisive in protecting Europe; it was simply the high probability that any large-scale use of force against a NATO country would set loose a chain of events that could lead to nuclear war. . . . The relative numbers of weapons have never been decisive in the credibility of the American deterrent in Europe." McGeorge Bundy, "To Cap the Volcano," *Foreign Affairs* 48, no. 1 (October 1969): 1–20; the quotation appears on p. 18. See also Andrew J. Pierre, "The SALT Agreement and Europe," *World Today* 28, no. 7 (July 1972): 281–288, esp. p. 285.

58. "Any examination of the defense of NATO runs into two problems. First, reasonable judgments about the Soviet Union, however alarmist, recognize that Moscow has no immediate national interest in starting large-scale military actions in Europe . . . The probability of war in Europe as judged by political leaders has always seemed low, and there is little sign that this judgment has changed. . . . The second problem in examining NATO defense is that it involves so many bizarre issues, especially when tactical nuclear weapons are brought into the picture, that an analysis of the problem in peacetime takes on an aura of either sterility or surrealism." Paul Bracken, "The NATO Defense Problem," *Orbis* 27, no. 1 (Spring 1983): 83–106; the quotation appears on p. 83.

59. Makins, "Bringing in the Allies," p. 94.

60. Thomas C. Schelling has argued that "the main difference between pre-1971 and post-1972 arms negotiations has been the shift of interest from the *character* of weapons to their *numbers*. . . . Until the emergence of a Strategic Defense Initiative (SDI) in 1983, for the last 13 years the focus of arms control has been on offensive weapons. I judge the proposals and negotiations on offensive weapons to have been mostly mindless, without a guiding philosophy. What guiding philosophy there used to be has got lost along the way" (italics in original). "What Went Wrong with Arms Control," *Foreign Affairs* 64, no. 2 (Winter 1985–86): 219–233; the quotation appears on p. 225.

61. Pierre Hassner has noted that this applies to West Europeans in general: "In a time of parity . . . Europeans worry (and are encouraged to do so by authoritative Americans) about the future of extended deterrence and fear U.S. strategic decoupling. On the other hand . . . [they] try even harder to decouple intra-European détente from conflicts in other parts of the world . . . and from Soviet-U.S. relations." Hassner, "Recurrent Stresses, Resilient Structures," in Robert W. Tucker and Linda Wrigley, eds., *The Atlantic Alliance and Its Critics* (New York: Praeger, 1983), pp. 61–94; the quotation appears on p. 73.

For a contrary view see Philip Windsor, who has argued that "the notion that 'détente is divisible' was never a West German one. Bonn still accepts that any continuing association with the GDR, even for limited common objectives, can be based only on a stable and enduring understanding of the rules of super-power relations." *Germany and the Western Alliance: Lessons from the 1980 Crises*, Adelphi Paper no. 170 (London: International Institute for Strategic Studies, 1981), p. 14.

One of the most striking examples of the German desire to separate détente from (plausible) deterrence is the speech delivered by Günther Gaus in November 1981 to members of the SPD in Berlin, in which he called for a return to a NATO policy of massive retaliation and a scrapping of flexible response, because this would allow the removal of U.S. nuclear weapons from Central Europe and thus enhance the prospects of East-West détente. See Theodore Draper, "The Phantom Alliance," in Tucker and Wrigley, *The Atlantic Alliance*, pp. 1–28, esp. pp. 12–13. Further on the German interest in the divisibility of détente see Wilhelm G. Grewe, *Deutsche Frage*, p. 128.

CHAPTER 4: *The Eurostrategic Balance, Arms Control, and SDI*

Epigraphs. William G. Hyland, "The Struggle for Europe: An American View," in Andrew J. Pierre, ed., *Nuclear Weapons in Europe* (New York: Council on Foreign Relations, 1984), p. 15; Robert W. Tucker, "The Nuclear Debate," *Foreign Affairs* 63, no. 1 (Fall 1984): 31.

1. Wilhelm G. Grewe, *Rückblenden, 1976–1951* (Frankfurt am Main: Propyläen, 1979), pp. 679–680.

2. On the programmatic origin of the SS-20 see Raymond L. Garthoff, "The SS-20 Decision," *Survival* 25, no. 3 (May-June 1983): 110–119. Garthoff did not see the SS-20 as an "interim ersatz deterrent, but as a key continuing element in a comprehensive structure of military forces," and suggested that "a clearer understanding of the reason for the Soviet deployment could have affected importantly the nature of the Western response." Raymond L. Garthoff, *Détente and Confrontation: American-Soviet Relations from Nixon to Reagan* (Washington: Brookings Institution, 1985), p. 872.

3. This notion of deterrence could possibly be redefined in the future, and might develop into a commitment to deter with U.S. nuclear weapons first use of theater nuclear weapons by the Soviet Union as part of a strategy in which conventional forces otherwise dominated.

4. Helmut Schmidt, "1977 Alastair Buchan Memorial Lecture," *Survival* 20, no. 1 (January-February 1978): 2–10. For the background and political context see Helga Haftendorn, "Das doppelte Missverständnis: Zur Vorgeschichte des NATO-Doppelbeschlusses von 1979," *Vierteljahreshefte für Zeitgeschichte* 33, no. 2 (February 1985): 244–287; Haftendorn, "Germany and the Euromissile Debate," *International Journal* 40, no. 1 (Winter 1984–85): 68–85; Raymond L. Garthoff, "The NATO Decision on Theater Nuclear Forces," *Political Science Quarterly* 98, no. 2 (Summer 1983): 197–214; James A. Thompson, "The LRTNF Decision: Evolution of US Theater Nuclear Policy, 1975–9," *International Affairs* 60, no. 4 (Fall 1984): 601–614; Lothar Ruehl, "Der Beschluss der NATO zur Einführung nuklearer Mittelstreckenwaffen," *Europa-Archiv* 35, no. 4 (1980): 99–110; David N. Schwartz, *NATO's Nuclear Dilemmas* (Washington: Brookings Institution, 1983), pp. 201–216. For a full account see Hubertus Hoffmann, *Die Atompartner Washington-Bonn und die Modernisierung der taktischen Kernwaffen: Vorgeschichte und Management der Neutronenwaffe und des Doppelbeschlusses der NATO* (Koblenz: Bernard & Graefe, 1986). Hoffmann's

central point is that the United States has for decades concentrated its efforts on strategic and tactical nuclear weapons, and since the mid-1960s sought a zero solution to the problem of medium-range missiles. See also Lothar Ruehl, *Mittelstreckenwaffen in Europa. Ihre Bedeutung in Strategie, Rüstungskontrolle und Bündnispolitik* (Baden-Baden: Nomos, 1987).

Even before Schmidt's speech, two NATO panels, one dealing with military aspects, the other with arms control, had begun deliberations on the issues raised by the Eurostrategic imbalance. On the more technical and strategic aspects of the Eurostrategic balance, François de Rose has argued that the need to introduce Pershing and cruise missiles stemmed from the increasing difficulty of NATO's air forces to penetrate Soviet defenses and was "justified less from a desire to counter-balance or equal the SS-20 than from a desire to reestablish the possibility of attacking the main enemy, and the only enemy to possess nuclear weapons, on their own ground. Consequently, even if the Soviet Union had not modernized her arsenal, the West would have had to modernize theirs. The real changes have taken place in the area of vulnerabilities. The vulnerability of Europe has worsened whereas that of the Soviet Union has continuously decreased." "Nuclear Forces and Alliance Relations: Updating Deterrence in Europe—Inflexible Response?" in Robert Nurick, ed., *Nuclear Weapons and European Security* (New York: St. Martin's for the International Institute for Strategic Studies, 1984), pp. 123–127; the quotation is from p. 124. See also in the same volume Christopher Makins, "TNF Modernization and Countervailing Strategy," pp. 128–135.

5. Zbigniew Brzezinski, President Carter's national security adviser, wrote: "I was personally never persuaded that we needed [the new weapons] for military reasons. I was persuaded reluctantly that we needed [them] to obtain European support for SALT. This was largely because Chancellor Schmidt made such a big deal out of the so-called Eurostrategic imbalance that was being generated by the Soviet deployment of the SS-20. To keep him in line we felt that some response in Europe on the intermediate level would be necessary." Quoted in Strobe Talbott, *Deadly Gambits* (New York: Alfred A. Knopf, 1984), p. 33.

For more on the American perspective see James R. Schlesinger, *The Theater Nuclear Force Posture in Europe: A Report to the United States Congress* (April 1975), repr. in Robert J. Pranger and Roger P. Labrie, eds., *Nuclear Strategy and National Security: Points of View* (Washington: American Enterprise Institute, 1977), pp. 167–188; Richard Burt, "The SS-20 and the Strategic Balance," *World Today* 33, no. 2 (February 1977): 43–51; Burt, "The Scope and Limits of SALT," *Foreign Affairs* 56, no. 4 (July 1978): 751–770; Zbigniew Brzezinski, *Power and Principle: Memoirs of the National Security Adviser, 1977–1981* (New York: Farrar, Straus and Giroux, 1983); Cyrus Vance, *Hard Choices: Four Critical Years in America's Foreign Policy* (New York: Simon & Schuster, 1983), esp. p. 67.

6. See Helga Haftendorn, *Security and Détente: Conflicting Priorities in German Foreign Policy* (New York: Praeger, 1985), pp. 142–143.

7. This difference in perception was expressed in official documents. While Bonn stressed those aspects of theater nuclear forces that coupled them with American strategic nuclear forces, Washington underlined the possibilities that theater nuclear weapons offered for delaying an American strategic response. See the German Defense Ministry's *White Paper, 1979: The Security of the Federal Republic of Germany and the Development of the Federal Armed Forces* (Bonn: Federal Minister

of Defence, 1979), p. 107: U.S. Department of Defense, Secretary of Defense, *Annual Defense Department Report, Fiscal Year 1980* (Washington: GPO, 1979), p. 84.

8. As Christoph Bertram has pointed out, however, "The limitations imposed by SALT on strategic forces would make regional imbalances more dangerous only if the remaining strategic forces were clearly insufficient to counter unfavorable regional asymmetries (and they are not) or if they implied that Soviet advantages could not be offset by commensurate U.S. force programs (they also do not). . . . Escalation dominance [moreover] suggests a tidiness of categories of nuclear weapons and a tidiness in nuclear escalation processes that belongs more to the theoretical scenarios of Western strategic analysts than to the realities of a world in crisis or at war." "Political Implications of the Theater Nuclear Balance," in Barry M. Blechman, ed., *Rethinking the U.S. Strategic Posture* (Cambridge, Mass.: Ballinger, 1982), pp. 101–128; the quotation is from p. 104.

9. In 1978 Defense Minister Hans Apel was reported to be "concerned that a new buildup of [intermediate-range weapons] in Western Europe to match the Soviets could eventually 'decouple' the U.S. commitment to defend Europe with long-range strategic weapons if necessary." *Washington Post*, December 1, 1978, sec. A, p. 29. See also Graeme P. Auton, "European Security and the INF Dilemma: Is There a Better Way?" *Arms Control* 5, no. 1 (May 1984): 3–53; Robert J. Art, "Fixing Atlantic Bridges," *Foreign Policy*, no. 46 (Spring 1982): 67–85, esp. p. 77; Glenn H. Snyder, "The Security Dilemma in Alliance Politics," *World Politics* 36, no. 4 (July 1984): 461–495, esp. pp. 491–495; J. Michael Legge, *Theater Nuclear Weapons and the NATO Strategy of Flexible Response* (Santa Monica: RAND Corp., 1983); Schwartz, *NATO's Nuclear Dilemmas*; Jeffrey D. Boutwell, Paul Doty, and Gregory F. Treverton, eds., *The Nuclear Confrontation in Europe* (Dover, Mass.: Auburn House, 1985).

After Schmidt's speech in London, the French foreign minister, Louis de Guiringaud, criticized Schmidt for having raised the issue, saying that he considered such arguments dangerous: "The Eurostrategic concept on which they are based presumes that a European theater-nuclear balance can exist that is separated and isolated from other elements of deterrence. This would lead directly to the decoupling that they are trying to avoid. That is, it would be equivalent to recognizing that the central strategic forces of the U.S. do not protect Western Europe." Cited in David S. Yost, "Beyond SALT II: European Security and the Prospects for SALT III," *Orbis* 24, no. 3 (Fall 1980): 625–655; the quotation appears on p. 644. David Owen, a former British foreign secretary, made a similar argument. See *Survival* 22, no. 3 (May–June 1980): 121–124.

10. See Henry Kissinger, "A Plan to Reshape NATO," *Time*, March 5, 1984, pp. 20–24, esp. p. 20.

11. Interview with author, October 14, 1982. With respect to Soviet political pressures stemming from the INF imbalance see also Karl Kaiser et al., "Nuclear Weapons and the Preservation of Peace," *Foreign Affairs* 60, no. 5 (Summer 1983): 1157–1170, esp. p. 1167.

12. For an argument stressing the consequences for military strategy of the Eurostrategic imbalance see Dennis M. Gormley, "A New Dimension to Soviet Theater Strategy," *Orbis* 29, no. 3 (Fall 1985): 537–569. On the Soviet air threat to Europe see Joshua Epstein, *Measuring Military Power* (Princeton: Princeton University Press, 1984), pp. 10–13, app. C.

13. For an analysis of the psychological and domestic political background on the INF issue in the Federal Republic see Stanley Hoffmann, "NATO and Nuclear Weapons: Reason and Unreason," *Foreign Affairs* 60, no. 2 (Winter 1981–82): 327–346; Thomas Risse-Kappen, *The Zero Option* (Boulder: Westview, 1988).

14. See *Strategic Survey, 1978* (London: International Institute for Strategic Studies, 1979), p. 10. See also Sherri L. Wasserman, *The Neutron Bomb Controversy: A Study in Alliance Politics* (New York: Praeger, 1983); Alex A. Vardamis, "German-American Military Fissures," *Foreign Policy*, no. 34 (Spring 1979): 87–106; Lothar Ruehl, "Die Nichtentscheidung über die 'Neutronenwaffe,'" *Europa-Archiv* 34, no. 5 (1979): 137–150.

15. See Theodor H. Winkler, *Arms Control and the Politics of European Security*, Adelphi Paper no. 177 (London: International Institute for Strategic Studies, 1982).

16. In a speech delivered in Moscow in June 1984, Horst Teltschik, a senior adviser to Chancellor Kohl on security and foreign affairs, said that "the last substantial proposals from the USA at the INF negotiations in Geneva, at the MBFR negotiations in Vienna and at the Geneva negotiations on the worldwide ban of chemical weapons were largely brought about by the Federal Government and other European partners who exercised a major influence on them." (Bonn-St. Augustin: Konrad-Adenauer-Stiftung, mimeographed, n.d.), p. 16.

17. Talbott, *Deadly Gambits*; Gregg Herken, *Counsels of War* (New York: Oxford University Press, 1987), esp. chap. 27.

18. Robert H. Johnson, "Periods of Peril: The Window of Vulnerability and Other Myths," *Foreign Affairs* 61, no. 4 (Spring 1983): 950–970.

19. The reluctance of the Reagan administration to make arms control a centerpiece of the summit in Geneva between the president and General Secretary Mikhail S. Gorbachev in fall 1985, and its stress instead on "bilateral" issues in the Third World, merely strengthened the Europeans' suspicions that Washington was fundamentally uninterested in détente and arms control. It was precisely these issues that had endangered the prospects of arms control and doomed détente in the 1970s. While Moscow was placing arms control at the center of its negotiating agenda with Washington (as it had also done during the Nixon and Carter administrations), the Reagan administration sought to broaden the focus to encompass the settlement of regional disputes (such as those in Afghanistan and Angola) and human rights.

20. "High Soviet officials, their aides, and their experts believe that President Reagan is determined to deny the Soviet Union nothing less than its legitimacy and status as a global power. This status, they thought, had been conceded once and for all by Reagan's predecessors, not to speak of America's allies. They believe President Reagan would deny them the respect and international influence due them as an inevitable consequence of what they see as the most important accomplishment in their postrevolutionary history—the achievement of military parity with the West. A rekindled sense of insecurity fires an angry and defiant response, a desire to lash out, to reassert self-esteem, to restore the diminished respect of others." Seweryn Bialer, "Danger in Moscow," *New York Review of Books*, February 16, 1984, p. 6.

21. U.S. Department of Defense, *Annual Report to the Congress: Fiscal Year 1983* (Washington, 1982), sec. I, pp. 13–17. For a list of some of the more strident views

expressed by the administration see Richard J. Barnet, "Annals of Diplomacy: Alliance-II," *New Yorker*, October 17, 1983, pp. 94–167. For the political importance of rhetoric to the Soviet Union and the debilitating effect in Moscow of the Reagan administration's verbal posturing see Bialer, "Danger in Moscow," p. 6.

22. Helmut Schmidt, *A Grand Strategy for the West: The Anachronism of National Strategies in an Interdependent World* (New Haven and London: Yale University Press, 1985), p. 21. Many Europeans considered the Reagan administration's view of the Soviet Union similar to the one Edmund Burke expressed about the French Revolution in his *Second Letter on a Regicide Peace*: "I never thought we could make peace with the [Jacobin] system; because it was not for the sake of an object that we pursued in rivalry with each other, but with the system itself, that we were at war. As I understood the matter, we were at war not with its conduct, but with its existence; convinced that its existence and its hostility were the same." For an early German assessment of the Reagan administration see Hartmut Wasser, ed., *Die Ära Reagan. Eine erste Bilanz* (Stuttgart: Klett-Cotta, 1988).

23. The abortive "walk-in-the-woods" compromise, which envisaged a significant leveling down of Eurostrategic systems on both sides, would have been acceptable to the Germans had they been asked. See Talbott, *Deadly Gambits*, esp. pp. 116–151. In 1985 Helmut Schmidt wrote, "In the summer of 1982, Nitze, in the course of the famous walk in the woods outside Geneva with his Soviet counterpart, introduced a compromise formula for an INF arms limitation agreement. I would still buy his formula at the drop of a hat, because it was a wise compromise. But without consulting, without even informing, their allies, both Moscow and Nitze's own administration in Washington rejected the compromise." *Grand Strategy*, p. 60.

24. In an interview on January 2, 1982, Chancellor Schmidt said of the NATO double-track decision: "For Germany it is a most difficult situation, for already we have some 5,000 American atomic weapons on our soil. Germany is about the size of Oregon, populated not by three million people but by over 60 million people. Think of a situation where an American Administration puts 5,000 nuclear rockets into Oregon and makes plans for adding some hundreds that could hit the Soviet Union and thereby make Oregon a great target area for Soviet missiles. It was a hard decision. I was instrumental in taking that decision and I am going to stick to it and I am not going to be inhibited by demonstrations.

"On the other hand, the attempts to scare the Europeans by the threat to withdraw American military forces from Europe is a futile effort. My first discussion on that subject took place over a quarter of a century ago. Such discussions come and go and come and go. You would abdicate from your leadership role in the Western world and I think that the political elites in the U.S. will always be sober enough not really to consider such a fatal move." *Documents on Disarmament, 1982* (Washington: U.S. Arms Control and Disarmament Agency, 1985), p. 1.

25. Should the Germans have required further demonstration of that reality, it was provided for them when in a speech to the *Bundestag* in January 1983, President François Mitterrand of France supported the Kohl government in its determination to implement the NATO double-track decision, while his fellow Socialists on the opposition benches were sitting on their hands amid the applause of the Christian Democrats.

26. Helmut Kohl, "Erklärung des Bundeskanzlers, 15 May 1987," *Bulletin*, no. 46 (Bonn: Presse- und Informationsamt der Bundesregierung, May 20, 1987), pp. 413–414.

27. Henry Kissinger reported that an eminent European said to him after the Reykjavík summit of 1986: "The [medium-range] missiles were a corset that ties Germany to the West. You are now destroying that corset and we will have to pay the price for it." *Newsweek*, October 12, 1987, p. 58. A similar sentiment was expressed by the *Economist* (January 23, 1988, p. 12), which editorialized that for the Federal Republic "going non-nuclear is near to going neutralist."

28. *New York Times*, February 10, 1988, p. 8Y.

29. Helmut Kohl, Address to the Chicago Council on Foreign Relations, October 23, 1986; repr. in *Bulletin*, no. 131 (Bonn: Presse- und Informationsamt der Bundesregierung, October 31, 1986): 1100–1104.

30. For a discussion of the problems connected with the MBFR negotiations in the 1980s and of the East-West Conference on Disarmament (CDE) at Stockholm see Jonathan Dean, "Arms Control in Europe: Prospects and Problems," in Wolfram F. Hanrieder, ed., *Arms Control, the FRG, and the Future of East-West Relations* (Boulder: Westview, 1987), pp. 49–60.

31. *NATO Review* 35, no. 3 (June 1987): 30.

32. G. Jonathan Greenwald, "Vienna: A Challenge for the Western Alliance," *Aussenpolitik* 38 (2d Quarter 1987): 155–167; the quotation appears on p. 167. Greenwald also provides a summary of the differing views within the Western alliance on the purposes and functioning of the third CSCE follow-up conference.

33. Sidney D. Drell, "Star Wars and Arms Control," in Hanrieder, *Arms Control*, pp. 77–84.

34. The declaration of an intent to shift to a "defense-dominant" strategy emanated primarily from the White House. The Pentagon was consistently more cautious, referring often to "intermediate" BMD architectures that would provide a defense only for hardened military assets, thereby bolstering rather than supplanting deterrence. See for example U.S. Department of Defense, *Report to the Congress on the Strategic Defense Initiative* (Washington: Department of Defense, 1985).

35. "[SDI] will introduce into a remarkably stable strategic relationship between East and West an unprecedented degree of uncertainty and nervousness. And it will introduce into the European-American relationship—a relationship that despite repeated strains and occasional dissent had on balance remained harmonious and well-functioning—a profound rift that could break up the Western alliance for good." Christoph Bertram, "Strategic Defense and the Western Alliance," *Daedalus* 114, no. 3 (Summer 1985): 281. For more on the German perspective see Ernst-Otto Czempiel, "SDI and NATO: The Case of the Federal Republic of Germany," in Sanford Lakoff and Randy Willoughby, *Strategic Defense and the Western Alliance* (Lexington, Mass.: D. C. Heath-Lexington Books, 1987), pp. 147–164; Paul E. Zinner, "German and U.S. Perceptions of Arms Control," in Hanrieder, *Arms Control*, pp. 11–28; Hans Günter Brauch, ed., *Star Wars and European Defense* (New York: St. Martin's, 1987), esp. chap. 6; Ivo H. Daalder, *The SDI Challenge to Europe* (Cambridge, Mass.: Ballinger, 1987), esp. pp. 17ff. (Reprinted in Daalder are the German-American agreements on German participation in SDI research and on technology transfers.)

36. To be sure, the strategic ideas and political aspirations reflected in the missile defense program were not totally new. In some ways, the debate occasioned by SDI was similar to the antiballistic missile debate of the late 1960s and early 1970s. Also, each American president beginning with Eisenhower had considered the feasibility of augmenting deterrence with defense, and each American administration had in some form expressed uneasiness about a nuclear strategy so dependent on the rationality of an opponent and carrying such a heavy risk for the American people. In a sense, SDI sought a return to the strategic situation of the 1950s, a view expressed by Secretary of Defense Caspar W. Weinberger: "If we can get a system which is effective and which we know can render their weapons impotent, we could be back in a situation we were in, for example, when we were the only nation with a nuclear weapon." Quoted in George W. Ball, "The War for Star Wars," *New York Review of Books*, April 11, 1985, p. 40.

37. At the conclusion of a meeting of the NATO Nuclear Planning Group in Turkey in 1984 Wörner expressed the view that SDI could destabilize the East-West military balance, decouple the United States from Europe, and split the Western alliance. (Interview, Associated Press and Deutsche Press-Agentur, April 8, 1984). For Rühle's concerns see "Löcher im Drahtverhau der Sicherheitsdoktrin. Das Defensivkonzept der Zukunft löst Europas Probleme kaum," *Christ und Welt/Rheinischer Merkur* 38, no. 13 (April 1, 1983): 3. For their changes of mind see Rühle, "Gorbachev's 'Star Wars,'" *NATO Review* 33, no. 4 (August 1985): 26–32; his interview "An die Grenzen der Technologie," *Der Spiegel* 39, no. 48 (1985): 155–159; "Wie kam es zu SDI?" *Standpunkte zu SDI in West und Ost* (Melle: Ernst Knoth, 1985), pp. 9–30; and the speech by Wörner at the *Wehrkundetag 1986* in Munich (*Süddeutsche Zeitung*, March 3, 1986, p. 6). In fall 1987 the German defense minister was placed in a similarly embarrassing position when he felt compelled once the double-zero proposal had been announced to welcome it at the autumn meeting of the Western defense ministers in Monterey, California, although he had strenuously opposed it during the spring meeting at Stavanger, Norway. See *New York Times*, November 4, 1987, p. 7Y. On the German Social Democrats' opposition to SDI see Czempiel, *SDI and NATO*, pp. 156–158; Schmidt, *Grand Strategy*, pp. 18, 39, 61, 63; Eckhard Lübkemeier, "Which SDI?" in Wolfram F. Hanrieder, ed., *Arms Control, the FRG, and the Future of East-West Relations* (Boulder: Westview, 1987), pp. 85–102. See also Andreas von Bülow, *Alpträume West gegen Alpträume Ost. Ein Beitrag zur Bedrohungsanalyse* (Bonn: Vorstand der SPD, Abteilung Presse und Information, 1984). On the political repercussions in Germany of von Bülow's paper see *Der Spiegel* 39, no. 38 (1985): 24.

38. When asked if he thought an exchange of nuclear weapons in Europe between the United States and the Soviet Union could be limited, or if escalation was inevitable, President Reagan replied: "I could see where you could have the exchange of tactical weapons in the field without it bringing either one of the major powers to pushing the button." *Washington Post*, November 1, 1981.

39. See Schmidt, *Grand Strategy*, pp. 36–37.

40. For a hopeful view of the technological benefits of SDI for Western Europe see Konrad Seitz, "SDI: Die technische Herausforderung für Europa," *Europa-Archiv* 40, no. 13 (1985): 381–390. For a critique of Bonn's waffling on SDI see Uwe Nerlich, "Folgerungen aus SDI für Strategie. Rüstungskontrolle und Politik. Zum

Entscheidungsbedarf der Bundesrepublik Deutschland," *Europa-Archiv* 41, no. 4 (1986): 88–98.

See also the study by Wolfgang Schreiber, *Die Strategische Verteidigungsinitiative. Vorgeschichte, Konzeption, Perspektiven*, Forschungsberichte, vol. 45 (Melle: Ernst Knoth, 1985), undertaken by the Konrad-Adenauer-Foundation. This study is especially interesting because of its rather positive if guarded view of SDI, and yet it concludes that the Federal Republic should expect the United States to scrap its policy of deterring the Soviet Union through the threat of nuclear weapons. This argument, at the conclusion of a 140-page study, practically accepts as a given the nuclear decoupling of the United States from Europe.

41. Already in the 1960s the Federal Republic of Germany's ambassador to Washington (and later to NATO) noted that "integration is without a doubt an effective hegemonial instrument of the most powerful in the alliance," and that NATO "is in a phase in which it fulfills its defense functions only in a reduced measure, in which its . . . functions in East-West relations are not noticeable, but in which its control function over the German partner has moved more strongly into the foreground." Grewe, *Rückblenden*, pp. 791, 797.

42. See McGeorge Bundy et al., "Nuclear Weapons and the Atlantic Alliance," *Foreign Affairs* 60, no. 4 (Spring 1982): 753–768. For a German response see Karl Kaiser et. al., "Nuclear Weapons." See also Robert S. McNamara, "The Military Role of Nuclear Weapons: Perceptions and Misperceptions," *Foreign Affairs* 62, no. 1 (Fall 1983): 59–80.

43. Michael Howard, "Reassurance and Deterrence: Western Defense in the 1980s," *Foreign Affairs* 61, no. 2 (Winter 1982–83): 309–314; the quotation is from p. 354. See also Hedley Bull, "European Self-Reliance and the Reform of NATO," *Foreign Affairs* 61, no. 4 (Spring 1983): 874–892; Gen. Bernard W. Rogers, "The Atlantic Alliance: Prescription for a Difficult Decade," *Foreign Affairs* 60, no. 5 (Summer 1982): 1145–1156; Rogers, "Greater Flexibility for NATO's Flexible Response," *Strategic Review* 11, no. 2 (Spring 1983): 11–19; Bundy et al., "Nuclear Weapons"; Report of the European Security Study, *Strengthening Conventional Deterrence in Europe: Proposals for the 1980s* (New York: St. Martin's, 1983); John D. Steinbruner and Leon V. Sigal, eds., *Alliance Security: NATO and the No-First-Use Question* (Washington: Brookings Institution, 1983), esp. the two chapters by William W. Kaufmann; Samuel P. Huntington, "Conventional Deterrence and Conventional Retaliation in Europe," *International Security* 8, no. 3 (Winter 1983–84): 32–56; John J. Mearsheimer, *Conventional Deterrence* (Ithaca: Cornell University Press, 1983). Initially, President Reagan's speech on SDI of March 1983 was also to have called for a Conventional Defense Initiative, based on sophisticated conventional weaponry. See Herken, *Counsels of War*, pp. 343–344.

44. Schmidt, *Grand Strategy*, pp. 40–41, 56–57. For a sharp attack on the idea of a Franco-German security condominium (and Helmut Schmidt's support of it) see Thomas-Peter Gallon, "Lieber stocknüchtern als 'frankophil.' Ketzerisches über die Voraussetzungen eines fruchtbaren französisch-deutschen Führungsverhältnisses," *Die Neue Gesellschaft/Frankfurter Hefte* 34, no. 8 (August 1987): 743–749; see also Robbin F. Laird, *France, the Soviet Union and the Nuclear Weapons Issue* (Boulder: Westview, 1985).

45. See Huntington, "Conventional Deterrence and Conventional Retaliation"; Richard K. Betts, "Conventional Deterrence: Predictive Uncertainty and

NOTES TO PAGES 127–128

Policy Confidence," *World Politics* 37, no. 2 (January 1985): 153–179. For a generally skeptical view of the possibilities of conventional deterrence see James R. Golden et al., eds., *Conventional Deterrence: Alternatives for European Defense* (Lexington, Mass.: D. C. Heath, 1984). On the difficulties of weapons standardization see Keith Hartley, *NATO Arms Cooperation* (Boston: George Allen & Unwin, 1983). See also the discussion in chap. 1 of the problem connected with conventional deterrence. For a French perspective see Françoise Manfrass-Sirjacques, "Null— und was dann? Die deutsch-französischen Beziehungen in der Perspektive eines nuklearwaffenfreien Europas," *Die Neue Gesellschaft/Frankfurter Hefte* 34, no. 8 (August 1987): 734–743.

46. See Thomas Schelling, "What Went Wrong with Arms Control," *Foreign Affairs* 64, no. 2 (Winter 1985–86): 219–233, esp. p. 232.

47. Robert W. Tucker, "The Nuclear Debate," *Foreign Affairs* 63, no. 1 (Fall 1984): 1–32; the quotation appears on p. 31. See also by the same author *The Nuclear Debate: Deterrence and the Lapse of Faith* (New York: Holmes & Meier, 1985).

48. On the unilateralist potential of SDI see Townsend Hoopes, "Star-Wars: A Way of Going It Alone," *New York Times*, January 2, 1986, p. 19Y. But Europeans also objected to American unilateralism of a different kind and on a smaller scale. The Germans in particular were disturbed when the United States, without consulting or even informing them, used military facilities in the Federal Republic for the air raid in April 1986 against Libya and again in June 1986 (as the report of the Tower Commission revealed) to sell arms to Iran.

49. For example, Gary Wills points out how SDI "fits Reagan's foreign-policy pattern of aggressive withdrawal." *Reagan's America: Innocents at Home* (Garden City, N.Y.: Doubleday, 1987), p. 360.

50. This line of thinking is especially pronounced with Americans who urge an American diplomacy more oriented toward the Pacific, an attitude deeply rooted in the present administration as well as in some segments of the Republican party, and which also tends to be connected with a preference for a maritime strategy. See the speech made in 1951 by Sen. Robert Taft (*97th Congressional Record*, 82d Cong., 1st sess.), pp. 54–61; Wolfram F. Hanrieder, "Grundprobleme der deutsch-amerikanischen Beziehungen," *Merkur* 37, no. 5 (July 1983): 518–530. For a European perspective see Eberhard Rhein, "Die pazifische Herausforderung. Gefahren und Chancen für Europa," *Europa-Archiv* 39, no. 4 (1984): 101–110.

51. Robert W. Komer, "Maritime Strategy vs. Coalition Defense," *Foreign Affairs* 60, no. 5 (Summer 1982): 1124–1144; the quotation appears on p. 1130. Colin S. Gray has argued that the Reagan administration has not sought a unilateralist maritime alternative to a continental coalition strategy. See "Keeping the Soviets Landlocked: Geostrategy for a Maritime America," *National Interest*, no. 4 (Summer 1986): 24–36, esp. p. 35 n. 10. For more on the debate see John J. Mearsheimer, "A Strategic Misstep: The Maritime Strategy and Deterrence in Europe"; Linton F. Brooks, "Naval Power and National Security: The Case for the Maritime Strategy," both in *International Security* 11, no. 2 (Fall 1986): 3–57, 58–88; Robert W. Komer, *Maritime Strategy or Coalition Defense?* (Cambridge, Mass.: Abt, 1984); Capt. Peter M. Swartz, "Contemporary U.S. Naval Strategy: A Bibliography," suppl. to *Proceedings* [U.S. Naval Institute] 112, no. 1 (January 1986): 41–47.

The navy has historically preferred the Pacific theater over the European one. See Vince Davis, *Postwar Defense Policy and the U.S. Navy, 1943–1946* (Chapel Hill: University of North Carolina Press, 1962), pp. 76–80. In the mid-1950s Adm. Arleigh Burke, former chief of naval operations, noted: "Naval forces, because of the Pacific Ocean and the geographical positions of the potential enemy, will be the primary sources of U.S. strength in the Western Pacific, whereas in the European Theater, other elements of this and other nations' armed forces would most surely predominate." Quoted in Lt. Cdr. Joseph A. Sestak, Jr., "Righting the Atlantic Tilt," *Proceedings* [U.S. Naval Institute] 112, no. 1 (January 1986): 66.

52. As long ago as the 1930s, the fundamental differences in the Atlantic and Pacific orientations of American diplomacy were analyzed by Charles and Mary Beard, who labeled them "collective internationalism" and "imperial isolationism" respectively. See *America in Midpassage* (New York: Macmillan, 1939). See also Alexander DeConde, ed., *Isolation and Security* (Durham: Duke University Press, 1957). The best historical account of these powerful compulsions remains Selig Adler's *The Isolationist Impulse: Its Twentieth-Century Reaction* (New York: Free Press, 1957). Adler points in particular to the historical connection between the isolationist impulse and a Pacific-oriented geopolitical orientation. Speaking of the latter part of the nineteenth century, Adler notes that "Americans seemed far less afraid of entanglement in the Orient. Here we could spread the Gospel, extend trade, urge reform, and diffuse American ideas without danger of *immediate* political involvement. There was no fear of being contaminated by Asiatic ideas" (italics in original). Of the 1950s Adler writes, "It is no accident that a group of present-day isolationists . . . think of the Far East and not Europe as our primary line of defense against the Communist thrust. American isolationism and an exaggerated American concern for Asia bear a close historical relationship" (pp. 24–25). For a more recent argument along the same lines see Joseph Nye, Jr., "Farewell to Arms Control?" *Foreign Affairs* 65, no. 1 (Fall 1986): 1–20, esp. pp. 19–20.

53. On the other hand, Robert E. Osgood saw in 1981 the revitalization of containment as the core of the Reagan administration's foreign policy, even though he also pointed to the unilateral aspect of Washington's defense buildup, its stress on sea power, and its turning away from a "Eurocentered" American strategy. Osgood also noted that "Secretary Weinberger explicitly rejected the artificial constraints implied by previous commitments to a 1½- or 2½-war strategy. If one took his repeated statements about the need to meet Soviet aggression in one location by responding to points of vulnerability elsewhere—a concept soon dubbed 'horizontal escalation'—as a strategy with operational significance, this would put an even higher premium on a multi-theater capability. For no one could reasonably assume in the 1980s that the threat to respond at 'places of our choosing' would—as John Foster Dulles seemed to hope when he used the same phrase in the 1950s—so enhance deterrence as to obviate the necessity of fighting local wars at all." "The Revitalization of Containment," *Foreign Affairs* 60, no. 3 (special issue: "America and the World, 1981"): 465–502, esp. pp. 476, 482; see also Paul Seabury, "Containment Redivivus: Playing a More Aggressive Game," *International Security Review* 6, no. 1 (Spring 1981): 57–78.

54. Some would not consider disengagement a calamity. For example, Robert W. Tucker notes: "A great nuclear state, able to destroy any other state or com-

bination of states, is no longer dependent on balance-of-power considerations for its core security. It possesses what was heretofore considered unachievable: a surfeit of deterrent power. And although in the extreme situation it is absolutely vulnerable with respect to its great nuclear adversary, this vulnerability cannot be significantly affected by alliances and allies. On the contrary, while allies cannot improve one's core security, they may threaten it, since the prospect of using nuclear weapons is most likely to arise as a result of threats to their security." "The Nuclear Debate," p. 30. For a somewhat less drastic view see Eliot A. Cohen, "Do We Still Need Europe?" *Commentary* 81, no. 1 (January 1986): 28–35. Cohen argues that Europe has declined "as a strategic stake and asset in the competition with the Soviet Union," that it "has become more of a strategic liability to the United States," and that for reasons of strategic geography "it is the flanks of NATO that are becoming increasingly important, primarily because of the rise of Soviet maritime power, because of changes in military technology, and because of threats in the Persian Gulf" (p. 34). See also the dim view of the alliance expressed by Theodore Draper, "The Phantom Alliance," in Robert W. Tucker and Linda Wrigley, eds., *The Atlantic Alliance and Its Critics* (New York: Praeger, 1983), pp. 1–27; and the various contributions in Ciro E. Zoppo and Charles Zorgbibe, eds., *On Geopolitics: Classical and Nuclear* (Dordrecht: Martinus Nijhoff, 1985). David P. Calleo has argued that "the real grievance of NATO's right-wing critics is that NATO entangles, whereas the driving force behind their world policy is a heroic denial of American dependence on any other country. In this view, the European connection is a source of weakness, not strength. . . . But the real obstacle to unilateral liberty is not that the United States still has allies, but that it needs them more than ever. The United States no longer has the resources to impose its will alone. NATO's function is no longer to organize the dominion over others, nor to replace their strength with American strength, but to mobilize their forces for shared purposes." "NATO's Middle Course," *Foreign Policy*, no. 69 (Winter 1987–88): 135–147; the quotation is from p. 144.

55. Some analysts have argued for a more independent nuclear role for the Federal Republic. See David Garnham, "Extending Deterrence with German Nuclear Weapons," *International Security* 10, no. 1 (Summer 1985): 96–110; Melvin Krauss, *How NATO Weakens the West* (New York: Simon & Schuster, 1986). For some earlier speculations see Horst Mendershausen, "Will West Germany Go Nuclear?" *Orbis* 16, no. 2 (Summer 1972): 411–434; Robert L. Rothstein, "Nuclear Proliferation and American Policy," *Political Science Quarterly* 82, no. 1 (March 1967), esp. pp. 15ff. On July 10, 1968, Secretary of State Dean Rusk told the Senate Foreign Relations Committee that if NATO were to dissolve, some states such as West Germany might well consider this the kind of "extraordinary event . . . jeopardizing their supreme interests" that would justify withdrawal from the NPT, in accordance with Article 10 of the treaty. It is also interesting that the original restrictions placed on the Federal Republic by its membership in the WEU in 1954 were understood to hold only under the principle of *rebus sic stantibus*. See Konrad Adenauer, *Erinnerungen*, vol. 2, *1953–1955* (Stuttgart: Deutsche Verlags-Anstalt, 1965), p. 347.

56. "It does not matter that the neutralist impulse seeks safety in the escape from power while unilateralism glories in its reassertion. Nor does it matter that the one may be driven by fear whereas the other is fueled by a heady sense of

newfound determination. For in both cases, the leitmotiv is retraction and insulation—from the grating demands of dependence, from the troubles of a strained partnership, from commitment to uncertain allies who exact loyalty with a vengeance but yield little of their jealously guarded freedom of action." Josef Joffe, "Europe and America: The Politics of Resentment," pt. 2, *Foreign Affairs* 61, no. 3 (special Issue: "America and the World, 1982"): 569–590; the quotation is from p. 570.

INTRODUCTION TO PART II

Epigraph. George F. Kennan, *American Diplomacy, 1900–1950* (Chicago: University of Chicago Press, 1951), p. 50.

1. Ludwig Dehio, *Germany and World Politics in the Twentieth Century* (New York: W. W. Norton, 1967), pp. 126–127. See also Hajo Holborn, *Germany and Europe* (Garden City, N.Y.: Doubleday, 1970); A. W. DePorte, *Europe between the Superpowers: The Enduring Balance* (New Haven and London: Yale University Press, 1979), esp. chaps. 1–9; Hans Gatzke, *Germany and the United States: A "Special Relationship"?* (Cambridge: Harvard University Press, 1980); Klaus Hildebrand and Reiner Pommerin, eds., *Deutsche Frage und europäisches Gleichgewicht. Festschrift für Andreas Hillgruber zum 60. Geburtstag* (Cologne: Böhlau, 1984); Fritz Stern, *Dreams and Delusions: The Drama of German History* (New York: Alfred A. Knopf, 1987); Renata Fritsch-Bournazel, *Das Land in der Mitte. Die Deutschen im europäischen Kräftefeld* (Munich: Iudicium, 1986).

2. The originator of the concept of containment, George F. Kennan, offered the classic statement of its rationale: "Today, standing at the end rather than the beginning of this half-century, some of us see certain fundamental elements on which we suspect that American security has rested. We can see that our security has been dependent throughout much of our history on the position of Britain . . . and that Britain's position in turn, has depended on the maintenance of a balance of power on the European Continent. Thus it was essential to us, as it was to Britain, that no single Continental land power should come to dominate the entire Eurasian land mass. Our interest has lain rather in the maintenance of some sort of stable balance among the powers of the interior, in order that none of them should effect the subjugation of the others, conquer the seafaring fringes of the land mass, become a great sea power as well as land power, shatter the position of England, and enter—as in these circumstances it certainly would—on an overseas expansion hostile to ourselves and supported by the immense resources of the interior of Europe and Asia." *American Diplomacy, 1900–1950* (Chicago: University of Chicago Press, 1951), pp. 4–5.

On the origins of the Cold War and containment see Harry S. Truman, *Memoirs*, vol. 2, *Years of Trial and Hope, 1946–1952* (New York: Doubleday, 1956); Dean Acheson, *Present at the Creation: My Years in the State Department* (New York: New American Library, 1970); Charles Bohlen, *Witness to History, 1929–69* (New York: W. W. Norton, 1973); George F. Kennan, *Memoirs*, 2 vols. (Boston: Little, Brown, 1967, 1972); Kennan, *Realities of American Foreign Policy* (New York: W. W. Norton, 1966); Arno Mayer, *Political Origins of the New Diplomacy, 1917–1918* (New Haven and London: Yale University Press, 1959); John Lewis Gaddis, *The United States and the Origins of the Cold War, 1941–1947* (New York: Columbia University

Press, 1972); Gaddis, *Strategies of Containment: A Critical Appraisal of Postwar American National Security Policy* (New York: Oxford University Press, 1982), pp. 25–88; Gaddis, "Containment: A Reassessment," *Foreign Affairs* 55, no. 4 (July 1977): 873–887; Gaddis, *The Long Peace: Inquiries into the History of the Cold War* (New York: Oxford University Press, 1987); Terry L. Deibel and John Lewis Gaddis, eds., *Containment: Concept and Policy* (Washington: National Defense University Press, 1986); Louis Halle, *The Cold War as History* (New York: Harper & Row, 1967); Eric F. Goldman, *The Crucial Decade: America, 1945–1955* (New York: Alfred A. Knopf, 1956); Daniel Yergin, *Shattered Peace: The Origins of the Cold War and the National Security State* (Boston: Houghton Mifflin, 1978); Walter Lippmann, *The Cold War: A Study in U.S. Foreign Policy* (New York: Harper & Row, 1947); Herbert Feis, *From Trust to Terror* (New York: W. W. Norton, 1970); Joseph M. Jones, *Fifteen Weeks: February 21-June 1, 1947* (New York: Harcourt, Brace & World, 1964); Hugh Thomas, *Armed Truce: The Beginnings of the Cold War, 1945–1946* (New York: Atheneum, 1987); Deborah Welch Larson, *Origins of Containment: A Psychological Explanation* (Princeton: Princeton University Press, 1985).

The implications for Germany are treated in Lucius D. Clay, *Decision in Germany* (Garden City, N.Y.: Doubleday, 1950); Wolfgang Krieger, *General Lucius Clay und die amerikanische Deutschlandpolitik* (Stuttgart: Klett-Cotta, 1987); Erika Fischer and Heinz-D. Fischer, *John J. McCloy und die Frühgeschichte der Bundesrepublik Deutschland. Presseberichte und Dokumente über den Amerikanischen Hochkommissar für Deutschland, 1949–1952* (Cologne: Verlag Wissenschaft und Politik, 1985); Ernst Nolte, *Deutschland und der Kalte Krieg* (Munich: Piper, 1974); Hans-Peter Schwarz, *Vom Reich zur Bundesrepublik. Deutschland im Widerstreit der aussenpolitischen Konzeptionen in den Jahren der Besatzungsherrschaft, 1945–1949* (Neuwied and Berlin: Luchterhand, 1966); Wilhelm Grewe, *Deutsche Aussenpolitik der Nachkriegszeit* (Stuttgart: Deutsche Verlags-Anstalt, 1960); John H. Backer, *The Decision to Divide Germany: American Foreign Policy in Transition* (Durham: Duke University Press, 1978); Anne Weiss-Hartmann, *Geschichte der deutschen Spaltung, 1945–1955* (Cologne: Pahl-Rugenstein, 1975); Wolfram F. Hanrieder, *West German Foreign Policy, 1949–1963: International Pressure and Domestic Response* (Stanford: Stanford University Press, 1967). On British policy see Claus Scharf and Hans-Jürgen Schröder, eds., *Die Deutschlandpolitik Grossbritanniens und die Britische Zone, 1945–1949* (Wiesbaden: Franz Steiner, 1979). See also John Gimbel, *The American Occupation of Germany: Politics and the Military, 1945–1949* (Stanford: Stanford University Press, 1968); Hermann Graml, *Die Alliierten und die Teilung Deutschlands. Konflikte und Entscheidungen, 1941–1948* (Frankfurt am Main: Fischer Taschenbuch-Verlag); F. Roy Willis, *France, Germany and the New Europe, 1945–1967* (New York: Oxford University Press, 1968); Ferenc A. Vali, *The Quest for a United Germany* (Baltimore: Johns Hopkins University Press, 1967); Lawrence L. Whetten, *Germany's Ostpolitik: Relations between the Federal Republic and the Warsaw Pact Countries* (London: Oxford University Press for the Royal Institute of International Affairs, 1971); William E. Griffith, *The Ostpolitik of the Federal Republic of Germany* (Cambridge: MIT Press, 1978).

On Moscow's postwar policy toward Germany see Renata Fritsch-Bournazel, *Die Sowjetunion und die deutsche Teilung: Die sowjetische Deutschlandpolitik, 1945–1979* (Opladen: Westdeutscher Verlag, 1979); Walrab von Buttlar, *Ziele und Zielkonflikte der sowjetischen Deutschlandpolitik, 1945–1947* (Stuttgart: Klett-Cotta,

1980); Thomas W. Wolfe, *Soviet Power and Europe, 1945–1970* (Baltimore and London: Johns Hopkins University Press, 1970); Klaus Erdmenges, *Das folgenschwere Missverständnis. Bonn und die sowjetische Deutschlandpolitik, 1949–1955* (Freiburg: Rombach, 1967); J. P. Nettl, *The Eastern Zone and Soviet Policy in Germany, 1945–1950* (London: Oxford University Press, 1951); Horst Duhnke, *Stalinismus in Deutschland. Die Geschichte der sowjetischen Besatzungszone* (Cologne: Verlag für Politik und Wissenschaft, 1955).

3. See W. W. Rostow, *The Division of Europe after World War II: 1946* (Austin: University of Texas Press, 1981).

4. John P. Mackintosh, "Britain in Europe: Historical Perspective and Contemporary Reality," *International Affairs* 45, no. 2 (April 1969): 246–257, esp. p. 250.

5. Raymond Poidevin and Jacques Bariéty, *Deutschland und Frankreich. Die Geschichte ihrer Beziehungen, 1815–1975* (Munich: C. H. Beck, 1977); Joseph Rovan and Werner Weidenfeld, eds., *Europäische Zeitzeichen. Elemente eines deutsch-französischen Dialogs* (Bonn: Europa-Union-Verlag, 1982); Robert Picht, ed., *Das Bündnis im Bündnis. Deutsch-französische Beziehungen im internationalen Spannungsfeld* (Berlin: Severin and Siedler, 1983); Ernst Weisenfeld, *Welches Deutschland soll es sein? Frankreich und die deutsche Einheit seit 1945* (Munich: C. H. Beck, 1986); Hans-Peter Schwarz, ed., *Adenauer und Frankreich: die deutsch-französischen Beziehungen 1958 bis 1969* (Bonn: Bouvier, 1985).

6. For a comparison of the institutional, political, and cultural developments in the two German states see Henry Ashby Turner, Jr., *The Two Germanies since 1945* (New Haven and London: Yale University Press, 1987); Eckhard Jesse, ed., *Bundesrepublik Deutschland und Deutsche Demokratische Republik. Die beiden deutschen Staaten im Vergleich* (Berlin: Colloquium, 1980).

7. For the long-range implications of containment for the Continent, the classic dialogue between George F. Kennan and Walter Lippmann is still useful. See the contributions by Kennan, Lippmann, and W. W. Rostow in "Containment: 40 Years Later," *Foreign Affairs* 65, no. 4 (Spring 1987): 827–890.

8. This political symmetry masked an underlying geostrategic asymmetry that became increasingly significant as the United States showed signs of wearying of the burdens entailed by its European commitments, raising the fear in Western Europe that America remained susceptible to the periodic expansion and contraction of its diplomatic interests and energies.

9. Vaclav Havel et al., *The Power of the Powerless: Citizens against the State in Central-Eastern Europe* (London: Hutchinson, 1985); George Konrad, *Antipolitics: An Essay* (New York: Harcourt Brace Jovanovich, 1985). See also the essay by Timothy Garton Ash (in which he reviews these two books as well as others) "Does Central Europe Exist?" *New York Review of Books*, October 9, 1986, pp. 45–51; and the comments by Vladyslav Bartoszewski (made at the Berlin Conference of the Aspen Institute in October 1987), in which he argues that another kind of "European mutuality" exists apart from that of the Western European Community, and that the inhabitants of Budapest, Prague, Warsaw and Cracow, and Leipzig and Dresden also regard themselves as "joint heirs of an all-European tradition." *German Tribune*, no. 1298 (November 8, 1987): 5. For a cautious view of what the two Germanies could contribute to the reestablishment of "Central Europe" see Dietrich Stobbe, "Der Traum von der 'Wiederherstellung der europäischen Mitte,'" *Die Neue Gesellschaft/Frankfurter Hefte* 33, no. 7 (July 1986):

586–589. See also the contributions by Peter Glotz, Gerhard Heimann, Dieter Hoffmann-Axthelm, György Konrad, and Friedrich Naumann in the same issue; and Leonhard Reinisch, ed., *Dieses Europa zwischen Ost und West. Eine geistige Ortsbestimmung* (Munich: Kindler, 1982).

10. Pierre Hassner does not see this interest as being very pronounced in Western Europe, saying that the Federal Republic "is the only Western country that really cares deeply about at least one part of Eastern Europe, the GDR; that really has an interest in challenging the division of Europe; and that really possesses a strategy to that end." "The Shifting Foundation," *Foreign Policy*, no. 48 (Fall 1982): 3–20; the quotation appears on p. 12.

11. In November 1984 Honecker noted: "There are two sovereign German states, independent of one another. They are an indispensable element of the European balance of power and thus indispensable also for a peaceful European order. All European peoples can live with the existence of two German states." *Neues Deutschland* (East Berlin), November 23, 1984, p. 4. In an interview with *Die Zeit*, February 6–7, 1986, Honecker said in response to a question about "keeping open the German question," "I consider this discussion to be superfluous. If one approaches this problem . . . with an open mind, I would say that it is actually fortunate for mankind that there are two German states. Pangermanism was always a misfortune for the peoples of Europe, and not only for them." When President François Mitterrand of France was on a state visit to the German Democratic Republic in June 1985, Honecker explicitly underlined the common French and East German interest in a divided Germany. See the interview with *Le Monde*, repr. in *Neues Deutschland*, June 8, 1985.

12. For an account of Germany's historical vacillations in the European state system and the domestic forces that propelled them see Klaus Hildebrand, "Der deutsche Eigenweg. Über das Problem der Normalität in der modernen Geschichte Deutschlands und Europas"; and Kurt Sontheimer, "Der 'Deutsche Geist' als Ideologie. Ein Beitrag zur Theorie vom deutschen Sonderbewusstsein," both in Manfred Funke et al., *Demokratie und Diktatur. Geist und Gestalt politischer Herrschaft in Deutschland und Europa* (Düsseldorf: Droste, 1987), pp. 15–34, 35–45. See also Bernd Faulenbach, " 'Deutscher Sonderweg.' Zur Geschichte und Problematik einer zentralen Kategorie des deutschen geschichtlichen Bewusstseins," *Aus Politik und Zeitgeschichte*, suppl. to *Das Parlament*, B 33/81 (August 15, 1981), pp. 3–21; Joseph Rovan, "Verändertes Nationalbewusstsein? Ein Beitrag zur Entspezifizierung der deutschen Frage," *Deutschland Archiv* 17, no. 10 (October 1984): 1032–1042; Hagen Schulze, *Weimar-Deutschland 1917 bis 1933* (Berlin: Severin und Siedler, 1982); Michael Stürmer, *Das ruhelose Reich. Deutschland, 1866–1918* (Berlin: Severin und Siedler, 1983); Andreas Hillgruber, *Deutsche Grossmacht- und Weltpolitik im 19. und 20. Jahrhundert* (Düsseldorf: Droste, 1977); Hillgruber, *Die Last der Nation* (Düsseldorf: Droste, 1984); Josef von Becker and Andreas Hillgruber, eds., *Die deutsche Frage im 19. und 20. Jahrhundert* (Munich: Ernst Vögel, 1983); Wolf D. Gruner, *Die deutsche Frage. Ein Problem der europäischen Geschichte* (Munich: C. H. Beck, 1985); David Calleo, *The German Problem Reconsidered* (New York: Cambridge University Press, 1978).

13. Michael Stürmer noted that in 1948–49 "the founding fathers of the Basic Law understood the idea of German unity, at its core, as reunification—and they were compelled to see it as such. Today, hope is directed more toward [the idea]

of the nation than of the nation-state." "Die deutsche Frage in der europäischen Geschichte," in Klaus Lange, ed., *Aspekte der deutschen Frage* (Herford: Busse-Seewald, 1986), pp. 21–34; the quotation appears on p. 34.

CHAPTER 5: *Reunification and the European Political Order*

Epigraphs. Otto von Bismarck, quoted in Peter Bender, *Neue Ostpolitik. Vom Mauerbau bis zum Moskauer Vertrag* (Munich: Deutscher Taschenbuch-Verlag, 1986), p. 9; Ludwig Dehio, *Germany and World Politics in the Twentieth Century* (New York: W. W. Norton, 1967), p. 138.

1. Dr. Karl Pfleiderer, a prominent FDP politician, noted in a speech in Waiblingen in June 1952: "And now I ask you: do you believe that such a gigantic, immensely powerful state as the Soviet Union is prepared to stake its political and economic position in Germany (one of its most important in the world) on the uncertain outcome of an election—that is, on whether the Germans cast their vote one way or the other? And if the outcome of the election is *not* uncertain, because one must assume that a majority of the people would vote against Soviet rule—do you then believe that the Soviet Union will allow elections at all?" (italics in original).

In accordance with this line of thinking, Pfleiderer proposed in October 1952 that a neutral zone be established between East and West Germany from which all NATO and Soviet troops would be withdrawn, and which would serve as the basis for negotiations over reunification. See Karl Georg Pfleiderer, *Politik für Deutschland. Reden und Aufsätze, 1948–1956* (Stuttgart: Deutsche Verlags-Anstalt, 1961). A similar argument was made by Jakob Kaiser, a prominent CDU politician and minister for all-German affairs in Adenauer's cabinet, who favored a "bridge building" concept in East-West relations, leading to his falling out with Adenauer's determined Westpolitik. See Dietrich Thränhardt, *Geschichte der Bundesrepublik Deutschland* (Frankfurt am Main: Suhrkamp, 1986), pp. 81–82. See also Richard Meyer von Achenbach, *Gedanken über eine konstruktive deutsche Ostpolitik. Eine unterdrückte Denkschrift aus dem Jahr 1953*, ed. Julius H. Schoeps (Frankfurt am Main: Athenäum, 1986); Christian Hacke, ed., *Jakob Kaiser. Wir haben Brücke zu sein. Reden, Äußerungen und Aufsätze zur Deutschlandpolitik* (Cologne: Verlag Wissenschaft und Politik, 1988).

2. On the risk for the Soviet Union of losing control over Eastern Europe see Christoph Royen, *Die sowjetische Koexistenzpolitik gegenüber Westeuropa. Voraussetzungen, Ziele, Dilemmata* (Baden-Baden: Nomos, 1978).

3. Josef Foschepoth, ed., *Kalter Krieg und Deutsche Frage. Deutschland im Widerstreit der Mächte, 1945–1952* (Göttingen and Zurich: Vandenhoeck & Ruprecht, 1985).

4. For discussions of the relevance of China to West Germany see William E. Griffith, "European Communism, 1965," in William E. Griffith, ed., *Communism in Europe*, vol. 2 (Cambridge: MIT Press, 1966), esp. p. 23; Rudolf Augstein, "Wege zu einer neuen Politik," *Der Spiegel* 19, no. 39 (1965): 18–25, esp. p. 20; Richard Löwenthal, "Der Einfluss Chinas auf die Entwicklung des Ost-West Konflikts in Europa," *Europa-Archiv* 22, no. 10 (1967): 339–350; Hans-Georg Studnitz, *Bismarck in Bonn* (Stuttgart: Seewald, 1965), p. 146; Jean Edward Smith, "Two Germanies and Two Chinas," *Reporter*, May 19, 1966, pp. 36–38. On Adenauer's view on the

China connection see Ernst Majonica, "Adenauer und China" in Dieter Blumen-witz et al., eds., *Konrad Adenauer und seine Zeit. Politik und Persönlichkeit des ersten Bundeskanzlers. Beiträge von Weg- und Zeitgenossen*, Beiträge der Wissenschaft, vol. 2 (Stuttgart: Deutsche Verlags-Anstalt, 1976), pp. 680–697.

Otto Kirchheimer called this the "Chinese projection game": as early as the 1950s some Germans speculated about how the Sino-Soviet split could be exploited for the cause of German unity—for example, by an alignment between China and Europe. Perhaps as a result of de Gaulle's recognition of the People's Republic of China in 1964, the Erhard government sought to nurture economic relations with Peking, but had to drop the plan for a trade agreement in the face of strong objections from Washington.

5. As Rudolf Augstein noted in reviewing Peter Koch's biography *Konrad Adenauer. Eine politische Biographie* (Reinbek: Rowohlt, 1985), "Adenauer after all was not only the chancellor of the Allies but also the chancellor of a solid majority of German voters in the Federal Republic and West Berlin." *Der Spiegel* 39, no. 41 (1985): 99. Augstein is of course referring here to the SPD's cutting characterization of Adenauer as "the chancellor of the Allies."

6. There were influential American draftsmen as well. See Eberhart Pikart, "Auf dem Weg zum Grundgesetz," in Richard Löwenthal and Hans-Peter Schwarz, eds., *Die zweite Republik. 25 Jahre Bundesrepublik Deutschland—Eine Bilanz* (Stuttgart: Seewald, 1974), pp. 149–176; Hans-Jürgen Grabbe, "Die deutsch-alliierte Kontroverse über den Grundgesetzentwurf im Frühjahr 1949," *Viertel-jahreshefte für Zeitgeschichte* 26, no. 3 (July 1978): 393–418.

7. The Basic Law was promulgated with the express reservation that it was a provisional arrangement, a "transitorium" (as it was called by Theodor Heuss, the first German Federal president) toward a reunified Germany that would then replace the Basic Law with a permanent constitution.

8. See Claus Arndt, "Legal Problems of the German Eastern Treaties," *American Journal of International Law* 74, no. 1 (January 1980): 122–133. Arndt notes that "the interpretation of the Constitution generally accepted by the Parliament (*Deutscher Bundestag*), the Federal Government, and the Federal Constitutional Court is that [the German Reich] was not extinguished in 1945, or in 1949, or subsequently—and therefore exists even today. Undeniably, it is currently unable to act under International law—as, similarly, were Poland between its partition at the end of the 18th century and 1918, and Austria between 1938 and 1945—because it lacks state organs capable of functioning. The sovereignty of the Federal Republic is further limited by the Occupation Statute to the extent that the rights and responsibilities of the United States, France and Great Britain with respect to Berlin and to Germany as a whole, which includes the questions of reunification and a peace treaty, are at issue. The Federal Republic expressly recognized this situation in Article 2 of the revised Treaty on the Relationship between the Federal Republic of Germany and the Three Powers (signed May 26, 1952, revised October 23, 1954)" (p. 124).

The call for the German borders of 1937 persists among German conservatives. See for example the preface by Franz-Josef Strauss in Klaus Lange, ed., *Aspekte der deutschen Frage* (Herford: Busse-Seewald, 1986), pp. 9–12: "The decision of the Constitutional Court of July 31, 1973 [affirming the compatibility of the Basic Treaty with the Basic Law] says unequivocally that the Basic Law has given us obligatory tasks (*Vorgaben*), which nobody may call into question. Included are the juridical continuation of the German *Reich* within the borders of 1937 and the continuing Four-Power responsibility for all of Germany, i.e., the openness of the German question. Nor have the Eastern Treaties changed the situation of Germany under international law and the Four-Power responsibility for all of Germany. Above all, the Eastern Treaties are not treaties which recognize borders under international law. ("Vor allem sind die Ost-Verträge keine Grenzanerkennungs-Verträge völkerrechtlicher Art.") A final decision about Germany's border must await a peace treaty with a united Germany" (p. 11).

   See also Michael Schmitz, *Die Rechtslage der deutschen Ostgebiete. Die Oder-Neisse-Grenze im Blickpunkt des Völkerrechts* (Cologne: Verlag Wissenschaft und Politik, 1986), which contains an extensive bibliography. Schmitz points out that the Basic Law does not lay claim to the territorial expanse of Germany in 1937, and that the obligation to seek unification has no territorial, spatial dimension but rather lays a claim to the unity of the German people (p. 65). See also Georg Bluhm, *Die Oder-Neisse-Linie in der deutschen Aussenpolitik* (Freiburg: Rombach, 1963); Herbert Kraus, *Die Oder-Neisse-Linie. Eine völkerrechtliche Studie* (Cologne: R. Müller, 1959); Hans Buchheim, *Deutschlandpolitik, 1949–1972. Der politisch-diplomatische Prozess* (Stuttgart: Deutsche Verlags-Anstalt, 1984), pp. 94–95.

   For a more recent reiteration of the importance the Germans attached to the legal aspects of the German question see the articles by Alois Mertes, "Die deutsche Frage bleibt offen"; and Kurt Plück, "Die deutsche Frage aus der Sicht der Bundesregierung," both in Lange, *Aspekte der deutschen Frage*, pp. 187–197, 307–322. See also Wolfgang Schäuble, "Die deutsche Frage im europäischen und weltpolitischen Rahmen. Deutschland-Politik im Kontext der Ost-West-Beziehungen," *Europa-Archiv* 41, no. 12 (1986): 341–348, esp. p. 341.

   9. This also meant that the Federal Republic sought to establish a constructive relationship with Israel. See Lilly Gardner Feldman, *The Special Relationship between West Germany and Israel* (London: George Allen & Unwin, 1984); Rolf Vogel, ed., *Deutschlands Weg nach Israel* (Stuttgart: Seewald, 1967); Nana Sagi, *Wiedergutmachung für Israel. Die deutschen Zahlungen und Leistungen* (Stuttgart: Busse-Seewald, 1981). For a monumental account (in seven volumes) of the Federal Republic's restitutions to victims of Nazi Germany see Bundesminister der Finanzen and Walter Schwarz, eds., *Die Wiedergutmachung nationalsozialistischen Unrechts durch die Bundesrepublik Deutschland* (Munich: C. H. Beck, 1974–85).

   10. The use of this debilitating term persisted into the mid-1980s. See Plück, "Deutsche Frage." For an account of the political purposes and consequences of linguistic political concepts see Wolfgang Bergsdorf, *Herrschaft und Sprache. Studie zur politischen Terminologie der Bundesrepublik Deutschland* (Pfullingen: Neske, 1983).

   11. See Thränhardt, *Geschichte der Bundesrepublik Deutschland*, esp. pp. 9, 30.

   12. See Hans-Peter Schwarz, "Adenauer und Russland," in Friedrich J. Kroneck and Thomas Oppermann, eds., *Im Dienste Deutschlands und des Rechtes. Festschrift für Wilhelm G. Grewe* (Baden-Baden: Nomos, 1981), pp. 365–387; Konrad Adenauer, *Teegespräche, 1955–1958*, Rhöndorfer Ausgabe, ed. Rudolf Morsey and Hans-Peter Schwarz (Berlin: Siedler, 1986). See also Hans-Peter Schwarz, *Adenauer. Der Aufstieg: 1876–1952* (Stuttgart: Deutsche Verlags-Anstalt, 1986), esp.

pp. 727ff; Hans-Peter Schwarz, ed., *Entspannung und Wiedervereinigung. Deutsch-landpolitische Vorstellungen Konrad Adenauers 1955–58* (Stuttgart and Zurich: Belser, 1979). On November 13, 1949, Adenauer seems to have expressed worry that the Soviet Union would *withdraw* from East Germany, allowing the East German policy forces and the East German communist party "to annex themselves" to West Germany. See Herbert Blankenhorn, *Verständnis und Verständigung* (Frankfurt am Main: Propyläen, 1980), pp. 75, 111.

13. Peter Bender, *Neue Ostpolitik. Vom Mauerbau bis zum Moskauer Vertrag* (Munich: Deutscher Taschenbuch-Verlag, 1986), p. 25.

14. Bonn's other "reunification" project, the return of the Saar territory to Germany, was brought to a successful conclusion precisely because it could be accomplished within the context of the Western alliance, where Bonn's influence was increasing steadily. After the Second World War the Saar territory was placed under international control, but was administered by France because it was situated in the French zone of occupation. Although France had by 1948 incorporated the Saar economically, and had attempted to solidify the Franco-Saar economic union politically and contractually, Adenauer's government managed by 1956 to negotiate the return of the Saar to Germany by skillfully exploiting the opportunities of the Cold War, which provided Bonn with considerable leverage vis-à-vis France within the Western alliance. See Wolfram F. Hanrieder, *West German Foreign Policy, 1949–1963* (Stanford: Stanford University Press, 1967), pp. 24–27, 62–66, 85–88; Jacques Freymond, *The Saar Conflict, 1945–1955* (New York: Praeger, 1960); Per Fischer, *Die Saar zwischen Deutschland und Frankreich* (Frankfurt am Main: Metzer, 1959).

15. See Immanuel Birnbaum, *Entzweite Nachbarn. Deutsche Politik in Osteuropa* (Frankfurt am Main: A. Scheffler, 1968); Hans-Adolf Jacobsen, ed., *Misstrauische Nachbarn. Deutsche Ostpolitik, 1919–1970. Dokumentation und Analyse* (Düsseldorf: Droste, 1970); Klaus Mehnert, *Der deutsche Standort* (Frankfurt am Main: Deutsche Verlags-Anstalt, 1971); Ernst Majonica, *Möglichkeiten und Grenzen der Deutschen Aussenpolitik* (Stuttgart: W. Kohlhammer, 1969). See also Buchheim, *Deutschland-politik*, p. 130.

16. Christoph Klessmann, *Die doppelte Staatsgründung. Deutsche Geschichte, 1945–1955* (Göttingen: Vandenhoeck & Ruprecht, 1982); Werner Weidenfeld, ed., *Die Identität der Deutschen* (Munich and Vienna: Carl Hanser, 1983).

17. Adenauer's willingness in 1958 to accept the neutralization of the GDR (following the model of Austria) also implied his readiness to give up German demands on the Oder-Neisse border. As early as 1955 Adenauer is reported to have privately told SPD chief Erich Ollenhauer: "Oder-Neisse, Eastern territories, etc.—they are gone! They don't exist anymore! Whoever will have to negotiate that . . well, it will not be me anymore." Quoted in Ludwig Elsing, "Polenpolitik der SPD, 1960 bis 1970," in Werner Plum, ed., *Ungewöhnliche Normalisierung. Beziehungen der Bundesrepublik Deutschland zu Polen* (Bonn: Verlag Neue Gesellschaft, 1984), pp. 55–65; the quotation appears on p. 57. See also Hans Georg Lehmann, *Der Oder-Neisse Konflikt* (Munich: C. H. Beck, 1979).

18. Not surprisingly, these differing elements of Bonn's foreign policies met with favor and disfavor from different political constituencies in Germany. Comparing ancient Greece with modern Europe, Ludwig Dehio wrote in 1953: "In both cases we find the tenacious but sterile survival of obsolete instincts. We find

particularist trends devoid of any sense of proportion, growing ever pettier and ever more outworn, while pursuing their squabbles over scraps of land—the worst possible obstacle to the establishment of a great new order." *Germany and World Politics in the Twentieth Century* (New York: W. W. Norton, 1967), p. 141.

19. Werner Link, "Die aussenpolitische Staatsräson der Bundesrepublik Deutschland," in Manfred Funke et al., eds., *Demokratie und Diktatur. Geist und Gestalt politischer Herrschaft in Deutschland und Europa* (Düsseldorf: Droste, 1987), pp. 400–416, esp. p. 407.

20. Blankenhorn notes that a major purpose of Adenauer's trip to Washington in April 1953 was "to make sure, once and for all, that an accommodation between East and West would not occur at the expense of Germany—in other words, that the status which the Federal Republic had obtained in its negotiations with the Western allies would not be diminished and that Germany would not relapse into new isolation. His anxieties in this respect, which he articulated openly, were especially great. They were considerably . . . strengthened by the conciliatory gestures of the new Soviet policy." *Verständnis und Verständigung,* p. 146.

21. Hans-Peter Schwarz, "Adenauer's Ostpolitik," in Wolfram F. Hanrieder, ed., *West German Foreign Policy, 1949–1979* (Boulder: Westview, 1980), pp. 127–144, esp. pp. 136ff.

22. This has led over the decades to a contradictory stance on the part of the Soviet Union. On the one hand, the Warsaw Pact's position is that the border arrangements of Europe, including the division of Germany, are permanent. On the other hand, the Soviet Union wishes to preserve its right as a victorious power to deal with all-German questions. In the mid-1980s, when the GDR's media spoke of the "Group of Soviet Armed Forces in the GDR," they were corrected by the Russians, who pointed out that the correct name was "Group of Soviet Armed Forces in Germany." See Peter Danylow, "Der aussenpolitische Spielraum der DDR. Wechselnde Grenzen der Handlungsfreiheit im östlichen Bündnissystem," *Europa-Archiv* 40, no. 14 (1985): 433–440, esp. p. 438. See also Wolfgang-Uwe Friedrich, "The German Question between West and East," *Aussenpolitik* 38, no. 3 (1987), esp. p. 249.

23. Article 7.2 of the Germany Treaty of 1952–54 states: "The signatory states will cooperate to achieve by peaceful means their common aim of a reunified Germany enjoying a liberal democratic constitution, like that of the Federal Republic, and integrated within the European community." As Peter Bender has pointed out, "Bonn and the Western powers were agreed: one could consider unity only if it connected the GDR to the West. One had created a task which could not be executed." *Neue Ostpolitik,* p. 41. For a full discussion of these qualification of Western support see Wilhelm G. Grewe, *Die deutsche Frage in der Ost-West-Spannung. Zeitgeschichtliche Kontroversen der achtziger Jahre* (Herford: Busse-Seewald, 1986), esp. pp. 14, 54, 57, 70–74.

For the negotiations leading to the *Deutschlandvertrag* see Arnulf Baring, *Aussenpolitik in Adenauers Kanzlerdemokratie. Bonns Beitrag zur Europäischen Verteidigungsgemeinschaft* (Munich and Vienna: R. Oldenbourg, 1969), pp. 124–163.

24. Beate Ruhm von Oppen, ed., *Documents on Germany under Occupation, 1945–1954* (London: Oxford University Press, 1955), pp. 522–527.

25. U.S. Senate, Committee on Foreign Relations, *Documents on Germany, 1944–1961* (Washington: GPO, 1961), p. 87.

26. Ibid., p. 88.

27. George F. Kennan, *Memoirs*, vol. 2, *1950–1967* (Boston: Little, Brown, 1972), p. 161; see also the passage preceding this quotation. On Kennan's opposition to NATO see John L. Gaddis, *Strategies of Containment: A Critical Appraisal of Postwar American National Security Policy* (New York: Oxford University Press, 1982), pp. 72–73. For more on Kennan's views see Gerd Bucerius, "Verpasste Chancen für die Abwendung unserer Teilung?" *Die Zeit*, April 20, 1984.

28. Because of the defeat of the EDC Treaty in the French National Assembly, the Contractual Agreement of 1952 did not come into force until May 1955, after the ratification of the Paris Treaties of October 1954, which provided for the Federal Republic's admission to NATO.

29. See William G. Hyland, "The Soviet Union and Germany," in Hanrieder, *West German Foreign Policy, 1949–1979*, pp. 111–126, esp. pp. 114ff.

30. U.S. Senate, *Documents on Germany*, pp. 117–123.

31. Alastair Buchan and Philip Windsor, *Arms and Stability in Europe* (New York: Praeger, 1963), pp. 38–39.

32. See Paul Sethe, *Zwischen Bonn und Moskau* (Frankfurt am Main: Scheffler, 1956), pp. 104–106.

33. *Keesing's Contemporary Archives*, vol. 10, p. 14059.

34. In later years the question of whether the notes of March 1952 offered a genuine opportunity for German unification or were a propaganda ploy of the Kremlin obtained a certain historiographic notoriety and remained hotly debated. For various assessments of the "missed opportunities" of March 1952 see Sethe, *Zwischen Bonn und Moskau*; Rolf Steininger, *Eine vertane Chance. Die Stalin-Note vom 10. März 1952 und die Wiedervereinigung* (Berlin and Bonn: J. H. W. Dietz, 1985); Hermann Graml, "Die Legende von der verpassten Gelegenheit. Zur sowjetischen Noten-Kampagne des Jahres 1952," *Vierteljahrshefte für Zeitgeschichte* 29, no. 3 (July 1981): 307–341; Wilhelm G. Grewe, "Ein zählebiger Mythos: Stalins Note vom März 1952," *Frankfurter Allgemeine Zeitung*, March 10, 1982, p. 11; Andreas Hillgruber, "Adenauer und die Stalin-Note vom 10. März 1952," in Blumenwitz et. al., *Konrad Adenauer und seine Zeit*, pp. 111–130; Gerhard Wettig, "Die sowjetische Deutschland-Note vom 10. März 1952. Wiedervereinigungsangebot oder Propagandaaktion?" *Deutschland Archiv* 15, no. 2 (1982): 130–148; Hans-Peter Schwarz, ed., *Die Legende von der verpassten Gelegenheit. Die Stalin-Note vom 10. März 1952*, Rhöndorfer Ausgabe, vol. 5 (Stuttgart and Zurich: W. J. Siedler, 1982). Peter Diehl-Frappe wrote in the *Süddeutsche Zeitung* in August 1981, "Even if Adenauer had assessed the Soviet note differently than the Allies, the story wouldn't have ended differently," because of the severe limitations placed on the German government. Cited in Herman Kahn and M. Redepenning, *Die Zukunft Deutschlands. Niedergang oder neuer Aufstieg der Bundesrepublik* (Munich: Molden, 1982), p. 217; Knud Dittmann, *Adenauer und die deutsche Wiedervereinigung. Die politische Diskussion des Jahres 1952* (Düsseldorf: Droste, 1981). On the early phases of German reunification policy see Werner Feld, *Reunification and West German-Soviet Relations* (The Hague: M. Nijhoff, 1963).

35. Blankenhorn, *Verständnis und Verständigung*, pp. 132–133; Konrad Adenauer, *Teegespräche, 1950–1954*, Rhöndorfer Ausgabe, ed. Rudolf Morsey and Hans-Peter Schwarz (Berlin: Siedler, 1984).

36. Referring to a secret note in British archives (dating back to December 1955), Richard Löwenthal has argued that "it proves what many critics of Ade-

nauer have always believed: he was opposed to reunification negotiations not because he thought they could not then succeed and because he wanted to wait for a situation of greater Western strength, as he declared time and again, but because he did not want them to succeed. He lacked confidence that the Germans, should they be reunited in a 'Reich,' would find their way back permanently to their European origins. I must say frankly that I do not consider this a dishonorable motive on subjective grounds—even though it is certain that Adenauer hid this motive from public opinion and in that sense consciously misled it in order to implement [his purpose]. But I believe that he was wrong on objective grounds, because I am convinced that the return of the Germans to their European roots was already much more secured than Adenauer would have considered possible." "Vom Weg der Deutschen. Vorgestern, gestern und heute," Introduction to David P. Calleo et al., *Geteiltes Land—Halbes Land?* (Frankfurt am Main: Ullstein, 1986), pp. 7–43; the quotation appears on pp. 32–33. See also Marion Gräfin Dönhoff, "Von der Schwäche starker Politik," *Die Zeit*, March 21, 1986, p. 3; and Lothar Rühl's discussion of a conversation among Adenauer and the foreign ministers of Belgium and Luxembourg in *Der Spiegel* 17 (1954).

This interpretation of Adenauer's motives remains a touchy subject in Germany. For example, Wilhelm Grewe reacted to it with some consternation, although his own analysis of Adenauer's intentions and of the international circumstances tends to confirm rather than contradict it. Grewe, *Deutsche Frage*, pp. 132ff.

37. The German *Sonderweg* was deeply ingrained in German history: "Choosing neither North or South, Luther or the pope, Habsburg or France, Russia or England, capitalism or communism, America or the Soviet Union: this belonged to the tradition of German striving for neutrality and which the Prussians and, respectively, the Germans considered necessary for the preservation of their autonomy." Klaus Hildebrand, "Der deutsche Eigenweg. Über das Problem der Normalität in der modernen Geschichte Deutschlands and Europas," in Manfred Funke et al., eds., *Demokratie und Diktatur. Geist und Gestalt politischer Herrschaft in Deutschland und Europa* (Düsseldorf: Droste, 1987), pp. 15–34; the quotation is from p. 29. See also Gordon Craig, *The Germans* (New York: New American Library, 1982). Ludwig Dehio notes pungently: "On two occasions, Germany has produced ideas that have spread: the Reformation and Marxism. But neither contributed anything to German politics." *Germany and World Politics*, p. 37.

38. In 1966, at the age of ninety, Adenauer still worried about the "unreliable Americans," the "dangerous Russians," and the "even more dangerous" Chinese. See Blankenhorn, *Verständnis und Verständigung*, p. 499.

39. Blankenhorn noted in 1950 that Adenauer had worried all along that the Western allies would exploit Soviet readiness to create a neutral Germany (ibid., pp. 92–93). For Adenauer's general suspicions about American reliability, even during the Eisenhower administration, see Rudolf Morsey and Konrad Repgen, eds., *Adenauer-Studien III* (Mainz: Matthias-Grünewald-Verlag, 1974).

40. But Adenauer also suspected France of trying to reach an accommodation with the Soviet Union. The signing of the Franco-German Friendship Treaty in January 1963 was for Adenauer an attempt to obviate diplomatic isolation, the only way to prevent a Franco-Soviet rapprochement over the head of the Germans. See Blankenhorn, *Verständnis und Verständigung*, p. 438–439. Adenauer's concern about America's reliability was also an important reason for signing the

treaty (although some advisers had cautioned him about its implications) and for his diplomatic attachment to France.

41. Perhaps Chancellor Adenauer's major political strength was that he strove for something attainable. But when Rudolf Augstein, the editor of *Der Spiegel*, made a remark to this effect to Adenauer, the chancellor (then out of office) replied: "More important was that I always thought in simple terms." ("Wichtiger war, dass ich immer so einfach gedacht habe.") *Der Spiegel* 21, no. 18 (1967): 28.

42. Buchheim, *Deutschlandpolitik*, p. 13. Adenauer distrusted the political circumspection of his fellow Germans so much that he might have preferred a united Germany to be associated with the Warsaw Pact rather than being neutral. Buchheim notes in this connection: "Characteristic of this [attitude] is the provision of the 'Globke-Plan' of 1958–59—a plan approved by Adenauer—that a reunited Germany decide whether it would belong to NATO or the Warsaw Pact, 'but not also if it wanted to become neutral'" (p. 13 n. 9; see also pp. 101–103).

43. This did not mean that the Germans could not be highly critical of American leadership. After the Hungarian uprising, Herbert Blankenhorn (a close advisor to Adenauer and Bonn's first ambassador to NATO, 1955–58) noted in his diary the dangers he perceived in the principle of "peaceful coexistence" and in Washington's New Look. Even President Eisenhower and Secretary of State John Foster Dulles were not immune to German wrath. On the day of President Eisenhower's reelection triumph (November 6, 1956), Blankenhorn wrote: "Required is a clear and energetic leadership in Washington. Many regret that President Eisenhower returns to the White House on November 7. I believe he is not up to the responsibilities which the global power America has to shoulder, lacking the physical and even the necessary mental (*geistig*) capabilities." *Verständnis und Verständigung*, p. 257; see also p. 372. In November 1957 Blankenhorn complained about Dulles's tendency to sustain the status quo and lack of "initiative." Ibid., pp. 278, 288. These sentiments were undoubtedly shared in Bonn and prompted Adenauer to view American policies with growing suspicion. See Buchheim, *Deutschlandpolitik*, esp. chap. 16; Grewe, *Rückblenden*, p. 442.

44. Löwenthal, "Vom Weg der Deutschen," p. 33.

45. Robert E. Osgood, *NATO: The Entangling Alliance* (Chicago: University of Chicago Press, 1962), pp. 332–333. See also George F. Kennan, *Memoirs*, vol. 1, *1925–1950* (Boston: Little, Brown, 1967), esp. pp. 365, 415ff., 453, 462; Kennan, *Memoirs*, vol. 2, esp. pp. 161, 253–254, 260–261. On American reunification policy see also Andreas Hillgruber, "Ein Pfad und drei Holzwege. Was Amerika in der deutschen Frage falsch gemacht hat," *Deutschland Archiv* 17, no. 4 (1984): 368–373; Alfred Schickel, "Washington war nicht dagegen. Wie die USA ein neutralisiertes Deutschland sahen. Die Geheimakte 6993," *Deutschland Archiv* 17, no. 6 (1984): 590–593; Peter Bender, "Amerikanische Deutschlandpolitik. Ein realistisches Wiedervereinigungskonzept hat es nie gegeben," *Deutschland Archiv* 17, no. 8 (August 1984): 830–833. For the official position of the West German government see *Efforts of the German Government and its Allies in the Cause of German Unity, 1955–1966* (Bonn: German Federal Foreign Office, 1966). Axel Frohn points out, however, that until the 1950s some circles in Washington remained committed to an all-German "neutral" solution, fearing the rise of German nationalism. *Neutralisierung als Alternative zur Westintegration. Die Deutschlandpolitik der Vereinigten*

Staaten von Amerika, 1945–1949 (Frankfurt am Main: Alfred Metzer, 1985). For a critique of Frohn's argument see the review of his book by Werner Link in *Frankfurter Allgemeine Zeitung*, September 16, 1986.

46. See Bennet Kovrig, *The Myth of Liberation: East-Central Europe in U.S. Diplomacy and Policies since 1941* (Baltimore: Johns Hopkins University Press, 1973).

47. Donald Watt, "Germany," in Evan Luard, ed., *The Cold War: A Reappraisal* (New York: Praeger, 1964), pp. 84–119; the quotation appears on p. 118. William G. Hyland noted in 1980: "If one were to make a list of the five most urgent international issues, the German question would almost certainly *not* be one of them. But if this same list had been composed twenty years ago, the German question would probably have been at the top, and thirty years ago it would have been *the* issue. The passing of the German question symbolizes in a broad sense the withering away of the most virulent phases of the Cold War: the struggle over Germany was indeed the Cold War." "The Soviet Union and Germany," p. 111.

48. Schwarz, "Adenauer und Russland," esp. p. 383.

49. On September 14, 1955, Blankenhorn wrote: "We had the impression that the Soviet position had hardened considerably and that the Russians would not for a very long time release the Eastern zone from their sphere of power. Their entire policy is aimed toward strengthening [the East German] regime and their own position." *Verständnis und Verständigung*, pp. 234–244.

50. See Hans-Peter Schwarz, "Supermacht und Juniorpartner. Ansätze amerikanischer und westdeutscher Ostpolitik," in Hans-Peter Schwarz and Boris Meissner, eds., *Entspannungspolitik in Ost und West* (Cologne: Carl Heymanns, 1979), p. 162.

51. John Lukacs, "The Soviet State at 65," *Foreign Affairs* 65, no. 1 (Fall 1986): 21–36; the quotation appears on p. 29. It is in my view questionable whether the Austrian State Treaty showed the way toward a solution of the German question. I rather hold with Nikita Khrushchev's reported view that a small country like Austria can be "tied with a piece of paper," but that Germany cannot. On another occasion, Khrushchev supposedly said to Prime Minister Guy Mollet of France that the Soviets preferred to have 18 million Germans on their side rather than 70 million against them or, at best, neutral. See Adenauer, *Erinnerungen*, vol. 3, *1955–1959*, pp. 131ff; Buchheim, *Deutschlandpolitik*, pp. 61–62. In March 1958 Adenauer proposed to Moscow to give the GDR the status of Austria, neutral and democratic. See Adenauer, *Erinnerungen*, vol. 3, p. 377ff. For a discussion of the special circumstances leading to the Austrian State Treaty see William H. Bader, *Austria between East and West* (Stanford: Stanford University Press, 1966); Ernst Görlich, *Österreichs Weg zur Neutralität. Eine Sinndeutung der Österreichischen Geschichte* (Lübeck: M. Schmidt/Römhilb, 1959).

52. In 1961 Kurt Birrenbach complained that after the Geneva conference of 1959 the Western powers no longer perceived the former linkage between security issues and German reunification. "The interest in disarmament and in the cessation of atomic tests . . . is so great in the United States and Britain that one cannot overlook the danger that disarmament and security issues will be separated from a solution of political problems in Central Europe." Kurt Birrenbach, *Meine Sondermissionen* (Düsseldorf and Vienna: Econ, 1984), p. 71.

53. Alfred Grosser wrote in 1963: "If every French Government since 1947 has lived in the hope of a Summit Conference it is because a relaxation of tension has seemed to be in France's interest. Why? Because whenever there has been tension between East and West, the attractions of the Federal German Republic have increased in the eyes of the United States while dissension has grown in France, where, as the Pentagon knew, a quarter of the electors voted Communist. On the other hand, when tensions relaxed, Federal Germany relapsed into the role of a pawn on the international chessboard while France again became one of the Big Four discussing the German problem." Alfred Grosser, "General de Gaulle and the Foreign Policy of the Fifth Republic," *International Affairs* 39, no. 2 (1963): 198–213. For more on the lack of American interest in the German question see Andreas Hillgruber, "Westorientierung, Neutralitätsüberlegungen, gesamtdeutsches Bewusstsein," in Henning Köhler, ed., *Deutschland und der Westen. Vorträge und Diskussionsbeiträge des Symposions zu Ehren Gordon A. Craig* (Berlin: Colloquium, 1984), pp. 159–168. Hillgruber also quotes the oft-mentioned comment that John Foster Dulles made to Willy Brandt, then lord mayor of Berlin, to the effect that whatever divided America from the Soviet Union, they were agreed that a united and rearmed Germany should not be left to drift between East and West. As Gordon A. Craig has noted in referring to the Eisenhower and Dulles years, "The globalization of the American engagement relativized the German question to such an extent that what happened in Quemoy and Matsu appeared to be as important as anything that might happen in Berlin." "Amerikanische Aussenpolitik und Deutschland, 1919–1983," in Köhler, *Deutschland und der Westen*, pp. 200–213; the quotation appears on p. 209.

54. Buchheim, *Deutschlandpolitik*, pp. 76–77. Adenauer had been suspicious all along of British "softness" on the German question, especially when Winston Churchill seemed prepared in 1953 to negotiate German neutrality with the Soviet Union. For an analysis and citations from the relevant documents see Josef Foschepoth, "Wie Adenauer Churchill austrickste," *Die Zeit*, May 4, 1984, p. 32. See also Karl Kaiser and Roger Morgan, eds., *Britain and West Germany: Changing Societies and the Future of Foreign Policy* (London: Oxford University Press, 1971).

55. George Kennan notes that Raymond Aron, in a critique of Kennan's BBC-Reith lectures of 1957, argued that nobody wanted to change the division of Germany, a view shared by Walter Lippmann: "This, the fact that no one in authority in Europe or America really wanted to see the division of Europe removed—that the pious lip service to the cause of German unification on the part of all Western statesmen from Adenauer down was the sheerest hypocrisy—was the point that Lippmann was to make, with even more powerful effect, in his articles of a year hence. And it was, of course, vital to the entire argumentation of my lectures. I have often thought that we might all have been spared a lot of trouble if someone in authority had come to me before these lectures were given and had said: 'Look here, George, the decision to leave Europe divided—and divided for an indefinite time to come—has already been taken, even if it hasn't been announced; the talk about German unification is all eyewash; and there isn't the faintest thing to be gained by your attempting to change the situation.'" Kennan, *Memoirs*, vol. 2, pp. 253–254. (The articles by Lippmann to which Kennan refers are in the *New York Herald Tribune*, April 6, 7, 8, and 9, 1959.) Kennan also notes that "the German Foreign Minister, Herr Brentano, was

quoted as saying, in some confidential inner-German meeting, 'Whoever says such things [as I had said] is no friend of the German people' " (p. 250). Kennan went on to say, "The Western powers were now embarked on a path for which I had no stomach. In the effort to solve the problems of Europe by perpetuating its division, and the effort to remove the dangers of nuclear weapons by an all-out competition with the Russians in their development, I could not be an effective guide; I had no confidence in either undertaking" (p. 261).

56. Konrad Adenauer, interview by William Randolph Hearst, *Frankfurter Allgemeine Zeitung*, April 28, 1958. See also Adenauer, *Erinnerungen*, vol. 3, pp. 34ff; Wilhelm Cornides, "Abrüstungsverhandlungen und Deutschlandfrage seit der Genfer Gipfelkonferenz von 1955," *Europa-Archiv* 15, no. 4 (1960): 103–116, esp. p. 110.

57. *Newsweek*, June 9, 1958, p. 15.

58. Walter Lippmann, *Western Unity and the Common Market* (Boston: Little, Brown, 1962), p. 32.

59. In the late 1950s the Western allies, although they formally reiterated in the Berlin Declaration of July 29, 1957, their commitment to a united, democratic Germany on the basis of free elections and the claim of "sole representation" of the Federal Republic, nonetheless showed readiness to accept the partition. Adenauer responded with a belated attempt to reenergize Bonn's unification policy and fashioned a "two-track" diplomacy. This consisted of an insistence on strict legalism in the West and more flexibility in the East, apparently going so far as to raise in March 1958 the possibility of obtaining for East Germany the status of Austria. Buchheim, *Deutschlandpolitik*, pp. 98–104; Adenauer, *Erinnerungen*, vol. 3, pp. 376ff, 449ff.

60. Buchheim, *Deutschlandpolitik*, p. 77.

61. For background discussions see Jean Edward Smith, *The Defense of Berlin* (Baltimore: Johns Hopkins University Press, 1963); John Mander, *Berlin: Hostage for the West* (Baltimore: Johns Hopkins University Press, 1962).

62. See Buchheim, *Deutschlandpolitik*, pp. 88ff.

63. Grewe, *Rückblenden*, p. 364.

64. Buchheim, *Deutschlandpolitik*, p. 91; see also Birrenbach, *Meine Sondermissionen*, chap. 1.

65. See Richard Merritt, "A Transformed Crisis: The Berlin Wall," in Roy C. Macridis, ed., *Modern European Governments: Cases in Comparative Policy Making* (Englewood Cliffs, N. J.: Prentice-Hall, 1968); Hans-Peter Schwarz, ed., *Berlinkrise und Mauerbau* (Bonn: Bouvier, 1985); Jack M. Schick, *The Berlin Crises, 1958–1962* (Philadelphia: University of Pennsylvania Press, 1971); Elisabeth H. Barker, "The Berlin Crisis, 1958–1962," *International Affairs* (London) 39, no. 1 (1963): 59–73. On the implications of the Berlin crisis of 1958–59 for the trilateral relationship of Germany, France, and the United States and its effect on NATO developments see Philip Windsor, *Germany and the Management of Détente* (New York: Praeger for the Institute of Strategic Studies, 1971), esp. pp. 47–48.

CHAPTER 6: *Toward Diplomatic Isolation*

Epigraphs. Ludwig Erhard, quoted in *Efforts of the German Government and Its Allies in the Cause of German Unity, 1955–1966* (Bonn: German Federal Foreign

Office, July 1966), p. 55; Wilhelm G. Grewe, *Die deutsche Frage in der Ost-West Entspannung. Zeitgeschichtliche Kontroversen der achtziger Jahre* (Herford: Busse-Seewald, 1986), p. 40.

1. There was a deep historical irony in this. After opposing for more than a decade the basic premise of Adenauer's integrative Western policies, in summer 1960 the SPD in effect accepted it. This was a personal and political triumph for Adenauer. One year later the Berlin Wall and the weak Western reaction to it demonstrated the total failure of Bonn's Eastern policies.

2. Willy Brandt later noted that on August 13, 1961, "a curtain was removed and showed us an empty stage. . . . One can put it more bluntly: We were robbed of illusions. . . . Ulbricht was permitted to deal a bad blow against the shin of the West's superpower—while the United States merely frowned. In subsequent years, my political calculations were importantly shaped by my experiences of that day. What was called my Ostpolitik was formed against this background. . . . Traditional formulas of Western policies had been shown to be ineffective and unrealistic." *Begegnungen und Einsichten. Die Jahre 1960–1975* (Hamburg: Hoffmann und Campe, 1976), p. 17.

3. See Honoré M. Catudal, *Kennedy and the Berlin Wall Crisis: A Case Study in U.S. Decision Making* (Berlin: Berlin Verlag, 1980); Kurt L. Schell, *Bedrohung und Bewährung. Führung und Bevölkerung in der Berlin-Krise* (Cologne and Opladen: Westdeutscher Verlag, 1965); Walther Stützle, *Kennedy und Adenauer in der Berlin-Krise, 1961–1962* (Bonn-Bad Godesberg: Verlag Neue Gesellschaft, 1973). See also Herbert Blankenhorn, *Verständnis und Verständigung* (Frankfurt am Main: Propyläen, 1980), p. 419.

4. "Already for the Kennedy administration détente . . . in Central Europe meant quite clearly a normalization within the framework of the status quo. Later administrations continued on this course in the hope that the German government would on its own initiative take over this course in the foreseeable future." Hans-Peter Schwarz, "Supermacht und Juniorpartner. Ansätze amerikanischer und westdeutscher Ostpolitik," in Hans-Peter Schwarz and Boris Meissner, eds., *Entspannungspolitik in Ost und West* (Cologne: Carl Heymanns, 1979), pp. 147–191; the quotation appears on p. 164. On the general question of Bonn's isolation with respect to its Eastern policies see p. 177. See also the contribution by Andreas Hillgruber, "Westorientierung, Neutralitätsüberlegungen, gesamtdeutsches Bewusstsein," in Henning Köhler, ed., *Deutschland und der Westen. Vorträge und Diskussionsbeiträge des Symposions zu Ehren von Gordon A. Craig* (Berlin: Colloquium, 1984), pp. 159–168.

5. For an intriguing speculation that links the Cuban missile crisis to the German question see Adam B. Ulam, *Expansion and Coexistence* (New York: Praeger, 1968), pp. 668–669. Ulam suggests that the Soviets installed missiles in Cuba to negotiate a deal, to be announced at the United Nations in November, that would have included a German peace treaty, an absolute prohibition of nuclear arms for Germany, and a nuclear-free zone in the Pacific designed primarily to contain the People's Republic of China.

6. For the most powerful articulation of this view see A. W. DePorte, *Europe between the Superpowers: The Enduring Balance* (New Haven and London: Yale University Press, 1979). See also the contributions by Kurt Sontheimer, Theo Sommer, and Frédéric Hartweg in Werner Hill, ed., *Befreiung durch Niederlage. Die*

deutsche Frage: Ursprung und Perspektiven (Frankfurt am Main: Fischer, 1986), all of which argue that the Germans, given the choice, would opt for freedom rather than unity. For a reiteration of DePorte's views and a thoughtful critique by Pierre Hassner see A. W. DePorte, "The Uses of Perspective"; and Pierre Hassner, "Recurrent Stresses, Resilient Structures," both in Robert W. Tucker and Linda Wrigley, eds., *The Atlantic Alliance and Its Critics* (New York: Praeger, 1983), pp. 29–60, 61–94, esp. pp. 65ff. See also Kenneth Waltz, "The Stability of a Bipolar World," *Daedalus* 93 (1964): 881–909; Wolfram F. Hanrieder, "Germany and the Balance of Power," *Polity* 13, no. 3 (Spring 1981): 495–504.

A similar attitude and intention on the stability of the European order seemed to have governed the much-debated ideas expressed by Helmut Sonnenfeldt in a meeting in London of U.S. ambassadors in December 1975. Suggesting that dissension in Eastern Europe could cause an East-West conflagration, Sonnenfeldt recommended a U.S. policy that would respond to East European aspirations for autonomy "within the context of a strong Soviet geopolitical influence." Such a policy would "influence the emergence of Soviet imperial power so that it will not remain founded in sheer power alone by making the base more natural and organic." Completing the "sphere of influence" argument, Secretary of State Kissinger warned at the meeting of the danger of increasingly influential communist parties in Western Europe and asserted that their dominance would be unacceptable. For texts of Sonnenfeldt's and Kissinger's speeches see *New York Times*, April 6, 1976, p. 14; April 7, 1976, p. 16. For a balanced West European reaction see *Manchester Guardian Weekly*, April 11, 1976, p. 9.

7. See the interview of President Kennedy conducted on November 25, 1961, by Aleksei I. Adzhubei (Kruschchev's son-in-law), in "A New Venture in 'Personal Diplomacy': What Kennedy Told the Russian People," *U.S. News and World Report*, December 11, 1961, pp. 84–90. Kennedy was quoted as saying, "If the relations between our countries can be normalized, there will be less military build-up on both sides, but we cannot now withdraw our troops from Europe, way back across the Atlantic ocean, when you merely withdraw your troops to the Soviet Union which is only a few hundred miles away. That is why we need some understanding of what is going to be the situation in Berlin and in Germany" (p. 88). President Kennedy also said he "would hope that, rather than attempting to talk about conditions in Germany as they were 20 years ago, we would look at them as they are today. We have had peace, really, in Europe for 15 years. The problem now is to see if we can reach a negotiation which can settle this matter for another 15 years. Nobody knows what is going to happen in the world over the long run, but at least we ought to be able to settle this matter of Berlin and Germany" (p. 90).

8. Blankenhorn, *Verständnis und Verständigung*, p. 491. In 1984 Walther Leisler Kiep professed to believe that "on the whole it can be said that the Western allies take a positive attitude toward the German Question. The task of German policy now is to persuade the various governments of the practical value to them in making German unity a central element of their policies." Walther Leisler Kiep, "The New Deutschlandpolitik," *Foreign Affairs* 63, no. 2 (Winter 1984–85): 316–329; the quotation is from p. 328.

9. Arthur M. Schlesinger notes, "The German Ambassador to Washington, Wilhelm Grewe, so bored the White House with pedantic and long-winded

recitals that word was finally passed to his government that his recall would improve communication." *A Thousand Days* (Boston: Houghton Mifflin, 1965), p. 403. See also Theodore Sorenson, *Kennedy* (New York: Harper & Row, 1965), p. 559; Hugh Sidey, *John F. Kennedy, President* (New York: Atheneum, 1963), p. 266. For Grewe's side of the story see *Rückblenden, 1976–1951* (Frankfurt am Main: Propyläen, 1979), pp. 442ff. See also the account of Kurt Birrenbach's dealings with John Kenneth Galbraith in Kurt Birrenbach, *Meine Sondermissionen* (Düsseldorf and Vienna: Econ, 1984), pp. 60–62.

10. Under the heading "The Continual Shrinking Process at the Expense of Germany" Wilhelm Grewe traces the progressive narrowing of the German question by way of pointing out the major topics of East-West summits: (1) the postwar European order, especially for Germany and Eastern Europe; (2) Germany as a whole, and Berlin; (3) West Berlin and the status of the GDR; (4) détente in Europe and conflict avoidance in non-European areas of tension; and (5) nuclear arms control. See *Die deutsche Frage in der Ost-West Spannung. Zeitgeschichtliche Kontroversen der achtziger Jahre* (Herford: Busse-Seewald, 1987), esp. p. 88.

I agree with Grewe that points 1–3 amounted to a narrowing of the German question. But points 4 and 5, which became so closely linked in East-West diplomacy, signified not a narrowing but a broadening of the German question. It is precisely the simultaneous narrowing of the German question (to Berlin) and its broadening (to Europe) that posed such diplomatic problems for Bonn.

11. Peter Bender, *Neue Ostpolitik. Vom Mauerbau bis zum Moskauer Vertrag* (Munich: Deutscher Taschenbuch-Verlag, 1986); the quotation appears on p. 61.

12. See Buchheim, *Deutschlandpolitik*, pp. 98–104.

13. For an account of these changes see Pierre Hassner, "German and European Reunification: Two Problems or One?" *Survey*, no. 61 (October 1966): 14–37.

14. As quoted by Zbigniew Brzezinski, *Alternative to Partition: For a Broader Conception of America's Role in Europe* (New York: McGraw Hill, 1965), p. 95.

15. Gerhard Schröder, "Germany Looks at Eastern Europe," *Foreign Affairs* 44, no. 1 (October 1965): 15–25, esp. p. 21.

16. On the material (as well as less tangible) costs of Bonn's nonrecognition policy toward the GDR see Heinrich End, *Zweimal deutsche Aussenpolitik. Internationale Dimensionen des innerdeutschen Konflikts, 1949–1972* (Cologne: Verlag Wissenschaft und Politik, 1973); Peter Bender, *Zehn Gründe für die Anerkennung der DDR* (Frankfurt am Main: Fischer, 1968).

17. See Pierre Hassner, "German and European Reunification," p. 18. See also Hans-Dieter Schulz, "Moskaus wichtigster Partner. Die Stellung der 'DDR' im Ostblock," *Europa-Archiv* 18, no. 21 (1964): 785–794; Kurt P. Tudyka, "Die DDR im Kräftefeld des Ost-West-Konflikts," *Europa-Archiv* 21, no. 1 (1966): 16–27.

18. See "Sowjetzone," *Der Spiegel* 19, no. 26 (1965): 26; "DDR," *Der Spiegel* 20, no. 19 (1966): 47–48.

19. See "Rednertausch," *Der Spiegel* 20, no. 19 (1966): 41–43; "Wiedervereinigung," *Der Spiegel* 20, no. 20 (1966): 23–34; "Rednertausch," *Der Spiegel* 20, no. 23 (1966): 32; "Rednertausch," *Der Spiegel* 20, no. 28 (1966): 15–16; Gerhard Wettig, "Der Dialog zwischen SPD und SED in der kommunistischen Deutschland-Politik," *Aus Politik und Zeitgeschichte*, suppl. to *Das Parlament*, B 9/67 (March 1, 1967). The East Germans may also have been restrained by the Russians; see Willy Brandt, interview by Jürgen Engert, *Christ und Welt*, July 8, 1966.

20. For the text of the Peace Note of March 25, 1966, and several international responses see *Europa-Archiv* 21, no. 7 (1966): 171–175; no. 18 (1966): 465.

21. For a discussion of Soviet motives see Fritz Ermarth, *Internationalism, Security, and Legitimacy: The Challenge to Soviet Interests in East Europe, 1964–1968* (Santa Monica: RAND Corp. Memorandum RM-5909-PR, March 1969); Thomas W. Wolfe, *Soviet Power and Europe, 1945–1970* (Baltimore: Johns Hopkins University Press, 1970), pp. 158–171; W. Hyland and R. W. Shryock, *The Fall of Khrushchev* (New York: Funk and Wagnalls, 1968), pp. 158–183.

22. See Gerhard Wettig, "Moskau und die Grosse Koalition in Bonn," *Aus Politik und Zeitgeschichte,* suppl. to *Das Parlament,* B 10/68 (March 6, 1968). On the importance of the German question for Soviet arms control proposals see Thomas B. Larson, *Disarmament and Soviet Policy, 1964–1968* (Englewood Cliffs, N.J.: Prentice-Hall, 1969).

23. William G. Hyland, "The Soviet Union and Germany," in Wolfram F. Hanrieder, ed., *West German Foreign Policy, 1949–1979* (Boulder: Westview, 1980), pp. 111–126, esp. p. 118.

24. George Liska, *Europe Ascendent* (Baltimore: Johns Hopkins University Press, 1962), p. 80.

25. See Karl E. Birnbaum, "Ways toward European Security," *Survival* 10, no. 6 (June 1968): 193–199, esp. p. 196. See also Wilhelm Cornides, "German Unification and the Power Balance," *Survey,* no. 58 (January 1966): 140–148; "Deutschland-Erklärung," *Der Spiegel* 19, no. 19 (1965): 27–28.

26. See Alfred Grosser, *French Foreign Policy under de Gaulle* (Boston: Little, Brown, 1965), esp. pp. 2–5.

27. DePorte, *Europe between the Superpowers,* p. 240.

28. Some critics of the Erhard government not only feared diplomatic isolation but envisaged the possibility of diplomatic "encirclement." See for example the remarks by Konrad Adenauer and the article "Ost-Locarno, ohne uns?" in *Die Zeit,* October 19, 1965. In his memoirs Henry Kissinger used even stronger words. Speaking of Willy Brandt's Ostpolitik, to which he was by no means totally devoted (see chapter 7), Kissinger wrote, "The Adenauer policies on reunification were bound to bring the Federal Republic into increasing conflict with both allies and the nonaligned. Bonn would have faced a possible crisis with the East practically alone had it held to its earlier course. It was to Brandt's historic credit that he assumed for Germany the burdens and the anguish imposed by necessity." Henry Kissinger, *White House Years* (Boston: Little, Brown, 1979), pp. 409–410.

29. The rivalry extended even to their China policies. After de Gaulle's recognition of the People's Republic in 1964, the Erhard government sought to nurture economic relations with Peking, but had to drop the plan for a trade agreement in the face of strong American objections. Generally, Chancellor Erhard seemed to have a somewhat exaggerated expectation of what German economic prowess could accomplish for German diplomacy. Willy Brandt recounts that when he was lord mayor of Berlin, Ludwig Erhard asked him how many billions he thought it would cost for the Russians to let go of the GDR. See the interview with Brandt in *Der Spiegel* 38, no. 37 (1984): 26.

30. "De Gaulle's preoccupation with East Europe reveals the strong element of 'sacro egoismo' and deception in his policy. Since his concept of Europe is one

led by France, it follows that the two alternatives for France are (1) Europe divided on the Elbe, in which a divided Germany depends on France for eventual reunification, or (2) a united Europe including not only a 70-million-strong Germany but also East Europe (and even Russia), for the latter combined with France would more than balance Germany while East Europe remained in the hands of a hostile and perhaps fearful Russia." Brzezinski, *Alternative to Partition*, pp. 108–109.

31. Alfred Grosser says that his theory about the "gentlemen's agreement" between Adenauer and de Gaulle on this reciprocal arrangement "was confirmed on December 31, 1963, at 8:30 p.m. in a single phrase spoken by General de Gaulle during his New Year's address. Indeed, in naming Pankow [East Berlin] among the capitals of totalitarian states—totalitarian, but states—he was serving notice to Chancellor Erhard: 'If you don't respect your promise of support in Atlantic policy, I can change my terms concerning the German problem.' In my view, these simple words provided a sort of confirmation of the Adenauer-de Gaulle 'deal' dating back to 1958." Grosser, *French Foreign Policy*, pp. 60–61.

32. Philip Windsor, *Germany and the Management of Détente* (New York: Praeger for the Institute for Strategic Studies, 1971), p. 61.

In 1966 Pierre Hassner noted: "Four relatively lasting elements besides the person of de Gaulle and his general policies on the international scene give France a political advantage over Germany, despite the latter's superior population and resources: the sympathy it enjoys in Eastern Europe, the fear and hostility still evoked by Germany in several countries (above all in Poland and Czechoslavakia), the possession by France of a nuclear force which is forbidden to Germany, finally the division of Germany. Of the four, it is the last which seems most important." "German and European Reunification"; the quotation appears on pp. 33–34.

33. See John Herz, "The Formation of the Grand Coalition," in James B. Christoph and Bernard E. Brown, eds., *Cases in Comparative Politics*, 2d ed. (Boston: Little, Brown, 1969).

34. With respect to the reunification issue and the government's new Ostpolitik, at least two opposing views were effectively represented in the Cabinet. As Karl Kaiser wrote in 1968: "To the first [view], Bismarck's *kleindeutsche Lösung* ['small-German' solution] of a unitarian German state, a *Reich*, remains a relevant model to guide German policy. Its support is diffuse, but there are identifiable pockets of strength among conservative Protestants, older civil servants (notably diplomats), refugees, and the extreme right. The second conception—partly as a reaction to the first—is groping for a different solution of the German problem, if necessary in the form of a radical departure from the concepts of past decades and of former German regimes. Its contours remain somewhat indistinct, but the common factor is a willingness to accept a political organization of Germany based on separate political entities, linked with each other and neighbouring entities in various forms of association, co-operation, confederation, etc. Its supporters can be found particularly among Catholics, Protestants left of centre, and more frequently in the younger generation than in the older.

"The impossibility of immediate unification in one state makes the new *Deutschland*—and *Ostpolitik*—acceptable to the 'Neo-Bismarckians' and imperative to the reform-minded 'associationists.' The truce between them is made possible by implementing a policy based on association between the two German states for the *near* future, while proclaiming a unitarian German state as its eventual goal for the *distant* future" (italics in original). *German Foreign Policy in Transition: Bonn between East and West* (London: Oxford University Press, 1968), pp. 125–126. See also Theo Sommer, "Bonn's New Ostpolitik," *Journal of International Affairs* 22, no. 1 (1968): 59–78; James L. Richardson, "Germany's Eastern Policy: Problems and Prospects," *World Today* 24, no. 9 (September 1968): 375–386.

35. See Hans-Jürgen Grabbe, *Unionsparteien, Sozialdemokratie und Vereinigte Staaten von Amerika, 1945–1966* (Düsseldorf: Droste, 1983).

36. For the political significance of the linguistic changes that accompanied the Grand Coalition's Ostpolitik (and later Willy Brandt's) see Wolfgang Bergsdorf, *Herrschaft und Sprache. Studie zur politischen Terminologie der Bundesrepublik Deutschland* (Pfullingen: Neske, 1983).

37. Although Bonn had officially disavowed any claims to the Czechoslovakian territory that was ceded to Nazi Germany in 1938 and returned to Prague in 1945, it refused until December 1966 to declare the Munich Agreement legally invalid, because doing so would have turned the Germans expelled from Czechoslovakia after the Second World War into Czech citizens. After the public outcry that occurred in summer 1964 when Hans Seebohm, West German minister of transport and a leader of the expellee movement, insisted that the Munich pact was still valid, Chancellor Erhard declared that Germany had "no territorial claims whatsoever with regard to Czechoslovakia and separates itself expressly from any declarations which have given rise to a different interpretation." It was symptomatic of Bonn's legalistic foreign policy conceptions, as well as of its sensitivity to pressure from refugee groups, that even the Grand Coalition did not declare the Munich Agreement invalid from the very beginning, which is what Prague wanted in order to preclude the possibility that a combined German claim of "right to the homeland" and self-determination would lead to future demands for border revisions.

38. Willy Brandt, "German Policy toward the East," *Foreign Affairs* 46, no. 3 (April 1968): 476–486; Sommer, "Bonn's New Ostpolitik," esp. p. 60 (see also pp. 70–78). On the contacts between Bonn and East Berlin see "Bemühungen der Bundesregierung um innerdeutsche Regelungen," *Europa-Archiv* 22, no. 14 (1967): D325–330; no. 20 (1967): D472–478; and Dietrich Schwarzkopf, "Die Idee des Gewaltverzichts. Ein Element der neuen Ostpolitik der Bundesrepublik," *Europa-Archiv* 22, no. 24 (1967): 893–900. For an English translation of Kiesinger's and Stoph's exchange of letters see "Efforts of the Government of the Federal Republic of Germany towards Intra-German détente" (Bonn: German Federal Foreign Office, mimeographed).

39. In late 1967 and early 1968 Bonn and Moscow held discussions on multilateral declarations abdicating the use of force in international relations, but they failed, in large part because the Soviet Union insisted on raising highly controversial political issues, such as the recognition of East Germany and the existing European borders, the permanent nuclear abstention of West Germany, and the Kremlin's claim as one of the victors of the Second World War to have the residual right to check the forces of "militarism and neo-Nazism" in West Germany.

For a discussion of Moscow's response to the Grand Coalition see Gerhard

Wettig, "Moskau und die Grosse Koalition in Bonn," *Aus Politik und Zeitgeschichte*, suppl. to *Das Parlament*, B 10/68 (March 6, 1968).

40. For examples of how Bonn used foreign aid programs to induce Third World countries to adhere to the Hallstein Doctrine see *Der Spiegel* 19, no. 12 (1965): 29–33.

The Hallstein Doctrine had also led to a considerable embarrassment for the Erhard administration in spring 1965, when Bonn canceled economic aid to Egypt because Gamal Abdel Nasser had nurtured increasingly cordial relations with East Germany, culminating in a state visit to Egypt by Ulbricht. As a consequence of this half-hearted application of the Hallstein Doctrine, most Arab states broke off diplomatic relations with Bonn. See Wolfgang Wagner, "Der Rückschlag der Bonner Politik in den arabischen Staaten," *Europa-Archiv* 20, no. 10 (May 25, 1965): 359–370; Roger P. Morgan, "The Scope of German Foreign Policy," *The Yearbook of World Affairs* (New York: Praeger, 1966), pp. 78–105, esp. pp. 100–102.

41. See "Dokumente zu den Beziehungen zwischen der Bundesrepublik Deutschland und Osteuropa," *Europa-Archiv* 22, no. 5 (1967): D97–116; no. 6 (1967): D117–135; no. 8 (1967): D187–196; no. 18 (1967): D431–434; 23, no. 5 (1968): D107–108. Sommer, "Bonn's New Ostpolitik," esp. pp. 65ff; "Ostpolitik," *Der Spiegel* 21, no. 6 (1967): 17–18; "Die Ergebnisse der Tagung des Warschauer Pakts in Bukarest," *Europa-Archiv* 21, no. 16 (1966): D413–424.

42. See Wolfgang Berner, "Das Karlsbader Aktionsprogramm," *Europa-Archiv* 22, no. 11 (1967): 393–400; Kurt Birrenbach, "Germany Re-enters the Arena," *Reporter*, May 16, 1968, pp. 9–19.

43. See Bender, *Neue Ostpolitik*, pp. 140–141.

44. See also Willy Brandt, "German Policy toward the East." Brandt suggests that "perhaps the declarations we have offered regarding the renunciation of force can be formulated and safeguarded in such a way that the present borders of Poland can be recognized for the period for which the Federal Republic can commit itself, i.e., until a peace settlement. Thus, in the interest of both nations, the border question would no longer stand in the way of a détente or of a European security system. At the same time, this would prevent this question from being used any longer as a pretext for those who oppose a German-Polish settlement" (pp. 484–485).

In May 1969 Gomulka, in a remarkably dispassionate speech reviewing German-Polish relations, categorically rejected the provisional nature of the recognition formula implied in Brandt's position. Gomulka called for a bilateral Polish-West German treaty recognizing the Oder-Neisse line (a treaty identical with the Polish-East German treaty of Görlitz of 1950) and argued that Brandt's formulation was not fundamentally different from the official government position, since it merely formalized Bonn's de facto acceptance of the Oder-Neisse line but still contained a revisionist element by postponing a final settlement until the signing of a peace treaty.

45. Karl E. Birnbaum, *Peace in Europe: East-West Relations 1966–1968 and the Prospects for a European Settlement* (New York: Oxford University Press, 1970).

46. See for example the interview with Herbert Wehner, then minister of all-German affairs, in *Der Spiegel* 22, no. 35 (1968): 31–32; and the remarks of Willy Brandt quoted in *Die Zeit*, February 18, 1969, p. 7.

47. See Hansjakob Stehle, "Die blockierte Ostpolitik. Wechselwirkungen

zwischen Bonns Bemühungen und Prager Reformkurs," *Die Zeit*, December 10, 1968, p. 8; William E. Griffith, *Eastern Europe after the Soviet Invasion of Czechoslovakia* (Santa Monica: RAND Paper P3983, October 1968).

48. The Soviet invasion, which destroyed some major assumptions underlying French and German policy toward Eastern Europe, gave rise to serious recriminations between General de Gaulle and Chancellor Kiesinger: de Gaulle echoed the Soviet argument that West Germany was to blame for the invasion, because its aggressive economic policy and great economic power would have exerted an irresistible drawing power on an independent Czechoslavakia, and Kiesinger remonstrated that de Gaulle's encouragement of centrifugal tendencies in the Soviet bloc had caused more trouble than had any German policies. See *New York Times*, October 6, 1968.

49. Lawrence L. Whetten, *Germany East and West: Conflicts, Collaboration, and Confrontation* (New York: New York University Press, 1980), pp. 47ff.

50. Fritz Ermarth, *Internationalism, Security, and Legitimacy*, pp. 121–122.

51. See Laszlo Görgey, "Emerging Patterns in West German-East European Relations," *Orbis* 10, no. 3 (1966): 911–929; Mario Levi, "Les relations économiques entre l'Est et l'Ouest en Europe," *Politique Etrangère* 32, nos. 4–5 (1967): 477–492; Fritz Erler, "The Alliance and the Future of Germany," *Foreign Affairs* 43, no. 3 (April 1965): 436–446, esp. p. 438; James Bell, "The Fall of the House of Krupp," *Fortune* 76, no. 2 (August 1967): 72–77; *New York Times*, February 3, 11, and 14, 1967; Konstantin Pritzel, "Der Interzonenhandel," *Aus Politik und Zeitgeschichte*, suppl. to *Das Parlament*, B 48/67 (November 29, 1967).

52. "One senior German diplomat recalls that [President] Johnson told [Chancellor] Kurt G. Kiesinger . . . that the United States 'would no longer fight a war of unification [of the two Germanies]. If you want to live in peace in Europe, you have to look for an alternative.' The German official says that such discussions were no secret inside the top strata of the governments in Washington and Bonn in the late 1960s." Seymour M. Hersh, *The Price of Power: Kissinger in the White House* (New York: Summit, 1983), p. 416. A similar view is expressed by Herbert Blankenhorn, who also argued that the two superpowers were not interested in a solution of European issues. See *Verständnis und Verständigung*, p. 558.

53. The Grand Coalition's refusal to recognize East Germany officially was also directed at the Western powers, in the hope of keeping German unity on the diplomatic agenda. James Richardson, "Germany's Eastern Policy: Problems and Prospects," *World Today* 24, no. 9 (September 1968): 375–386, esp. p. 380.

The self-defeating consequences of the Hallstein Doctrine and the difficulty of scrapping it entirely were again demonstrated in spring 1969, when Iraq, Cambodia, and the Sudan recognized the East German regime. The Cambodia episode touched off a new controversy within the Bonn government that was finally resolved with a compromise: Bonn did not formally break relations with Cambodia but permanently recalled the German ambassador. Now the West German presence in Cambodia was downgraded while East Germany was fully represented by an embassy—an exact reversal of the situation existing previously. (Bonn considered taking less "drastic" action against Cambodia, such as canceling foreign aid and development credits, but it ultimately rejected these as ineffective because of the relatively insignificant amounts involved.)

54. In 1968 Alard von Schack noted: "The more time has passed, and the more the German Democratic Republic has succeeded in consolidating its state structure—succeeded not only in exercising governmental functions but in developing a certain independence from the former occupation power, and in fashioning a greater correspondence with the will of the people and granting them some freedoms and rights—the more the Federal Republic's policy needed to recognize this and modify [previously enunciated doctrines]." Von Schack also called for recognizing the GDR as "at least partially a subject of international law." See "Zum nächsten Abschnitt deutscher Ostpolitik," *Aussenpolitik* 19, no. 2 (February 1968): 81–89, esp. p. 88. See also Jan Hoesch, "Verfassungsrechtliche Aspekte der Deutschland-Politik," *Europa-Archiv* 22, no. 4 (1967): 125–134, esp. pp. 128–130; *Der Spiegel* 21, no. 51 (1967): 27–29; and the proposal by Wilhelm Wolfgang Schütz, chairman of the Committee for Indivisible Germany, in *Die Zeit*, December 8, 1967, p. 9.

55. The term *acceptance without recognition* is from Richardson, "Germany's Eastern Policy," p. 379.

CHAPTER 7: *A New Ostpolitik for the 1970s and 1980s*

Epigraphs. Willy Brandt, speech at the SPD party convention in Saarbrücken, May 13, 1970 (Vorstand der SPD, *Protokoll*, p. 470). The first part of Henry Kissinger's comment is from *Years of Upheaval* (Boston: Little, Brown, 1982), p. 146; the second is from *White House Years* (Boston: Little, Brown, 1979), p. 410.

1. See Arnulf Baring, *Machtwechsel. Die Ära Brandt-Scheel* (Stuttgart: Deutsche Verlags-Anstalt, 1982).

2. On the continuity of these policies see Wilhelm Bruns, *Deutsch-deutsche Beziehungen. Prämissen, Probleme, Perspektiven* (Opladen: Leske, 1984); Peter Bender, "Die Ostpolitik der Regierung Kohl," *Die Neue Gesellschaft/Frankfurter Hefte* 33, no. 10 (October 1986): 884–888; Christian Hacke, *Die Ostpolitik der CDU/CSU: Wege und Irrwege der Opposition seit 1969* (Cologne: Verlag Wissenschaft und Politik, 1975). Actually the term *Wende* was initially applied by the German foreign minister Hans-Dietrich Genscher to changes in economic policy (in a party circular of the FDP in summer 1982).

3. On the difficulties of connecting Soviet-American bilateral détente with multilateral Western détente see J. Robert Schaetzel, *The Unhinged Alliance: America and the European Continent* (New York: Harper & Row, 1975).

4. George F. Kennan, *Memoirs*, vol. 1, *1925–1950* (Boston: Little, Brown, 1967), p. 417.

5. Peter Bender, *Neue Ostpolitik. Vom Mauerbau bis zum Moskauer Vertrag* (Munich: Deutscher Taschenbuch-Verlag, 1986), esp. p. 166.

6. This did not mean of course that the fundamental contradiction between Bonn's aim of integration into the West and the goal of national unity had become reconciled. As E. H. Albert pointed out at the time, "The West Germans want two kinds of greater unity: on the one hand national union and on the other hand political union comprising the nations of Western Europe. These two goals are contradictory, and though no West German politician can admit this in so many words, they must all know it at heart. The closer Western European union is forged, the deeper the gulf between the two parts of Germany must become—

unless Soviet power in Eastern Europe were to collapse. In that case the situation in the West would also be transformed; for the European Communities are based on partnership, while a new German giant could not help dominating Western Europe." "The Brandt Doctrine of Two States in Germany," *International Affairs* 46, no. 2 (April 1970): 293–303; the quotation appears on p. 302. For a thoughtful consideration of the same dilemmas many years later see Theo Sommer, "Die Einheit gegen Freiheit tauschen," *Die Zeit*, July 3, 1987, p. 1.

7. Helmut Schmidt, "Germany in the Era of Negotiations," *Foreign Affairs* 49, no. 1 (October 1970): 40–50; see esp. pp. 45–46. "Ostpolitik in fact involved no diminution of West German ties to the United States and the West. It tended even to strengthen them insofar as it reaffirmed the division of Germany and Europe between the two blocs without removing the weight of Soviet power overshadowing Western Europe." A. W. DePorte, "The Uses of Perspective," in Robert W. Tucker and Linda Wrigley, eds., *The Atlantic Alliance and Its Critics* (New York: Praeger, 1983), pp. 29–59; the quotation appears on p. 35. For a similar point of view see Henry Kissinger, *White House Years* (Boston: Little, Brown, 1979), p. 411.

8. It is interesting to note the differing justifications for their respective détente policies put forth by Washington and Bonn. Whereas Willy Brandt traced his own interest in a dynamic German détente policy to the building of the Berlin Wall in 1961, Henry Kissinger claimed that it was Bonn's Ostpolitik that had energized Western détente policies. This argument must have surprised those Germans who in the 1960s had seen everyone in the West pursue East-West détente policies. See Willy Brandt, *Begegnungen und Einsichten. Die Jahre 1960–1975* (Hamburg: Hoffmann und Campe, 1976), p. 17; Henry Kissinger, *Years of Upheaval* (Boston: Little, Brown, 1982), esp. pp. 145–146. See also Seymour Hersh, *The Price of Power: Kissinger in the White House* (New York: Summit, 1983), esp. chap. 2.

9. For a listing of some of the opponents and an editorial comment see *New York Times*, January 3, 1971. See also Martin J. Hillenbrand, "The United States and Germany," in Wolfram F. Hanrieder, ed., *West German Foreign Policy: 1949–1979* (Boulder: Westview, 1980), pp. 73–91, esp. pp. 82–83. On French reservations see Raymond Poidevin, "Der unheimliche Nachbar. Die deutsche Frage aus französischer Sicht," in David P. Calleo et al., eds., *Geteiltes Land—Halbes Land?* (Frankfurt am Main: Ullstein, 1986), pp. 127–196, esp. pp. 187ff. See also Renata Fritsch-Bournazel, "The French View," in Edwina Moreton, ed., *Germany between East and West* (Cambridge: Cambridge University Press, 1987), pp. 64–82, esp. pp. 73–76.

10. See for example Günther Schmid, *Entscheidung in Bonn. Die Entstehung der Ost- und Deutschlandpolitik, 1969/1970* (Cologne: Verlag Wissenschaft und Politik, 1979). See also Schmid, "Henry Kissinger und die deutsche Ostpolitik. Kritische Anmerkungen zum ost- und deutschlandpolitischen Teil der Kissinger-Memoiren," *Aus Politik und Zeitgeschichte*, suppl. to *Das Parlament*, B 8/80 (1980), pp. 10–20.

11. Kissinger, *White House Years*, p. 410. "The four-power negotiations offered a subtle instrument with which the dynamic of the Social-Liberals' Ostpolitik could be monitored, if needed be, held in check." Helga Haftendorn, *Security and Détente: Conflicting Priorities in German Foreign Policy* (New York: Praeger, 1985), p. 211.

12. See Richard Löwenthal, "Vom Kalten Krieg zur Ostpolitik," in Richard Löwenthal and Hans-Peter Schwarz, eds., *Die Zweite Republik. 25 Jahre Bundesrepublik Deutschland—Eine Bilanz* (Stuttgart: Seewald, 1974), pp. 604–699, esp. pp. 681ff.

13. Raymond L. Garthoff, *Détente and Confrontation: American-Soviet Relations from Nixon to Reagan* (Washington: Brookings Institution, 1985).

14. For a contrary view see Kenneth Dyson, "The Conference on Security and Cooperation in Europe: Europe before and after the Helsinki Final Act," in Kenneth Dyson, ed., *European Détente: Case Studies of the Politics of East-West Relations* (New York: St. Martin's, 1986), pp. 83–112, esp. p. 84.

15. For an authoritative treatment of these two treaties see Claus Arndt, *Die Verträge von Moskau und Warschau. Politische, verfassungsrechtliche und völkerrechtliche Aspekte* (Bonn: Verlag Neue Gesellschaft, 1982).

16. By the end of 1971, however, the American position had softened considerably, for it had become apparent that a majority of NATO members favored the convening of the conference, provided the Berlin issue could be resolved satisfactorily. After the Four Power accord on Berlin of September 1971, Secretary of State William Rogers suggested in early December that "concrete preparations" for the conference be undertaken by the Western allies, and outlined a basic American approach. He said the conference should "encourage the reconciliation of sovereign European states, not confirm their division," stress "substance over atmosphere" and take specific steps to "encourage the freer movement of people, ideas and information," but leave such complex issues as arms control to be discussed in forums "less general and highly visible." See *New York Times*, December 2, 1971, p. 16. See also Wichard Woyke, Klaus Nieder, and Manfred Görtemaker, *Sicherheit für Europa? Die Konferenz von Helsinki und Genf* (Opladen: Leske, 1974).

17. For a discussion of the effects of the Warsaw treaty on relations between Bonn and Warsaw see Hans-Adolf Jacobsen, *Fünf Jahre Warschauer Vertrag. Versuch einer Bilanz der Beziehungen zwischen der BRD und der Volksrepublik Polen, 1970–1975* (Berlin: Berlin Verlag, 1976). On Ostpolitik and Poland see W. W. Kulski, *Germany and Poland: From War to Peaceful Relations* (Syracuse: Syracuse University Press, 1976), esp. chaps. 8–12. For a Polish perspective see Júzef Kokot, *The Logic of the Oder-Neisse Frontier* (Poznan: Wydawnictwo Zachodnie, 1959); Alfons Klafkowski, *The Polish-German Frontier after World War II* (Poznan: Wydawnictwo Poznanskie, 1972).

18. Lawrence L. Whetten, "Appraising the Ostpolitik," *Orbis* 15, no. 3 (Fall 1971): 856–878, esp. pp. 870–871.

19. Bender, *Neue Ostpolitik*, esp. p. 164.

20. Willy Brandt, "German Foreign Policy," *Survival*, no. 12 (December 1969): 370–372, esp. p. 370. See also E. H. Albert, "Bonn's Moscow Treaty and Its Implications," *International Affairs* 47, no. 2 (April 1971): 316–326, esp. p. 319. For an early argument for the legal recognition of East Germany as a separate state see Thomas Oppermann, "German Unity and Peace," *Europa-Archiv* 26, no. 3 (1971): 83–90; trans. in *Survival* 13, no. 7 (July 1971): 239–243. See also Hans Buchheim, *Deutschlandpolitik, 1949–1972. Der politisch-diplomatische Prozess* (Stuttgart: Deutsche Verlags-Anstalt, 1984), pp. 166–167.

Referring to the various treaty arrangements of the 1970s and the Helsinki accord, one German commentator noted sardonically that "only erudite international law specialists can still perceive a juridical difference between [the various treaty provisions] and the full recognition under international law." Wilhelm G. Grewe, *Die deutsche Frage in der Ost-West Spannung. Zeitgeschichtliche Kontroversen der achtziger Jahre* (Herford: Busse-Seewald, 1986), p. 38; see also p. 65. Waldemar Besson already pointed out in 1970, however, that "the question of the recognition of the GDR under international law has for a long time been completely overestimated by both its opponents and its advocates. The decisive factor is solely how much independence the GDR can allow herself in her own German policy. The fact that the GDR is now the one that is practising Adenauer's policy of isolation can be quite easily explained by her lack of actual independence and stability. If her relations with West Germany were normalized, many of the grounds for keeping GDR citizens under political tutelage would disappear. The question is simply whether the leadership of the GDR will be able boundlessly to sustain its isolation combined with unbending attitudes if at the same time West Germany's normalization of relations with Eastern Europe and the Soviet Union continues apace." "The Federal Republic's National Interest," *Aussenpolitik* 21 (1970), pp. 128–129.

21. This remnant of the Hallstein Doctrine (which Brandt's and Scheel's foreign policy team explicitly rejected as outmoded) was intended to serve two purposes. First, it was to be a counterweight to East Germany's "Ulbricht Doctrine," which formulated the demand that Bonn would have to recognize East Germany fully before Eastern European countries could enter into diplomatic relations with West Germany. Second, it was intended to deny East Germany diplomatic recognition by a majority of states until the Federal Republic and German Democratic Republic had arrived at a legally binding intra-German modus vivendi, that is, a general treaty (*Generalvertrag*) normalizing the relations between the two states. Like the Hallstein Doctrine, Bonn's position, dubbed the "Scheel Doctrine," ran into several difficulties. In the first place, during the first two years of Brandt's and Scheel's government, sixteen countries (among them Egypt, Algeria, Ceylon, and Chile) exchanged ambassadors with the GDR, and whereas Bonn had still responded with a cutback in aid when Somalia recognized the GDR in 1970, Chile's recognition of East Germany in 1971 caused hardly a ripple in Bonn. Moreover, by 1972 progressively more countries were ready to enter into diplomatic relations with East Germany as they saw the intra-German dialogue intensifying, and the exclusion of the GDR from important international gatherings (such as the United Nations conference on the human environment in Stockholm in 1972) looked like an increasingly outmoded remnant of the Cold War years. That more and more Third World countries recognized the GDR did not greatly affect East and West German trade. About 17 per cent of West German exports went to the Third World, compared with about 5 per cent of East German exports, and since 1955 West Germany had given about twenty times as much credit assistance to Third World countries as had East Germany. Wilhelm Grewe later wrote that the Hallstein Doctrine was the "weakest point" of Bonn's Germany policy. See Grewe, *Die Deutsche Frage*, p. 32.

22. On the Federal Republic's role in the United Nations see *Aussenpolitik* 36, no. 3 (1985) (Special issue: "Forty Years of the United Nations: Peace-keeping and Peace-making Activities: The Role of the Federal Republic of Germany"). For the background see Ernst-Otto Czempiel, *Macht und Kompromiss. Die Beziehungen der*

Bundesrepublik Deutschland zu den Vereinten Nationen 1956–1970 (Düsseldorf: Bertelsmann Universitätsverlag, 1971); Wilhelm Bruns, "Zehn Jahre Vollmitgliedschaft der beiden deutschen Staaten in den Vereinten Nationen," *Aus Politik und Zeitgeschichte*, suppl. to *Das Parlament*, B 36/83 (September 10, 1983), pp. 17–30.

23. Ernest D. Plock, *The Basic Treaty and the Evolution of East-West German Relations* (Boulder: Westview, 1986), p. 58.

24. For the text of the treaty, as well as explanatory notes and a historical background, see *The Quadripartite Agreement on Berlin of September 3, 1971* (Bonn: Press and Information Office of the Federal Government, 1971); Honoré Catudal, Jr., *The Diplomacy of the Quadripartite Agreement on Berlin* (Berlin: Berlin Verlag, 1977); David M. Keithly, *Breakthrough in the Ostpolitik. The 1971 Quadripartite Agreement* (Boulder: Westview, 1986). For subsequent developments, which by and large stabilized the situation in West Berlin, see Martin J. Hillenbrand, ed., *Die Zukunft Berlins* (Berlin: Ullstein Verlag, 1981); Gerhard Wettig, *Das Vier-Mächte-Abkommen in der Bewährungsprobe. Berlin im Spannungsfeld von Ost und West* (Berlin: Berlin Verlag, 1981).

25. "The Agreement on Berlin," *World Today* 27, no. 10 (October 1971): 416–417, esp. p. 417.

26. The intra-German accord of December 1971 was not the final step in the settlement of the Berlin issue: the agreement still required completion by the Four Powers in a final protocol (with the Soviet Union holding out for ratification by the Bundestag of the Moscow and Warsaw treaties), as well as additional agreements between West Berlin officials and East German officials on technical details.

27. Gerald R. Livingston, "East Germany between Moscow and Bonn," *Foreign Affairs* 50, no. 2 (January 1972): 279–309.

28. "Until 1973 the GDR was, in its relations with the Soviet Union, not much more than a protectorate. . . . [But] in the time period of détente . . . and during the CSCE-process . . . the GDR obtained an enlargement of its possibilities for actions (*Handlungsmöglichkeiten*)—not tremendously, but in any case a little bit. And then, one notices, until 1980, the GDR rose from being a protectorate . . . to a highly dependent junior partner of the Soviet Union." Eberhard Schulz, "Wie gross ist der aussenpolitische Spielraum der DDR?" in Klaus Lange, ed., *Aspekte der deutschen Frage* (Herford: Busse-Seewald, 1986), pp. 43–56; the quotation appears on p. 53.

29. Jonathan Dean, "The Future of Berlin," in Edwina Moreton, ed., *Germany between East and West* (Cambridge: Cambridge University Press, 1987), pp. 157–179, esp. pp. 158, 160, 169.

30. Plock, *Basic Treaty*, p. 61

31. For a thorough treatment of the implications of the Basic Treaty see Georg Ress, *Die Rechtslage Deutschlands nach dem Grundlagenvertrag vom 21. December 1972* (Heidelberg: Springer, 1978); Otto Kimminich, *Grundvertrag: Vertrag über die Grundlagen der Beziehungen zwischen der Bundesrepublik Deutschland und der Deutschen Demokratischen Republik mit Zusatzvereinbarungen und Begleitdokumenten* (Hamburg: J. Heitman, 1975); Plock, *Basic Treaty*; Jens Hacker, *Deutsche unter sich. Politik mit dem Grundvertrag* (Stuttgart: Seewald, 1977).

32. William E. Griffith, *The Ostpolitik of the Federal Republic of Germany* (Cambridge: MIT Press, 1978), pp. 218–219.

33. Whether or not the Federal Republic gave up its claim to sole representation in the Basic Treaty remains a matter of dispute among analysts. For the view that the Basic Treaty abrogated this right see Eric G. Frey, *Division and Détente: The Germanies and Their Alliances* (New York: Praeger, 1987), esp. p. 15; Griffith, *Ostpolitik*, esp. pp. 218–219. For a more qualified view see Buchheim, *Deutschlandpolitik, 1949–1972*, esp. pp. 164–165. For discussions of the ambiguity of the Basic Treaty see Plock, *Basic Treaty*; Lawrence L. Whetten, *Germany East and West: Conflicts, Collaboration, and Confrontation* (New York: New York University Press, 1980), esp. pp. 83–85.

34. Plock, *Basic Treaty*, p. 145.

35. Griffith, *Ostpolitik*, p. 222–223.

36. Philip Windsor, *Germany and the Western Alliance: Lessons from the 1980 Crises*, Adelphi Paper no. 170 (London: International Institute for Strategic Studies, 1981), esp. pp. 5–6.

37. See A. James McAdams, *East Germany and Détente: Building Authority after the Wall* (Cambridge: Cambridge University Press, 1985); Frey, *Division and Détente*.

38. There was yet a further irony in the new Ostpolitik: "Indeed Adenauer himself laid the basis for what he regarded as a particular threat to West Germany: the danger of isolation from the West. The SPD-FDP government, as Brandt observed, had to defend an axiom of Adenauer's early policy against his political heirs who adamantly opposed the new *Ostpolitik*. And even after the transition to Chancellor Schmidt, the problem persisted as witnessed in the reception of the Helsinki accords, which the German opposition rejected, making it the only democratic party in the West to do so. It was the new *Ostpolitik* that brought the Federal Republic back into the mainstream of Western policy." Karl Kaiser, "The New Ostpolitik," in Wolfram F. Hanrieder, ed., *West German Foreign Policy, 1949–1979* (Boulder: Westview, 1980), pp. 145–156; the quotation appears on p. 148.

39. See François Duchene, "SALT, die Ostpolitik und die Liquidierung des Kalten Krieges," *Europa-Archiv* 17, no. 4 (1970): 639–653. For more general treatments of détente see Harry Gelman, *The Brezhnev Politburo and the Decline of Détente* (Ithaca: Cornell University Press, 1984); Robert S. Litwak, *Détente and the Nixon Doctrine: American Foreign Policy and the Pursuit of Stability* (Cambridge: Cambridge University Press, 1984); Garthoff, *Détente and Confrontation*; Manfred Görtemaker, *Die unheilige Allianz. Die Geschichte der Entspannungspolitik, 1943–1979* (Munich: C. H. Beck, 1979); Richard Melanson, ed., *Neither Cold War Nor Détente?* (Charlottesville: University of Virginia Press, 1982); Alvin Z. Rubinstein, "The Elusive Parameters of Détente," *Orbis* 19, no. 4 (Winter 1976): 1344–1358; Adam B. Ulam, "Détente under Soviet Eyes," in Wolfram F. Hanrieder, ed., *Arms Control and Security: Current Issues* (Boulder: Westview, 1979), pp. 87–98; Kenneth Dyson, ed., *European Détente. Case Studies of the Politics of East-West Relations* (New York: St. Martin's, 1986).

40. For arguments that détente could not be expected to work in Third World contexts see the contributions by Arthur M. Schlesinger and Hans J. Morgenthau (who see détente as a function of the balance of power) in George Schwab and Henry Friedlander, *Détente in Historical Perspective: The First CUNY Conference on History and Politics* (New York: Cyrco, 1975). See also Richard J. Barnet, *The Giants: Russia and America* (New York: Simon & Schuster, 1977); Fred Warner Neal,

Détente or Debacle: Common Sense in U.S.-Soviet Relations (New York: W. W. Norton, 1979).

41. For a Soviet view of détente see Leonid Brezhnev, *On the Policy of the Soviet Union and the International Situation* (Garden City, N.Y.: Doubleday, 1973), pp. 230–231. For a concise list of American grievances see John Lewis Gaddis, *Strategies of Containment: A Critical Appraisal of Postwar American National Security Policy* (New York: Oxford University Press, 1982), pp. 310–311. See also Garthoff, *Détente and Confrontation*; Boris Meissner, "Das Entspannungskonzept der Hegemonialmacht: Entspannungsbegriff und Entspannungspolitik aus der Sicht der Sowjetunion," in Hans-Peter Schwarz and Boris Meissner, eds., *Entspannungspolitik in Ost und West* (Cologne: Carl Heymanns, 1979), pp. 1–54. This volume also contains contributions on the détente concepts of the GDR, Poland, Czechoslovakia, Yugoslavia, Rumania, the Federal Republic, the United States, France, and Italy. See also John Van Oudenaren, *The Soviet Union and Eastern Europe: Options for the 1980s and Beyond* (Santa Monica: RAND Corp., 1984); John Lewis Gaddis, "Containment: Its Past and Future," *International Security* 51, no. 4 (Spring 1981): 74–102, esp. pp. 89–93.

42. The Helsinki Final Act called for review conferences to be held at five-year intervals. The first began in Belgrade in October 1977 and ended in March 1978. At this meeting, Carter was able to persuade the NATO partners to use the opportunity to show the poor human rights record of the Soviet Union and Eastern European countries. At the second, held in Madrid from November 1980 to September 1983, the emphasis was on the formation of a separate conference on European disarmament. In the final communiqué of the meeting, there was a mandate for the Conference on Confidence- and Security-Building Measures and Disarmament in Europe (CDE), to begin in Stockholm in January 1984. One of the requirements imposed by the Reagan administration as a condition of its supporting this conference was that it be held under the auspices of the CSCE Conference, in order not to diminish the relevance of human rights measures. In addition, the CDE was to focus on confidence-building measures, not only security measures, to keep it separate from the MBFR talks. A third follow-up meeting to the CSCE Accords began in November 1986 in Vienna. See Jonathan Dean, *Watershed in Europe* (Lexington, Mass.: Lexington Books, 1987), esp. pp. 110–115, chap. 8. See also Vojtech Mastny, *Helsinki, Human Rights, and European Security* (Durham: Duke University Press, 1986).

43. For an extensive bibliography on Bonn's Germany policy since 1980 see Joachim Held, *Ostpolitik der Bundesrepublik Deutschland. Literatur seit 1980* (Ebenhausen: Stiftung Wissenschaft und Politik, 1987).

44. These demands were reiterated in Erich Honecker's so-called Gera demands in 1980, in which he called for the full recognition of East German citizenship, the conversion of the standing representatives in Bonn and East Berlin into embassies, the settlement of the Elbe border issue, and the dismantling of the West German human rights monitoring center at Salzgitter. See Peter Jochen Winters, "Erich Honecker in der Bundesrepublik," *Deutschland Archiv* 20, no. 10 (October 1987): 1009–1016, esp. p. 1012. For a discussion of the transformation of the national question for the East Germans see Roland W. Schweizer, "Die DDR und die Nationale Frage. Zum Wandel der Positionen von der Staatsgründung bis zur Gegenwart," *Aus Politik und Zeitgeschichte*, suppl. to *Das Parlament*, B 51–52/85 (December 21, 1985), pp. 37–54.

45. The United States and Western Europe (especially the Federal Republic) perceived the meaning of détente differently. "The East-West détente in Europe had different origins, wider impact, and deeper roots than the American-Soviet détente of the 1970's had. But it was only after Afghanistan and the US effort to make Soviet behavior a touchstone of East-West relations that the full extent of the difference, and its significance in both East-West and American-Europe relations, became evident. While the Europeans saw Soviet behavior in Afghanistan as reprehensible, they saw détente in Europe as working—and working to their benefit." Garthoff, *Détente and Confrontation*, p. 977. For a discussion of the benefits of détente for West Germany see Horst Ehmke, "A Second Phase of Détente," *World Policy* 4, no. 3 (Summer 1987): 363–382. For a highly negative German view of the results of détente see Hans-Peter Schwarz, "Die Alternative zum Kalten Krieg? Bilanz der bisherigen Entspannung," in Schwarz and Meissner, *Entspannungspolitik*, pp. 275–303. Schwarz is especially critical of what he considered misguided attempts to enlarge trade relations between East and West Germany; see pp. 294–295.

For an account of the difficulties the GDR faced within its own alliance on account of its détente policies see McAdams, *East Germany and Détente*, esp. chaps. 5–7. See also Gerhard Wettig, *Die Sowjetunion, die DDR und die Deutschland-Frage, 1965–1976* (Stuttgart: Bonn aktuell, 1976); Peter C. Ludz, *Die DDR zwischen Ost und West* (Munich: C. H. Beck, 1977); Kurt Sontheimer and Wilhelm Bleek, *Die DDR: Politik, Gesellschaft, Wirtschaft* (Hamburg: Hoffmann und Campe, 1979).

46. See Siegfried Kupper, "Festhalten an der Entspannung. Das Verhältnis der beiden deutschen Staaten nach Afghanistan," *Deutschland Archiv* 16, no. 10 (October 1983): 1045–1065.

47. The importance of Berlin in keeping the German question "open" should not be underestimated. Without the official Four Power status of the city, the German question might have lost its day-to-day relevance for the Western powers. Indeed, the lack of follow-up to President Reagan's ill-considered proposal for the internationalization of the city (made at the festivities marking its 750th anniversary) attests to the unwillingness of the occupying powers and of the West Germans themselves to alter the status quo in Berlin. See "Berlin. Amateure am Werk," *Der Spiegel* 42, no. 3 (January 1988): 34–37. See also Edwina Moreton, "The German Question in the 1980s"; and Jonathan Dean, "The Future of Berlin," both in Edwina Moreton, ed., *Germany between East and West* (Cambridge: Cambridge University Press, 1987), pp. 3–20, 157–179; Udo Wetzlaugk, *Berlin und die deutsche Frage* (Cologne: Verlag Wissenschaft und Politik, 1985); Ronald A. Francisco and Richard L. Merritt, eds., *Berlin between Two Worlds* (Boulder: Westview, 1986); Gerd Langguth, "Innerdeutsche und internationale Aspekte der Berlin-Politik," *Aus Politik und Zeitgeschichte*, suppl. to *Das Parlament*, B 33–34/86 (August 16, 1986), pp. 36–46.

48. See Pierre Hassner, "The Shifting Foundation," *Foreign Policy*, no. 48 (Fall 1982), esp. p. 13. Even before the Soviet intervention in Poland, Zbigniew Brzezinski, then American national security adviser, wrote on October 29, 1980, "The Germans have told us . . . that détente should not be the victim of such intervention; in other words, the Germans are saying that in the event of a Soviet intervention the Germans would be prepared to continue with their East-West relationship. This was the best proof yet of the increasing finlandization of the

Germans." "White House Diary, 1980," *Orbis* 32, no. 1 (Winter 1988): 32–48; the quotation appears on p. 34.

49. For a discussion of the tensions between Bonn and Moscow see Hannes Adomeit, "The German Factor in Soviet *Westpolitik*," *Annals*, AAPSS [American Academy of Political and Social Sciences], no. 481 (September 1985): 15–28.

50. Richard Löwenthal, "The German Question Transformed," *Foreign Affairs* 63, no. 2 (Winter 1984–85): 303–315; the quotation is from p. 313. Most likely, the domestic and international legitimacy that accrued to East Germany because of intensified inter-German relations was a primary motivation to leaders of the GDR. "The leaders of the GDR were wary of the idea of any kind of détente with the West because it seemed to undermine their efforts to generate domestic authority; but by the 1980s, they seemed to welcome the process precisely because it served those ends." McAdams, *East Germany and Détente*, p. 6. See also Fred S. Oldenburg, "East German Foreign and Security Interest," in Edwina Moreton, ed., *Germany between East and West* (Cambridge: Cambridge University Press, 1987), pp. 108–122.

51. For an account of the intensified human, economic, and financial contacts between the two Germanies in the 1980s see Ernst Martin, *Zwischenbilanz. Deutschlandpolitik der 8oer Jahre* (Stuttgart: Bonn aktuell, 1986); Ottfried Hennig, "Zum Stand der innerdeutschen Beziehungen," *Politische Studien* 37, no. 289 (September-October 1986): 494–502; Dorothee Wilms, *The German Question in Inner-German Relations*, Occasional Paper Series, no. 8-87 (Bonn: Konrad Adenauer Stiftung, 1987); Renata Fritsch-Bournazel, *Das Land in der Mitte. Die Deutschen im europäischen Kräftefeld* (Munich: Iudicium, 1986). See also Eckhard Jesse, "Die deutsche Frage rediviva. Eine Auseinandersetzung mit der neueren Literatur," *Deutschland Archiv* 17, no. 4 (April 1984): 397–414; Wilhelm Bruns, "Die deutsch-deutschen Beziehungen in der zweiten Hälfte der achtziger Jahre," *Aus Politik und Zeitgeschichte*, suppl. to *Das Parlament*, B 51–52/85 (December 21, 1985), pp. 23–35.

52. On the symbolic and political implications of Honecker's visit see Theo Sommer, "Deutschland: Gedoppelt, nicht getrennt. Honeckers Besuch in Bonn: Worum es geht." *Die Zeit*, September 11, 1987; Peter Jochen Winters, "Erich Honecker in der Bundesrepublik," *Deutschland Archiv* 20, no. 10 (October 1987): 1009–1016; Wilhelm Bruns, "After the Honecker Visit—And What Now?" *Aussenpolitik* 38, no. 4 (1987): 344–353.

53. For an overview of renewed European anxieties about the "German question" see Eberhard Schulz and Peter Danylow, eds., *Bewegung in der deutschen Frage? Die ausländischen Besorgnisse über die Entwicklung in den beiden deutschen Staaten*, 2d ed. (Bonn: Forschungsinstitut der Deutschen Gesellschaft für Auswärtige Politik, 1985); Hannelore Horn and Siegfried Mampel, eds., *Die deutsche Frage aus der heutigen Sicht des Auslandes* (Berlin: Duncker & Humblot, 1987).

Eric Frey notes that when the interests of both German states seem to coincide at the expense of European security interests (the Germanization of détente) the German problem resurfaces: "In popular political thought the danger of the "German question' is almost always based on the link between German nationalism and defection from the alliances." Frey, *Division and Détente*, p. 86.

54. This second phase of Ostpolitik was especially problematic for the government because of the subgovernmental foreign policy being conducted by the

SPD with the SED of East Germany on security issues. See Edwina Moreton, "The German Question in the 1980s"; and William E. Griffith, "The American View," both in Edwina Moreton, ed., *Germany between East and West* (Cambridge: Cambridge University Press, 1987), pp. 3–20, 49–63.

55. Robert E. Osgood, *American and European Approaches to East-West Relations* (Washington: Johns Hopkins Foreign Policy Institute, 1982), p. 8. See also Uwe Nerlich and James A. Thomson, eds., *Das Verhältnis zur Sowjetunion. Zur politischen Strategie der Vereinigten Staaten und der Bundesrepublik Deutschland. Eine Untersuchung der RAND Corporation, Santa Monica, und der Stiftung Wissenschaft und Politik/SWP, Ebenhausen* (Baden-Baden: Nomos, 1986).

56. For the negative political consequences of the Reagan administration's security and arms control policies in the Federal Republic see Jonathan Dean, "How to Lose Germany," *Foreign Policy*, no. 55 (Summer 1984): 54–72, esp. p. 54; Werner J. Feld, *Arms Control and the Atlantic Community* (New York: Praeger, 1987). For a discussion of the disjuncture between political purpose and strategic preparations in the Reagan administration see Barry R. Posen and Stephen W. Van Evera, "Reagan Administration Defense Policy: Departure from Containment," in Kenneth A. Oye, Robert J. Lieber, and Donald Rothchild, eds., *Eagle Resurgent? The Reagan Era in American Foreign Policy* (Boston: Little, Brown, 1987), pp. 75–114. For a German view see Hartmut Wasser, ed., *Die Ära Reagan. Eine erste Bilanz* (Stuttgart: Klett-Cotta, 1988).

"In the 1980s and 1990s growing worries about security and defence issues among Western publics in general and the West German public in particular mean that a failure to manage properly the issue of security in Europe could well generate new and profound problems for the Western alliance. Because of West Germany's special position as a front line state, the problem could become very specifically German. Thus has the nature of the German problem changed. The question is no longer how the German national question itself will affect European politics over the next ten to fifteen years, but how European politics will affect the disposition of the two Germanies." Moreton, "The German Question in the 1980s," p. 20.

57. See Wolfgang Venohr, "Deutschlands Mittellage. Betrachtungen zur ungelösten deutschen Frage," *Deutschland Archiv* 17, no. 8 (August 1984): 820–829; Fritz Stern, "Germany in a Semi-Gaullist Europe," *Foreign Affairs* 58, no. 4 (Spring 1980): 867–886; Günter Gaus, *Wo Deutschland liegt. Eine Ortsbestimmung* (Berlin: Severin and Siedler, 1983).

58. To refer to the concepts of *Sonderweg*, *Mittellage*, and *Mitteleuropa* in their original German rather than to translate them as "special path," "location in the middle," and "Central Europe" is itself an indication of how they lose in translation the deeply rooted, complex historical and psychological connotations that have grown around them not only in German and European historiography but also in the public political discourse.

Yet another term that defies translation is *Sonderbewusstsein*, as distinguished from the German *Sonderweg*. Karl Dietrich Bracher makes this distinction, reserving the latter for the outrages committed by the Nazi regime and protecting the concept of *Sonderbewusstsein* from these negative connotations. Karl Dietrich Bracher, *Deutscher Sonderweg—Mythos oder Realität?* (Munich: Institut für Zeitgeschichte, 1982), pp. 46–53. See also Kurt Sontheimer, "Ein deutscher Sonderweg?" in Werner Weidenfeld, ed., *Die Identität der Deutschen* (Munich: Karl Hanser, 1983), pp. 324–336.

Already in 1951, Ludwig Dehio noted that he rejected interpretations that "regard the history of Germany . . . as growing, like a tree, out of purely German roots and which overlook the extent to which German history has been entangled with the history of other nations. . . . I am also departing from those interpretations that take a broader view of events and emphasize contemporary analogies. There is some truth in both these views, but both require amplification. This is especially true of the interpretation (more popular abroad) that isolates Germany. This view tends to over-emphasize Germany's peculiar characteristics, whereas the second view tends to disregard them. Those who acknowledge that Germany has in our time exercised supreme power will avoid both these errors. They will see that, in her role of supremacy, Germany was essentially different from her fellows in the family of nations, but they will not regard this as proof that Germany has always possessed this distinct personality." *Germany and World Politics in the Twentieth Century* (New York: W. W. Norton, 1967), p. 12.

59. Timothy Garton Ash, "Does Central Europe Exist?" *New York Review of Books*, October 9, 1986, pp. 45–52; the quotation appears on p. 45. For a contending view see Zbigniew Brzezinski, "The Future of Yalta," *Foreign Affairs* 63, no. 2 (Winter 1984–85): 279–302. See also Peter Bender, "Mitteleuropa—Mode, Modell oder Motiv?" *Die Neue Gesellschaft/Frankfurter Hefte* 34, no. 4 (April 1987): 297–304. See also the literature cited in n. 9 to the introduction to pt. 2.

60. Wilhelm Bruns, "Die deutsch-deutschen Beziehungen: Vom Sonderkonflikt zum Sonderkonsens?" *Politische Bildung* 20, no. 1 (1987): 38–52; Peter Bender, "Erträgliche Beziehungen. Über die beiden deutschen Staaten und ihr Verhältnis zueinander," *Die Neue Gesellschaft/Frankfurter Hefte* 34, no. 10 (October 1987): 868–870. See also Peter Bender, *Das Ende des ideologischen Zeitalters. Die Europäisierung Europas* (Berlin: Severin und Siedler, 1981).

61. Richard von Weizsäcker, "Probleme der Deutschland- und Europapolitik," interview by Deutschlandfunk, August 19, 1984, *Informationen* 17 (Bonn: Bundesminister für innerdeutsche Beziehungen, 1984). See also the interview with Willy Brandt ("Wir können nicht an den Grossen vorbei") in *Der Spiegel* 38, no. 37 (1984): 25–28.

62. For an eloquent plea to overcome the integrated systems of both parts of Europe, perhaps within the framework of the CSCE, see Werner Weidenfeld, "The European Community and Eastern Europe," *Aussenpolitik* 38, no.2 (1987): 134–143. For an account of how the United States persists in opposing the CSCE framework see G. Jonathon Greenwald, "Vienna: A Challenge to the Western Alliance," Ibid., pp. 155–167. See also Ehmke, "A Second Phase of Détente," esp. pp. 378–379.

INTRODUCTION TO PART III

Epigraphs. Hans J. Morgenthau, *Politics among Nations: The Struggle for Power and Peace*, 5th ed. (New York: Alfred A. Knopf, 1973), p. 32. Helmut Schmidt, interview with the Swiss journal *Finanz und Wirtschaft* 49 (February 1975), quoted in Edwin Hartrich, *The Fourth and Richest Reich* (New York: Macmillan, 1980), p. 5.

1. For example, Karl Hardach has noted that in the Germany of this century,

"economic events—indeed the entire economic system—have to a large degree been formed by political decisions . . . [and] the course of economic events during the last half century or so . . . has been determined by politics at the highest level." *The Political Economy of Germany in the Twentieth Century* (Berkeley: University of California Press, 1980), pp. xi, 6; original German ed.: *Wirtschaftsgeschichte Deutschlands im 20. Jahrhundert* (Göttingen: Vandenhoeck & Ruprecht, 1976). See also Gerd Hardach, *Deutschland in der Weltwirtschaft, 1870–1970: Eine Einführung in die Sozial- und Wirtschaftsgeschichte* (Frankfurt am Main: Campus, 1977); Dieter Grosser, ed., *Der Staat in der Wirtschaft der Bundesrepublik* (Opladen: Leske, 1985).

Similarly, the German Democratic Republic's economic, political, and social order was shaped by its association with the Soviet Union. Each German state reflected the economic and political systems of its superpower ally, and the subsequent integration of both in their respective alliances further sharpened these divergences. See Hardach, *Political Economy*, p. 7. See also Martin Schnitzer, *East and West Germany: A Comparative Economic Analysis* (New York: Praeger, 1972); U.S. Congress, Joint Economic Committee, *Economic Developments in Countries of Eastern Europe* (Washington: GPO, 1970); Gert Leptin, *Die deutsche Wirtschaft nach 1945. Ein Ost-West Vergleich* (Opladen: Leske, 1970); Wolfgang F. Stolper, *The Structure of the East German Economy* (Cambridge: Harvard University Press, 1960); Karl C. Thalheim, *Die wirtschaftliche Entwicklung der beiden Staaten in Deutschland* (Opladen: Leske, 1978); Werner Obst, *Reiz der Idee—Pleite der Praxis. Ein deutschdeutscher Wirtschaftsvergleich* (Osnabrück and Zurich: Interfrom, 1983).

2. This makes for an interesting comparison between the Federal Republic and Japan, for Japanese trade and monetary policies, although frequently criticized, are usually not seen as reflecting fundamental political purposes.

There are other differences in Germany's and Japan's economic reconstruction and security efforts that are equally striking. In contrast to Japan, the Federal Republic's economic recovery took place in the regional context of West European integration, and German security policies were shaped by the multilateral collective defense arrangements of NATO. The unresolved issue of Germany's division and the Cold War competition over Central Europe had a profound effect on the Federal Republic's economic and defense policies and compelled the Germans, unlike the Japanese, to acquiesce in rearmament in return for the restoration of political sovereignty. See Wolfram F. Hanrieder, "Security and Economics: German Defense Policy and Prosperity in the Postwar Period," in Haruhiro Fukui et al., eds., *Japan and West Germany: Political Management of Economic Change* (mimeographed, 1985). See also Michael Schaller, *The American Occupation of Japan: The Origins of the Cold War in Asia* (New York: Oxford University Press, 1985); Yonosuke Nagi and Akira Iriye, eds., *The Origins of the Cold War in Asia* (New York: Columbia University Press, 1977); Theodore Cohen, *Remaking Japan: The American Occupation as New Deal*, ed. Herbert Passin (New York: Free Press, 1987); Arnulf Baring and Masamori Sase, eds., *Zwei zaghafte Riesen. Deutschland und Japan seit 1945* (Stuttgart: Belser, 1977); Karl Hax and Willy Kraus, eds. *Industriegesellschaften im Wandel. Japan und die BRD* (Düsseldorf: Bertelsmann, 1970).

3. Antony J. Blinken, *Ally vs. Ally: America, Europe, and the Siberian Pipeline Crisis* (Westport, Conn.: Greenwood, 1987); Reimund Seidelmann, "Die sowjetischen Energieimporte in die Bundesrepublik Deutschland—Abhängigkeit oder politische Zusammenarbeit?" *Beiträge zur Konfliktforschung* 12, no. 1 (1982).

4. Reinhold Biskup, *Deutschlands offene Handelsgrenze. Die DDR als Nutzniesser des EWG-Protokolls über den innerdeutschen Handel* (Berlin: Ullstein, 1976); Rudolf Morawitz, "Der innerdeutsche Handel und die EWG nach dem Grundvertrag," *Europa-Archiv* 28, no. 10 (1973): 353–362; Ulrich Dietsch, *Aussenwirtschaftliche Aktivitäten der DDR* (Hamburg: Weltarchiv, 1976); Siegfried Kupper, "Politische Aspekte des innerdeutschen Handels," in Claus-Dieter Ehlermann et al., *Handelspartner DDR—Innerdeutsche Wirtschaftsbeziehungen* (Baden-Baden: Nomos, 1975); Heinrich End, *Zweimal deutsche Aussenpolitik. Internationale Dimensionen des innerdeutschen Konflikts, 1949–1972* (Cologne: Verlag Wissenschaft und Politik, 1973); Bernhard May, *Kosten und Nutzen der deutschen EG-Mitgliederschaft* (Bonn: Europa-Union-Verlag, 1982).

5. On the remarkable continuity of the political intent of Germany's Eastern trade policies see Hans-Jürgen Perrey, *Der Russlandausschuss der deutschen Wirtschaft. Die deutsch-sowjetischen Wirtschaftsbeziehungen der Zwischenkriegszeit* (Munich: R. Oldenbourg, 1985).

6. From the German perspective, enlargement of trade appears desirable on both grounds. The Federal Republic's trade with the Soviet Union has a large potential because of complementary needs and pronounced comparative advantages (the Germans export finished goods and technology and import raw materials and energy), and although these large economic complementaries are absent between the Federal Republic and Eastern Europe (mainly because most East European exports are not suitable for Western markets), political considerations will suggest the continuation and enlargement of West German trade with Eastern Europe, even if it requires credit guarantees and other measures to ease the East Europeans' hard currency shortages.

From the perspective of the Soviet Union, the issue of East-West trade remains complicated. Whereas the Soviet Union and East European countries are becoming less insular economically, a large political question is unresolved or only ambiguously and revocably resolved: for what degree of economic autarky or interdependence the Soviet bloc will aim. This question will have an important impact on German-Soviet relations throughout the 1990s. Whatever the Soviet Union's decision on the matter of autarky turns out to be, and it will most likely be a decision that is incremental and hedged, it will carry a major import for the Soviet Union, Eastern Europe, and the future of the overall European order. For a prospective discussion of the 1980s see Lawrence Y. Caldwell and William Diebold, *Soviet-American Relations in the 1980s: Superpower Politics and East-West Trade* (New York: McGraw Hill, 1981).

The literature on the politics of West Germany's trade with the East is large. See Robert W. Dean, *West German Trade with the East: The Political Dimension* (New York: Praeger, 1974); Heiner Ernst, *Der Osthandel—Eine politische Waffe?* (Stuttgart: J. Fink, 1964); Michael Kreile, *Osthandel und Ostpolitik* (Baden-Baden: Nomos, 1978); Rolf Krengel, *Die Bedeutung des Ost-West Handels für die Ost-West Beziehungen* (Göttingen: Vandenhoeck & Ruprecht, 1967); Angela E. Stent, *Economic Relations with the Soviet Union: American and West German Perspectives* (Boulder: Westview, 1985); Stent, *From Embargo to Ostpolitik: The Political Economy of West German-Soviet Relations, 1955–1980* (Cambridge: Cambridge University Press, 1981); Klaus Bolz, Hermann Clement, and Petra Pissulla, *Die Wirtschaftsbeziehungen zwischen der BRD und der Sowjetunion. Entwicklung, Bestimmungsfaktoren und Perspektive* (Hamburg: Weltarchiv, 1976); Connie M. Friesen, *The Political Economy of East-West Trade* (New York: Praeger, 1976); Stanislaus Wasowski, ed., *East-West Trade and the Technology Gap* (New York: Praeger, 1970); Samuel Pisar, *Coexistence and Commerce: Guidelines for Transactions between East and West* (New York: McGraw-Hill, 1970); Atlantic Council, *East-West Trade: Managing Encounter and Accommodation* (Boulder: Westview, 1977); M. M. Kostecki, *East-West Trade and the GATT System* (New York: St. Martin's for the Trade Policy Research Centre, 1978); Marshall Goldman, *Détente and Dollars: Doing Business with the Soviets* (New York: Basic Books, 1975); Franklin D. Holzman and Robert Levgold, "The Economics and Politics of East-West Relations," in C. Fred Bergsten and Lawrence B. Krause, eds., *World Politics and International Economics* (Washington: Brookings Institution, 1975); Roger E. Kanet, "East-West Trade and the Limits of Western Influence," in Charles Gati, ed., *The International Politics of Eastern Europe* (New York: Praeger, 1976); Karl-Heinz Gross, "Der innerdeutsche Handel aus internationaler Sicht," *Deutschland Archiv* 19, no. 10 (1986): 1075–1084; Matthias Schmitt, "Ökonomische Perspektiven in der Ostpolitik," *Aussenpolitik* 22, no. 4 (1971): 193–208; Heinrich Machowski, "Zur politischen Ökonomie der Beziehungen zwischen dem RGW und der EWG," *Aus Politik und Zeitgeschichte*, suppl. to *Das Parlament*, B 12/82 (March 27, 1982), pp. 33–44; Wolfram F. Hanrieder, "Germany as Number Two?" *International Studies Quarterly* 26, no. 1 (March 1982): 57–86.

7. See for example Joachim Hütter, "Die Stellung der Bundesrepublik Deutschland in Westeuropa. Hegemonie durch wirtschaftliche Dominanz?" *Integration* 1, no. 3 (1978): 103–113; Ernst-Otto Czempiel, "Die Bundesrepublik—Eine heimliche Grossmacht?" *Aus Politik und Zeitgeschichte*, suppl. to *Das Parlament*, B 26/79 (June 30, 1979), pp. 3–19; Michael Kreile, "Die Bundesrepublik Deutschland—eine 'économie dominante' in West Europa?" *Politische Vierteljahresschrift*, suppl. 9 (1978): 236–256. For the origin of the concept see François Perroux, "Esquisse d'une théorie de l'économie dominante," *Economie Appliquée* 1 (1948): 243–300; for a critique see Mark Blaug, 'A Case of Emperor's Clothes: Perroux' Theories of Economic Domination," *Kyklos* 17, no. 4 (1964): 551–563.

8. C. Fred Bergsten, "Die amerikanische Europa-Politik angesichts der Stagnation des Gemeinsamen Marktes. Ein Plädoyer für Konzentration auf die Bundesrepublik," *Europa-Archiv* 29, no. 4 (1974): 115–123; Bergsten, "The United States and Germany: The Imperative of Economic Bigemony," in C. Fred Bergsten, *Toward a New International Economic Order: Selected Papers of C. Fred Bergsten, 1972–1974* (Lexington, Mass.: Lexington Books-D. C. Heath, 1975), pp. 333–344.

Over the years Bergsten seems to have given up on the possibility of a German-American "bigemony," calling instead for a Japanese-American economic condominium. See C. Fred Bergsten, "What to Do about the U.S.-Japan Economic Conflict," *Foreign Affairs* 60, no. 5 (Summer 1982): 1059–1075; and in particular "Economic Imbalances and World Politics," *Foreign Affairs* 65, no. 4 (Spring 1987): 770–794, esp. pp. 789–794. See also Robert Gilpin's argument that after the decline of American financial leadership it is Japan's turn to assume it. *The Political Economy of International Relations* (Princeton: Princeton University Press, 1987), esp. pp. 340, 376 ff.

On the more general question of joint economic hegemony see Charles P. Kindleberger, "Dominance and Leadership in the International Economy," *International Studies Quarterly* 25, no. 3 (June 1981): 242–254, esp. p. 252.

For a cautionary German attitude see Otmar Emminger, *Verteidigung der* DM. *Plädoyers für stabiles Geld* (Frankfurt am Main: Fritz Knapp, 1980), esp. pp. 40, 122–125. In 1985 Helmut Schmidt wrote that the United States expected its economic allies to "perform ridiculous feats," such as pulling "the vast economy of the United States out of its inflationary and unemployment mess in the late 1970s." *A Grand Strategy for the West: The Anachronism of National Strategies in an Interdependent World* (New Haven and London: Yale University Press, 1985), p. 17.

9. Margaret Sharp, ed., *Europe and the New Technologies* (Ithaca: Cornell University Press, 1986); Andrew J. Pierre, ed., *A High Technology Gap? Europe, America and Japan* (New York: Council on Foreign Relations, 1987). For projections of Germany's economic future see Bruno Tietz, *Optionen bis 2030. Szenarien und Handlungsalternativen für Wirtschaft und Gesellschaft in der Bundesrepublik Deutschland* (Stuttgart: Poller, 1986); *Die Bundesrepublik 1990/2000/2010*, Prognos-Report no. 12 (Stuttgart: Poller, 1986). For an argument of how West European economies have become "deindustrialized" since the mid-1970s see Staffan Burenstam Linder, *The Pacific Century: Economic and Political Consequences of Asian-Pacific Dynamism* (Stanford: Stanford University Press, 1986). For political programs on how to deal with issues of growth and redistribution of income see Kurt H. Biedenkopf, *Die neue Sicht der Dinge* (Munich: Piper, 1985); Lothar Späth, *Wende in die Zukunft* (Reinbek: Rowohlt, 1985); Peter Glotz, *Manifest für eine neue politische Linke* (Berlin: Siedler, 1985); Wolfgang Roth, *Der Weg aus der Krise* (Munich: Kindler, 1985).

10. Fritz Stern, "Germany in a Semi-Gaullist Europe," *Foreign Affairs* 58, no. 4 (Spring 1980): 867–885, esp. p. 875.

11. For a view that sees in contemporary German economic dynamism an unrelieved expression of historic German expansionism see Raymond Poidevin, *L'Allemagne et le monde au XXe siècle* (Paris: Masson, 1983). For a presentation of highly diverse views on the political implications of the German economic role in Europe see Gabriele Weber, ed., *Die europapolitische Rolle der Bundesrepublik Deutschland aus der Sicht ihrer EG-Partner*, Materialien zur Europapolitik, vol. 6 (Bonn: Europa-Union-Verlag, 1984).

12. Generally speaking, monetary policies tend to be more amenable to governmental direction than are trade issues, which is a major reason why my subsequent discussion tends to focus on them. For a full argument see Gernot Volger, *Die Zahlungsbilanzpolitik der Vereinigten Staaten. Dominanz und Dependenz im internationalen Währungssystem*, Schriften zu internationalen Wirtschaftsfragen, vol. 4 (Berlin: Duncker & Humblot, 1976), esp. pp. 191ff.

13. On the concept of economic culture see Wolfram F. Hanrieder, "Dissolving International Politics: Reflections on the Nation-State," *American Political Science Review* 72, no. 4 (December 1978): 1276–1287, esp. p. 1283. See also Neil J. Smelser, *The Sociology of Economic Life* (Englewood Cliffs, N.J.: Prentice-Hall, 1963); James Clyde Sperling, "Economic Culture and Economic Management in an Open Economy: A Conceptual Analysis" (mimeographed, 1987); Ronald Inglehart, *The Silent Revolution* (Princeton: Princeton University Press, 1977); Kendall Baker, Russell J. Dalton, and Kai Hildebrandt, *Germany Transformed* (Cambridge: Harvard University Press, 1981); Peter Reichel, "Politische Kultur. Zur Geschichte eines Problems und zur Popularisierung eines Begriffes," *Aus Politik und Zeitgeschichte*, suppl. to *Das Parlament*, B 42/85 (1985), pp. 13–26; Paul Egon

Rohrlich, "Economic Culture and Foreign Policy: The Cognitive Analysis of Economic Policy Making," *International Organization* 41, no. 1 (Winter 1987): 61–93; Peter L. Berger, *The Capitalist Revolution: Fifty Propositions about Prosperity, Equality, and Liberty* (New York: Basic Books, 1986); T. J. Jackson Lears, "The Concept of Cultural Hegemony: Problems and Possibilities," *American Historical Review* 90, no. 3 (June 1985): 567–593; Clifford Geertz, *The Interpretation of Cultures* (New York: Basic Books, 1973).

14. "There's a series of concentric influences beginning with the work process and moving outwards through political, cultural attributes, all of which bear on, accelerate or decelerate, encourage or discourage, the possibilities of accumulation." Robert L. Heilbroner, "The Future of Capitalism," *Challenge* 25, no. 5 (November-December 1982): 32–39; the quotation appears on p. 33. See also Fernand Braudel, *Afterthoughts on Material Civilization and Capitalism* (Baltimore: Johns Hopkins University Press, 1977), p. 68.

15. Michael von Klipstein and Burkhard Strümpel, "Wertewandel und Wirtschaftsbild der Deutschen," *Aus Politik und Zeitgeschichte*, suppl. to *Das Parlament*, B 42/85 (1985), pp. 19–38, esp. pp. 31ff.

16. Otmar Emminger, long-time president of the Bundesbank, spoke, like Dostoevsky, of money as "coined liberty." Emminger, *Verteidigung der DM*, pp. 43–44.

17. For a general discussion of the clash between economic interdependence and political autonomy see Gilpin, *Political Economy*, esp. p. 167. The conflict between domestic autonomy and international monetary stability is treated in John Gerard Ruggie, "International Regimes, Transactions, and Change: Embedded Liberalism in the Postwar Economic Order," *International Organization* 36, no. 2 (Spring 1982): 379–416; and Richard Cooper, "Is There a Need for Reform?" in Federal Reserve Bank of Boston, *The International Monetary System Forty Years after Bretton Woods* (proceedings of a conference held at Bretton Woods, New Hampshire, May 1984), esp. p. 220.

18. For a discussion of the importance for the Federal Republic's economic vitality of its membership in the Community see Rudolf Hrbek and Wolfgang Wessels, eds., *EG-Mitgliedschaft. Ein vitales Interesse der Bundesrepublik Deutschland?* Europäische Schriften des Instituts für Europäische Politik, vol. 62 (Bonn: Europa-Union-Verlag, 1984). For the Community's importance for Germany's foreign and security policies see Bernhard May, *Kosten und Nutzen der deutschen EG-Mitgliedschaft*, Schriften des Forschungsinstituts der Deutschen Gesellschaft für Auswärtige Politik (Bonn: Europa-Union-Verlag, 1982). On the cushioning effect against global capital transactions provided by the large volume of German trade within the EEC see Otmar Emminger, *The Dollar's Borrowed Strength*, Occasional Papers, no. 19 (New York: Group of Thirty, 1985), esp. p. 7.

CHAPTER 8: *Political and Economic Reconstruction, 1950s*

Epigraphs. The Politics of Aristotle, trans. Ernest Barker (Oxford: Oxford University Press, 1952), bk. 1, sec. 9, pp. 7–8; Charles P. Kindleberger, *Power and Money: The Politics of International Economics and the Economics of International Politics* (New York: Basic Books, 1970), p. 117.

1. On the period 1945–49 and its impact on the future direction of German

foreign policy see Wolfram F. Hanrieder, *West German Foreign Policy, 1949–1963* (Stanford: Stanford University Press, 1967), esp. pp. 13–22. See also John F. Golay, *The Founding of the Federal Republic of Germany* (Chicago: University of Chicago Press, 1958); Peter H. Merkl, *The Origin of the West German Republic* (New York: Oxford University Press, 1963); Alfred Grosser, *The Colossus Again* (New York: Praeger, 1955); Norbert Toennies, *Der Staat aus dem Nichts* (Stuttgart: Constantin, 1954); Kurt Zentner, *Aufstieg aus dem Nichts, 1945–1953*, 2 vols. (Cologne: Kiepenheuer & Wietsch, 1953). On Western occupation policy see Lucius D. Clay, *Decision in Germany* (Garden City, N.Y.: Doubleday, 1950); W. Friedmann, *The Allied Military Government of Germany* (London: Stevens & Sons, 1947); Edward H. Litchfield et al., *Governing Postwar Germany* (Ithaca: Cornell University Press, 1953); John Gimbel, *The American Occupation of Germany: Politics and the Military, 1945–1949* (Stanford: Stanford University Press, 1968); Harold Zink, *American Military Government in Germany* (New York: Macmillan, 1947); James K. Pollock and James H. Meisel, *Germany under Occupation: Illustrative Materials and Documents* (Ann Arbor: Wahr, 1947).

2. Karl Kaiser, *German Foreign Policy in Transition: Bonn between East and West* (London: Oxford University Press, 1968), p. 1. See also the Bonn government's cabinet deliberations during the first year of the Federal Republic. Hans Booms, ed., *Die Kabinettsprotokolle der Bundesregierung*, vol. 1, *1949* (Boppard: Harald Boldt, 1982)

3. See Kurt Sontheimer, *Die verunsicherte Republik* (Munich: Piper, 1979), p. 14.

4. See Werner Weidenfeld, *Konrad Adenauer und Europa. Die geistigen Grundlagen der westeuropäischen Integrationspolitik des ersten Bonner Bundeskanzlers* (Bonn: Europa-Union-Verlag, 1976); Heinrich August Winkler, ed., *Politische Weichenstellung im Nachkriegsdeutschland, 1945–1953*, Geschichte und Gesellschaft, special issue no. 5 (Göttingen: Vandenhoeck & Ruprecht, 1979). For discussions of the period before 1949 see Josef Becker, Theo Stammen, and Peter Waldmann, eds., *Vorgeschichte der Bundesrepublik Deutschland. Zwischen Kapitulation und Grundgesetz* (Munich: Fink, 1979); Institut für Zeitgeschichte, *Westdeutschlands Weg zur Bundesrepublik, 1945–1949* (Munich: C. H. Beck, 1976); Claus Scharf and Hans-Jürgen Schröder, eds., *Politische und ökonomische Stabilisierung Westdeutschlands, 1945–1949. Fünf Beiträge zur Deutschlandpolitik der westlichen Alliierten* (Wiesbaden: Franz Steiner, 1977); Claus Scharf and Hans-Jürgen Schröder, eds., *Die Deutschlandpolitik Frankreichs und die französische Zone, 1945–1949* (Wiesbaden: Franz Steiner, 1983).

5. See the introduction by Richard Löwenthal to David P. Calleo et al., eds., *Geteiltes Land—Halbes Land?* (Frankfurt am Main: Ullstein, 1986), esp. pp. 32–33.

6. See Ernst-Otto Czempiel, ed., *Die anachronistische Souveränität* (Cologne and Opladen: Westdeutscher Verlag, 1969). Indeed, with respect to the Federal Republic it would be best to place qualifying quotation marks around the term "sovereignty." See also my discussion in pt. 1 of the importance of equality and integration to the Federal Republic's policies within NATO.

7. Charles de Gaulle, *Discours et messages: Pendant la guerre, juin 1940–janvier 1946* (Paris: Plon, 1970), p. 617. Like the United States, France needed to follow its own double-containment policy. With the outbreak of the Cold War, French security goals toward Germany (Alfred Grosser has called them the "goals of

1944") needed to be adjusted to the "goals of 1947," or security from the Soviet Union. See Alfred Grosser, *French Foreign Policy under de Gaulle* (Boston: Little, Brown, 1965), pp. 2–5; Wolfram F. Hanrieder and Graeme P. Auton, *The Foreign Policies of West Germany, France and Britain* (Englewood Cliffs, N.J.: Prentice-Hall, 1980), esp. chap. 5. See also Raymond Poidevin, "Der unheimliche Nachbar. Die deutsche Frage aus französischer Sicht," in Calleo et al., *Geteiltes Land*, pp. 127–196, esp. pp. 142–148.

8. See Hans Buchheim, *Deutschlandpolitik, 1949–1972. Der politisch-diplomatische Prozess* (Stuttgart: Deutsche Verlags-Anstalt, 1984), esp. p. 51.

9. The major obstruction to fulfilling the pledge of the Potsdam agreement to unify the German economy came from France rather than the Soviet Union. See John Gimbel, "On the Implementation of the Potsdam Agreement: An Essay on U.S. Postwar German Policy," *Political Science Quarterly* 87, no. 2 (June 1972): 242–269; Robert L. Messer, *The End of an Alliance: James F. Byrnes, Roosevelt, Truman, and the Origins of the Cold War* (Chapel Hill: University of North Carolina Press, 1982); Josef Foschepoth, ed., *Kalter Krieg und Deutsche Frage. Deutschland im Widerstreit der Mächte* (Göttingen and Zurich: Vandenhoeck & Ruprecht, 1985).

10. The literature on socioeconomic and political developments in the Western zones of occupation is growing and has given rise to a certain historiographic "revisionism" relative to the amount of pressure and influence on these developments exerted by the Western powers, especially the United States. See Eberhard Schmidt, *Die verhinderte Neuordnung, 1945–1952. Zur Auseinandersetzung um die Demokratisierung der Wirtschaft in den westlichen Besatzungszonen und in der Bundesrepublik Deutschland* (Frankfurt am Main: Europäische Verlags-Anstalt, 1970); Manfred Overesch, *Deutschland, 1945–1949. Vorgeschichte und Gründung der Bundesrepublik* (Düsseldorf and Königstein: Athenäum, 1979); Ute Schmidt and Tilman Fichter, *Der erzwungene Kapitalismus. Klassenkämpfe in den Westzonen, 1945–1948* (Berlin: Klaus Wagenbach, 1971).

11. Charles S. Maier, "Production and Rehabilitation: The Economic Bases for American Sponsorship of West Germany in the Postwar Atlantic Community," in Frank Trommler and Joseph McVeigh, eds., *America and the Germans: An Assessment of a Three-Hundred-Year History*, vol. 2, *The Relationship in the Twentieth Century* (Philadelphia: University of Pennsylvania Press, 1985), pp. 59–73; the quotation appears on p. 71. See also Volker R. Berghahn, *The Americanization of West German Industry, 1945–1973* (New York: Cambridge University Press, 1986).

12. This was the primary American purpose in establishing the Organization for European Economic Cooperation (OEEC), the coordinating agency through which Marshall Plan funds were channeled. In 1960 the OEEC was superseded by the Organization for Economic Cooperation and Development (OECD), of which the United States and Canada became members, and through which the United States sought to induce the now affluent European countries to share the burden of aid to underdeveloped countries.

13. See Manfred Knapp, ed., *Die deutsch-amerikanischen Beziehungen nach 1945* (Frankfurt am Main: Campus, 1975); John H. Backer, *Priming the German Economy: American Occupational Policies, 1945–1948* (Durham: Duke University Press, 1971); Werner Abelshauser, *Wirtschaft in Westdeutschland, 1945–1948. Rekonstruktion und Wachstumsbedingungen in der amerikanischen und britischen Zone* (Stuttgart: Deutsche Verlags-Anstalt, 1975); Warren F. Kimball, *Swords or Ploughshares? The*

Morgenthau Plan for Defeated Nazi Germany, 1943–1946 (Philadelphia: J. B. Lippincott, 1976); Bruce Kuklick, *American Policy and the Division of Germany: The Clash with Russia over Reparations* (Ithaca: Cornell University Press, 1972).

14. This influence extended even into the area of social policy. See Hans Günther Hockerts, *Sozialpolitische Entscheidungen im Nachkriegsdeutschland. Alliierte und deutsche Sozialversicherungspolitik, 1945 bis 1957* (Stuttgart: Klett-Cotta, 1980). See also Volker Hentschel, "Das System der sozialen Sicherung in historischer Sicht 1880 bis 1975," *Archiv für Sozialgeschichte*, vol. 18 (1978), pp. 307–352.

15. See Harry B. Price, *The Marshall Plan and Its Meaning* (Ithaca: Cornell University Press, 1955); John Gimbel, *The Origins of the Marshall Plan* (Stanford: Stanford University Press, 1976). See also the comment by Manfred Knapp in "Das Deutschlandproblem und die Ursprünge des Europäischen Wiederaufbauprogramms. Eine Auseinandersetzung mit John Gimbels Untersuchung 'The Origins of the Marshall-Plan,' " *Politische Vierteljahresschrift* 19, no. 1 (1978): 48–65; Manfred Knapp, "Reconstruction and West-Integration: The Impact of the Marshall Plan on Germany," *Zeitschrift für die gesamte Staatswissenschaft* 137, no. 3 (1981): 415–433; Erich Ott, "Die Bedeutung des Marshall-Plans für die Nachkriegsentwicklung in Westdeutschland," *Aus Politik und Zeitgeschichte*, suppl. to *Das Parlament*, B 4/80 (1980), pp. 19–37; Werner Link, "Der Marshall-Plan und Deutschland," *Aus Politik und Zeitgeschichte*, suppl. to *Das Parlament*, B 50/80 (1980).

Dean Acheson quotes Will Clayton, Under Secretary of State for Economic Affairs, as having urged: "Surely the plan would be a European plan and come—or, at any rate, appear to come—from Europe. *But the United States must run the show.* And it must start running it now" (italics in original). *The Struggle for a Free Europe* (New York: W. W. Norton, 1971), p. 24.

16. See Klaus Knorr, *The Power of Nations: The Political Economy of International Relations* (New York: Basic Books, 1975), pp. 25–26.

17. For a full account of the EPU see Robert Triffin, *Europe and the Money Muddle: From Bilateralism to Near-Convertibility, 1947–1956* (New Haven and London: Yale University Press, 1957), esp. pp. 161–179, 199–208. On the phenomenal extent of bilateral trade in Western Europe and the extent of governmental control over the economy, especially in France, see Isaiah Frank, *The European Common Market: An Analysis of Commercial Policy* (New York: Praeger, 1961), pp. 42, 61; Gardner Patterson and Judd Polk, "The Emerging Pattern of Bilateralism," *Quarterly Journal of Economics* 62, no. 1 (November 1947): 118–142.

18. See Fred Hirsch and Michael Doyle, "Politicization in the World Economy: Necessary Conditions for an International Economic Order," in Fred Hirsch, Michael Doyle, and Edward L. Morse, *Alternatives to Monetary Disorder* (New York: McGraw-Hill, 1977), esp. pp. 31–32.

19. In the notes he prepared for himself before he accompanied Secretary of State Dean Acheson to Paris for the Foreign Ministers Conference of June 1949, John Foster Dulles writes of the "natural affinity" of dynamic regimes with one another, which would make it natural for the new German government in Bonn to be attracted to the Soviet Union. Therefore, positive alternatives would have to be found. See Lloyd C. Gardner, "Economic Foreign Policy and the Quest for Security," in Norman A. Graebner, ed., *The National Security: Its Theory and Practice, 1945–1960* (New York: Oxford University Press, 1986), pp. 76–102; the

quotation appears on p. 91. Gardner also notes that "Acheson's handling of the German trade question was perhaps the best illustration of the intricate subtleties of economic policy in the Cold War" (p. 99). On the American determination to guide European reconstruction on the basis of capitalist principles see Jeremy Leaman, *The Political Economy of West Germany, 1945–1985: An Introduction* (New York: St. Martin's, 1988), esp. chaps. 1–3.

20. See Nathan Reich, *Germany's Labor and Economic Recovery*, Proceedings of the Academy of Political Science, vol. 36 (New York: Academy of Political Science, Columbia University, 1955); Wolfgang Hirsch-Weber, *Gewerkschaften in der Politik* (Cologne: Westdeutscher Verlag, 1959); Andrei S. Markovits, *The Politics of West German Trade Unions: Strategies of Class and Interest Representation in Growth and Crisis* (Cambridge and New York: Cambridge University Press, 1986). See also André Piettre, *L'Economie allemande contemporaine, 1945–1952* (Paris: Génin, 1952); Frederick G. Reuss, *Fiscal Policy for Growth without Inflation: The German Experiment* (Baltimore: Johns Hopkins University Press, 1964); Karel Holbik and Henry Myers, *Postwar Trade in Divided Germany: The Internal and International Issues* (Baltimore: Johns Hopkins University Press, 1964).

21. This last point has led some analysts to see as the primary reason for Germany's economic resurgence the socioeconomic tabula rasa they perceived in postwar Germany. See for example Mancur Olson, Jr., *The Rise and Decline of Nations: Economic Growth, Stagflation, and Social Rigidities* (New Haven and London: Yale University Press, 1982), esp. pp. 9ff.

22. Henry C. Wallich, *Mainsprings of the German Revival* (New Haven and London: Yale University Press, 1955), p. 17. See also Julia Dingwort-Nusseck, "Economic Growth, Economic Policy, and Foreign Affairs," in Wolfram F. Hanrieder, ed., *West German Foreign Policy, 1949–1979* (Boulder: Westview, 1980), pp. 213–228.

23. Some analysts draw a distinction between monetary systems and monetary orders (or regimes), the latter being governed by a specific set of rules and procedures. See Robert A. Mundell, "The Future of the International Financial System," in A. L. K. Acheson et al., *Bretton Woods Revisited* (Toronto: University of Toronto Press, 1973), pp. 91–104.

24. For a discussion of the provision concerning capital flows in Article VI, Section 3, of the IMF Articles of Agreement see Kenneth W. Dam, *The Rules of the Game: Reform and Evolution in the International Monetary System* (Chicago: University of Chicago Press, 1982), p. 133. As Charles P. Kindleberger has pointed out, however, although it was agreed at Bretton Woods that interference with trade was bad, control over capital movements was given assent. *Power and Money* (New York: Basic Books, 1970), p. 170.

25. John H. Williams, *Postwar Monetary Plans and Other Essays* (New York: Alfred A. Knopf, 1944).

26. For a discussion of the basic contradictions between providing continuous liquidity through U.S. balance-of-payments deficits and simultaneously sustaining confidence in the dollar see Robert Triffin, *Gold and the Dollar Crisis: The Future of Convertibility* (New Haven and London: Yale University Press, 1960).

27. This was not achieved without cost to the Germans. Speaking of "export hypertrophy and its consequences," Patrick M. Boarman has noted that "the exchange and gold surplus position really represented a loss business for two

reasons. First, the countries with inflated currencies could, because of the more stable purchasing power of the mark, buy too cheaply in Germany, whereas the Germans had to pay too high prices for what they received. Secondly, a large part of German exports was being exchanged, in effect, for mere money; persistent export surpluses were equivalent to an uncompensated outflow of German 'substance.'" Patrick M. Boarman, *Germany's Economic Dilemma: Inflation and the Balance of Payments* (New Haven and London: Yale University Press, 1964); the quotation is from p. 89.

28. Thomas L. Ilgen, *Autonomy and Interdependence: U.S.-Western European Monetary and Trade Relations, 1958–1984* (Totowa, N.J.: Rowman & Allanheld, 1985), p. 23.

29. In fact, the establishment of NATO was also seen as helping the Marshall Plan. Acheson said years later that by mid-1948 there was a crisis of confidence with respect to the progress of the European Recovery Program: "You want to have capital brought back from out of the country and people who own factories to build anew. In 1948 two things happened which scared them to death— Czechoslavakia and Poland. The whole Marshall Plan business just stopped. The airlift's going on in Berlin. What's going to happen? No one will build factories in Paris as long as that's going on. George Kennan had a group meet in the State Department to hash this whole thing over. It seemed clear to them that some kind of important political step had to be taken to offer them economic help and make businessmen believe there was security there, that they would not be rolled over by a Russian tank division. . . . NATO was conceived of first as a political act." Quoted in Gardner, "Economic Foreign Policy," p. 86. See also Robert A. Pollard, *Economic Security and the Origins of the Cold War, 1945–1950* (New York: Columbia University Press, 1985), esp. chaps. 4, 5, 7.

30. See Walter LaFeber, *America, Russia and the Cold War, 1945–1984*, 5th ed. (New York: Alfred A. Knopf, 1985), p. 62. Some analysts have argued that Washington connected the concepts of economic interdependence and national security as early as the period between the fall of France and Pearl Harbor. See Carlo Maria Santoro, *La perla e l'ostrica: Alle fonti della politica globale degli Stati Uniti* (Milan: Franco Angeli, 1987).

31. See Fred L. Block, *The Origins of International Economic Disorder: A Study of United States International Monetary Policy from World War II to the Present* (Berkeley: University of California Press, 1977). Block goes so far as to argue that "the U.S. goal of a multilateral, world economy, which was dependent upon a revived and economically liberal Western Europe, was endangered by the possibility of accommodation with the Soviet Union in 1949–1950. Rearmament proved a useful means to intensify the polarization of Europe, and the idea of negotiation from strength gave the United States a justification for avoiding a settlement that would endanger its goals" (pp. 106–107). See also William Diebold, Jr., "The United States in the World Economy: A Fifty Year Perspective," *Foreign Affairs* 62, no. 1 (Fall 1983): 81–104, esp. pp. 87–88.

32. The term itself, implying effortless and perhaps undeserved results, met with disapproval on the part of many Germans. See Albert Hunold, ed., *Wirtschaft ohne Wunder* (Zurich: E. Reutsch, 1953); Wolfgang Zank, "Das Wunder liess sich nicht vermeiden. Die Wirtschaftshistoriker streiten noch heute über den Neubeginn," *Die Zeit*, June 24, 1988, pp. 25–26. Further, "By contemporary

international standards, the German economic comeback after 1948 was not exceptional, since in per capita production Germany was still about 12 percent behind France and 3 percent behind Great Britain in 1952. However, these and other European countries had a headstart of about three years, as their peacetime reconstruction had not been delayed until the middle of 1948." Karl Hardach, *The Political Economy of Germany in the Twentieth Century* (Berkeley: University of California Press, 1980), p. 161. Other analysts speak of three "economic miracles": the period of reconstruction (1948–52), the shift from chronic balance-of-payments deficits (until 1952) toward chronic surpluses, and the shift from having the smallest foreign currency holdings to having the largest (after 1972). See Wilhelm Hankel, *Der Ausweg aus der Krise* (Düsseldorf and Vienna: Econ, 1975), p. 105.

33. See Otmar Emminger, *D-Mark, Dollar, Währungskrisen* (Stuttgart: Deutsche Verlags-Anstalt, 1986), esp. chap. 1.

34. Wolfgang Hager, "Political Implications of US-EC Economic Conflicts (II): Atlantic Trade: Problems and Prospects," *Government and Opposition* 22, no. 1 (Winter 1987): 49–63.

35. As Dean Acheson noted in a speech delivered on May 8, 1947: "[What] we must do in the present situation is to push ahead with the reconstruction of those two great workshops of Europe and Asia—Germany and Japan—upon which the ultimate recovery of the two continents so largely depends." *Struggle for a Free Europe*, p. 35. See also Pollard, *Economic Security*.

36. "Hegemony rests on the subjective awareness by elites in secondary states that they are benefitting, as well as on the willingness of the hegemon itself to sacrifice tangible short-term benefits for intangible long-term gains." Robert O. Keohane, *After Hegemony: Cooperation and Discord in the World Political Economy* (Princeton: Princeton University Press, 1984), p. 45.

37. During the Pax Britannica and the Pax Americana many countries other than the hegemonic one prospered, in some cases more than the hegemon. See Robert Gilpin, *U.S. Power and the Multinational Corporation* (New York: Basic Books, 1975), p. 85; Gilpin, *War and Change in World Politics* (Cambridge: Cambridge University Press, 1981): 175–185.

38. See Alfred Müller-Armack, "Die Anfänge der Sozialen Marktwirtschaft. Zugleich eine Dokumentation ihrer Entwicklung in den Jahren 1945, 1946, 1947, 1948," in Richard Löwenthal and Hans-Peter Schwarz, eds., *Die zweite Republik. 25 Jahre Bundesrepublik Deutschland—Eine Bilanz* (Stuttgart: Seewald, 1974), pp. 123–148; Horst Friedrich Wünsche, *Ludwig Erhards Gesellschafts- und Wirtschaftskonzept. Soziale Marktwirtschaft als politische Ökonomie* (Landsberg: Bonn aktuell, 1986); Erika Blomenthal-Lampe, *Der Weg in die soziale Marktwirtschaft. Referate, Protokolle, Gutachten der Arbeitsgemeinschaft Erwin von Beckerath 1943 bis 1947* (Stuttgart: Klett-Cotta, 1986). Ludwig Erhard's views can be found in the collection of his essays covering the 1940s and 1950s entitled *The Economics of Success* (Princeton: D. Van Nostrand, 1963).

The social market economy was based on the following theses: "(1) A competitive market economy is the best social order (the state is to enforce its prerequisites). (2) Such an economy requires corrections in favor of all who suffer economic disadvantages (redistribution in general). (3) The corrections must benefit wage earners in particular (an industrial constitution). (4) The entire economic process must be supervised and steered, partly for the very purpose of maintaining a competitive market economy (monetary, fiscal, cartel, agricultural and other policies). All of these viewpoints, contradictory or complementary, have left their imprint on the evolution of the economic structure of the Federal Republic." Horst Mendershausen, *Two Postwar Recoveries of the German Economy* (Amsterdam: North-Holland Publishing Company, 1954), pp. 71–72 n. 1. Mendershausen is here quoting from Gert von Eynern, "Soziale Marktwirtschaft," in Institut für Deutsche Konjunkturforschung, *Beiträge zur empirischen Konjunkturforschung* (Berlin: Duncker & Humblot, 1950).

39. Historically, German merchants and German historians had considered long-distance trade (*Fernhandel*) a commercial activity superior to trade where the distance between production and consumption was short. *Fernhandel* escapes more easily from political interference and supervision and offers more flexibility, because it can be shifted readily from one distant market to another. See Fernand Braudel, *Afterthoughts on Material Civilization and Capitalism* (Baltimore: Johns Hopkins University Press, 1977), pp. 53–54.

40. Hankel, *Ausweg aus der Krise*, pp. 110–111. Hankel also notes the impact of the division of Germany, which pushed the efforts of West German industry toward world markets, because it had lost a large portion of its former domestic markets. (For example, in 1936 the territories that later became West Germany "exported" almost 60 percent of their products to the other parts of Germany.) The GDR, on the other hand, needed to replace its former "imports" from these territories (approximately 85 percent of all imports) through new production or other sources in Eastern Europe; see pp. 105, 107–108. On the German and Japanese proclivities for export surpluses see also Hans O. Schmitt, "Mercantilism: A Modern Argument," *Manchester School of Economic and Social Studies* 47, no. 2 (1979): 93–111.

41. See Gardner Patterson, *Discrimination in International Trade: The Policy Issues, 1945–1965* (Princeton: Princeton University Press, 1966), esp. pp. 181–188.

42. Benjamin J. Cohen, "The Revolution in Atlantic Economic Relations: A Bargain Comes Unstuck," in Wolfram F. Hanrieder, ed., *The United States and Western Europe: Political, Economic and Strategic Perspectives* (Cambridge, Mass.: Winthrop, 1974): 106–133.

43. George F. Kennan, *Memoirs*, vol. 1, *1925–1950* (Boston: Little, Brown, 1967), p. 452.

44. For full accounts see Ernst B. Haas, *The Uniting of Europe* (Stanford: Stanford University Press, 1958); William Diebold, *The Schuman Plan* (New York: Praeger, 1959).

45. Gardner, "Economic Foreign Policy," p. 88. Gardner is here quoting from Jean Monnet, *Memoirs* (Garden City, N.Y.: Doubleday, 1978), p. 292.

46. See Leon Lindberg, *The Political Dynamics of European Economic Integration* (Stanford: Stanford University Press, 1963).

47. For the literature on inter-German trade and the Community see n. 4 to the introduction to pt. 3.

48. Hankel, *Ausweg aus der Krise*, pp. 119–121. For a full account of the intricate negotiations leading to the treaty and the various national perspectives see F. Roy Willis, *France, Germany and the New Europe, 1945–1967* (Stanford: Stanford University Press, 1968), esp. pp. 242–272. Willis takes a more positive

view of the long-range economic benefits for France stemming from membership in the Community.

49. *Economic Conditions in the Federal Republic of Germany*, Report no. EC (56) (Paris: OEEC, 1956), pp. 5–12.

50. The economy's rate of growth had slowed and the real gross national product had increased by only 5 percent in 1957, compared with 6.4 percent in 1956 and almost 12 percent in 1955. *Economic Conditions in Member and Associated Countries of the OEEC: Federal Republic of Germany*, Report no. EC (58) 9 (Paris: OEEC, 1958): 5. See also Uwe W. Kitzinger, *The Politics and Economics of European Integration* (New York: Praeger, 1963), esp. p. 18.

51. In February 1959 a tax of twenty D-Marks a ton was imposed on ECSC imports, except for a duty-free contingent; in May 1959 a tax of twenty-five D-Marks a ton was imposed on heavy fuel oil. *Economic Conditions in Member and Associated Countries of the OEEC: Federal Republic of Germany*, Report no. EC (59) 25 (Paris: OEEC, 1959): 9; Report no. EC (60) 25 (Paris: OEEC, 1960): 7.

52. *Economic Conditions in Member and Associated Countries of the OEEC: Federal Republic of Germany*, Report no. EC (60) 25 (Paris: OEEC, 1960): 19–24.

53. Steven J. Warnecke, "The European Community after British Entry: Federation or Confederation?" in Steven Joshua Warnecke, ed., *The European Community in the 1970's* (New York: Praeger, 1972), pp. 3–28, esp. pp. 5–6.

54. For a discussion of the early tensions and contradictions within the Community, which are remarkably similar to those of the 1980s, see Hans von der Groeben, *Aufbaujahre der Europäischen Gemeinschaft—Das Ringen um den Gemeinsamen Markt und die Politische Union (1958–1966)* (Baden-Baden: Nomos, 1982); Hans Jürgen Küsters, *Die Gründung der Europäischen Gemeinschaft* (Baden-Baden: Nomos, 1982); Peter Weilemann, *Die Anfänge der Europäischen Atomgemeinschaft. Zur Gründungsgeschichte von Euratom, 1955–1957* (Baden-Baden: Nomos, 1982).

55. For a sharp critique of Western Europe's integrative failures and a skeptical view of its prospects see von der Groeben, *Aufbaujahre der Europäischen Gemeinschaft*.

56. See Stanley Hoffmann, "Toward a Common European Foreign Policy?" in Wolfram F. Hanrieder, ed., *The United States and Western Europe: Political, Economic and Strategic Perspectives* (Cambridge, Mass.: Winthrop, 1974), pp. 79–105. For a discussion of how the founding of the community was tied to large international developments, including the crisis of confidence within the Western alliance resulting from the Suez crisis of 1956 see Küsters, *Die Gründung der Europäischen Gemeinschaft*. See also Robert Picht, ed., *Deutschland, Frankreich, Europa* (Munich: Piper, 1978).

CHAPTER 9: *The German-American Connection, 1960s*

Epigraphs. Karl Blessing, quoted in Otmar Emminger, *Verteidigung der DM. Plädoyers für stabiles Geld* (Frankfurt am Main: Fritz Knapp, 1980), p. 100; Charles P. Kindleberger, *Power and Money: The Politics of International Economics and the Economics of International Politics* (New York: Basic Books, 1970), p. 168.

1. See F. Roy Willis, *France, Germany and the New Europe, 1945–1967*, rev. ed. (London: Oxford University Press, 1968), pp. 265–266; Uwe W. Kitzinger, *The Politics and Economics of European Integration* (New York: Praeger, 1963), pp. 120–143. See also Emile Benoit, *Europe at Sixes and Sevens* (New York: Columbia

University Press, 1961), p. 86; Isaiah Frank, *The European Common Market: An Analysis of Commercial Policy* (New York: Praeger, 1961).

2. Emile Benoit, *Europe at Sixes and Sevens*, p. 86.

3. Hans Buchheim, *Deutschlandpolitik 1949–1972. Der politisch-diplomatische Prozess* (Stuttgart: Deutsche Verlags-Anstalt, 1984), esp. p. 54.

4. Heinrich Bechtoldt, "Germany and the German Market," *India Quarterly* 16, no. 3 (1960): 249–258, esp. p. 251. Bechtoldt suggests that "After the Soviet ultimatum of 28 November 1958, De Gaulle . . . proved himself so reliable, even on the question of Berlin, that Dr. Adenauer was compelled to let the continuation of the close political cooperation with France outweigh his disappointment over the shelving of the negotiations regarding the Great Free Trade Zone."

5. Benoit, *Europe at Sixes and Sevens*, pp. 92–95. See also Randall Hinshaw, *The European Community and American Trade* (New York: Praeger, 1964).

6. Benoit, *Europe at Sixes and Sevens*, pp. 86–87.

7. Bechtoldt, "Germany and the German Market," pp. 256–257 n. 46.

8. As could be expected, the Hallstein Plan, which was generally well received in the Community on its economic merits, met with considerable opposition in West Germany because it required rapid increases in German tariffs against non-EEC markets. The final program, which was approved in May 1960, provided a concession to German industrial interests in that only half the unilateral cuts in German tariff would have to be restored during 1960, the other half by the end of 1961. Benoit, *Europe at Sixes and Sevens*, pp. 89–91; Herbert Nicholas, *Britain and the U.S.A.* (Baltimore: John Hopkins University Press, 1963), chap. 10.

9. Kitzinger, *Politics and Economics*, pp. 140–141.

10. Hinshaw, *European Community*, chap. 4; William Diebold, Jr., "Economic Aspects of an Atlantic Community," in Francis O. Wilcox and H. Field Haviland, Jr., eds., *The Atlantic Community* (New York: Praeger, 1963), pp. 145–164; George Lichtheim, *The New Europe* (New York: Praeger, 1963), pp. 51–59.

11. In September 1962 the government published figures of aid granted by the Federal Republic between 1950 and 1962. The total amounted to 19.2 billion D-Marks, of which 15.2 billion D-Marks were for bilateral aid, and 4 billion D-Marks for multilateral aid. See *Bulletin* (Bonn: Presse- und Informationsamt der Bundesregierung, October 9, 1962), pp. 3–4.

12. See Kurt Birrenbach, *Meine Sondermissionen* (Düsseldorf and Vienna: Econ, 1984), esp. pp. 167–176.

13. See Fritz R. Allemann, *Zwischen Stabilität und Krise* (Munich: Piper, 1963), pp. 57–69, 70–80, 289–309.

14. Willis, *France, Germany and the New Europe*, p. 312.

15. For example, in 1964 de Gaulle warmly celebrated the twentieth anniversary of the Franco-Soviet alliance, extended seven-year credits to the Soviet Union through a new trade agreement, and generally exhibited great cordiality toward the Soviet Union and Eastern European countries. In his press conference of February 4, 1965, de Gaulle stressed that reunification was a European problem that would have to be settled largely by Germany's neighbors, implying that Germany and the United States would play a secondary role in a settlement.

16. See Hinshaw, *European Community*; and Werner Feld, "External Relations of the Common Market and Group Leadership Attitudes in the Member States," *Orbis* 10, no. 2 (1967): 564–587.

17. Willis, *France, Germany and the New Europe*, p. 343.

18. Miriam Camps, *European Unification in the Sixties: From the Veto to the Crisis* (New York: McGraw-Hill, 1966), pp. 117–118; see also John Newhouse, *Collision in Brussels: The Common Market Crisis of 30 June 1965* (New York: W. W. Norton, 1967)

19. "The German economic interest clearly lay in British Common Market membership. Yet [Prime Minister] Wilson found the Germans reluctant to press Britain's case at the risk of jeopardizing the 'special relationship' with France which the Kiesinger Government had striven to restore. . . . For another reason, however, the Germans had reservations about British EEC entry. With her accession at the Rome Treaty, Britain might replace Germany as the principal French ally in Western Europe. Collaboration in the development of advanced technology, the possibility of creating an Anglo-French nuclear force, and the prospect of agreement on major political issues might lead to a new Franco-British entente, isolating Germany." Robert L. Pfaltzgraff, Jr., "Britain and the European Community: 1963–1967," *Orbis* 12, no. 1 (1968): 87–120; the quotation appears on p. 107.

20. Professor Hallstein, a devoted advocate of European integration and the president of the EEC Commission from its establishment in 1958, had frequently incurred de Gaulle's displeasure for attempting to enlarge the functions of the Common Market (and the Brussels Commission) beyond economic integrative measures toward a coordinated program for common social, commercial, and fiscal policy, and ultimately toward a supranational political union. When the French finally agreed on a fixed time for the fusion of the executive bodies of the Common Market, the Coal and Steel Community, and Euratom in 1967 (the merger treaty had been signed as early as April 1965 and was ratified by the six parliaments by October 1966) one of their conditions was that Hallstein would not become the head of the integrated commission. Hallstein's successor, Belgium's Jean Rey, was not much more to de Gaulle's liking: Rey was also fully committed to European economic and political integration.

21. *New York Times*, October 6, 1968.

22. For a balanced description of the French economy during 1967 see OECD *Economic Surveys: France* (Paris: OECD, 1968).

23. For the French aspect see Henrik Schmiegelow and Michèle Schmiegelow, "The New Mercantilism in International Relations: The Case of France's External Monetary Policy," *International Organization* 29, no. 2 (Spring 1975): 367–392.

24. In its pungent way, *Der Spiegel* noted that "through the loss of value incurred by exchanging sound D-Marks into consumptive lire and francs, West Germany involuntarily finances Italy's development program in Southern Italy and Sicily as well as de Gaulle's expensive dream to become the world's fourth atomic mushroom." *Der Spiegel* 18, no. 27 (1964): 28. No doubt de Gaulle's military expenditures (especially the costly force de frappe) and his reorientation of economic planning toward measures that would complement French foreign policy contributed to inflationary trends in France and exacerbated the sociopolitical problems that erupted during the general strike in spring 1968. See Richard B. DuBoff, "The Decline of Economic Planning in France," *Western Political Quarterly* 21, no. 1 (March 1968): 98–109; Karl Albrecht, "Die Reservewährung, das Währungssystem und die Politik der EWG," *Europa-Archiv* 23, no. 15 (1968): 543–556; Jan S. Prybyla, "The French Economy: Down the Up Staircase and into the Market," *Current History* 54, no. 3 (March 1968): 135–142.

25. Germany was reported to have offered France even before the Bonn conference a unilateral loan of $1 billion, which was apparently turned down because Germany refused to revalue and demanded that additional anti-inflationary measures be imposed on the French economy. Of the $2 billion loan made to France in November, Germany contributed $600 million, the United States $500 million, and Italy $200 million; the balance, in smaller amounts, came from the conference's other participants. *New York Times*, November 23, 1968.

26. For a detailed account of the French cutback in military programs see *Der Spiegel* 23, no. 9 (1969): 122–124; Michael M. Harrison, *The Reluctant Ally: France and Atlantic Security* (Baltimore: Johns Hopkins University Press, 1981).

27. See Wolfram F. Hanrieder, *The Stable Crisis: Two Decades of German Foreign Policy* (New York: Harper & Row, 1970), pp. 186–190. See also Arnulf Baring, *Machtwechsel. Die Ära Brandt-Scheel* (Stuttgart: Deutsche Verlags-Anstalt, 1982), pp. 142–147.

28. There was another option, unsuccessfully advocated by the Dutch in the face of strong French opposition: the imposition of purely internal French tax measures. This option was partly incorporated in the compromise reached over whether France or the EEC would control the apparatus for isolating the French market. The agreement provided that the French government would tax farm exports and subsidize farm imports, and that by January 1, 1971, prices for two hundred French agricultural products would be allowed to rise by half the amount that the franc had been devalued, with a second, equal increase allowed by January 1, 1972.

29. See Hans von der Groeben, "Zum 25. Jahrestag der Unterzeichnung der Rom-Verträge," *Aus Politik und Zeitgeschichte*, suppl. to *Das Parlament*, B 12/82 (March 27, 1982), pp. 3–16. For later reflections on the unsatisfactory progression of Western Europe toward unity by von der Groeben (who was one of the founding fathers of the Community) see Hans von der Groeben, *Die Europäische Gemeinschaft und die Herausforderungen unserer Zeit* (Baden-Baden: Nomos, 1987); von der Groeben, *Legitimationsprobleme der Europäischen Gemeinschaft* (Baden-Baden: Nomos, 1987).

30. At the Bretton Woods Conference, John Maynard Keynes had worried that there might come about a "contractionist pressure on world trade," and later such economists as Robert Triffin feared that a system that relied on creating dollar liabilities for its liquidity would ultimately face serious monetary shortages. Of course the system did the very opposite: it allowed excess inflation rather than deflation and provided excess liquidity in the process.

31. "A gold-exchange standard is built on the illusion of convertibility of its fiduciary element into gold at a fixed price. The Bretton Woods system, though, was relying on deficits in the U.S. balance of payments to avert a world liquidity shortage. Already, America's 'overhang' of overseas liabilities to private and official foreigners was growing larger than its gold stock at home. The progressive deterioration of the U.S. net reserve position, therefore, was bound in time to undermine global confidence in the dollar's continued convertibility. In effect, governments were caught on the horns of a dilemma. To forestall speculation against the dollar, U.S. deficits would have to cease. But this would confront governments with the liquidity problem. To forestall the liquidity problem, U.S. deficits would have to continue. But this would confront governments with the confidence problem. Governments could not have their cake and eat it too."

Benjamin J. Cohen, *Organizing the World's Money: The Political Economy of International Monetary Relations* (New York: Basic Books, 1977), p. 99. See also C. Fred Bergsten, *Dilemmas of the Dollar* (New York: New York University Press, 1975); Alfred E. Eckes, Jr., *A Search for Solvency: Bretton Woods and the International Monetary System, 1941–1971* (Austin: University of Texas Press, 1975); John S. Odell, *U.S. International Monetary Policy: Markets, Power, and Ideas as Sources of Change* (Princeton: Princeton University Press, 1982). On the increase in the late 1950s of U.S. investments in Western Europe, encouraged by currency convertibility, see Robert Solomon, *The International Monetary System, 1945–1976: An Insider's View* (New York: Harper & Row, 1977), esp. pp. 23–24.

32. Patrick M. Boarman, *Germany's Economic Dilemma: Inflation and the Balance of Payments* (New Haven and London: Yale University Press, 1964).

33. See Michael Hudson, "Epitaph for Bretton Woods," *International Affairs* 23, no. 2 (1969): 266–301.

34. For a discussion of the theories of hegemonic stability and the consequences of hegemonic decline see Robert Gilpin, *The Political Economy of International Relations* (Princeton: Princeton University Press, 1987), esp. pp. 90–91.

35. Otmar Emminger, *Verteidigung der DM*, pp. 230–231. For the effect of this development on the American power position see Stephen D. Krasner, "American Policy and Global Economic Stability," in David P. Rapkin and William P. Avery, eds., *America in a Changing World Political Economy* (New York: Longman, 1982), pp. 29–48. De Gaulle's decision of 1965 to convert surplus holdings of dollars into gold was also a demonstration of Europe's recovery. See Fred Hirsch, Michael Doyle, and Edward L. Morse, *Alternatives to Monetary Disorder* (New York: McGraw-Hill, 1977), p. 39. For a more technical discussion of the issue see Phillip Cagan, *Persistent Inflation: Historical and Policy Essays* (New York: Columbia University Press, 1979), esp. pt. 2.

36. Eugene A. Phillips, "American Investment in West German Manufacturing Industries, 1945 to 1959," *Current Economic Comment* 22, no. 2 (May 1960): 29–44. Other studies of foreign investment pointing to the positive contributions U.S. investments made to the German economy include Heinz Hartmann, *Amerikanische Firmen in Deutschland* (Cologne: Westdeutscher Verlag, 1963); Rudolf Matthias, *Die amerikanischen Auslandsinvestitionen in der Nachkriegszeit* (Winterthur: P. G. Keller, 1966); and Winfred Schmitz, *Auslandskapital in der deutschen Wirtschaft* (Bonn: Heinz Möller, 1969). See also Solomon, *International Monetary System*, esp. pp. 23–24.

37. See Robert Triffin, *Gold and the Dollar Crisis: The Future of Convertibility* (New Haven and London: Yale University Press, 1966).

38. Jacques Rueff, *The Monetary Sin of the West* (New York: Macmillan, 1972). In later years some analysts characterized the United States as a "predatory hegemon"; see Gilpin, *Political Economy*, p. 345, quoting John A. C. Conybeare.

39. David L. Grove, *A Proposed Solution for the Dollar Overhang Problem* (Tübingen: J. C. B. Mohr, 1972).

40. See Charles P. Kindleberger, "Dominance and Leadership in the International Economy: Exploitation, Public Goods, and Free Rides," *International Studies Quarterly* 25, no. 2 (June 1981): 242–254.

One reason why the United States tolerated an increasingly overvalued dollar and a declining trade balance was the need to retain a central fixed-rate currency in the Bretton Woods monetary system (this was the problem of the so-called N-1 countries). See John Williamson, *The Open Economy and the World Economy* (New York: Basic Books, 1983), pp. 334–335.

41. See Robert E. Hudec, *The GATT Legal System and World Trade Diplomacy* (New York: Praeger, 1975).

42. See Susan Strange, "The Politics of Economics: A Sectoral Analysis," in Wolfram F. Hanrieder, ed., *Economic Issues and the Atlantic Community* (New York: Praeger, 1982), pp. 15–26.

43. Emminger, *Verteidigung der DM*, p. 19.

44. Otmar Emminger noted in 1975 that the Bundesbank tried every conceivable defense to stanch imported inflation: (1) compensating for excessive foreign demand (self-defeating); (2) ambivalent monetary policy, that is, a combination of restricting liquidity and slowing capital inflows with low interest rates (neither fish nor fowl); (3) compensatory capital exports (works only if sustained by real market forces, not when arranged artificially by government or central bank); (4) curtailing capital inflows with zero-interest rates or government permits (mixed results); (5) changing the par-value (always too little, too late; incapable of dealing with huge destabilizing capital inflows). See Emminger, *Verteidigung der DM*, p. 181. For the technicalities involved see *OECD Economic Surveys: Germany* (Paris: OECD, 1971), pp. 21–23.

45. *OECD Economic Surveys: Germany* (Paris: OECD, 1967), esp. pp. 24–31. See also the survey on Germany published by the OECD in April 1968.

46. See Frederich G. Reuss, *Fiscal Policy for Growth without Inflation: The German Experiment* (Baltimore: Johns Hopkins University Press, 1964).

47. Herbert Giersch, then the director of the Institute for European Economic Policy in Saarbrücken, said in an interview: "Our export offensive, which we subsidize with the undervaluation of the D-Mark, threatens to become a sort of substitute nationalism. When I think of the arguments put forth recently . . . I cannot help but feel that our old political-military nationalism revives as an export nationalism." *Der Spiegel* 23, no. 21 (1969), p. 52. On the costs connected with Germany's "export hypertrophy" with respect to internal demand and domestic economic substance see Boarman, *Germany's Economic Dilemma*, esp. chap. 6.

48. David P. Calleo and Benjamin Rowland, *America and the World Political Economy* (Bloomington: Indiana University Press, 1976).

49. International Monetary Fund, *Annual Report of the Executive Directors for the Fiscal Year Ended April 30, 1964* (Washington, 1964), p. 28.

50. Wolfram F. Hanrieder, "Germany as Number Two?" *International Studies Quarterly* 26, no. 1 (March 1982): 57–86; see also Emminger, *Verteidigung der DM*, p. 185.

51. In spring 1971 former Bundesbank president Karl Blessing said in an interview how much he regretted not having "rigorously" exchanged accumulated dollars into gold, and instead had promised the American envoy John J. McCloy in 1967 not to convert dollars (he did so under pressure because of German-American negotiations on the stationing of American troops). This question is also connected to that of the so-called Blessing Letter to Mr. William McChesney Martin, chairman of the U.S. Federal Reserve. See Emminger, *Verteidigung der DM*, p. 186 n. 11; Leo Brawand, *Wohin steuert die deutsche Wirtschaft?* (Munich: Kurt Desch, 1971), p. 61. See also John Yochelson, "The American

Military Presence in Europe: Current Debate in the United States," *Orbis* 15, no. 3 (Fall 1971): 784–807, esp. p. 803.

CHAPTER 10: *The Community and the New Monetary Regimes, 1970s*

Epigraphs. Otmar Emminger, *Verteidigung der DM. Plädoyers für Stabiles Geld* (Frankfurt am Main: Fritz Knapp, 1980), p. 252; Aristotle, *Ethics*, bk. 5, chap. 5.

1. "The precondition for de Gaulle's aloof policies toward the United States or Britain was in any event disappearing with the advent of the Brandt government in West Germany as a result of the elections of September 1969. Brandt was on record as favoring Britain's entry into the Common Market; his new policy towards the East (*Ostpolitik*) raised the specter of a more independent and more national course by Germany. All of this made Britain's participation in Europe seem more attractive to the French." Henry Kissinger, *The White House Years* (Boston: Little, Brown, 1979), p. 389. The British in turn argued in Washington that their membership might check the German nationalist ambitions that they claimed to see in Bonn's new *Ostpolitik* (see p. 416).

2. Helmut Schmidt wrote in 1985: "On balance, I have come to think that General De Gaulle was right in his belief that the British are not really prepared to cast their lot with the rest of the European nations. . . . The British will join the club only if they cannot prevent it from being successful." *A Grand Strategy for the West: The Anachronism of National Strategies in an Interdependent World* (New Haven and London: Yale University Press, 1985), pp. 52–53.

3. On the symbolic and practical importance of trade for the Germans see Wolfgang Hager, "Germany as an Extraordinary Trader," in Wilfrid L. Kohl and Giorgio Basevi, eds., *West Germany: A European and Global Power* (Lexington, Mass.: Lexington Books, 1980), pp. 3–19. For the changes taking place in the "rules of the game" governing the international monetary relations see Kenneth W. Dam, *The Rules of the Game: Reform and Evolution in the International Monetary System* (Chicago: University of Chicago Press, 1982). This set of concerns and objectives was brought to the fore with the decision in 1971 to float the D-Mark. See James Clyde Sperling, "Three-Way Stretch: The Federal Republic of Germany in the Atlantic Economy, 1969–1976" (Ph.D. diss., University of California, Santa Barbara, 1986), pp. 255ff.

4. On the theory of optimum currency areas see Robert A. Mundell, "A Theory of Optimum Currency Areas," *American Economic Review* 51, no. 4 (September 1961): 657–665. See also Edward Tower and Thomas D. Willett, *The Theory of Optimum Currency Areas and Exchange Rate Flexibility*, Special Papers in International Economics, no. 11 (Princeton: International Finance Section, Princeton University, 1976).

For an account of the various proposals for monetary and economic union see Peter Coffey and John R. Presley, *European Monetary Integration* (London: Macmillan, 1971); Giovanni Magnifico, *European Monetary Integration* (London: Macmillan, 1973); and Peter Coffey, *Europe and Money* (London: Macmillan, 1977). Factors within and without the Community affecting European monetary union are analyzed in Loukas Tsoukalis, *The Politics and Economics of European Monetary Integration* (London: George Allen & Unwin, 1977); Sperling, "Three-Way Stretch," pp. 467–468; Deutsche Bundesbank, "The Balance of Payments in the Federal Republic of Germany in 1973," *Monthly Report* 26 (March 1974): 18.

5. Rainer Hellmann, *Gold, the Dollar, and the European Currency Systems* (New York: Praeger, 1979), pp. 21–22. See also Norbert Kloten, "Germany's Monetary and Financial Policy and the European Community," in Kohl and Basevi, *West Germany*, pp. 177–199.

6. Herbert Blankenhorn, *Verständnis und Verständigung* (Frankfurt am Main: Propyläen, 1980), p. 341.

7. Carl F. Lankowski has argued that, in effect, the target of Bonn's strategy was "the social wage (wages, fringe, and public-sector spending directly benefitting the working class) in other EC countries. The strategy was implemented by reorganization of international monetary relations and refocusing these relations on Europe. . . . It was carried out both by promising substantial support for compliance and by a series of vetoes over counterproposals inconsistent with West German strategy. Insofar as this strategy was orchestrated through the institutions of the EC and insofar as its unfolding accounts for most of the programmatic development of the EC in the 1970s, one cannot escape the conclusion that *Modell Deutschland* is inextricably bound up with the regional extension of the West German state." "*Modell Deutschland* and the International Regionalization of the West German State in the 1970s," in Andrei S. Markovits, ed., *The Political Economy of West Germany: Modell Deutschland* (New York: Praeger, 1982), pp. 90–115; the quotation appears on p. 93.

8. For an overview of German economic and monetary policies in the 1970s see K. H. F. Dyson, "The Politics of Economic Management in West Germany"; and Jonathan Story, "The Federal Republic: a Conservative Revisionist," both in William E. Paterson and Gordon Smith, eds., *The West German Model: Perspectives on a Stable State* (Totowa, N.J.: Frank Cass, 1981), pp. 35–55, 56–86.

9. In other words, Prime Minister Heath agreed to support the French position that "in the case of very important interests the discussion must be continued until unanimous agreement is reached." This was a deviation from the Community treaty regulations, which France pushed through in January 1966 as a precondition for ending the Common Market crisis of 1965–66.

10. See Benjamin Cohen, *The Future of Sterling as an International Currency* (New York: Macmillan, 1971), esp. pp. 88ff.

11. Although Washington disliked the Common Market's economic involvement in the Mediterranean it welcomed its political consequences, which were seen as compensating in some measure for the growing Soviet naval and political presence in the area. Generally, the State Department was more sympathetic toward the political and economic aims of the Community, whereas the Treasury and Commerce departments inclined toward a harder line on the economic controversy between the United States and the EEC.

12. On the connection between monetary matters and a growing sensitivity to trade balances in the transatlantic relationship in the late 1960s and early 1970s see Thomas L. Ilgen, *Autonomy and Interdependence: U.S.-Western European Monetary and Trade Relations, 1958–1984* (Totowa, N.J.: Rowman & Allanheld, 1985), esp. chap. 4.

13. Harold van Buren Cleveland, "How the Dollar Standard Died," *Foreign Policy*, no. 5 (Winter 1971–72): 41–51. For the overriding domestic political considerations that guided the American decision see Joanne Gowa, *Closing the Gold Window: Domestic Politics and the End of Bretton Woods* (Ithaca: Cornell University Press, 1983); John S. Odell, "The U.S. and the Emergence of Flexible Exchange

Rates: An Analysis of Foreign Policy Change," *International Organization* 33, no. 1 (Winter 1979): 57–81.

14. Gowa, *Closing the Gold Window*; John Odell, *U.S. International Monetary Policy* (Princeton: Princeton University Press, 1982).

15. For example, David Calleo argues that the global monetary system led by the United States is in effect used to force the Europeans and Japanese to pay for their own defense indirectly, because they are not willing to do so directly. See "Deutschland und Amerika. Eine amerikanische Sicht," in David P. Calleo et al., eds., *Geteiltes Land—Halbes Land?* (Frankfurt am Main: Ullstein, 1986), pp. 45–96, esp. p. 79. See also Elke Thiel, "Dollarkrise und Bündnispolitik," *Europa-Archiv* 28, no. 11 (1973): 373–381, esp. pp. 377ff. On the general alliance problems of the mid-1970s see Ernst-Otto Czempiel and Dankwart Rustow, eds., *The Euro-American System: Economic and Political Relations between North America and Western Europe* (Boulder: Westview, 1976); Karl Kaiser and Hans-Peter Schwarz, *America and Western Europe: Problems and Prospects* (Lexington, Mass.: Lexington Books, 1977); Wolfram F. Hanrieder, ed., *The United States and Western Europe: Political, Economic and Strategic Perspectives* (Cambridge, Mass.: Winthrop, 1974).

16. For example, the EEC executive committee issued an information sheet that showed the value of American corporate investment in EEC countries to have risen from $1.9 billion in 1958 to $13 billion in 1970, earning $1 billion annually in repatriated profits, whereas the EEC's direct investment in the United States was only one-third that amount. In addition, the Community had a big trade deficit with the United States—$2.4 billion in 1970—which reflected the extensive and profitable nature of American trade with the Community, and the Common Market's tariffs averaged less than those of the United States (6 percent compared with 7 percent).

17. Robert Z. Aliber, *The International Money Game*, 5th ed. (New York: Basic Books, 1987), p. 7.

18. The French were constantly worried that the innovation of German industrial structures, a "new German economic miracle," would put them at a deep disadvantage (*Le Figaro*, July 6–7, 1985). For an account of French anxieties see Raymond Poidevin, *Die unruhige Grossmacht. Deutschland und die Welt im 20. Jahrhundert* (Freiburg: Ploetz, 1985); Poidevin, "Der unheimliche Nachbar: Die Deutsche Frage aus französischer Sicht," in Calleo et al., *Geteiltes Land*, pp. 127–196, esp. pp. 158ff; Renata Fritsch-Bournazel, "Gefahren für die Entspannung in Europa," in Josef Föllenbach und Eberhard Schulz, eds., *Entspannung am Ende? Chancen und Risiken einer Politik des Modus vivendi*, Internationale Politik und Wirtschaft 43 (Munich and Vienna: R. Oldenbourg, 1980): 35–70, esp. p. 51.

19. Robert Gilpin, "The Politics of Transnational Economic Relations," *International Organization* 25, no. 3 (Summer 1971): 413–414.

20. C. Fred Bergsten, *Toward a New International Economic Order: Selected Papers of C. Fred Bergsten* (Lexington, Mass.: Lexington Books, 1975), p. 61.

21. David P. Calleo, *The Imperious Economy* (Cambridge, Mass.: Harvard University Press, 1982), pp. 5–6. See also Joanne Gowa, "State Power, State Policy: Explaining the Decision to Close the Gold Window," *Politics and Society* 13, no. 1 (1984): 91–117, esp. pp. 98–101.

22. The EEC Executive Commission recommended narrowing the EEC currencies' margins of fluctuation, and on the eve of the formal agreement in January

1972 expanding the Community to ten members, Foreign Minister Scheel proposed three steps for strengthening the operating procedures of the EEC: (1) that each member appoint a "Europe Minister" who would sit in his own national cabinet as well as at EEC headquarters in Brussels—a proposal first made by President Pompidou; (2) that the powers of the president of the Common Market's Ministerial Council be enlarged and that his tenure of office be extended to one year; and (3) that the various EEC commissions take over long-range planning from the member governments.

23. Hellmann, *Gold*, p. 63.

24. On March 1, 1973, the Bundesbank in a single day had to convert on the basis of its intervention obligations almost 2.7 billion dollars—at the rate then current, almost 8 billion D-Marks! Emminger, *Verteidigung der DM*, p. 219. There is some evidence that without the actions of foreign banking operations the crisis of February 1973 either would not have occurred, or would have been much less serious. In March 1973 the German central bank estimated that two-thirds of the currency flows in the crisis were related to changes in payments involving multinationals. See also Sieghardt Rometsch, "Multinationale Unternehmen und nationale Währungspolitik," *Handelsblatt*, March 29, 1973, pp. 25, 28.

25. Strictly speaking, it is inaccurate to speak of the demise of the Bretton Woods monetary system: it was the principles of dollar-gold parity and of more or less fixed exchange rates that broke down. What remained of the Bretton Woods system was significant: the International Monetary Fund, the consultative and coordinating mechanisms that helped make it work, and the general principle that the solution or at least the attenuation of monetary problems requires an institutional setting that compels a measure of sustained cooperation.

26. Floating exchange rates were not officially sanctioned by the IMF until the conference in Jamaica of 1976. See Tom de Vries, "Jamaica or the Non-reform of the International Monetary System," *Foreign Affairs* 54, no. 3 (April 1976): 577–605; Dam, *Rules of the Game*, p. 255ff. For an overview of the Federal Republic's policies after 1973 see Armin Gutowski, Hans-Hagen Härtel, and Hans-Eckart Scharrer, "From Shock Therapy to Gradualism: Anti-inflationary Policy in Germany from 1973 to 1979," *Intereconomics* 16, no. 2 (March-April 1981): 90–96.

27. Emminger, *Verteidigung der DM*, p. 223. By 1975 France and the United States also supported the new principle that domestic economic stability should precede stability in exchange rates. See Dam, *Rules of the Game*, pp. 256–257.

28. See Stephen D. Cohen, *The European Community and the General Agreement on Tariffs and Trade* (Washington: European Community Information Service, 1975), esp. p. 23.

29. See Alexandre Lamfalussy, "A Plea for an International Commitment to Exchange Rate Stability," in Gregory Flynn, ed., *Economic Interests in the 1980's: Convergence or Divergence* (Paris: Atlantic Institute, 1982), pp. 44–53. On the realignments within the European currency snake see Hellmann, *Gold*, pp. 65ff.

30. For example, Helmut Schmidt did not hesitate in spring 1976 to criticize what he viewed as the inability of Italy's conservative parties to implement much-needed economic and social reforms, thus enabling the Communist party to reach the threshold of sharing power in the Italian government. Although Chancellor Schmidt and Henry Kissinger were not agreed on the threat posed by Eurocommunism (which the Germans thought was not nearly as threatening as

Kissinger made it out to be), the German chancellor nevertheless showed that he did not relish the prospect of its fruition; his remarks of course disgruntled the Italians.

31. Emminger, *Verteidigung der DM*, p. 259. For a German perspective on the importance of interest rate differentials relative to monetary reserves see Gerhard Zeitel, "Foreign Policy and Monetary Policy," in Wolfram F. Hanrieder, ed., *West German Foreign Policy, 1949–1979* (Boulder: Westview, 1980), pp. 197–211, esp. p. 208.

32. On the use of the ECU in the private sector see Robert Triffin, "The European Monetary System and the Dollar in the Framework of the World Monetary System," *Banco Nazionale del Lavoro Quarterly Review* 35, no. 142 (September 1982): 245–267, esp. pp. 256ff.

33. See Hellmann, *Gold*.

34. Helmut Schmidt was profoundly skeptical of the prospects for Europe: he speaks of "the abdication of Europe," the "lack of internal cohesiveness and leadership," and the absence of "political vitality." See Schmidt, *Grand Strategy*, pp. 21, 31–65.

35. See Susan Strange, "Germany and the World Monetary System," in Kohl and Basevi, *West Germany*, pp. 45–62, esp. p. 57.

36. See Otmar Emminger, *Verteidigung der DM*, pp. 90–91, 258.

37. Washington's measures to prop up the dollar had ambiguous implications for U.S. monetary and trade policies: "The question of whether the international role of the dollar is a special burden or, in the words of General de Gaulle, an exorbitant privilege, has intermittently complicated U.S.-European relations for several decades. The end of the Bretton Woods system in 1971 meant that the accumulation of dollars by other nations through exchange market intervention is now voluntary rather than mandatory, but this has not abolished the problem. In fact, both sides continue to display a certain amount of schizophrenia regarding the role of the United States as the world's banker and of the dollar as the leading international currency. The Europeans and the Japanese, for their part, insist that the United States must become more competitive and bolster its current account position, but often appear unwilling to accept a concomitant weakening of their own trade and current account positions. The United States, for its part, insists that the dollar should have the same freedom of exchange-rate movement as any other currency to eliminate imbalances in our external position. At the same time, we seem reluctant to contemplate a reduction in the reserve currency role of the dollar, a role which places a premium on dollar stability." Marina v. N. Whitman, "A Year of Travail: The United States and the International Economy," *Foreign Affairs* 57, no. 3 (special issue: "America and the World, 1978"): 527–554; the quotation appears on p. 540. See also Edgar L. Feige and James M. Johannes, "Was the United States Responsible for Worldwide Inflation under the Regime of Fixed Exchange Rates?" *Kyklos* 28, no. 2 (Summer 1984): 329–339.

38. Emminger, *Verteidigung der DM*, p. 91.

39. Ibid., p. 208. In the mid-1970s monetary relations between Paris and Washington were troubled as well. "As far as exchange rates were concerned, the differences of opinion increasingly threatened to become a Franco-American dispute. The United States wanted full legalization of floating now, and the absence of any obligation or moral pressure to return to a par value in the future.

NOTES TO PAGES 304–305

Since the U.S. authorities do not intend to reestablish a par value for the dollar for as far ahead as they can see, they were, quite rightly, adamant in refusing to accept any obligation to do so. The French, on the other hand, were not prepared to agree to the elimination from the Fund's Articles of future obligations relating to the observance of par values, a regime to which they remain strongly and fundamentally attached, and continue to hope to return to." De Vries, "Jamaica"; the quotation appears on p. 588.

40. Speaking of the meeting of the IMF and the World Bank, the *New York Times* noted: "The West Germans also came with a message, which they were not too discreet in stating, that they represented, at least financially, the strongest power in Europe and that the rest of the world, particularly the United States, should accept the kind of discipline that had brought them their success." Clyde H. Farnsworth, "A Message from Germany," *New York Times*, October 7, 1979, sec. F, p. 17.

41. On the growth in reserve holdings of the D-Mark and the Germans' resistance to having the D-Mark play a reserve currency role see Dam, *Rules of the Game*, pp. 316–318. Susan Strange noted at the time: "The basic strategy [of the EMS] is clear enough: one of collective self-defense against the continuing and threatened depreciation of the dollar, a kind of Lone Rangers Incorporated role, played jointly by the members of the Community. It cannot, however . . . succeed except by keeping the dollar stable, which is too difficult and costly a task for Europeans to undertake unless they have the full cooperation of the United States." Strange, "Germany and the World Monetary System," p. 57.

42. The French were highly sensitive when the Federal Republic presented its stability-oriented *Modell Deutschland* as an example to be emulated by others, and they interpreted it as a German attempt to obtain a dominant position in Europe, reflecting a sort of German "currency imperialism." See Henri Ménudier, "L'Allemagne Fédérale: Puissance et dépendence," in Alfred Grosser et al., eds., *Les Politiques extérieures européennes dans la crise*, Travaux et recherches de science politique, vol. 43 (Paris: Presses Fondation Nationale de Science Politique, 1976), pp. 125ff. See also Ménudier, *Das Deutschlandbild der Franzosen in den 70er Jahren* (Bonn: Europa-Union-Verlag, 1981); Klaus Manfrass, ed., *Paris-Bonn. Eine dauerhafte Bindung schwieriger Partner. Beiträge zum deutsch-französischen Verhältnis in Kultur, Wirtschaft und Politik seit 1949* (Sigmaringen: Jan Thorbecke, 1984); Manfrass stresses German economic advantages in French-German relations.

In 1978, "for the first time since World War II Germany began to claim political rights that would match its economic ascendancy. The main practical manifestation of this was . . . the scheme for the EMS, but in many smaller ways Germany's partners in the European Community noted an increasing tendency on the part of the Germans to demand automatic deference to their interests in a fashion hitherto monopolized by the French." David Watt, "The European Initiative," *Foreign Affairs* 57, no. 3 (special issue: "America and the World, 1978"): 572–588; the quotation is from p. 587. Watt also notes that "in 1978, a West German government thought and acted for the first time on Gaullist, or at least semi-Gaullist, principles" (p. 573).

43. This issue was demonstrated again in the controversy over West Germany's decision to provide Brazil with an installation for uranium enrichment, a nuclear reactor, and a reprocessing plant for nuclear fuel. In light of criticism by

the United States that the export of such sensitive technology should be checked, because it made possible the manufacture of nuclear weapons, the Germans in turn argued that American motives were political and economic, and unjustifiable in light of America's own export of nuclear power plants to Brazil.

44. Benjamin J. Cohen, "The Revolution in Atlantic Economic Relations: A Bargain Comes Unstuck," in Hanrieder, *United States and Western Europe*, pp. 106–133.

45. On the first point see Robert O. Keohane, "The International Politics of Inflation," in Leon N. Lindberg and Charles S. Maier, eds., *The Politics of Inflation and Economic Stagnation: Theoretical Approaches and International Case Studies* (Washington: Brookings Institution, 1985), pp. 78–104, esp. p. 97; on the second see Gowa, *Closing the Gold Window*.

46. For an overview of the monetary issues of the early 1970s see Patrick M. Boarman and David G. Tuerck, eds., *World Monetary Disorder. National Policies vs. International Imperatives* (New York: Praeger, 1976); Cohen, "The Revolution in Atlantic Economic Relations"; William Diebold, Jr., "Economics and Politics: The Western Alliance in the 1970s"; David A. Walker, "Some Underlying Problems for International Monetary Reform"; Edward L. Morse, "European Monetary Union and American Foreign Economic Policy," all in Hanrieder, *United States and Western Europe*, 134–163, 164–186, 187–210.

47. Manfred Knapp, "Bonn-Washington: Co-operation and Competition," *Aussenpolitik* 29, no. 4 (1978): 387–400.

CHAPTER 11: *The Politics and Economics of the 1980s*

Epigraphs. Fernand Braudel, *The Mediterranean and the Mediterranean World in the Age of Philip II*, vol. 2 (New York: Harper & Row, 1972), p. 661; John Updike, *Hugging the Shore: Essays and Criticism* (New York: Alfred A. Knopf, 1983), p. xix.

1. For an overview of the Reagan administration's economic policies and their impact on the global political economy see Robert Gilpin, *The Political Economy of International Relations* (Princeton: Princeton University Press, 1987), chaps. 9, 10. For a discussion of American debts see Lawrence Malkin, *The National Debt* (New York: Henry Holt, 1987); Alfred L. Malabre, Jr., *Beyond Our Means* (New York: Random House, 1987); Daniel Bell and Lester Thurow, *The Deficits: How Big? How Long? How Dangerous?* (New York: New York University Press, 1986). For a more sanguine view see Robert Eisner, *How Real Is the Federal Deficit?* (New York: Free Press, 1986). In fiscal year 1987–88, the public debt (which had swollen from $1 trillion to more than $2.5 trillion in the preceding seven years) entailed annual interest payments of $144.7 billion. See *New York Times*, February 12, 1988, p. 30Y.

2. William Greider, *Secrets of the Temple: How the Federal Reserve Runs the Country* (New York: Simon & Schuster, 1987).

3. The Eisenhower administration (in 1953) and the Kennedy and Johnson administrations (in 1963–64) cut taxes to sustain economic recovery, and Congress persuaded the Ford administration in 1974 to put together an antirecession policy package of tax rebates and Federal expenditures. On the Ford Administration's economic policies see A. James Reichley, *Conservatives in an Age of Change: The Nixon and Ford Administrations* (Washington: Brookings Institution, 1981).

4. John T. Woolley, *Monetary Politics: The Federal Reserve and The Politics of Monetary Policy* (Cambridge: Cambridge University Press, 1984).

5. Otmar Emminger, *The Dollar's Borrowed Strength*, Occasional Papers, no. 19 (New York: Group of Thirty, 1985), pp. 3 and 4.

6. Helmut Schmidt, *A Grand Strategy for the West* (New Haven and London: Yale University Press, 1985), p. 48.

7. James Tobin, "How to Think about the Deficit," *New York Review of Books*, September 25, 1986, pp. 43–46; the quotation is from p. 46.

8. The Germans were less comfortable with Washington's argument that the American trade balance was not a problem, a conclusion that the United States reached by definition: technically, trade deficits pose a problem only if joined by a current account deficit and a depreciating currency, and neither condition held for the United States. In 1981 the United States enjoyed a modest current account surplus, due in large part to the weakness of the dollar during the Carter administration, and the dollar was appreciating. Given these criteria, the United States could be said to be making a positive contribution to the world economy. See U.S. Congress, Joint Economic Committee, *The 1982 Economic Report of the President: Hearings before the Joint Economic Committee*, 97th Cong., 2d sess. (Washington: GPO, 1982), p. 179.

9. "The overvaluation of the dollar had accelerated the process of de-industrialization of the American economy, both through its effect on trade competitiveness and through the induced dissemination of American technology via direct foreign investment in Europe and off-shore Asia," Wolfgang Hager, "Political Implications of US-EC Economic Conflicts (II): Atlantic Trade: Problems and Prospects," *Government and Opposition* 22, no. 1 (Winter 1987): 49–65.

10. This view was shared by the IMF, which rebuked the American reliance on monetary policy as a cure for inflation and noted that volatile exchange rates suggested that "the stability of exchange rates could be enhanced by a more balanced and coordinated mix of monetary and fiscal policies in industrial countries." International Monetary Fund, *Annual Report, 1982* (Washington, 1983), p. 49. See also *IMF Annual Meeting Summary Proceedings* (Washington, 1981), p. 38.

11. The Bundesbank, for example, complained in 1983 that it and other central banks had "little other choice in the past two years than to follow the monetary policy of the United States. In order to work against a depreciation of the currency and the associated danger of inflation, others had to follow a restrictive course." This view was shared by the Federal Reserve Board. See Deutsche Bundesbank, *Annual Report, 1982–83* (Frankfurt am Main: Bundesbank 1983), secs. 20, 21, 151; U.S. Federal Reserve Board, *69th Annual Report, 1982* (Washington: GPO, 1983), p. 24.

12. At the summit in Williamsburg in May 1983, the major industrialized nations agreed on the need to reduce interest rates and the structural components of their budget deficits by cutting government expenditures. The United States admitted the connection between the budget deficit and high interest rates, and by implication between the budget deficit and volatile exchange rates. But although the Germans, British, and Japanese made good on their promise to reduce the structural component of their budget deficits, the United States did not fulfill its own.

13. International Monetary Fund, *Annual Report 1982*, pp. 62–63.

14. Emminger, *Dollar's Borrowed Strength*, p. 13.
15. See Herbert Giersch, "The Age of Schumpeter," *American Economic Review* 74, no. 2 (May 1984): 103–109, esp. p. 106. See also Roland Vaubel, *Internationale Absprachen und Wettbewerb in der Konjunkturpolitik?* (Tübingen: J. C. B. Mohr, 1980). For a somber assessment of trade developments after the Tokyo Round see Gilbert R. Winham, *International Trade and the Tokyo Round Negotiation* (Princeton: Princeton University Press, 1986); John Quinn and Philip Slayton, eds., *Non-tariff Barriers after the Tokyo Round* (Montreal: Institute for Research on Public Policy, 1982). On the long-standing and continuing problems between the United States and Western Europe on agricultural markets see Nicholas Butler, "The Ploughshares War between Europe and America," *Foreign Affairs* 62, no. 1 (Fall 1983): 105–122.
16. Schmidt, *Grand Strategy*, p. 147. See also Helmut Schmidt, *Menschen und Mächte* (Berlin: Siedler, 1987).
17. *Bundestag Debates*, Stenographic Record, May 14, 1985, no. 10189C (Bonn: Bundestag Publications, 1985).
18. Otmar Emminger, "Konjunktur, Geldpolitik, Geldwertstablität," *Verteidigung der DM. Pädoyers für stabiles Geld* (Frankfurt am Main: Fritz Knapp, 1980), pp. 76–85. For Emminger's general views see his memoirs, *D-Mark, Dollar, Währungskrisen. Erinnerungen eines ehemaligen Bundesbankpräsidenten* (Stuttgart: Deutsche Verlags-Anstalt, 1986).
19. "Treasury and Federal Reserve Foreign Exchange Operations," *Federal Reserve Bulletin* 73, no. 7 (July 1987): 552ff.
20. Ibid., pp. 425ff.
21. See the interview with the Bundesbank's chief, Karl Otto Pöhl, "Da werden wirklich Nägel mit Köpfen gemacht," *Der Spiegel* 41, no. 36 (1987): 51–62.
22. *New York Times*, October 30, 1987, p. 33Y.
23. *First Annual Arthur F. Burns Memorial Lecture* (New York: American Council on Germany, 1987).
24. Kenneth King, *U.S. Monetary Policy and European Responses in the 1980s*, ed. Royal Institute of International Affairs, Chatham House Papers, no. 16 (London: Routledge & Kegan Paul, 1982), esp. pp. 29ff. See also Robert Triffin, "The European Monetary System and the Dollar in the Framework of the World Monetary System," *Banco Nazionale del Lavoro Quarterly Review* 35, no. 142 (September 1982): 245–267, esp. p. 249.
25. Mario Sarcinelli, "The EMS and the International Monetary System: Towards Greater Stability," *Banco Nazionale del Lavoro Quarterly Review* 39, no. 156 (March 1986): 57–83; the quotation appears on p. 62.
26. See Emminger, *Dollar's Borrowed Strength*, pp. 4–7; and the interview with Pöhl, "Da werden wirklich Nägel mit Köpfen gemacht," esp. p. 59. For a highly skeptical German view of the prospects for a new global economic "regime" see Karl Heinz Frank and Herbert Giersch, eds., *Gegen Europapessimismus. Weltwirtschaftliche Perspektiven* (Stuttgart: Deutsche Verlags-Anstalt, 1986). The Germans also opposed target zones for the major currencies, arguing that they would "not present a practical alternative to the existing system, since the fundamental causes of exchange rate distortions have not been moved out of the way." Deutsche Bundesbank, *Annual Report, 1987–88* (Frankfurt am Main: Bundesbank, 1988), sec. 39.

27. Elke Thiel, "Macroeconomic Policy Preferences and Coordination: A View From Germany," (paper presented at the Interdisciplinary Conference on the Political Economy of International Macroeconomic Policy Coordination, Andover, Mass., November 6–7, 1987).

28. See Pierre-Alain Muet, "Economic Management and the International Environment, 1981–1983," in Howard Machin and Vincent Wright, eds., *Economic Policy and Policy-making under the Mitterrand Presidency, 1981–1984* (New York: St. Martin's, 1985), pp. 70–95; DeAnne Julius, "Britain's Changing International Interests: Economic Influences on Foreign Policy Priorities," *International Affairs* 63, no. 3 (Summer 1987): 375–393.

29. Robert Triffin, "The European Monetary System." For a critical assessment of West European progress toward policy coordination see Karl Kaiser et al., eds., *The European Community: Progress or Decline?* (London: Royal Institute of International Affairs, 1983).

30. This was one reason why the Bundesbank remained skeptical of the institutional prospects of the EMS, noting the insufficient degree of economic convergence among the EMS states, the nonparticipation of the United Kingdom in the scheme, the 6 percent band of fluctuation enjoyed by the Italian lira, a two-tier exchange rate market in Belgium, a plethora of capital controls (especially in France), and the continued divergence between the inflation rates of West Germany and the EMS (the gap ranged from almost 9 percent in 1980 to 5.2 percent in 1984). Deutsche Bundesbank, *Annual Report, 1984* (Frankfurt am Main: Bundesbank, 1985), p. 68.

31. For a diverse assessment of the problems and prospects of the Community see Werner Weidenfeld and Wolfgang Wessels, eds., *Wege zur Europäischen Union. Vom Vertrag zur Verfassung* (Bonn: Europa-Union-Verlag, 1986). See also Werner J. Feld, ed., *Western Europe's Global Reach: Regional Cooperation and Worldwide Aspirations* (New York: Pergamon, 1980).

32. See Alan Butt Philip, *Implementing the European Internal Market* (London: Royal Institute of International Affairs, 1988). For the Community's own assessment see the EC Commission's report *Research on the Cost of Non-Europe* (Brookfield, Vt.: Gower Press, 1988).

33. *Der Spiegel* 42, no. 28 (1988): 68–69. See also *Economist*, June 25, 1988, p. 11.

34. For a balanced assessment of these problems see Paul Taylor, *The Limits of European Integration* (New York: Columbia University Press, 1983); George Stephen, *Politics and Policy in the European Community* (New York: Oxford University Press, 1985); Robert S. Jordan and Werner Feld, *Europe in the Balance* (London: Faber and Faber, 1986). For an account of the treaty of 1984 on European Union and the evolution of the Community's parliamentary initiatives see Juliet Lodge, ed., *European Union: The European Community in Search of a Future* (New York: St. Martin's, 1986).

35. Karl Hardach, *The Political Economy of Germany in the Twentieth Century* (Berkeley: University of California Press, 1980), p. 1.

36. Helen Wallace, William Wallace, and Carole Webb, eds., *Policy-Making in the European Communities* (London: John Wiley and Sons, 1977). On the continuity of the Community's problems and for a deeply skeptical view of whether they can be resolved see Herbert Müller-Rorschach, *Die deutsche Europapolitik, 1949–1977*

490

(Bonn: Europa-Union-Verlag, 1980). See also Ernst B. Haas, *The Obsolescence of Regional Integration Theory*, Institute of International Studies, Research Series, no. 25 (Berkeley, 1975).

37. "Under the stimulus of economic nationalism . . . nations may also occasionally act against the multilateral framework. . . . Nationalism might have been expected to reduce interdependence. It might be argued that, if nations seek only to achieve their own goals without reference to the rest of the system, the linkage between units must decline. If nationalistic goals depend on supportive actions by other members of the international community, however, nationalism cannot be achieved in isolation. Not only does interdependence not decline in such circumstances, aggressive nationalism may lead to higher negative interdependence. The greater nationalism of the twentieth century therefore need not entail a reduction of interdependence." Richard Rosecrance and Arthur Stein, "Interdependence: Myth or Reality?" *World Politics* 26, no. 1 (October 1973): 1–27, esp. pp. 21–25. See also Werner Link, ed., *The New Nationalism: Implications for Transatlantic Relations* (New York: Pergamon, 1979).

38. Hajo Holborn, "American Foreign Policy and European Integration," *World Politics* 6, no. 1 (October 1953): 1–30; the quotation appears on pp. 29–30.

39. See Weidenfeld and Wessels, *Wege zur Europäischen Union*.

40. For an account of the stagnation of the EMS and its inability to progress toward its "second stage" see Norbert Kleinheyer, *Die Weiterentwicklung des Europäischen Währungssystems. Überlegungen zur stabilitätsorientierten Ausgestaltung der "Zweiten Stufe"* (Berlin: Duncker & Humblot, 1987). See also Loukas Tsoukalis, *The Politics and Economics of European Monetary Integration* (London: George Allen and Unwin, 1977).

41. "That both France and Britain have continued to oppose Monnet-style integration is a wry tribute to their confidence that there is no need to strengthen the community to contain the growing power of the Federal Republic because the Atlantic arrangement does the job so effectively, in economic as in security matters. But of course the limitations on the community in this respect further strengthened the importance of the Atlantic arrangements which contain the Federal Republic—not what de Gaulle wanted. American policymakers were slow to grasp that the real alternative to an integrated Europe of their dreams, which de Gaulle blocked, was not his European Europe but the Atlantic Europe which they themselves had created." A. W. DePorte, *Europe between the Superpowers: The Enduring Balance* (New Haven and London: Yale University Press, 1979), p. 226.

42. This has led some analysts to suggest a "mixed" national-supranational economic strategy, with highly discrete responsibilities. For an argument that urges revitalization of the Community through a growth and investment strategy led by Brussels (that is, "permissive" policies on the international level), which would be kept in balance by anti-inflationary policies of member states (that is, "repressive" policies on the national level) see Michel Albert, *Un pari pour l'Europe* (Paris: Editions du Seuil, 1983).

43. See Henry R. Nau, "From Integration to Interdependence: Gains, Losses, and Continuing Gaps," *International Organization* 33, no. 1 (1979): 119–147.

44. On the decline of American hegemony see Mancur Olson, *The Rise and Decline of Nations: Economic Growth, Stagnation, and Social Rigidities* (New Haven

and London: Yale University Press, 1982); Gilpin, *Political Economy*; Richard Rose-crance, *The Rise of the Trading State: Commerce and Conquest in the Modern World* (New York: Basic Books, 1986); David P. Calleo, *Beyond American Hegemony: The Future of the Western Alliance* (New York: Twentieth Century Fund-Basic Books, 1987); Robert W. Cox, *Production, Power, and World Order: Social Forces in the Making of History* (New York: Columbia University Press, 1987); Paul Kennedy, *The Rise and Fall of the Great Powers: Economic Change and Military Conflict from 1500 to 2000* (New York: Random House, 1987); Joshua S. Goldstein, *Long Cycles: Prosperity and War in the Modern Age* (New Haven and London: Yale University Press, 1988).

45. David Calleo, *The Imperious Economy* (Cambridge, Mass.: Harvard University Press, 1982).

46. See Lester C. Thurow, *The Zero-Sum Society: Distribution and the Possibilities for Economic Change* (New York: Basic Books, 1980).

47. See Rosecrance, *Rise of the Trading State*.

48. "The question we must raise is why we are allowing our economic position to deteriorate at an unprecedented rate. The answer is painfully clear: we have been abandoning our economic superiority in order to achieve military superiority. We have been borrowing abroad to finance rearmament. The current account of the U.S., which reflects the balance of trade, declined by $155 billion between 1980 and 1986, while the defense budget rose by $138 billion between the same years. . . . Fortuitously, President Reagan embarked on a huge rearmament program while cutting taxes at the same time. The resulting budget deficit saved the world economy from depression by providing much-needed fiscal stimulus. In an ironic twist of fate the United States became, in effect, both the borrower and the spender of last resort." George Soros, "A Global New Deal," *New York Review of Books*, August 13, 1987, p. 52. See also the comments by Felix Rohatyn, "On the Brink," *New York Review of Books*, June 11, 1987, p. 3.

49. "In the closing decades of the twentieth century the United States has found itself caught between its many commitments and decreased power, the classic position of a declining hegemon. As Soviet military power expanded, the United States had assumed increased costs to maintain its hegemonic political and military position; simultaneously the rise of new industrial competitors and the loss of former economic monopolies in energy, technology, and agriculture had decreased the capacity of the United States to finance its hegemony. With a decreased rate of economic growth and a low rate of national savings, the United States was living and defending commitments far beyond its means." Gilpin, *Political Economy*, p. 347. See also Robert Heilbroner, "Hard Times," *New Yorker*, September 14, 1987, pp. 96–109, esp. p. 105.

50. Gilpin, *Political Economy*, pp. 348–350. See also Hager, "Political Implications," pp. 49–65.

51. See Robert B. Reich, "The Economics of Illusion and the Illusion of Economics," *Foreign Affairs* 66, no. 3 (special issue: "America and the World, 1987–88"): 516–528. For the "complicity" between state and electorate in a consumer-oriented economy see James D. Savage, *Balanced Budgets and American Politics* (Ithaca: Cornell University Press, 1988).

52. See Samuel P. Huntington, "Coping with the Lippmann Gap," *Foreign Affairs* 66, no. 3 (special issue: "America and the World, 1987–88"): 453–477. See also James Chace, *Solvency: The Price of Survival* (New York: Random House, 1981).

53. Walter Lippmann, for example, noted in addition to pointing to other deficiencies that the continuing exertions and patient application that this policy required would turn out to be too taxing for American institutions and the American people. See "The Cold War," *Foreign Affairs* 65, no. 4 (Spring 1987): 869–884, esp. pp. 872–873. See also George F. Kennan, *American Diplomacy, 1900–1950* (Chicago: University of Chicago Press, 1951).

54. See Seyom Brown, *The Faces of Power: Constancy and Change in United States Foreign Policy from Truman to Johnson* (New York: Columbia University Press, 1968).

55. For a treatment of the interrelatedness of finance and foreign policy and the encouragement of German prosperity by the United States see Benjamin J. Cohen, *In Whose Interest? International Banking and American Foreign Policy* (New Haven and London: Yale University Press, 1986).

56. See Marc Weiss and Martin Gellen, "The Rise and Fall of the Cold War Consensus," in Judith Carnoy and Marc Weiss, eds., *A House Divided* (Boston: Little, Brown, 1973), pp. 14–36; John G. Tower, "Congress versus the President: The Formulation and Implementation of American Foreign Policy," *Foreign Affairs* 60, no. 2 (Winter 1981–82): 229–246; Charles H. Percy, "The Partisan Gap," *Foreign Policy*, no. 45 (Winter 1981–82): 3–15; Lee H. Hamilton and Michael H. Van Dusen, "Making the Separation of Powers Work," *Foreign Affairs* 57, no. 1 (Fall 1978): 17–39; Douglas J. Bennet, Jr., "Congress in Foreign Policy: Who Needs It?" *Foreign Affairs* 57, no. 1 (Fall 1978): 40–50; Lloyd N. Cutler, "To Form a Government," *Foreign Affairs* 59, no. 1 (Fall 1980): 126–143; Warren Christopher, "Cease-Fire between the Branches: A Compact in Foreign Affairs," *Foreign Affairs* 60, no. 5 (Summer 1982): 989–1005.

57. Henry A. Kissinger, *Years of Upheaval* (Boston: Little, Brown, 1982), p. 91.

58. This gave rise to a spate of books on the "mysteries" of the Germans' transatlantic partner. See for example Herbert von Borch, *Amerika. Dekadenz und Grösse* (Munich: Piper, 1981); Klaus Harpprecht, *Der fremde Freund. Amerika: Eine innere Geschichte* (Stuttgart: Deutsche Verlags-Anstalt, 1982); Helmut Ahrens, *Reagans Amerika. Vorwärts nach Gestern* (Augsburg: Hofmann, 1982); Norbert Muehlen, *Amerika—Im Gegenteil: antiamerikanische und andere Ansichten* (Stuttgart: Seewald, 1972); Walther Leisler Kiep, *Good-bye Amerika—Was dann?* (Stuttgart: Seewald, 1972); Hans Rühle, Hans-Joachim Vehn, and Walter F. Hahn, eds., *Der Neo-Konservatismus in den Vereinigten Staaten und seine Auswirkungen auf die Atlantische Allianz* (Melle: Ernst Knoth for the Konrad-Adenauer-Stiftung, 1982); Klaus Harpprecht, *Amerikaner* (Munich: Deutscher Taschenbuch-Verlag, 1984); L. L. Matthias, *Die Kehrseite der USA* (Reinbek: Rowohlt, 1985); Hartmut Wasser, *Die Vereinigten Staaten von Amerika. Porträt einer Weltmacht* (Stuttgart: Deutsche Verlags-Anstalt, 1980); Peter Merseburger, *Die unberechenbare Vormacht. Wohin steuert die USA?* (Munich: Bertelsmann, 1983); Dieter Kronzucker, *Unser Amerika* (Reinbek: Rowohlt, 1987); Peter von Zahn, *Verlässt uns Amerika?* (Frankfurt am Main: Ullstein, 1987); Marion Gräfin Dönhoff, *Amerikanische Wechselbäder* (Stuttgart: Deutsche Verlags-Anstalt, 1983).

INTRODUCTION TO PART IV

Epigraph. Kurt Schumacher, "Die Staatsgewalt geht von den Besatzungsmächten aus" (SPD pamphlet, n.d. [probably 1948]).

1. John Gimbel quotes Hans Simon, a close observer of the scene, as saying

that the Basic Law was "made primarily for international purposes," and that the Western powers wanted it "in order to provide a partner for the western European integration, a better-equipped situation for Marshall aid, and primarily in order to strengthen a friction point which could not be left soft any longer." John Gimbel, *The American Occupation of Germany: Politics and the Military, 1945–1949* (Stanford: Stanford University Press, 1968), p. 256. Gimbel is here quoting from Hans Simon, "The Bonn Constitution and Its Government," in Hans J. Morgenthau, ed., *Germany and the Future of Europe* (Chicago: University of Chicago Press, 1951), p. 114.

2. See Alexander Mitscherlich, *Hauptworte, Hauptsachen. Zwei Gespräche: Heimat, Nation*, ed. A. M. Kalow and Gert Kalow. (Munich: Piper, 1971); Ralph Giordano, *Die zweite Schuld oder von der Last Deutscher zu sein* (Hamburg: Rasch and Röhring, 1987); Rüdiger Altmann, *Der wilde Frieden. Notizen zu einer politischen Theorie des Scheiterns* (Stuttgart: Deutsche Verlags-Anstalt, 1987); Dietrich Güstrow, *In jenen Jahren. Aufzeichnungen eines befreiten Deutschen* (Munich: Deutscher Taschenbuch-Verlag, 1985); Margaret Boveri, *Tage des Überlebens* (Munich: Piper, 1985).

3. For general treatments of the domestic response to the changing international context see Rudolf Wildenmann, *Macht and Konsens als Problem der Innen- und Aussenpolitik* (Frankfurt am Main: Athenäum, 1963); Wolfram F. Hanrieder, *West German Foreign Policy, 1949–1963: International Pressure and Domestic Response* (Stanford: Stanford University Press, 1967), chaps. 4, 7; Hanrieder, *The Stable Crisis: Two Decades of German Foreign Policy* (New York: Harper & Row, 1970), chap. 4.

4. On the Right's need to adjust on the German question see Werner Weidenfeld, "Ratloses Nationalgefühl? Fragen an die Deutsche Frage," *Deutschland Archiv* 17, no. 6 (June 1984): 586–589, esp. p. 586; Wilhelm Bruns, *Deutsch-deutsche Beziehungen. Prämissen, Probleme, Perspektiven* (Opladen: Leske & Budrich, 1984), pp. 146–152; Peter Bender, "Die Ostpolitik der Regierung Kohl," *Die Neue Gesellschaft/Frankfurter Hefte* 33, no. 10 (October 1986): 884–888; Eberhard Schulz and Peter Danylow, "Bewegung in der deutschen Frage? Die ausländischen Besorgnisse über die Entwicklung in den beiden deutschen Staaten," Arbeitspapiere zur internationalen Politik 33 (Bonn: Europa-Union-Verlag, 1985): 154; Wilhelm G. Grewe, *Die deutsche Frage in der Ost-West-Spannung. Zeitgeschichtliche Kontroversen der achtziger Jahre* (Herford: Busse-Seewald, 1986), esp. pp. 124–125.

5. See Theo Sommer, "Die Einheit gegen Freiheit tauschen," *Die Zeit*, July 3, 1987, p. 1. Some German analysts play down this contradiction. For an account of these views see Werner J. Feld, *West Germany and the European Community: Changing Interests and Competing Policy Objectives* (New York: Praeger, 1981), pp. 111–112.

6. See Peter Bender, *Neue Ostpolitik. Vom Mauerbau bis zum Moskauer Vertrag* (Munich: Deutscher Taschenbuch-Verlag, 1986). Bender describes the period 1963–69 as one of "transition and adjustment." For a similar periodization see Dietrich Thränhardt, *Geschichte der Bundesrepublik Deutschland, 1949–1984* (Frankfurt am Main: Suhrkamp, 1986).

CHAPTER 12: *From Dissent to Convolution, 1949–69*

Epigraph. The comment by Herbert Wehner was made in a speech to the Bundestag. See *Verhandlungen*, June 30, 1960, sec. 46, pp. 7052–7070.

1. For example, Dr. Gustav Heinemann, then the CDU's minister of the interior, later an SPD cabinet member (minister of justice) in the Grand Coalition, and later still the president of the Federal Republic, resigned over the issue of rearmament and helped organize protest meetings throughout West Germany. Jakob Kaiser, minister for all-German affairs (1949–57), strongly opposed as well Adenauer's sterile reunification policy. On the former see Helmut Lindemann, *Gustav Heinemann. Ein Leben für die Demokratie* (Munich: Kösel, 1978); and Helmut Gollwitzer, "Politik an den Grenzen des Bürgertums. Zur Gesamtausgabe der Reden und Schriften Gustav W. Heinemanns," *Evangelische Theologie* 37 (March-April 1977): 185ff. On the latter see Christian Hacke, ed., *Jakob Kaiser. Wir haben Brücke zu sein. Reden, Äusserungen und Aufsätze zur Deutschlandpolitik* (Cologne: Verlag Wissenschaft und Politik, 1988).

2. For a treatment of the German chancellors see Wilhelm von Sternburg, ed., *Die deutschen Kanzler von Bismarck bis Schmidt*, 2d ed. (Königstein: Athenäum, 1985). For a survey of policy statements made by them see Klaus von Beyme, ed., *Die grossen Regierungserklärungen der deutschen Bundeskanzler von Adenauer bis Schmidt* (Munich: Hanser, 1979). For the institutional and bureaucratic setting of the Federal Republic's foreign policymaking see Helga Haftendorn, ed., *Verwaltete Aussenpolitik. Sicherheits- und entspannungspolitische Entscheidungsprozesse in Bonn* (Cologne: Verlag Wissenschaft und Politik, 1978).

For a discussion of the composition and program of the CDU see Ernst Deuerlein, *CDU/CSU, 1945–1957*, Beiträge zur Zeitgeschichte (Cologne, 1957); Arcadius R. L. Gurland, *Die CDU/CSU. Ursprünge und Entwicklung bis 1953*, ed. Dieter Emig (Frankfurt am Main: 1980); Geoffrey Pridham, *Christian Democracy in Western Germany: The CDU/CSU in Government and Opposition, 1945–1976* (London, 1977); Dorothee Buchhaas, *Die Volkspartei. Programmatische Entwicklung der CDU, 1950–1973*, Beiträge zur Geschichte des Parlamentarismus und der politischen Parteien, vol. 68 (Düsseldorf: Droste, 1981); Wolf-Dieter Narr, *CDU-SPD. Programm und Praxis seit 1945* (Stuttgart, 1966).

3. For a general account of the development of the FDP see Richard S. Cromwell, *The Free Democratic Party in German Politics, 1945–1956: A Historical Study of a Contemporary Liberal Party* (Ph.D. diss., Stanford University, 1961); Kurt J. Korper and Jörg Michael Gutscher, *Die Entwicklung der FDP von ihren Anfängen bis 1961* (Meisenheim am Glan: A. Hain, 1967). On the economic policies of the FDP see Max Gustav Lange, "Der FDP-Versuch einer Erneuerung des Liberalismus," in Max Gustav Lange et al., *Parteien in der Bundesrepublik* (Stuttgart: Ring Verlag for Institut für Politische Wissenschaft, 1955). For the FDP's view on rearmament see Dietrich Wagner, *FDP und Wiederbewaffnung. Die wehrpolitische Orientierung der Liberalen in der Bundesrepublik Deutschland 1949–1955*, Militärgeschichte seit 1945, vol. 5 (Boppard: Harald Boldt, 1978).

4. Although they did not oppose European integration as such, the Social Democrats' objections to the European Coal and Steel Community were sweeping. In general, they attacked the Schuman Plan as an international conspiracy to impede unification and handicap Germany's ability to compete with France on world markets. By 1955, however, the Social Democrats advocated internationally coordinated investment policies and business-cycle controls, and began criticizing the ECSC for not having gone far enough in this direction. See Ernst Haas, *The Uniting of Europe* (Stanford: Stanford University Press, 1958), p. 138. See

also Wolfram F. Hanrieder, *West German Foreign Policy, 1949–1963: International Pressure and Domestic Response* (Stanford: Stanford University Press, 1967), esp. pp. 119–121. This led to concerns by conservatives that economic integration would have the potential for socialist planning. See Herbert Blankenhorn, *Verständnis und Verständigung* (Frankfurt am Main: Propyläen, 1980), p. 108.

5. See Gordon A. Craig, "NATO and the New German Army," in William W. Kaufmann, ed., *Military Policy and National Security* (Princeton: Princeton University Press, 1956), pp. 194–232.

6. For example, in the 1950s the so-called Königsteiner Kreis, a group of intellectuals concerned primarily with the economic dimensions of unification policy, spelled out some of the severe problems that would have followed the combining of the two German economies. See the discussion in the *Handelsblatt*, November 23, 1951, p. 3; Wolfgang F. Stolper, *Germany between East and West* (Washington: National Planning Association, 1960).

7. For public opinion survey data see Erich P. Neumann and Elisabeth Noelle, *Antworten* (Allensbach am Bodensee: Verlag für Demoskopie, 1954). See also Gerald Freund, *Germany between Two Worlds* (New York: Harcourt Brace Jovanovich, 1961), p. 95. Of all the organized interest groups, the trade union movement was the only one that lent active political support to the cause of reunification, believing that unification could revitalize the rather flabby German trade union movement. But cross-pressures prevented the trade unions from becoming an effective interest lobby for reunification. See Otto Kirchheimer, "West German Trade Unions: Their Domestic and Foreign Policies," in Hans Speier and W. Phillips Davison, *West German Leadership and Foreign Policy*, 2d ed. (New York: St. Martin's, 1981), pp. 174–176, 179–185.

Business circles were also unwilling to exert influence on behalf of a foreign policy program that assigned the highest priority to unification. Unification would have required integrating two economic systems that had evolved in different directions, and the uncertainties and risks involved appeared high to West German entrepreneurs. See Gabriel Almond, "The Politics of German Business," in Speier and Davison, *West German Leadership*, pp. 195–241.

8. See Sebastian J. Glatzeder, *Die Deutschlandpolitik der FDP in der Ära Adenauer. Konzeptionen in Entstehung und Praxis* (Baden-Baden: Nomos, 1980).

9. For an account of the changes taking place within the SPD on the party's NATO policy, European integration, and Ostpolitik see Hartmut Soell, *Fritz Erler. Eine politische Biographie* (Bonn-Bad Godesberg: J. H. W. Dietz, 1976); Abraham Ashkenasi, *Reformpartei und Aussenpolitik. Die Aussenpolitik der SPD* (Cologne: Westdeutscher Verlag, 1968); Udo Loewke, *Für den Fall dass: SPD und Wehrfrage, 1949–1955* (Hannover: Verlag für Literatur und Zeitgeschichte, 1967); Joachim Hütter, *SPD und nationale Sicherheit. Internationale und innenpolitische Determinanten des Wandels der sozialdemokratischen Sicherheitspolitik, 1959–61* (Meisenheim am Glan: A. Hain, 1975); Gordon D. Drummond, *The German Social Democrats in Opposition, 1949–1960* (Norman: University of Oklahoma Press, 1982); Stephen J. Artner, *A Change of Course: The West German Social Democrats and NATO, 1957–1961* (Westport, Conn.: Greenwood, 1985); Peter Arend, *Die innerparteiliche Entwicklung der SPD, 1966–1975* (Bonn: Eichholz, 1975); Douglas A. Chalmers, *The Social Democratic Party of Germany: From Working-Class Movement to Modern Political Party* (New Haven and London: Yale University Press, 1964); Lothar Wilker, *Die Sicher-*

heitspolitik der SPD, *1956–1966. Zwischen Wiedervereinigungs- und Bündnisorientierung* (Bonn-Bad Godesberg: Neue Gesellschaft, 1977); William E. Paterson, *The* SPD *and European Integration* (Lexington, Mass.: Lexington Books, 1974); Rudolf Hrbek, *Die* SPD, *Deutschland und Europa. Die Haltung der Sozialdemokratie zum Verhältnis von Deutschlandpolitik und West-Integration (1945–1957)* (Bonn: Europa-Union-Verlag, 1972); David Childs, *From Schumacher to Brandt* (Oxford: Pergamon Press, 1966).

10. See Wolfram F. Hanrieder, *The Stable Crisis: Two Decades of German Foreign Policy* (New York: Harper & Row, 1970), esp. pp. 151–152.

11. For a treatment of the West German antinuclear movement see Hans-Karl Rupp, *Ausserparlamentarische Opposition in der Ära Adenauer* (Cologne: Pahl-Rugenstein, 1970).

12. This plan was so accommodating to the Soviet Union that it could not even marshal the support of all elements of the SPD. See Fritz René Allemann, *Zwischen Stabilität und Krise. Etappen der deutschen Politik, 1955–1963* (Munich: Piper, 1963). On the connection between the SPD's Germany Plan and the East-West disengagement proposals of the late 1950s, and the disappointments engendered by the Soviet reaction to the plan, see Hans-Jürgen Grabbe, *Unionsparteien, Sozialdemokratie und Vereinigte Staaten von Amerika, 1945–1966* (Düsseldorf: Droste, 1982), pp. 245ff.

13. See Drummond, *German Social Democrats*, esp. p. 280. In 1962 Blankenhorn agreed that there was no longer any difference between the SPD's and the government's foreign policy conceptions (*Verständnis und Verständigung*, p. 418).

14. See Raymond Aron, *The Great Debate* (Garden City, N.Y.: Doubleday, 1965), esp. p. 90.

15. See Gerard Braunthal, "The Free Democratic Party in West German Politics," *Western Political Quarterly* 13, no. 2 (1960): 332–348.

16. Grabbe, *Unionsparteien*, esp. chap. 7.

17. Horst Osterheld, *"Ich gehe nicht leichten Herzens. . . ." Adenauer's letzte Kanzlerjahre—Ein dokumentarischer Bericht*, Adenauer Studien, vol. 5, ed. Rudolf Morsey and Konrad Repgen (Mainz: Matthias-Grünewald-Verlag, 1986); Allemann, *Zwischen Stabilität und Krise*, pp. 57–80; Gerald Braunthal, "The Succession Crisis of 1959," in James B. Christoph, ed., *Cases in Comparative Politics* (Boston: Little, Brown, 1965), pp. 209–240; Peter H. Merkl, "Equilibrium, Structure of Interests, and Leadership: Adenauer's Survival as Chancellor," *American Political Science Review* 56, no. 3 (1962): 634–650.

18. This was due in part to the uproar caused by the so-called Spiegel affair, in which leading staff members of the weekly magazine *Der Spiegel*, long a gadfly to the government and especially to Defense Minister Franz-Josef Strauss, were arrested for publishing allegedly secret evaluations of West Germany's and NATO's preparedness. The arrests were carried out in a constitutionally questionable manner and led to the resignation of Strauss, who had worked behind the scenes to clamp down on *Der Spiegel*.

19. For a full account see Daniel Koerfer, *Kampf ums Kanzleramt. Erhard und Adenauer* (Stuttgart: Deutsche Verlags-Anstalt, 1987).

20. Reimund Krönert, *Die Deutschlandpolitik der* FDP *1961 bis 1969* (Frankfurt am Main, 1978); Peter Juling, ed., *Programmatische Entwicklung der* FDP *1946 bis 1969*, Studien zum politischen System der Bundesrepublik Deutschland, vol. 19

(Meisenheim am Glan: A. Hain, 1977); Hans Hotter, *Der Wandel der FDP seit 1966 im Hinblick auf Selbstverständnis, Programmatik und Parteipolitik* (Berlin, 1971).

21. Fritz René Allemann, "The Changing Scene in Germany," *World Today* 23 (February 1967): 49–62, esp. p. 54. See also Grabbe, *Unionsparteien*, esp. chaps. 8, 9.

22. See Volkhard Laitenberger, *Ludwig Erhard. Der Nationalökonom als Politiker* (Göttingen: Muster-Schmidt, 1986).

23. See John Herz, "The Formation of the Grand Coalition," in James B. Christoph and Bernard E. Brown, eds., *Cases in Comparative Politics*, 2d ed. (Boston: Little, Brown, 1969).

24. The first quotation is from Theo Sommer, "Bonn Changes Course," *Foreign Affairs* 45, no. 3 (April 1967): 477; the second is from *Die Zeit*, June 27, 1969, p. 1.

25. Most SPD members and CDU moderates favored German participation in the treaty because they realized the cost of rejecting it. As a vocal opponent of the treaty, however, Franz-Josef Strauss called it a "Versailles of cosmic proportions." Other CSU and CDU leaders opposed the treaty (including ex-chancellor Adenauer), seeing it as another example of Soviet-American complicity damaging to vital German national interests and impairing Bonn's present and future mobility. For a well-argued presentation of this position see Franz Horner, "Der Atomsperrvertrag—Politischer Idealismus oder Realismus?" *Politische Studien* 18, no. 176 (November–December 1967): 691–704. On the clash over monetary policy see Hanrieder, *Stable Crisis*, esp. pp. 186–190.

26. Klaus Hildebrand, *Von Erhard zur Grossen Koalition, 1963–1969*, vol. 4 of Karl Heinz Bracher et al., eds., *Geschichte der Bundesrepublik Deutschland* (Stuttgart: Deutsche Verlags-Anstalt, 1984), esp. pp. 365–383; see also Hanrieder, *Stable Crisis*, pp. 190 ff.

CHAPTER 13: *Convergence at the Center, 1969–89*

Epigraphs. Wilhelm G. Grewe, *Die deutsche Frage in der Ost-West-Spannung. Zeitgeschichtliche Kontroversen der achtziger Jahre* (Herford: Busse-Seewald, 1986), p. 75; Henry Kissinger, *Newsweek*, October 12, 1987, p. 57; Helmut Schmidt, *A Grand Strategy for the West* (New Haven and London: Yale University Press, 1985), pp. 147–148.

1. For full accounts of the origins of the coalition and its Ostpolitik see Arnulf Baring, *Machtwechsel. Die Ära Brandt-Scheel* (Stuttgart: Deutsche Verlags-Anstalt, 1982); Günther Schmid, *Entscheidung in Bonn. Die Entstehung der Ost- und Deutschlandpolitik, 1969–1970* (Cologne: Verlag Wissenschaft und Politik, 1979). See also Reimund Krönert, *Die Deutschlandpolitik der FDP 1961 bis 1969* (Frankfurt am Main, 1978); and Wolfgang Schollwer, *Der Weg zur Entspannung. Deutschlandpolitik der F.D.P. seit 1952* (Bonn, 1972).

2. See Christian Hacke, *Die Ost- und Deutschlandpolitik der CDU/CSU. Wege und Irrwege der Opposition seit 1969* (Cologne: Verlag Wissenschaft und Politik, 1974); David M. Keithly, *Breakthrough in the Ostpolitik* (Boulder: Westview, 1986), chap. 12.

3. See Werner Link, "Aussen- und Deutschlandpolitik in der Ära Brandt, 1969–1974," pt. 2 (pp. 163–282) of Karl Dietrich Bracher, Wolfgang Jäger, and

Werner Link, *Republik im Wandel, 1969–1974. Die Ära Brandt*, vol. 5 of Karl Dietrich Bracher et al., eds., *Geschichte der Bundesrepublik Deutschland* (Stuttgart: Deutsche Verlags-Anstalt, 1986), esp. pp. 206–213.

4. For an elaboration on the opposition's concerns see Gerhard Schröder, " 'Nein' zu den Ostverträgen," *Die Zeit*, February 8, 1972. For a measured German critique of the Moscow Treaty see Kurt Birrenbach, *Meine Sondermissionen* (Düsseldorf and Vienna: Econ, 1984), pp. 309–431. On the constitutional and procedural issues involved see Eberhard Menzel, "Bundesrat—Bremse gegen Ostverträge?" *Die Zeit*, August 31, 1971, p. 8; and the articles by Carl Christian Kaiser and Rolf Zundel in *Die Zeit*, December 21, 1971, and January 25, 1972.

5. For an account of Schmidt's close ties in economic policy-making with industrial leaders, especially Ernst Wolf Mommsen, head of the Krupp concern, see "Ernst Wolf Mommsen: A Close Advisor to Chancellor Schmidt," *German Tribune*, December 12, 1974, p. 4. For Schmidt's views on a variety of political, military-strategic, and economic issues (and an extensive bibliography on Schmidt) see Wolfram F. Hanrieder, ed., *Helmut Schmidt: Perspectives on Politics* (Boulder: Westview, 1982).

6. Kurt Sontheimer, *Zeitenwende? Die Bundesrepublik Deutschland zwischen alter und alternativer Politik* (Hamburg: Hoffmann und Campe, 1983).

7. Ralf Dahrendorf, "The Europeanization of Europe," in Andrew J. Pierre, ed., *Domestic Change and Foreign Policy: A Widening Atlantic?* Europe/America 4 (New York: Council on Foreign Relations, 1986): 5–56, esp. p. 30.

8. It is striking how the Federal Republic's chancellors seemed suited to their times in office, almost as if their lives' experiences had been an unconscious preparation for their historical tasks. One thinks of Jacob Burckhardt's remark "Zeit und Mensch treten in eine grosse, geheimnisvolle Verrechnung." Adenauer was great by Cavour's standard of having *le tacte des choses possibles*; he bent necessity to his will and transformed it into choice, was distrustful of everyone, above all his fellow Germans, and was in Isaiah Berlin's sense a hedgehog rather than a fox (although the latter became his sobriquet), knowing one thing truly well—the need to tie Germany to the West. Erhard, bruised by foreign and domestic setbacks, was yet sustained by a belief that an invisible hand would right things in politics as well as in economics, and that everything would turn out well if, like the market, it was left to itself. He had a deep and warm bonhomie, was somewhat sentimental, and was protected by a refusal to listen to the bad news of his time. Kiesinger was courtly and restrained, as suitable in the role of intermediary between France and the United States as anyone else could have been, gracious with his coalition partners, a perfect chancellor of transition. Brandt was articulate on the outside, silent within, wounded early and not fully healed, sensuous in politics and life, by political background and temperament almost predestined to make the opening to the East. Schmidt was acerbic and sensitive; his political and aesthetic imagination was curbed by intelligence and a deep aversion to ideology, a justified self-absorption (conversing with him amounted to exchanging his ideas with him), a cool exterior and warm interior; he was prepared by intellect and experience to face the military-strategic, economic, and monetary issues that confronted Germany in the 1970s and early 1980s.

9. The selection of Strauss by the CDU and CSU in the expectation that he

would fail may have been a deliberate attempt to remove him from politics in Bonn. See William E. Paterson, "The Christian Union Parties," in Wallach and Romoser, *West German Politics*, pp. 60–80, esp. p. 76. See also Peter Pulzer, "What the 1980 Election Did Not Solve," in William E. Paterson and Gordon Smith, eds., *The West German Model: Perspectives on a Stable State* (London: Frank Cass, 1981), pp. 124–133.

10. See Christian Soe, "The Free Democratic Party," in H. G. Peter Wallach and George K. Romoser, eds., *West German Politics in the Mid-Eighties: Crisis and Continuity* (New York: Praeger, 1985), pp. 112–186, esp. pp. 144, 148; R. E. M. Irving and W. E. Paterson, "The Machtwechsel of 1982–83: A Significant Landmark in the Political and Constitutional History of West Germany," *Parliamentary Affairs* 36, no. 4 (Autumn 1983): 417–435, esp. p. 427; Ralf Dahrendorf, "Die Leitsterne unserer Politik erlöschen," *Die Zeit*, August 26, 1977, p. 3; Dahrendorf, *Die Chancen der Krise. Über die Zukunft des Liberalismus* (Stuttgart: Deutsche Verlags-Anstalt, 1983). On the conservative policy trend see Rolf Zundel, "Bilan d'une politique intérieure conservatrice," *Documents. Revue des questions allemandes*, September 1976, pp. 38–46.

11. For a critique by SPD moderates of the leftist trend of the SPD's security policy see Jürgen Maruhn and Manfred Wilke, eds., *Wohin treibt die SPD?* (Munich: Olzog, 1983). See also David S. Yost and Thomas C. Glad, "West German Party Politics and Theater Nuclear Modernization Since 1977," *Armed Forces and Society* 8, no. 4 (Summer 1982): 525–560.

12. For a discussion of the changes in the salience of foreign and domestic policy issues within the German electorate between the elections of 1980 and 1983 see Russell J. Dalton and Kendall L. Baker, "The Contours of West German Opinion"; and Arthur M. Hanhardt, Jr., "International Politics and the 1983 Election," both in Wallach and Romoser, *West German Politics*, pp. 24–59, 219–234.

13. Robert Gerald Livingston, "The 1983 National Elections: Three Winners and a Loser," in R. G. Livingston, ed., *The Federal Republic of Germany in the 1980s* (New York: German Information Center, 1983), pp. 43–59, esp. pp. 50–51.

14. See Kjell Goldmann, *Détente: Domestic Politics as a Stabilizer of Foreign Policy* (Princeton: Center of International Studies Publication, 1984), esp. pp. 38, 54. Goldmann also points out that this was a major difference between the United States and Germany. In the United States this institutionalization of détente did not take place, and there were conceivable alternatives, such as a renewal of containment policies resembling those of Reagan. See also Peter H. Merkl, "The Evolution of West German Public Opinion on Détente Since 1970," in Wolfram F. Hanrieder, ed., *Arms Control, the FRG, and the Future of East-West Relations* (Boulder: Westview, 1987), pp. 29–47.

15. "Until the beginning of the seventies, détente was but one of many possibilities for foreign policy. Today détente has become a national political necessity, which, if pursued realistically and with circumspection, can count on a far-reaching domestic consensus." Christian Hacke, "Von Adenauer zu Kohl. Zur Ost- und Deutschlandpolitik der Bundesrepublik 1949–1985," *Aus Politik und Zeitgeschichte*, suppl. to *Das Parlament*, B 51–52 (December 21, 1985), pp. 3–22; the quotation appears on p. 21. See also David P. Conradt, "West Germany's Center Coalition," *Current History* 86, no. 529 (November 1986): 357–360, 389–391; Peter H. Merkl, "The Role of Public Opinion in West German Foreign Policy," in

Wolfram F. Hanrieder, ed., *West German Foreign Policy, 1949–1979* (Boulder: Westview, 1980), pp. 157–180.

16. For a general treatment of West German domestic politics during the 1980s, including their role in foreign policy, see Paterson and Smith, *West German Model*; Wallach and Romoser, *West German Politics*; Gebhard Schweigler, *Grundlagen der aussenpolitischen Orientierung der Bundesrepublik* (Baden-Baden: Nomos, 1985); Schweigler, *West German Foreign Policy: The Domestic Setting* (New York: Praeger, 1984). See also Berthold Meyer, *Der Bürger und seine Sicherheit. Zum Verhältnis von Sicherheitsstreben und Sicherheitspolitik* (Frankfurt am Main: Campus, 1983).

17. The opposition of the SPD to INF deployment and to the Reagan administration's grudging arms control policies manifested itself in the formulation of the "second phase of Ostpolitik," what Helmut Kohl disparagingly called a parallel foreign policy. Although the governing coalition expressed its willingness to accept the "special responsibility" of the two German states for peace in Europe, the SPD sought closer relations with the East German Sozialistische Einheitspartei Deutschlands (SED) and with other East European parties in matters of arms control. In addition to "the alliance partnership in the West," the SPD promoted a "security partnership with the East." These negotiations resulted in a draft treaty for a Central European corridor free of nuclear and chemical weapons. See Ronald D. Asmus, "The SPD's Second Ostpolitik with Perspectives from the USA," *Aussenpolitik* 38, no. 1 (1987): 40–55; and the contributions by Thomas Meyer, Dieter Haack, Jürgen Schnappertz, and Martin Kriele in "Zum SED-SPD-Papier," *Deutschland Archiv* 21, no. 1 (January 1988): 32–52.

18. Johannes Gross, *Unsere letzten Jahre. Fragmente aus Deutschland* (Stuttgart: Deutsche Verlags-Anstalt, 1980), pp. 65–69; Gordon Smith, "The Changing West German Party System: Consequences of the 1987 Election," *Government and Opposition* 22, no. 2 (Spring 1987): 131–144.

19. Theo Sommer, "Die Einheit gegen Freiheit tauschen," *Die Zeit*, July 3, 1987, p. 1. Jonathan Dean notes that when Western security policies conflict with Eastern policies, the West Germans have consistently chosen the NATO alliance and integration into the West. See Jonathan Dean, *Watershed in Europe* (Lexington, Mass.: Lexington Books, 1987), esp. pp. 249–250.

20. For discussions of the peace movement see Harold Mueller and Thomas Risse-Kappen, "Origins of Estrangement: The Peace Movement and the Changed Image of America in West Germany," *International Security* 12, no. 1 (Summer 1987): 52–88; Josef Joffe, "Peace and Populism: Why the European Anti-nuclear Movement Failed," *International Security* 11, no. 4 (Spring 1987): 3–40; Karl-Werner Brand, ed., *Neue soziale Bewegungen in Westeuropa und den USA. Ein internationaler Vergleich* (Frankfurt am Main: Campus, 1985), esp. the contributions by Roland Roth (on West Germany) and Herbert Kitschelt (on the United States); Wilfried von Bredow and Rudolf N. Brocke, *Krise und Protest. Ursprünge und Elemente der Friedensbewegung in Westeuropa* (Opladen: Westdeutscher Verlag, 1987).

On the Greens see Peter Gatter, *Die Aufsteiger. Ein politisches Porträt der Grünen* (Hamburg: Hoffmann und Campe, 1987); Wilfried von Bredow and Rudolf N. Brocke, "Dreimal Deutschlandpolitik. Deutschlandpolitische Ansätze der Partei der Grünen," *Deutschland Archiv* 19, no. 1 (January 1986): 52–61. For the position of the "new Right" see Margret Feit, *Die "Neue Rechte" in der Bundesrepublik. Organisation-Ideologie-Strategie* (Frankfurt am Main: Campus, 1987).

21. *Newsweek*, October 12, 1987, p. 57.

22. In 1983 NATO had adopted a decision at Montebello, Canada, which called for the withdrawal of approximately 1,400 nuclear munitions and pledged NATO members to modernize the remaining tactical nuclear systems. The decision did not draw much public attention at the time but became highly significant in the wake of the INF accord of 1987–88, which provided for the withdrawal of Soviet and American intermediate-range and shorter-range missiles from Europe. By way of compensation, NATO (and especially the United States and Britain) were now determined to implement the Montebello decision. (See also chapter 4).

23. These apprehensions were reinforced by a newly issued Pentagon study on "discriminate deterrence" that implied a revival of the old idea (always anathema in Bonn) that NATO should be equipped to fight a limited nuclear war. See Fred C. Iklé and Albert Wohlstetter, eds., *Discriminate Deterrence: Report of the Commission on Integrated Long Term Strategy* (Washington: GPO, 1988). For a critical comment on the Pentagon study see Paul Kennedy, "Not So Grand Strategy," *New York Review of Books*, May 12, 1988, pp. 5–8. On the attitudes of the West German public and political parties toward these matters see Barry M. Blechman and Cathleen S. Fisher, *The Silent Partner: West Germany and Arms Control* (Cambridge, Mass.: Ballinger, 1988).

24. See Pierre Hassner, "Recurrent Stresses, Resilient Structures," in Robert W. Tucker and Linda Wrigley, eds., *The Atlantic Alliance and Its Critics* (New York: Praeger, 1983), pp. 61–94.

25. Stanley Hoffmann, "Coming Down from the Summit," *New York Review of Books*, January 21, 1988, pp. 21–25, esp. p. 25.

26. See Volker Rittberger, "Basic Patterns and Recurrent Contradictions in West German Foreign Policy" (February 1986, mimeographed).

27. For a look at the darker side of Germany's economic success see Stephan Leibfried and Florian Tennstadt, eds., *Politik der Armut. Die Spaltung des Sozialstaats* (Frankfurt am Main: Suhrkamp, 1985).

28. On the conflict between achieving monetary stability and low unemployment levels, especially in the 1970s, see Peter Reichel, ed., *Politische Kultur in Westeuropa. Bürger und Staaten in der Europäischen Gemeinschaft* (Frankfurt am Main: Campus, 1984); Fritz W. Scharpf, *Sozialdemokratische Krisenpolitik in Europa* (Frankfurt am Main: Campus, 1986).

29. Wilhelm Hankel, "Germany: Economic Nationalism in the International Economy," in Wilfrid L. Kohl and Giorgio Basevi, eds., *West Germany: A European and Global Power* (Lexington, Mass.: Lexington Books, 1980), pp. 21–43; the quotation appears on p. 23.

30. Günther Schatz, "Macht Wohlstand Unpolitisch?" *Der Monat* 17, no. 196 (January 1965): 36–40.

31. Stephen F. Szabo, ed., *The Successor Generation: International Perspectives of Postwar Europeans* (London: Butterworth, 1983); Szabo, "The New Generation in Germany," *Transatlantic Perspectives*, no. 7 (December 1982): 10–12; Klaus Mehnert, *Jugend im Zeitbruch* (Stuttgart: Deutsche Verlags-Anstalt, 1976); Kendall Baker, *Germany Transformed* (Cambridge: Harvard University Press, 1981); Alan Platt, ed., *The Atlantic Alliance: Perspectives from the Successor Generation* (Santa

Monica: RAND Corp., 1983); Gerd Langguth, "Wie steht die junge Generation zur deutschen Teilung?" *Politische Studien* 37, no. 289 (September-October 1986): 524–542.

32. Michael Howard, "A European Perspective on the Reagan Years," *Foreign Affairs* 66, no. 3 (special issue: "America and the World, 1987–88"): 478–493.

33. For a similarly skeptical view of the importance of the "generation gap" see Theodore C. Sorenson, "A Changing America," in Ralf Dahrendorf and Theodore C. Sorenson, *A Widening Atlantic? Domestic Change and Foreign Policy* (New York: Council on Foreign Relations, 1986), pp. 57–107, esp. pp. 102–103.

34. In the Federal Republic complaints about the unpredictability of U.S. policy ranged across the entire political spectrum. For two examples see the remarks by Helmut Schmidt in the *Washington Post*, May 5, 1983, and Franz-Josef Strauss in *Der Spiegel* 42, no. 3 (1988): 16.

35. See Manfred Henningsen, *Der Fall Amerika* (Munich: List, 1974). For prescient reflections on the nature of relations between America and Europe see Eugen Kogon and Walter Dirks, "Europa und die Amerikaner," *Frankfurter Hefte* 6, no. 2 (February 1951): 73–80.

36. See Joseph S. Nye, Jr., and Whitney MacMillan, eds., *How Should America Respond to Gorbachev's Challenge?* (New York: Institute for East-West Security Studies, 1987); Marion Gräfin Dönhoff, "Die Weltpolitik vor der Wende? Gorbatschows 'Neues Denken' verlangt eine Antwort vom Westen," *Die Zeit*, February 5, 1988, p. 1.

37. See Willi P. Adams and Knud Krakau, eds., *Deutschland und Amerika. Perzeption und historische Realität* (Berlin: Colloquium, 1985); Horst Ehmke, Interview, *Die Zeit*, April 17, 1981, p. 5.

38. See Richard Löwenthal, "The German Question Transformed," *Foreign Affairs* 63, no. 2 (Winter 1984–85): 303–315, esp. pp. 311–312.

39. Kurt Sontheimer, "How Real is German Anti-Americanism? An Assessment," in Frank Trommler and Joseph McVeigh, eds., *America and the Germans: An Assessment of a Three-Hundred-Year History*, vol. 2, *The Relationship in the Twentieth Century* (Philadelphia: University of Pennsylvania Press, 1985), pp. 117–132.

EPILOGUE

1. For a fuller argument see Wolfram F. Hanrieder, "Dissolving International Politics: Reflections on the Nation-State," *American Political Science Review* 72, no. 4 (December 1978): 1276–1287.

2. Daniel Bell, "The Future World Disorder: The Structural Context of Crises," *Foreign Policy*, no. 27 (1977): 109–135. See also Eric A. Nordlinger, *On the Autonomy of the Democratic State* (Cambridge: Harvard University Press, 1981).

3. See John Herz, *International Politics in the Atomic Age* (New York: Columbia University Press, 1959).

4. See Wallace J. Thies, *The Atlantic Alliance, Nuclear Weapons and European Attitudes*, University of California Institute of International Affairs, Policy Paper no. 19 (Berkeley, 1983).

5. "Nothing can change the fundamental fact that the Soviet Union has a dual nature. It is, at the same time, a European country and a great world power. There is no European security system without it, but if the other great world

power does not play a role in the system, there is Soviet domination in place of security. However, if the United States is included, it is no longer a European system; it is simply a subsystem of the global system of balance of power." Alfred Grosser, "Europe: Community of Malaise," *Foreign Policy*, no. 15 (Summer 1974): 169–182; the quotation is from p. 172.

6. This mutual reliance is an issue that dates back to the years of Charles de Gaulle. See A. W. DePorte, *Europe between the Superpowers: The Enduring Balance* (New Haven and London: Yale University Press, 1979), p. 226.

7. See Jonathan Dean, "How to Lose Germany," *Foreign Policy*, no. 55 (Summer 1984): 54–72, esp. pp. 71–72.

8. See George Liska, "From Containment to Concert," *Foreign Policy*, no. 62 (Spring 1986): 3–23; Liska, "Concert through Decompression," *Foreign Policy*, no. 63 (Summer 1986): 108–129. Liska calls for the United States to replace its policy of containment ("compression") with a policy of "decompression."

9. "If the United States simply 'acts like a superpower,' it will be perceived simply as a superpower—that is, another rogue elephant on the political scene from whose ravages other members of the international community will seek protection, either by some kind of communal non-alignment, or by a policy of maneuver between the two blocs." Michael Howard, "A European Perspective on Reagan," *Foreign Affairs* 66, no. 3 (special issue: "America and the World, 1987–88"): 478–493; the quotation appears on p. 490.

10. Robert W. Tucker, "The Atlantic Alliance and Its Critics," in Robert W. Tucker and Linda Wrigley, eds., *The Atlantic Alliance and Its Critics* (New York: Praeger, 1983), pp. 155–188; the quotation appears on p. 188.

11. Aside from its intrinsic importance, the task of thinking about a new Germany policy is urgent in case the Soviet Union should at some point propose confederation to both German states, a withdrawal of Soviet troops from East Germany, and withdrawal of Western allies' troops from the Federal Republic. See Fred Oldenbourg, "Neues Denken in der sowjetischen Deutschlandpolitik?" *Deutschland Archiv* 20, no. 11 (November 1987): 1154–1160; Eberhard Schulz, "Sowjetische Deutschland-Politik: Noch immer unentschlossen?" *Deutschland Archiv* 20, no. 9 (September 1987): 940–949.

12. "U.S. political leadership in the world cannot be sustained if confidence in the American economy continues to be undermined by substantial trade and budget deficits. . . . Convincing economic discipline, clear and publicly supported long-term economic strategies, as well as equitable budget reductions, must be applied quickly if we are to halt the erosion of our international position. It is increasingly obvious that our military prowess and even our nuclear capabilities do not by themselves contribute to the struggle for our international markets." Henry Kissinger and Cyrus Vance, "Bipartisan Objectives for American Foreign Policy," *Foreign Affairs* 66, no. 5 (Summer 1988): 899–921; the quotation appears on p. 910.

13. "The inflationary cost to the Germans of [their] special relationship caused it to weaken in 1973 and eventually to fracture in 1979. The Germans were in turn replaced by the Japanese, who subsequently provided the financial underwriting of American hegemony." Robert Gilpin, *The Political Economy of International Relations* (Princeton: Princeton University Press, 1987), p. 380.

14. For a Franco-German dialogue on these issues see Karl Kaiser and Pierre

504 NOTES TO PAGES 383–385

Lellouche, eds., *Deutsch-französische Sicherheitspolitik* (Bonn: Verlag Europa Union, 1986). See also Bernard Brigouleix and Josef Rovan, eds., *Que devient l'Allemagne?* (Paris: Editions Anthropos, 1986).

15. See Josef Joffe, "Europe's American Pacifier," *Foreign Policy,* no. 54 (Spring 1984): 64–82, esp. pp. 78–81. See also Richard H. Ullman and Mario Zucconi, eds., *Western Europe and the Crisis in U.S.-Soviet Relations* (New York: Praeger, 1987).

16. This attitude was particularly noticeable at the WEU conference at The Hague in October 1987, where the Germans won from the French the concession "to defend any member country at its border," but where both Britain and Italy expressed reservations about a French-German "WEU-directorate." On the prospects of the German-British security connection see Karl Kaiser and John Roper, eds., *Die Stille Allianz. Deutsch-Britische Sicherheitskooperation* (Bonn: Europa-Union-Verlag, 1987), esp. chaps. 5, 10.

17. For a discussion of the prospects of a West European Ostpolitik see the contributions by Klaus Bloemer, Peter Brandt, Thomas-Peter Gallon, Klaus Hänsch, Françoise Manfrass-Sirjacques, Günter Minnerup, and Christiane Rix in *Die Neue Gesellschaft/Frankfurter Hefte* 34, no. 8 (August 1987).

18. For a highly skeptical view by the former French ambassador to Moscow and Bonn see Henri Froment-Meurice, *Europa als eine Macht* (Cologne: Verlag Wissenschaft und Politik, 1986). For a sober but ultimately optimistic assessment of the prospects for West European unity see Werner Weidenfeld et al., *Europäische Defizite, europäische Perspektiven—Eine Bestandsaufnahme für morgen* (Gütersloh: Bertelsmann Stiftung, 1988).

19. On the concept of a semi-Gaullist Europe see David Watt, "The European Initiative," *Foreign Affairs* 57, no. 3 (special issue: "America and the World, 1978"): 572–588, esp. p. 573; Fritz Stern, "Germany in a Semi-Gaullist Europe," *Foreign Affairs* 58, no. 4 (Spring 1980): 867–886.

20. See Hans-Peter Schwarz, *Die gezähmten Deutschen. Von der Machtbesessenheit zur Machtvergessenheit* (Stuttgart: Deutsche Verlags-Anstalt, 1985); Christian Hacke, *Weltmacht wider Willen. Die Aussenpolitik der Bundesrepublik Deutschland* (Stuttgart: Klett-Cotta, 1988). For an earlier argument that the Germans had obtained their own *Staatsräson* and should be prepared to act on it see Waldemar Besson, *Die Aussenpolitik der Bundesrepublik. Erfahrungen und Masstäbe* (Munich: Piper, 1970).

21. On the peculiar mix of pessimism and optimism, anxiety and self-satisfaction, nationalism and internationalism, and other German contradictions, with an ultimately encouraging assessment, see Walter Laqueur, *Germany Today: A Personal Report* (London: Weidenfeld and Nicholson, 1985).

Index

Acheson, Dean, 68, 199
Adenauer, Konrad: and arms control, 86–88; and Berlin crisis of 1958, 257; British membership in EEC viewed by, 255–62; and German Gaullism, 183, 256–57, 267; and German control of nuclear weapons, 38–48; nonproliferation treaty viewed by, 93; Ostpolitik of, 18, 86–88, 171–78, 182–83, 190–93, 233; political and economic recovery of West Germany and, 223–53, 260–62, 338–45; and rearmament, 9, 38–42, 223; reunification policy of, 8–11, 17, 86–88, 145–69, 197–98; and West European integration, 6–7, 13–14, 255–62, 288
Adjustment Controls, Agreement on, 236
Allied High Commission, 5, 232, 241
Andropov, Yuri, 214
Antiballistic Missile Defense (ABM), 34, 73, 95–97, 103, 108, 115, 118, 122–30. See also Strategic Defense Initiative
Antiballistic Missile Treaty, 115. See also Strategic Arms Limitation Talks
Atlantic Alliance. See North Atlantic Treaty Organization
Austria, 256; State Treaty of, 161

Bahr, Egon, 101, 204
Bangemann, Martin, 315
Basic Law, 141, 144, 232
Basic Treaty, 202–09
Belgium, 246–48, 251, 270, 283–87
Berlin, 86, 104, 152, 165–69, 214, 234, 257; 1948 blockade of, 166, 241; 1961 crisis of, 17, 52, 72, 170–71; Four Power negotiations over, 98, 102, 175–

77, 187–89, 198, 200–19; Quadripartite Agreement on, 101–02, 202–09
Bonn Conventions, 234. See also Paris Agreements
Brandt, Willy, 17, 79, 267, 283, 288, 298, 342; and arms control, 93–94, 101–03; British membership in EEC viewed by, 284–85; Ostpolitik of, 19–20, 171–77, 186–87, 190, 195–98, 334–35
Bretton Woods Monetary system, 16, 269, 273; erosion of, 22, 283–306, 309–13; implementation of, 10, 238–40, 253
Brezhnev, Leonid, 102, 182, 201, 204
Brzezinski, Zbigniew, 106
Bulgaria, 178, 188–89, 209
Bundesbank, 243, 269, 278, 286, 297–306, 351–52; and European monetary union, 288, 314–20. See also Deutsche Mark
Bundeswehr, 29, 37–62, 249

Canada, 182, 210, 257–58
Carlucci, Frank C., 120, 365
Carter, Jimmy, 22, 33; and dollar stabilization, 302–03, economic policy of, 306; and limited nuclear war, 108; and Presidential Review Memorandum 10, 79–80; and SALT II, 106, 110–12, 115; Schmidt's relations with, 78–80, 106, 113
Chernenko, Konstantin, 214–15
China, 143, 204, 212
Christian Democratic Union/Christian Social Union (CDU/CSU), 244, 283, 288; and double-zero option, 119; and Franco-German relations, 267; and Ostpolitik and reunification, 175, 180,

505

Rühle, Hans, 124
Rumania, 178, 181–2, 187–88

Scheel, Walter, 94, 102, 283; Ostpolitik
of, 19, 75, 195, 203
Schiller, Karl, 288, 293–94, 351–54
Schlesinger, James R., 77–78
Schmidt, Helmut: Carter's relations with,
78–79, 105–06, 113; economic policy
of, 23, 221, 298–301, 305; and European Monetary System, 309–12; Eurostrategic balance viewed by, 22, 103,
110–12, 114, 117–18; Ostpolitik of, 116,
195, 358–59; SALT viewed by, 103–05;
U.S. strategy viewed by, 58
Schröder, Gerhard, 14, 48, 91, 178–80,
182, 189, 262–63, 267, 346–47
Smithsonian Agreement, 290–99
Social Democratic party (SPD): Adenauer's relations with, 6, 156, 237, 241,
244; EEC viewed by, 255, 288; and nuclear weapons, 42, 116, 119, 175, 216;
Ostpolitik of, 19, 99, 181, 190, 195, 199,
209–11, 214; rearmament viewed by, 7,
39, 175; in West German party politics,
171, 175, 332–65. See also Brandt, Willy;
Ostpolitik; Schmidt, Helmut
Soviet Union: attempts to dissolve NATO,
89, 200–01; deterrence of, and arms
control, 29–35, 96–106; Czechoslovakia
invaded by, 17, 74, 184, 191, 268; and
division of Europe, 17, 30, 56; EEC's relations with, 225; German reunification
viewed by, 8–11, 67, 141–69, 197–219,
261; Hungary invaded by, 44, 74, 159,
161; and nonproliferation treaty, 15;
Ostpolitik viewed by, 20, 24, 171–94;
Sputnik launched by, 44; friendship
treaty with East Germany, 180; treaty
with West Germany, 101, 202–09, 356–
57. See also United States: nuclear parity with Soviet Union
Special Drawing Rights (SDRS), 295, 301–
02
Stalin, Josef, 154
Stoltenberg, Gerhard 314–20
Stoph, Willi, 187, 206, 351
Strategic Arms Limitation Talks (SALT),
22, 78, 102–06, 110; SALT I, 73, 95, 97–
98, 100–03, 110, 115, 201, 211; SALT II,
97, 100, 102–04, 106, 110, 112, 114–15,
201, 213
Strategic Arms Reduction Talks (START),
103, 114, 118
Strategic Defense Initiative (SDI), 34, 108,
122–30. See also Antiballistic Missile
Defense

Strauss, Franz-Josef, 51, 93, 215, 267,
359–60

Test Ban Treaty, 72, 89, 92, 263
Thatcher, Margaret, 318–20
Third World, 3, 24, 97, 173, 188, 201,
205–06, 212, 226, 304–05
Tito, Josef, 160, 188
Truman, Harry, 158
Turkey, 109

Ulbricht, Walter, 187–8, 207; Ulbricht
Doctrine, 188
Union of Soviet Socialist Republics
(USSR). See Soviet Union
United Kingdom. See Great Britain
United Nations, 153, 167
United States: arms control policy of, 4,
35, 59–60, 83–106; balance of payments of, 16, 239, 258, 261, 271, 276–
77, 280, 290; European integration policy of, 15, 256–81; hegemonic decline
of, 3–4, 13, 22, 323–28, 367–72; international economic policy of, 7–8, 76,
223–53, 269, 283–306; Ostpolitik
viewed by, 133–219; nuclear parity
with Soviet Union, 4, 13, 56, 65–66, 70,
73–76, 78, 97, 109–10, 172, 201; nuclear
superiority of, 31, 128; strategic doctrine of, 37–130; trade deficit of, 276,
324–28; unilateralism of, 128–30

Vietnam, 17, 46–47, 73, 76, 89–90, 92, 98,
183, 263, 277, 282, 292

Warsaw Pact, 21, 53, 57, 73–74, 77–78,
80, 85, 88–90, 100, 103, 127, 143, 182,
188–89, 193, 205, 207, 210; cohesion of,
17–18, 172; East German membership
in, 10, 59, 159
Weizsäcker, Richard von, 218
Werner Plan, 285–88, 296–97, 303
West European integration, 48, 148, 152,
184, 200, 230, 245–90, 384; stagnation
of, 316–23
West European Union (WEU), 40, 234
West German-Czechoslovakian Treaty,
202–09
West German-Polish Treaty, 202–09, 356–
57
West German-Soviet Treaty 101, 202–09,
356–57
Wörner, Manfred, 58, 103, 124, 360

Yugoslavia, 160, 187–88